Camardese

PSYCHODYNAMIC SOCIAL WORK

PSYCHODYNAMIC SOCIAL WORK

JERROLD R. BRANDELL

COLUMBIA UNIVERSITY PRESS   NEW YORK

COLUMBIA UNIVERSITY PRESS
Publishers Since 1893
NEW YORK, CHICHESTER, WEST SUSSEX

Library of Congress Cataloging-in-Publication Data
Brandell, Jerrold R.
Psychodynamic social work / Jerrold R. Brandell.
p. cm. — (Foundations of social work knowledge)
Includes bibliographical references and index.
ISBN 0-231-12636-0 (cloth: alk. paper) — ISBN 0-231-12637-9 (pbk. : alk. paper)
1. Psychiatric social work. 2. Psychoanalysis. I. Title. II. Series.

HV689.B68 2004
362.2′0425—dc22

2004051953

Columbia University Press books are printed on permanent and
durable acid-free paper.
Printed in the United States of America

c 10 9 8 7 6 5 4 3 2 1
p 10 9 8 7 6 5 4 3 2 1

To Esther, Andrea, Joey, and Stevie

CONTENTS

ACKNOWLEDGMENTS

THE CREATIVE PROCESS that culminates in the production of a new work must always begin with a simple idea. In this instance the original idea belonged not to the author but to Dr. Frederic Reamer, series editor for Columbia's Foundations of Social Work Knowledge, whose invitation to write a book on psychodynamic practice for social workers I gratefully accepted in 2001. Since signing on with Columbia, I have also had the distinct pleasure of working with John Michel, senior executive editor, whose good humor and consummate professionalism have proved to be a steadying influence over the past three years.

A portion of the research for this book was completed during a semester-long sabbatical leave I was granted during the fall of 2002. For this I am indebted to Dean Phyllis I. Vroom of the Wayne State University School of Social Work, whose strong endorsement of clinical scholarship and research on practice is deeply appreciated. I would also like to acknowledge with gratitude the support of my university, which awarded me the Board of Governors' Distinguished Faculty Fellowship in 2002.

Although many of the cases used to illustrate this volume are taken from my own clinical practice, I believed that the inclusion of diverse case material derived from different practice venues would enhance the volume's generalizability. I therefore invited a number of colleagues and former students to contribute clinical case examples. Although in each instance I bear final responsibility for the case descriptions as well as for the discussions that follow each case illustration, I acknowledge with deep appreciation the contribution of the following individuals, who so generously agreed to share their clinical work: Jim Baetz, MSW, BCD; Carleen Miller, MA, LFMT, LMHC; Agron Myftari, MSW, BCD; Christina Repay, MSW, CSW; and Mark Somerstein, MSW, CSW. In addition, I would like to thank William Meyer, MSW, BCD, for permission to use and comment on the case of "Sarah" in chapter 4, an earlier version of which appeared in his 2001 article "Why They Don't Come Back: A Clinical Perspective on the No-Show Client," *Clinical Social Work Journal* 29.4 (Fall 2001), pp. 325–339. I also thank Ted Varkas, MSW, CSW, for his willingness to permit me to adapt and comment on the treatment of "Mark" in chapter 10, whose therapy was originally chronicled in "Childhood Trauma and Posttraumatic Play: A Literature Review and Case Study," published in *Psychoanalytic Social Work* 5.3 (Summer 1998), pp. 29–50.

I wish to make special mention of Drs. Jerry Floersch and Jeffrey Longhofer, coauthors of chapter 13, "Psychodynamic Case Management." I believed it essential to include a chapter on dynamically informed clinical case management in this volume, but, unfortunately, considered this specialized field to be well beyond my area of expertise. I therefore invited Dr. Floersch, an expert on psychodynamic case management who teaches on the faculty of Case Western Reserve University's Mandel School of Applied Social Services, and his colleague, Dr. Longhofer, to contribute this important chapter.

I am deeply indebted to my wife, Esther, for her interest, encouragement, and ongoing assistance, which took so many different forms, throughout the life of this project. I would also like to thank my good friends and colleagues, Drs. Roberta Ann Shechter and Ann Alvarez, for their thoughtful comments and suggestions for early drafts of several chapters. Although the review process at Columbia is an anonymous one, I take this opportunity to express my gratitude to both the social work scholars who read the original prospectus and chapter outline. Their incisive observations and helpful recommendations have significantly altered and enhanced the scope and content of this project. Likewise, I thank Dr. Barbara Simon, of the Columbia University School of Social Work, for her enthusiastic response to this material.

Portions of the first three chapters are derived from a previously published chapter, "Psychoanalytic Theory," that originally appeared in my edited book, *Theory and Practice in Clinical Social Work*, published in 1997 by Free Press/Simon and Schuster. I am in debt to the Free Press and to Dr. Rick Perlman, who was my coauthor on the original chapter, for their permission to adapt this material for republication. I would like to thank Basic Books, Incorporated, for permission to use case material and other portions of a chapter published originally in my 2000 book, *Of Mice and Metaphors: Therapeutic Storytelling with Children*, in a section of chapter 10 of the current work. In addition, I gratefully acknowledge permission to incorporate clinical material previously published as "Countertransference as Communication: Intersubjectivity in the Treatment of a Traumatized Adolescent Patient," in *Smith College Studies in Social Work* 69 (Spring 1999), pp. 405–427, in chapter 5 of this work. I also wish to thank *Families in Society* for permission to include portions of my paper, "Focal Conflict

Theory: A Model for Teaching Dynamic Practice," *Social Casework* 68 (May 1987), pp. 299–310, in chapter 14 of this book.

Perhaps the greatest contribution to this project has come from my psychoanalytic and psychotherapy patients, from whom I have learned so much about the unique intimacy of the clinical encounter. I shall never be able to repay the debt I owe to my psychoanalytic mentors, particularly Joseph G. Kepecs and the late Erika Fromm, both of whom taught me so much about psychodynamic theory and practice. Finally, I would like to express my gratitude to the many graduate students and clinical supervisees whose penetrating questions about theoretical psychoanalysis and the dynamic treatment process have shaped and stimulated my own thinking and development as a clinician, educator, and supervisor.

I FIRST BECAME ACQUAINTED with psychoanalysis when, in my sopho-more year of college, a comparative literature instructor assigned Freud's 1916 essay, "Some Character-Types Met with in Psychoanalytic Work," as a companion piece to Ibsen's *Rosmersholm*. Although most of my classmates regarded this reading assignment as nothing special, or perhaps as slightly more onerous than our other readings, I had a very different reaction. I found Freud's ideas fascinating, a passion that launched me along a career trajectory that led first to clinical social work training and practice, later to a social work doctorate and a career in clinical social work education, and finally to training as a psychoanalyst. In an important sense this book represents the culmination of those intervening thirty years of study, teaching, and clinical practice. Within its pages are topics that I believe have special salience for social work trainees and for those who have recently begun postgraduate clinical practice.

Psychoanalysis is a complex body of theories, clinical teachings, and research literature that began in the late nineteenth century and continues into the present. During the first years of the twentieth century, the majority of psychoanalysts and others who incorporated psychoanalytic thinking into their clinical practice adhered to the tenets of classical psychoanalysis, the theoretical framework most intimately associated with Sigmund Freud. His revolutionary schema, which consisted of such concepts as *libido*, the *unconscious*, and *intrapsychic conflict*, was for the most part accepted by his followers, and for a brief time psychoanalytic thinking seemed fully to be defined by such classical ideas. However, the illusion of a unitary theoretical framework for psychoanalysis gradually disappeared with the introduction of a continuing series of theoretical challenges—both within and outside the psychoanalytic movement—to many of Freud's theories. While some of these challenges proved nonsubstantive, neither standing the test of time nor leading to new ways of thinking, others, as we shall see in the first section of this book, attained the status of theories and gradually became incorporated into the existing framework of psychoanalytic knowledge.

This is a book about psychoanalysis written specifically for social workers, both advanced graduate students and recent postgraduates. Reflecting the heterogeneous nature of contemporary psychoanalytic theory, it is not written from a single theoretical vantage point, but instead incorporates a number of different psychoanalytic psychologies. I do not make the claim that the book is truly "integrative" because I do not believe such a framework to be possible. I have come to accept that the psychoanalytic theories of such writers as Freud, Klein, Sullivan, and Kohut represent radically different traditions with fundamentally dissimilar, indeed frequently irreconcilable positions on matters of development, pathology, technique, and clinical process. In contradistinction, my preference is to characterize this work, as well as my own framework for practice, as *transtheoretical*. Although I have the greatest respect for colleagues who are able to operate confidently and exclusively out of a particular framework, be it classical, object relational, self psychological, or Lacanian, I have, personally, never found this to be an appealing alternative. For me each of these different psychoanalytic traditions holds a piece of the truth, a unique wisdom not replicated by any of the others. As readers will note, certain cases within these pages are examined from the theoretical perspective of ego psychology, others are approached from the vantage point of self psychology, while still others are considered from a relational-intersubjective position. The framework that I advocate for dynamic assessment (as explicated in chapter 6) also incorporates ideas derived from multiple psychoanalytic psychologies (e.g., ego psychology, psychology of the self, and object relations theory). While this certainly adds to the framework's complexity, I would submit that it reminds us of the value of competing explanations and hypotheses as well as the limitations of the theoretical systems from which they are derived. I would like to underscore the idea, however, that a transtheoretical framework does *not* mean multiple theoretical positions are *always* taken with a given set of clinical data. Rather, the student is free to apply a particular psychoanalytic theory *or* to use different psychoanalytic psychologies in combination to illuminate or explain a clinical phenomenon. The essential requirement is that, whichever theory or theories are used, the application reflect intellectual rigor and conceptual clarity. Although this sometimes requires more work, thoughtful extrapolation from various psychoanalytic theoretical frameworks according to the requirements of particular case situations often proves to be enriching and generative.

A word about the title of this book, *Psychodynamic Social Work*. Although the terms *psychoanalytic* and *psychodynamic* are often used somewhat interchangeably (as indeed they are in these pages), my reasons for titling the book as I did are twofold. First, I believe that it is in keeping with this book's transtheoretical framework, since *psychodynamic* often connotes a more expansive theoretical base than that of *classical* theory—a term that for many years was used coextensively with the term *psychoanalytic*. Furthermore, *psychodynamic* implies the distillation of psychoanalytic ideas into psychotherapeutic approaches *aside* from that of psychoanalysis and, in consequence, the potential to reach a greater range of clinical problems and a more diverse clientele. Although in the right clinical circumstances I strongly endorse the idea that psychoanalysis may be profoundly beneficial and valid as a method of treatment, the great majority of clinical applications in social work will be psychotherapeutic in nature.

The design of the book. This book is replete with brief clinical vignettes as well as more detailed clinical examples derived from an assortment of practice venues, including inpatient and outpatient mental health, family service, residential treatment, corrections, and private practice. The cases, furthermore, represent the diversity that has come to be associated with psychodynamic social work practice; they involve adults, adolescents, and children of varied ethnocultural backgrounds and sexual orientations, voluntary as well as involuntary clients, whose presenting problems range from suicidal depression to pathological narcissism.

The book is divided into four sections. In part 1, "The Psychodynamic Perspective," the unique relationship between social work and psychoanalysis is explored, including important controversies that have surrounded this theoretical framework almost since its inception. Other chapters in this section highlight the specific contributions that the various psychoanalytic psychologies have made to our understanding of both psychosocial development and dysfunction and the central ideas of transference and countertransference. In part 2, "The Process of Dynamic Therapy," our focus is on clinical process from assessment through termination. Because clinical assessment in social work is often not dynamically based, we review those particular elements that contribute to a dynamic perspective during this critical pretreatment phase. In subsequent chapters we examine such concepts as initial engagement, the holding environment, the real relationship, and the formation of the therapeutic alliance; resistance, working through, what constitutes dynamic technique; and the process and technique of terminating treatment. Part 3, "Special Clinical Populations and Adaptations of the Psychodynamic Approach," focuses on some of the special requirements and technical adaptations associated with dynamic treatment of children and adolescents and also includes chapters on brief and time-limited dynamic therapy as well as on dynamically oriented case management. In part 4, "Research on Dynamic Treatment," we begin by considering the case for and against psychoanalysis as an empirical science, continuing with a review of extant research in the psychoanalytic field that assesses both clinical process dimensions and treatment outcomes. Finally, an instrument that has been used for clinical instruction, as well as in supervision and single-case research, the *focal conflict model*, is presented in depth.

PSYCHODYNAMIC SOCIAL WORK

PART 1

The Psychodynamic Perspective

1

Enter Freud:
Psychodynamic Thinking and Clinical Social Work

PSYCHOANALYTIC THEORY IS NOT a unified body of knowledge; rather, it is composed of multiple theories, models, and schemata pertaining to development, psychopathology, and clinical method and technique. It is a literature of vast scope whose evolution now spans more than a century. In this chapter a concise history of psychoanalytic and psychodynamic ideas and their gradual incorporation into the mainstream of clinical social work theory and practice is offered. Beginning with the contributions of important social work theorists such as Richmond, Garrett, Hollis, Smalley, Robinson, Taft, Perlman, as well as the more recent contributions of Strean, the Blancks, Sanville, Applegate, and others, the historical relationship between psychoanalysis and clinical social work is assayed. This history is actually fraught with points of convergence and dissonance, and important issues and controversies surrounding the use of dynamic principles in assessment and treatment is, accordingly, a principal chapter theme. In addition to a brief review of significant controversies within the psychoanalytic movement and among intellectual historians, several key criticisms of the psychodynamic perspective (e.g., that it is not an empirically valid body of knowledge, is antifeminist, pathologizes clients, and is not sufficiently appreciative of the role of the environment) will be explored.

The historical relationship between clinical social work and psychoanalysis is both fascinating and extremely complex. Classical psychoanalytic theory and, later, ego psychology stand in relation to social work theory in much the same way that the theory of relativity stands in relation to modern-day theoretical physics. In each case the introduction of a new and radical theory has had far-reaching ramifications for the existing framework of knowledge.

It was following Freud's historic 1909 visit to the United States to lecture at Clark University accompanied by then disciples Carl Jung and Sandor Ferenczi that English translations of important early works such as *Three Essays on the*

Theory of Sexuality, The Interpretation of Dreams, and *Studies on Hysteria* became available. Though these early translations of Freud's books and essays, particularly those works translated by American psychiatrist A. A. Brill, were uneven and, "at times, fearfully inaccurate" (Gay 1988:465),[1] their impact was palpable, pervading not only the fields of psychiatry and psychology but also the popular culture.[2] Ideas that a life beneath consciousness might exist, of which an individual may be only dimly aware, or that intrapsychic conflict was inherent in mental life, that past experiences might continue to influence the present, and that passionate expressions of love might conceal equally passionate feelings of hatred seemed both powerful and transformative. They were especially appealing to American intellectuals, such as G. Stanley Hall (Freud's host at Clark University), who found that Freud's radical theories of human development and psychopathology offered a fresh, indeed daring, alternative to the prevailing thought in the social and behavioral sciences.

PSYCHOANALYSIS AND CLINICAL SOCIAL WORK

By the early part of the twentieth century social work practice was already showing signs of a bifurcation between clinical and macro-level practice traditions, a state of affairs that appears, if anything, to have become even further entrenched as we enter the second century of modern social work practice.[3] On the one hand, the experience of "friendly visitors" with the charity organization societies in both England and America in latter part of the nineteenth century had gradually evolved into an early, though fundamentally nondynamic form of social casework, largely owing to the pioneering work of Mary Richmond (Richmond, 1899, 1917). A coterminous development was the settlement house movement, which offered social work interventions at the level of neighborhood and community and has spawned such developments as social group work and what, in more contemporary patois, is known as community practice. The settlement house movement tended to place a greater emphasis on the responsibility of society for the conditions in which people lived, a position that has given rise to social work's advocacy of social reform and social legislation as well as to various preventive programs (Goldstein 1995).

The earliest historical influence of psychoanalytic ideas on the social work field seems to have occurred in the late 1920s. Strean (1993, 1996) observes that the professional climate in social work favored the introduction of social work ideas at this time, inasmuch as caseworkers had begun to recognize the limitations of advice giving, moral suasion, and manipulation of the environment in their work with clients.[4] Beginning in the early 1920s, with the advent of the child guidance movement, and work with such clinical populations as the shell-shocked victims of World War I, the context for social work practice shifted dramatically. Many social workers began to work in hospitals and clinics, thereby extending their exposure to psychiatrists and psychiatric thinking (Goldstein 1995). In fact, the influence of psychiatric thinking so dominated social work during this period that it led one historian to describe it as the "Psychiatric Deluge" (Woodroofe 1971). Freud's theories, in particular, stimulated great interest among social workers, a significant number of whom sought psychoanalytic treatment, thereby initiating a trend that endured for several generations.

Psychoanalytic theory placed emphasis on the individual and imputed meaning to pathological symptoms. It presumed the existence of an unconscious and of universal experiences in early childhood development (such as the Oedipus complex) that, failing adaptive resolution, might persist into later development and serve as a basis for psychopathology. It also provided a model for understanding the tendency of individuals to translocate and to repeat early childhood conflicts in adult relationships, even extending to the client-worker relationship (Goldstein 1995; Woods and Hollis 2000).

Annette Garrett, in a publication that appeared in 1940, became one of the first social work authors to comment on the transformative impact of Freud's work on social work theory and practice. She observed that the concepts of *social diagnosis* and *social treatment,* originally derived from the pioneering work of Mary Richmond, had gradually evolved into *psycho*social diagnosis and *psycho*social treatment. The incorporation of Freudian ideas into social work practice thus enabled social workers to individualize the person-in-environment configuration; each client was regarded as having a unique set of personal experiences, specific strengths and weaknesses peculiar to him or her, and highly individualized, idiosyncratic ways of operating in the world (Strean 1993).

During the past seventy-five years psychoanalysis has exerted a powerful and at times revolutionary influence on the field of clinical social work, a phenomenon paralleled in other social and behavioral sciences. Although it can be argued that the impact of psychoanalytic thinking has pervaded a variety of clinical social work approaches, three that are classic to social casework may illustrate this influence most clearly: the diagnostic or psychosocial school, the functional school, and the problem-solving model.

THE DIAGNOSTIC OR PSYCHOSOCIAL SCHOOL

Mary Richmond, perhaps the best-known exponent of what came to be known as the *diagnostic school*, was the first to articulate the dual focus on *person and environment,* an idea that is arguably as distinctive a feature of contemporary clinical social work practice as it was over eighty-five years ago, when her book *Social Diagnosis* was first published (1917). Guided by sensitivity and compassion, as well as a determined effort to create a scientific approach to the practice of social casework, Richmond's model was, nevertheless, primarily sociological in nature, locating causality in the transactions between clients and their reference groups (Strean 1993, 1996). Oftentimes the focus of the caseworker's interventions involved the very real material needs of clients, although social guidance, child-rearing advice, and other forms of *direct treatment* were also freely proffered. It was Richmond who first differentiated *indirect treatment,* consisting of environmental interventions, from *direct treatment,* the influence of "mind upon mind" (Woods and Hollis 2000).

Although Mary Richmond is often credited with having originated the diagnostic or psychosocial approach to casework, there were a number of other early contributors. Gordon Hamilton, Bertha Reynolds, Charlotte Towle, Fern Lowry, Marion Kenworthy, Betsey Libbey, Annette Garrett (as per above), and Florence Hollis are among those whose teaching and scholarship helped to shape this approach to casework (Hollis 1970).

An important link between psychoanalysis and the psychosocial approach is in the latter's use of Freudian personality theory as a basic organizing framework.[5] According to Hollis (1970:36), dynamic personality theory, augmented by ego psychological principles, provided the most useful approach to an understanding of the individual and his or her relative success or failure in adaptive functioning.

The influence of psychoanalytic theory is especially evident in the psychosocial school's view of diagnosis. Diagnosis is conceived of as having three equally important facets: *dynamic diagnosis,* in which the individual's interplay with others in his or her environment is examined; *etiological diagnosis,* where the focus is on both current and historically remote features of the person-environment matrix; and *classificatory diagnosis,* in which an effort is made to classify various aspects of the individual's functioning, typically including a clinical diagnosis (Hollis 1970:52). Other psychoanalytic ideas, such as resistance, transference, and countertransference, have also been integrated into the psychosocial perspective.

THE FUNCTIONAL SCHOOL

The functional theory of casework, developed by Virginia Robinson and Jessie Taft at the Pennsylvania School of Social Work in the 1930s, was also linked to psychoanalysis. The functionalists, however, rejected the classical psychoanalytic ideas that the psychosocial school had embraced, characterizing them as "mechanistic, deterministic view(s) of man . . . [who is seen as] . . . prey to the dark forces of an unconscious and . . . the harsh restrictive influences of internalized parental dicta in the early years" of development (Smalley 1970:82–83). Freud's disciple, Otto Rank, whose theories emphasized human growth, the development of the self, and the will as a controlling and organizing force, became an important force in functional theory as a member of the teaching faculty at the University of Pennsylvania. Rank's work also emphasized such ideas as the use of relationship to facilitate growth and the significance of time as a factor in the helping process, ideas that Taft and others used as the basis for the functional model.[6] Robinson, in fact, noted that the Rankian concept of the psychoanalytic situation was a dynamic one "in which the patient works out his own "will," his conscious desires and unconscious and unaccepted strivings, against the attitude of the analyst" (Robinson 1930:122). Like Taft and other exponents of the functionalist school, she believed this view of the analytic relationship closely paralleled aspects of the social casework relationship.

One of Rank's unique contributions, according to Smalley, was his theory of birth trauma.[7] "Rank emphasized the development of life fear and death fear out of the birth experience and saw all individuals as experiencing and expressing these two fears throughout life . . . the fear of not living, not experiencing, not realizing potential which may be thought of as the death fear; and the fear of separation, of independent existence outside of the womb" (Smalley 1970:92–93).

Functional theory has also drawn from Erik Erikson's model of psychosocial and psychosexual development and, to some extent, from the work of Karen Horney and Erich Fromm. Although such fundamental tenets of the functional approach as the function of agency and the use of time as a dimension in the casework relationship are not especially psychoanalytic, the emphases on separation and individuation and on developmental crises and adaptations appear to have an unmistakable psychoanalytic cast.

THE PROBLEM-SOLVING MODEL

The problem-solving model was developed by Helen Harris Perlman in the 1950s at the University of Chicago. Perlman's model has been described by one author as an effort to traverse the often contentious debate that had erupted between the functional school and the diagnostic school by the 1950s, although she was largely unsuccessful in achieving this objective (Goldstein 1995:37). Perlman's model of casework is very closely tied to ego psychological theory, and she views the casework process itself as a "parallel to the normal problem-solving efforts of the ego" (1953:308–15). With the use of such concepts as *partializing* (breaking down large problems into smaller, more manageable tasks), Perlman attempted to "translate ego psychology into action principles" (Perlman 1970:135).

The problem-solving model also emphasized the significance of relationship, and Perlman did write of such relational phenomena as transference and countertransference. However, she was always careful to make clear distinctions between casework and depth psychology. Casework always aimed to "maintain the relationship on the basis of reality," to keep client and caseworker firmly anchored in their joint purpose, aware of "their separate and realistic identities," and their goal of achieving "a better adaptation between the client and his current problem-situation" (1957:78). Such goals stand in marked contrast to those of psychoanalysis and psychoanalytic psychotherapy, where there is considerably greater emphasis and attention given to remote or distal causes of intercurrent symptoms and failures in adaptation and to the intrapsychic basis of conflict in general. Furthermore, whereas the transference relationship is promoted in psychoanalysis and in certain psychoanalytic psychotherapies, in the problem-solving approach the effort is "to so manage the relationship and the problem-solving work so as to give minimum excitation to transference" (Perlman 1957).

BEYOND THE CLASSICAL CASEWORK MODELS: CONTRIBUTIONS TO THE EVOLVING RELATIONSHIP BETWEEN PSYCHOANALYSIS AND SOCIAL WORK

Beginning in the early 1960s, important changes both within and outside the social work profession led both to renewed interest in social action and social programming, and to a corresponding deemphasis of social casework's theoretical focus on the individual. The important initiatives of the Kennedy and Johnson administrations, including such programs as Operation Head Start and the War on Poverty, rekindled interest and optimism in the value of macrosystemic approaches to the amelioration of social problems (Goldstein 1995). In such a climate the influence of classical formulations advanced by Richmond, Taft, Perlman, and others waned, a development that may have been accelerated by the publication of a spate of studies questioning the effectiveness of social casework (Mullen, Dumpson and associates 1972; Fischer 1976; Goldstein 1995). At the same time, unfamiliar if not entirely new theoretical systems (e.g., generalist social work practice, behavioral treatment, humanistic-existential therapies, and family systems approaches) were being introduced into graduate social work curricula and, in some cases, simply replacing traditional casework altogether.

During this turbulent period, which seems only to have ended with the unmistakable shift in the political climate and national priorities of the 1980s, psychodynamic ideas, while increasingly unpopular, remained alive at the fringes of social work graduate education. Florence Hollis, in particular, continued to revise and update her classical text on the psychosocial method of casework, *Casework: A Psychosocial Therapy*, and, in consequence, this approach retained a certain vitality that may have been less true of other casework approaches. A few newer authors, most notably Herbert Strean and Gertrude and Rubin Blanck, made important, enduring contributions to the psychodynamic literature during the 1970s and 1980s. Strean and the Blancks began their careers as social work clinicians, but later sought out psychoanalytic training and in so doing represented the vanguard of a new group of deeply committed postgraduate social work clinicians determined to undergo formal psychoanalytic training.[8]

Herbert S. Strean (1931–2001), a practicing clinical social worker and psychoanalyst, was also a full-time graduate social work instructor, director of a psychoanalytic training institute, and the author of some thirty-five books. Although he often wrote for an interdisciplinary audience of social workers, psychologists, and psychiatrists, Strean was deeply committed to clinical social work education and to psychodynamic thinking within a social work tradition. He wrote on a variety of clinical themes and topics: psychoanalytic education and supervision, marriage and marital conflicts, resistance, counterresistance, transference, countertransference, inter alia. Mindful of the critical reception psychodynamic ideas appeared to be generating in the mid-1970s, Strean's book, *Clinical Social Work: Theory and Practice* (1978), attempted to integrate then contemporary social work models and theories into a fundamentally ego psychological framework. The contribution of environmental influences, the use of family assessment and interventions, social systems and role theory, double-bind theory, and other fundamentally nondynamic models and paradigms are acknowledged and incorporated in Strean's work, but not at the expense of the psychodynamic perspective basic to his view of the clinical process. The result was that, even in publications intended for a social work readership, psychoanalytic ideas such as the metapsychological perspectives, the worker-client relationship, the working-through process, and the phenomena of resistance, transference, and countertransference are often highlighted and illustrated with cases extracted from a traditional social work practice context.

Social worker-psychoanalysts Gertrude Blanck (1914–2001) and her husband, Rubin Blanck (1914–1995), like Herbert Strean, also directed an interdisciplinary psychoanalytic training course. They held visiting faculty appointments at Smith College School for Social Work and published five books, the most influential of which was probably *Ego Psychology: Theory and Practice* (1974, 1994). This scholarly work, a detailed discussion and analysis of the conceptual scheme that joins classical psychoanalytic ideas with contemporary ego psychology and object relational concepts, exemplifies the Blancks' talent for intellectually rigorous theory formulation. They paid close attention to the role of early object relationships in the formation of ego development and, after Mahler, emphasized the importance of the differentiation of self from object as a prerequisite for healthy development. Another significant aspect of this work, one that was equally true of their postgraduate teaching, is the ongoing effort to distinguish psychoanalysis as a treatment method from that of psychoanalytic psychotherapy. Inasmuch as many of their students worked in social service agency settings and with clinical populations for whom traditional psychoanalysis would not have been either possible or beneficial, this proved critical. Among the Blancks' unique contributions was their formulation of a *developmental diagnosis*, a diagnostic schema that proved especially successful as a guide to the treatment of the less structured personality (Edward 2002).

Jean Sanville, author of *The Playground of Psychoanalytic Therapy* (1991) and numerous other publications, also served as editor of *Clinical Social Work Journal* for many years. Like Strean and the Blancks, Sanville has maintained close ties to both clinical social work education and the training of psychoanalysts. A frequent visiting instructor at Smith College, she also founded the Institute for Clinical Social Work in California and helped to establish the first psychoanalytic training institute on the West Coast to accept nonmedical applicants. Sanville's publications have focused on a number of themes, including creativity and play, the supervisory relationship, the process of termination, and the sociocultural surround as well as the special challenges of psychoanalytic psychotherapy with children.

Other contemporary figures have also played a prominent part in further defining and distilling psychoanalytic ideas and applying them to social work practice.

Jeffrey Applegate, author of a number of articles and coauthor (with Jennifer Bonovitz) of *The Facilitating Partnership* (1995), has presented key Winnicottian ideas about development and treatment within a clinical social work treatment context. Eda Goldstein has published an ego psychology text (1995) and a more recent one on object relations and self psychology (2001), both of which approach psychodynamic theories from within an explicit framework of social work practice. Still others include Carolyn Saari (1991, 2002), whose published work has focused on narratology, constructivism and the concept of the environment; Judith Mishne (1983, 1986, 2002), a self psychologist and child and adolescent psychotherapist who has also written on transcultural psychotherapy; and Joseph Palombo (2001), whose recent work explores the relationship of neurocognitive deficits to selfobject disorders in children and adolescents.

CRITIQUES OF THE PSYCHOANALYTIC PERSPECTIVE

EARLY CONTROVERSIES IN THE PSYCHOANALYTIC MOVEMENT

Psychoanalysis and its derivative forms (principally psychodynamically oriented treatment approaches) are no strangers to controversy. Indeed, beginning with Freud's earliest forays into the treatment of hysteria in the late nineteenth century, disbelief, denial, dismissal, and condemnation have been familiar if unwelcome companions at nearly every juncture. As one of Freud's biographers has noted, "In developing the theory of psychoanalysis, Freud was to have more enemies, and fewer friends, than he wanted. Failure was probable; hostility and ridicule were virtually certain" (Gay 1988:55–56). Examples abound: Freud's legendary clash with his former mentor and professor, Theodore Meynert, in large measure occasioned by Freud's interest in the use of hypnosis (a method he soon abandoned) in work with hysterical patients, the antagonistic reception of the Viennese medical community to the 1895 publication of Freud and Breuer's *Studies on Hysteria*, a work generally acknowledged as the first *psychoanalytic* publication (Jones 1953:252–53), and a similarly icy reception to the claim of a sexual etiology to the neuroses, are but a few among many such early examples.

As what is now referred to as *classical psychoanalytic theory*—the work of Freud and such early adherents as Karl Abraham, Sandor Ferenczi, Otto Fenichel, Hans Sachs, and Carl Jung—gradually took shape, incrementally, over a period of forty-some years, there were also celebrated controversies from *within* the psychoanalytic movement. Several prominent followers of Freud, among them Carl Jung, Alfred Adler, and Otto Rank, eventually broke with Freud. Jung disputed a cornerstone of Freudian theory, the central role of sexuality, en route to developing a comprehensive psychology of his own, which he later termed *analytical psychology*. Adler, whose theory was "essentially one of the ego" (Jones 1955:131), rejected Freud's theory of the *Oedipus*, and placed correspondingly greater emphasis on the distribution of power in relationships, popularizing the concepts of *inferiority complex* and *superiority complex*. Rank's efforts to shorten the length of psychoanalyses through *active therapy*,[9] in combination with the publication of *The Trauma of Birth* (see note 6, this chapter) brought him, also, into conflict with Freud.

RECENT CONTROVERSIES INVOLVING FREUD'S LEGACY

Has psychoanalysis remained as controversial, some sixty-five years after Freud's death, as it appears to have been during his lifetime? After all, one might argue, psychoanalysis has gradually been expropriated, absorbed, and popularized, pervading both our intellectual life and our common culture. And yet such signal psychoanalytic precepts as dynamic motivation, unconscious fantasies, oedipal desire, separation anxiety, or the notion of intrapsychic conflict and defense have remained as disquietingly powerful in contemporary times as they were for Freud's detractors and adversaries in the last century. Two recent examples may serve as an illustration.

In 1984, in a book titled *The Assault on Truth: Freud's Suppression of the Seduction Theory*, Jeffrey Masson argues that Freud's "abandonment" of the seduction theory was a deliberate, scientifically dishonest move calculated to end the isolation from the Viennese medical establishment that resulted from his revolutionary ideas. Masson's controversial thesis soon led to a contentious debate, waged not only in the professional journals but also in the popular media (Malcolm 1983). According to Peter Gay, an intellectual historian and psychoanalyst, Masson's argument is "preposterous" for two reasons. Not only did Freud, in subsequent years, continue to propose equally radical ideas, but he also acknowledged, though painfully, that real seduction and rape were indisputable facts in at least a few cases of which he had direct knowledge (Gay 1988:751).

An even more recent example involves the exhibition "Freud, Conflict and Culture," originally scheduled for display at the Library of Congress in the fall of 1996 but subsequently postponed until 1998 because of the controversy that erupted after the exhibition was first announced.[10] Soon after the Library of Congress made public its plans for the exhibition in 1995, a group of approximately fifty researchers, several of whom had consistently challenged fundamental psychoanalytic premises as well as Freud's status in intellectual history, forwarded a petition to the director of the library. This petition requested the appointment of a legislative attorney to ensure full representation of the petitioners' "collective interests and concerns" so that the exhibition would "suitably portray the present status of knowledge and adequately reflect the full spectrum of informed opinion about Freud's contributions" (Swales et al. 1995). It was widely perceived as a coercive effort to influence the library and the very nature of the exhibition, and there were prominent protests, counterpetitions, and public debates. Under such pressure the library initially announced plans to cancel the exhibition altogether, but reversed itself shortly thereafter, and "Freud: Conflict and Culture" was finally displayed in Washington as well as in a number of other public venues in the United States and abroad.

CONTEMPORARY CRITIQUES OF PSYCHOANALYSIS
AND PSYCHODYNAMIC IDEAS

In this section we will consider carefully four rather specific criticisms of psychodynamic thinking: "Psychoanalysis is not empirically valid," "Psychoanalysis is antifeminist," "Psychoanalysis pathologizes clients," and "Psychoanalysis is not sufficiently appreciative of the role of the environment."

CRITICISM 1: "PSYCHOANALYSIS IS NOT EMPIRICALLY VALID"

Psychoanalysis, while employing empirical methods, is not an experimental science, an apparent dissymmetry that forms the basis of the "peculiar and complex" relations that have existed between psychoanalysis and normative science since Freud's earliest psychoanalytic publications (Galatzer-Levy et al. 2000). Freud, in fact, was very eager to link his clinical findings with the quantitative science that prevailed in late nineteenth-century Europe (Galatzer-Levy et al. 2000; Holtzman 1998; Sulloway 1979; Jones 1953), associated with such scientists as von Helmholtz, Fechner, and Brucke.[11] Freud's attempts, however, to treat psychoanalytic data analogously to findings from the biological sciences, as well as his efforts to create a psychological theory modeled after the physical sciences, were less than successful (Galatzer-Levy et al. 2000).

Contemporary psychoanalytic investigations are, with some notable exceptions, principally not quantitative in nature. Some have argued that relative absence of experimental data in psychoanalytic research, the failure to present psychoanalytic data in an experimentally testable form equivalent, for example, to data derived from other nondynamic forms of therapy, invalidates it as an empirical discipline. The formidable methodological challenges involved in testing findings that possess the complexity and subtlety of psychoanalytic data aside, this view of empirical science rests upon a narrow and restrictive definition. In fact, its stringent application would also exclude such sciences as astronomy and geology, both of which also depend greatly on the observational method and the "conceptualizing (of) relations among phenomena that are observed to vary" (Holtzman 1998:5). Nevertheless, in consequence of its predominately qualitative and nonexperimental research base, psychoanalysis, as a clinical discipline, has been disadvantaged in a scientific community that has placed a disproportionate value on *nomothetic* research—research typically grounded in an epistemology of positivism and designed to confirm or refute a hypothetical proposition (Cournoyer and Powers 2002). This disadvantage has been magnified to some extent by the fact that the effects of other therapeutic approaches, such as cognitive or behavioral therapy, are readily measured and their efficacy supported by quantitative methods. Although the nature of psychoanalytic findings is indisputably empirical, the absence of data specifically in support of the claims of the therapeutic efficacy of psychoanalytic and psychodynamic treatments has probably led to a decline in their status.[12]

The picture, however, is far from bleak. In their recent review of research on psychoanalytic treatment, Galatzer-Levy and his colleagues reviewed most of the important studies undertaken by psychoanalysts and other researchers examining clinical process and therapeutic efficacy over the last half century. They examined a variety of research studies, including extensive large-scale investigations, methodologies for investigating psychoanalytic and psychodynamic processes, and the single case method. Large-scale studies, such as the Menninger Foundation Psychotherapy Research Project (Wallerstein 1986), the Boston Psychoanalytic Institute Studies (Kantrowitz, Katz, and Paolitto 1990a, b), the Anna Freud Center Study (Fonagy and Target 1994, 1996; Target and Fonagy 1994), the New York Psychoanalytic Institute Studies (Erle 1979; Erle and Goldberg 1984), and the Columbia Psychoanalytic Center Research Investigation (Weber, Bachrach, and Solomon 1985a, b), despite certain methodological limitations, tended to provide support for the belief that psychoanalytic treatment may be an effective treatment for certain clients. Studies that examined psychodynamic and psychoanalytic processes, such as the Core Conflictual Relationship Theme Method (Luborsky and Crits-Cristoph 1990), the Patient's Experience of the Relationship with the Therapist (Gill and Hoffman 1982), and Control Mastery Theory (Weiss, Sampson, and Mount Zion Psychotherapy Research Group 1986), also demonstrated qualified support for assumptions about the efficacy and action of psychoanalytic treatment. However, the most promising methodology for investigating psychoanalytic and psychodynamic processes and effects, in their view as well as that of the author's, appears to be that of the single-case study.

Single-case research is actually a variant of a well-established psychoanalytic convention, the *narrative case study*, first used to advantage by Breuer and Freud in their clinical case illustrations of hysteria (Breuer and Freud 1893–95). The narrative case study is defined as the intensive examination of an individual unit (although such units need not be limited to individual persons). Such case studies are also held to be *idiographic* (i.e., the unit of study is the individual unit); multiple variables are investigated; and generalization is fundamentally analytic, inferential, and impressionistic rather than statistical and probabilistic (Brandell and Varkas 2001). Case studies may also serve a variety of purposes: they may be descriptive, predictive, generative, explanatory, or used for hypothesis testing (Runyan 1982) and, in these ways, are especially well-suited for the clinical complexities of the analytic clinical situation. When characterized by a careful design describing what the investigation is intended to accomplish, the methods to be used, the situation under study, the logic that connects observations with conclusions, and criteria for determining to what degree that link is satisfactory, such single-case investigations can culminate in empirically rigorous, meaningful research on a range of treatment variables (Brandell and Varkas 2001; Galazter-Levy et al. 2000).

CRITICISM 2: "PSYCHOANALYSIS IS ANTIFEMINIST"

It is of historical interest that among the academics and physicians in attendance at Freud's 1909 Clark University lectures was none other than Emma Goldman, the anarchist and advocate of free love whose notoriety made her presence worthy of a newspaper story in the Boston papers the following day. What is of even greater interest is that Goldman counted herself "among his (Freud's) most ardent admirers," later publishing a brief essay "specifying the affinity between psychoanalysis and feminism: the recognition of sexuality as preeminent in the makeup of women as well as men" (Buhle 1998:1–2). But Goldman's high valuation of psychoanalysis and of Freud was not predicated solely on the analytic emphasis on sexuality and the sexual emancipation it appeared to promise women in particular. She also regarded psychoanalysis and feminism as irrepressible forces "standing together on the brink of modernity," both of which promised a "definitive break with past endeavors" in the historical quest for female subjectivity (ibid).

The views of early feminists such as Goldman notwithstanding, psychoanalytic theory has, with at least the same frequency, been reviled for its supposed depiction of women as psychologically and morally inferior to men and for its oppressive gender-role prescriptions. Beginning with the publication of Betty Friedan's manifesto of liberation, *The Feminine Mystique* (1963), psychoanalysis was soon identified as a principal agent of women's oppression, and Freud was vilified as one of the twentieth century's most notorious misogynists. By the early seventies psychoanalysis had been described derisively as "our modern Church" (Firestone 1970:42) and as a "magic formula more powerful than any fence" (Figes 1970:133), and Freud had been called "the strongest individual counterrevolutionary force in the ideology of sexual politics" (Millett 1970:178; Buhle 1998).

At the heart of these spirited attacks were several important issues. Classical psychoanalysis, in the first place, provided an incomplete and unsatisfying picture of female psychosexual development, particularly in light of the far more comprehensive perspective it offered in regard to the psychosexual development of males. Freud, for example, had suggested in "On Narcissism" (1914) that early in development infants of both sexes love themselves and the caregiver on whom they are dependent for feeding and protection, although the paths of little girls and boys soon diverge. Males renounce their self-love, instead seeking out love objects of the attachment or anaclitic variety; whereas an innate, biologically driven, narcissistic propensity guides females to desire male love objects who desire *them*. In other words, according to Freud, the renunciation of infantile narcissism fails to take place developmentally for most women, thus permitting them to retain a certain "self-contentment and inaccessibility" (Freud 1914a:89).

The concept of penis envy, linked to several essays of Freud (e.g., 1914a; 1917; 1919; 1920) and most clearly enunciated in "Some Psychical Consequences of the Anatomical Distinction Between the Sexes" (1925), was also elaborated on by early disciples such as Karl Abraham (1922). Penis envy, as formulated by Freud, is a natural consequence of the "momentous discovery" that boys possess an external sexual organ that girls do not, and they immediately "recognize it as the superior counterpart" of their own clitoris (Freud 1925:252). The psychical sequelae of this narcissistic injury, Freud advised, are "various and far-reaching." They include a sense of inferiority, jealousy, and a loosening of the girl's tie to her mother as a love object principally owing to the latter's being held responsible for the girl's "castration." Ultimately, Freud proclaims that the psychologically and socially adaptive substitution of the wish for a penis with the wish for a child, coextensive with the girl's psychic shift to father as her love object, makes possible the development of true femininity.

It is in this same essay that Freud declares females to possess an inherently weaker superego owing to the fact that their resolution of the oedipal dilemma can never be analogous to that of the male, in whom castration anxiety (sexual guilt) ushers in the formation of the superego. "Their superego," he states, "is never so inexorable, so impersonal, so independent of its emotional origins as we require it to be in men" (ibid:258). This was a view of women as both anatomically inferior and psychologically and morally deficient. In fact, the meaning of these distinctions even extends to the goals of psychoanalytic work, according to Freud. In one of his last essays, "Analysis Terminable and Interminable," Freud avers that the goal of psychoanalysis for male patients is the further development of their capacities, sexual or otherwise, although for female patients the goal is resignation to their deficiencies (Buhle 1998).

In discussing Freud's views of feminine development and female sexuality, one must be careful to take note of the fact that Freud himself seemed less than fully satisfied with his understanding of women, whose sexual life he once described as a "dark continent for psychology" (1925:212). Later in this essay, ("Anatomical Distinctions") he acknowledges that his ideas about female sexual development are only valuable to the degree that "my findings, which are based on a handful of cases, turn out to have general validity and to be typical" (258). And finally, he cautions readers at the conclusion of the chapter on femininity in

the *New Introductory Lectures* (1933), "If you want to know more about femininity, enquire from your own experiences of life, or turn to the poets, or wait until
science can give you" better answers (135).

A number of psychoanalysts, many of them women, began in the 1920s to
challenge Freud's conclusions about the nature of femininity as well as the biological determinism in which these suppositions were rooted. One of his earliest
critics, Karen Horney, was perhaps the first to openly assert that Freud's ideas
about psychosexual development and femininity were tainted by virtue of their
phallocentrism. Indeed, Horney complained, this masculine perspective seemed
to predominate in psychoanalytic scholarship, thus leading to a distorted interpretation of female psychology (Horney 1926; Buhle 1998). As early as 1922, at a
meeting of the International Psycho-Analytical Congress, Horney took exception to the pivotal significance of penis envy, declaring instead that it represented
merely a transitory jealousy, one that, in the outstanding majority of cases, possessed no lasting developmental significance (Horney 1924; Buhle 1998). Ultimately Horney articulated a model of female development that was at fundamental variance with Freud's classical schema. Horney's theory, which gradually
took shape between the early 1920s and the middle 1930s, posits female sexuality
as a "primal, biological principle" (Horney 1967 [1924]:65; Muller 1932) that, furthermore, requires no shift from clitoral to vaginal erotism. The vagina, Horney
asserted, was always the seat of pleasurable sensations, the clitoris far less
strongly cathected with libido from day one.[13] Horney also hypothesized a basic
male envy of the female capacity for reproduction and disputed Freud's claim
that the wish for a baby represented a compromise solution to the girl's inability
to acquire a penis. Motherhood, she announced, represented a psychological
bedrock of sorts, and then hypothesized the existence of a corresponding biological principle, an instinct for procreation.

Later, in the mid-1930s, Horney attributed increasing significance to environmental forces in the shaping of the personality and, in particular, the course of
female development. She, along with like-minded colleagues such as Clara
Thompson and Erich Fromm, came to represent the *culturalist* tradition in psychoanalysis, gradually setting aside her ideas about innate biological impulses in
favor of environmental influences (Horney 1951; Buhle 1998). Horney was influenced in this to a considerable degree by Harry Stack Sullivan, whose early
emphasis on object relations in his theory of personality development furnished
her with a framework for her most radical assertions about the nature of femininity. Horney's final position on the topic, one that defined the culturalist
school of psychoanalysis, was that femininity, as a product of culture, does not
as such exist. What Freud has termed *feminine masochism* (which he and Helene
Deutsch had assumed to be a primal, biologically determined aspect of female

development), feelings of inferiority, dependency, indeed neurosis itself—none of these were immutable but rather culture specific (Buhle 1998).

There are a number of other feminists, both academicians and psychoanalysts, whose contributions to the study of femininity and female psychosexual development are judged to be significant. Among them are Jane Sherfey (1966), Natalie Shainess (1975), Jean Strouse (1974), Juliet Mitchell (1974), and Nancy Chodorow (1978, 1989), though arguably the most influential member of this group is Jean Baker Miller, who, like Horney, was also heavily influenced by Sullivanian ideas. Baker Miller's book, *Toward a New Psychology for Women* (1976) was instrumental in launching what has been termed the *self-in-relation* model, which has become an important model for understanding women's development. Self-in-relation theory has, inter alia, emphasized the importance of the original mother-daughter relationship and such relational phenomena as affiliativeness, nurturance, empathy, and compassion. Baker and her colleagues believe that empathy, in fact, serves as a central organizer or structure of the female personality, explaining a great deal about both normality and dysfunction in the lives of women. While Freud's Oedipus may have continued salience as a model for illuminating the development of males, advocates of self-in-relation theory, continuing in part along a pathway first established by Horney, argue that an entirely new model is required to make sense of female development.

Is psychoanalysis antifeminist? If the answer rests on the premise that there have been no significant psychoanalytic contributions to this issue since 1930, one would have to respond in the affirmative. On the other hand, as I have shown, there is a wealth of psychoanalytic and psychodynamic literature that challenges Freud's schemata regarding femininity and female psychosexual development. If one takes into account this voluminous literature, the illusion of clarity disappears. In fact, many contemporary psychoanalysts would now assert that psychoanalytic theories of development, as they are currently conceived, are decidedly *not* antifeminist. Indeed, feminist writers such as Juliet Mitchell have argued for some time that psychoanalysis is an indispensable tool and, somewhat along the lines of Emma Goldman and her contemporaries, an instrument of liberation rather than one of oppression.

CRITICISM 3: "PSYCHOANALYSIS PATHOLOGIZES CLIENTS"

In recent years the broad appeal of what is termed the "strengths perspective" in social work education and practice is attested to not only by its rapid incorporation into our practice and scholarly literature but also our professional lexicon. Although advocates of the strengths perspective readily acknowledge that the principle of "building on clients' strengths" is neither new nor novel, their rendering of the concept is described as "a dramatic departure from conventional social work practice" (Saleebey 2002:1). Declaring that many such earlier claims to build on the strengths of clients evince little more than professional dishonesty, Saleebey proceeds to discuss what distinguishes a contemporary strengths perspective from its precursors:

Strengths

- It has a new lexicon. Terms such as *empowerment, membership, resilience, healing* and *wholeness, dialogue* and *collaboration,* and *suspension of disbelief* are used to highlight the worker's "appreciation of the assets" of the clients with whom she or he works.
- There is an abiding focus on the clients' personal narratives and the worker's response to them. It is not only the worker's capacity to listen, but to listen for the client's strengths in surmounting adversity and misfortune that will pave the way for "transformation and growth."
- Trauma and abuse, illness, handicaps, and other personal struggles may reflect injury but can also serve as sources of challenge and opportunity. Workers must be ever vigilant that they may help clients to discover and use to greater advantage existing resources, strengths, and capabilities.
- The work is always collaborative, and the real expertise resides in the client. The worker is a collaborator or consultant who may be a source of some specialized knowledge but has by no means cornered the market on wisdom (Saleebey 2002:1).

Contrasting the strengths model with a "pathology model," further distinctions are made. These include the view of treatment as being "possibility focused" rather than "problem focused" and that personal accounts and narratives are viewed as a route to knowing and appreciating the person from her or his own unique perspective as opposed to being greeted with professional skepticism and used diagnostically. Moreover, in contradistinction to the traditional model, which assumes that pathology limits choices, personal development, and so forth, the strengths perspective leaves such choices and possibilities open. Although psychoanalytic theories are not always named specifically in these discussions, at times they "have been criticized for placing too great an emphasis on client weaknesses, such as a client's problem or abnormality" (Greene 2002:15–16).

Insofar as psychoanalysis and psychodynamic thinking seem to have been implicated in this critique, or at least to embody the characteristics of a pathology-based or deficit model, further examination seems warranted. In my opinion several contemporary developments argue against the assumption of legitimacy of such unqualified claims against psychoanalysis. The first development is the gradual ascendancy of the "two-person" model in psychoanalysis and psychoanalytic psychotherapy. Although traditional (classical) psychoanalysis was

nomena), it is possible to speak of a "constancy principle" which regulates the distribution of energy in an individual [the economic hypothesis in Freud's metapsychology].

3. The origin of every human activity can be traced ultimately to the demands of drive.

4. There is no inherent object, nor preordained tie to the human environment; the object is "created" by the individual out of the experience of drive satisfaction and frustration (Greenberg and Mitchell 1983).

Social ties are of secondary importance in such a framework, and then only insofar as others may be able to assist the individual in discharging drive tensions. Although Freud continued to emphasize the role of constitution in favor of environmental forces in his developmental theory, he assigned a far greater role to object relations in *The Ego and the Id* (Freud 1923). This essay, a critically important work that signaled Freud's "strategy of accommodation," was initially undertaken as a response to the dissension of Alfred Adler and Carl Jung (Greenberg and Mitchell 1983).

It is with the contribution of the culturalists, theorists such as Horney, Fromm, Sullivan, ego psychologists like Hartmann and Erikson, and exponents of the "middle tradition," most notably Winnicott, that important shifts in the role imputed to the extramural environment became more obvious. Others, such as Spitz and Mahler, early developmentalists whose clinical work and research investigations focused on infant-mother interactions and pathology, also figure prominently in the evolving status of environment as it was represented in the psychoanalytic theories of the 1940s, 1950s, and 1960s.

Environment is, of course, a difficult concept to define inasmuch as it represents a very large and complex domain. Object relations theorists, for example, may tend to characterize environment as it is represented by the external or real interactions with other individuals, but even then may emphasize fantasied relations with objects and their internal representations as having equal importance to actual object relations. Ego psychologists such as Hartmann describe the environment in rather broad terms, attributing influence to it but almost invariably linking it to the reality principle without elucidating its qualities or precise nature.[17] Margaret Mahler, a developmentalist whose separation-individuation theory (discussed in chapter 3) exerted such a profound influence, struggled to portray relational concepts and the interactions of infants with caregivers in drive psychology terms, leading one author to depict her as an "accommodation" strategist (Greenberg and Mitchell 1983). Mahler's observations of mother-infant interaction, too, seem to have been modified to fit theoretical assumptions, so that infants were described as "autistic" and as needing to emerge from a symbiotic orbit with their mothers en route to physical separation and concomitant psychic individuation. Such ideas, however, are not well-supported by current infant research.

Winnicott (also discussed in chapter 3) is generally acknowledged as having been among the first psychoanalytic theorists to devote serious attention to the role of environment. His view of the environment, which may have presaged ideas associated with constructivism and intersubjectivity theory (Saari 2002), is notable for its designation of a transitional realm of experience serving to link objective, reality-based experiences with those that are exclusively subjective.

Others have shaped the contemporary psychoanalytic perspective on the environment as well. These include Bowlby (1969), who systematically investigated attachment phenomena, Loewald (1980), whose work attempted to explicate the complexities of the ego in its commerce with external reality, and Kohut (1977) and his followers, whose self psychological formulations attributed considerable importance to the reality dimension of thwarted self/selfobject relations.[18] More recently, psychoanalytic researchers such as Stern (1985) and Emde (1992) have, through systematic observation, offered views of environmental phenomena that seem far less encumbered by theory than Mahler's studies at the Masters Children's Center in the 1960s.

It may be rather optimistic to conclude that more recent psychoanalytic formulations have satisfactorily elucidated the role of environment in development or with respect to the process of treatment. However, at the same time, it does not overstate the case to observe that cumulative evidence exists for both greater interest in the person-environment matrix among many analytic authors and even a willingness to consider different theoretical positions (e.g., social constructivism) in the quest for improved understanding.

A RELATIONSHIP REAPPRAISED

As psychoanalysis celebrates its centenary, much has changed. Multiple psychoanalytic psychologies, each with its own vision of human development, psychopathology, and the treatment process, now stand alongside Freud's classical formulations. Challenges made to the empirical basis of psychoanalytic treatment and its formulations about development and dysfunction have spawned a new and more promising body of research. The shift from a one-person to a two-person psychology, the gradual ascendancy of relational ideas, as well as interest and sensitivity in the environmental surround, have likewise been momentous developments. Once the dominant force in American psychiatry, psychoanalysis has, as a medical specialty, all but disappeared, even as it has been "feminized"

with the gradual introduction of social workers and psychologists to its professional ranks.[19]

These are a few of the more significant changes that mark the beginning of the
second century of psychoanalytic thought. Social work too has changed in many
ways since its earliest attempts to employ psychoanalytic concepts in better
understanding and serving its clientele. Although psychoanalytic ideas once held
a revered status among clinical social workers and casework theorists, this has
been altered by the introduction of newer nondynamic treatments, the changing
requirements of the agencies and clients we serve, and an overriding focus on
short-term engagement, to name but several influences. Perhaps it is time for a
reappraisal of psychoanalysis and what it may offer the social work clinician. In
the chapters that follow both the rationale and formula for such a rapprochment
are presented in detail.

2

Psychoanalytic Theories of Development and Dysfunction: Classical Psychoanalytic Theory

SINCE FREUD'S INTRODUCTION of the genetic principle—that the past persists into the present—psychoanalytic theorists have emphasized different aspects of development in childhood and adolescence. In this chapter and the one that follows, various psychoanalytic conceptions of development (Freud's theory of libidinal development, Erikson's epigenetic theory, Bowlby's attachment theory, Mahler's separation-individuation theory, Sullivan's interpersonal theory, Winnicott's object relations model, Kohut's selfobject theory, inter alia) are presented. Inasmuch as all later psychoanalytic theories of development are derived at least in part from Freud's original ideas, the principal focus of this chapter will be classical psychoanalytic conceptions of development, with other developmental frameworks, schemata, and theories to be explored in chapter 3.

Alongside psychoanalytic theories of development are corresponding psychodynamic conceptions of psychopathology. Because psychoanalytic theories, unlike other nondynamic theories of human development, have relied considerably upon reconstructed data obtained from the psychoanalyses of adults,[1] dynamic ideas about psychopathology, somewhat akin to the double helix structure of DNA, have been historically difficult to extricate from dynamic conceptions of development. Accordingly, these two chapters have been organized in an integrative fashion, so that developmental ideas and conceptions of psychopathology do not need to be artificially separated.

Although there are significant differences between the various theories of psychopathology presented here, each appears to be rooted in Freud's dictum that we are all located, inescapably, somewhere on a continuum that runs from the normal to the psychotic. Historically, psychodynamic theorists and practitioners have been less interested in the categorization of mental illness per se than they have been in understanding its origins, which are generally presumed to involve both proximal or intercurrent factors as well as distal events and scenarios from childhood. That each life is also a story from which important meanings may be extrapolated, decoded, and ultimately understood remains the essence of any psychodynamic understanding of psychopathology. With this in mind, widely divergent psychodynamic ideas regarding intrapsychic conflicts and defenses, neurosis, disorders of character, trauma, and psychosis will also be considered in these two chapters.

FOUNDATIONS OF THEORETICAL PSYCHOANALYSIS

Sigmund Freud (1856–1939) was a Viennese neurologist whose pioneering studies of hysteria, obsessional illness, and other obscure disorders of unknown etiology led him from the practice of neurology to the creation of a new form of treatment based on the investigation of the individual sufferer's mental life, psychoanalysis. Freud's discovery that certain mental illnesses occurred when the sufferer's personality was permeated by the intrusion of powerful and mysterious impulses from deep within the psyche was a radical one and placed him at odds with explanations derived from traditional psychological theories. At one time Freud thought these mysterious impulses were delayed reactions to traumas—in particular, sexual traumas—that had been experienced in early childhood and subsequently dissociated. He soon discovered, however, that these mysterious impulses were not necessarily the reactions of individuals to untoward events of childhood; instead, they were expressions of instinctual drives at the core of the psyche.[2] Normally these instinctual forces are repressed, Freud wrote, but in neurosis they rise up menacingly like demonic forces that have been awakened from the deep. A whole variety of neurotic symptoms, including the hysterical paralyses, amnesias, obsessions, and phobias could be seen as the battleground where the forces of the invading instinctual drives became locked in combat with the defending forces of the embattled personality.

Freud devoted his entire professional life to the study of these invading instinctual forces: their origins in the mind and their influence on mental life. He gradually began to think of the mind as an organization of hierarchical mental systems in which higher systems (i.e., those associated with mature development) regulate the activity of lower systems, which are more primitive. Instinctual forces, he believed, emanated from the unconscious (later, the id), often portrayed as the great darkness at the center of psychic life. He struggled to identify the elemental instinctual forces, to trace their development, and to understand their influence not only on the individual but also on the cultural life of humankind. During his career Freud continually modified his investigative-therapeutic techniques, writing extensively about his discoveries. These discoveries were applied not only to problems of psychopathology and pathogenesis but also to the psychology of dreams, mythology, creativity, and love and to critical issues in anthropology, developmental psychology, religion, and political science.

The structure of Freud's psychoanalytic enterprise was exceedingly complex. Freud conceived of psychoanalysis as a research method, a therapeutic technique, a theory of mental functioning, a theory of psychopathology, and a theory of human development. Each of these theories was intimately connected with all of the others; as a result of clinical discoveries the entire network of theories was continually modified. In the course of his lifetime Freud propounded three theories of the instincts (1905b, 1914b, 1920a), two theories of anxiety (1895a, 1926), and two different models of the mind (1900, 1923).

One of the most important trends in the development of Freudian theory was the progressive expansion of his focus from the study of instinctual drives and of the unconscious to the investigation of higher strata of the mind responsible for processing and regulating the instincts in accordance with realistic and moral considerations. Freud initially was little interested in the higher functions of the mind, which he thought were easily understood through introspection. His expanding clinical experience, however, yielded new data that dramatically disconfirmed this naive assumption. Many patients, he learned, suffered from feelings of guilt of which they were utterly unaware and over which they could exert no control. He also discovered that defensive functioning was largely unconscious. These discoveries revealed that the higher stratum of the mind was largely unconscious and far more complex in its functioning than he had originally recognized. Freud's early work may be characterized as a *psychology of the id* or *depth psychology*, while the later work is usually summarized by the term *ego psychology*.

One of the most interesting features of Freud's scientific style was that he never systematized his ideas or categorically renounced any of his earlier points of view, even when he propounded new ideas that contradicted the old. As a result, his students could hold different "Freudian" positions, each the product of a different phase of Freud's theoretical development.

In the years since Freud's death, psychoanalysts around the world have reshaped Freud's theory in accordance with their own views and empirical data.[3] The result has been a proliferation of psychoanalytic theories, a process paralleled by efforts to identify their most salient common characteristics. Some have paid special attention to the problem of object relations,[4] characterizing these theories as having either a drive/structure or relational/structure basis (Greenberg and Mitchell 1983). Others have grouped psychoanalytic theories into several dominant psychologies or orientations of psychoanalytic thought, which collectively have been referred to as the *four psychologies of psychoanalysis* (Pine

1988). Although each of these psychological systems or orientations—drive theory, ego psychology, object relations theory, and the psychology of the self—has certain distinctive features, it is arguable whether any of the four can be thought of as an essentially separate psychological system (Pine 1990).

CLASSICAL PSYCHOANALYTIC THEORY

Classical psychoanalytic theory derives from the *structural model* or viewpoint of psychoanalysis (Freud 1923). It represents an integration of Freud's theories of instinctual life with his later understanding of the ego and its development. Classical psychoanalytic treatment techniques emphasize self-knowledge or insight as the essential curative factor in psychotherapy. Classical psychoanalytic theory has been refined among each generation of Freud's followers. The most influential proponents of the classical position have included theorists like Otto Fenichel, Anna Freud, Annie Reich, Bertram Lewin, Leo Rangell, Jacob Arlow, and Charles Brenner. Much of the following exposition of classical theory comes directly from Freud. The more contemporary views discussed here derive largely from the views of Brenner and his collaborators. Because Brenner's thinking includes a number of significant modifications, it is often characterized as *contemporary classical* or *contemporary structural theory.*

Psychoanalytic theory posits that the mind is a product of evolutionary development, which functions to ensure adaptation and survival. Mental activity is governed by a fundamental propensity to seek pleasure and avoid pain. Freud called this the *pleasure-unpleasure principle* or sometimes, simply, the *pleasure principle.* It is likely that the pleasure principle is favored by natural selection because pain is associated with injury, which threatens survival, while pleasure is associated with the satisfaction of needs, which promotes survival. Organisms failing to seek pleasure and avoid pain would probably be prone to extinction.

Freud held that the mind is moved to activity by the pressure of genically determined motivations, or *instinctual drives*, whose satisfaction is pleasurable. The automatic pursuit of pleasurable satisfactions is modified by successive developmental experiences in which pleasure seeking is paired with aversive contingencies that provoke affects of unpleasure. This may be exemplified by the normal experiences of socialization in which primitive infantile pleasures are disrupted by parental discipline. Socialization challenges the pleasure principle by creating situations in which the child learns that the pursuit of instinctual pleasures will be met by aversive contingencies such as punishment or the withdrawal of affection. As a result, urges to pursue those instinctual pleasures trigger contradictory affective signals motivating contradictory tendencies toward both approach and avoidance. This approach-avoidance dilemma may be characterized as a condition of psychic conflict.

Psychoanalytic research reveals that mental life is characterized by the pervasive presence of psychic conflict. This is a consequence of the prolonged dependency of the child on his or her parents and, later, the extended family and wider social environment. As a result of this extensive dependency, a child undergoes a protracted process of development and socialization during which many innate desires for pleasurable activity and human relatedness are subject to the idiosyncratic responsiveness and disciplinary reactions of the child's significant caretakers. When these responses to the child's behavior are repetitive and painful, they eventually precipitate psychic conflict in the child who both wants to gratify her pleasurable inclinations yet avoid the painful consequences she expects her behavior to elicit. Psychic conflict challenges the mind to produce new patterns of pleasure seeking that will gratify desires while avoiding or minimizing expected aversive consequences.

Freud discovered that psychological symptoms and character pathologies are complex structures, unconsciously produced by the mind in order to avoid or minimize unpleasure. He characterized these structures as *compromise formations.* The concept of compromise conveys the discovery that psychological symptoms and character problems, however painful or crippling, are intended to achieve a measure of pleasure while averting a measure of pain.

At one time psychoanalysts believed that psychic conflict and compromise formation were features of mental illness, while mental health was characterized by the absence of psychic conflict. Psychoanalytic data, however, have revealed this to be an inaccurate view of mental health. Analysis of the healthy aspects of any individual's mental functioning, such as a happy vocational choice or the pursuit of a pleasurable hobby, regularly reveals the influence of the same desires and conflicts that determine the patient's symptoms and character pathology (Brenner 1982). Freud's own view of normality, along somewhat similar lines, was that it constituted "an ideal fiction," and his preference was to think of pathology and normality as continuous rather than operating in a discrete or mutually exclusive fashion.

CONFLICTS, COMPROMISE FORMATIONS, AND THEIR AFTERMATH

The analysis of compromise formations requires a familiarity with their basic anatomy. Psychoanalytic data reveal that compromise formations regularly include wishes of childhood origin that are associated with, and therefore arouse, aversive affects, such as anxiety and guilt, and psychological defenses that function to reduce the unpleasure of these aversive affects. This section will provide a more detailed description of these components.

WISHES OF CHILDHOOD

Childhood wishes are formed by the interaction of biological and social-experiential factors. In the first days of infancy, biologically rooted needs produce tension states that are devoid of psychological content. These diffuse tensions acquire structure when caretakers provide "experiences of satisfaction" appropriate to the infant's actual need. As a result, diffuse tensions are gradually transformed into wishes to repeat these experiences of satisfaction (Freud 1900). Because these experiences entail specific activities with specific persons, wishes always include representations of these activities and persons. These aspects of the wishes are called their *aims* and *objects*. Every individual's wishes are unique and personal, because they are formed by unique personal experiences.

Classical psychoanalysts have traditionally employed a theory of drives (or instinctual drives) to conceptualize the biological sources of mental life. The psychoanalytic concept of instinctual drives, however, differs from the ethological concept of instincts. In lower animals instincts are "specific action potentials" with genically determined, prestructured patterns of action (Thorpe 1956). The evolution of higher vertebrates, however, includes the progressive substitution of learned behavior for these preprogrammed action patterns (Lorenz 1957 [1937]). In the classical theory, instinctual drives give rise to tensions, but not to specific programs for action. Wishes, which arise when these tensions are structured by experiences of satisfaction, are specific schemata for action. Because they represent the motivational pressure of drives, wishes are also referred to as *drive derivatives*. Drives themselves, however, are not observable and must be regarded as hypothetical constructs (Brenner 1982). Psychoanalytic theory has traditionally employed the related idea of drive energy to conceptualize the driving force of wishes in mental life. Although some contemporary theorists reject these energic ideas (Greenberg and Mitchell 1983; Mitchell 1988; Klein 1976), other psychoanalysts find them useful because they provide a means for conceptualizing the fluctuating intensities with which wishes are invested.

Psychoanalytic theorists since Freud have wrestled with the challenge of identifying and classifying the basic drives. Many different drives have been suggested over the years. Freud himself posited basic drives for sex and self-preservation (Freud 1905b) and, later, for life and for death (1920a). Other theorists hypothesized drives for power and masculinity (Adler 1927), individuation (Jung 1967a,

1967b), aggression (Hartmann, Kris, and Lowenstein 1949), mastery (Hendrick 1942), attachment (Bowlby 1969), effectance (White 1963), safety (Sandler 1960), empathy (Kohut 1971, 1977), and so on. Are all these drives primary motivations, or may some be better understood as derivative expressions of more basic drives? Most theorists believe that science is best served if primary drives can be identified. No scientific consensus about primary motivations to date has been achieved. Most classically trained or traditional analysts, however, recognize the existence of two primary drives: the sexual and the aggressive. This classification is extrapolated from clinical findings in which a certain prominence in the role of sexual and aggressive wishes is regularly revealed in the psychodynamics of symptoms and other pathology.

THE SEXUAL DRIVE

In psychoanalytic thought, sex has a broader meaning than it does in everyday discourse. In psychoanalysis, the word *sexual* connotes a broad range of pleasures that are not necessarily connected with sexual intercourse or even with overtly sexual conduct. The semantic extension of the terms *sex* and *sexuality* highlights the plasticity of the sexual drive and the continuity of sexual development from childhood to adulthood. In accordance with Freud's view, human sexuality does not arise in adulthood or even in adolescence, but in early childhood. Although the sexual wishes of childhood differ from those of adulthood, they are predecessors of adult sexuality, and their motivational influence is discernible when the sexual wishes of adulthood are studied. Although adult sexuality supersedes childhood sexuality, it does not entirely replace it. Childhood sexual wishes are absorbed into the larger network of adult desires and may in some cases substitute for adult desires. Because some childhood sexual wishes are inevitably conflictual, their role in adult sexuality often results in disturbances of sexuality and love life. Adult sexuality, then, cannot be adequately understood without an appreciation of its roots in the sensual desires of childhood.

Childhood sexuality (or *infantile sexuality*) is composed of numerous sensual pleasures, experienced in relation to sensitive parts of the body, such as the skin, the mouth, the anus, and the genitals (the *erogenous zones*). Classical psychoanalysis ultimately developed a phase model to characterize the progression of the libido across these erogenous zones. Freud believed that such libidinal pleasures are initially stimulated by the activities of baby care, such as holding, feeding, touching, and bathing, and then subsequently pursued as ends in their own right. He also believed that the maturation of the sexual drive through childhood entailed a sequenced intensification of oral, anal, and phallic (clitoral) sexual

Stages of Development

wishes (Freud 1905b). The *oral stage*, according to this model, represented the earliest stage of libidinal development, commencing at birth and continuing until approximately eighteen months. Divided by some authors into an *early oral* or *sucking* and a *later oral-sadistic* or cannabalistic stage, this developmental period is dominated by oral needs, perceptions, and expressive modes that are principally focused on the mouth, lips, and tongue. The *anal stage*, which extends from approximately one to three years of age, is initiated by the neuro-muscular maturation of the anal sphincters, an important milestone that permits the infant substantially greater voluntary control over the expulsion or retention of feces. The pleasure associated with anal functions, referred to as *anal erotism*, is experienced both with respect to the infant's capacity for retaining fecal products as well as in offering them to the parents as precious gifts. The *phallic stage* of development, which occurs between the third and sixth years of life, is characterized by a shift in erotic pleasure to the secondary sexual organs— the "discovery" of the penis/vagina—and the associated pleasures of stimulation of the genital region. Often, the child's stimulation of the genitals occurs in connection with unconscious sexual fantasies having to do with the opposite-sex parent (discussed in the following section on the Oedipus complex). Somewhere between five or six and eleven years, children enter a *latency* period during which there is relative quiescence or inactivity of the libidinal drive, a situation that permits a fuller resolution of oedipal or triangular conflicts (Meissner 2000). The final stage of the libido is the *genital stage*, which commences at the onset of puberty and extends to young adulthood. Characterized by continuing maturation of genital/sexual functioning, it is also associated with hormonal and other bodily changes.

OEDIPUS COMPLEX

The Oedipus complex is often referred to as the *nuclear neurosis of childhood* in classical psychoanalytic literature, which attests to its pivotal importance in classical developmental theory. It is thought of as a configuration of psychological forces characterized by the concentration of sexual wishes on one parent, usually of the opposite sex, and the emergence of hostile feelings for the remaining parent, who becomes the child's rival in love. Numerous variations in this typical pattern occur under different familial conditions. Siblings, for example, may become objects of oedipal desire, through early displacement away from a loved parent, or when a child's relations with parents thwart typical oedipal development (Abend 1984; Sharpe and Rosenblatt 1994). The Oedipus complex typically entails feelings of inadequacy, fears of the rival parent's retaliation, and feelings of defeat. Such painful consequences ordinarily motivate a retreat from Oedipal strivings and efforts to limit awareness of persisting Oedipal desires, a process that leads to the latency phase of development, during which sexual wishes are relatively dormant. The Oedipus complex actually consists of both positive oedipal and negative oedipal strivings. The "positive" Oedipus complex reflects the child's wish for a sexual relationship with the opposite-sex parent and a concomitant wish for the demise of the same-sex parent. Due to the child's sense of vulnerability and fundamental ambivalence, however, "negative" oedipal strivings coexist with the positive ones. In effect, the child also desires a sexual union with the parent of the same sex, a wish that gives rise to feelings of rivalry with the opposite-sex parent for the former's affections. In most instances the positive Oedipus complex supersedes the negative Oedipus complex, a condition that traditional psychoanalytic theory stipulates is necessary for the emergence of a heterosexual orientation and cohesive identity in adulthood (Moore and Fine 1990). Sexual desire reemerges as a prominent motivation under the hormonal impetus of adolescence, which introduces the genital pleasure of orgasm. The sexual wishes of adulthood provide a context for the gratification of childhood sexual wishes as well. These are normally evident in the activities of foreplay, which typically include kissing, touching, anal stimulation, and other such features that derive from childhood sensual experience. The influence of infantile sexual wishes is also evident when the person chosen as a partner in adulthood (*object choice*) resembles a primary object of childhood sexuality.

THE AGGRESSIVE DRIVE

Most psychoanalysts recognize that destructive wishes play an important role in mental life. Although there is little dispute about the centrality of aggression, there is widespread disagreement about how best to understand it. Analysts differ on whether the aggressive drive exerts a continuous pressure for discharge, as does the sexual drive, or, whether aggression is a "reactive instinct" (Fine 1975), triggered by frustration, perceived threats, or other noxious conditions. Freud and many of his followers believed that the aggressive drive generates a more or less continuous flow of destructive impulses (Freud 1920a; Hartmann, Kris, and Loewenstein 1949). Friedman and Downey (1995) have recently argued that aggression is related to the organizing influence of male hormones on the fetal brain and is thus a typical feature of male psychology, evidenced by rough-and-tumble play among boys. They suggest that aggression in males may express genically determined strivings for dominance over other males. Other important theorists conceptualize aggression as a reaction to threats or injuries to self-esteem (Kohut 1972; Rochlin 1973), for example, or to physical or mental pain (Grossman 1991), to the experience of "ego weakness" (Guntrip 1968), to the frustration of dependency needs (Fairbairn 1952; Saul 1976), or to "the internally felt experience of excessive unpleasure" (Parens 1979), among others.

Psychological data support the view that hostile aggression is a reaction to pain, frustration, and feelings of endangerment. These mental states can be episodic and situational, but they may also be chronic features of mental life. Traumatic events, for example, often leave emotional "lesions," which give rise to a continuous stream of aggressive wishes. Captain Ahab's unrelenting hatred for Moby Dick, the great whale that bit off his leg, is a good example.[5] All children experience frustrations and disappointments and are prone to feel small, powerless, damaged, or unloved, at least at times. Oedipal strivings, for instance, normally entail feelings of anxiety and guilt, which may persist as feelings of doom or endangerment. The ultimate failure of oedipal ambitions may lead to a feeling of inferiority. In this view, aggression is an inevitable aspect of mental life since everybody suffers to some extent from the painful residue of childhood conflicts. Moreover, this position would attribute a more central role to aggression in mental life in accordance with the degree to which such painful states dominate subjective experience. It may also be observed that people who endure a great deal of pain or frustration as a result of maladaptive compromise formations are also prone to be aggressive as a consequence of their unhappiness. Aggression, therefore, is not only a component of psychic conflict; it may also be a consequence of it.

UNPLEASURES

Psychic conflict occurs when wishes become associated with painful affects of unpleasures in the course of development. Freud (1926) discovered that childhood wishes were regularly associated with anxiety (i.e., fear). He believed that these fears fall into one of four basic categories, each representing a specific danger: loss of the object (mother or primary caretaker), loss of the love of the object, punishment, especially by genital mutilation (castration), and fear of being a "bad" child who deserves to be punished (fear of conscience or superego). When a wish is associated with any of these dangers, the impulse to enact it triggers mounting anxiety. This may reach traumatic levels, if not alleviated by the reassurance of protective caretakers or by independent measures. Over time the child gradually learns various ways to reduce anxiety, called defenses. One important defense is repression, which entails a shifting of attention away from tempting but dangerous wishes. As awareness of the wish diminishes, the associated fear is also reduced. Eventually the child learns to recognize the onset of anxiety and to employ defenses to curtail its development. When anxiety is employed as a signal of danger, it is termed *signal anxiety*. Since signal anxiety involves only a small modicum of anxiety and is therefore not immobilizing, it permits the individual to take some sort of expedient (defensive) action.

Contemporary psychoanalysts have offered many additions and refinements to Freud's 1926 theory. Many theorists have proposed additions to the classification of psychological dangers and anxieties: fear of loss of the personality or "aphanisis" (Jones 1948a [1911]), fear of being eaten (Fenichel 1929), fear of ego disintegration (Freud 1936), engulfment by persecutory objects (Klein 1975 [1946]), ego dissolution (Bak 1943), narcissistic injuries, such as humiliation or disillusionment with an ideal object (Kohut 1966), dissolution of self (Frosch 1970) or fragmentation anxiety (Kohut 1971), separation anxiety (Mahler 1968, 1972), and annihilation anxiety (Hurvich 1989, 1991), to name a few. There is no arbitrary limit to the number of childhood fears that may be identified, although the attribution of certain fears or anxieties to children might represent adultomorphic errors—assumptions made about the psychology of childhood based upon adult psychology. The fear of one's own death, for example, is not regarded as a fear of early childhood inasmuch as young children cannot conceive of death—a final, irreversible ending—in the adult sense of this term. In children's thought, death signifies known dangers, such as bodily damage or separation from loved ones. The study of childhood fears is complicated by the fact that some fears are disguised expressions of more basic anxieties. The theoretical desideratum is to identify the elemental fears, which at present remains something of an unsettled issue.

An important theoretical innovation follows from the discovery that anxiety is not the only painful affect with which childhood wishes are associated. Brenner (1974) has demonstrated that depressive affects (or "miseries") also instigate psychic conflict. He has proposed an important revision in the psychoanalytic theory of affects and their relation to psychic conflict (Brenner 1975, 1982). In his view all affects are composed of two components, sensations of pleasure and unpleasure, which are innate potentials, and ideas of gratification and calamity, which derive from experience. Pleasurable affects include sensations of pleasure in conjunction with ideas of gratification. Unpleasurable affects include sensations of unpleasure in conjunction with ideas of misfortune or calamity. The ideational component also entails a temporal dimension: gratification or calamity may occur in the future, in the present, or in the past. Happy reminiscences, for example, pertain to the past gratifications, while excited anticipation pertains to future expectations. Similarly, anxiety includes the anticipation of future calamities, while depressive affect includes calamities that have occurred.

In Brenner's view the ideational components of anxiety and depressive affect are identical. These are the four dangers Freud described, conceptually reformatted as the calamities of childhood (Brenner 1982).

Brenner's revised theory expands the range of dynamic thinking and better explains certain clinical data. In Brenner's view both anxiety and depressive affect are recurring components of psychic conflict. Psychic conflict occurs when wishes are associated with depressive affect, just as when they are associated with anxiety (Brenner 1982). This is a normal aspect of the mourning process, during which every wish for reunion with the lost object elicits a wave of misery. It is also typical of many pathological conditions, especially depressive conditions, in which psychic conflict is characterized by prominent feelings of loss, of being unloved, of being punished or morally condemned, and of being inferior (Brenner 1982). Both anxiety and depressive affect typically include ideas pertaining to more than one calamity. A child who fears that he will be viciously attacked by a punitive parent, for example, is also likely to feel either anxious or miserable about the loss of the parent's love. Insofar as depressive affect is a motivational factor in psychic conflict, the term *signal affect* may be a superior alternative to the term signal anxiety (Jacobson 1994).

DEFENSE

The third component of psychic conflict is defense. The theory of defense is a cornerstone of psychoanalytic theory (Freud 1894). The theory of defense has undergone numerous changes and revisions, and like the other aspects of psychoanalytic theory it is subject to numerous controversies. Defenses may be defined as psychological activities that reduce the unpleasure of psychic conflict by blocking, inhibiting, or distorting awareness of disturbing mental contents. Defenses are traditionally conceptualized as methods for blocking or disguising the expression of the drive derivatives that arouse unpleasure. Contemporary theorists, however, recognize that the unpleasure associated with drive derivatives may be warded off independently of the drive (Abend 1981; Brenner 1981, 1982). This is particularly important in clinical work with impulsive clients who habitually "forget" about the consequences of their conduct. Of course, defenses against negative affects may also be adaptive, for example, in situations where anxieties are unrealistic and unduly inhibiting or in circumstances that require courage or fortitude in the face of unpleasure.

The traditional concept of defense mechanisms entails the assumption that defenses are discrete mental functions that can be observed and classified. In the course of his career Freud described at least ten different defenses. Anna Freud (1936), in her pioneering study of the ego, listed nine defenses: regression, repression, reaction formation, isolation, undoing, projection, introjection, turning against the self, and reversal, although (1936) she also identified other defensive operations (e.g., intellectualization, identification, and sublimation). In the years that followed this list grew to include twenty-two major and twenty-six minor defenses (Laughlin 1979). Contemporary structural theory explains this proliferation as a consequence of the idea that defense requires special mechanisms. In fact, what are cited as defense mechanisms are simply ego functions that are deployed in situations of psychic conflict to reduce unpleasure. "Whatever ensues in mental life that results in diminution of unpleasurable affects—ideally in their disappearance—belongs under the heading of defense. . . . The ego can use for defense whatever lies at hand that is useful for the purpose" (Brenner 1981:558). Affects, ideas, attitudes, alterations of attention, and even wishes (drive derivatives) may serve as defenses. Brenner thus concludes: "Modes of defense are as diverse as psychic life itself" (561).

THE GENESIS OF PSYCHIC CONFLICTS AND COMPROMISE FORMATIONS

The analysis of psychological conflicts and compromise formations also requires a knowledge of the genesis of psychic conflict. Psychic conflict comes into existence during the course of individual development as a result of childhood experiences and the way that these are interpreted by the child. Childhood normally entails many pleasurable experiences, which give rise to wishes for an expanding variety of pleasures. These are often felt as desires of great urgency and power and are often irresistible to the immature child. Even as these wishes reach new levels of intensity, however, every child must undergo a succession of socialization experiences, such as weaning and toilet training, in which their expression is limited, restricted to special circumstances, or utterly forbidden. Discipline often entails punishment and temporary withdrawals of the parent's loving attentiveness, interactions that are threatening to the child. The character of the child's subjective perception may be quite distorted because of his emotional reactions to discipline and as a result of immature cognitive functioning. Whenever a parent punishes a child or restricts a child's pleasure, especially a pleasure in which the child is highly invested, the child is prone to become frustrated and angry. The angrier the child becomes, the more likely he or she is likely to believe that the parent is equally angry. Parents who discipline, even lovingly, may thus come to be perceived as fantastical figures of devastating power. These distorted representations of the parent's aggressive intentions are an aspect of the child's *psychic reality.*

"Psychic reality" is the "true" context of existence, that perspective on experience about which the child has conviction (Freud 1900). Psychic reality, of course, is only partially determined by objective events. Wishes, affects, and related cognitive distortions result in the formation of a privately constructed universe in which highly unrealistic wishes, such as the wish to be both sexes or the wish to marry the parent, may appear quite reasonable. Accompanying these wishes, fears of horrendous dangers, such as abandonment or castration, may appear equally real and imminent. Sometimes aspects of psychic reality may be recognized as fantastical in nature, an insight that dissipates their compelling quality. The situation is more complicated when the construction of psychic reality includes memories, however fragmentary, disguised, or elaborated, of seduction and incest, or of other threatening or horrifying events. When psychic reality has been shaped by such objective events, fantastically exaggerated elaborations of these memories tend to exert a persistent influence over the person, based on an enduring sense of actuality. Psychic conflicts are thus bound to be particularly damaging and intractable when parents are actually abusive or when childhood is characterized by the occurrence of unusual traumas, such as a death in the family, a serious accident or illness, or surgery.

No matter how entangled in psychic conflict a child's wishes may be, they exert a persistent pressure toward gratification, thus motivating an unending succession of efforts to achieve fulfillment, in both fantasy (imaginary action) and action. In the course of these efforts, childhood wishes are shaped and reshaped by the impact of aversive contingencies on the one hand and by the discovery of pleasurable substitutes on the other. Repetitive trials eventually produce compromise solutions. The best compromises confer a maximum of pleasure with a minimum of unpleasure. These compromises are valued and retained as preferred schemata or blueprints for future gratifications of the wish. They may be repeated with numerous variations whenever the wish arises, in both fantasy and action. Of course, the inexorable process of socialization soon imposes new restrictions and unpleasures, which in turn necessitate the construction of new compromise formations.

THE METAPSYCHOLOGICAL PERSPECTIVES

What is referred to as the Freudian *metapsychology is* actually a collection of six axiomatic principles that serves as the explanatory basis for Freud's most important formulations about human behavior and psychopathology. The term *metapsychology* came to be used to refer to this framework because it emphasized phenomena that went beyond the extant psychological systems of Freud's time. The six viewpoints or perspectives are the *topographical, structural, dynamic, economic, genetic,* and *adaptive.* Some authors have suggested that the genetic and adaptive perspectives, unlike the first four perspectives, were not as clearly explicated by Freud as by later theorists, although there is a general consensus that these two perspectives are nevertheless implicitly represented in Freud's writings (Moore and Fine 1990).

THE TOPOGRAPHICAL PERSPECTIVE

According to the topographical model (Freud 1900), the mind is composed of three systems: the system unconscious, the system preconscious, and the system conscious. The system unconscious, which represents the primitive core of instinctual strivings, functions entirely according to the pleasure principle and is incapable of delaying or inhibiting pleasure seeking. It generates desires for which it seeks representation in conscious thought and fulfillment in action. The unconscious is developmentally superseded by a higher system, the preconscious, which functions in tandem with the system conscious. The preconscious is composed of contents and thought activities that are readily identifiable and accessible to consciousness, and it is therefore also referred to as the preconscious-conscious. The preconscious is capable of realistic thought, moral self-evaluation, and conscious regulation of pleasure seeking according to the reality principle. Most important, the preconscious inhibits the primitive impulsivity of the unconscious by blocking the mental representations of unconscious desires through repression and other defenses. The preconscious performs this function because certain primitive impulses, which are pleasurable in the system unconscious, are experienced as unpleasurable in the (more realistic) system preconscious. Finally, the system conscious is conceptualized as a sense organ, capable of perceiving outer stimuli, bodily sensations (including emotions), and the mental contents of the preconscious. In this early formulation Freud conceptualized psychic conflict as occurring between the unconscious and the preconscious-conscious.

THE STRUCTURAL PERSPECTIVE

Freud employed the topographical model until it became clear that it did not accurately match the clinical data. The topographical model predicts that the anti-instinctual activities of the preconscious should be accessible to conscious awareness. Clinical data revealed, however, that some aspects of defensive and moral functioning (unconscious defenses and unconscious guilt), both anti-instinctual features of the preconscious, are in fact inaccessible to consciousness. Accordingly, Freud developed a revised model, which has come to be known as the structural model (Freud 1923). According to the structural model, the mind is constituted by three agencies—the id, the superego, and the ego—each serving a different set of functions. The id is a new term for the older system unconscious, which continuously generates primitive impulses that press for satisfaction. The superego, a mental system composed of internalized representations of parental authorities, functions as an inner supervisor, providing love and approval for moral behavior as well as condemnation and criticism for immoral desires and conduct. The ego is the executive system of the mind, responsible for the organization of mental life and the management of social conduct. The ego functions to integrate the demands of the id and the superego with the conditions and contingencies of external social reality. The ego is the seat of consciousness, although aspects of ego functioning (unconscious thoughts, ego defenses) are unconscious. The structural model permits the conceptualization of psychic conflict between the three systems, each of which pursues potentially contradictory aims. In accordance with the structural model, the terms *unconscious, preconscious,* and *conscious* may be used as adjectives to describe the accessibility to consciousness of specific mental contents rather than as nouns to denote mental systems.

THE DYNAMIC PERSPECTIVE

The dynamic perspective, which can be traced to *Studies on Hysteria* (Breuer and Freud 1893–1895), postulates that behavior is motivated; it is lawful, has an identifiable cause, and is purposive (Holzman 1998). The dynamic perspective is necessary to understand not only neurotic symptoms and other forms of psychopathology but also the neurotic meaning of ostensibly insignificant behavioral acts associated with everyday living (also termed *parapraxes*),[6] such as slips of the tongue, forgetting names, misreadings, and bungled actions (Freud 1901, Holzman 1998). It is an especially important and facilitative viewpoint in psychoanalytic efforts to understand the latent meaning of dreams.

In *The Psychopathology of Everyday Life* (Freud 1901) the dynamic perspective is brought to life by literally hundreds of examples of parapraxes. A representative vignette follows:

I forbade a patient to telephone to the girl he was in love with—but with whom he himself wanted to break off relations—since each conversation served only to renew the struggle about giving her up. He was to write his final decision to her, though there were difficulties about delivering letters to her. He called on me at one o'clock to tell me he had found a way of getting round these difficulties, and amongst other things asked if he might quote my authority as a physician. At two o'clock he was occupied in composing the letter that was to end the relationship, when he suddenly broke off and said to his mother who was with him: "Oh! I've forgotten to ask the professor if I may mention his name in the letter." He rushed to the telephone, put through his call and said into the instrument: "May I speak to the professor, please, if he's finished dinner?" In answer, he got an astonished: "Adolph, have you gone mad?" It was the same voice which by my orders he should not have heard again. He had simply "made an error," and instead of the physician's number he had given the girl's.   (222)

THE ECONOMIC PERSPECTIVE

It is not possible to explain mental life solely on the basis of qualitative variables. All the motivations already described vary in their intensities at different times, resulting in an endless shifting in the balance of psychological forces within the mind. The economic perspective is an outgrowth of Freud's observations concerning the strength of the drives and other mental phenomena that seemed to require a quantitative explanation. In his early clinical work Freud had been impressed by the power of intrusive ideas and the compelling character of rituals in obsessive-compulsive neurosis, the refractory nature of conversion symptoms to even the most aggressive medical interventions, and the potency of paranoid delusions. These forms of psychopathology, as well as his experience with the resistance of his neurotic patients, convinced him that a quantitative factor underlies much of behavior, pathological or otherwise (Holzman 1998). The mechanisms of displacement and condensation, both of which Freud had originally discussed in connection with the concepts of primary and secondary process and dream analysis (Freud 1895b, 1900), were also conceived of quantitatively. Displacement is the intrapsychic operation whereby the intensity or interest of an idea that is anxiety generating is shifted onto a second idea that has an associative connection to the first but is less anxiety arousing. Condensation is an unconscious defensive operation through which a single image, as in a dream, actually serves to represent multiple ideas or meanings.

THE GENETIC PERSPECTIVE

The genetic point of view, like the topographical, economic, and dynamic viewpoints, is anchored in Freud's earliest papers and several lengthier works, for example, *Studies on Hysteria* (Breuer and Freud 1893–1895) and *The Interpretation of Dreams* (1900). The genetic viewpoint asserts that a meaningful psychological understanding of the adult is of necessity predicated on a thorough comprehension of that person's childhood experiences. Stated in slightly different terms, the genetic perspective postulates that the past persists into the present (Holzman 1998). This particular viewpoint, which has been expropriated by popular culture to a greater degree than perhaps any other, has given rise to the somewhat simplistic notion that dysfunctional behavior and psychopathology in adulthood are almost invariably linked to unhappy childhood experiences.

Freud actually never regarded past experiences as the sole criterion for the development of later psychopathology. He did propose that the historical legacy of experiences acquired meaning as a consequence of a "mutual interaction between and integration of constitutional factors and environmental events" (Holzman 1998:56). In other words, such constitutional factors as the strength of the drives and various individual endowments and capabilities exert influence and are, in turn, influenced by the nature of the individual's experiences in his or her environmental milieu.

THE ADAPTIVE PERSPECTIVE

The adaptive perspective, chiefly concerned with the relationship of the individual to the surrounding environment, highlights the influence of both interpersonal and societal forces. This has been termed the individual's "commerce with the real world" (Holzman 1998:58). Although the adaptive perspective was present in a nascent form in Freud's early formulations of drive theory (1900, 1905b), it was not until his publication of *The Ego and the Id* (1923) that the importance of the extramural environment was emphasized. The development of Freud's concept of the ego and its relationship to the environment opened the way for dramatic developments in psychoanalytic theory.

In this chapter we have examined the theoretical foundation of classical psychoanalysis: the nature and function of the instincts; the role and mediation of intrapsychic conflict; the idea of compromise formation; the importance attached to the Oedipus complex; the concept of pleasure and unpleasure; and the theory of defense. We have also briefly reviewed the six metapsychological perspectives and their unique place in Freud's theoretical edifice.

In much the same way that an individual's past exerts a continuing influence on her life in the present, the ideas derived from Freud's original theories of mental functioning, human development, and psychopathology continue to influence and shape contemporary thinking in psychoanalysis and psychodynamic psychology. All those who have followed him—ego psychologists, object relations theorists, self psychologists, intersubjectivists, Lacanians—are heavily indebted to the psychological truths first revealed in this rich and elaborate theoretical system, retrospectively identified as that of "classical" psychoanalysis. In this sense it matters less whether such classical theorems represent a basis for the accrual of additional data affirming Freud's original propositions (e.g., Brenner's contemporary classical theory) or merely a point of reference for dissenting theories (e.g., the self psychological ideas of Kohut). In the next chapter we will explore the work of Freud's successors, authors of the important theories of development and psychopathology that have evolved since the articulation of Freud's classical ideas.

3

Psychoanalytic Theories of Development and Dysfunction:
Ego Psychology, Object Relations Theories, the Psychology of
the Self, and Relational Psychoanalysis

EGO PSYCHOLOGY

The relationship of classical psychoanalysis to ego psychology, which some would argue is far more intimate than that of classical theory to any of the other major psychoanalytic psychologies, is already partially revealed in the last chapter, which examined such ideas as compromise formations, defense theory, and the metapsychological perspectives. In the early stages of his career Freud was primarily concerned with exploring the depths of the mind in an effort to discover its primordial origins. He saw mental life as the refracted expression of primitive strivings. His first view of the curative process in psychoanalysis rested on the assumption that bringing these strivings to life (i.e., making the unconscious conscious) would permit them to be dealt with in a more adaptive way. Accordingly, he had little interest in studies of consciousness, which he regarded as superficial. However, with the introduction of structural theory in 1923 the importance of the preconscious was expanded, and the psyche was depicted as having greater complexity.

The 1923 formulation of structural theory was epochal, permitting various problems in normal development as well as the influence of environmental variables and the character of the infant's earliest relationships to caregivers to be studied in entirely new ways. It also paved the way for the gradual emergence and more systematic development of a general psychology of the ego, which paralleled the translocation of focus from the ego's functions to the place of the ego in an expanding sociocultural context (Meissner 2000). At the same time, ego psychological theorists have managed to preserve, more or less intact, Freudian drive theory, which may differentiate this school from either object relational or self psychological theories (Mitchell and Black 1995). The more prominent architects of ego psychology are Anna Freud, Heinz Hartmann, Rene Spitz, Margaret Mahler, Erik Erikson, and Edith Jacobson. It is to certain of their contributions that we now turn.

ANNA FREUD AND DEFENSE THEORY

Perhaps Anna Freud's most significant contribution to ego psychology was her clarification of defense theory and specification of the principal mechanisms of defense. She was also considered a pioneer in the field of child psychoanalysis and devoted much energy to studying the psychoanalytic treatment process and to developing research instruments such as the Hampstead Profile, a comprehensive, developmentally based instrument for assessing a patient's ego functioning and object relations. Anna Freud's efforts to explicate the structural model and Sigmund Freud's revised theory of anxiety (Freud 1926), and to make these consonant with a superordinate focus on the ego and its functions, led her to consider such problems as the "choice of neurosis" and "motives" for defense. In fact, she distinguished four principal motives for defense against the drives: superego anxiety (or guilt), objective anxiety (in children), anxiety about the strength of drives, and anxiety stemming from conflicts between mutually incompatible aims (Freud 1936). On the basis of her extensive observations of and psychoanalytic work with young children, Anna Freud later developed the concept of developmental lines (Freud 1963), a variegated developmental schedule that permitted the clinician-researcher to follow important changes in sexual, aggressive, and social developmental "lines" from infancy to adolescence.

THE EGO AND ADAPTATION

Heinz Hartmann's contributions were designed to enhance and expand the scope of psychoanalytic theory, with the objective of transforming it into a system of general psychology (Goldstein 1995; Mitchell and Black 1995). A central argument of Hartmann's most important work, *Ego Psychology and the Problem of Adaptation* (1939), was that the human infant was born with innate "conflict-free ego capacities" that would be activated in an "average expectable environment," thereby ensuring the infant's survival and adaptation. The capacities to which Hartmann referred included language, perception, memory, intention, motor activity, object comprehension, and thinking. Hartmann's notion of conflict-free ego capacities contrasted with more traditional psychoanalytic ideas, where adaptation is achieved only as an outcome of frustration and conflict. Hartmann also proposed the twin concepts of *alloplastic adaptation,* the individual's efforts to alter external realities to meet various human needs, and autoplastic adaptation, which refers to the individual's efforts to accommodate to external realities.

THE DEVELOPMENTALISTS:
RENE SPITZ, MARGARET MAHLER, AND ERIK ERIKSON

Spitz and Mahler, both of whom began their professional careers as pediatricians, are well recognized for their important contributions to developmental ego psychology. Working as a consultant in a foundling home during World War II, Spitz first described the dramatic sequelae of a syndrome that exacted a profound developmental toll on the infants he studied. Although the nutritional needs of these infants were met quite adequately and care was provided for them in hygienic environments, they were deprived of interaction with maternal caregivers. Seemingly as a direct consequence of the absence of mother-infant interaction, they became withdrawn, failed to achieve developmental milestones, and had very high morbidity and mortality rates (Spitz 1945).[1] Spitz characterized this syndrome as *anaclitic depression* (depression associated with thwarted dependency needs). Spitz later identified what he termed the three psychic organizers: the baby's social response at approximately three months, the emergence of stranger anxiety at eight months, and the child's "no" response, first observed at about fifteen months (Spitz 1965). Spitz's greatest contribution may have been his systematic effort to identify the particular facilitative environmental conditions that spur the development of the "innate adaptive capabilities" Hartmann had previously described (Mitchell and Black 1995).

Mahler's work was also principally with young children, although the original focus of her clinical research was psychotic youngsters. Mahler believed that the nature of the ego pathology she observed in psychotic children was inadequately addressed within the traditional framework of drive theory. She proposed that these children suffered from defects or failures in the organization of internalized self and object representations and experienced a corresponding difficulty in differentiating self from not-self; in consequence, such children were largely incapable of acquiring an enduring sense of self that is distinct and separable from others. This, in turn, suggested to Mahler that the infant's "mediating human partner," as Spitz had also maintained, had a highly significant role in the evolution of the infantile ego. Ultimately Mahler turned to the study of normal infant development. Mahler's theory of the separation-individuation process, later criticisms notwithstanding (Horner 1985; Stern 1985), introduced a schema that transformed not only the study of infant pathology but has also served as the theoretical basis for a psychoanalytic approach to the psychother- apy of adults with borderline personality disorder (Masterson and Rinsley 1975).[2] On the basis of her longitudinal investigations of maternal-infant pairs in a nursery setting, Mahler portrayed a process that begins at birth and continues into the child's fourth year (Mahler, Pine, and Bergmann 1975). Characterizing infants as essentially nonrelated or objectless at birth (the autistic phase), she described their gradual emergence via a period of maternal-infant symbiosis into four relatively discrete stages of separation and individuation: differentia- tion (five to nine months), practicing (nine to fifteen months), rapprochement (fifteen to twenty-four months), and the development of the object constancy (twenty-four to thirty-six months and beyond).

Erikson's greatest contributions to ego psychology involved his theory of psy- chosocial and psychosexual epigenesis and the detailed attention he gave to the concept of ego identity.[3] Whereas Spitz and Mahler had focused their attentions on the earliest developmental processes of the infant's emerging ego, Erikson's psychosocial epigenetic theory examined ego development across the entire life span and highlighted social-environmental factors to a greater degree than any existing ego psychological model. In Erikson's view, healthy ego development was contingent on the mastery of specific developmental tasks and normative crises associated with each of eight life cycle stages he identified:

1. *Basic trust versus basic mistrust.* Coterminous with Freud's oral phase, the principal experiential mode in this stage is oral-receptive. In optimal cir- cumstances there is a preponderance of positively valenced experiences with one's mother, which culminate in basic trust.

2. *Autonomy versus shame and doubt.* Coincides with the anal stage in Freud's model of the libidinal stages; emphasis on the child's newly emerging autonomy, coextensive with increased radius of locomotor activity and maturation of the muscle systems. Success in this phase results in the child's pleasure in independent actions and self-expression, failure, in shame and self-doubt.

3. *Initiative versus guilt.* Corresponds to Freud's phallic stage. Sexual curiosity and oedipal issues are common, competitiveness reaches new heights, and the child's efforts to reach and attain goals acquires importance. Danger arises when the child's aggression or manipulation of the environment trig- gers an abiding sense of guilt.

4. *Industry versus inferiority.* Occurs during the latency period in Freud's model; associated with the child's beginning efforts to use tools, his sense of being productive and of developing the capability to complete tasks.

5. *Identity versus identity diffusion.* Ushered in by adolescence. This stage is perhaps the most extensively developed in the Eriksonian model; stable identity requires an integration of formative experiences "that give the child the sense that he is a person with a history, a stability, and a continuity that is recognizable by others" (Holzman 1998:163). Erikson also enumerated seven aspects of identity consolidation (Erikson 1959) that are critical codeterminants of success or failure in this stage: 1. a time perspective, 2. self-certainty, 3. role experimentation, 4. anticipation of achievement, 5. sexual identity, 6. acceptance of leadership, and 7. commitment to basic values.

6. *Intimacy and distantiation versus self-absorption.* The major developmental task of this phase, which occurs during early adulthood, is the individual's capacity for healthy sexual and nonsexual intimacy while still retaining a firm sense of personal identity. Should such intimacy be impossible, there is a "regressive retreat to exclusive concern with oneself" (Holzman 1998).

7. *Generativity versus stagnation.* This penultimate phase of the adult life cycle involves the adult in the critical tasks and responsibilities of parenting. Parenthood is not inextricably tied to generativity, however; just as there are adults who relinquish or are otherwise unable to fulfill parental responsibilities, so too there are childless adults whose generativity involves the pursuit of creative or artistic initiatives.

8. *Integrity versus despair and disgust.* Ego integrity is the culmination of ego identity (Erikson 1959; Goldstein 1995). It reflects a level of maturity signaling the individual's acceptance of the past, particularly past disappointments and mistakes.

JACOBSON: THE SELF AND THE OBJECT WORLD

The daunting task of summarizing the considerable scope of Edith Jacobson's contributions to the psychoanalytic literature has been previously discussed (Greenberg and Mitchell 1983). Jacobson attempted to integrate the Freudian emphasis on constitutional factors in development (including instinctual drives) with the growing recognition of the potent imprint of life experience. In a series of papers that culminated in the publication of *The Self and the Object World* (1964), Jacobson revised and reformulated Freud's theory of psychosexual development and various aspects of classical metapsychology, particularly the economic principle. Although she never actually disputed the primacy of the drives, she theorized that the mother-infant relationship had complementarity with innate maturational forces and, furthermore, that the distinctive features of the infant's instinctual drives acquire meaning only within the milieu of the caregiving relationship. In Jacobson's model of early development, a complex reciprocal interchange between the infant's ongoing experience with caregivers and the maturational unfolding of the drives leads to the formation of self images and object images. These images have different hedonic valences, and it is the infant's gradual capacity for integrating good and bad experiences of objects and of self that is finally necessary for mature affectivity. The phenomenology of affective disorders was also of considerable interest to Jacobson, whose book *Depression: Comparative Studies of Normal, Neurotic, and Psychotic Conditions* (1971) continued her exploration of the complex relationship between affectivity and the inner representational world.

OBJECT RELATIONS THEORY

None of the psychoanalytic theory groups discussed in this chapter actually constitutes a fully separate psychoanalytic psychology. This is perhaps especially true of object relations theory, a general heading under which is subsumed several distinct groups of theories, each possessing distinctive theoretical premises and complementary approaches to psychoanalytic treatment.

Grotstein (1996) traces the psychoanalytic use of the term *object* to a series of six papers written by Freud: "Three Essays on the Theory of Sexuality" (1905b), "Family Romances" (1909a), "On Narcissism: An Introduction" (1914a), "Mourning and Melancholia" (1917a), "A Child Is Being Beaten" (1919a), and "The Ego and the Id (1923). In the original use of this term (1905b:135–36), Freud had sought to minimize the importance of the infant's caretakers, who were viewed with respect to their inhibition or facilitation of the child's instinctual wishes rather than as human beings in their own right. Gradually, however, Freud demonstrated increasing interest in the role of objects, which we can glean from "his conception of the ego-ideal, the superego, and the Oedipus Complex itself . . . contributions [where the object is conceived] as being incorporated into the psychic structure" (Grotstein 1996:91). In Freud's essay on the mourning process (1917a), there was further exploration of the relationship between external object loss and the internal process through which the object is established as an identification in the mourner's ego. Freud also made use of object relations ideas in his examination of the role that sadism and masochism played in pathological narcissism.

A number of theorists have shaped object relations thinking since Freud: Karl Abraham (1924a), whose model of object relations was embedded in an eloquent paper on the development of the libido; Sandor Ferenczi (1950a [1913]), whose postulation of an infantile desire to return to a prenatal symbiotic state anticipates the work of Maragaret Mahler; Ian Suttie (1935), who wrote that the infant comes into the world with an innate need for companionship, nonsexual love, and security, all of which evolve in the mother-infant relational matrix (Mishne 1993); Imre Hermann (1933, 1936), who hypothesized that there was a human instinct to cling that paralleled the instinctual behavior of other primates;[4] and Michael Balint and Alice Balint, among whose theoretical contributions were the instinct of "primary object love" (A. Balint 1949)[5] and "the basic fault" (M. Balint 1949, 1968), a concept that designated a primary breach in the ego arising during the preoedipal period.

Contemporary object relations theories, however, have been especially influenced by several major theorists: Harry Stack Sullivan, Melanie Klein, and Donald Winnicott.

INTERPERSONAL PSYCHOANALYSIS:
THE WORK OF HARRY STACK SULLIVAN

worked @ Chestnut Lodge

Interpersonal psychoanalysis derives from the clinical work and theoretical formulations of Harry Stack Sullivan (1892–1949), an American psychiatrist who pioneered the psychotherapeutic treatment of severely disturbed individuals. Sullivan, who studied medicine in Chicago, was greatly impressed by the exciting intellectual developments in philosophy and the social sciences at the University of Chicago. He was particularly influenced by the work of such social thinkers as George Herbert Meade, Edward Sapir, John Dewey, and other proponents of the American pragmatist school of philosophical thought. Sullivan's distinctive approach to psychotherapy and psychiatry reflected his profound immersion in this intellectual milieu (Chapman 1976; Mullahy 1970; Perry 1982).

Sullivan was deeply dissatisfied with existing psychoanalytic theory. He distrusted the abstract, metaphorical concepts of Freudian theory, which, in his view, pertained to mental systems and structures that are not observable and hence only hypothetical in nature. In contrast to Freudian theorists, Sullivan, who was greatly influenced by Bridgman's "operationalism" (Bridgman 1945; Sullivan 1953), believed that psychiatric theories should, to the greatest extent possible, employ "operational" terms with definable and empirical referents. Sullivan also found that Freudian theory (as it existed during his formative years of psychiatric practice) was inadequate to the understanding and treatment of the severely mentally ill patients with whom he worked. As a result, Harry Stack Sullivan's clinical and theoretical contributions to psychiatric and psychoanalytic thought are strikingly original, couched in his own highly idiosyncratic terminology.

Over the years Sullivan came to reject basic features of Freudian theory. Most important, Sullivan repudiated Freud's belief that human motivations are determined by instinctual drives. In opposition to Freud's classical drive theory, Sullivan posited that human motivations are primarily interpersonal in nature, determined by relationships, especially the relationships of childhood and adolescence, and understandable only in terms of such relationships. Sullivan believed that human beings respond to two sets of motivations. One set is characterized as the satisfaction of bodily and emotional needs, including sexuality and intimacy. A second set of motivations is related to the experience of anxiety and related strivings for security. Both the satisfaction of needs and the achievement of security are interpersonal events occurring in relation to other persons. In contrast to the Freudian conception of personality as the characteristic way that the individual organizes the competing claims of id, ego, and superego, Sullivan conceptualized personality as the characteristic ways that the individual interacts with other people in the pursuit of satisfactions and security. Mental illness, he argued, can best be understood as a disturbance of interpersonal relations. Sullivan's efforts to employ operational concepts and his concomitant emphasis upon interpersonal relations gradually gave rise to a new psychoanalytic orientation in which the primary focus was on interpersonal relations rather than intrapsychic events.

Sullivan's approach to treatment reflected this shift of emphasis. If, he reasoned, mental illness and other malformations of personality are the consequence of pathogenic interpersonal relationships, then mental health is best promoted by the creation of healthy interpersonal relationships. In the late 1920s Sullivan implemented this idea at Sheppard and Enoch Pratt Hospital in Baltimore, where he developed an unusual inpatient psychiatric unit for male schizophrenics in which ward staff were specially trained to interact with patients and to foster comfortable and emotionally rewarding interpersonal relationships with them in order to help correct their unhealthy relationship patterns. Sullivan also developed a distinctive method of conducting individual therapy with patients. Abandoning the free association method of classical psychoanalysis, Sullivan employed a conversational approach to patients, conceptualizing his role as that of a participant-observer in the relationship with the patient. His goal was to engage the patient in a collaborative study of the patient's interpersonal relationships so that the patient's unhealthy patterns of relating to others could be discovered and understood. Most important, Sullivan stressed the importance of establishing a healthy relationship with the patient in order to correct habitual maladaptive interpersonal patterns. Employing these techniques, Sullivan achieved unparalleled therapeutic gains with patients that had previously been regarded as hopeless and untreatable. As his work was more widely disseminated, Sullivan became one of America's most respected and admired psychiatrists. He acquired a growing circle of collaborators that included some of the leading thinkers in psychoanalysis, such as Clara Thompson, Erich Fromm, and Frieda Fromm-Reichman, all of whom contributed to the development of the interpersonal school of psychoanalysis.

Sullivan never attempted to establish a comprehensive theoretical system, and contemporary therapists working within the interpersonal tradition have introduced their own technical and theoretical innovations (Arieti 1974; Chrzanowski 1977; Fromm-Reichman 1950; Havens 1976, 1986; Levenson 1972; Thompson 1964; Witenberg 1973). Interpersonal psychoanalysis is best described as "a set of different approaches to theory and clinical practice ... with shared underlying assumptions and premises" (Greenberg and Mitchell 1983:79). These include Sullivan's rejection of Freudian instinct theory, his basic view of psychopathology as a disturbance of interpersonal relationships, his belief in the interpersonal roots of mental illness, and his emphasis upon the curative importance of healthy interpersonal relationships. Interpersonal psychoanalysis has often been criticized by exponents of traditional psychoanalysis as being superficial or lacking in depth because of its focus on the interpersonal field and its rejection of drive concepts. However, Sullivan's ideas are now believed to have exerted a profound and far-reaching influence on contemporary psychoanalytic thinking (Havens and Frank 1971).

An overarching theme in Sullivan's writings is that the human infant is born into a relational milieu; relational configurations in his theoretical model evolve out of actual experience with others. Sullivan repeatedly underscored the assertion that human beings can be understood only within the "organism-environment complex" and consequently are incapable of "definitive description in isolation" (Sullivan 1962b [1930]:258).[6] In Sullivan's developmental model a superordinate importance is placed on the interpersonal field together with the efforts that children devise to maintain relatedness with significant others.

Needs for satisfaction are "integrating tendencies" that impel the individual to seek physical and emotional contact with others. The integration of relationships in the pursuit of satisfactions is complicated, however, by the arousal of painful affective states that Sullivan characterized as anxiety. Sullivan's notion of anxiety differs from Freud's view of anxiety in two principal ways. In his mature formulation (Freud 1926) Freud conceptualized anxiety as a kind of fear related to specific typical danger situations of childhood (loss of the mother, loss of the mother's love, castration, and guilt). Sullivan used the term anxiety to include any form of mental suffering, distress, or anguish aroused in an interpersonal situation. A second difference pertains to the manner in which anxiety is generated.

In Freudian theory anxiety is a signal of danger, typically aroused by the mobilization of repressed wishes associated with specific danger situations. Accordingly, "drives and reality are inextricably linked as sources of danger to the ego" (Holzman 1998:143). In Sullivan's theory the infant's experience of anxiety is aroused by anxiety (in its more narrowly defined sense) or by other strong affects of distress in the caregiver. Babies are exquisitely sensitive to the moods of others, and, through a phenomenon Sullivan termed *empathic linkage*, experience the caregiver's anxiety as if it were their own. While needs for satisfaction are integrating tendencies that foster relatedness, anxiety and other forms of emotional suffering are aversive experiences that impair interpersonal relations. Excessive anxiety in infancy and childhood predisposes the affected individual to experience anxiety in the context of his or her adult relationships. This vulnerability to anxiety contributes to disturbances of interpersonal relationships that are usually referred to as psychopathology or mental illness.

Sullivan believed that the most basic differentiation for the infant was "not between light and dark, or between mother and father, but between anxious states and non-anxious states" (Mitchell and Black 1995:68). During development the child forms schematic impressions or "personifications" of himself and of his mother. Pleasurable experiences give rise to impressions of the "good mother" and the "good me," while experiences of anxiety produce impressions of the "bad mother" and the "bad me." Extremely painful or terrifying interpersonal situations elicit representations of the "evil mother" and the "not me." The memories of such experiences are vigorously avoided and may be terrifying when they are aroused. "Evil mother" and "not me" experiences are associated with severe mental illness.

Sullivan introduced the term *self-system* to collectively characterize the myriad psychological activities which the individual employs to avoid anxiety ("bad me" and "not me") and to ensure feelings of security ("good me"). In Sullivan's writing, security is defined as the absence of anxiety. The self-system is an expansive system of mental states, symbols, and coordinated activities that functions to promote feelings of security by assessing the safety of interpersonal situations, anticipating the arousal of anxiety, and minimizing anxiety through the activation of security operations. Security operations roughly parallel the concept of defense in the traditional Freudian system: they operate covertly, out of the individual's awareness, serving to diminish anxiety and other feelings of emotional distress associated with the "bad me" or "not me," and to restore feelings of security and well-being that are the affective concomitants of the "good me." However, the concept of security operations also differs from the traditional Freudian concept of defenses in significant ways. In classical Freudian theory defenses are mental activities designed to reduce anxiety arising from intrapsychic conflict (i.e., conflict between id, ego, and superego). In Sullivan's theory security operations are intended to diminish the anxiety and emotional distress that arise from disturbances in interpersonal relationships. While defenses are best understood as intrapsychic phenomena, security operations entail an interpersonal dimension. Security operations promote relatedness and facilitate the satisfaction of emotional needs by preserving security in interpersonal situations.

Security operations develop and become increasingly sophisticated as the child matures. Typical security operations of early childhood include apathy and somnolent detachment, both of which reflect a process of disengagement from an anxiety-arousing interpersonal situation, such as an anxious or anguished mother. As the child develops progressive cognitive capabilities, other security operations become possible. A typical security operation of later development is selective inattention, a tactical redeployment of focal attention from disturbing aspects of interpersonal experience to aspects that enhance the individual's feelings of self-esteem or security. As a result of selective inattention, disturbing aspects of interpersonal phenomena are excluded from experience and memory. An individual's security operations include complex patterns of interpersonal activity that manifest as typical aspects of the individual's interpersonal relationships. For example, habitual compliance or placating behavior, aggressive bullying or dominating, emotional withdrawal or constriction, pomposity and self-centeredness may be conceptualized as complex security operations intended to avoid anxiety in interpersonal situations, that is, to maintain the vulnerable individual's sense of comfort and security. Sullivan summarized such patterns of interpersonal conduct as the dramatization of roles, or the repetitive enactment of emotionally safe relational configurations, interpersonal patterns Sullivan called *me-you patterns* (Sullivan 1953).

In sum, Sullivan's interpersonal approach to psychoanalysis is prototypical of psychoanalytic schools of thought that diverge from classical Freudian theory by positing that human motivations and personality structure derive from the interpersonal experiences of development rather than from the unfolding influence of instinctual drives. Other psychoanalytic theorists who shared this point of view are Fairbairn (1952) and Guntrip (1968, 1971). Greenberg and Mitchell (1983) have designated these schools of thought, collectively, as the *relational/structure* model.

In addition to his enduring impact on psychoanalytic theory, Sullivan's contributions have had a major impact on the understanding and treatment of schizophrenia (Sullivan 1962a). Sullivan was passionate in his arguments against professional "objectivity" and "detachment" in the psychotherapy of schizophrenic clients, since he believed that the distorted interpersonal relations of the schizophrenic originally developed from a matrix of disordered relationships between the client and members of the client's family. ~~Although a relational approach to the psychotherapy of schizophrenia has enjoyed less popularity since the recent ascendancy of biological psychiatry,~~ Sullivan's emphasis upon the social context of psychopathology remains a viable theoretical premise.

Current

THE WORK OF MELANIE KLEIN

Some have asserted that Melanie Klein (1882–1960) and her theory of object relations have exerted an influence on the contemporary world of psychoanalysis second only to that of Freud (Mitchell and Black 1995). Though this claim is arguable, most would concede that Klein's theoretical positions were at the center of a protracted debate in the British psychoanalytic establishment that ultimately led to the creation of three separate schools of psychoanalysis in that country. Klein was also the first psychoanalyst to treat children with the psychoanalytic method, "a project . . . long overdue . . . [that] aroused considerable interest in the psychoanalytic community" when her first paper was published in 1919 (Greenberg and Mitchell 1983). Although the history of psychoanalysis is replete with controversies over theory and technique, perhaps none has attained the notoriety and divisiveness or equaled the profound ramifications of the prolonged disagreement between Melanie Klein and Anna Freud.

The schism that developed between Klein and Anna Freud began in the mid- to late 1920s over issues of technique in child analysis.[7] A fundamental premise of Klein was that the play of young children was equivalent to the free associations of adult clients; so long as the meaning of their play was interpreted to them, children, like adults, were suitable subjects for psychoanalytic treatment. Anna Freud's position, however, was that small children could not be analyzed owing to an inherently weak and rudimentary ego that would be incapable of managing deep interpretations of instinctual conflict (Mitchell and Black 1995). Klein published a number of theoretical and clinical papers and several books over a period of some forty years. Although she steadfastly maintained that her observations and psychoanalytic work with children were intended as confirmations and extensions of Freud's hypotheses, her discoveries led her to portray the mind "as a continually shifting, kaleidoscopic stream of primitive, phantasmagoric images, fantasies, and terrors," a vision that ~~seemed very unlike that~~ of Freud (Mitchell and Black 1995:87). In Freud's model of the mind, the Oedipus complex has a developmentally profound, transformative impact on the psyche that yields the creation of new conflict-mediating structures (~~the mature ego~~ and superego), which have stability and coherence. An almost inexorable progression of the libido culminates in the six-year-old's genital sexuality and the accompa-

Play

A. Freud
children

Klein

Freud

nying oedipal dilemma; this, for Freud, constitutes the core conflict or nuclear complex of the neuroses. In fact, Klein never questioned the primacy of the Oedipus complex, but located it at a much earlier point in development than did traditional psychoanalytic theory. Klein's fundamental view of the nature of oedipal phenomena also differed from the traditional perspective. For Klein "the very nature of the Oedipus complex changed from a struggle over illicit pleasures and the fear of punishment, to a struggle for power and destruction and the fear of retaliation" (Greenberg and Mitchell 1983:123).

Sigmund Freud had theorized that infants proceed from a state of primary narcissism to object love via autoerotism; in effect, true object love is not possible until the libido progresses to the oedipal stage. The Kleinian infant, by contrast, is both psychologically separate and object seeking from the moment of birth (Klein 1964b; Grotstein 1996). Klein went further, however, proposing that infants as young as three weeks of age are subject to a primitive anxiety state, which she called *persecutory anxiety*. She believed this configuration of anxiety was linked to schizoid mechanisms (e.g., splitting, projective identification, idealization, and magic omnipotent denial) and that such intrapsychic experience resulted in the infant's first developmental organizer, the *paranoid-schizoid position* (1964b). In the paranoid-schizoid position "*paranoia* refers to the central persecutory anxiety, the fear of invasive malevolence, coming from the outside. . . . *Schizoid* refers to the central organizing defense: splitting, the vigilant separation of the loving and good breast from the hating and hated bad breast" (Mitchell and Black 1995:93). The infant who is operating out of the paranoid-schizoid position has a bifurcated and fragmented experience of objects; "the child attempts to ward off the dangers of bad objects, both external and internal, largely by keeping images of them separate and isolated from the self and the good objects" (Greenberg and Mitchell 1983:125). Relations with objects are, by definition, always partial and either all good or all bad, but never composed of both good and bad parts. According to Klein, however, the infant gradually begins to integrate the experiences of good and bad breast-other, so that whole object relations ultimately become possible (Klein 1964a [1935]). Klein has termed this important shift in intrapsychic experience, which begins at approximately three to four months, the *depressive position*.

The depressive position (the second developmental organizer of infancy) is initiated by the infant's growing concern for the welfare of the libidinal object who has been the recipient of hateful fantasies of vengeance and annihilation characteristic of the paranoid-schizoid position.[8] Concomitant with the infant's newly emerging capacity for whole object relations is an ability to experience ambivalence or both good (loving) and bad (hateful) feelings toward the same object. Although this represents a critical developmental achievement for the infant, it simultaneously creates new dangers since

> the whole mother who disappoints or fails the infant, generating the pain of longing, frustration, desperation, is destroyed in the infant's hateful fantasies, not just the purely evil bad breast (with the good breast remaining untouched and protected). The whole object (both the external mother and the corresponding internal whole object) now destroyed in the infant's rageful fantasies is the singular provider of goodness as well as frustration. In destroying the whole object, the infant eliminates her as a protector and refuge . . . [which leads to] . . . intense terror and guilt.   (Mitchell and Black 1995:95)

[margin note: object = external + internal]

The target of the infant's destructive urges is also a deeply loved figure toward whom the infant feels profound gratitude (Klein 1964a). These feelings, coupled with the child's regret and sorrow over her or his destructiveness, serve as the basis for fantasies of reparation. Such fantasies are intended to repair the damage and transform the annihilated object into a whole object once again.

The concept of projective identification, which some believe to be a sine qua non for the understanding and treatment of borderline and other severe personality disorders, is also attributed to Klein (1975a [1946], 1952). Projective identification represents not simply a strategy of defense but is a significant though developmentally primitive mode of interaction. In projective identification the subject projects unwanted parts of the self into others for "safekeeping." Ogden, a contemporary Kleinian, has defined the concept in the following manner: "Projective-identification is a concept that addresses the way in which feeling states corresponding to the unconscious fantasies of one person (projector) are engendered in and processed by another person (the recipient), that is, the way in which one person makes use of another person to experience and contain an aspect of himself" (Ogden 1982:1).

[margin note: Proj. Identif. Borderline Tx]

[margin note: P.I.]

Klein and her theories have been criticized for a number of reasons. A basic premise of Klein is that the infant is capable of a complex fantasy life from birth, a contention that receives little support from either cognitive psychology or the neurosciences (Tyson and Tyson 1990). Others have noted that in Klein's framework, where mental life is viewed as fragmented and chaotic, there is "considerable fuzziness concerning the relationship between fantasy and the establishment of character or psychic structure" (Fairbairn 1952; Kernberg 1980; Mishne 1993). At the same time, the magnitude of Klein's influence is indisputable and of particular importance for our discussion of the theorist whose work we now consider, D. W. Winnicott.

THE MIDDLE TRADITION AND D. W. WINNICOTT

There was considerable divisiveness within the British psychoanalytic community by the early 1940s, principally due to theoretical differences between Anna Freud and Melanie Klein, which had given rise to an increasingly contentious and acrimonious professional environment. Ernest Jones was the official head of the psychoanalytic movement in Britain at the time, and he had worked diligently to foster a professional climate of "creative exploration, inclusiveness, and openness to emerging ideas," an ambience that had made possible relative quiescence, if not harmony, between Melanie Klein and adherents of mainstream psychoanalysis—at least until the arrival of the Freuds from Vienna in 1938 (Borden 1995).[9] As relations between those faithful to Anna Freud's views and those who pledged loyalty to Melanie Klein began to deteriorate, Jones worked to uphold the integrity of the British Psycho-Analytic Society. In 1943 and 1944 he organized what have come to be known as the "controversial discussions," a series of formal theoretical debates, the original intent of which were to provide Melanie Klein with an opportunity to clarify her position on Sigmund Freud's metapsychology (Kohon 1986; Mishne 1993; Borden 1995) and to explore the nature of theoretical differences between the Kleinians and (Anna) Freudians. The result of these discussions,[10] which failed to remedy deep theoretical differences between the two camps, was the organization of the British psychoanalytic community into three distinct groups: the Kleinians, the Freudians, and a middle or independent group.

The independent group consisted of a number of seminal thinkers, among them D. W. Winnicott, W. R. D. Fairbairn, John Bowlby, Michael Balint, and Harry Guntrip. Each of these theorists developed object relations theories based on Klein's basic postulate of an infant who is object seeking from the moment of birth. At the same time "they also all broke with Klein's premise of constitutional aggression . . . proposing instead an infant wired for harmonious interaction and nontraumatic development but thwarted by inadequate parenting" (Mitchell and Black 1995:114–15). D. W. Winnicott (1896–1971) is regarded by many as the best-known representative of the independent group (Grotstein 1996; Borden 1995). Winnicott, like Spitz and Mahler, was originally trained as a pediatrician and spent over forty years working with infants and mothers. His careful observations of infants and their mothers led him to assert that "there is no such thing as an infant. There is only the infant and its mother" (Winnicott 1965c [1960]:39). This declaration, which is truly axiomatic for Winnicott, underscores the critical importance that he attributed to the earliest object relations between infant and caregiver.

Winnicott is especially well known for his ideas about primary maternal preoccupation, good-enough mothering, and the holding environment, his formulation of the true self and the false self, and the concept of the transitional object.

PRIMARY MATERNAL PREOCCUPATION, GOOD-ENOUGH MOTHERING AND THE HOLDING ENVIRONMENT

Winnicott believed that the emergence of a health-promoting psychological milieu for each human infant depends on her or his mother's capacity for what Winnicott termed *primary maternal preoccupation.* The state of primary maternal preoccupation, which gathers considerable momentum in the last trimester of pregnancy, reflects each mother's natural absorption with the baby growing inside her. The expectant mother becomes "increasingly withdrawn from her own subjectivity . . . and more and more focused on the baby's movements, on the baby's vitality. . . . The mother finds her own personal interests, her own rhythms and concerns fading into the background" (Mitchell and Black 1995:125). Winnicott has also characterized this as mother's identification with the infant (Winnicott 1965).

Good-enough mothering, which commences with the mother's primary maternal preoccupation, initially requires that mother meet the symbiotic needs of her newborn. If she is well attuned with her baby, whatever she offers the baby is provided at the "right time" for her baby rather than being timed to meet her own needs. As her baby faces experiences that evoke frustration, aggression, or loss, the good-enough mother is able to provide empathically attuned support or *holding.* Winnicott stresses that good-enough mothering is a natural and spontaneous process that evolves out of each mother's intuitions and leads to the creation of a facilitative or holding environment on which each infant depends. He also observed that the extensive adaptations and accommodations that a mother makes to her infant gradually diminish; the result is brief lapses that teach baby that mother is not omnipotent (Moore and Fine 1990). Such maternal failures in empathy coincide with significant advances in the infant's psychomotor development; while infantile omnipotence is lost, there is newfound delight in the infant's exciting forays into the object world outside the infant-mother matrix (Winnicott 1958a, 1965b).

TRUE SELF AND FALSE SELF

Winnicott wrote that all individuals begin life with a true self, an "inherited potential" that represents the infant's core self or essence. In a facilitative environment the true self, which has been equated with the spontaneous expression of the id, continues to develop and becomes firmly established. The false self, on the other hand, is a facade that the infant-child erects so as to achieve compliance with mother's inadequate adaptations, whether these maternal failures are in the form of deprivations or impingements on the child's growth (Goldstein 1995). Infants exposed to such repeated deprivations or impingements are able to survive, but in Winnicott's estimation they are able to do so only at the cost of "living falsely" (Winnicott 1965b, 1965c [1960]; Mishne 1993). Although Winnicott emphasized that the partition or distribution of self experience into "true" and "false" is always present in varying degrees (even in normal infants), the false self has an almost palpable presence in various forms of child and adult psychopathology. Winnicott treated a number of patients with basic pathology of the self, individuals who might have been diagnosed with schizoid or borderline disorders. What impressed him most about such patients was their profound inner alienation. In such patients "subjectivity itself, the quality of personhood, is somehow disordered" (Mitchell and Black 1995:124). Winnicott gradually came to understand that these adult patients suffered from "false self disorders," and the bridge he "constructed between the quality and the nuances of adult subjectivity and the subtleties of mother-infant interactions provided a powerful new perspective for viewing both the development of the self" and the process of treatment (Mitchell and Black 1995:125).

THE TRANSITIONAL OBJECT

Winnicott's concept of the transitional object is perhaps the best known of his theoretical ideas, though its popularization may have contributed to a blurring of its original meaning (Mitchell and Black 1995). The transitional object is typically a blanket, teddy bear, or other inanimate but nevertheless cherished possession of the infant. The soothing and calming qualities with which it is endowed are especially evident during stressful separations from caregivers and at bedtime (Winnicott 1951). Its odor and tactile characteristics hold a special significance, in that they are believed to be reminiscent of mother. In mother's absence it is the transitional object that enables the infant to sustain the illusion of a calming, comforting mother. Because the transitional object is a creation of the infant and, unlike mother, remains under her control, it serves to promote the infant's increased autonomy and independence (Moore and Fine 1990). The blanket or teddy bear, however, is not simply a symbolic re-creation of mother, designed to facilitate the infant's transition from symbiotic merger to relative autonomy; it is rather a "developmental way station,"

a special extension of the child's self, halfway between the mother that the child creates in subjective omnipotence and the mother that the child finds operating on her own behalf in the objective world. The transitional object . . .

cushions the fall from a world where the child's desires omnipotently actualize their objects to one where desires require accommodation to and collaboration of others to be fulfilled. (Mitchell and Black 1995:128)

Although Winnicott originally presented the concept of the transitional objects and transitional experience in the context of early infant development (1958b [1951]), he later broadened this framework to include aspects of adult experience. The transitional experience for the child is embedded in a capacity for play, whereas, for the adult, transitional experience is a "protected realm" where there exist opportunities to "play with" new ideas and fantasies and cultivate one's own creative impulses (Greenberg and Mitchell 1983).

Winnicott's theories, unlike those of Freud, Klein, or Sullivan, have never attained the status of a school of thought, nor did Winnicott ever make the claim that his theories, taken together, represented "a comprehensive theory of object relations" (Bacal and Newman 1990:185). His papers, many of which were originally presented as talks (Greenberg and Mitchell 1983), have a stylistic informality and poetic quality that at times can be almost seductive to the reader; at other times, however, these same inherent ambiguities and his idiosyncratic, discursive style make Winnicott difficult, even frustrating, to read. Despite this, and despite recent criticisms of Winnicott's distortion of traditional psychoanalytic ideas (Greenberg and Mitchell 1983), his influence has remained strong. Winnicott's vision has enriched our understanding not only of infant development but also of the significant relationship between environmental failures in early life and the phenomenology of certain disorders of adulthood. Perhaps more so than other psychoanalytic theorists, Winnicott's work, with its abiding object relational emphasis on the person-environment matrix, has been especially appealing to social work clinicians. Nevertheless, some feminist scholars have been critical of Winnicott and other object relations theorists for a "matrifocal" theoretical emphasis which they believe promotes patriarchal thinking and, in consequence, contributes to gender inequities in child care, mother blaming, and the devaluation of women in the culture (Okun 1992; Applegate and Bonovitz 1995).

THE PSYCHOLOGY OF THE SELF

The psychology of the self, introduced by Heinz Kohut, has only recently emerged from a vigorous and at times rancorous debate within psychoanalytic circles. The evolution of Kohut's self psychology is represented in a series of books and papers published between 1959 and 1984. Kohut originally introduced "his theoretical and technical innovations *within* the framework of classical drive theory" (Greenberg and Mitchell 1983:357) but subsequently presented a significantly expanded and revised framework (Kohut 1977, 1984) that has become the basis for an important and distinctive theory of psychoanalytic psychology.

Heinz Kohut (1913–1981) received a traditional psychoanalytic education and worked for many years in the classical tradition with his analytic clients. The original impetus for the development of his theory came from his clinical experiences with clients, particularly those who seemed unable to make use of interpretations that followed the classical formulas. Kohut had noted that, despite his most concerted efforts, these clients frequently evinced no benefit from his interpretive work and, in many cases, their symptoms actually became worse (Leider 1996). After repeated efforts to revise and refine his formulations proved unsuccessful, Kohut surmised that the essential difficulty was not poorly timed interpretations or an overly narrow or global focus but the fundamental theoretical assumptions of classical theory. These theoretical premises, Kohut argued, were useful in the treatment of the classical neuroses (e.g., hysterical, obsessive-compulsive, and phobic disorders), but by the latter part of the twentieth century such cases were no longer seen with the same frequency that they had been in Freud's day. If classical neurotic cases were modal in the 1920s, clients with borderline and narcissistic personality disorders, in particular, seemed to be diagnosed with increasing frequency by the 1960s and 1970s.

Kohut's vision of the human condition gradually evolved into something quite different from that of Freud. The Freudian view of humankind can be characterized as an ongoing battle between primitive desires and civilized precepts for behavior, a struggle that is repeated anew with each succeeding generation. In such a perspective guilt represents a supreme accomplishment, a painful though essential ingredient for the renunciation of instinct, which is a sine qua non for socialization. Kohut, on the other hand, addressed himself not to battles but to

isolation . . . painful feelings of personal isolation. . . . Kohut's man in trouble was not riddled with guilt over forbidden impulses; he was moving through a life without meaning. . . . He looked and acted like a human being, but experienced life as drudgery, accomplishments as empty. Or he was held captive on an emotional roller coaster, where exuberant bursts of creative energy alternated with painful feelings of inadequacy in response to disrupting perceptions of failure. The creative process was short-circuited. . . . Relationships, eagerly, even desperately pursued, were repeatedly abandoned with an increas-

[ing feeling of pessimism at ever getting what one really "needs" from another. (Mitchell and Black 1995:149)]

Kohut asserted that one of the most fundamental distinctions between self psychology and classical psychoanalytic theory concerned human nature. Kohut believed that classical psychoanalysis was chiefly concerned with Guilty Man, "whose aims are directed toward the activity of his drives . . . and who lives within the pleasure principle," attempting "to satisfy his pleasure-seeking drives to lessen the tensions that arise in his erogenous zones" (Kohut 1977:132). Kohut's concept of Tragic Man, however, illuminates "the essence of fractured, enfeebled, discontinuous human existence" (Kohut 1977:238). It represents Kohut's effort to explain such clinical phenomena as the schizophrenic's fragmentation, the pathological narcissist's efforts to cope with diffuse and painful vulnerabilities, and the despair of those approaching old age with recognition that important ambitions remain unfulfilled, and ideals unattained.[11]

"Tragic Man" (margin annotation)

Kohut and his adherents have introduced several terms and concepts that are associated with psychoanalytic self psychology, each of which we shall explore in some detail: *mirroring, idealizing,* and *partnering selfobjects,* the *tripolar self,* the *self types, empathy* and *transmuting internalization, cohesion, fragmentation,* and *disintegration anxiety,* and *compensatory structures.*

MIRRORING, IDEALIZING, AND PARTNERING SELFOBJECTS

Kohut used the term *selfobject* to refer to a particular kind of object relationship in which the object is actually experienced as an extension of the self, without psychological differentiation. He observed that "the expected control over such [selfobjects] . . . is then closer to the concept of control which a grownup expects to have over his own body and mind than to the . . . control which he expects to have over others" (Kohut 1971:26–27). Kohut believed that infants are born into an interpersonal milieu that optimally provides them with three distinctly different though equally necessary kinds of selfobject experiences. One kind of experience calls for mirroring selfobjects "who respond to and confirm the child's innate sense of vigor, greatness and perfection." A second variety of self-object experience requires the powerful and reassuring presence of caregivers "to whom the child can look up and with whom he can merge as an image of calmness, infallibility, and omnipotence" (Kohut and Wolf 1978:414). Kohut later introduced a third selfobject realm, referred to as alter ego or partnering selfobjects. This third variety provides a range of experiences through which children acquire a sense of belonging and of essential alikeness within a community of others.

Infant 3 selfobject (margin annotation)

1 (margin annotation)

2 (margin annotation)

THE TRIPOLAR SELF

The tripolar self is the intrapsychic structure over which are superimposed the three specific selfobject experiences we have described. The first pole, that of grandiose-exhibitionistic needs, is associated with the need for approval, interest, and affirmation (mirroring). The second pole, the idealizing pole, is associated with developmental needs for closeness and support from an (omnipotent) idealized other (Leider 1996).[12] The third pole is that of the alter ego, and it involves the ongoing need for contact with others who are felt to bear likeness to the self. These three poles are "structures that crystallize as a result of the interaction between the needs of the self and the responses of those important persons in the environment who function as selfobjects" (Leider 1996:141).

THE SELF TYPES

Kohut and other exponents of psychoanalytic self psychology believe that the self is most usefully understood within the intersecting matrices of developmental level and structural state. Four principal self types that have been identified are 1. the *virtual self,* an image of the newborn's self that originally exists within the parent's mind and evolves in particular ways as the parental "selfobjects empathically respond to certain potentialities of the child" (Kohut 1977:100); 2. the *nuclear self,* a core self that emerges in the infant's second year, serving as the basis for the child's "sense of being an independent center of initiative and perception" (Kohut 1977:177); 3. the *cohesive self,* the basic self structure of a well-adapted, healthily functioning individual, characterized by the harmonious "interplay of ambitions, ideals, and talents with the opportunities of everyday reality" (Leider 1996:143); and 4. the *grandiose self,* a normal self structure of infancy and early childhood that develops originally in response to the selfobject's attunement with the child's sense of himself or herself as the center of the universe.

EMPATHY AND TRANSMUTING INTERNALIZATION

Kohut, whose theoretical contributions have focused on development of the personality, psychopathology, and psychoanalytic technique, placed a great deal of emphasis on the role of empathy in human development.[13] Self psychology defines empathy as "vicarious introspection," the immersion of oneself into the experience of an other; the capacity for empathic attunement in the child's selfobject milieu is considered to be of the utmost importance. At the same time, a critical impetus for healthy self-development involves what are described as minor, relatively nontraumatic lapses in parental empathy. Such lapses, because they are optimally frustrating, serve as a catalyst for the child's development of transmuting internalizations. Transmuting internalization is an intrapsychic process whereby the child gradually "takes in" functions associated with the self-object, which may range from self-calming and self-soothing to pride, humor, and stoicism in the face of adversity. In other words, through an almost imperceptible, bit-by-bit process of translocation, these functions gradually become enduring parts of the child's own self structure, though they are transformed to "fit" the child's unique self.[14]

COHESION, FRAGMENTATION, AND DISINTEGRATION ANXIETY

Cohesion is the term used in self psychology to refer to a self state that serves as the basis for robust, synchronous, and integrated psychological functioning. Self cohesion makes possible the harmonious interplay of ambitions, ideals, and talents in the context of everyday realities. It also protects the individual from regressive fragmentation in the face of adversity or obstacles that may interfere with the satisfaction of object or selfobject needs (Leider 1996). Individuals who are fragmentation prone (who tend, under stress, to develop such symptoms as hypochondriasis, hypomanic excitement, or disturbances in bodily sensation and self-perception) have been unable to acquire stable, consolidated, and enduring self structures. Whether this is a consequence of parental pathology, environmental vicissitudes, or a combination of the two, it is invariably associated with the unavailability of parental selfobjects to perform important selfobject functions. Such developmental deficiencies are associated with self or self-object disorders (e.g., narcissistic pathology, borderline states, depression, and psychosis). Disintegration anxiety is defined as the fear of the breaking up of the self, which, according to Kohut, is the most profound anxiety a human being is capable of experiencing. A related term, *disintegration products*, refers to various symptoms produced by an enfeebled, disharmonious self (e.g., paranoia, narcissistic rage, or exhibitionism).

COMPENSATORY STRUCTURES

When in the course of early development the parental selfobjects fail to respond adequately to a particular constellation of selfobject needs (whether for mirroring, idealizing, or partnering), it is sometimes possible to compensate for these deficiencies through more intensive structuralization of a second set of selfobject needs. As an example, an individual who has experienced developmental arrest in the area of ambitions (perhaps due to chronic disappointments in his or her efforts to evoke mirroring responses from a parent) may find the same selfobject to be far more accessible for the fulfillment of idealizing or partnering needs. The evolution of compensatory structures is motivated by the individual's need to rise above developmental obstacles and to repair defects in self structure (Leider 1996). Compensatory structures, however, are regarded as normative, and, as Kohut observes, "there is not one kind of healthy self—there are many kinds" (Kohut 1984:44)[15]

RECENT DEVELOPMENTS IN SELF PSYCHOLOGY

Self psychology is no longer the unitary theory it was during Kohut's lifetime, though most who are identified with his theories continue to subscribe to two basic features of his work: the central importance of the therapist's sustained, empathic immersion in the subjective experience of the client and the concept of selfobjects and the selfobject transference (Mitchell and Black 1995). There has been considerable divergence and ferment within self psychology in recent years, a situation that has prompted one well-known theorist to observe that "self psychologists no longer have a common language" (J. Palombo, personal communication).

The analyst and infant researcher Joseph Lichtenberg has addressed himself to Kohut's developmental concepts and their particular meaning in the light of important new developments in the field of infant research (Lichtenberg 1983, 1989). Infant research has also been of interest to Lachmann and Beebe, who have paid special attention to self psychological notions of self-regulation and transmuting internalization, expanding and extending Kohut's original formulations (Lachmann and Beebe 1992, 1994). Stolorow's intersubjectivity theory (Stolorow, Brandschaft, and Atwood 1987), while based on the organizing framework of Kohut's system, represents a more revolutionary paradigm. "Rather than the individual, isolated self, Stolorow's emphasis is on the fully contextual interaction of subjectivities with reciprocal, mutual influence" (Mitchell and Black 1995:167). Bacal (1995) and Basch (1986, 1988), and others too numerous to mention, have also shaped the burgeoning literature of psychoanalytic self psychology.

RELATIONAL PSYCHOANALYSIS:
AN EMERGING PSYCHOANALYTIC PSYCHOLOGY

Relational psychoanalysis, perhaps the newest theoretical school to emerge from within the psychoanalytic field in recent years, gained considerable momentum with the publication of two groundbreaking works, both of which appeared in 1983. The first of these was a paper written by Merton Gill in which the author took note of the sweeping changes in the field of psychoanalysis that had rendered Freud's energy discharge model highly problematic if not fundamentally flawed (Gill 1983). Gill proposed what he termed a "person point of view," which combined essential elements of Kleinian object relations theory, interpersonal psychoanalysis, and self psychology with Freudian clinical theory and aimed to establish an entirely new psychoanalytic orientation. The second work, Mitchell and Greenberg's landmark volume, *Object Relations in Psychoanalytic Theory*, explored the nature and underlying assumptions of existing psychoanalytic theories according to how each dealt with the problem of object relations. As we have noted previously, Greenberg and Mitchell's careful yet comprehensive analysis of psychoanalytic theoretical systems yielded two distinctive and mutually exclusive models of the mind that they termed, respectively, the *drive/structure* and *relational/structure* models (Ghent 1992).

Broadly speaking, relational theorists tend to share the view that, in character development as well as in the genesis of psychopathology, human relations play a superordinate role (Ghent 1992). Ghent has defined the relational perspective in somewhat greater detail:

Relational theorists have in common an interest in the intrapsychic as well as the interpersonal, but the intrapsychic is seen as constituted by the internalization of interpersonal experience mediated by the constraints imposed by biologically organized templates and delimiters. Relational theorists tend also to share a view in which both reality and fantasy, both outer and inner world, both the interpersonal and the intrapsychic, play immensely important and interactive roles in human life. . . . Due weight is given to what the individual brings to the interaction: temperament, bodily events, physiological responsivity, distinctive patterns of regulation, and sensitivity. . . . Relational theorists continue to be interested in the importance of conflict, although conflict is usually seen as taking place between opposing relational configurations rather than drive and defense. Relational theory is essentially a psychological, rather than a biological or quasi-biological, theory; its primary concern is with issues of motivation and meaning and their vicissitudes in human development, psychopathology, and treatment.   (Ghent 1992:xviii)

Although shaped by such earlier influences as Sandor Ferenczi's ideas about transference and countertransference, British object relations theory, Sullivanian interpersonal psychoanalysis, Kohut's self psychology, and infant developmental research, relational psychoanalysis is now considered distinctive among contemporary psychoanalytic psychologies. Like the interpersonalists and other object relations theorists whose work preceded their own, relational psychoanalysts also emphasize the importance of the individual's interactions with her or his social surround and internal as well as external interpersonal relations. However, unlike other psychoanalytic schools, relational theorists have focused on the interrelationships between physical, temperamental, motivational, and psychological processes, and have reinforced the importance of context and meaning (Ghent 1992). Relational theory has also explored the developmental significance of mutual regulation and self-regulation, psychopathology stemming from developmental barriers to the establishment of such regulatory processes, and the manner in which such processes are re-created in the clinical situation.[16] Perhaps most important, relational theorists are at the forefront of the contemporary psychoanalytic movement to effect a shift from the "one-person" psychology of traditional psychoanalysis to a "two-person" perspective of the clinical process—a fundamental change in perspective that many believe has transformed the theory and practice of psychoanalysis.

Many authors have contributed to the burgeoning relational literature, among them Stephen Mitchell, Jessica Benjamin, Neil Altman, Lewis Aron, and Philip Bromberg. Irwin Hoffman, an exponent of social constructivism, has also exerted a strong influence on the development of relational psychoanalysis (1983, 1991, 1992). A principal premise of the social constructivist model is that the observer always influences that which he or she observes.[17] Moreover, constructivists view knowledge as *perspectival* rather than *objective*, which permits one to account more fully for the personal psychic realities of therapist and patient as well their reciprocal, mutual influences upon one another. Hoffman has paid particularly close attention to the analyst's role in the creation of the patient's transference (Gordon et al. 1998:33). Hoffman's ideas regarding both transference and countertransference, like those of most other relational theorists, are in sharp contrast to earlier, classical conceptions of these phenomena. In classical theory, transference represents the displacement of repressed feelings associated with significant figures from the patient's historical past to the analytic relationship in the present, while countertransference represents an obstacle to treatment that must be overcome.[18] Relational psychoanalysts, however, conceive of transference and countertransference as *coconstructions* or mutual creations of the patient and psychoanalyst. Furthermore, each participant in the analytic process "is assumed to respond to the *actual* participation of the other, shaped by the internal dynamics and personal past of both" (Gordon et al. 1998:41).

It is perhaps too early to determine the full impact that relational thinking has had on psychoanalytic developmental theory or psychoanalytic views of psychopathology; furthermore, it remains unclear as to whether relational psychoanalysis can even be conceived of as a substantially separate and distinctive theoretical system. Nevertheless, as part of a larger postmodern development, the introduction and appeal of relational ideas in psychoanalysis appear to parallel changes in many other disciplines and fields of study.

This chapter examined a range of psychoanalytic systems, from ego psychology to relational psychoanalysis, emphasizing the important contributions made by leading exponents of each psychoanalytic psychology, theorists such as Anna Freud, D. W. Winnicott, Margaret Mahler, and Heinz Kohut. Because psychoanalytic theories of development are often closely linked to corresponding theories of psychopathology, both of these have been incorporated in the chapter. I have also attempted to highlight and explicate major theoretical disagreements in order to reveal more fully the richness and complexity of this vast body of literature. Although this chapter and the one preceding it represent excursions into the realm of "pure" theory, remaining chapters will tend to be far more "clinically" focused, thus permitting the practical application of ideas derived from different psychoanalytic frameworks.

4

Transference

FEW IF ANY IDEAS in the history of psychoanalytic thought have received more attention than the concept of transference. Transference reactions and the somewhat more stable transference relationship involve an unconscious displacement of important attitudes, affects, fantasies, desires, and conflicts from historically significant object relationships to the person of the therapist. In an earlier age social work clinicians were routinely cautioned against permitting transferences to take root in casework relationships, although these admonitions were based on a faulty premise: that the nature and intensity of transference reactions were subject to the rules of secondary process logic and could therefore be controlled. Transference, of course, is neither bound by the laws of logic nor capable of being created or destroyed. As all psychodynamic clinicians know, transference simply "happens." A range of clinical vignettes in this chapter will illustrate different conceptions of transference and distinctions between transference reactions, the transference relationship in expressive psychotherapy, and transference phenomena in psychoanalysis.

WHAT IS TRANSFERENCE?

The concept of transference has, since its discovery nearly a century ago, been regarded as a sine qua non of psychodynamic theory. The domain of transference has gradually expanded to accommodate those discrete reactions that are transferential in nature, the more enduring transference relationship, and the transference neurosis, a unique variant associated with psychoanalytic treatment. Although there are important differences between these transference phenomena, most definitions of transference have emphasized three key elements: 1. the historical translocation of past experiences to the present, 2. that such repetitions are made without conscious awareness, and 3. that what is "transferred" or displaced (e.g., ideas or affects) may seem illogical or even irrational.

For our purposes, transference (embodying both discrete transference reactions and the more stable transference relationship) is broadly defined as *a reflexive, unconscious repetition or revivification of varying combinations and patterns of ideas, fantasies, affects, attitudes, or behavior, originally experienced in relation to a significant figure from one's childhood past, that have been displaced onto an intercurrent interpersonal relationship.*

Transference neurosis is the term given by psychoanalysts to describe the recreation within the analysis of the client's "childhood neurosis." This has generally been regarded as possible only within an intensive treatment context in which the client's regression has been promoted and the analyst has remained relatively neutral and abstinent. The use of the couch, the basic adherence to the rule of free association, the therapist's relative anonymity, and the client's accruing frustration make possible the reemergence of infantile fantasies and conflicts and, ultimately, the transference neurosis. Such a development is unlikely though not impossible in less intensive psychodynamic treatment, and psychoanalysts today are divided as to whether, even in psychoanalysis, its occurrence is either inevitable or necessarily associated with successful treatment (Reed 1994).

Transference is not restricted to the relationship of client to therapist. Indeed, it is a universal feature of all object relationships, owing to the fact that our earliest, affectively charged attachments, whether to parents, grandparents, siblings, teachers, or others, serve as the basis for all "later editions." Phenomenologically speaking, transference is not easily differentiated with respect to the person onto whom it has been displaced, although transferences occurring in psychotherapy and psychoanalysis are usually distinguished by their greater limpidity, strength, and depth.

Since transference typically involves the intertwining of love and hate, its manifestations are both ambivalent and complex (Moore and Fine 1990). Nevertheless, it has sometimes proven useful to distinguish *positive* from *negative* transference, terms that characterize the basic affective tone of the transference at a particular time in the treatment. Positive transference is generally used to refer to those patterns that are manifestly benevolent, friendly, affectionate, or loving, while negative transference, to patterns that involve unfriendly, critical, demeaning, aggressive, or hostile feelings or behavior. As we shall see later in this chapter, transference may sometimes also be aptly characterized according to its childhood relational derivation (e.g., *maternal transference* or *paternal transference*) or to specific attributes or relational qualities sought by the client (e.g., *mirror transference* or *idealizing transference*).

ORIGINS OF THE CONCEPT IN PSYCHOANALYTIC THEORY

The discovery of transference, a concept at the very center of our understanding of the therapeutic process in psychoanalysis and psychotherapy, occupies a unique place among Freud's many epochal discoveries, which include the power of the unconscious, the concept of repression, and the phenomena of infantile sexuality. None, however, "has proved to be more heuristically productive or more clinically valuable than his [Freud's] demonstration that humans regularly and inevitably repeat with the analyst and with other important figures in their current lives, patterns of relationship, of fantasy, and of conflict with the crucial figures in their childhood" (Esman 1990:1). Freud's understanding of transference and its special function in the psychoanalytic treatment situation, however, evolved incrementally. He had originally conceived of transference as an "impediment" to the analysis, an essentially inconvenient obstacle to be surmounted so that the "real" work of analysis might then resume. Later, however, he came to regard transference, and the transference neurosis in particular, as central to the analysis.

The earliest references to transference appear in Freud and Breuer's collaborative work, *The Studies on Hysteria* (Breuer and Freud 1893–95), in Freud's concluding section on "Psychotherapy of Hysteria." When the *Studies* was written Freud was still convinced of the value of the "pressure technique"[1] and of the cathartic method, both of which are closely tied to the hypnotic method.[2] However, these techniques were not invariably successful, one specific reason being a "disturbance" in the "patient's relation to the physician" (301). Freud observed that, when such a disturbance arises, no reassurance or insistence from the therapist's side had the capability of counteracting it. Instead, such an "obstacle," the content of which involves distressing ideas arising from the analytic work that are transferred on to the analyst through a "false connection," required elucidation and interpretation.[3]

Consideration of the transference, originally characterized in pejorative language, and narrowly defined principally by virtue of its capability of disrupting the work of analysis, had at first "greatly annoyed" Freud owing to its potential to increase his psychological work. Gradually, however, Freud's perspective changed, so that by the time he wrote of his failed treatment of *Dora,* some ten years later, he proposed a significantly expanded role for this concept.

[Transferences] are new editions or facsimiles of the impulses and phantasies which are aroused and made conscious during the progress of the analysis; but they have this peculiarity . . . that they replace some earlier person by the person of the physician. To put it another way: a whole series of psychological experiences are revived, not as belonging to the past, but as applying to the person of the physician at the present moment. (Freud 1905a:116)

Freud noted that psychoanalysis is not responsible for the creation of transferences, "but merely brings them to light." That which seems ordained to be "the greatest obstacle" to the work of psychoanalysis, he continued, may be converted into its "most powerful ally," if only the analyst can remain alert to its manifestations and endeavor to explain them to the client each time they arise (ibid.).

Another seven years passed before Freud returned to theoretical considerations of the topic of transference, although there are various references in the intervening years, especially in connection with his discussion of the paradigmatic Rat Man case (Freud 1909c). In "The Dynamics of Transference," published in 1912, Freud characterizes transference as "the most powerful resistance" to psychoanalytic treatment, at the same time repeating his view that transference phenomena should not be mistakenly attributed to the analytic treatment itself but rather to the client's neurosis. The concept of transference, in this essay as well, ties in more closely to both the topographical and economic hypotheses (Esman 1990). Transference, Freud observes, will impel the analytic patient to "put his passions into action without taking account of the real situation." Perforce, it will lead the analyst to attempt to understand these emotional impulses in the context of the treatment and in relation to the patient's life history, culminating in a "struggle" between analyst and client: "This struggle between doctor and patient, between intellect and instinctual life, between understanding and seeking to act, is played out almost exclusively in the phenomena of transference . . . [on which field] victory must be won" (Freud 1912a:108).

The only other major essay Freud devoted to the topic of transference, written three years later, was "Observations on Transference-Love" (1915). It is in this important essay on analytic technique that Freud's frequently misinterpreted injunction for the analyst to carry out the treatment "in abstinence" is articulated.[4] Much stress is laid on the idea that the erotic transference, as would be true of any other clinical material emerging in the analysis, should neither be discouraged nor directly gratified.

Transference was not a topic about which a great deal was written for the next twenty years, although with the publication of James Strachey's groundbreaking 1934 paper "The Nature of the Therapeutic Action of Psycho-Analysis" this trend was gradually altered. The importance of Strachey's essay lay in its identification of "mutative interpretations" as the instrument through which psychoanalytic treatment can claim to be therapeutically effective. Such interpretations, by definition, contain the elements of emotional immediacy and specificity, and are directed to "an id-impulse . . . in a state of cathexis" or, put more simply, to the *transference* (Strachey 1934:148). Although Strachey did not discount the value of other kinds of interpretative work, his perspective that transference interpretations constitute the "ultimate operative factor in the therapeutic action of psychoanalysis" soon gave rise to an important debate that, in certain respects, continues today.

A number of other writers can be credited with broadening and deepening our understanding of transference phenomena and their clinical utilization both within and outside of the traditional psychoanalytic treatment. Anna Freud, August Aichhorn, Grete Bibring, and Richard Sterba are a few of those whose contributions have shaped contemporary perspectives on the transference. Anna Freud (1936) is credited with helping to elucidate the important distinctions that exist between the transference of libidinal impulses, defense transferences, and acting in the transference (Esman 1990). Aichhorn, an educator whose pioneering work with antisocial youth presaged the later work of social workers such as Fritz Redl and Rudolf Ekstein, advocated the exploitation of the positive transference as a basis for "social reeducation" (Aichhorn 1948 [1925]). Bibring (1936), in an important paper that adumbrates the intersubjective notion of reciprocal shaping of transference and countertransference by both analyst and client, suggested that the characteristics of the analyst might exert a profound effect on the nascent transference, to the extent that analysis could suffer permanent harm. Sterba, his professed allegiance to classical conceptions of the analytic process and to Freud's ideas about transference resistance notwithstanding, introduced two important concepts, which he later termed "observing ego" and "experiencing ego," in his 1940 paper "The Dynamics of the Dissolution of the Transference Resistance." It is with the client's observing ego that the analyst forms an alliance such that transference interpretations might achieve their desired therapeutic effect.

Between the late 1930s and early 1960s psychoanalytic authors increasingly turned their attention to transference. A number of writers, among them Frieda Fromm-Reichmann (1939), Janet Rioch (1943), Ida Macalpine (1950), Herman Nunberg (1951), Melanie Klein (1952), Phyllis Greenacre (1954), and D.W. Winnicott (1956), made significant contributions to this burgeoning literature. Important controversies also began to emerge, foremost among which was the question whether a phenomenological distinction existed between the analytic transference proper and what some authors were now referring to as "basic" transference, "therapeutic alliance," or "working alliance."[5] In more recent years the transference literature has grown in almost geometric proportions. Although this list could be far longer, important recent contributions have come from writers such as Leo Stone (1967), Hans Loewald (1971), Roy Schafer (1977), Merton Gill (1983), Otto Kernberg (1987), Arnold Cooper (1987), John Gedo (1989), James Fosshage (1994), Gail Reed (1994), Thomas Ogden (1995), and Glen Gabbard (1996).

THE SELFOBJECT TRANSFERENCE: CONTRIBUTIONS OF KOHUT'S SELF PSYCHOLOGY

In this section a theoretical approach to the understanding and clinical utilization of transference material, based on Heinz Kohut's psychology of the self, is presented. Psychoanalytic self psychology, acknowledged even by its critics as one of the most important new theoretical developments in psychoanalysis during the last thirty years, has contributed a great deal to our understanding of human development and psychopathology, as we have previously discussed in chapter 3. Kohut's formulations, some would argue, have also changed our understanding of what is curative in the therapeutic process. Because I believe self psychological ideas regarding the nature of transference and its mobilization in treatment to be sufficiently unique to set this theoretical system apart from other psychoanalytic frameworks, these ideas are presented here in greater detail.

Some have maintained that to consider transference in selfobject terms almost requires that one renounce classical ego psychology or object relations, inasmuch as they rely on a conception of drive not deemed central to selfobject theory or are rooted in *conflict theory* whereas self psychology is *deficit* based. I would submit, however, that the value of any theory or proposition is directly proportional to its ability to offer a satisfactory explanation for the clinical phenomena under investigation, and that one logically proceeds from the clinical data to a parsimonious theoretical formulation rather than the other way around.[6] In effect, this means that adherence to "pure" theoretical positions, particularly in the absence of compelling clinical data, becomes a far less likely outcome. Although such an approach to psychoanalytic theory cannot be considered truly "integrative," neither is it the equivalent of theoretical *eclecticism*, which typically connotes pragmatism and is defined as "selecting what appears to be the best from diverse sources" (*Webster's II New College Dictionary* 1995). Rather, it is a *transtheoretical* framework, which, as I suggested in the introduction, identifies important features associated with multiple theories and strives for both theoretical rigor and internal clarity.

In this regard we note that the original impetus for Kohut's development of self psychological theory came from his efforts to work with clients whose pathology did not seem to conform to classical schemata that presumed a neurotic personality organization. When Kohut encountered clinical problems, particularly in connection with the phenomena of transference, "that seemed opaque and intractable within the framework" of extant classical psychoanalytic theory, he began to think of transference and the process of dynamic treatment in increasingly different terms (Mitchell and Black 1995). As a direct consequence, self psychology appears to have illuminated particular transference configurations and the clinical process through which they are revealed and addressed therapeutically. In so doing, it has captured and examined, in depth and with clarity, dimensions of transference either not previously identified or to which other psychoanalytic theories have not attached major significance.

Self psychologists believe that the therapist's basic attitude of concern and compassionate acceptance, as well as his or her promotion of an ambience of emotional vitality and responsiveness, is necessary to bring about the therapeutic remobilization of various archaic selfobject needs, considered a sine qua non for meaningful psychotherapy. This therapeutic stance has often been presented in stark contrast to the "detached, cold, abstemious, surgeonlike demeanor" attributed to Freud and to his rendering of classical psychoanalytic technique (Freud 1912b; Leider 1996).

The interpretative process in self psychology consists of two basic phases: a phase of *understanding* superseded by a phase of *explanation and interpretation*. Both these phases are deemed essential to the therapeutic process (Kohut 1984). With the unfolding of the therapeutic process and the establishment of a selfobject transference, the client unconsciously perceives the therapist as fulfilling various selfobject needs. It is the client's dawning perception that the therapist has somehow failed to satisfy these selfobject needs (an unavoidable eventuality) that leads to fragmentation, archaic affect states, and other sequelae of misattunement. Such therapeutic breaches, however, are not only unavoidable, in the view of self psychology, but *necessary* for further psychological growth and structural repair (Kohut 1977; Wolf 1988; Leider 1996).

The phase of understanding commences with the therapist's recognition of the empathic rupture or breach, which the therapist then conveys to the client. Such therapeutic communications, accompanied by the therapist's attempt to reconstruct and characterize the events leading to the disruption, serve to reestablish psychological homeostasis (Kohut 1984). This makes possible explanation, in which the significance of the therapeutic breach is recast in dynamic-genetic terms, permitting the client and therapist to reconstruct the circumstances of childhood in which parental selfobjects were chronically unavailable, "analogous disruptions occurred, and the self was permanently injured" (Leider 1996:157).

TYPES OF SELFOBJECT TRANSFERENCES

Kohut focused his attention on the formation or malformation of the self, and the typology he developed for understanding transference phenomena is closely tied to the developmental model associated with psychoanalytic self psychology (as previously detailed in chapter 3). He believed that the clinical manifestations of transference were intimately related to a revivification of various distorted archaic needs arising from the individual's early self/selfobject milieu as well as the defenses erected against them.

Kohut (1971, 1977) and Wolf (1988), another leading self psychologist, have identified five selfobject transference types, each of which is described below.

MERGER TRANSFERENCE

In this primitive transference configuration, the individual attempts to reestablish an inchoate self/selfobject experience in which the selfobject is experienced as an extension of the client's self. In such a transference the therapist is not perceived as having her or his own sensibilities, initiative, or capacity for autonomous action but is rather regarded as being more like an appendage of the client. The merger transference may at times also be expressed defensively as the client's need to maintain distance as a protection against the possibility of overwhelming, traumatic disappointment, which is anticipated should the selfobject be unwilling to submit to the client's efforts at enmeshment and control.

CLINICAL EXAMPLE In a family service agency setting, weekly treatment was initiated for a twelve-year-old Mexican American boy who had been diagnosed with a pervasive developmental disorder. This child, it soon became evident, was neither interested in nor developmentally capable of participating in collaborative or competitive play and expressed no interest in talking, drawing, or any of the usual therapeutic play activities. Eventually he was able to express a preference for playing Pac-Man, a video arcade game. However, when he and his therapist played this game, the therapist's exclusive function was as a repository for quarters while the client played one game after another from the beginning to the end of each hour. In fact, the client rarely bothered to look behind him as he reached into the therapist's outstretched palm for the next quarter at the conclusion of each game. The therapist was not permitted to make any comments or in any way disturb the client's play until much later in the treatment, at which time a fuller range of play modalities became possible with this child.

IDEALIZING TRANSFERENCE

The recrudescence within the transference relationship of a client's need for merger with an infallible, calm, strong, soothing, and wise selfobject. This may be directly expressed positively, through the client's open admiration for the therapist, or defensively, through depreciation.

CLINICAL EXAMPLE   A fifty-two-year-old woman was referred for treatment by a colleague, complaining of anxiety symptoms and long-standing marital problems, the latter having proved refractory to several attempts at marital therapy. Within a relatively short time this client expressed deep satisfaction in her therapy, often remarking on what she regarded as her therapist's brilliant insights and understanding of the tortured childhood she had led in a small southern town. Her father was an emotionally weak individual who avoided family obligations by working long hours in a small retail business founded by the client's grandfather. The client's mother, whom she hated, had treated her in an emotionally abusive and at times sadistic manner until the client reached her middle teens, at which time she was finally able to liberate herself from her family. Her sycophantic admiration of the therapist and of the qualities she identified in him was in striking contrast to her unceasingly depreciative comments about her husband.

MIRROR TRANSFERENCE

The reactivation within the treatment relationship of an early developmental need for recognition, acceptance, and affirmation of the self. In the clinical self/selfobject milieu, such reawakened needs may involve efforts to elicit the therapist's interest, approbation, adulation, or ebullient participation in the client's emotional life.

CLINICAL EXAMPLE   A twenty-seven-year-old gay male artist who had originally sought couples treatment at a college counseling service with his domestic partner began individual treatment with a male therapist a short time later for a long-standing problem with depression. Within several weeks of beginning individual treatment, the client focused increasingly on his professional work. He also spoke with both bitterness and profound disappointment about his parents' lack of interest in his artistic creativity, a unique talent of which nearly everyone else seemed to be aware. As the transference relationship deepened, this client began periodically to arrive at his therapy sessions with a portfolio of recently completed etchings and woodcuts, eventually asking that the therapist look at these works so that he might better understand the client. It was of particular interest that these drawings, representing just one of many themes in this artist's ouevre, were exclusively of male nudes. Therapist and client gradually came to appreciate the client's presentation of these works to the therapist as a transference revival of a thwarted need for recognition and affirmation not only of the client's art but, more fundamentally, of his bodily self.

ALTER-EGO OR PARTNERING TRANSFERENCE

The remobilization within the treatment relationship of the client's need for an experience of essential likeness with another. Such clients frequently view the therapist as similar or identical to themselves with respect to manner, appearance, interests, or opinions.

CLINICAL EXAMPLE A forty-three-year-old single man, a regional sales director for a clothing manufacturer, sought treatment at a mental health outpatient facility because of a vague sense of dissatisfaction in his personal life. An alcoholic several years into recovery, this client soon revealed a series of short-lived romantic relationships with women who had broken up with him, complaining that he was inattentive and self-centered or primarily interested in satisfying his sexual appetite. His father had deserted the family when the client was in mid-latency, and there had been no subsequent contact with him. Seen for weekly treatment over a period of approximately four months, he soon began to comment on what he perceived to be similarities between the therapist and himself: the office decor, the therapist's choice of art work, even his coffee cup were so like those owned by the client. When he learned that the therapist owned a retriever, he observed that "fellows like us are just naturally attracted to big, friendly dogs." On another occasion, shortly after a presidential election, he expressed frustration that a majority of voters hadn't shared "our views" (though the therapist had neither expressed his political preferences nor even cast his vote for the same candidate).

ADVERSARIAL TRANSFERENCE

In this selfobject transference the client's efforts to enlist emotional support are coextensive with the need to establish one's autonomy and for the selfobject to be both responsive and accepting of this. In effect, the client simultaneously seeks the selfobject's opposition and support as a way of firming the self.

CLINICAL EXAMPLE A thirty-five-year-old woman was referred by her EAP for therapy to help her in managing her collegial relationships with greater success. This woman worked as a researcher in a university-affiliated hospital setting and, owing to her status as both a new employee and a recent doctoral graduate in her field, was required to undergo close supervision. She found this exasperating and often argued with her supervisor over both procedural and technical issues. This finally led to her consultation with the hospital's EAP social worker and referral to an affiliate agency social worker for brief treatment. The presenting complaint was soon recast in terms of the transference, as the client's need to openly disagree with her therapist. Digging in her heels, the client would adopt a position directly opposite that of the therapist, each time secretly believing that not to do so would make her appear small, helpless, and without opinions of her own. Although it was not possible to explore the genetic origins of this behavior owing to the brief nature of the therapeutic contact, this "ally-antagonist" (Wolf 1988) pattern was gently pointed out to the client, who became less adversarial both toward the therapist and her supervisor at work.

TRANSFERENCE IN THE TREATMENT OF CHILDREN

The nature, intensity, and technical handling of transference themes and reactions in child analysis and child psychotherapy have formed the basis of a protracted and passionate debate that began over seventy years ago.[7] Melanie Klein (1932) and Anna Freud (1926, 1965) were the first analysts to publish theoretical and clinical papers on the application of psychoanalytic techniques to clinical work with children. Their ideas about child development and child analytic technique were, however, radically different and led to the founding of two distinct schools of child treatment.

Melanie Klein (1932) maintained that children could be analyzed through direct interpretation of their play, which she took to be the equivalent of the adult patient's free associations. Her contention was that children were analyzable and capable of developing "a transference neurosis analogous to that of grown-up persons" (xvi). Anna Freud (1926) originally believed that children were incapable of forming transferences as a result of their ongoing relationships with their parents, whose continuing influence as primary objects was seen as an insurmountable obstacle. However, she later modified this early position, acknowledging that children were not only capable of forming transferences but might also experience reactions analogous to the adult client's transference neurosis (Freud 1965; Yanof 1996). Nevertheless, Freud continued to insist that important differences (e.g., those involving the dimensions of globalization, duration, and resolution) do exist between the child's transference neurosis and that of the adult (Freud 1965; Altman 1992; Yanof 1996).

Current thinking about transference issues is no less complicated today than it was for child analysts and therapists practicing in the early days of child treatment. Phyllis Tyson (1978; Tyson and Tyson 1986) and Joseph Sandler, Hansi

Kennedy, and Robert Tyson (1980), who have written extensively about transference phenomena in child treatment, consider transference to fall along a continuum that includes both transference proper and transferencelike phenomena (categorized as *externalizations projected onto the analyst, transference of habitual modes of relating, transferences of current relationships,* and *transference proper*). Many writers (e.g., Chused 1988, 1992; Abrams 1993; Fonagy et al. 1996) are in general agreement today that children can and do experience transference reactions, that a thorough understanding of transference themes and issues is essential to effective child treatment, and that the systematic analysis of transference is central to effective analytic work (Yanof 1996).

SOCIAL WORK AND THE IDEA OF TRANSFERENCE

It would probably not be an exaggeration to state that the field of social work has had a fundamentally ambivalent relation to the concept of transference since it was first introduced in the 1920s. Although acknowledging the substantial likelihood that transference reactions might arise in "casework" relationships, most social work theorists evinced discomfort with the idea. Helen Harris Perlman, whose problem-solving model (summarized in chapter 1) has influenced several generations of social workers, was certainly not alone when she advised,

> In casework practice our effort is to maintain the relationship on the basis of reality. . . . Transference manifestations need to be recognized, identified, and dealt with as they occur, but the effort is to so manage the relationship and the problem-solving work as to give *minimum excitation to transference* [emphasis mine]. . . . A client's loss of his sense of reality as to the purpose and nature of his relationship with the caseworker may set off a whole chain of unrealistic responses in him . . . [that] muddy or distort the client's vision.
>
> (Perlman 1957:78–79)

A safeguard against the inadvertent "rousing of transference," Perlman observed, was also provided through the worker's clarity of direction, role, and purpose of the casework encounter. Moreover, gentle acceptance of the "naturalness of relationship distortions" would enable a client to "face up to what he himself may then find 'foolish' or inappropriate in his behavior or feeling" (79).

There are a few elements embedded within Perlman's advisory to caseworkers worthy of additional attention. First is the intimation that transference is essentially an inconvenience, distracting both client and worker from the "real business" of the casework process. A second inherent possibility is that exploration of the transference will promote regression in the client, thereby making him or her neurotically dependent on the social work clinician and thus culminating in a "management problem." Finally, there is the suggestion that discussion of transference issues is not really within the legitimate province of social workers, being more properly suited to the psychoanalytic process.

Such distinctions between psychoanalysis and clinical social work psychotherapy at one time were rigidly maintained by psychiatric and psychoanalytic organizations through the exercise of powerful negative sanctions to prevent professional-role boundary transgressions. The demedicalization of psychoanalysis, together with the introduction of a panoply of nondynamic therapies in the past thirty-five years has certainly diminished the salience of such boundary disputes. However, many clinical social work educators continue to reinforce the notion that consideration or exploration of transference leads to complications or even derailment of the clinical social work treatment process, ideas that echo Perlman's admonitions from nearly half a century ago. In one recent direct practice text, for example, the authors discuss the importance of "managing" transference reactions:

> The question can be raised as to whether transference reactions can best be resolved by focusing on the past to enable clients to gain insight into their origin. . . . It is [usually] counterproductive to focus extensively on the past, as so doing diverts efforts from problem-solving in the present and unnecessarily prolongs treatment. Further, there is no evidence that focusing on the remote origin of unrealistic feelings, perceptions, and beliefs is more effective in modifying them than scrutinizing their validity in the here and now.
>
> (Hepworth, Rooney, and Larsen 1997:562–63)

If there is an essential difference between the clinical approaches described above and a psychodynamic approach to clinical social work practice, perhaps it lies both in the general significance imputed to transference phenomena as well as its potential to enhance the helping process. Exploration of the transference, including aspects of its historical origins, may prove critical to the clinical endeavor. Accordingly, transference reactions are not reflexively circumnavigated, and neither is dissolution of transference necessarily a goal. While it is perhaps generally true that the exploration of transference is inversely proportional to the duration or intensity of treatment, this is by no means a certainty. Transference reactions may be important to understand and address in some time-limited therapies and just as important to deemphasize in longer-term dynamically oriented case management (Kanter 1995).

In the following examples, derived from medical social work outpatient, agency, and private practice venues and representing both long-term and time-limited treatments, several different transference configurations are examined, the therapeutic responses highlighted.

CLINICAL CASE ILLUSTRATION 4.1: "SARAH"

Sarah was a tall, pretty, slender—though obviously pregnant—African American young woman who arrived with her well-cared for, equally pretty, three-year-old daughter at a high-risk obstetrics clinic for indigent clients. In speaking with her the clinician learned that she was a twenty-two-year-old woman pregnant for the third time and distressed about a number of problems. She was poor, uninvolved with the father of the baby she was carrying, and, as a result of the poor judgment of youth, she had recently lost her public housing when she let some irresponsible friends temporarily share her dwelling. She and her three-year-old daughter now lived in her mother's apartment, which also housed her mother's sometime boyfriend, her pregnant sixteen-year-old sister, and two younger sisters as well, a scenario that will be all too familiar to those who have worked in agencies that serve poor families.

Although this was Sarah's third pregnancy, her daughter was her only living child. Sarah had lost her first child, a baby boy, seven months after his very premature birth. His had been a short and ghastly hospital life as a result of being born with gastroschesis, a condition in which his intestines were external to his body. His survival was dependent on a plethora of invading tubes, needles, and other mechanical devices—the wonders and horrors of modern medicine—that can prolong the life of a very sick infant. Through those seven months Sarah more or less lived at her baby's bedside and since her baby's death struggled with considerable guilt, anger, and sadness. Frustrated by the circumstances of her life, she knew she wanted more for herself and her children.

Clinician and client chatted a bit, and the possibility of counseling was offered for the client to consider. The clinician believed that it could be helpful for her to have someone who could listen to the client discuss those areas in her life that troubled her. At this point the clinician told her that he could see her, without fee, once weekly throughout her pregnancy and perhaps for a while after the birth of her baby.

Sarah arrived quite late for the first session, affording only the briefest opportunity for conversation. The therapist extended the session by about ten minutes and told her it was unfortunate that they were unable to make better use of the time. Why, the therapist inquired, did she think she came in so late? It was only because she did not yet know the bus schedule, she replied.

Such excuses should always be viewed skeptically by the treating clinician. Although they are often at least partly true, other factors are almost always involved. On this occasion there was simply not time, and perhaps it would not have been timely to inquire further. Arrangements were made for another session the following week. Sarah neither came in nor called to cancel. After waiting twenty minutes into what would have been this hour, the clinician called her. She told him that she had intended to come in but her sister, also pregnant, thought she might be having contractions and asked her to stay nearby. Had she thought to call the clinician? Yes, she was going to, but then it turned out her sister didn't need her, and by that time half the day was gone. Clinician and client arranged an appointment for the following day.

Many therapists make a critical mistake by not exploring such situations further. After all, the "excuse" appeared plausible and would seem—on its own—to justify a missed appointment. But the transference implications should never be ignored. The next day, in what was now becoming a pattern, she came in quite late again. Although there was only time for a brief inter-action, the transference issues that were almost certainly shaping a troubling and most problematic treatment alliance could not wait. Therapist and client chatted briefly, but then the clinician said, "It is understandable that concerns about your sister and her pregnancy could keep you from our appointment, but do you think there may have been other reasons as well?"

Sarah paused and, for the first time, looked at the worker with quiet seri-ousness. "If you let other people get to know you they can destroy you," she said, "and besides, if I keep coming in you might start to care about me." The worker suggested that she might also be worried that she might start to care about him. "People can destroy you if they get close to you," she said. Obvi-ously, there was much for therapist and client to talk about, and the thera-pist underscored this fact.

Sarah's attendance over the next few sessions was erratic. Following one of the missed sessions the therapist deliberately waited several days to call her. The next time they met, he told her that if she missed any more sessions he would no longer contact her. It would be her responsibility to call him. She thought this reasonable and said she should be more responsible. The clinician gently emphasized the importance of their trying to understand her reasons for missing these sessions. Surely, he said, there were reasons.

Sarah did not miss any more appointments, but frequently she arrived late. Over the next several meetings Sarah would tell the therapist about the latest disappointment she experienced with her boyfriend or her mother's boyfriend. She would mock their words and mannerisms. It was always a performance. "Men are stupid," she would say pouting, imitating a young child. Her manner seemed to imply that it was all a joke to her and that her feelings were not to be taken seriously. The therapist suggested that this was how she dealt with troubling feelings—she did not trust others enough with the knowledge that something genuinely troubled her. Furthermore, he noted, perhaps she had worries that the therapist, yet another male, would let her down in some way. "I'm afraid you'll think I'm crazy," she said somewhat jokingly, "maybe you'll lock me up." He observed that even though she was saying this in a joking manner, it must be something she was really worried about. "Yes," she said, "that's what people say they do with crazy people." The clinician assured her that he had heard nothing to make him think about her being "locked up," but also thought there must be reasons for this possibility to occur to her.

During the next session she told the clinician that her boyfriend wanted to settle down with her. She wanted to get married, but only to a man who would do everything that she told him. "If I say go to the store, he will go to the store, if I say get me a soda, he will get me a soda." The therapist noted that it sounded as though she was worried about a man having an independent mind. She replied that if she gets involved with a man she can't control, he might leave her. That's what men do, she said conclusively, they leave you.

During the next appointment, Sarah again arrived late. Again, she said it was a problem with the bus. She and her sixteen-year-old sister were arguing, she said. This sister just had her baby and, unlike Sarah's past experience, everyone in Sarah's family was doting on her sister.

When Sarah was seventeen, she told the therapist, she had to tend to her sick baby by herself. Although her mother would drop her off at the hospital, she felt that no one really helped her. When her baby died, Sarah and the baby's father made preparations for the funeral by themselves. She paused, and for the first time, cried in the therapist's presence. The therapist told her that what happened was a terrible tragedy and an unbelievable ordeal for a seventeen year old to go through, especially when she felt so unsupported.

She said things were really going well now between her and her boyfriend, even though he was not the father of the baby she was now carrying. She was really starting to talk to him and he was talking to her. OK, Sarah said, so all men aren't stupid. She said she liked talking to the clinician and wanted to keep at it. The real problem wasn't the bus, she said, but that maybe he would think she's crazy. People who are crazy can have their children taken from them. The therapist suggested that the client and he needed to understand more about the reasons for this fear. As they went to set the next appointment time, the therapist opened his calendar and Sarah, with pride, pulled from her purse her very own newly purchased calendar. The therapist was heartened at this symbolic identification; both client and therapist now had calendars, a hopeful sign for their continued work.

On the day of the next scheduled appointment, the therapist received a call from one of the social workers on the mother-baby unit. Sarah had delivered her baby the night before and asked that he be notified. He rode the hospital tram and paid Sarah a brief visit. Her eyes lit up when she saw him. "What you won't do to avoid coming to your appointment," he gently teased. She laughed heartily and held up her beautiful baby boy for the therapist to admire, which he did enthusiastically. She told him that she wanted to keep her regular appointment in one week, and for that one and all subsequent appointments she showed up on time.

Over the next four visits—some with Sarah alone, some with baby in tow—Sarah revealed more about her background. She remembered a loving relationship with her father during the first years of her life. Her parents separated when she was four, and her mother became involved with an abusive man. "I lost my virginity to him at the age of six," she told the therapist without much visible affect. "Mother left him as soon as she found out. He's dead now," she said in the matter-of-fact tone frequently used by people whose formative years were marred by such tragedy. When Sarah was seven she spent a summer with her father, and she had mostly good memories of that experience. She was not to hear from him again, and he did not send any child support, but he did send her $100 for her sixteenth birthday.

The worst day of her life, she said, was the day of her baby's funeral. She was stunned and filled with mixed emotions to see her father and his girlfriend walking toward the gravesite. That he would come to be with her, on this most dreadful day, seemed momentarily to make up for all past hurts and disappointments. At the end of the funeral service, after the small crowd had thinned, her father asked her why she was not crying. She said that she didn't know, but, in truth, she was relieved that her baby was no longer suffering. In addition, what she did not tell him was that she had experienced an emotional catharsis several days earlier when the decision was made to disconnect her baby from all the wires and machines that had kept him alive. That day she held her baby for the first time and wept for hours.

"If you can't cry at your own baby's funeral, then you're no daughter of mine," her father bellowed. He kept repeating this. Perhaps he had been drinking. "If you can't show emotion, I'm not your father! Cry! You need to cry!" Confused, numb, and bewildered, she walked away while he was screaming, telling her to come back, listen to him—after all, he was her father!

Sarah and her therapist spoke of the pain and confusion she must have experienced that day and, further, of the horrors and deep disappointments she had known with men who were father figures in her life. "You don't know how many times I've killed them in my mind," she said, looking right at the therapist. "I'll bet you have," he said. How understandable that Sarah worried whether her therapist might think she was crazy! How clear it became why she would—for so many reasons—need to protect herself from him and why she would need to deal with him as though he would be "stupid" like the other men in her life. That Sarah and this therapist had a working relationship attested to the positive parenting she received, certainly from her mother and even from her earlier years with her father.

The therapist felt that he needed to demonstrate that he could be a reliable caregiver who, especially as a male, was different than those Sarah had known. Second, he needed to work with Sarah so that collaboratively they could put her fears, worries, and anxieties into words in order to examine what was getting in the way of their being able to work together. Neither actions nor words alone would have been sufficient to establish a therapeutic alliance.

For some months after the birth of the baby, therapist and client met weekly. She had taken the bus to all her appointments and had not missed one session, until one particular week. She neither came in nor called. The therapist was disappointed but not surprised, because *he* had been on vacation— had left her—the week before. Her absence reminded him that, in light of her past, it was still too early in the development of the relationship to take for granted a strong therapeutic alliance.

Near the conclusion of their work together, Sarah's therapist referred her to a program at a local university that works with young mothers interested in attending college.

DISCUSSION

In certain respects the foregoing case illustration represents a timeless casework encounter between client and clinician. This is due in part to the venue through which services are provided, a hospital-based clinic for indigent patients, but also to the traditional nature of the treatment itself, a time-limited therapeutic relationship more or less coterminous with Sarah's pregnancy. The clinical picture is classical in other respects, as well. The combination of Sarah's status as a poverty-stricken minority single mom, complicated by her history of traumatic loss and the ongoing issues with her family and boyfriend, collectively casts a giant shadow across this pregnancy. Perhaps as much as any client, Sarah is in urgent need of help; and yet, paradoxically, an obstacle, one difficult to apprehend except in dynamic terms, stands in the way of her receiving it. It would certainly be possible and relevant for the discussion of this case to consider matters of initial resistance, the promotion of the working alliance, or even the significance of the transracial treatment relationship. However, our focus here will be on the transference, the contribution it makes to the shaping of this clinical encounter, and how the therapist both understands it and makes use of this knowledge.

Sarah's difficulty in developing a stable working alliance with her therapist seems to reflect what in more traditional language has been termed the "negative transference." Negative transference was the term first used by Freud (Freud 1912a, 1917b), in his efforts to characterize a transference configuration in which aggressive or hostile features predominated. In an important sense Sarah begins this treatment relationship with two interrelated and very powerful unconscious assumptions. The first of these is that men will let you down, abandon you, or even destroy you, given half a chance, and, second, it is very important to control men in order to prevent such situations from occurring. Sarah's treatment is, of course, barely underway as the pattern of late arrivals and missed sessions begins. We are reminded of the distinction that Tyson and Tyson make between *transference proper* and *transference of habitual modes of relating* (1986), for Sarah's reactions seem much less a by-product of an intensive therapeutic encounter than a relational template, unconsciously activated prior to her first meeting with the therapist.

If the therapist fails to explore the historical significance of Sarah's negative transference reaction, it seems likely that her treatment might well be doomed from the outset. In fact, the cautions so often raised by social work theorists—that the client will become neurotically dependent on the therapist, such a "focus on the past" represents a diversion from problem-solving efforts in the present, or that the treatment process itself will be placed in jeopardy—seem somehow misplaced. In the first instance, that exploration of the transference might culminate in the client's neurotic dependency on the therapist, we see instead that a reliable working alliance between therapist and client becomes possible only *after* the topic of transference has been broached. In effect, the therapist's gentle insistence on exploration of Sarah's transferential issues not only has the effect of strengthening the alliance but also serves as an instrument of liberation, a means through which the client may acquire valuable insight about her desires and conflicts. Moreover, the failure to "focus on the past" in such an instance might be anticipated to result in a *repetition* of the past, but one that occurs without benefit of insight. One can easily imagine Sarah continuing to play out these issues in all subsequent relationships, but in a reflexive and automatic fashion, without the means to alter the template. Finally, it is important to recognize that exploration of the transference *is* the treatment process, no less so than the examination of the client's current problems or adaptations to them.

Nevertheless, there are important differences between the therapist's handling of transferential themes and issues in such a time-limited treatment encounter and in longer-term expressive psychotherapy or psychoanalysis. For one thing, the focus on Sarah's "habitual mode of relating" to men is not expressly geared toward an ongoing effort to shape this automatic reaction into a more stable transference configuration, as it would be in expressive psychotherapy or psychoanalysis. Rather, it is intended to lessen the possibility that the illusion of all men as unattuned, abandoning, or destructive will effectively sabotage the therapist's efforts to build a working alliance with her.

A second difference is the therapist's somewhat more *selective focus on the historical past*. The therapist is interested in the client's past relationships and in her historical narrative, but principally insofar as these have bearing on her current difficulties. This, however, is not the equivalent of asserting that such forays into the client's history and her troubled relationship with her father should be avoided lest the client and therapist become hopelessly mired in the past. In fact, it is likely that neither therapist nor client could have arrived at any useful understanding of the dynamic basis for Sarah's fears of abandonment or of the therapist's exertion of malevolent control over her without some consideration of these historical features.

Finally, Sarah's therapist's exploration of the negative transference is fundamentally designed to promote Sarah's mastery of a disruptive and ultimately self-defeating way of relating to others. The content of the therapist's transference "interpretations" is therefore technically parsimonious and expressly designed to lend support to Sarah's capacity for self-observation. In more traditional terms, such work is directed primarily at the client's ego, with correspondingly less emphasis on deeper aspects of the transference experience. Or, put in somewhat different language, the interpretative effort remains focal, designed neither to culminate in a regressive transference nor to expand into a transference neurosis in which there is a recrudescence of the original infantile trauma (Kepecs 1966).

CLINICAL CASE ILLUSTRATION 4.2: "PAM"

Pam, a forty-one-year-old single Caucasian woman, was referred by to a large outpatient mental health clinic with symptoms that included low energy, lack of motivation, outward signs of depression, and crying spells that were interfering with her ability to work. In addition, the EAP social worker expressed alarm over her suicidal thoughts. During intake, Pam revealed ongoing difficulty with sleep, a depressed appetite, and low self-esteem. She confirmed that she had suicidal ideation, although without a plan. A recent break up with a boyfriend she had known for four years had precipitated the outbreak of her symptoms. Another factor of potential significance was that her mother had been suffering for years from a degenerative neurological disorder and, within the last year, had lost her ability to speak or recognize even close friends and family.

To help stabilize her, Pam agreed to attend sessions twice weekly. After one month the session frequency was reduced to once weekly, although twice-weekly interviews have been used to advantage when, at several junctures in her (ongoing) over three-year course of therapy, Pam felt particularly troubled. In the first month Pam also consulted a psychiatrist for anti-depressant medication.

Pam was a mild mannered, soft-spoken woman who reflected, during one early session, that she had been sad all her life. She had been "in and out of counseling" since she was an adolescent, having been previously diagnosed as "clinically depressed." Pam was first prescribed antidepressants when she was twenty-one and reported that they were helpful. There was a history of depression in her family, Pam noted, especially on her mother's side; in addition, both grandfathers had serious problems with alcohol. Some years earlier she had been treated in a community mental health center where, on two separate occasions, her therapist made a unilateral decision to bring her treatment to termination. On both occasions the explanation she received was simply that "administrative problems" had required this action be taken. While in treatment at this CMHC (community mental health center) she had also suffered an adverse effect from a medication prescribed by the clinic psychiatrist. In consequence of these experiences, she stayed out of counseling for many years.

Pam recounted early in her treatment that she used to feel anger at her mother for not having protected her. Indeed, she felt neglected and unloved, as well, and never recalls actually having heard her mother say that she loved her. She does remember frequently feeling as a child that her "family was about to fall apart." Pam was the youngest of four children. Her two sisters are both much older than she is. The older of the two sisters, who had been like a surrogate mother to Pam, left home permanently when Pam was of preschool age. This loss was "devastating" to Pam and may well have represented her earliest experience of depression. Pam reported that she never got along with her older brother, two years her senior. Her father favored this brother, which represented a narcissistic injury to Pam that her father neither fully understood nor ever attempted to assuage. Interestingly, Pam's brother's importance in her father's eyes seemed to be emblematic of a greater issue in her family surrounding the devaluation of women and overvaluation of men. Her mother, for example, held the deep conviction that a wife must always place the needs of her husband before her own, a role she adopted in her own marriage despite the fact that many of her own emotional needs were chronically thwarted in consequence.

Pam recalled that throughout her childhood, she felt as though her father "hated" her. In early childhood she would fantasize longingly of her father reading to her and playing with her, activities that, in reality, rarely occurred. In fact, he daily belittled her, using the harshest criticisms, which included personal attacks on her character (e.g., calling her "stupid"). He would also yell at Pam's mother, who was typically reduced to tears. Pam's mother believed it was not "ladylike" to express anger and gradually became dependent on drugs, such as Valium, to cope with the unceasing psychological abuse from her husband. Because the family was poor, Pam and her siblings suffered chronic material deprivations and often had to wear old clothes. Many years later, as an adult, Pam learned that her mother had secretly saved a good deal of money, much of which she had quietly donated to the Church.

In addition to the chronic emotional privation and material deprivations of Pam's childhood, she was also a victim of intrafamilial sexual abuse. When Pam was four years old her uncle fingered her vagina; at the age of approximately nine her brother also began to fondle her genitals, and this continued for several years. When Pam complained to her mother about these sexual violations, her mother was dismissive, and Pam did not feel that she could she talk to anyone else about the abuse. Although her parents had been strictly opposed to her dating boys, Pam recounted with obvious self-satisfaction that she had nevertheless—since age twelve—always had a boyfriend or been in a relationship with a man. By her teens Pam had become sexually promiscuous, having gradually learned what she believed men wanted in order to procure their affection. She made some rather unfortunate choices, a factor that may have contributed to her having been sexually molested by dates. One of these boys actually raped her, although the crime was never reported to the police. Then, while in her freshman year at a Christian college, she became pregnant. She was not in love with the young man, but, in order to placate her parents, she finally gave in to their fervent demands to marry him so that the family would not be "shamed." Eight months after giving birth to her first son, Pam's weight dropped to eighty-five pounds, and at age nineteen she was hospitalized for anorexia, though without any follow-up treatment. Her marriage was troubled from the outset, and things gradually worsened as her husband became first emotionally and later physically abusive toward her. The marriage lasted four years, during which time she gave birth to another boy. Subsequently, she had an extramarital affair and shortly thereafter separated from her husband and filed for divorce.

Pam felt "ashamed" and "like a failure" over her first marriage, and she had no one with whom to share her feelings and financial worries. The loneliness was very difficult for her to bear, and not long after separating from her husband she became involved with another man whom she later married. This second marriage lasted eight years and produced no children. Pam supported the family; her second husband had a serious drinking problem and, like her ex-husband, was "mean" and physically and emotionally abusive. When asked why she stayed in the relationship so long, she replied that she had been "terrified to leave."

Five years ago, Pam became extremely sick from a bronchial virus, which seemed to worsen every winter. Subsequently, she was diagnosed with severe chronic asthma. She also had surgery to correct an abnormality that had caused chronic uterine bleeds, followed by a complete hysterectomy. In addition, Pam has suffered from weight problems and migraine headaches that were originally connected with her menses.

As the treatment relationship deepened, Pam's revelations about her troubled past revealed an interesting dynamic pattern. It seemed as though physical illness for Pam had served as a "condition of safety" through which she was able to satisfy important unrequited emotional needs. In the fifth grade, for example, Pam developed pneumonia and, for once, her mother was compassionate and caring. Pam's recollection was that she felt both "guilty and loved," a phrase that she used again in a subsequent treatment hour. She had been describing her deep depression, following the divorce from her second husband, and how her son had taken her to see a psychiatrist, lovingly put her to bed, and later brought her dinner. Although the therapist was able to help Pam identify and talk about this pattern, which had its analogue in the treatment relationship, such recognition seemed initially to have little impact on these early, and profound, unmet needs for love and attuned physical care.

Pam's treatment has actually consisted of a number of discrete episodes conducted over a three-year period. She was initially in therapy for a year and then left rather precipitously without discussing termination. She was not responsive at that time to repeated efforts by her therapist to make contact by phone or letter, although, some time later, Pam finally did return to therapy. Subsequently her pattern of involvement has been to attend therapy for five or six months, typically followed by spontaneous and unilateral decisions to suspend her sessions for periods of up to several months. In each instance her decision to return to therapy has generally followed a crisis involving her two sons or her grandson. For example, the last time she reentered therapy Pam had just learned from one son that he had tested positive for HIV. Although Pam's tentative involvement in treatment might be understood as a resistance, it seems most closely related to factors within the transference relationship.

Over the course of treatment Pam has gradually developed a limited capacity to discuss her feelings, especially those thematically related to her fear of emotional isolation and abandonment. In one memorable session, summoning great effort, she was able to tell the therapist that she had felt "rejected" by him following a recent session in which the two had discussed the limitations of her insurance coverage. She was able to see that this fear of rejection intensified as soon as she gave any thought to actually expressing her anger. However, she noted that the feeling of rejection lingered whereas her anger, if she were able to contain it, seemed to have a much shorter half-life and was, therefore, far more manageable. Pam had considerable difficulty not only in discussing her emotional reactions but also in being able to apprehend and translate signal affects into words. It is of relevant interest that, even when she believes she is very angry, Pam has reported that it "doesn't look like I'm mad to anyone else." Oftentimes, when Pam has become tearful in therapy sessions, she finds it exceedingly difficult to find words to express these powerful affect states.

Pam's mother's condition gradually worsened over the first two years of her therapy. When she was near death, in a family encounter Pam was later to describe as "toxic," her mother was essentially unconscious though in pain, and her father, in an undisguised display of sadistic cruelty, steadfastly refused to allow the doctors to disconnect his wife from life support. In the first session following this visit, Pam described a number of disturbing memories about her father that had resurfaced, feeling as though she were "in a free-fall, falling deeper and deeper into depression." During this same hour she also reflected, "If my father doesn't love me, who could?" and "It feels good to feel bad." The therapist and Pam then talked about her father's severe characterological limitations as well as his narcissistic way of expressing love. In effect, Pam's father had little capacity to love anyone, and this had been forcefully brought home when the family was briefly reunited at Pam's mother's bedside. Pam's remark that it "felt good to feel bad" was then examined. Therapist and client were able to arrive at an understanding of this as Pam's way of describing the relief afforded her through the mechanism of her guilt, an immediate reaction to the powerful though unconscious hatred she felt for her father. When her mother finally died, Pam had been in treatment for over two years. She showed little affect and recounted the details of her mother's death in an almost perfunctory way. Although Pam was now able to make the observation that it was her mother who had so little capacity to love Pam rather than Pam being unlovable, these statements were not made with deep emotional conviction.

Interestingly, Pam has revealed that even in the most difficult emotional times she has found ways to manage through her lifelong interest in the theater and in musical performance, both instrumental and vocal. Pam has, moreover, always worked, and within the past three years has had three promotions; she was recently nominated and voted in as the only woman on one of her company's important political action boards.

DISCUSSION

In the beginning of therapy Pam impressed her therapist as being like a little girl who took delight in the clinician's attention. In fact, her mannerisms, her innocent smile, her vocal intonations, even her posture, seemed at times to be very childlike. However, it was not until approximately two years into treatment that Pam began to talk about "having a crush" on her therapist. There was an unmistakably erotic component in Pam's transference reaction, although such feelings also aroused powerful negative reactions of guilt and shame, which were principally derived from the childhood molestation and abuse she had encountered within her family. Pam would later acknowledge that she was frightened of these erotic feelings and the accompanying fantasies for two reasons. The first was that such sensations in the past had always been associated with bad outcomes: exploitation, betrayal, and deep sadness and despair. The second was that she feared the strength of her own desire, which, she had concluded, ultimately made such abuse her responsibility in spite of the fact that logic told her otherwise. But even if she could trust herself, men could hardly be trusted, Pam concluded, inasmuch as even those who aren't sexually exploitative tend to be uncaring, self-centered, neglectful, or psychologically abusive. Furthermore, her past experiences with the psychiatric establishment and community mental health had convincingly demonstrated to Pam that therapists are capable of mistakes—even egregious medical errors—that could imperil not only her psychological well-being but also her physical health.

Pam's decisions to withdraw from treatment are, of course, directly related to the transference fantasies and feelings with which she had struggled since early in her therapy, which were also undoubtedly a factor in her precipitous withdrawal from therapy on at least two earlier occasions. She had considerable difficulty in exploring this, however, choosing instead to make a hasty exit from therapy each time the transference gained in strength. Pam's transference, however, was multifaceted and consisted of two distinct elements aside from the erotic-libidinal feelings toward her therapist. She also sought some sort of proof that the therapist recognized and understood the "little-girl" who had only wanted to be played with and read to, loved and doted on by her big daddy. Such transference fantasies were anxiety arousing, as well, for the wishes they represent had not only remained largely unfulfilled in the past but had instead seemed to evoke sadistic and verbally abusive responses. A third aspect of Pam's transference, one that has not been as accessible as these other two transference configurations, was Pam's abiding view of herself as a child whose mother could not love her. This, in certain respects, may be the most difficult and primordial transference of all, for the mother-infant relationship serves as the model for all subsequent relationships. In Pam's case not only did her mother fail to protect her from exploitation and abuse, but she also dismissed as fictions the truths Pam presented to her. Only when Pam was seriously ill was her mother able to show her kindness and love.

Pam and her emotional problems, as well as the nature of the complex transference that unfolded in her therapy, might be viewed in several different ways. The therapist, however, believed that Pam was a particularly good illustration of the *false self* organization, as described by Winnicott (see chapter 3). This was indeed how Pam had managed to survive such a traumatic childhood set against the backdrop of so bleak and impoverished an emotional environment. It was most transparently evident in the libidinous and childlike persona she had adopted in order to attract men while, at the same time, relegating her *true self*, one that longed for loving attention and affirmation of her intrinsic worth from a tender and affectionate father, to a subterranean existence. Pam had learned from her mother that women needed to be subservient to their husbands and had early on been disabused of the idea that little girls have as much right to attention and love as their male siblings. Having concluded that the only way out was to adopt such a false self persona, she nevertheless unconsciously selected sadistic, uncaring partners whose behavior reproduced these early childhood scenarios time and again, with nearly always the same unfortunate results.

Two aspects of the transference have to date received the greatest emphasis in treatment sessions. The first and more prominent is the nonlibidinous father transference, through which a basic affirmation and recognition of Pam's childhood needs for play and for indulgent fatherly attention have been expressed. The second is a libidinous false self transference, wherein Pam unconsciously repeats dreaded early scenarios involving sexual abuse and exploitation. For two reasons the maternal transference has not been a focus of the treatment. In the first place, the therapist's gender has made this transference configuration a somewhat less likely one; a female therapist would conceivably elicit a stronger maternal transference, and some have even questioned whether most male therapists can evoke and resolve a maternal transference (Schachtel 1986). Second, inasmuch as this treatment is primarily being conducted on a once-weekly basis, the therapist made a conscious decision not to interpret at the level of the maternal transference. His reluctance, though based for the most part on clinical intuition, may prove useful for us to consider in comparing how transference is approached in once-weekly versus more intensive treatment. Although such ideas should not be mistaken for axiomatic principles, the combination of the *history of failed therapy relationships*, the *client's difficulty in remaining consistently engaged in treatment*, and the *primordial nature of the mother transference* appear to reinforce the therapist's intuitive judgment here. If this material were thematically more prominent in the sessions, and were therapy conducted on a more intensive basis so that the client's reactions could be more accurately gauged, such cautions might not appear to be so necessary.

As a way of focusing on the nonlibidinous father transference, the therapist suggested to Pam that perhaps it wasn't the therapist Pam desired so much as the ways in which he had treated her. He posed this in a hypothetical way, wondered if exploring it might be of some value to Pam. By this point in her treatment, approximately twenty-six months, Pam seemed far more willing and capable of discussing these transference-based fantasies. She commented that, although she had felt a little guilty about it, she enjoyed being the center of the therapist's attention; this, in combination with the genuine interest he showed in her feelings and his nonjudgmental perspective, represented new experiences for Pam. Interestingly, as therapy has progressed she has also seemed somewhat more adultlike, and her "little girl" mannerisms seem to have receded. The libidinous false self transference has been less focal in Pam's ongoing treatment, although it contains a critically important transference theme; namely, that her erotized feelings translate into a vulnerability to exploitation, sexual or otherwise, by her male clinician. Although the concept of false and true selves has been discussed in connection with much of Pam's history as well as in relation to her ongoing relationships, it has only recently been explored with respect to the transference relationship.

CLINICAL CASE ILLUSTRATION 4.3: "JOE"

Joe, a slightly overweight, forty-seven-year-old, upper-middle-class Italian American Catholic man, originally came for treatment complaining of difficulty in establishing meaningful autonomy from his parents, a "joyless" marriage, and not being able to derive pleasure from his work. He pointedly offered that, unlike his father, he felt unable to "pull the trigger on business deals," believing that his indecisiveness had cost him dearly both at work and in his personal life. Joe had been in both individual and marital therapy before. In fact, his referral came from the female therapist with whom several years earlier he had concluded a three-year course of therapy. His complaints at that time had apparently been similar to the difficulties he was now experiencing. Although not sanguine as to the prospects of success, he was resigned to the idea of additional treatment, even willing to consider something more intensive, since he felt as troubled now as he had at the beginning of his previous therapy. I shared with him my sense that he seemed to be asking for a treatment that would help him to achieve more enduring personality change. After six meetings we decided on a course of psychoanalysis, with a session frequency of three times per week. This work continued for just over three years, at which time the analysis was brought to a mutually agreed upon termination.

Joe and his wife, Lisa, who was forty-three, had been married for nearly twenty years. They had four children: Don, twenty-two, who was Lisa's son from an earlier marriage, Robert, twelve, Tony, nine, and Mike, seven. Joe managed the family business, a small smelting and refining company founded by his father and his uncle some fifty years earlier, that was located in the industrial corridor of a large northeastern city. He was no longer involved in the day-to-day operations at the plant, but Joe's father called his son daily, asking for updates and frequently offering advice Joe was loathe to accept. Joe's father had been an aggressive and highly successful businessman, although in his personal life he was weak, ineffectual, and unable to lend Joe any modicum of real emotional support. Joe had never felt that he could count on his father when the chips were down or in a crisis. At such times Joe's father was alternately distant or critical and, in general, seemed largely incapable of any meaningful emotional connection with Joe. He was, moreover, unpredictable; he could "blow" at any moment. Worse yet, Joe believed that his father was contemptuous of him and had been since childhood.

Relations with his mother were also a source of disappointment and conflict for Joe. From the time he was very young, he found her to be both unreliable and unattuned. She would become very impatient with him when he clung to her at the babysitter's, often leaving him sobbing, and throughout his early and middle childhood seemed incapable of furnishing him with the emotional safety he required. In fact, he often found himself in the position of placating her, calming her down, and generally placing her needs before his in what amounted to a reversal if not a parody of the mother-child relationship. Another significant theme in this relationship was Joe's strong sense that his mother was unable to take delight in his appearance. In fact, she shunned him at times, which caused him to feel small, ashamed, and physically repulsive. His struggle to maintain a normal weight, beginning in early childhood, was in some measure due to hereditary factors but certainly compounded by the fact that food proved a reliable means for alleviating painful affect states and inner emptiness associated with thwarted selfobject needs in both of these relationships.

Early in the analysis Joe recounted several incidents that had occurred when he was seven years old, during an extended family trip abroad. Joe's father and his uncle, who had a competitive though close relationship at the time, had business to conduct in South America. A decision was made to travel with their respective families and lease a house near Rio de Janeiro and enroll the school-age children in an American school. On one weekend excursion to a mountain resort shortly after their arrival, the two families had gathered at the mountain summit and were enjoying the view from a scenic overlook. Joe had been playing hide-and-seek with his cousins when suddenly, without warning, his uncle, known for his brutish behavior, picked Joe up in a rage and threatened to throw him over the railing. The incident, evidently sparked by Joe's uncle's misinterpretation of a disagreement between the cousins, left an indelible impression not only because of the sheer terror he felt at the prospect of his falling several thousand feet to certain death but also because his parents were present at the time and neither protested. Joe also remembered his mother bringing him to the American school and making rather hasty arrangements with the school's administrator so that "she could basically get rid of me as quickly as possible." It soon became evident that this was not a safe environment for him, either physically or emotionally. Within a few weeks of starting at the school, Joe nearly drowned in the pool, largely as a result of the physical education instructor's inattentiveness. Moreover, Joe's teacher at the school, although it wasn't obvious at first, was gradually revealed to be sadistic. He humiliated Joe, calling on him purposely when he clearly didn't understand the question, making jokes at his expense, and, in other respects, treating him with insensitivity and cruelty. It was also during this long family trip that he witnessed a fatal accident involving a nine- or ten-year-old boy, who was struck by a car after he darted out into the street during a game of tag. He recalled hearing his parents, albeit shocked, remonstrating the young victim to each other for his "carelessness," in effect, making the child responsible for the tragedy that had befallen him. But Joe was especially struck by the fact that this boy, not that much older than he, was just out having fun and *no one had been able to protect him* from this tragic fate.

Shortly after we began treatment, Joe reported a dream in which a large dog that didn't belong to him "has taken an enormous dump . . . and made a huge mess. I end up helping the people (responsible for this dog) out of their problem." Joe's first association to this dream involved his own children and their dog and the fact that he often had to assume responsibility for the animal's care because "the kids aren't old enough." However, as we talked more about the dream's imagery and his feeling of being compelled to assist others with an unpleasant task, it brought to mind other thoughts. He associated to his relationship with his mother, who at critical junctures had relinquished her maternal role and forced Joe to take on responsibilities that were not legitimately his to assume. He then thought of the "messes" that his employees created for him at the office and how often he seemed to be called on to "deal with their shit," settling disputes, calming down angry clients, and so forth. We also contemplated the possibility that the dog, which in his dream belonged to someone else, may have actually represented a spilling over of Joe's own anger and resentment.

As treatment intensified, Joe began to focus more on his depression and despair. Interestingly, he had never thought of himself as depressed before starting analysis, though he now recognized many of his reactions, both at work and at home, as depressive in nature. Even when he was successful in cementing a lucrative business deal, for example, it wasn't enough to make him happy. He also acknowledged that raising his kids, which he believed should be a source of genuine gratification, was instead burdensome and draining. After six months of analysis, Joe revealed a recurring fantasy that for him was particularly disturbing and humiliating. In the fantasy he is travelling alone on a deserted stretch of highway and stops at an isolated rest area. He walks into the men's room and is rather surprised to find another man standing near the rear by the toilet stalls. This man cannot be seen clearly because he is in the shadows. Without hesitating, Joe kneels down in front of the other man, unzips his fly, and begins to perform fellatio. At first, he feels excitement, as the man's penis becomes erect, and then, at the moment of orgasm, a sense both of power and primal satisfaction. This is as far as the fantasy goes. Even though Joe has had this fantasy for years, he has spoken of it only once before, during a session with his former therapist. At that time he had expressed concern that it might mean he was gay. Although the therapist tried to reassure him that this seemed very unlikely to her, she "also moved off the topic pretty quickly."

DISCUSSION

Joe suffers from what has been most aptly characterized in self psychology as a "depletion depression." Depletion states and depletion depression, in contrast to the classical syndrome of "guilt" depression, are born neither of intrapsychic conflict nor of the problems associated with the discharge of aggression implicit in the classical model. Instead, such depression is regarded as a "disintegration product," one signaling a structural deficiency that is itself a developmental sequela of early problems in the subject's self/selfobject milieu. In self psychological terms Joe had failed to attain self-cohesiveness, owing to the unremitting series of traumatic disappointments that he had suffered in his relationships with both his parents. Indeed, Joe's history was replete with such selfobject failures, of a kind and to a degree that would appear to surpass the threshhold for the traumatogenic selfobject milieu hypothesized as being necessary for such deficits in the structure of the self to occur. Joe's mother, who was chronically overburdened, evinced a marked insensitivity and lack of attunement with her son's emotional needs, further compounded by her own pathological reliance on him as a soothing and calming selfobject. Joe's father, despite his many successes in the business world, had little wisdom to impart to his son and was rarely if ever able to serve as a fount of strength or steadfastness for Joe. Lacking in self-confidence and inner vitality, Joe had gradually come to feel an emptiness that could not be assuaged in his marriage; nor was his emptiness alleviated in interaction with his two children, nor even at work in his business relationships. He felt devitalized and impotent, was subject to mercurial fluctuations of mood, and was also markedly sensitive to narcissistic slights. Joe's capacity for the regulation of his self-esteem was minimal, inasmuch as he was highly reliant on the positive valuation of others.

But what of the transference? What form did it take and how was the thera-pist's understanding of it used to advantage in Joe's analysis? What if any impact did the therapist's interpretative efforts have on the process of treatment?

Within several months of beginning analysis, Joe developed a stable idealiz-ing transference to me, a transference configuration that endured throughout our work together. As the foregoing material suggests, however, this basic trans-ference configuration was at times augmented by both mirror and adversarial transference features. The mirror transference seemed closely linked to Joe's sense that even in infancy and early childhood his mother took little pleasure in his small body, "turning away" from him both literally and figuratively. At other times in his analysis, and especially in connection with issues involving his need to feel supported in autonomous decision making, adversarial features seemed to rise to the surface.

In the view of self psychology the transference revival of archaic selfobject needs does not call for a "corrective" therapeutic response. As Ernest Wolf has noted, "The analyst does not actively soothe; he interprets the analysand's yearn-ing to be soothed. The analyst does not actively mirror; he interprets the need for confirming responses" (Wolf 1976). It is not the active provision of selfobject responses by the therapist but "an accepting analytic ambience" that is the "sine qua non for making interpretations effective" so that they may strengthen the structural integrity of the self (Wolf 1988:133). The empathic breach in Joe's rela-tionship with his father had been profound and nearly continuous. "I wish that my father had given me loving direction, based on a deep understanding— rather than advice based on his meeting his own needs," Joe said during one early session. Some time later he remarked that, although he knew his father was a business powerhouse, none of that strength seemed available to Joe. "I always felt let down, disappointed. Dad never seemed to have the time to take me to ball games, or play cards with me, or listen to my complaints. He'd just wave me away, roll his eyes, or became furious at me. And, he never held me . . . ever." There was also the recurring fantasy of acquiring strength from a man via fellatio. Such comments, which Joe had begun to make with increasing frequency, set the stage for a recrudescence of these unfulfilled needs within the analysis itself.

Joe's idealizing transference gradually gained momentum as we neared the six-month mark in his analysis. He had been recalling a number of childhood memories in which his father had accidentally fallen on top of him, spilt hot soup on him, criticized him when he came for help, yelled at him for being clumsy, ignored him completely when the two were alone together, and so forth. He also had complained about the physical structure of the analysis itself, more specifically, of not being able to see me and of my being unable to see him—in particular the emotions his face might be registering. I made a series of interpretations emphasizing his fear that I would fail him in the same way his father had. Perhaps I would injure him by making the wrong interpretation or be unable or unwilling to lend him the emotional strength he required for his work in analysis. Maybe the very structure of the analysis would be a barrier to emotional intimacy between us, causing him to feel isolated. Worse yet, the possibility existed that I simply didn't care or was incapable of caring, a recapitulation of the great loneliness and despair he associated with the father of his childhood.

I believe such interpretations proved helpful to Joe, which is not, of course, the same thing as saying they were received painlessly. One might go so far as to say that this particular interpretation and its multiple variants became mutative for Joe in some measure *because* they exposed him to small, manageable doses of anxiety, a principle of analytic technique that is rooted in Strachey's original views on the subject (Strachey 1934). In fact, Joe complained at several junctures in the first year of his analysis that his depression seemed more intractable, his distress greater. Furthermore, he sometimes felt as though analysis was "just a lot of psychobabble." Nevertheless, he continued in analysis, producing new material in most sessions and making many more comments that were explicitly transferential or strongly suggestive of it as the analysis progressed.

It is of considerable significance that my understanding of Joe, both with respect to the transference and in relation to dynamic themes and issues not specifically linked to our relationship or to the analysis, was by no means invariably accurate. In fact, I often made minor errors in emphasis, used phraseology that he disliked, failed to comment on something he felt was important, or otherwise contributed to minor breaches in the therapeutic relationship. Such breaches in the analyst's empathy are both unavoidable and, in the view of self psychology, necessary in order to create the conditions in which self structure accrues and self cohesiveness becomes possible. These lapses, in the broad context of what Kohut originally termed optimal frustration and what Bacal has referred to somewhat more benevolently as the therapist's *optimal responsiveness* (Bacal 1985), furnish the motivation for a therapeutic process of *transmuting internalization*. Such a process, homologous though not identical to the developmental sequence described in chapter 3, culminates in the building up of missing or deficient self structures. In Joe's case analysis ultimately enabled him to resolve somewhat more satisfactorily the tremendous disappointments he had felt for so long with respect to his parents' limitations, particularly the injuries he sustained in the relationship with his father. His marital relations improved, he found that he had more time and energy to play with his children, and he no longer dreaded going to work. In fact, he found that he was able to handle personnel crises with somewhat greater equanimity and seemed more comfortable in making adaptive use of aggression in this context as well as in his personal life.

He was less successful in maintaining the weight loss he sought, although, as mentioned previously, this effort was likely complicated by nondynamic features. He occasionally felt anxious and continued to be subject to depressive episodes, but these seemed to him to be more manageable. Although transference was not the sole instrument through which these changes were initiated, it proved a durable and integral feature of the overall change effort with this client.

This chapter has examined the theme of transference in substantial detail, summarizing the historical literature in psychoanalysis and clinical social work as well as more contemporary dynamic perspectives on this clinical phenomenon. In particular, the contributions of psychoanalytic self psychology were examined, and several different transference configurations derived from this literature were highlighted. Transference in the treatment of children was also briefly reviewed. Three detailed case illustrations representing several different practice venues (medical, agency, and private practice) and therapeutic approaches (supportive, once-weekly, and intensive psychoanalytic) were then examined. Although these cases reveal important commonalties with respect to the way in which transference is understood, there are also certain differences as to how transference material is used in the clinical work. In the case of Sarah a clear though focal approach to transference served primarily to build and strengthen a treatment alliance that would otherwise have been imperiled at the outset because of the client's strong negative transference reaction. Other aspects of the transference, because they were somewhat less central to Sarah's treatment, may not have been explored in the same depth. Pam's therapist seemed to focus on transference ideas somewhat more consistently in his work with her, although not all aspects of the therapist's transference understanding were introduced in the treatment dialogue. Discussions with Pam of the nonlibidinous father transference and, to a lesser extent, the libidinous false self transference have proved very helpful in her continuing efforts to understand the problems she encounters in her ongoing relationships with both family members and her romantic relationships. Transference issues in Joe's treatment were an important and continuous feature of the analytic work, although the evidence for the existence of a transference neurosis is not incontrovertible even in this case. The consistency of the focus on transference, however, was likely promoted by reliance on the client's associative material and the use of the couch and further shaped by the client's motivation to understand the historical reasons for the deep dissatisfactions he experienced with interpersonal relationships at work and at home.

5

Countertransference

Viewed as an obstacle or hindrance to effective clinical work, interfering with the social worker's full participation in the treatment process or
compromising her or his professional role, countertransference was once judged
to represent a psychological defect or "blind spot" in the worker's perception of
the client. As psychodynamic views regarding the clinical significance and meaning of countertransference have changed, however, the clinician's subjective
experience of the client has gained a new level of respectability and acceptance.
This chapter begins with a brief descriptive review of the more common manifestations of countertransference, followed by a discussion of the ambivalence
this concept has historically elicited in the social work field. We then examine
three different models of countertransference (classical, totalist, and intersubjectivist) using adolescent and adult case illustrations derived from both family
service and private practice settings.

WHAT IS COUNTERTRANSFERENCE?

Perhaps no topic in dynamic theory has stimulated greater controversy nor been
defined in such radically different ways as that of countertransference, which
may be among the most commonly experienced yet least well understood
aspects of the treatment relationship. At times it has been narrowly defined to
include only specific reactions evoked by the client's transference. At other times
the definition is altered to encompass any displaced feelings and attitudes of a
therapist toward a client insofar as these are derived from earlier scenarios in the
therapist's life. Still other definitions are far more expansive, viewing the totality
of the therapist's emotional reactions to the client, whether conscious or unconscious, as the legitimate domain of countertransference. This last definition is, in

fact, the closest to that used in this volume. For our purposes, countertransference is defined as *the broad range of subjective reactions, whether conscious or unconscious, educed from the therapist in the context of ongoing therapeutic interaction with a client. These reactions may consist of fantasies, thoughts, attitudes, affects, counterreactions, counterresistances, behavior, and behavioral enactments. Although specific countertransference reactions may involve displacements of affective or ideational phenomena from historically important relationships of the therapist, this is neither a universal feature nor a requirement.*

The manifestations of countertransference are almost infinite in their variety and complexity, though it is emphasized that such manifestations are context dependent, and, when approached dynamically, the significance of even identically manifest reactions will reveal considerable variability. Countertransference manifestations may include:

- *Affective reactions of an unusual kind or degree* that are associated with a particular client, whether these are positively or negatively valenced. Examples are unusual interest or curiosity, concern, admiration, warmth, (non-sexual) love, sexual attraction, dislike, envy, irritation, boredom, competitiveness, anger, hatred, fear, anxiety, and dread.
- *Waking fantasies, thoughts, wishes, ideas, preoccupations, dreams, and other cognitions* associated with a particular client.
- *Forgetting of appointment times, mislaying of notes, sleepiness, fogginess, or inability to focus* in session with a client.
- *Unusual behavior* associated with a specific client. Examples would include overly solicitous actions, uncharacteristic gestures or bodily movements, and sexual or nonsexual physical contact.
- *Indirect countertransference: strong or unusual affective reactions, cognitions, attitudes, or behavior toward other family members of the client* (somewhat more commonly experienced in work with children and adolescents).

SOCIAL WORK AND THE IDEA OF COUNTERTRANSFERENCE

With but a few notable exceptions (e.g., Strean 1979; Gottesfeld and Lieberman 1979; Schamess 1981; Grayer and Sax 1986; Elson 1986; Sprung 1989), the social work literature has historically tended to regard countertransference in somewhat the same manner that it has the concept of transference and transference neurosis: as a potential *complication* in the treatment relationship that requires expeditious resolution. It is of some historical interest that older texts often substituted other language (e.g., *worker self-awareness*) and approached the topic implicitly rather than use the term countertransference at all. One reason for this convention was that the very use of the term may have suggested a level of therapeutic intensity associated with psychoanalysis or psychoanalytic psychotherapy, an impression that many social work practitioners and educators were anxious to avoid. But even in more recent social work publications that use the term explicitly, it is almost invariably negatively connoted, with frequent references to the "disruptive impact" of such reactions, their "irrational" nature, the urgent need for "handling" through introspection, insight, personal therapy, and so forth (e.g., Woods and Hollis 2000). Countertransference, another well-known social work textbook advises, "can damage helping relationships if not recognized and managed effectively" and, furthermore, "contaminates (the helping relationship) . . . by producing distorted perceptions, blind spots, wishes, and antitherapeutic emotional reactions and behavior" (Hepworth, Rooney, and Larsen 1997:565). Such views of countertransference, as we'll see in the sections that follow, are rooted in the earliest psychoanalytic conceptions of this phenomenon, although contemporary psychoanalysis has largely discarded this perspective.

ORIGINS OF THE CONCEPT IN PSYCHOANALYTIC THEORY

Countertransference, it may be argued, has only gradually achieved a level of respectability and acceptance in the psychoanalytic literature. The earliest classical formulations, in fact, view countertransference as an obstacle to analysis, a potential malignancy that must be excised lest it exert a more adverse and damaging influence over the course of treatment. The earliest references to the topic of countertransference in the psychoanalytic literature appear in three essays by Freud, "The Future Prospects of Psychoanalytic Therapy" (1910), "Recommendations to Physicians Practicing Psychoanalysis" (1912b), and "Observations on Transference-Love" (1915). In these essays Freud characterizes countertransference as a hindrance to effective psychoanalysis, a potential obstacle to analytic neutrality, and exhorts therapists to overcome any such impediment to their full participation in the therapeutic process. He also lays the groundwork for linking the therapist's countertransference to the client's transference. However, the point is forcefully made that any psychological "defects" of the therapist that "hold back from consciousness what has been perceived by his unconscious," any "unresolved repression(s)," constitute a "blind spot" in the therapist's perception of the client (1912b:116). An oft-quoted variation of Freud's prescription for the psychoanalyst's evenly suspended attention—that the analyst "must turn his unconscious like a receptive organ towards the transmitting unconscious of the patient" (ibid.)—appears in this same essay. The interweaving of these two schemes—that of the therapist's use of his or her own unconscious as an organ of reception and that of countertransference as an obstacle to treatment— appears as a "double helix throughout the historical development of psychoanalytic conceptions of countertransference" (Epstein and Feiner 1979:282).

One of the most theoretically troublesome aspects of the classical position on countertransference is the extent to which it reflects a view of the clinical process as scientifically determined and knowable. The classical conception of counter-transference, it has been argued (Hamilton 1993: Hanna 1998; Mitchell 1993), adheres to what is termed a *correspondence theory* of truth. In effect such a theory posits that all the critical dimensions of the client's subjective experience can be systematically scrutinized, if not measured, by the analyst/therapist scientist-observer. Such a perspective has also been characterized in the scientific literature as positivism, realism, objectivism, or fundamentalism (Hanna 1998). Within such an epistemology countertransference attitudes, fantasies, and particularly enactments constitute a serious threat, indeed a toxic contaminant to the unfolding of the therapeutic process. Such phenomena must be understood, but solely for the purpose of eliminating them from the analytic equation, inasmuch as they impair the therapist's capacity to function as a dispassionate scientist.[1]

POSTCLASSICAL CONTRIBUTIONS TO COUNTERTRANSFERENCE THEORY: THE TOTALISTS

Beginning with the seminal contributions of such writers as Heimann (1950), Winnicott, Little (1950, 1957), and Racker (1953, 1957, 1968), the countertransference literature gradually acknowledged and normalized what is assumed to be the universal influence of the therapist's subjectivity on the clinical process. This view has been called *totalistic* in light of its explicit assumption that the analytic field legitimately consists of subjective elements that arise from both participants, that the therapist's emotional reactions may occur in a transference-countertransference matrix or may exist more or less independently of the client's transference, and, furthermore, that the totality of the therapist's emotional reactions is a potentially meaningful source of diagnostic data relating to the therapeutic process. Our conception of *induced countertransference*, an idea heavily represented in the pioneering work of Racker, Searles, and others, owes a substantial debt to the totalistic premise that the therapist's subjective reactions are rarely a function solely of the therapist's own unresolved dynamic conflicts; rather, they are codetermined by the therapist's subjective experience of the patient (Hanna 1998).[2] Projective identification, a concept that was originally identified with

Melanie Klein (1975a [1946]) but that has been used by a number of other object relations theorists, is regarded by many who operate out of the totalistic tradition as a key component of countertransference. It is, in fact, considered by some contemporary theorists (e.g., Ogden 1982) to constitute a unique defense mechanism that, unlike other (intrapsychic) defenses, is fundamentally *interpersonal* and can also serve as a form of primitive communication between client and therapist. There is, however, no singular totalistic perspective on countertransference, as a cursory review of the work of these authors reveals. While some authors emphasize the importance of containment of the countertransference to facilitate the unfolding of the patient's transference, others (e.g.. Sandler 1976) advocate the examination of the therapist's countertransference enactments as a legitimate, indeed clinically necessary part of the analytic endeavor (Hanna 1998).

THE INTERSUBJECTIVE-RELATIONAL POSITION

As a number of authors have noted (e.g., Strean 2002; Gabbard 1995, 2000), the classical perspective seems gradually to have been replaced by a far more wholistic conception of countertransference, a development that signals what appears to be a normalization of countertransference within the psychoanalytic community. A further shift, of more recent origin, is what may be termed the *intersubjective-relational position*. Exponents of this paradigm emphasize not only the mutual contributions of therapist and client to a transference-countertransference matrix but also such ideas as coconstruction, the reciprocal shaping of transference and countertransference by therapist and client, the notion that transference and countertransference are inextricable elements in a dual unity created by the therapeutic dyad, and the value of selectively introducing countertransference elements into the therapeutic dialogue.

The reasons for this shift in perspective may, however, be somewhat more difficult to identify. The application to social phenomena of Heisenberg's "uncertainty principle," which, as we have noted previously, originally developed within the framework of the experimental sciences to account for the influence of the observer over his observations, may be one contributing factor. The influence of postmodernism on the behavioral sciences, with its emphasis on the creation of meaning within social and interpersonal contexts, is very likely another major influence. A coterminous development within psychoanalysis, which, as I have suggested elsewhere (Brandell 2002), may be traceable to contributions of the late French psychoanalyst and hermeneuticist Jacques Lacan, is the notion of *intersubjectivity*.

Over fifty years ago Lacan described psychoanalysis as a kind of intersubjective dialogue occurring between subjects, that "retains a dimension which is irreducible to any psychology considered as an objectification of certain properties of the individual" (Wilden/Lacan 1998:xi).[3] Intersubjectivity is now most often used to refer to the idea of reciprocal mutual influence in the analytic relationship or, more narrowly, the continuous interplay between the patient's transference and the analyst's countertransference. This perspective, a natural outgrowth of the shift from a one-person to a two-person psychology, appears to be a radical departure from traditional psychoanalytic ideas about the analytic process and the nature of healing. Thus some have characterized transference and countertransference, rather than as separate entities arising in response to one another, as instead being "aspects of a single intersubjective totality experienced separately (and individually) by analyst and analysand" (Ogden 1997:25*n*1). Adherents of an encompassing framework of intersubjectivism have gone even further, describing the intersubjective field as "an indissoluble system that constitutes the empirical domain of psychoanalytic inquiry" (Atwood and Stolorow 1984:64). Within this framework the effects of the analyst's countertransference on the patient's transference would appear to be no less significant nor less influential than the effects the patient's transference might exert on the therapist's countertransference.

The intersubjective system in psychoanalysis, as represented in the work of such authors as Stolorow, Brandschaft, Atwood, and Fosshage, is a newer approach to treatment historically linked to Heinz Kohut's self psychology. Based on the organizing framework of Kohut's system, it nevertheless, represents a revolutionary paradigm. "Rather than the individual, isolated self, Stolorow's emphasis is on the fully contextual interaction of subjectivities with reciprocal, mutual influence" (Mitchell and Black 1995:167). Atwood and Stolorow have defined the essential constituents of their approach in the following manner:

> In its most general form, our thesis . . . is that psychoanalysis seeks to illuminate phenomena that emerge within a specific psychological field constituted by the intersection of two subjectivities—that of the patient and that of the analyst . . . [P]sychoanalysis is pictured here as a science of the intersubjective, focused on the interplay between the differently organized subjective worlds of the observer and the observed. The observational stance is always one within, rather than outside, the intersubjective field . . . being observed, a fact that guarantees the centrality of introspection and empathy as the methods of observation . . . [pp. 41–42]. [C]linical phenomena . . . cannot be understood apart from the intersubjective contexts in which they take form.   (64)

Furthermore, there can be no certainty, no position of scientific remove from which to understand the client's pathology, or to mount interventions, but rather an intersubjective reality articulated from the therapist's sustained empathic immersion in the client's subjective experience. Ogden, whose position is in certain respects very close to the intersubjectivists, has defined countertransference as "the analyst's experience of and contribution to the transference-countertransference . . . [which] refers to an unconscious intersubjective construction generated by the analytic pair" (1997:95n1).[4] Operating within such a theoretical position, the therapist must assiduously avoid the pitfalls of assuming a hierarchical posture in which she or he becomes the arbiter of what is correct and what is distorted in the client's view (Schwaber 1992). Put more discretely in terms of transference-countertransference, the therapist must "acknowledge not only that the patient's view of reality has validity but also that the patient's view of the therapist in the transference has validity" (Hanna 1998:6).

Relational theory, which as we noted in chapter 3 contains elements of self psychology, British object relations, interpersonal psychoanalysis, and infant developmental research, has much in common with what we have here termed the intersubjective framework. With a view of the mind as essentially dyadic and interactive in nature, the relationalists underscore the dynamic shaping and reshaping of the therapeutic encounter through the continued participation of therapist and client "as well as by the coconstruction of meaning, authenticity, and new relational experiences" (Gordon et al. 1998:31). Accordingly, transference and countertransference are understood as mutual creations of the analytic/therapeutic dyad, though there is a concomitant emphasis on old relational patterns, including internalized object relations, and how these become interpolated into the transference-countertransference (ibid).

The therapeutic action of interpretation, one might then extrapolate, seems to occur within a specific relational interaction composed of the distinctive contributions of both subjects. As the intersubjectivists have observed, the client's transference and the therapist's transference (though by convention the latter is more commonly referred to as the countertransference) are usefully thought of as components of a larger system that is more accurately understood as an intersubjective field or context (Stolorow and Atwood 1996). Such a perspective, as I've suggested, is no longer viewed as unique to selfobject theorists, and the term *intersubjectivity* has gradually acquired a meaning apart from its discrete linkage with self psychology. Gabbard has recently observed that a new "common ground" has emerged in contemporary views of countertransference (1995, 2000). Classical analysts, modern Kleinians, relational theorists, and social constructivists all seem to have endorsed the view that the countertransference is jointly created by the mutual contributions of analyst and analysand. While important theoretical differences remain (e.g., regarding the usefulness of broadening Klein's concept of projective identification or the handling of countertransference enactments), Gabbard believes a significant agreement as to the value of countertransference in understanding the patient has emerged, one that transcends the traditional analytic orientations and schools. He writes:

> Over the past 100 years, countertransference has evolved from a narrow construct referring to the analyst's transference to the patient to a jointly created phenomenon that is ever-present in the psychotherapeutic situation. In recent years, a myriad of theoretical perspectives have begun to converge around the view that countertransference is partly determined by the therapist's preexisting internal object world and partly influenced by feelings *induced* (emphasis in the original) by the patient. Countertransference is now regarded as inevitable, and minor enactments of countertransference may provide valuable information about what is being recreated in the therapist-patient dyad.
>
> (2000:983)

COUNTERTRANSFERENCE ENACTMENTS AND THERAPIST SELF-DISCLOSURES

No discussion of countertransference would be complete without some reference to the concept of *countertransference enactment* and the parallel concept of *self-disclosure*. Enactment, previously referred to as *acting in, acting out,* and *disjunctive countertransference,* has been defined in several different ways, though Maroda's definition is a particularly good one. She defines enactment as "an affectively driven repetition of converging emotional scenarios from the patient's and the analyst's lives . . . necessarily a repetition of past events . . . buried in the unconscious due to associated unmanageable or unwanted emotion" (Maroda 1998:520). Though defined differently by other writers, there seems to be general consensus that enactments are spontaneous in nature, invariably involve the elicitation of strong, unconscious affect superseded by some behavior, and are probably inevitable in the course of psychotherapeutic treatment. Moreover, enactments are a special form of transference-countertransference interplay owing to the fact that the strong affects are mutually educed/stimulated (ibid.). These unique characteristics may also limit the value of the more traditional methods for addressing countertransference (e.g., self-analysis, consultation, and further personal analysis) since they are fundamentally intrapsychic, when in fact interpersonal techniques that "allow for constructive interaction" between therapist and client are called for. In fact, Maroda has gone so far as to assert that the working through of very difficult or even traumatic enactments may not be possible without recourse to such interpersonal techniques (ibid.).

This is, of course, very complicated and potentially dangerous terrain and is intimately tied to current debate about the use of self-disclosure in psychotherapy. Renik (1993a, 1993b, 1995, 1999), Jacobs (1999), and Goldstein (1997) are just a few of the authors to address this theme. There are several different varieties of self-disclosure. Self-disclosures may involve slips, errors, or other nonverbal phenomena outside the therapist's conscious awareness, but they may also represent deliberate actions, for example, the decision to share various subjective experiences or to respond to questions, requests for information about the therapist, and so forth (Strean 2002). An emerging viewpoint in this literature is that when self-disclosures are of the latter variety, there may be a great deal to be gained through their introduction into the therapeutic dialogue, with the proviso that the focus remains on the client. Such a recommendation should not, of course, be misconstrued as granting clinicians permission to share anything, at any time, about oneself with a client.

CLINICAL CASE ILLUSTRATION 5.1: "DIANA"

Diana, a thirty-one-year-old graduate student in political science referred by a colleague, initially requested therapy because she felt vaguely unhappy, had become increasingly anxious when alone, and feared that she would "go careening out of control." She reported panic attacks that occurred on an almost daily basis, during which she would have to remind herself who she was, where she was, what she was doing, and so forth. She quickly identified three factors that seemed to contribute to her distress. Diana and her boyfriend, Pat, were living in different parts of the country; she had recently been involved in a serious auto accident; and her grandmother, of whom she had been very fond, had died less than three months earlier. Diana insisted that while she had always felt happy before, she was now unable to concentrate. In particular, she reported being distracted by intrusive thoughts of her boyfriend either having been with another woman or contemplating such a sexual liaison, though she admitted she had no grounds for suspicion.

Diana was a tall, attractive woman with blond hair, the second in a sibship of five. She initially characterized her family life as a very happy one, but soon acknowledged an atmosphere of "dynamic tension" in her home when she was growing up. Although usually friendly, there were constant debates and arguments between Diana, her siblings, and their parents. Her father, Theodoros, a first generation Greek American, believed that service to others must always precede the gratification of one's own needs. He had been known, Diana noted proudly, to "lend his last dime" to someone in need, never pausing for a moment to consider the consequence of his own impoverishment. Diana's mother, Tina, was not of the same philosophy and in fact was uncomfortable with her husband's largesse, which occasionally led to bitter arguments between them. In spite of her admiration for her father, Diana revealed that he could also be petulant if not hostile, quarrelsome, and given to biting sarcasm, especially with Diana and other family members. "He's not your huggy-bear type," she observed. There was also a flip side to her father's oft-articulated philosophy of selflessness: never expect anything back in return. One is simply supposed to give, unhesitatingly, unquestioning.

Diana's mother, whom she described as "a perfect example of your very compulsive Greek homemaker type," had also suffered from periodic bouts of depression as far back as Diana could remember, and had for some years been on prescription antidepressants. Diana recalled that, beginning when she was two, her mother operated a family childcare business out of their home. She acknowledged that, while her mother's attention was divided between Diana, her brother, and the other children, this wasn't usually a problem for her. In fact, she felt rather privileged to be her mother's "special helper" from the time she was three or four. At some juncture in her later development, Diana's status as a special helper began to feel more like a liability. Her mother had suffered a miscarriage when Diana was very little, which she recalled as a highly significant event, one that evidently contributed quite substantially to her mother's depression. As a young adult, when she sought out her mother for emotional support, Diana would often feel as though their roles had become somehow reversed. Her mother would respond, with a mournful sigh, that she hadn't been a very "good Mommy" to Diana, and then, beseechingly, ask to be forgiven for her failings. Diana, almost reflexively, would make an impassioned claim to the contrary, offering both reassurance and forgiveness. Her mother usually felt better; Diana, burdened by her mother's despair, typically felt worse.

Diana had a close relationship with Dan, her thirty-two-year-old older brother, dating back to early childhood. Diana, in fact, often functioned in the role of an intermediary between Dan and other family members when the two were small, in part owing to her precocious speech but also because of Dan's rather passive, shy nature and his anxiety proneness in social situations. The other three siblings, two younger sisters and a younger brother, were twenty-one, twenty-three, and twenty-five, respectively. Although Diana felt that she had remained relatively close to them, from the time she was nine or ten until late adolescence, it was expected that she would provide much of the childcare for these siblings, which at times, proved a burdensome responsibility.

Because Diana had planned to spend the summer with her boyfriend on the East Coast, treatment was necessarily brief and consisted of twenty meetings. However, we decided to meet on a twice-weekly basis owing to the magnitude of her anxiety. Diana spoke in an accelerated, almost driven, manner as we got underway in what I assumed, at first, to be a manifestation of the anxiety of which she had complained. I soon recognized this, however, as Diana's characteristic style of presentation. The principal theme during the first couple of sessions, as well as in several subsequent ones, was Diana's tremendous difficulty in trying to relate to Pat over the phone. "He doesn't know which questions to ask," she complained, responding to her "directness" by withdrawing or behaving defensively. This was intolerable for her. Although Pat was at first "very supportive" in their relationship, things had changed. Now, when they were able to spend a long weekend together, there were missed cues, misunderstandings, quarreling. Although their sex life used to be uncomplicated, neither seemed to be enjoying sexual intimacy as both had earlier in the relationship. She also had concerns about Pat's emotional health. He had a very unstable family growing up, one ravaged by divorce and the strong suggestion of family incest. A younger sister developed a psychoticlike disturbance, and has had multiple hospitalizations, and Pat himself has been subject to recurrent mild depressions.

Another theme emerging in the first few weeks of treatment was Diana's earlier relationship with David, a former boyfriend with whom she had been in a committed, monogamous relationship. In this relationship, too, there had been a history of missed cues and unacknowledged pain and disappointments. David, now involved with another woman, had recently written Diana, she felt, to "seek my forgiveness." Instead, she was furious with him, accusing him not only of remarkable insensitivity but also of being self-serving and remorseless. After one session in which she complained bitterly about David, she had a dream in which she found herself in the awkward position of "offering reassurance to his girlfriend," as a sort of older and wiser sibling. In a second dream, reported a few sessions later, Diana and Pat had been hospitalized, though the reason for this was unclear. Then, with no apparent transition, the two were recast in the role of the helpers, offering assistance to a family involved in a serious accident. Diana remembered one part of the dream in which she consoled the two daughters while their father "ranted and raved" about something.

By now several dynamic themes had emerged in Diana's treatment. The first concerned the difficulty Diana experienced as a child in obtaining necessary emotional supplies from her mother and father. Her mother was obsessional and depressed, often preoccupied with Diana's younger siblings or the other children in her charge. Her father was argumentative and adversarial, rarely approachable except on an intellectual basis. A second issue, represented in the manifest content of both dreams described above, was Diana's role within her family as a surrogate parent, a family role designation into which she had been coercively inducted. Furthermore, Diana's mother's tendency to seek comfort from her represented a subversion of the usual mother-daughter relationship. As suggested previously, although this was undoubtedly a source of some gratification to Diana, such pleasures were far outweighed by the emotional burden this created for her. In Diana's adult life this seemed to play out in a tendency to become involved with emotionally needy individuals who placed their own needs ahead of hers as well as her deep resentment of this fact. Perhaps one distinguishing characteristic of these intercurrent relationships, in contradistinction to that with her mother, is that Diana seemed to be actively rebelling against this eventuality even as she reproduced the same dynamic with each successive new object encounter. There was little if any conscious awareness of such a pattern, with vigorous denials following any efforts on the therapist's part even to suggest the possibility.

Though she often reported feeling deeply hurt and enraged following conversations or encounters with Pat and others, Diana had considerable difficulty in describing other emotional reactions, to the point where I began to suspect that the normal range and magnitude of emotional states may have simply been unavailable to her. Such difficulties in experiencing, identifying, and ultimately, in giving expression to affects have been collectively referred to as *alexithymia* (Krystal 1993) or *disaffectation* (McDougall 1984, 1985, 1989). In individuals so affected a sort of psychological foreclosure of potential affects and affect representations occurs, such that people become psychologically separated from their emotions "and may indeed have 'lost' the capacity to be in touch with psychic realities" (McDougall 1989:103).

Indeed, Diana tended to use an array of "primitive" defenses, among them denial, projection, displacement, and externalization. I also suspected that a tremendous amount of psychic energy was necessarily consumed both to preserve the "good" parts of her relationships with both parents and to defend them from annihilation, inasmuch as her rage at both appeared to be so profound. What is perhaps more to the point is that my work with this client, which was of a planned, time-limited nature, evoked a specific countertransference reaction, detailed below.

DISCUSSION

Diana was neither an easy person with whom to work nor was she especially likable. She often complained endlessly, projecting blame onto virtually everyone except herself. If her boyfriend protested that she was being unfair or excessively critical, she would become frustrated, angered that he seemed unable to grasp the essential truth of her remarks. Though she often thought of herself as "bending over backwards" for others, at these times she seemed peculiarly unempathic. She registered agreement when I suggested she was tired of "taking a back seat" when it came to the satisfaction of her emotional needs and of being cast more or less permanently in the role of her mother's special helper. Oftentimes, however, she would talk from the moment she arrived at her sessions until her time was up, rarely permitting an opening for me to comment or ask questions. This was typically followed by an iteration of her frustration in not getting specific advice from me, solutions for the problems that she had so clearly and painstakingly outlined. She almost invariably experienced any comments I did manage to interpolate between her breathless narratives and complaints about my passivity as attacking or simply unhelpful. My efforts to bring this pattern within the treatment relationship to her attention were, in the main, fruitless. Although I had at first felt sympathy for this client, who since early childhood had shouldered the onerous burden of serving as a calming and soothing, reassuring self-object for her mother, my attempts to remain attuned with her psychological distress became increasingly difficult to sustain.

In fact, within several weeks of Diana's beginning treatment I felt exhausted and depleted by the end of each hour. Her critical and dismissive comments combined with her ceaseless complaints, her expectation that sooner or later people would fail her, had been recreated in the transference-countertransference. In this respect a phenomenon that Racker has termed *complementary identification* seemed to have occurred (Racker 1953, 1957, 1968). In such a countertransference configuration the therapist feels as though he or she is being treated as an internalized object of the client, with whom the therapist becomes partly identified. Diana's efforts to rid herself of what I now believe to represent unwanted parts of her self had, via a silent process that might also be characterized as projective identification, culminated in my experiencing these split off and projected parts of her personality as affects, attitudes, and impulses of my own. In the transference-countertransference I now began to feel much as I imagine Diana must have, listening to her mother's unending complaints, personal revelations, and the like. I began to dread her appointments and regretted the fact that I had agreed to see her at substantially less than my usual fee. I felt as though she were *taking something away from me* as each hour ended and sometimes had the urge to counteract this internal experience by consuming a snack or drinking cappucino.

I never disclosed very much about my countertransference to Diana, although at other times and with other clients I have found this to be very helpful. My reasons for this were twofold: first, I don't believe my understanding of these reactions was complete until we were well into what, at the outset, had been designated a planned brief therapy. Second, I believed that such disclosure with this client might easily have been misinterpreted within the transference as yet another instance of the maternal role reversal previously described. Nevertheless, I found that this understanding could be used somewhat less directly. For example, I commented at one juncture that I could easily imagine how exhausting it must have been for Diana to spend an hour on the phone with her mother, listening to her complain, *since I felt exhausted just listening to her description of the conversation.* At another juncture Diana had been describing the feeling of being "held against your will," relating it to a friend who had been molested and to her own feeling of being in vulnerable situations over which she could not exercise much control. Suddenly aware of how "paralyzed" I felt in this treatment, I wondered aloud whether she might be feeling something akin to this in the psychotherapy, in addition to the other situations she had mentioned. Diana was silent for a moment, one of few reflective moments in this twenty-session treatment. She smiled and offered that, while she didn't feel this exactly, she did find my chair "rather uncomfortable."

Interpretations, reflective comments, even simple observations so challenged Diana's fragile psychic equilibrium that virtually any comment could be perceived as an interference with her autonomy, a coercive demand, or a potential betrayal of trust. Although treatment helped Diana to maintain a tenuous stability so that she was able to finish out her term in graduate school, these basic issues and the history they embodied were not possible to address with any notable success. Shortly before we ended our work, Diana and I agreed that continued treatment would be helpful after she returned to school following the summer break.

COUNTERTRANSFERENCE THEORY IN THE CHILD AND ADOLESCENT LITERATURE

Countertransference in the dynamic treatment of children and adolescents, a topic that might be expected to evoke intense theoretical and clinical curiosity, has been historically relegated to a role of comparative insignificance. The scant attention paid to this theme in the child and adolescent literature appears to be in marked contrast to a burgeoning literature in the domain of adult psycho-analysis and psychotherapy in which every conceivable theoretical position has been explicated and virtually every clinical manifestation of countertransfer-ence examined in detail. Other authors who have reviewed the child and ado-lescent literature have arrived at fundamentally the same conclusion (Anasta-sopoulous and Tsiantis 1996; Berlin 1987; Brandell 1992; Christ 1964; Kohrman et al. 1971; Marshall 1979; Palombo 1985; Schowalter 1986). Several reasons for the paucity of contributions in this critical area of clinical practice have been suggested.

Kohrman, Fineberg, Gelman, and Weiss (1971) have discussed the dearth of literature on countertransference in child treatment, which they believe is closely linked with the difficulties child therapists have in acknowledging emotional reactions evoked by child patients in general. Palombo has summarized these issues rather succinctly:

1. Children may arouse intense infantile longings in the therapist.
2. Therapists come to be considered by children as substitute parents, which induces in therapists a parenting response rather than a purely therapeutic response.
3. Children's communications are often primitive and action-oriented: these forms of communication may evoke defensive reactions in the therapist that cloud the perception of the child's transference.
4. Children's regressions may lead the therapist to identify with the child patient and therefore not deal therapeutically with the regression.
5. The fact that contact with parents is often obligatory in work with children adds to the complications of the treatment process (Palombo 1985:40).

Kohrman and associates, Wolf (1972), and Marshall (1979) have suggested other factors that may have contributed to the failure of early child therapists to develop a theory of countertransference. Anna Freud had maintained for many years that children were incapable of developing a transference neurosis (Freud 1926). Although she amended this declaration somewhat in later years (Freud 1965), she continued to insist that there were important qualitative differences in the transferences formed by children as compared with those formed by adults in treatment. It is possible to adduce from Anna Freud's work on transference that countertransference reactions, therefore, would also be of a somewhat dif-ferent nature owing to the diminished scope and intensity of the transference relationship. In any event, neither she nor Melanie Klein ever addressed coun-tertransference issues directly in their writings, a situation that may have "deterred less courageous therapists from formal exploration" (Marshall 1979:596). Anna Freud (1926) also observed that "the negative impulses toward the analyst are essentially inconvenient and should be dealt with as soon as possible. The really fruitful work always takes place with a positive attachment" (Marshall 1979:596). Marshall makes the compelling observation that such pronouncements could easily have engendered anxiety or guilt in child and adolescent therapists who might otherwise have been willing to discuss their "negative" countertransference reactions.

Some have argued that countertransference issues encountered in psychotherapy with the adolescent patient are sufficiently unique to set them apart from both children and adults, though this literature is even more modest than the child countertransference literature. Gartner (1985) points to the adolescent's unique ability in restimulating the therapist's own adolescent conflicts, which she feels has in part to do with the existence of powerful cultural stereotypes regarding adolescent aggression, sexual feelings, and impulse life. Countertransference reactions that involve narcissistic injuries are also likely to be activated by the adolescent's undisguised boredom, incessant complaints of not being helped, and devaluation of the therapist's technique or person. Giovacchini observes that, while "countertransference problems are as complex and varied as are the personalities of different therapists," there may nonetheless be "some homogeneous features to our reactions which go beyond personal idiosyncrasies" (1975:356). He observes that countertransference issues with adolescents tend to involve a range of reactions that may include therapist guilt and/or inadequacy for failing to help the patient; the wish for the patient to remain as he is; and the therapist's resistance to change, which becomes especially problematic in light of the rapid change and growth that characterize adolescent development. Anastasopoulous and Tsiantis (1996) believe that intense countertransference reactions may also result from the "mingling of components from different developmental stages and the massive use of splitting and projective identification" (91). Adolescents, they observe, may have a tenuous tie to reality, tend to be regression-prone, and are especially inclined toward acting and acting out. Such characteristics may indeed be further exacerbated by the adolescent's ubiquitous conflicts with adult authority.

A final point in attempting to explain the neglect of this concept resides in a nearly universal value in protecting, nurturing, and giving guidance to children and adolescents. Marshall (1979) has observed that formidable defenses protect adults, therapists included, from awareness of destructive and sexualized impulses, fantasies, and feelings toward children. I would submit, however, that such defenses are as likely to be activated in our work with adolescents. These taboos, in fact, are no less powerful and may be even more absolute for child and adolesce. 'therapists than for other adults outside the psychotherapy profession. Kohrman, r ... berg, Gelman, and Weiss refer anecdotally to an experience that one of the authors had while participating in a clinical discussion of a child analytic case at a national conference. This therapist had suggested at an opportune moment that a puzzling aspect of the case under discussion might be illuminated by examining the therapist's contributions to the clinical situation, which appeared to signal a possible countertransference issue. At this point the moderator intervened, declaring emphatically, "We don't talk about such things" (1971:488).

What is especially fascinating about this 1971 anecdote is that it is both *time bound* and equally *timeless.* Such a comment does indeed reflect a perspective on countertransference heavily influenced by classical theory and the (then) prevailing one-person model of the psychoanalytic process (even Kohrman's pioneering article was subtitled *"problems* of countertransference"—emphasis mine). At contemporary presentations of *adult* case material, therapists have at times been overheard to complain that the transference-countertransference matrix often seems to be all that we talk about. Yet even now this does not seem to be as true for child and adolescent cases, in which the countertransference dimension is by convention seldom discussed with the explicitness found in adult cases. Can it be that, thirty-some years later, we still "do not talk about such things"?

In the lengthy case illustration and discussion that follow, I have selected an adolescent client whose treatment proved to be particularly challenging, in large measure owing to the nature and intensity of the transference-countertransference. It also raised a number of provocative questions. What, for example, are the implications of an intersubjective approach to countertransference in psychotherapy with adolescent clients and how universal is such a framework? Indeed, can such an approach, developed by psychoanalysts working with adult clients, be successfully adapted for use in clinical work with adolescents? In what ways does it alter our understanding of our clients, of the clinical process, and of the manner in which we participate in it? More specifically, how might such an approach alter our understanding of and responsiveness to phenomena that we identify as transference based? What impact might it have on deepening the therapeutic alliance? Inasmuch as this chapter is intended to be an introduction to the topic of countertransference, comprehensive consideration of these issues is beyond its purview. Nevertheless, I hope to highlight several of these issues and examine them by focusing on a clinical case, which involved a severely traumatized late adolescent patient seen over a period of two years.

CLINICAL CASE ILLUSTRATION 5.2: "DIRK"

Dirk was in his late teens when he first requested treatment at a family service agency for long-standing insomnia and a "negative outlook on life." He often felt as though he might "explode," and he suffered from chronic anxiety that was particularly pronounced in social situations. He reluctantly alluded to a "family situation" that had exerted a dramatic and profound impact on his life, and, as the early phase of his treatment began to unfold, the following account gradually emerged. When Dirk was perhaps thirteen years old his father (who shall be referred to as Mr. S) was diagnosed with cancer of the prostate. Unfortunately, neither parent chose to reveal this illness to Dirk, his two older brothers, or his younger sister for nearly a year and a half. Mr. S, an outdoorsman who had been moderately successful as a real estate developer and entrepreneur, initially refused treatment, and his condition gradually worsened. By the time he finally consented to surgery, some eighteen months later, the cancer had metastasized and his prognosis was terminal. A prostatectomy left him impotent, increasing the strain in a marriage that had already begun to deteriorate.

Within several months of his father's surgery, when Dirk was perhaps fourteen or fifteen years old, Ms. S (Dirk's mother) began a clandestine affair with a middle-aged man who resided nearby. The affair intensified, and presumably as a consequence of Ms. S's carelessness, Mr. S learned of the affair. He also learned that his wife was planning a trip around the world with her lover. Although narcissistically mortified and enraged, he chose not to confront her right away, instead plotting secretly to murder her. On a weekday morning when Dirk and his younger sister were at school (his older brothers no longer resided in the family home), Mr. S killed his wife in their bedroom with one of his hunting rifles. He then carefully wrapped her body up, packed it in the trunk of the family car, and drove to a shopping center where he took his own life. The news was, of course, devastating to Dirk and his siblings and, if it were possible, even more injurious because of the relentless media coverage the crime received. Every conceivable detail of the murder-suicide was described on television and in the local press. Suddenly, Dirk and his siblings were completely bereft of privacy, and there was no adult intercessor to step forward and protect them from the continuing public exposure, humiliation, and pain.

These traumatic injuries were compounded by the reactions of neighbors and even former family friends, whose cool reactions to Dirk and his siblings bordered on social ostracism. The toll on Dirk's family continued over the next several years. First, the elder of Dirk's two brothers, Jon, committed suicide at the age of twenty-seven in a manner uncannily reminiscent of his father's suicide. Some months later, Dirk's surviving brother, Rick, a polysubstance abuser, was incarcerated after being arrested and convicted for a drug-related felony. Finally, Dirk and his younger sister gradually became estranged from each other and, by the time he began treatment, were barely speaking to one another. Dirk, in fact, had little contact with anyone. After his parents' deaths, he spent a couple of years at the homes of various relatives, but eventually he decided to move back into the family home, where he lived alone. Dirk had been provided for quite generously in his father's will. He soon took over what remained of the family business, which included a strip mall and a small assortment of other business properties. At the time he began weekly psychotherapy, Dirk had monthly contact with some of his tenants when their rent became due and made occasional trips to the grocery store. He had not dated since high school and had only episodic contact with his paternal grandmother, whom he disliked. He slept in his parents' bedroom, which had not been redecorated after their deaths. There was even unrepaired damage from the shotgun blast that had killed his mother. He did not at first appear discomfited by this fact and maintained that it was not abnormal or even especially noteworthy. He explained that he was loathe to change or repair anything in the house, which he attributed to a tendency toward "procrastination." Efforts to explore this theme, however, seemed to arouse anxiety in both Dirk and myself, in large measure because, I thought, of its frankly macabre nature. We gradually came to understand Dirk's need to maintain his residence in this house as representing a kind of selfobject phenomenon. People were unreliable, but his house, despite the carnage that had occurred there, remained a stabilizing force. Change was loathsome because it interfered with the integrity of important memories of the house and of the childhood lived within its walls. Nevertheless, this failed to explain to my satisfaction why he chose to continue to sleep in his parents' bedroom.

Dirk was quite socially isolated and had a tremendous amount of discretionary time, two facts that he found alternately frightening and reassuring. Although he wanted very much to become more involved with others and, eventually, to be in a serious relationship with a girl, he trusted no one. He believed others to be capable of great treachery and from time to time revealed conspiratorial ideas that had a paranoid if not psychotic delusional resonance to them. He lived in a sparsely populated semirural area and, for the most part, involved himself in solitary pursuits, such as stamp collecting, reading, or fishing. He would hunt small game or shoot at targets with a collection of rifles, shotguns, and handguns that his father had left behind. He spoke at times with obvious pleasure of methodically skinning and dressing the small animals he trapped or killed. There was little or no waste; even the skins could be used to make caps or mittens. He maintained that hunting and trapping animals was by no means unkind; indeed, it was far more humane than tacitly permitting their overpopulation and starvation. Occasionally, he would add that he preferred the company of animals, even dead ones, to humans. They, unlike people, didn't express jealousy and hatred.

As the treatment intensified Dirk began to share a great deal more about his relationships with both parents. Sometimes, he would speak with profound sadness of his staggering loss. Needing both to make sense of the tragedy and to assign responsibility for it, he would then become enraged at his mother's lover. It was *he* who was to blame for everything that had happened, Dirk would declare. At other times he described both of his parents as heinous or monstrous, having had total disregard for the rest of the family's welfare.

Things had never been especially good between Dirk and his mother. She had a mild case of rubella during her pregnancy with Dirk, which he believed might have caused a physical anomaly as well as a congenital problem with his vision. Perhaps, he thought, she had rejected him in his infancy when the anomaly was discovered. The manner in which his mother described the anomaly, which was later removed, made him feel as though his physical appearance displeased, perhaps even disgusted her. Although he spent a great deal of time with her growing up, he recalled that she was often emotionally distant or upset with him. When his childhood enuresis didn't resolve in latency as the pediatrician had predicted it would, his mother became increasingly frustrated and irritated with him. It was taking too long, and she became convinced that Dirk's enuresis was the result of another congenital deformity. She demanded a complete urological workup and surgery, if necessary. The pediatrician was simply mistaken, and there must be a physical cause. Finally, Dirk's father stepped in; he declared that there would be no urological examination and expressed confidence that Dirk would simply "grow out of it," which he later did.

From this time onward he gradually became less trusting of his mother, growing closer to his father, whom he emulated in a variety of ways. He had often noted that he and his father were much alike. He had thought the world of this strong, "macho" man who demanded strict obedience but was also capable of great kindness, particularly in acknowledgment of Dirk's frequent efforts to please him. It was quite painful for Dirk to think of this same strong father as a cuckold. It was even more frightening to think of him as weakened and castrated and profoundly traumatic to believe that he could have been so uncaring about Dirk and his siblings as to actually carry out this unspeakably hateful crime of vengeance.

Early in his treatment Dirk was able to express anger and disappointment with his mother for her lack of warmth and the painful way in which she avoided him, even shunned him. She had made him feel defective, small, and unimportant. This material was mined both for its preoedipal and oedipal significance and also for what it revealed of the nature of Dirk's relational (selfobject) needs. We gradually learned how his mother's own limited capacity for empathy interfered with the development of Dirk's capacity for pleasure in his own accomplishments, for healthy self-confidence and the exuberant pursuit of important personal goals. In fact, Dirk avoided virtually any social situation where he thought others might disappoint him, where mother's inability to mirror his boyhood efforts and accomplishments might be traumatically repeated. This was an important theme in our early explorations of Dirk's contact-shunning adaptation to the world outside his family home. However, this dynamic issue was not at the core of the transference-countertransference matrix that gradually evolved in my work with Dirk. It was only through a set of experiences culminating in a psychoticlike countertransference reaction that we were both able to come to an understanding of the role Dirk's profoundly powerful and conflict-laden feelings toward his father played in the development of his illness and in our relationship as well.

During the early spring, about five months into his treatment, Dirk began to reveal more details of his relationship with his father. His father, he observed, was really more like an employer than a parent, forever assigning Dirk tasks, correcting his mistakes, and maintaining a certain aloofness and emotional distance from him. Although up until this point Dirk had tended to place more responsibility for the murder-suicide on the actions of his mother and her lover, he now began to view his father as having a greater role in the family tragedy. For the first time, he sounded genuinely angry. Awareness of this, however, proved exceedingly painful for him, and depressive thoughts and suicidal fantasies typically followed such discussions: "My father could have shot me . . . in fact, sometimes I wish he had blown me away."

During this same period burglars broke into the strip mall that Dirk had inherited from his father's estate. This enraged Dirk, almost to the point of psychotic disorganization. He reacted to it as though his personal integrity had been violated, and reported a series of dreams in which burglars were breaking into homes or he was being chased, with people shooting at him.

He associated these dreams with his father, whom he described as a "castrating" parent with a need to keep his three sons subservient to him. He observed for perhaps the first time that his father may have been rather narcissistic, lacking genuine empathy and interest in his three boys. He was beginning to think of himself and both his older brothers as really quite troubled, though in different ways. He then recounted the following dream:

> (A man who looked like) Jack Benny was trying to break into my house to steal my valuables. He wanted me to think that he had rigged some electrical wire with a gas pipe to scare me, and thereby force me to disclose the hiding place where my valuables were. . . . He was a mild-mannered man.

Later the same night, he dreamt of "seeing a girl lying naked on a bed." This was actually a dream fragment that, blushing, he referred to as a "snatch" of a dream. Dirk's initial associations to the first dream were of "my father trying to ruin my life." At first, I believed the dream suggested strongly that one basis for Dirk's paranoia was intimately connected to the sudden and unexpected fulfillment of his oedipal desires, including the vanquishing of his chief rival without Dirk having any complicity in the commission of the crime. An obvious problem with this explanation is that Dirk's mother, the object of his oedipal desire, perished at the same time, effectively precluding the possibility of any such "oedipal victory." Yet, in another sense, with his father out of the way, no longer there to regulate his behavior, many things were now possible that he could only have fantasized about before. We then hypothesized that Jack Benny, a mild-mannered Jewish comedian whose initials were identical to my own, might also represent me, or in any event, aspects of Dirk's experience of the treatment process. In an important sense I was asking Dirk to reveal the hidden location of treasured memories, feelings, and fantasies that he had worked unremittingly to conceal not only from others but from himself as well. These interpretations seemed to make a good deal of sense to both of us, yet my recollection at the end of this hour was that I was somehow vaguely troubled.

It was also approximately at this point in Dirk's treatment that I began to take copious notes. I rationalized that this was necessary because I felt unable to reconstruct the sessions afterward without them. However, I now believe that this note taking was also in the service of a different, fundamentally unconscious motive. From time to time Dirk would complain that I was physically too close to him in the office or that I was watching him too intently during the hour, which made him feel self-conscious and ashamed. On several occasions I actually had moved my chair further away from him at his request. Again, in response to his anxiety, I had made a point of *looking away* from him precisely during those moments when I would ordinarily want to feel *most* connected to a patient (e.g., when he had recalled a poignant experience with his father or was talking about the aftermath of the tragedy). I also noted that it was following "good" hours, hours characterized by considerable affectivity and important revelations, that he would request our meetings be held on a biweekly basis. When this occurred, probably a half dozen times over the two years he was in treatment with me, I recall feeling both disappointed and concerned. My efforts to convince him of the therapeutic value in exploring this phenomenon rather than altering the frequency of our meetings were not simply fruitless; they aroused tremendous anxiety, and Dirk several times threatened to stop coming altogether if I persisted. In effect, my compulsive note taking represented an unconscious compliance with Dirk's articulated request that I titrate the intensity of my involvement with him. At times our interaction during sessions bore a marked similarity to his interactions with both parents, particularly his father. Like his father, I had become increasingly distant and aloof. On the other hand, Dirk exercised control over this relationship, which proved to be a critical distinction for him as the treatment evolved.

Interestingly, in the next hour Dirk reported a dream fragment in which he was watching or participating in a clandestine effort to expropriate stolen goods from a shopping mall with secret passageways. The passageways were coated with a slippery, icelike substance, and "it was a lot of fun to go through them—whee-e-e-ee!" His sense of personal boundary violation following the mall break-in and burglary seemed to have undergone a further transformation in this dream, i.e., the loss of personal boundaries may not inevitably lead to trauma. On the contrary, exciting and potentially gratifying, positive experiences may be associated with such boundary diffusion. Dynamically, this dream was almost transparently oedipal, filled with both erotic imagery and the consonant affects of thinly disguised sexual excitement and sexual guilt. Alongside, or perhaps behind, the oedipal material and the depiction of sexual intercourse, however, seemed to be the somewhat more primitive representation of an intrauterine fantasy, although this was not addressed in any depth. Dirk had appeared reasonably satisfied with the oedipal meaning at which we had arrived. It was during this hour, which occurred in late July, some nine months into treatment, that I reminded Dirk of my upcoming vacation. As we ended our session, he remarked for the first time how similar we seemed to each other. I did not comment on this observation since we had reached the end of the hour. However, I believe that I felt rather uneasy about it.

In the next hour, our last meeting prior to my vacation, Dirk reported that he was getting out more often and had been doing a modest degree of socializing. He was making a concerted effort to be less isolated. At the same time, he expressed a considerable degree of hostility when speaking of his (then incarcerated) brother, whom he described as "exploitative and deceitful." Toward the end of this hour he asked where I would be going on vacation. On one previous occasion Dirk had sought extratherapeutic contact with me; that had been some months earlier when he called me at home, quite intoxicated, at two or three in the morning. However, during his sessions he had rarely asked me questions of a personal nature. I remember feeling compelled to answer this one, which I believed represented an important request. "We'll be vacationing in New York," I told Dirk. He shrugged his shoulders, and simply commented, "New York City is an unappealing place to visit." Although he had mistakenly assumed I meant New York City when I had said "New York," I didn't correct him.

When I left with my wife for our trip to the South Fork of Long Island, she was six months pregnant with our first child. Although we were vacationing in New York to visit with my wife's family, they were staying in the city, and it had been agreed that we would spend the first night or two by ourselves in their newly purchased Long Island summer home and that they would join us shortly thereafter. The house was nestled among a half-dozen fruit trees in a beautiful though isolated waterfront setting on a small island connected by a causeway to the main village. As it turned out, my in-laws had been doing substantial renovation in this house, and consequently the rooms were rather spare and building materials were strewn about the first floor. Although the phone seemed to be connected, there was a great deal of static on the line, making conversation difficult if not impossible. I remember feeling rather disconcerted by this, wondering if we would be able to call for assistance *should we require help in an emergency.* I mentioned this to my wife, who was not especially troubled by this fact since she anticipated no such emergency arising. I was not reassured, however. By mid-evening storm clouds began to roll ominously across Great Peconic Bay. Later it began to rain heavily, and our view of the red warning lights that guided boats through the inlet, less than fifty feet from the back of the house, became almost completely obscured by the downpour. The storm then seemed to be almost directly overhead and, after one particularly brilliant flash of lightning and an accompanying thunderclap of Wagnerian intensity, the lights went out. From what I could see, the power failure had affected the entire neighborhood, though the red warning lights along the inlet were still visible. After anxiously rifling through the kitchen drawers, I managed to find a flashlight and some candles. It was now rather late, and my wife was exhausted. She went to bed, but I remember thinking that it was very important, indeed critical, that I remain awake. It was then that the thought occurred to me: *Dirk knew where I was.* At any moment, I would see his tortured face on the other side of the glass slider, illuminated in a ghastly fashion by the lightning overhead. I couldn't stop the thoughts. I imagined that he had followed me, some three hundred miles, and was waiting for this moment to murder us all: me, my wife, and our unborn child. I felt defenseless, small, and terrified. Fortunately, my terror was soon replaced by more manageable anxiety as it dawned on me that I was experiencing some kind of unusual countertransference reaction, the sort of thing one hears about from more experienced colleagues. I vowed that as soon as I returned from vacation I would explore the entire experience with our agency's clinical consultant. While that helped a little—and I remember consoling myself with such thoughts a number of times over the next four or five hours—I nevertheless continued my candlelight vigil by the back door. I think I must finally have fallen asleep as the storm subsided and the first light appeared. My wife, I might add, slept quite soundly.

DISCUSSION

Although Dirk was not an easy patient to treat, he was likable. I felt this way from our first meeting and believe that this basic feeling for him permitted our work to continue despite his paranoia and a number of disturbing developments along the transference-countertransference axis. During the first weeks of therapy I recall that, though I found his story fully believable, I also felt shocked, overwhelmed, and at times, even numbed by it. It was difficult, if not impossible, to conceive of the impact of such traumata occurring *ad seriatim* in one family.

Although I wanted very much to feel moved by his story and to be able to convey this to Dirk, his manner of narrating it was a powerful signal to me that he would not find this helpful, at least for the time being. It was as though he could not take in such feelings nor allow me to be close in this way. I wasn't especially troubled by this and felt as though my principal task was simply to listen, to make occasional inquiries, and provide a climate of acceptance. I did make interpretations from time to time, but these were primarily of intercurrent experience (e.g., linking paranoid reactions or somatic complaints to hostile wishes and fantasies) and tended not to address transference themes.

I believe my discomfort with Dirk cumulated silently during those first few months of treatment, although an important threshold was crossed with Dirk's revelation that he continued to sleep in his parents' bedroom. I found this not only bizarre but also frightening. When we attempted to discuss this, he was dismissive. I, on the other hand, was quite willing to let the matter rest, and it was only much later in his treatment that we were able to return to this dialogue. This fact, in combination with my awareness of Dirk's nearly obsessive love of hunting and trapping, led me to begin to view him not so much as a victim of trauma than as a heartless and potentially dangerous individual. It did not occur to me until months later that each time he killed a muskrat or a raccoon it may have served as a disguised reenactment of the original trauma while simultaneously permitting him to identify with an admired part of the father who had taught Dirk how to hunt and trap. Dirk, after all, had observed in an early session that he and his father were really quite similar. It may, of course, be argued that his paranoia and penchant for hunting, trapping, and skinning animals, in combination with my knowledge of the traumas he had endured, had helped to shape my countertransference-driven withdrawal and compulsive note taking. He had also requested, somewhat urgently, that I exercise caution lest he feel "trapped": I was to pull my chair back, not make eye contact, and the like. But soon I felt trapped as well; I had altered my therapeutic modus operandi and I became aware of experiencing mild apprehension on those days Dirk came in for his appointments. Some of Dirk's sessions seemed interminable, and, if I were feeling this way, I think it likely that he was feeling something similar. Perhaps, in this additional sense, *both* of us were feeling trapped.

As Dirk became increasingly aware of the depth of the injury that he believed his mother had caused him and of the rage he felt toward his father, the extent of his developmental arrest became more comprehensible. Dirk continued to live in his parents' home, as noted earlier, in an effort to preserve the integrity of childhood memories associated with this house. However, the house remained *exactly* as it had been at the time of the murder-suicide, and he slept in the very room where the carnage had occurred. I believe that there was an additional reason for this, one intimately connected with Dirk's feelings toward both parents and his father, in particular.[5] I had noted to myself at several junctures that Dirk spoke of his father as though he were living. In an important sense Dirk had been unable to bury either parent. He was haunted by them and yet unable to relinquish his torturous tie to them.

As Dirk developed greater awareness of the rage he felt for his father, a feeling he had worked so hard to project, dissociate, and deny, he seemed to demonstrate greater interest in me and in our relationship. When he commented with some satisfaction that the two of *us* seemed to be similar, I suddenly recalled Dirk's earlier comment about how similar he and his father were. When he had observed that his father behaved more like an employer than a parent, assigning him tasks, correcting his mistakes, and otherwise maintaining an emotionally distant, aloof posture, I felt as though I recognized parts of myself in his description. Yet this was a distorted reflection, more akin to that of the fun house mirror. His dreams, too, seemed to equate me with his father: his first association to the dream of Jack Benny had been of his "father trying to ruin" his life. Like his father, I might attempt to trick him into a relationship where he was chronically exploited and mistreated and reduced to a kind of helpless, indentured servitude. Although the oedipal significance of this dream was not inconsequential, with its reference to hidden valuables, I don't believe this was the most salient dynamic issue insofar as our relationship was concerned. As mentioned earlier, I ended that hour feeling vaguely troubled in spite of Dirk's agreement that the interpretation was helpful. Though the dream was manifestly paranoid, an important truth about the asymmetry of the therapeutic relationship is also revealed. I was apprehensive because Dirk's associations had signaled the presence of a danger, and that danger was now perceived in some measure as coming from me.

Dirk's report that he was "getting out more" and was less reclusive should have been good news, though I recall reacting with only mild enthusiasm when he informed me of this shortly before my vacation. Dirk was just fine to work with so long as his paranoid fears prevented him from venturing out very far into the world of "real" relationships. However, the thought of Dirk no longer confined to a twilight existence, coupled with his increasing capacity both to feel and express rage, was an alarming one. What ultimately transformed this countertransference fantasy into a dramatic (and disjunctive) countertransference *reaction* was the haunting parallel—partially transference based, partly grounded in reality—that had emerged in Dirk's view of me as fundamentally similar both to him and his father. I now believe that my intensive countertransference reaction while on vacation in New York had accomplished something that had simply not been possible despite careful introspection and reflection. I finally came close to experiencing Dirk's terror, though in my own idiosyncratic way. Like Dirk, I felt small, vulnerable, and alone. I was isolated and helpless, in unfamiliar surroundings, and cut off from commerce with reality and the intersubjective world. Dirk was frightening, but it was even more frightening to *be* Dirk. As his therapist, I had been the hunter; suddenly, I was the hunted. I was convinced I had betrayed Dirk in much the same way his father had betrayed him, the trauma reenacted in his treatment. In effect, in this psychoticlike countertransference reaction, I felt not only as Dirk felt, but as I believe he might have wished his father to feel—the dreaded and hated father against whom he sought redress for his grievances. Dirk, of course, had enacted both roles daily for well over five years; I had enacted them but for a single night.

Did Dirk's paranoia induce this powerful, psychoticlike reaction in me, as some might argue? Was it an instance of projective identification, with the therapist's evident failure to absorb and metabolize the unwanted, projected parts of the patient's self? Was my reaction principally the residuum of my own pathology and unworked-through issues? I cannot with certainty refute these possibilities, though I am inclined to suggest an alternative explanation. I believe that my reaction was the culmination of a series of overdetermined, intersubjective transactional events shaped by Dirk's transference fantasies and feelings, my idiosyncratic reactions to those transference fantasies and feelings, and his unconscious efforts to incorporate my countertransference attitudes and behavior in the evolving transference relationship to me. The abject terror I felt was therefore a coconstruction. It wasn't really Dirk's terror, nor was it mine: it was *ours*.

My relationship with Dirk changed a good deal after my vacation experience in New York. I sought consultation, which I found most helpful. I began to feel increasingly comfortable with him, and, I believe, he with me. I stopped taking notes. I was able to find a way of adjusting the intensity of my affective involvement with him without pulling back and becoming emotionally distant and aloof. He complained a bit less of somatic preoccupations and, after endless ruminations, finally asked a girl out for a date. He was quite apprehensive about this, but it seemed much more a picture of normative adolescent anxiety than paranoid dread. He began to speak of going back to school and wondered what career path he might finally take. He started to give serious consideration to selling off the strip mall, perhaps even moving out of his house. The world seemed filled with new possibilities, and Dirk permitted himself to ponder his future. He even tried, though without marked success, to cultivate a closer relationship with his younger sister. Although I continued to meet with Dirk for nearly another year, our work came to a premature conclusion when I accepted an academic position requiring that I relocate out of state. I lost track of Dirk soon afterward.[6]

In this chapter we have explored the topical terrain of countertransference. The burgeoning treatment literature on countertransference was briefly reviewed, and the unique theoretical and clinical contributions of various orientations (classical, totalistic, and intersubjectivist) discussed. The neglect of countertransference in the child and adolescent treatment literature was also examined, and some of the special countertransference issues linked to this population were described. Finally, two clinical illustrations were provided. The first involved the twice-weekly privately conducted treatment of an adult woman with a disorder of character, and the second an agency-based course of once-weekly therapy with a severely traumatized late adolescent. Although the cases are quite different from each other, both offer an opportunity for distilling and applying certain conceptual schemata derived from the intersubjective relational frame to illuminate aspects of countertransference.

PART 2

The Process of Dynamic Therapy

6

Dynamic Assessment

In this chapter, the question of what makes an assessment "dynamic" is considered in depth. We begin with an overview of this theme as it is has been represented in the psychoanalytic literature, identifying key components that are deemed integral to the assessment process. A comprehensive framework for conducting a dynamic clinical assessment is then presented and described.[1] Using a detailed clinical case example derived from early interviews with a thirty-two-year-old incarcerated man, the value of understanding the precise nature of a client's presenting complaint, the relevance of particular historical antecedents, as well as the importance of the client's characteristic defenses, strategies, and adaptations for alleviating or binding anxiety are extensively described and illustrated. Other topics include assessment of the client's ego functions and self-cohesiveness, assembling the object relations history, the mental status examination, specific areas of competence and effectance, the nature of the clinician's subjective experience of the client, and, finally, the construction of a dynamic-genetic formulation and plan for treatment.

PSYCHOANALYTIC IDEAS REGARDING ASSESSMENT

Although ideas about dynamic assessment are presumably important to all psychoanalytic schools, they tend to be "embedded" in discussions of developmental principles, various selection processes for determining an individual's personal suitability for psychoanalysis or psychoanalytic psychotherapy, treatment methods or specialized dynamic treatment techniques, and clinical illustrations of psychopathology. It is of some significance that psychoanalysis, with its roots in human biology and physicalistic science, originally approached assessment and diagnosis by focusing on patterns of symptoms and etiologic agents (Greenspan and Polk 1980). Sigmund Freud, as noted earlier, had trained as a physician and practiced neurology prior to the early experiments that led to his discovery of psychoanalysis. Perhaps it should not come as a surprise that many of his early clinical papers reflect such a medical-empirical method for clinical assessment. Freud's carefully detailed descriptions of hysterical patients and his emphasis on anamnesis, or case history, seem to epitomize this model. Each subsequent psychoanalytic school, moreover, has tended to filter ideas about clinical assessment through its own unique lens, so that ego psychologists are inclined to place greater emphasis on ego functions, object relations theorists on attachment issues and the topography of an individual's object world, and self psychologists on the structure and cohesiveness of the self. Just as there are distinctive psychoanalytic theories of development, psychopathology, and the clinical process, much the same might be said of psychoanalytic conceptions of clinical assessment.

The model of clinical assessment that is presented in the remainder of this chapter attempts to extract and integrate important ideas from each of these major traditions in psychoanalysis. Adherents of a particular psychoanalytic school might argue that, in addition to being distinctive, their conception of human development, psychopathology, or view of intrapsychic contents or processes is irreconcilable with other psychoanalytic psychologies. For example, the same "symptoms" that classically trained analysts might be inclined to regard as compelling evidence of intrapsychic conflict could represent for the self psychologist the "break-down products" of a disintegrating self. Similarly, exponents of Kleinian theory would be far more likely to impute meaning to early developmental phenomena arising from the subject's negotiation of the *schizoid* and *depressive* positions than would, for example, ego psychologists, who may not even accept the existence of such object relational phenomena. It is certainly not my intention to dispute the legitimacy of any such claims; rather, I would submit that the most important organizing principle for a thorough dynamic assessment is that it be *inclusive* and *multifaceted*. This might be understood as an analogue to our acceptance of the classical psychoanalytic principle of "multideterminism." Multideterminism is a construct that asserts a psychic event or aspect of behavior may have multiple causes and "may serve more than one purpose in the psychic framework and economy" (Moore and Fine 1990:123). A framework that encourages the clinician to adopt multiple dynamic perspectives in the gathering and assimilating of clinical data also reinforces the notion that each of our psychoanalytic theories may yield an important clinical "truth" or contribute in some unique way to our understanding of the client.

A MODEL FOR COMPREHENSIVE DYNAMIC ASSESSMENT

The realities of contemporary practice often dictate that clinical assessment is conducted with a rapidity and efficiency that is probably not possible and, even were it possible, not desirable. Oftentimes, clinicians in agency and other settings are asked to provide their clinical assessment after only a single meeting with the client, although in such instances it is likely that a disproportionate value is placed on the *descriptive* diagnosis. Such descriptive diagnoses, derived from an ever increasing list (currently numbering 340) of psychological disorders appearing in the American Psychiatric Association's *Diagnostic and Statistical Manual* (*DSM-IV*) have become the shorthand by which psychological problems are understood and clinical interventions launched. Very specific diagnostic criteria inform the clinician, for example, that a client suffers from "panic disorder without agoraphobia" or "bipolar I disorder." Such a system of classification, unfortunately, prompts us to think of clients principally with respect to the nature and severity of their symptomatology. Concise clinical description is of course important, but must be counterbalanced by thoughtful attention to a range of other variables (e.g., ego functions, defenses, object relations history, etc.) as well as by the clinician's abiding interest in the client's personal "story." Should descriptive diagnosis become such a superordinate organizer, the clinician may be much less inclined to focus on complex dynamic issues or to extract the humanizing personal narratives that permit immersion in a client's experience of the world, a sine qua non for the comprehensive model of assessment presented here.

In clinical social work practice clinical assessment has traditionally been geared not only to evaluating psychopathology, developmental derailments, and dysfunction, but also a client's strengths and assets. Furthermore, social work has tended to place far more emphasis historically on the environment, its resources, and its role in the clinical treatment situation than have its counterparts in psychiatric medicine or clinical psychology. In the outline that follows there is an effort to balance the contributions attributable to history, intercurrent situation, and intraspsychic features. In addition, the role of the subject's environmental milieu is both explicitly and implicitly considered, as are the individual's talents, skills, and other personality strengths.

The outline consists of eight principal components: a diagnostic summary, results of the mental status examination, assay of specific ego/superego functions and object relational capacities, self/selfobject relations and self structure, specific areas of competence and effectance, nature of the clinician's subjective experience of the client, the genetic-dynamic formulation, and the treatment plan. It is emphasized, however, that this is an outline for *gathering and organiz-*

ing data rather than a prescriptive format for the conduct of the interview itself. Assessment interviews, as the clinical illustration that follows should demonstrate, are always more effective when they emerge from a natural discourse between clinician and client. It is also a distinct possibility that certain data will either not exist (e.g., medical history for a foster or adopted child) or not be readily available (e.g., early memories). Furthermore, the clinician may be required, because of inevitable clinical priorities, to defer collection of certain information until a later point in the treatment.

The concept of *diagnosis* in this book is used not in its conventional descriptive sense but as a multitiered process that represents equally a) formal descriptive or classificatory diagnosis, b) dynamic diagnosis, and c) etiological diagnosis.[2] The formal descriptive or *clinical diagnosis* is perhaps most commonly represented by what *DSM IV* has labeled "Axis I" or "Axis II" disorders. *Dynamic diagnosis* is here used to refer to significant ongoing adaptive and maladaptive features of the client-environment transactional milieu, which are hypothesized to influence, shape, or act on the client's problems in demonstrable ways (e.g., ongoing marital conflict that exacerbates a client's preexisting problem with anxiety). *Etiological diagnosis*, as the term suggests, is directed at the more distal or remote causes of a particular complaint or presenting problem (e.g., arriving at a more satisfactory understanding of a recent bout of depression in an eleven-year-old child whose early history also includes abandonment by her birth parents). Finally, although it is optimal for a reasonably thorough assessment to be conducted prior to the beginning of treatment, assessment and diagnosis are most usefully thought of as ongoing throughout the period of therapeutic engagement. Ideally, as one's understanding of a client deepens over the course of treatment, various "missing" elements of the original assessment may be "filled in" and other portions revised to reflect a clinical picture that has gained in accuracy. Nevertheless, much of the information represented in the following clinical assessment outline is possible to obtain in an interview process consisting of approximately three-four sessions.

THE DYNAMIC CLINICAL ASSESSMENT: AN OUTLINE

1. *DIAGNOSTIC SUMMARY* OF AN INDIVIDUAL CHILD, ADOLESCENT, OR ADULT TREATMENT CASE. PLEASE INCLUDE THE FOLLOWING INFORMATION:

a) *Identifying data* (physical description of the client, gender, age, school/work status, parents' ages and occupations, siblings' ages, current living arrangement, cultural/ethnic background, religious/spiritual beliefs, sexual orientation, other relevant demographic data in re: self, family, neighborhood, community, etc.);

b) *Context of service* (description of the practice venue in which assessment is being completed and/or treatment offered);

c) *Presenting complaint(s)/concern(s)* (relevant [descriptive] symptomatology);

d) *History of presenting complaint/concern* (how long the person has experienced these particular problems, identifiable precipitants, including recent changes or transitions in the subject's life);

e) *Previous problems and their resolution* (including past experiences in therapy);

f) *Pertinent history* (developmental, family, social, medical, school/work, as required).

Note: Detailed developmental information, particularly in the case of children, is always very useful when it is possible to obtain. Data in regard to conception, pregnancy and delivery, postpartum experiences, early attachment, important developmental milestones, separation-individuation experiences, and peer relationships represent a few of the more important areas.

g) Earliest memory(ies).

2. MENTAL STATUS EXAMINATION PRESENTED IN SUMMARY FORM:

a) *General appearance*: Description of client's appearance. Please note whether client is well dressed, neatly groomed, if there are abnormalities in gait, posture. What was client's general attitude toward the clinician (cooperative, friendly, hostile or aggressive, indifferent, bored, etc.)? In the case of a child, did the child and/or mother/father/other adult experience difficulty in separating from each other in early interviews?

b) *Behavior*: Description of client's psychomotor activity level. Was the client anxious, relaxed, lethargic, exuberant, agitated, pacing? Were there changes in the level/nature of behavior during the interview(s)? If so, did these seem related to particular themes/content? Did the client make eye contact with the clinician? Was there evidence of tics, unusual mannerisms, gestures (deliberate or involuntary)?

c) *Mood*: Deduced from the clinician's observation as well as the client's report. Mood is a "baseline" emotional state that is generalizable to the whole personality and psychic life. Terms used to describe mood include *euthymic, anxious, depressed, petulant, euphoric*, etc.

d) *Affect*: Affect, unlike mood, is derived only from immediate observations and may fluctuate during the interview in association with different content and specific memories. The subjective feeling component of affects is best understood as existing along a pleasure-unpleasure continuum. Important affects include surprise, interest, joy, distress, anger, fear, shame, contempt, and disgust. An individual's affectivity may be qualitatively described in the following ways:

- Broad: characterized by a normal fluctuation in emotional expressiveness as respresented in verbal tone, gestural communications, and facial expressions
- Labile: involving sudden and inexplicable changes in affective expression
- Restricted: notable decrease in both the availability and intensity of affect
- Blunted: clinical presentation sometimes seen in severely depressed individuals in which affective responses are extremely limited in range
- Flat: seen in schizophrenia and other severely disturbed clients who are incapable of any discernible affective response (e.g., little or no gestural communication, verbalizations made in a monotone)
- Inappropriate: reflecting a dyssynchrony between the content of client's thoughts and his or her emotional responses (e.g., busting into laughter without explanation when discussing a sad experience)

e) *Speech*: The quality and quantity of speech are important aspects of any mental status examination. Speech also provides us with data regarding intelligence, possible psychological confusion, anxiety, mania, and psychosis. Here one notes the kind of expressive language (e.g., taciturn vs. loquacious, overly general or vague vs. supererogatory, expansive vs. discrete), and whether the speaker is domineering or compliant. Is speech understandable or are there problems with enunciation/articulation? Is speech pressured or slow and deliberate? Is there any difficulty finding words, evidence of stuttering, vocal tics (e.g., the coprolalia of Tourette's syndrome). Does the client use subvocalizations? Is there a noticeable lisp? Are there neologisms or a blending of languages?

f) *Thought content*: Quite simply, describe the contents of the person's thoughts. Is there a normal range of interests appropriate to particular circumstances? Do thoughts seem to be dominated by fantasy, delusions, bizarre ideas, ruminations, obsessions or preoccupations, suicide, homicide, or other morbid themes? If so, please furnish examples.

Note: Suicidal or homicidal thoughts, particularly when reported by children or adolescents, signify potentially serious problems requiring thorough evaluation.

g) *Thought process*: In this part of the mental status exam, the intent is to identify the existence of any formal thought disorder through an assessment of the flow of thoughts. Thought disorders are typically identified as being one of three primary types: 1. illogical thinking, 2. loose or bizarre associations (e.g., "word salad") or tangential thinking, and 3. lack of interactive cohesiveness, which presents as a breakdown of the normal back and forth flow of conversation. In the third type, one is particularly struck by the disjointed, fragmented, or obscure meaning that characterizes the speaker's thought process.

Note: Thought disorders are relatively rare in children.

h) *Perceptions*: In this portion of the mental status exam, the principal focus is the client's orientation to reality. Is the world perceived in a normal, consensually based manner? Is there evidence of any perceptual distortions (olfactory, tactile, gustatory, auditory, or visual hallucinations)? Does the client appear to be responding to or preoccupied with internal or unseen stimuli? Does the client report conversations with deceased people or aliens? Describe being bothered by "voices" at various times? Report that bodily parts are degenerating (in the absence of diagnosable organic illness) or falling off?

i) *Judgment*: The focus here is on those deficiencies in judgment unrelated to known organic causes or to mental retardation. The operating premise is that although the individual understands the difference between the right and wrong thing to do, she or he may not behave in a manner consistent with that knowledge. For example, is this person subject to injuries due to careless behavior? Is the person properly attired for the external weather conditions?

j) *Sensorium*: The concept of *sensorium* involves both perception and the individual's orientation to reality. Orientation to reality generally involves four axes: *person, place, time,* and *situation.* Does the client know who he or she is, where he or she is, the date, and understand the reason for his or her visit? The client's general alertness is also described here (alert, hypervigilant, drowsy, catatonic, etc.).

Note: Developmental age is taken into account for younger children.

k) Cognition:

[1] Memory: This is a complicated function that may be compromised by anxiety, depression, or even lack of sleep, inter alia. Oftentimes, anxious or depressed individuals will report memory problems directly. At other times such problems may not be reported directly by the client, though they may have become noticeable to other family members or coworkers who note that the capacity for recall of events, situations, or conversations has changed. When there are memory problems, it is useful important to try to make a distinction between long-term (remote), near-term (recent), and immediate.

[2] Concentration: This is related to the individual's ability to use energy to sustain focus and attention on a given task. It can be formally assessed through serial counting and repetitive math computations, but is often reported by individuals as a symptom of depression or anxiety. In children problems in concentration may be revealed in the child's inability to engage in sustained play with a small number of toys (instead moving abruptly from one activity to another).

[3] Intellectual function: In the absence of formal test data, one can roughly estimate an individual's intellectual level by noting word usage, vocabulary, the

ability to comprehend and use concepts and abstractions as well as demonstrate a general fund of knowledge about the world. Moreover, educational achievement is often positively correlated with intelligence.

[4] Capacity for insight/Capacity for play:

Capacity for insight: In work with the adolescent or adult client, the capacity for insight is that ability to apprehend the nature of a particular situation or one's own problems. More specifically, it indicates the individual's capacity for understanding those dynamic factors that have culminated in the person's conflicts. This presumes the existence of specific capacities for self-observation, reflection, and contemplation, in turn linked to the ego's synthesizing and integrative functions.

Capacity for play: This is the corollary to the adult's capacity for insight and may be considered a measure of the child's ability to participate fully in the expressive process of dynamic play therapy. It is used here in its progressive, creative, developmental sense.[3] For example, some traumatized children are not able to develop stories and themes in their play. Their play possesses repetitive and ruminative features, and frequently unsuccessful adaptations, qualities that have led some professionals to term such play *posttraumatic.* Children who have experienced severe early deprivation may be largely incapable of playing, as may children suffering from depression.

3. ASSAY OF SPECIFIC EGO/SUPEREGO FUNCTIONS AND OBJECT RELATIONAL CAPACITIES:

a) Regulation and control of drives, affects, and impulses: Described in relation to four basic criteria:

[1] Directness of impulse expression (ranging from primitive acting out to neurotic acting out to relatively indirect forms of behavioral expression).

[2] Evidence of capacity for experiencing/tolerating guilt.

[3] The effectiveness of delay and control and the degree of frustration tolerance.

[4] Mitigating environmental features, either historical or ongoing.

b) Defensive functioning/adaptive coping strategies:

[1] Taking into account the subject's chronological age, note developmental level of defensive functioning (i.e., primary or "primitive" defensive operations such as projection, omnipotent control, primitive idealization/devaluation, or projective identification vs. secondary or "higher order" defensive operations such as regression, isolation, turning against the self, undoing, reaction formation, or sublimation).

[2] Note specific qualities of defenses, such as stability, flexibility, selectivity, and effectiveness.

[3] Describe specific adaptive strategies the individual employs for coping with interpersonal or other problems.

c) Relationship potential: In this category the individual's capacity for relationships with others is assessed, relying in part on the history of early object relations, later relationship patterns, and current patterns, as well as the quality of affect and relatedness during the interview. Predominant aspects of the individual's characteristic relationships with others should be assessed. These may include a range of qualities or dimensions (e.g., autistic, need satisfying, insecure, ambivalent, narcissistic, symbiotic, sadomasochistic, borderline, dependent). Relationships may also reveal a mature capacity for sharing and loving.

d) Synthetic-integrative functioning: Here we note the person's relative success in reconciling or integrating discrepant or potentially contradictory attitudes, values, affects, behavior, self-representations, and object-representations.

e) Environmental mastery-competence: In this category the person's performance in relation to the ability to interact with and master her or his environment as well as the sense of competence (how well the person believes she or he can do) is assessed. One may also wish to note the quality and availability of environmental supports and resources (both institutional and personal) that can be used in conjunction with any therapeutic efforts.

4. SELF/SELFOBJECT RELATIONS AND SELF STRUCTURE:

Relevant observations about an individual's developmental experiences as these are organized along the dimensions of *mirroring, idealizing,* and *partnering* as well as how these features may be related to the nascent transference relationship may be described in this section.[4] One is especially interested in ascertaining the nature and cohesiveness of the self. Is there evidence, for example, of selfobject pathology, as represented by poor self-esteem regulation, grandiosity, impaired capacity for empathy, depletion states, or various "disintegration products"? Or does the individual's self structure appear to be reasonably well-integrated and cohesive, evidenced by healthy, vital, and fulfilling experiences with others and in various activities? Knowledge of the individual's intercurrent environment, especially in the case of children, is important to include. (It is, however, recognized that such data may be incomplete or fragmentary during the period of assessment.)

5. SPECIFIC AREAS OF COMPETENCE AND EFFECTANCE:

In this section of the assessment, particular areas of competence, special skills or abilities (e.g., scholastic, musical, or occupational performance), interests, and talents are noted. These may be based upon the individual's report, that of collateral sources, or actually demonstrated during the clinical interview.

[6. NATURE OF THE CLINICIAN'S SUBJECTIVE EXPERIENCE OF THE CLIENT:]

In this section the clinician highlights her/his own subjective reactions to the client during the interview. Such commentary is not necessarily designed to highlight that which may more often be termed *countertransference* in ongoing therapy, although strong reactions to a client in an early interview are always worth noting. This section may take the form of a process summary, but is principally geared toward highlighting thoughts and emotional reactions of the clinician that may, in themselves, have diagnostic or treatment significance.

[7. GENETIC-DYNAMIC FORMULATION:]

Drawing on sections 1 through 6, the clinician presents a genetic-dynamic understanding of the case. The basic idea, of course, is to furnish a narrative overview of the case, taking into account the presenting complaints, the contribution of the client's environment, relevant historical features, findings from the mental status examination, specific observations regarding ego/superego functions, object relatedness, and self/selfobject relations, and the client's areas of competence and/or effectance, as well as one's own subjective reactions. Attention is always paid to the client's *strengths and assets* as well as to features of psychopathology (e.g., the individual's efforts to resolve a problem often reflect a combination of less adaptive defenses and adaptive coping strategies). The genetic-dynamic formulation is intended to be *creative and generative* rather than perfunctory and conclusive; *conjecture and hypothetico-deductive reasoning are an essential part of a useful genetic-dynamic formulation.* One should be able to consider the basic question, "What historical and ongoing issues seem to have combined to produce this specific problem, occurring in this specific way at this particular time?"

8. TREATMENT PLAN:

In this final section of the clinical assessment, several key questions are addressed.

a) First and foremost, there must be an explicit description of the client's understanding of the problem(s), her or his specific objectives or plan for treatment, and the outcomes desired. (In the case of children or some court-mandated clients, the existence of a "problem" may itself be in dispute, a fact that should be plainly acknowledged.)

b) In addition to noting the individual's capacity for undertaking dynamically oriented work, it is useful to assess her or his motivation for treatment and the nature and extent of environmental/interpersonal supports available to her or him.

c) Treatment objectives are useful to identify; these may range from the resolution of highly specific problems (e.g., anxiety associated with sexual performance) to characterological change (e.g., enduring structural change in a client with a borderline personality organization).

d) The means by which such change(s) will be measured (in dynamically oriented treatment, generally a combination of the client's subjective report and therapist's clinical assessment).

e) Finally, the form that the treatment will take (e.g., once-weekly individual therapy, intensive psychotherapy, individual child treatment with adjunctive parental guidance sessions, etc.) should be clearly described.[5]

CLINICAL CASE ILLUSTRATION 6.1: "PATRICK"

1. DIAGNOSTIC SUMMARY

Patrick was a tall, attractive, muscular thirty-two-year-old white male, single, never married and childless, who was admitted to the Mental Health Outpatient (MHO) program of a large metropolitan correctional facility, following a two-week stay in the jail's quarantine unit. Patrick complained of feeling "under the weather" and also reported difficulty sleeping. Patrick's physical appearance was unremarkable with the exception of two tattoos: a skull with crossbones on his right shoulder and a fire-breathing dragon on his left arm. A reddish scar bore testimony to a knife stab suffered in a fight when he was twenty-one. Patrick has one older brother, age thirty-seven, and another, age twenty-nine, both of whom reside in different states and with whom he has "pretty much lost touch." His father is deceased. He has maintained a relationship with his sixty-one-year-old mother, visiting her on a monthly basis. Patrick's father was a first-generation American of French Canadian ancestry and his mother's background was English and German.

Patrick was assessed at County Jail, a fourteen-story building that houses nearly one thousand inmates, of whom approximately one hundred live in the residential units. Another fifty-seventy are in the Mental Health Outpatient (MHO) program, housed in the general population throughout the jail. This twenty-four-hour daily program includes enhanced supervision and the intensive support necessary to manage individuals with serious mental illness. It also offers evaluation and referral for Jail Diversion Services for detainees with a mental illness or developmental disability and a history of nonviolence who are charged with a nonviolent felonious offense. General health and medical care, laboratory and diagnostic testing, special dietary, spiritual, and ancillary services are offered to these inmates in a supportive milieu. Despite the presence of a diagnosable psychiatric disorder requiring regular mental health follow-up, recipients of mental health services may be housed in the general population should a mental health professional determine that enhanced therapeutic placement is not needed. These clients, who may or may not receive psychotropic medicines, are also seen by a psychiatrist every four to six weeks and by the MHO social work clinician on an as-needed basis (at least once monthly).

In the first diagnostic interview Patrick told the clinician that he felt as though he might "explode" and added that the smell and noise level of the "screeching monkeys in here is driving me nuts!" Despite his boyish countenance, Patrick's intense stare and icy hazel eyes betrayed seething anger and resentment at his plight. In the initial encounter the client was informed of the scope of services available through the outpatient program and apprised of the maximum duration of treatment (twelve months), at which time he would either be released or, following a jury trial and sentencing, spend additional time in the state prison. He appeared pleased when the clinician informed him that the psychiatrist would meet with him every four to six weeks. He seemed more ambivalent when the social work clinician suggested that they meet on a twice-weekly basis, although he expressed some interest when informed that the sessions would be conducted in a classroom setting in the absence of deputies, adding, "At least I'll be able to get out of my shit-hole cell." After his initial consultation with the psychiatrist, Patrick was prescribed Serzone. He did meet twice weekly with the social work clinician, and the sessions were conducted in a classroom setting, generally lasting from thirty to forty-five minutes without a sheriff's deputy present.

Guarded, aloof, suspicious, and reticent, Patrick disclosed very little in the first half-dozen or so encounters. He found it extremely difficult to open up and talk about himself and his feelings. Even after the clinician interceded on Patrick's behalf with the social services specialist to arrange visitation and telephone privileges, he continued to be uncooperative, in the main nodding and giving monosyllabic answers.

He revealed that he had completed high school and had attended college for a "a year and a half or so." Patrick's interests had been in "mechanical, fixing-with-your-hands subjects." He hated math and English and, ultimately, couldn't handle the structure and demands of college. Patrick dropped out and worked at a number of odd jobs, including bartending, construction, landscaping, and auto repair. When he was arrested, Patrick was working as a millwright. After prompting, Patrick divulged that he had been arrested and charged with criminal sexual conduct against a young woman after having a few drinks with her at a bar. Immediately prior to this incident, his girlfriend of seven months ("a nice girl") left him "for some computer programmer." In a phone conversation she told Patrick not ever to call her again and that she had notified the police. He added, with a trace of bitterness in his voice, that "she said she was terrified of me." He was enraged after the phone conversation and, impulsively, went to his favorite bar, where he met a "bar girl, a loose woman." They had a "few drinks" together and drove to her place, where Patrick claimed they had consensual sex. He subsequently refused to discuss his case with the clinician because of "legal complications," adamantly maintaining that he did not force himself upon the young woman, a position from which Patrick never deviated.

He disclosed a long history of aggressive behavior, which included numerous fights at school, acts of vandalism, home invasion, shoplifting, alcohol and drug use (marijuana, cocaine), numerous previous convictions for violent offenses, especially physical violence toward female partners, and several DUI arrests and convictions. He reported a long history of explosive outbursts of temper (often accompanied by heavy drinking) and partner battering. His violent assaults had led to several different incarcerations in the county jail as well as mandated community service. At the age of thirteen years he unintentionally "grazed" his finger and injured an accomplice when a gun the two had discovered in a home they were burglarizing accidentally discharged. They were apprehended, and Patrick subsequently spent eighty-four days at a camp for juvenile offenders. At age fifteen he was sentenced to two years at a state correctional school for youthful offenders for "strong armed robbery," a place where "they had a positive peer culture program; if you acted out, your peers would restrain you." He studied drafting and auto repair, and obtained his graduate equivalency diploma. At age seventeen he spent ninety days at another correctional facility after he assaulted his father and threatened him with a knife. Although Patrick didn't stab his father, he knifed the family dog, which later died of its wounds. He has also attended several mental health and dual diagnosis outpatient programs since his earliest incarcerations as an adolescent.

Patrick described his father as a strict disciplinarian, the "cock of the roost." His father, who had a high school education, was moody and drank heavily. He was often both physically and psychologically abusive to Patrick and took little if any interest in Patrick's social and educational development. Patrick's father worked in a factory for as long as Patrick could remember and died when he was twenty-three years old. His mother, a devoutly religious woman who had received a strict Catholic upbringing, was timid and passive, almost never contradicting her emotionally uninvolved husband. Upon his death, she too began to drink, though not heavily. Until her retirement she worked for an air freight company as a scheduler. She has not remarried. Inasmuch as his mother worked evenings and his father rarely stayed at home unless he was too inebriated to go out, Patrick recalled that, from the time he was six or seven years old, he and his brothers were often left alone without any adult supervision. Although he minimized its significance, he intimated that he often felt lonely and frightened at these times. A picture emerged of a mother who could be cold and unloving and of a relationship principally built around her unceasing admonitions and moral proscriptions. Patrick added that she gave him no feeling of warmth and affection but had always been there to confront him with his badness. Patrick revealed that he was very dependent upon her. Although he was loathe to criticize her, he indicated that she had probably hindered him in his efforts to exercise initiative or act autonomously; at the same time, he felt unable to make important occupational or other life decisions without her direct advice and suggestions. He found his work monotonous and unfulfilling, and whenever he tried to find something more meaningful or gratifying she would ridicule his plans, dampening if not defeating his initiative before he could even attempt to put such plans into action. He disclosed highly ambivalent feelings toward her; although he felt dependent on her, he was also terrified of her.

Patrick revealed that he started to masturbate at age eight and began having sexual intercourse with girls at age fifteen. He recalled his first heterosexual experience as "somewhat traumatic." When he was nine years old a slightly older girl initiated him into sexual play, leaving him with the understanding that all girls like to be sexually fondled. While playing with a younger neighborhood girl a few weeks afterward, Patrick fondled her and "fingered her vagina," believing that this was what she desired. The girl ran home and told her parents; an hour later her enraged father appeared at Patrick's front door and confronted his father. Patrick remembered feeling deeply ashamed and then his father gave him "a whipping I'll never forget." From that point on, his father belittled him and made him feel "dirty and perverted." This was even more likely to occur when his father was inebriated. Patrick began to see himself as unattractive, unlikable, and socially and sexually aberrant, with little opportunity for self-expression or creativity. His sense of loneliness increased, and he became shy and increasingly inept at social interaction.

Although Patrick was sexually active from the age of fifteen, his relationships were typically only with "loose girls" and invariably short-lived. Over time a pattern developed in which Patrick would find evidence of his girlfriend's promiscuity; this would lead to a violent assault not only on the girlfriend but, on occasion, her current sexual partner. Patrick's earliest difficulty with anger and aggression probably dated to his latency years, although it was in his early and middle adolescence that his aggressive behavior finally came to the attention of school and legal authorities.

Patrick's physical examination was normal, and he tested negative for HIV, hepatitis, and tuberculosis. He reported having sustained a head injury and several broken ribs from different fights, though he had suffered no recent injuries. Chest and skull X-rays and electroencephalogram results were normal. As reported above, Patrick has a scar from a knife wound and two tattoos.

Patrick's earliest memories were of his younger brother's birth, at which time he was not quite three, and of "one time waiting for my Mom to come in the middle of the night when I woke up scared." Patrick was not able to say exactly how old he might have been on this second occasion, although as he anxiously awaited his mother's appearance he recalled that he was clutching the gate on the side of his crib, which meant "I had to be less than three."

2. MENTAL STATUS EXAMINATION

Patrick's personal appearance was unremarkable with the exceptions noted earlier. He wore mandated prison attire, had good personal hygiene, and always appeared neatly dressed. He tended to shuffle, taking as much time as possible to walk from the holding cell area to the conference room, but this is not considered remarkable in an inmate population.

His attitude toward the clinician vacillated between boredom and indifference to petulance and mild hostility. He was typically less than fully cooperative during most of the assessment interviews except on those occasions when he believed the clinician might be able to offer him a tangible reward or arrange for his grievances to be addressed. Patrick's mood was downcast and anxious. Suspicious and reticent, his disclosures were minimal if not parsimonious, and his irritation with the clinician, at times, palpable. Occasionally, his voice would grow loud, raucous, and demanding as Patrick complained about the quality of food or his inability to shower often enough in the unit. His rate of speech was unremarkable, although when he addressed certain topics (e.g., "loose women," his mother, etc.), he could become explosive, and his speech less coherent. Although he was nearly mute during significant portions of each interview, at particular times

Patrick could become highly verbal and interactive, dominating the conversation. He was, at other times, fidgety, and his affect often shifted abruptly from indifference to flippancy or irritation. He seldom made direct eye contact and would have revealed few details, were it not for the clinician's persistence. Particularly during the early interviews, he complained of "feeling under the weather" and having considerable difficulty falling asleep.

Patrick denied any history of suicidality. He was visibly peeved by his fellow inmates and surroundings, but denied harboring any intent to harm others. There was no overt sign of psychosis. Although guarded, Patrick voiced coherent, logical cognitions. His sensorium seemed intact; he was focused and oriented to all four domains, generally well-grounded in reality, and exhibited no signs of a formal thought disorder. Patrick did evince a moderately poor capacity to channel impulsive actions, based in large part on his history. His capacity to deploy sound judgment, especially in light of his tendency to translate impulses into action without evident consideration of their consequences, appeared to have been poor, though again this was based to a greater extent on the history than on observations made during the assessment interviews.

Patrick exhibited impoverishment in his ability to fantasize. In subsequent sessions it emerged that any kind of adverse stimulus led directly to behavior without mediating thought, ruminations, or fantasies. In general, Patrick acted first and thought about the consequences afterward. He lashed out verbally or went out and got drunk and then violently assaulted people.

Patrick revealed no obvious limitations in his capacity for recall of immediate, recent, and remote events and experiences, nor was there evidence of problems in his ability to concentrate. His capacity for insight was judged to be limited, as will be further detailed below.

3. ASSAY OF SPECIFIC EGO/SUPEREGO FUNCTIONS AND OBJECT RELATIONAL CAPACITIES

Patrick reveals significant limitations in his capacity to modulate and control drives, affects, and impulses, as previously suggested. Owing to an impoverishment in the capacity for trial action, Patrick tends to discharge impulses directly via behavioral enactment. These enactments are often very primitive displays and furthermore reveal very little capacity for tolerating either frustration or guilt. This pattern appears to have its origins in Patrick's early development and is probably related at least in part to the harsh and punitive family environment in which he was raised.

Patrick's defensive functioning is most aptly described as primitive and unstable. He makes use of a range of primary defense mechanisms and strategies, including but not limited to projection, projective identification, splitting, omnipotence, massive denial, displacement, devaluation/idealization, identification with the aggressor, and defensive hostility directed outward. It is noted that these defenses are used in ways that reveal neither flexibility nor effectiveness; in fact, inasmuch as acting out often preempts other, more adaptive efforts to manage anxiety or other threatening affects, Patrick's use of defenses seems to be largely unsuccessful. There is a corresponding lack of discrimination in his defensive functioning, further underscoring the general impoverishment in this aspect of ego functions; accordingly, Patrick reveals little of what might be termed either higher-order defenses (e.g., repression, undoing, reaction-formation) or relatively conflict-free adaptations (e.g., stoicism, humor, or self-observation). *Inability to describe emotions in a verbal manner*

Patrick's difficulty in identifying his own affective states may signify alexithymia, frequently a posttraumatic adaptation observed in individuals who like Patrick, have been raised in a family milieu in which unremitting neglect or physical and psychological abuse compound extant severe parental limitations or pathology. Patrick often claimed he didn't know when he was angry and seemed unable to distinguish the subtler nuances of his feelings. Negative affects were usually not differentiated, but rather perceived in a globally unpleasant way.

Patrick gives evidence of a developmental arrest in his object relations, which are principally geared toward the satisfaction of immediate needs and the alleviation of tensions or anxieties that threaten to overwhelm him at various times. There is evidence both of dependency wishes and counterdependent reactions in many of his interpersonal interactions as well as a tendency to split aspects of both his self-experience and relationships with others according to whether these are predominantly "good" or "bad." Patrick's *Splitting* characteristic manner of relating to others also reveals such attributes as narcissistic entitlement, grandiosity, and haughty condescension, and, not surprisingly, little capacity for mature object-relating.

Insofar as Patrick's synthetic-integrative functioning is concerned, there is abundant evidence of flagrant discrepancies in his view of himself and attitudes/behavior toward others. For example, Patrick's naughty condescension and grandiosity appear to furnish him with some protection from the inner experience of vulnerability and emptiness; likewise, his hyperaggressiveness and counterdependent behavior may represent an effort to counteract an image of the self as small and vulnerable or, perhaps, offer a modicum of pro-

tection from the core experience of abandonment anxiety/depression. However, his capacity to reconcile such discrepant and contradictory aspects of his
behavior and self-experience remains relatively primitive, with little evidence
of harmonious functioning.

Patrick has tended to master environmental challenges through manipulative or aggressive behavior. There is, moreover, little evidence of a sense of
competence except in a few isolated areas of his life (e.g., his ability to work
with his hands). It should also be noted that few environmental supports
have been available to Patrick, which has, of course, hampered his efforts to
address and master environmental challenges and obstacles. It is also noteworthy that Patrick, albeit tentatively, has recently voiced some interest in
being able to use therapy to longer-term advantage rather than simply in the
interest of short-term gratifications.

4. SELF/SELFOBJECT RELATIONS AND SELF-STRUCTURE

Patrick appears to have suffered a series of traumatic disappointments in his
childhood relations with primary selfobjects, the cumulative impact of
which was an arrest in the development of the self. Patrick's father was himself a seriously disturbed individual, largely incapable of expressing love or
interest in his son; furthermore, he was psychologically and physically abusive and took sadistic pleasure in humiliating Patrick. His mother, owing to
limitations in her own psychological makeup, was unable to offer Patrick
psychological protection, praise, or affirmation of his childhood efforts at
mastery or displays of competence. She expressed little confidence in her son
and frequently undermined his efforts at individuation, independence, self-
assertiveness, and creativity, though she was not completely incapable of
expressing loving feelings toward Patrick.

More specifically, Patrick appears to suffer from structural deficiencies in
all three selfobject domains. One might hypothesize that idealizing experiences in which either parent was able to lend empathically attuned, uplifting
care to assuage Patrick's anxiety and restore inner homeostasis were more
often the exception than the rule. This likelihood in combination with his
father's frank abuse and his mother's failure to protect Patrick from her husband's sadism and violence, which had evidently begun by the time he was
three or four years old, probably led to an early developmental derailment in
the idealizing domain. The culmination of such traumatic disappointments
in this sphere was Patrick's failure to develop a reliable internal structure for
restoring internal homeostasis, for calming and soothing the self. This seems
most evident in Patrick's tremendous difficulty in modulating and moder-

ating his own affectivity and in his inability to make adaptive use of signal affects. Childhood needs for affirmation of his innate worth, for acknowledgment of skills, talents, or special attributes appears to have suffered a similar fate. Praise and parental interest or investment was rarely forthcoming from his father and were inconsistently available from Patrick's mother. Patrick's ongoing difficulty in maintaining his self-esteem, and in pursuing important goals (e.g., occupational or educational), are probably tied to the malformation of this aspect of self-structure. Patrick's childhood needs for partnering, which comprise the third selfobject domain, were also less than satisfactory. By early adolescence he tended to see himself as "sort of a loner," with few friends and without ties to any kind of peer group. Many of his relationships were with other antisocial adolescents, none of them enduring, or very brief sexual encounters with girls, most of which could not even be described as relationships.

Patrick also presents a range of symptoms that might be usefully thought of as "disintegration products": inflated sense of self-worth, grandiosity, entitlement, haughty condescension, inability to tolerate guilt or anxiety, hyper-aggressivity and physical violence, impaired capacity for empathy, manipulative interpersonal behavior, antisocial behavior, and so forth. The combination of this symptomatology and what is known of his early history strongly suggest that Patrick has been unable to attain self-cohesiveness and likely also suffers from a primary disorder of the self. Although the clinical assessment has only recently been completed and treatment is just now underway, certain transference manifestations of these selfobject needs, principally idealizing and secondarily in the mirroring realm, have already been observed. Patrick has, for example, already exhibited a tendency to use the therapist to regulate his internal tensions, to help him calm down. He also occasionally speaks of his criminal exploits with a sort of pride, at times in an apparent effort to elicit both interest and affirmation from the clinician of the dangers he confronted, the clever ruses and deceptions he used, and so forth. Partnering needs have not found any obvious expression as of the present, although these may be anticipated as the transference relationship evolves.

5. SPECIFIC AREAS OF COMPETENCE AND EFFECTANCE

Although his school career was discontinuous owing to Patrick's criminal exploits and incarcerations, he showed an early and impressive physical agility and was judged a very good athlete by his instructors in elementary school. As he grew older he became less inclined to participate in competitive group sports, although his athletic prowess is still evident. He began power-lifting when he was in his late teens, and continues to the present. Patrick revealed that he completed high school, attended college for a "year and a half or so," and displayed an interest and adroitness in "mechanical, fixing with your hands subjects." Although his work history has been unstable, he has shown proficiency for a variety of different jobs and is characteristically able to learn new tasks and skills quickly. Patrick has actually worked at over a dozen odd jobs since dropping out of college. These have included bartending, construction, landscaping, and auto repair; he has also worked as a cinema attendant and, just before his arrest, as a millwright.

6. NATURE OF THE CLINICIAN'S SUBJECTIVE EXPERIENCE OF THE PATIENT

Powerfully built and over six feet tall, Patrick was an imposing figure. However, for reasons of confidentiality and in order to foster trust, he was seen alone, with no sheriff's deputies present, in a large, jail-type classroom. Although the possibility of physical assault was not a great likelihood with this client, it remained a distinct possibility. This led the clinician on occasion to take the path of least resistance, at times appeasing Patrick rather than commenting on or dealing more directly with his hostile-aggressive attitude. On one occasion, during the formal clinical assessment, the clinician believed himself to be in imminent danger of physical assault, when Patrick's anger escalated to rage over a perceived slight. With few other options available, the clinician abruptly terminated the interview, summoning the deputies to escort Patrick back to his cell and place him in "lock down."

At other times Patrick would allude to a deep sense of inadequacy and vulnerability, a core conviction that he was unlovable. The clinician's subjective experience of these painful revelations was, of course, entirely different. At these times the clinician felt profoundly moved by the client's words and affects such as sadness, depression, and resignation became internally available to him.

7. GENETIC-DYNAMIC FORMULATION

Patrick, a thirty-two year old, single, white male of French Canadian and European ancestry, was admitted to the Mental Health Outpatient (MHO) program by the clinical social worker after spending two weeks in the jail's quarantine unit. He complained of "feeling under the weather" and of having difficulty sleeping, and felt he might explode because of the sickening odor and unremitting noise in the unit. He found it extremely difficult to open up and talk about himself and his feelings. Charged with criminal sexual conduct against a young woman, Patrick was assessed and treated in the MHO program at County Jail. Aside from the barest essentials, Patrick steadfastly refused to discuss his case with the clinician, fearing that "legal complications" might arise were he to do so.

Patrick grew up being emotionally and physically abused by a moody, alcoholic father who showed no interest in his social and educational development. His religious mother was cold and unsupportive, offering him little in the way of warmth or affection; in addition, she unfailingly confronted him with his badness. Growing very dependent on her, he felt thwarted in his efforts to exercise initiative or independence. Gradually, Patrick began to see himself as unattractive, unlikable, and socially and sexually aberrant. His sense of loneliness, which bordered on desolation, gradually increased, and he became shy and increasingly inept and uncomfortable in social interactions outside the immediate family.

These problems may be more fully understood in reference to the theoretical frameworks of self psychology, ego psychology, and object relational thinking. Patrick's self/selfobject relationships reveal deficiencies in all three of the major configurations of the self (mirroring, idealizing, and partnering), and may also account for the range of symptoms he has presented during this assessment (e.g., problems in modulating affectivity; explosive behavior; core depression; entitlement; grandiosity, etc.). In consequence Patrick has probably not attained self-cohesiveness. His ego functions, on examination, also reveal significant and substantial defects. Poor judgement, impulsivity, deficient moral reasoning, a rigid reliance on primary defenses, impoverishment of the capacity for fantasy and trial action, and impairments in the synthetic-integrative function, represent some of the more serious difficulties observed in ego functioning. In addition, Patrick may suffer from alexithymia, which is frequently a posttraumatic adaptation; Patrick often claimed he didn't know when he was angry and seemed unable to distinguish the subtler nuances of his feelings. Negative affects were usually not differentiated but rather perceived in a globally unpleasant way. Patrick's object relations tend toward the narcissistic or borderline end of the spectrum, reflecting concern with the alleviation of internally arising tensions or the satisfaction of particular needs. He also makes prominent use of such defenses as splitting and projective identification, both of which are characteristic of persons who have not attained the capacity for mature object relations.

Patrick had been severely punished at the age of nine for undressing and fondling a younger neighborhood girl. In retrospect, this experience also proved a historical marker for a shift in the way Patrick's father treated him. His father had for some time belittled and humiliated Patrick, but these sadistic attacks seemed to increase in both frequency and magnitude after Patrick's sexual experimentation with the neighbor girl. In his later pattern of victimization and physical assault on others, Patrick has demonstrated what might be termed a classic instance of "identification with the aggressor." In this context one might understand such crimes as representing the unconscious repetition of his father's original "crimes" against him, which always involved abuse commingled with such features as humiliation, uncontrolled rage, and sadism. Patrick began to enter short-lived relationships with sexually active and oftentimes promiscuous young women. A pattern emerged whereby Patrick would feel sexually betrayed and then abruptly terminate his involvement, typically by violently assaulting his girlfriends and, on occasion, their partners. Patrick's difficulties in modulating or otherwise adaptively managing aggressive impulses and feelings seemed to typify his behavior throughout adolescence up until the present. He built up a long list of criminal offenses: fights at school, acts of vandalism, shoplifting, alcohol, and drug use, numerous convictions for violent offenses, especially toward female partners, several DUI's, and the most recent charge of criminal sexual conduct against the young woman he had met at the bar.

Upon release from a residential training school for adjudicated minors who have committed felonious offenses, Patrick obtained his graduate equivalency diploma and attended college for about a year and a half. His interest and dexterity for repairing mechanical things was more fully revealed at this time. However, he detested required subjects such as math and English and felt unable to accommodate to the structure and demands of college. Patrick dropped out. He subsequently drifted from one job to the next, and although he worked at a variety of different jobs, none lasted longer than a couple of years. It is noteworthy that Patrick was usually a "quick study," though, just as characteristically, he would begin to lose interest soon after mastering the essentials of a particular job, which in some measure accounts for his checkered work record.

Patrick tended to view the world and his relationships in a black and white way. Relationships with others were discriminated on the basis of whether or not they were useful to him. In fact, the clinician believed that Patrick's narcissism, his demanding nature and evident disregard for others' feelings and needs served both to conceal an unconscious belief that he was neither lovable nor admirable and to offer protection against a core feeling of depression and anxiety associated with the possibility of the loss of self-object supplies or of abandonment. This highly narcissistic and antisocial individual had great needs for others but even greater anxiety about the consequences should these persons prove defective, untrustworthy, uncaring, or abandoning.

Patrick has demonstrated that he can be an engaging and interesting client. He obviously possesses a certain aptitude for mechanical repair and, when not complaining, out of control, or behaving in a manipulative fashion does seem capable of engaging in conversation with the clinician, although the range of topics is rather limited.

8. TREATMENT PLAN

Patrick's assessment was challenging for a number of reasons. He was secretive, unwilling to cooperate, and generally distrustful of perceived authority figures. He often plunged the sessions into long silences, placing the clinician in the somewhat uncomfortable position of using a very active therapeutic modus operandi to elicit material from him. He was, in fact, reluctant much of the time to acknowledge that he had a problem at all. Nevertheless, he sought short-term relief both from his sleeplessness and from a vague problem he had simply described as "feeling under the weather." Patrick had little if any insight into the distal causes of his ongoing difficulties, nor would this have constituted a legitimate treatment objective for such a client.

Instead the clinician focused on his most immediate concerns. Treatment, it was mutually decided, would be undertaken to help Patrick cope more successfully with his strong emotional reactions to the prison setting and to the other inmates, which seemed to figure prominently in his insomnia and may also have been linked to his dysphoria. Through a combination of meetings with the clinician and with the psychiatrist, who prescribed a tricyclic antidepressant (Serzone) for his depression, Patrick might experience some relief from these symptoms.

Another important focus of Patrick's treatment would be that of assisting him in better identifying and grasping the reasons for his emotional reactions; Patrick expressed less interest in this objective but did acknowledge that he sometimes couldn't understand exactly what might cause him to fly into a rage so quickly. Because Patrick experienced his violent behavior as a dystonic event, as something unpleasant, he seemed willing to include this as an additional objective for treatment. Such an effort might begin with assisting Patrick to describe certain changes experienced in connection with his changing affective states: sensations within his body, his muscle tone, and felt inner experience. Focal attention to inner subjective states would certainly be something new for Patrick, though it should be noted that the direct *expression* of affects was not really the immediate goal here. A more proximal goal for Patrick would be to enhance his capacity to *recognize* and *describe* strong affects, a necessary step toward strengthening such ego functions as signal anxiety and perception and, ultimately, toward somewhat better impulse control and reasoning. Finally, his capacity for mentalization, to interpose thought and fantasy between impulse and action, might also be enhanced by such a focus.

In the treatment of antisocial clients, certain basic principles that underlie good clinical technique may be helpful to elaborate. These principles include that the therapist be stable, persistent, and thoroughly incorruptible, that he or she be able repeatedly to confront the client's denial and minimization of antisocial behavior, and that he or she offer consistent help to enable the client to connect actions with internal states. Generally speaking, confrontations of here-and-now behavior are more effective than interpretations of unconscious material from the past. The clinician's countertransference must be rigorously monitored to preclude disjunctive reactions, and therapists must also avoid having unrealistic expectations for improvement. The clinician recognized that specific techniques, such as role-playing, mediate catharsis,[6] direct guidance, and intercession on the client's behalf with the supervisory personnel in the County Jail system, would likely also be part of any ongoing treatment effort with Patrick.

The nature of the change effort would of necessity be modest, inasmuch as Patrick's incarceration at County Jail would not last beyond twelve months and could conceivably be much shorter. Treatment would be offered on a twice-weekly basis; it would be psychodynamically based, principally ego supportive in nature, and consist of several different therapeutic aims. These would include offering Patrick symptomatic relief from the complaints he had presented at intake, strengthening and extending his repertoire of coping strategies, augmenting his capacity for mentalization in place of behavioral enactment, and enhancing his capacity for identifying emotions and using such information to greater adaptive advantage.

The concept of assessment has always been central to effective dynamic treatment. In this chapter we have explored various psychoanalytic and clinical social work perspectives on the function of clinical assessment and the value that such a process may hold for the dynamic therapist undertaking the treatment of a given client. A thorough dynamic clinical assessment, as the case material in this chapter has demonstrated, can be a most revealing and useful prelude to formal treatment. It can tell us about the client's strengths and weaknesses, inform us about salient aspects of the client's history, identify the most critical objectives for treatment, and, in general, prepare us for the task of therapy. It may also capture important features of the client's narrative somewhat more completely than is usually possible through nondynamic instruments designed to measure the client's presenting symptoms, their severity, and so forth. Although this model does require more of the clinician than the usual combination of behavior checklists and other tools for "rapid assessment," it may also yield clinical data of far greater complexity and richness.

Beginning Treatment:
Initial Engagement, the Holding Environment, the Real
Relationship, and Formation of the Therapeutic Alliance

WHEN DOES TREATMENT BEGIN? How do clients and therapists get started? What are the most crucial tasks of the initial phase of therapy? With these questions in mind, this chapter explores the process of treatment as it gets underway. We begin with a review of the idea of the casework relationship as it has evolved in the social work literature and then consider various psychoanalytic perspectives on relationship and initial engagement, including the transformative idea of a therapeutic holding environment. Using a case illustration involving a middle-aged mother of three who had recently emigrated from Russia, the critical significance of the establishment of therapeutic "holding" and its contribution to the clinician's efforts to overcome an empathic breach that had occurred in the first hour is illustrated. The importance of the rudimentary alliance and its transformation into a therapeutic alliance with distinctive properties that set it apart from both transference-linked phenomena and the real relationship is then discussed. In this regard, a far more extensive rendering of the therapeutic alliance, that of Meissner's, is examined in depth. Finally, two further clinical examples are presented. The first explores special challenges to the creation of a solid therapeutic alliance with a suicidal young adult, the second the process of initial engagement and alliance building with a depressed, middle-aged Hispanic client who sought assistance in improving her relationships with men.

HISTORICAL PERSPECTIVES IN SOCIAL WORK

Since its inception as a profession, social work has identified and promoted two distinctive and equally critical tasks, both of which must be successfully completed before treatment can be said to be fully underway. The first of these stresses the importance of psychosocial or biopsychosocial study and represents a tradition traceable to the earliest case work theorists, but one that is faithfully preserved in the contemporary dynamic clinical social work literature (e.g., Woods and Hollis 2000; Goldstein 2001). The second postulate is that the formation of a relationship between client and worker represents a necessary precondition for effective clinical intervention.

It is generally acknowledged that even the most systematic and comprehensive data gathering, absent efforts to build a basic or rudimentary alliance or working relationship, offers little assurance that the treatment process will be successful. This approach perhaps is roughly analogous to the medical aphorism that "the operation was a success, but the patient died." Conversely, most dynamically trained clinicians believe that, no matter how skillfully done, a treatment relationship entered into without the benefit of meaningful assessment or effort to understand the dynamic basis of a client's difficulties is unlikely to culminate in either clinical clarity or treatment success. In this instance the surgeon acts to relieve the patient's acute distress but is clueless as to the nature and cause of the patient's problem, a medical practice that would be neither confidence inspiring nor conducive to a medical "cure."

Since we have discussed and presented a framework for conducting a comprehensive dynamic assessment in the previous chapter, our focus here is on the relational aspects of the early phase of treatment.[1] Relationship has long been emphasized in the social casework literature, although it was originally conceived in a nondynamic way. Mary Richmond, writing over one hundred years ago, noted that

> friendly visiting means intimate and continuous knowledge of and sympathy with a poor family's joys, sorrows, opinions, feelings, and entire outlook upon life. The visitor that has this is unlikely to blunder about relief or any detail; without it he is almost certain, in any charitable relations with members of the family to blunder seriously.   (Richmond 1899:180)

In this early view, one that is framed in the language of the charity organization movement, relationship is not conceived of as a dynamic, interactive process, but as something akin to a friendship. As a matter of fact, it wasn't until 1930 that the term *relationship* was finally adopted as a way of characterizing the encounter between the worker and client (Robinson 1930; Biestek 1957). Although other terms such as *empathy* and *rapport* were subsequently introduced to enhance this early characterization, these conceptions of relationship lacked dimension. When, in the late 1920s, the psychoanalytic concept of transference was first used in the social casework lexicon, thereby adding considerable complexity to the simple formula originally provided by Richmond, it may have furnished additional impetus to efforts to define the nature of the casework relationship.[2]

In the late 1950s Felix Biestek published a now classic volume, *The Casework Relationship*. In this book he outlined seven principles of relationship distilled from a comprehensive analysis of the extant casework literature. These consisted of: *individualization, purposeful expression of feelings, controlled emotional environment, acceptance, nonjudgmental attitude, client self-determination,* and *confidentiality* (Biestek 1957). One might argue that these principles are in basic synchrony not only with important psychoanalytic concepts emerging in the mid-1950s regarding nontransferential aspects of the analytic relationship but also presage the work of Carl Rogers and his colleagues on the "facilitative conditions"[3] for effective psychotherapy. Biestek's focus on a professional relationship emphasizing the creation of an interpersonal climate, in which clients are encouraged to express their feelings openly and workers respond with nonjudgmental acceptance, also calls to mind the object relations notion of the "holding environment."

THE HOLDING ENVIRONMENT

We have previously summarized some of D.W. Winnicott's more notable contributions to psychoanalytic developmental psychology (in chapter 3), which, as often proves to be the case with psychoanalytic ideas about development, have an analogue in the clinical situation. The Winnicottian "holding environment" may be one of the best illustrations of this principle. Though originally used to describe the facilitative maternal environment through which the *good-enough mother* is able to offer her infant emotional security, which ultimately affords him or her protection against the inevitable failures in maternal attentiveness or empathy, this concept also possesses a unique currency in the treatment situation. In the broad context of social services, "holding" may be defined to include the provision of material goods, such as food, housing, or financial assistance, family preservation programs or respite care, or even removal of children who have been subject to abuse or neglect (Applegate and Bonovitz 1995). In the clinical milieu the *good-enough parent* is, of course, the therapist, the holding metaphorical rather than literal. What elements, however, are associated with such therapeutic holding?

Foremost among these would be the creation of a safe emotional environment in which the client can feel relative comfort and security in disclosing the details of her personal life. Oftentimes such a safe environment is possible only through therapeutic containment, whereby elements of the client's rudimentary identity, as well as rage, violent projections or fantasies, and other internally arising dangers are "absorbed" and "therapeutically metabolized" by the clinician *Containment* (Bion 1962, 1963; Klein 1974; Ogden 1982; Meissner 1996). The therapeutic effect of such containment is to assure the client that the therapist cannot be destroyed and that she or he is a "good" container for such dangerous thoughts, wishes, or impulses, thus furnishing the client with a "safe context for emotional discharge" (Meissner 1996:20). The safety of the therapeutic environment may also be enhanced or managed through various external structures such as institutional rules or even psychotropic medications that function to diminish frightening thoughts or impulses (Applegate and Bonovitz 1995). The therapist's genuine interest and concern for the client, her ability to listen attentively to the client's story as it unfolds, and reasonable efforts to remain affectively attuned and empathically resonant are clearly also of importance. Although his remarks were specific to the analytic relationship, Winnicott's comments about holding seem readily applicable to the psychotherapeutic relationship. Writing in 1963, he observed, "The analyst is *holding* the patient, and this often takes the form of conveying in words at the appropriate moment something that shows that the analyst knows and understands the deepest anxiety that is being experienced, or that is waiting to be experienced" (Winnicott 1963:240).

Meissner has observed that the Winnicottian holding environment helped to explain how therapeutic rapport might be possible with psychoanalytic patients incapable of developing a transference neurosis or of forming a therapeutic alliance. The concept of a holding environment permitted a shift of focus "from Strachey's model of mutative interpretation to the affective relatedness between analyst and patient, providing a safe context for the analytic process" (Meissner *Personality* 1996:19). The concept of the holding environment helped particularly to illumi- *disorder* nate the nature of the therapeutic action in more primitively functioning, personality-disordered clients who could not immediately make use of conventional analytic interpretive work. "Holding thus provides an illusion of safety and protection from dangers both within and without" (19), Meissner suggests, although the operationalization of this concept is not risk free.[4]

At times special measures may be necessary to create and maintain the illusory holding environment. Goldstein (2001) has suggested that the use of tran- *trans* sitional objects and other transitional phenomena may assist certain clients with *objects* impaired object-relational capacities to preserve an emotional connection with the therapist that would otherwise be impossible to sustain between appointments. These may consist of the therapist's telephone number or an item associated with the therapist or the office in which she works, the therapist's email address, and so forth. Although such practices were at one time dismissed as unconventional "treatment parameters" by the psychoanalytic establishment, their value in clinical work with very disturbed clients is now well established. However, therapeutic holding cannot be easily reduced to specific technical parameters or formulae, leading one author to conceive of it as a "non-specific supportive continuity," established in part through "the regularity of visits, rituals of coming and going, the underlying empathy, the steadiness of voice, and the very continuity of the objects, spaces, and textures" of the meeting-room (Moore and Fine 1990:206).[5]

It is through the combined effect of such experiences of being held in treatment that clients' fears of the annihilation of both self and object can be relieved (Klein 1974) and a greater capacity to tolerate frustrations caused by the unavoidable discontinuities in the process of therapy is acquired. Such discontinuities are, of course, as often as not due to breaches in the treatment relationship itself, which may in turn be linked to technical errors or misattunement on the therapist's part.

to leak
frustration

CLINICAL CASE ILLUSTRATION 7.1: "OLGA"

Olga Sverdlov, a forty-six-year-old, divorced Russian immigrant mother of three, employed as a line worker at a local automobile assembly plant, had been referred by her female gynecologist for treatment after she became inconsolably anxious and tearful during a routine pelvic exam. Olga explained that she had experienced such anxiety attacks before but had managed to recover without professional help. This last time, however, seemed worse than previous experiences. The therapist wondered what might have contributed to this change, since Olga confessed she was at a loss to account for it. However, the therapist's obvious interest in hearing Olga's story and her kindly manner seemed to help Olga to relax. As she began to let down halfway through the first interview, Olga also revealed other symptoms that suggested a mixed clinical picture of anxiety and long-standing depression. She acknowledged that, although she had planned for some time to seek counseling for herself, she tended to regard treatment as an extravagance her family could ill afford. The therapist then inquired whether in light of Olga's considerable distress she might not be feeling some relief over her decision to follow through with the gynecologist's referral. Olga didn't respond directly but began instead to talk a little about her childhood. In a voice that seemed both measured and nearly devoid of affect, she described being sexually abused by her father for a period of nearly five years starting at age four. She also mentioned that two days prior to her ninth birthday, her father, without explanation or even so much as a goodbye, abandoned the family, which consisted of Olga, her mother, and three younger siblings. Efforts to locate him were fruitless, and neither Olga nor other family members ever heard from him again. The therapist commented that Olga must have felt very confused and hurt by her father's actions and that such feelings in combination with those she had about her sexual victimization must have been a great burden for her to carry for so long a time. Olga nodded and drew a deep breath.

Clinic procedures and policies were then briefly discussed, including those regarding cancellations and missed appointments. Olga seemed to accept this without any difficulty, but then, near the end of the hour, asked whether there was a clinic policy regarding missed appointments by *therapists*. The therapist noted that, when she asked this question, Olga's tone was almost adversarial, which took her therapist by surprise. In part because it was near the end of the hour, but also due to the therapist's failure to connect this question to the discussion that had preceded it, she responded matter-of-factly. Therapists, she replied, were of course, expected to keep their appointments with clients, although conceivably there might be unique circumstances, such as a family emergency, that could supervene to make this impossible. Olga seemed satisfied with the therapist's response, and therapist and client then agreed to meet at the same time the following week. Olga expressed relief and gratitude to the therapist, feeling that she was finally about to receive the gift of treatment she had denied herself for so many years.

The day before her next appointment, Olga left a voicemail message for her therapist indicating that she had been feeling much better and no longer needed additional treatment. Besides, she reasoned in the message, her health plan only covered a portion of the therapy, and it would be too expensive to continue. The therapist, sensing that she wasn't getting the entire story, returned the telephone call and gently suggested that Olga and she meet at least one more time to explore her reaction; if afterward Olga still felt the need to discontinue, her therapist would be respectful of this decision. Olga did return for her second appointment, as well as a third and fourth; in fact, she remained in therapy for over two years. Over a period of time, Olga and her therapist were able to discern the meaning of the strong reaction she had after her first visit. The sense of assuagement Olga felt in having finally taken the step of beginning treatment served as a powerful reminder of complex and conflict-laden memories she had about her father. On the one hand, Olga had experienced an incredible sense of relief when he abandoned the family, for it meant the end of the secret sexual affair that had always felt so wrong to her. However, this "gift" was counterbalanced by her abiding sense of shame and guilt over his precipitous departure, of which, in her nine-year-old mind, she had been the principal agent. A further complication was the yearning she felt for him, since the sexual intimacy was often followed by special "gifts" and favors. Quite naturally, no one had been in a very festive mood for her birthday two days later, and in the disorganization that followed her father's sudden departure, there was neither a cake nor gifts. Olga gradually recognized that, ever since this time, simply the thought of receiving a gift, tangible or otherwise, had stirred up an admixture of powerful guilt, shame, and anxiety. The anxiety reaction she now attributed to the sense of impending loss. It had been forever associated in her mind with her father's abandonment just before her birthday, ordinarily a time of celebration and pleasure. Although, at the time of the second interview, Olga was only vaguely aware of her profound anxiety that this scenario might somehow be repeated in the relationship with her therapist, it was sufficiently troubling for her to cancel the appointment.

DISCUSSION

This vignette might be used to illustrate a variety of clinical phenonena, among which are the revival of traumatic memories, resistance to initial engagement, negative transference, pathogenic beliefs, and the long-term sequelae of sexual victimization. However, we will focus more specifically on the issue of containment and holding, the therapist's role in creating such an ambience in the clinical setting, and the significance of her empathic breach in the first hour. From the information that we have, the therapist appears to have conducted the interview in a competent and professional manner. She conveys both interest and concern for Olga and supports her client's sound judgment in following through with the first appointment. Discussion of the client's immediate concerns seems nicely counterbalanced by Olga's mention of salient family history, including the abandonment and abuse by her father. The therapist also makes a point of weaving into the discussion a brief mention of clinic policies and procedures, which, as previously mentioned, may be viewed as a significant structural component of the therapeutic holding environment. So what went wrong? What led Olga to cancel her second hour? Part of the answer seems to be connected to Olga's abiding fear of retraumatization through abandonment by the therapist; in essence, history can repeat itself. This was her motive, of course, for the question about clinic policies having to do with "therapist cancellations." The therapist's response

[margin note: no empathy?]

to this question, while accurate, makes no acknowledgment of this possible connection; furthermore, it could be argued that Olga gives no indication she is dissatisfied with the therapist's factual response.

What the therapist might have done at this juncture is to raise the possibility of a link between Olga's history and her query to the therapist. "I'm thinking of what you said a little earlier about your father, Olga. Do you think that you might possibly have similar concerns about how reliable I'm going to be?" Whether or not Olga confirms this dynamic understanding is probably not so important as the therapist's recognition of the possibility and willingness to bring it into the therapeutic dialogue. The therapist's failure to make this connection likely has multiple determinants. One factor was her realization that as the end of the hour was near she needed to wrap things up rather expeditiously. But her response also seems to have been influenced by the subjective surprise she felt at her client's sudden adversarial tone. Only some time later was Olga able to say it was at this moment that she felt as though she had made a huge mistake in coming in for the appointment. If, however, we assume that the therapist has unwittingly erred here, it is even more important to determine what has set the therapy back on track.

[margin note: relate question back to client]

On receiving the voicemail message, Olga's therapist feels unconvinced of her client's claim of improvement and makes an important effort to contact her and invite her to return for at least one more hour, no strings attached. Olga recalled some time after that she was very moved by the therapist's expression of concern and her unwillingness to take "no" for an answer; her interest in understanding Olga's reaction seemed genuine, as well, and this contributed to Olga's impression that her therapist was indeed trustworthy. In effect, it was not only the therapist's initial efforts to establish a therapeutic holding environment, but her recognition that a rupture had occurred and her efforts to assuage it that made continued treatment possible with this client.

[margin note: to correct lack of connection to dad + lack of empathy]

THE REAL RELATIONSHIP

In addition to those aspects of the therapeutic holding environment discussed in the previous sections, the treatment relationship in both psychoanalysis and psychodynamic therapy has often been thought to possess three major dimensions: the transference-countertransference relationship, the therapeutic alliance, and the real relationship. We have already defined and discussed transference and countertransference in the first part of the book but have yet to distinguish these relational phenomena from either the real relationship or the therapeutic alliance.

As most social workers will freely admit, clinical work that does not take note of the realities to which both client and clinician are subject is unlikely to be highly successful. The geographic setting in which treatment is conducted, the agency venue, the physical characteristics of the therapist's office, its decor and furnishings, each exert some influence over the client's perceptions of the therapist. Other factors, such as the client's personal finances, employment responsibilities, participation in a health plan that provides for outpatient psychotherapy coverage, and the various extraneous forces that may have combined to pressure the client into therapy—whether or not it was mandated—are likewise important to gauge (Meissner 1992).

An even greater consideration is the reality of "who" each of these two participants is within this relationship. Both therapist and client possess objective characteristics that, properly speaking, belong neither to the therapeutic alliance nor to the domain of transference. Such characteristics include but are not limited to gender, physical attractiveness, behavior, personality characteristics, speech style, mannerisms, attitudes, prejudices, personal beliefs and values, and political views (Lester 1990; Meissner 1992), all of which help to create and shape the unique encounter between a particular client and her particular therapist. Greenson (1967), whose contribution to elaborating the therapeutic alliance will be discussed below, suggested there are certain "realistic reactions" of a therapist to a client, or of a client to a therapist, that deserve to be classified as belonging to the real relationship. This, Greenson contended, represented the "realistic and genuine relationship" between therapist and client (1967:217) and deserved its own special category. Perhaps a brief clinical vignette will illustrate:

A therapist whose work I had been supervising was referred a case involving a very attractive nine-year-old African American child whose history included physical abuse and maternal abandonment and who had witnessed the murder of his much-beloved uncle by members of a neighborhood street gang. He was a small, rather quiet child who rapidly formed a close attachment to his young female therapist. For a time the therapy seemed to proceed reasonably well. However, the therapist soon reported that she had reached an impasse in her work, a result, she believed, of her client's strong negative transference to her as a woman approximately his mother's age and, secondarily, owing to his distrust of her as a white person. The client had become resistant and nonproductive in therapy, and the treatment seemed stalled. She believed it would be best for this client if the case were transferred to another therapist, preferably a man and, if at all possible, someone who was also African American. I was somewhat surprised by the supervisee's strong conviction about transferring the case, especially in light of the fact that she had been meeting with her young client for less than two months. Furthermore, just several sessions earlier, he had presented her with a picture of a sun-drenched field in which two hearty flowers blossomed— an image we took to represent the therapist and client—and appeared to thrive despite their being surrounded by a field of weeds.

As we began to examine her reactions more closely, however, a different or rather, more complete picture began to emerge. The client seemed to have had a strong positive transference and attachment to his therapist, some- thing that was apparent from their very first encounter. He also had a tem- perament that might be termed phlegmatic; his pace was slow, he was not especially oriented to task, but simply enjoyed being with the therapist. The therapist, on the other hand, found such qualities distracting if not irritating and continually tried to quicken the pace of his treatment and otherwise manage their time together so that she and the client "were getting some- where." In consequence, the client had become disaffected and withdrawn, but more as a response to the therapist's imposition of her own treatment agenda than for any other reason. The therapist acknowledged that she had felt similarly toward other clients, both children and adults, and always felt she was being more effective when the treatment didn't "get bogged down" in the relationship and she could stay focused on "strategies for change."

In this case example the client has reacted *realistically* to the therapist's need to superimpose her own agenda on the therapy (a philosophical position that could be said to reside completely in the therapist) by becoming "resistant." As it turned out, my supervisee ultimately decided that the slower pace of insight- oriented work and the focus on the relationship was not an especially good "fit" with her therapeutic "style" and philosophy of change. She subsequently became interested in cognitive-behavioral treatment and no longer considers herself to be psychodynamic.

THE THERAPEUTIC ALLIANCE

The concept of the therapeutic alliance, whose origins can be traced to Freud and Sterba, was later elaborated by a number of psychoanalysts and, while remaining a controversial idea, gradually acquired a position of respectability (Meissner 1996). It has been variously defined, although most definitions have emphasized three factors:

- The contractual arrangements through which the logistics of treatment are specified (e.g., scheduling, fee setting and payments, confidentiality, etc.)
- Consensus as to how therapist and client will work together and with what objectives in mind
- An understanding and acceptance of the specific roles and responsibilities assigned to each.

Social work practice arose from a tradition in which the idea of alliance and alliance-building is almost inextricable from conceptions of treatment. Paradoxically, because this idea is so embedded, the result has been considerable development devoted to its molecular components, such as contracting, treatment objectives, worker and client roles, although with somewhat less attention to the more encompassing *concept* of alliance. For psychoanalysts the development of a theory emphasizing the therapeutic alliance appears to have been belated, only gaining real momentum in the 1950s and 1960s with the work of such authors as Zetzel (1970 [1956]), Stone (1961), and Greenson (1965a, 1967). There are undoubtedly several reasons for this, not the least of which is the superordinate role and strength psychoanalysts historically attributed to the *unconscious* in mental life and psychopathology, in general, and in the psychoanalytic treatment process, specifically. That important aspects of the treatment relationship might be influenced or shaped by forces residing closer to consciousness would have been incompatible with this early classical view of the unconscious. A related difficulty is that psychoanalysis was originally an id psychology in which the principle of psychic determinism was an a priori assumption, and the concept of "alliance," in which an individual's self-determination is a central element, appears to be at least partly at variance with this principle. Yet another factor may have been the gradual transformation from a predominantly classical vision of the analytic treatment process, often referred to as a one-person psychology, to a greater range of clinical and theoretical perspectives in which the "human" dimension was elevated (e.g., Sullivan 1953; Fromm-Reichmann 1950). Finally, the disentangling of the notion of alliance from that of transference has proven to be a formidable task for psychodynamic theorists.

Freud was not unmindful of the necessity of forging an alliance with his patients, a theme that emerges as early as the *Studies on Hysteria* (Breuer and Freud 1893–95) in which he speaks of the necessity of fashioning the analytic relationship as a collaborative one (Meissner 1996). This theme resurfaces on at least three other occasions in Freud's oeuvre (Freud 1912a, 1937, 1940). Freud's conception of alliance is, however, never "disentangled" fully from his ideas regarding transference. In the *papers on technique* what he had earlier referred to as a collaboration with the patient is recast as the "unobjectionable positive transference" (Freud 1912a), language that seems firmly to establish the alliance as a "form of libidinal attachment, an aspect of positive transference" (Meissner 1996:10). Near the end of his life, in "Analysis Terminable and Interminable," one of his last two strictly psychoanalytic essays, Freud does speak of making a "pact" with the patient's ego so that portions of the id not yet subject to control may be "subdued" (Freud 1937:235). But, as Kanzer (1981) has noted, collaboration as Freud conceives of it in his final thoughts on the nature of the therapeutic process is still almost indissolubly linked to ideas of resistance and transference. However, Sterba's (1940) formulation of the "observant ego," although still incorporating aspects of the positive transference, placed greater emphasis on the "union of purpose" between analyst and client (Meissner 1996). As such, it served as a bridge between the "analytic pact" of Freud and later elaborations of alliance subsequently advanced by Zetzel, Greenson, and others.

Zetzel's (1970 [1956]) distillation of the concept framed the working alliance as a component within a more encompassing, though bifurcated, vision of the transference relationship. In the Zetzel version the therapeutic alliance repre- *Zetzel* sented a non-neurotic aspect of the transference and required the client to summon "more mature and autonomous ego functions" in order to "preserve the real object relationship" with the therapist despite the distorting effect of the transference neurosis (Meissner 1992:1061). Greenson's idea of the "working alliance," also clearly influenced by Sterba's formulation of a rational alliance "between the patient's reasonable ego and the analyst's analyzing ego" (Greenson 1965a:46), is in most respects similar to the formulation Zetzel had proposed nearly a decade earlier. He believed that, in tandem with the client's neurotic suffering, the establishment of the working alliance impelled the analytic client to submit to the requirements of analytic work. The analyst, the client, and the analytic setting all contributed, in Greenson's view, to the formation and maintenance of the working alliance. Without its "benign influence," an analytic "atmosphere" is not possible, interpretations cannot be fully understood or integrated, and the transference neurosis cannot be successfully analyzed.

A number of authors have been critical of the view of the therapeutic alliance espoused by Zetzel and Greenson. Meissner (1992, 1996) claims that, at the conceptual level, the alliance is neither sufficiently well developed nor clearly differentiated from the real relationship, on the one hand, or the transference, on the other. Brenner (1979), Abend (2000), and Hoffer (2000) have each arrived at an understanding of the therapeutic alliance as essentially a compromise formation principally derived from the positive transference (Jacobs 2000). In this view the therapeutic alliance is a meaningless term or, in any event, represents a phenomenon that is already completely subsumed under the general heading of transference.

Meissner, whose creative scholarship has done a great deal to restimulate contemporary psychoanalytic interest in the therapeutic alliance, has attempted to address such criticisms by developing a multidimensional model of the alliance. Central to his thinking is the idea that the therapeutic alliance resides not only in the client but rather involves an interactive process to which both participants contribute. Although he agrees that there is a complex commingling of the transference, the real relationship, and the therapeutic alliance in the crucible of therapeutic process, he also believes these are distinguishable if not substantially discrete entities.

In his model of the therapeutic alliance, Meissner includes not only such features as mutual empathic attunement, the therapeutic contract or framework, and mutual responsibilities within the treatment relationship; he also identifies such qualitative dimensions as freedom, trust, autonomy, initiative, and ethics as operational factors. Meissner's model of the therapeutic alliance is important chiefly because it places the alliance at the center of the therapeutic effort. He believes it is considerably more complex than the formulations of Sterba, Zetzel, and Greenson suggest, with their focus on the notion of collaboration and rational cooperation. Acknowledging the complex nature of the alliance, which is in appreciable measure a product of the interpenetration of the dimensions described above, Meissner concludes that the therapeutic alliance is "vital to the beneficial outcome of any therapeutic process, analytic or not" (1992:1084).

In the examples that follow, the process through which initial engagement leads to the development of a rudimentary alliance and ultimately coalesces into a reliable therapeutic alliance is described in detail.

CLINICAL CASE ILLUSTRATION 7.2: "IAN"

Ian, a twenty-one-year-old college student in his senior year at a small northeastern college, was referred for treatment of depression by a psychiatrist from his hometown. Ian had been in treatment twice before, in his freshman and sophomore years, and at various times had also been prescribed three different antidepressants, although he had discontinued his most recent medication some five months earlier. Ian's parents were divorced, and he lived with his father and his stepfamily during summers and vacation breaks from school. He also had three older siblings: a twenty-three-year-old brother and two sisters, one who was twenty-five and a second who was nearly twenty-eight. Ian revealed that he and his brother had a close though rivalrous relationship, but felt that he had little in common with his sisters, particularly Kate, the twenty-five year old, with whom conversations rarely included more than an exchange of amenities. Ian's father was a businessman, and his mother a public health nurse who was then coordinator of an ongoing research project involving the psychosocial adjustment of adolescents with chronic health problems. Ian felt closer to his father than to his mother, who had certain "limitations" that had made him less likely to confide in her. He was a handsome young adult who was, nevertheless, pale and rather thin, his hair tousled though not unkempt. Dressed in faded jeans and an oversized shirt, he looked pretty much like any other college student. Ian was deferential almost to the point of sounding apologetic as he entered the office and asked where he might put his backpack. I noted also that he somehow took up less space than I might have expected when he finally seated himself. He indicated that he hadn't been sleeping as well as usual, often awakening several times throughout the night and early morning hours. He also complained that even his favorite foods didn't taste as good as they used to and thought he may have "dropped a few pounds" as a result. As I listened to Ian I was aware of feeling not simply fatigued but drained; when he spoke of feeling tired much of the time, and of being unable to concentrate, I found myself wondering when I had last felt well-rested and really able to focus my energy on tasks. I was also aware of feeling sad, although I hadn't been aware of this prior to meeting with Ian. I commented something to the effect that Ian seemed to be on "automatic," that he was going through the motions but felt little energy or enthusiasm for things that usually gave him pleasure. He then appeared even more depressed, slumping in his chair, sighing audibly, and casting his eyes downward. It was at this juncture that I began to wonder whether Ian might be suicidally depressed, a possibility always worth considering where depressive symptoms are involved.

THER: I guess I'm wondering how bad it gets. Have you thoughts about killing yourself?

IAN: Yes. I have thoughts about it. I might jump from one of those tall buildings downtown near the trade center. The idea is that it would somehow be empowering. But, on the other hand, I don't feel that I'd ever get to the point where I'd actually just do it.

THER: What is it that stops you from actually committing suicide?

IAN: I don't think I'd ever get that desperate. I guess it would make my parents feel incredibly guilty . . . but then, after a while, people would just forget about it. I don't know, maybe my mother never would . . .

So Ian had given more than a passing thought to committing suicide; he had even selected a method, though he seemed anxious to convince us both that he was extremely unlikely ever to "go through with it." Though I hardly felt comforted by such reassurance, Ian later expressed relief over having told me of this fantasy. We spent most of the remaining time in that first hour talking about how Ian would cope with these disturbing thoughts, should they intensify and feel threatening to him. On the one hand, I didn't wish to convey alarm over what he had confided in me. On the other, I believed it critically important to take seriously the possibility of suicide and to convey this concern to Ian. A collaborative plan was worked out with several key components. In the first place, should Ian be in crisis and fail to reach me, he would immediately call either the suicide hotline or the local hospital emergency room. We also decided that Ian would be evaluated by a psychiatric colleague, both so that we might have a second opinion but also for Ian to explore whether he might not want to try a different antidepressant medication. I was somewhat relieved when he indicated that he was by no means bereft of support. Not only were there one or two close friends, his ex-girlfriend, and others whose help he felt he could count on in a crisis, but he was not averse even to the idea of accepting his parents' help. After all, he reasoned, wasn't it his mother who had gotten my number from the psychiatrist in the first place? We also talked about the important matter of confidentiality. I reinforced the fact that Ian's communications to me in his therapy hours would remain completely confidential and private, with but one exception. Should I feel at any time that his well-being was endangered by the suicidal ideas he had mentioned earlier, I might wish to contact his parents so that his safety would be ensured. I emphasized, however, that, even if I deemed this to be necessary, we would approach it as we would any other task in therapy, collaboratively. Ian told me he had no objection to this. We talked some about Ian's expectation from therapy and what we would actually do during our meetings together. Perhaps because he had been in treatment previously, Ian seemed familiar and reasonably comfortable with the treatment process. His goal was both to understand what was making him feel so badly and to experience some sort of relief from the depression that had been weighing him down. He could discuss anything he liked; real-life experiences, fantasies, dreams, whatever he felt like mentioning on a given day. My job would be to assist in this process, working with him to extricate meaning from his thoughts, symptoms, experiences in the outside world, and so forth. I suggested that we meet on a three-times-weekly basis, at least for the time being. Although I anticipated some resistance from Ian as I made the suggestion, I felt that sessions spaced too far apart might be risky. I was rather surprised when, pulling out an appointment book from his overstuffed backpack, he nodded in agreement and then simply asked, "What days do we meet?"

Over the next three sessions a more complete picture began to emerge. It turned out that Ian's parents had divorced when he was only eighteen months old and that his father had "cheated" on Ian's mother near the end of their marriage, a fact of which he had become aware only years later. At the time Ian felt angry that his father hadn't been able to "commit" to the marriage, though he recognized in himself a similar inability to commit to a relationship with a woman. Just after the divorce, Ian's father relocated to a southeastern city over twelve hundred miles away. When his father returned several years later, Ian understandably reacted to him as though he were a stranger; in fact, one of his earliest memories was of his father coming to pick Ian up for a weekend visit. Ian recalled that he screamed and cried as his father led him to the car. "If I wasn't with my mother, I guess it just didn't feel safe," he observed. However, the atmosphere was tense in his mother's home, with frequent fights and lingering bad feelings, especially between Ian's mother and his older brother, John. When Ian was about six, John and his oldest sister, Rebecca, moved out of his mother's home to live with his father. Ian and Kate stayed behind. Ian recalled that this seemed unfair to him, and he wondered why it was that John and Rebecca "got to go" but that he "had to stay." Just before he entered high school, Ian also went to live with his father, who was by then remarried, with several stepchildren. Not too long afterward, his father was diagnosed with a life-threatening medical condition, which required several months of intensive medical treatment and convalescence at home. Ian found it very difficult to watch his father, who had always been vigorous if not athletic, reduced to a weakened and feeble condition, as much by the treatment he was receiving as by the medical condition itself. Ian noted that, though he should "probably have been more frightened," he instead was aware of feeling both contempt and anger, which he found distressing and over which he experienced considerable guilt. He also began to talk about a "critical inner voice" during these hours, one that could never be fully appeased and seemed to spoil experiences others would find gratifying. I questioned him rather carefully about this, but felt satisfied that he was not actually "hearing voices" and was instead using the word metaphorically. When he arrived for his fourth hour, Ian looked uncomfortably tense.

IAN: Listen, I want you to know that there are certain things I'm not comfortable revealing to you . . . at least until we have more of a relationship.
THER: I guess I can understand that. After all, we've only known each other for a week. (At this, he seemed to relax a bit and paused for a moment.)

IAN: I feel like I really should be sharing things with my mother first. I ought to feel guilty about it, but I don't . . . which seems strange. I mean, here I am, instead, talking with you about all this stuff.

THER: Maybe some of this doesn't feel safe to share with her, at least for now.

IAN: You mean, like it would be a burden to her? You're right, I'd be dumping on her, and that would be selfish.

THER: That wasn't exactly what I meant. I was thinking more of you, that there are certain things she might not be able to help you with right now . . . because of her "limitations," as you put it a couple of sessions back.

IAN: Yeah, I did say that, didn't I?

THER: Uh hmm.

In the next hour Ian first mentioned that his "critical voice" seemed to have quieted down for a brief while. He then talked about a friend who had visited him the previous evening and described a story about a college student who sells all of his belongings, treks to Alaska, and does "the Siddhartha thing." Things end very badly, however. The young man ultimately dies of starvation and exposure. Ian can't decide whether this is a fictional story or a veridical account, though he seems somewhat troubled by it. I sensed that the story held a special meaning for Ian and encouraged him to explore any feelings he might have about it. In one respect Ian seemed to view the young man as stoic and strong, although he was also able to acknowledge that his actions were self-destructive. This led Ian to thoughts of men who are stoic and strong in their sexual identity, and then to his desire to be able to discuss sex more openly with his father. Ian recalled that, when he about twelve years old, his father had initiated one of the few discussions they'd ever had about sexual matters by advising Ian to "be on the watch-out for older men" who might be "sexual perverts." Near the end of the hour, Ian mentioned that he and his ex-girlfriend, Michelle, had started seeing each other again, although the issues in the relationship hadn't really been worked out. As we ended the hour, he casually mentioned that he had met with the psychiatrist whose name I had given him the week before, liked him, and had just started on a new antidepressant medication.

DISCUSSION

Ian, who is, developmentally speaking, on the "bridge" between adolescence and young adulthood, appears to suffer from a depression that is predominantly of the superego or "introjective" variety (Anthony 1970; Blatt 1974; Bemporad and Gable 1992). Introjectively depressed adolescents and young adults have difficulty availing themselves of the usual gratifications and freedom that are ordinarily a part of this developmental epoch. As their universe expands to furnish them with novel opportunities for pleasure, new relationships, or new beliefs, "they recoil from their own stimulated desires with shame, guilt, and a sense of betrayal of their loyalty to their families" (Bemporad and Gable 1992:123). Such clients also appear to be their own worst critics, at times evincing a dark despair and self-loathing that may lead them to consider suicide as their only viable option. It seemed unclear to me whether or not Ian's depression was purely "introjective," though his propensity to guilt and shame, his contemplation of suicide, as well as my own subjective reaction to him, suggested this as a strong possibility.

Although my effort to establish a rudimentary working alliance with Ian from which might be fashioned a more enduring therapeutic alliance extended beyond the five sessions I've described here, much of the work was completed during these early meetings. I felt that I was charged with several tasks during those sessions. It was important first of all to understand the nature and extent of Ian's depression and to assess the lethality of his suicidal thoughts. Was there any evidence of psychosis? Would outpatient therapy even be a viable option for Ian? I felt reasonably confident midway into our first meeting that Ian was a suitable candidate for outpatient treatment, although I didn't yet know him well and believed it essential to address these issues before we ended our first hour. Collectively, these considerations can be thought of as providing a foundation for the nascent therapeutic alliance. We talked very openly about his suicidal thoughts. At times clients will present such concerns without being asked, though in my experience there is a greater likelihood that this critical bit of information may not be volunteered. My retrospective impression, however, is that Ian "cued" me. In consequence this question seemed to arise almost naturally from the cumulative effect of Ian's recital of rather classical depressive symptoms, his body language and personal appearance, the history of prior difficulties with depression, as well as the thoughts and feelings that Ian's clinical picture seemed to educe in me. Although he tended right away to play down the significance of what he had said, the information was now "out there" in the discourse between us, which had the effect of making it more palpable, more "real." As I mentioned, Ian later revealed that being able to talk about this early on relieved some of the anxiety this fantasy had evoked. But the concern at this point was to establish a safe holding environment within which the rudimentary alliance could take root and develop. We therefore talked about how Ian might cope with an intensification of his suicidal thoughts, arriving at a jointly created plan that assuaged both his anxiety and my own.

guilt over aggressive concerns of Ian's

One of the dynamic issues that seems to echo in much of the material Ian presented, especially in connection with his suicide fantasy, is that of guilt over aggressive wishes. I hasten to add that Ian seemed only to have awareness of the guilt that his hostility stirred up, not of the hostile feelings themselves, but it also appeared that such guilty feelings may have had a role in preventing him from carrying out any suicidal plan. When Ian observed that it would make his parents "feel incredibly guilty" and that his mother might never recover from the loss, an interesting dynamic complexity is revealed. Not only can we infer the guilt reaction Ian experienced at having entertained such thoughts but also the unconscious motive that appears to lie behind it—the disguised wish to *cause* his parents to suffer. Although Ian didn't believe he would become sufficiently desperate to enact his fantasy of committing suicide by leaping from the top of a skyscraper, neither of us wished to assume unnecessary risks. I suggested a specific plan in the event of a crisis, and we also agreed on multiple weekly sessions in addition to a psychiatric consult. The matter of therapist-client confidentiality is especially important here, since suicidal threats constitute one of the very few reasons for breaching the rule of confidentiality. It is my belief that this discussion, however, further strengthened the alliance between us, perhaps in part because I attempted to present the idea as another facet of the collaborative treatment relationship.

suicide wish: unconscious wish to cause parents harm

We spent some time discussing the process of therapy, with reference to the frequency and timing of our meetings as well as the role that each of us will have within the treatment relationship. Although evidently neither of Ian's former therapy experiences were with psychodynamically oriented clinicians, he seemed broadly acquainted and reasonably comfortable with the process of treatment. During the fourth hour, however, Ian seemed anxious to convey to me that he might not choose to reveal the details of his innermost thoughts just yet. This seemed utterly reasonable to me, a thought that I shared with him. When, a moment later, he once again seemed to express guilt (or rather, guilt over *not* feeling guilty) that he was sharing such personal information with me, a stranger, rather than with his own mother, he appeared to misinterpret my response. Since Ian had just a few meetings earlier mentioned that his mother had certain emotional limitations, I saw this as a good opportunity to underscore yet another quality germane both to the therapeutic holding environment and the therapeutic alliance to which it is intimately connected. One important reason contributing to the "safety" of the treatment relationship and the formation of an alliance is the therapist's remove from both historical and intercurrent dynamic conflicts and tensions that characterize virtually all the client's close relationships outside of treatment. The relationship with his mother was of course far too close for him realistically to be able to share such material with her. It is of interest that his misinterpretation led him immediately to chastise himself for even having momentarily considered the possibility of sharing such burdensome material with her. Although my comment is subsequently clarified, I was left with the impression that Ian would not be easily induced to exchange such superego condemnation, which obviously serves an important function in his psychic economy, for a more benevolent view of himself.

In the fifth hour Ian started out by mentioning that his "critical voice" had quieted down, a seemingly positive development. He then shared his friend's account of the young man who abandoned the world of human relationships in order to contemplate the meaning of life. My understanding of this material was severalfold. First, I sensed that Ian was strongly identified with the young man and his quest for personal meaning. Furthermore, there was an unmistakable stylistic similarity between the story character and Ian in that Ian, too, seemed to withdraw from human contacts when he felt most troubled. Another interesting parallel is suggested by the fate of those who might elect to do "the Siddhartha thing." The college student in the story possesses certain characteristics of what Balint (1959) might have termed a *philobat*, a "person who dislikes attachments but loves the spaces between them" (Fonagy 2000). At the same time, however, his actions suggest a less than adaptive effort to resolve dependency strivings by adopting a basic attitude of counterdependency, in this instance with tragic consequences. Ian also gave evidence of such an internal struggle in comments he had made about his mother, his decision to move out of her home in early adolescence, and so forth. But might the consequences of such a decision be emotional starvation or worse? These seemed to be important questions for later exploration. Ian's thoughts about the young man's strength and stoicism formed a segue to the idea of sexual strength and ultimately to thoughts about his father's admonitions against "sex perverts." Although I suspected that this material had several different meanings, the most obvious connection then seemed to be that of Ian's relationship with me, a grown man who has expressed interest in hearing the intimate details of Ian's life, sexual and otherwise. Could I indeed be trusted?

In the foregoing material I have examined various developments associated with the process of initial engagement and alliance formation. Issues having to do with therapeutic containment and holding were highlighted in both the client's process and in the therapist's response. Basic matters such as the client's physical safety, the nature of the therapeutic relationship, confidentiality, and other details having to do with the setting and conditions of treatment were addressed. By the fifth session the client seems to have given a good indication of his willingness and ability to comply with the terms that will constitute the architecture of this basic alliance. This impression is based, in part, on Ian's regular attendance, his willingness to begin the painful process of sharing details of his troubled inner life, his casual report in the fifth hour that he has met with the psychiatrist and started on a new antidepressant medication, and so forth.

CLINICAL CASE ILLUSTRATION 7.3: "JUANA"

Juana, a Hispanic woman in her early fifties, originally from Costa Rica but already resident in the U.S. for twenty-three years, came to my office. She had been referred by an insurance company to which I had indicated my availability and expertise in helping people with difficulties in relationships. After asking, "What do I do?" (to which I responded, "Begin at the beginning"), Juana began her presentation in an almost impassioned way. It reflected, to my mind, the depth of her feeling and concern about her relations with men. She was now alone, she said, and not only feeling lonely but also awakening daily with a cold, empty feeling. Juana also reported changes in mood from "clarity to darkness" and frequent crying spells. I understood these things as indications of depression.

I asked Juana if she could recall how and when these feelings began. Her reply led her into her relational history, almost spontaneously. She had been together with a man, as sweethearts and then as a married couple, for twelve years; she had a son with this man. Her husband, however, began an affair with the baby-sitter, which was discovered due to the pregnancy of the latter. Juana separated from her husband, attempted a reconciliation of a year's duration, but ultimately secured a divorce from him and returned to live in her parents' home. I did not feel this experience as the one that brought Juana to see me; she was married very young and seemed to have "worked it through." The quality of her delivery was more descriptive/historical than emotionally active, but it did alert me to a possible pattern of relating with men that might prove important.

Although she did not seem to need much prompting, I assured Juana of confidentiality, so that there would not be a bar to her expressing herself freely. I also verified that she had not had therapy before, except for an extremely brief interlude (no more than one or two sessions while she still resided in Costa Rica) at the time of her divorce. Juana, now working as a

---

Although I did not personally conduct this treatment, I have decided in this instance to preserve the author's use of the first person, since it seems to lend a certain immediacy to the narrative that I believe would otherwise be absent.

dental hygienist, also assured me that she was in good health and had no medical issues. Proceeding with her history, Juana answered my question about home life by telling me about growing up the eldest of five siblings and the only girl. She described her early life as being normal, with its appropriate share of rivalry but without anything extraordinary. Her mother was a timid, frightened woman, restricted in her life, always at home for the children. If Juana's father were away, she would sleep with the children until he returned. Father, in turn, was a very fair person, decent ("He didn't scream or hit"), with discipline usually coming through Mother. Father did not show affection openly or publicly. Although Juana said she knew she was loved, both parents were very reserved people, and Juana knew of their love almost indirectly, through their parental actions, rather than through open demonstration. Juana did not recall her parents ever fighting in front of the children and also noted that her parents were able to provide her with whatever she needed or wanted. Juana was educated through high school in the Catholic system, which presumably required a greater outlay of resources than the average schooling received in Costa Rica. I made a mental note to refer back to Juana's experience of her mother at another time.

After her divorce, and spending some time as an adult in her parents' home, Juana ultimately made the decision to come to the United States. After some initial ambivalence, expressed in several trips to and fro, Juana finally settled here in 1980, at the age of thirty. I noted that this must have been a courageous act, as Juana did not at that time have any family members here. In fact, aside from her son (with whom she gets along quite well) and her grandson, this remains largely true even today. After being here for some time, Juana became interested in Pablo, a Mexican-born coworker of Juana's at the factory where she was employed. Juana found him quite attentive and eventually married him. Everything went very well at first, Juana related, but, after a while, things deteriorated. Pablo began keeping late hours, staying away from home, taking things that didn't belong to him, becoming argumentative and abusive. Juana's worst fears were confirmed when she found out that Pablo was heavily involved in narcotics. He contracted AIDS and died of this illness in 1991. I inquired about Juana's feelings at the end of this second attempt at marital harmony:

THER: What were your feelings about your husband Pablo?
JUANA: Shame. Disgust. I was embarrassed to go to the funeral, because I was afraid some of the things that he did would get out, and I didn't want anyone to know.
THER: Did you have any subsequent relationships?

JUANA: Yes. After some time, I began to go out again, and I found myself going with married men. Let me tell you about the last two, who are the most important now. I met Jose, who was married but not staying with his wife. We started to go out, and I liked him. He said he liked me, and I thought he was going to get a divorce. He then told me I was too good for him and that he was going back to his wife. I did not believe him. I knew he was going to go with someone else, not his wife. I hear that a lot now, "I'm not good enough for you."

THER: Was there anyone else?

JUANA: Yes. I met George, who was separated from his wife. I thought he really was going to get a divorce.

THER: What was that relationship like?

JUANA: Very good. I know he really liked me, and I know it wasn't only sexual.

THER: How did you know?

JUANA: Because he helped me out a lot—with schoolwork, books, encouragement and support of me. He helped me become a dental hygienist.

THER: What happened?

JUANA: He also reconciled and went back to his wife.

I interrupted the process to ask Juana if it was all right for me to take notes while she was speaking. She gave her permission readily. I also made her aware that I am a Spanish speaker and indicated that, although her English was very good, should she want to express herself in her native tongue she could do so and be understood. As this had already been a long session, I went over routines (payment, appointment times, missed appointments, how we work together). Juana understood, and we came to agreement. Before she left, Juana asked for homework, something she could do to practice putting herself first, before she came to the next session. While I generally do not give homework assignments, I understood this as something Juana wanted/needed to maintain a connection until her return, and I did suggest that she treat herself at her next purchase, for example, to a topflight brand of cosmetic or something for herself that she would not usually get.

Juana arrived punctually at her next session, and we continued from our previous conversation. I had already gotten some ideas about Juana's current choices of men as well as her personality and stance toward men based on her history. I therefore opened up the discussion in the following way, after a brief recap:

THER: Why do you think it is so difficult for you to hold on to men these days?

JUANA: My friends tell me, my coworkers tell me, my son tells me, you are too trusting, you are too giving, you never say no.

THER: Do you agree?

JUANA: Yes. When I love, I love with a full heart, but I don't understand why the men don't respond in the same way.

I said that this is difficult to understand, but that there is something in people that becomes lax and exploitative under those conditions. I also asked if she would like to go about her relationships differently. Juana definitely agreed that it would be better to change her approach, but wondered how. I remarked that it was a good thing in itself to talk about these things, especially since they were causing her pain, and that we would explore together and see what in her personality and character were operative in her winding up in her present, lonely condition. I also asked her if she thought her choices of men who had other ties had something to do with her losing them. Juana understood this and agreed that although George was separated and appeared on the way to divorce, he was not completely available to her. I made a mental note to broaden this idea to include the idea of safety, insofar as I believed that Juana, because of her recent experiences and also, in part, because of her early life, was angry and afraid of what intimacy could bring. In effect, she seemed to be choosing men whose path to intimacy and commitment presented some obstacle. Juana then asked me if calling George on the phone was a good idea. I replied that if she truly wanted to be free, to start again in a different way, that it was not a good idea. Juana understood that feelings could be restimulated by contact but wondered why she had such a great desire, such a compulsion to call and be in contact with him. I asked her if it weren't the feeling she had, when she was with him, of being taken care of, of being in a safe, warm, good place, that she wished to recall, rather than truly participating in the current, limited experience. I remarked that we do this many times, seeking the connection to something/someone good that we had in our past rather than what was really in front of us in the present.

JUANA: That's right. I know the experience can't be the same. He's with his wife, he can't be with me. But the temptation is so strong.

THER: Yes, it is. It is very difficult for us to "let go" of such an experience. But we must do it if we are to go forward.

Juana repeatedly told me to ask any question and that she would listen to any advice that would help her let go of her attachment to her recent boyfriends and her feelings of low self-esteem, loneliness, and undesirability. I replied that we would continue to explore the ways to do this. I also mentioned that I had asked her a lot of questions; were there any she wanted to ask me? There were not at this time. Before she left, Juana remarked, "Before I came, my friend said that you don't make a connection with a therapist. You just come and talk and that's it. But I think I have made a connection here." I immediately responded that that was wonderful, that I also felt we had a connection, and that it boded well for our future work together.

DISCUSSION

Juana's reasons for seeking treatment were manifestly due to a pattern of problematic relationships with men, although, like Ian, her narrative also reveals a core depression. Juana's depression, however, which consisted of such symptoms as "cold, empty feelings," frequent crying spells, and diminished self-esteem, seemed linked to an unconscious and reflexive pattern of self-defeating behavior. Over a period of many years she had repeatedly involved herself with men who were married or, like her second husband, emotionally unavailable to her. While the therapist has not speculated on the original dynamic motives influencing Juana's object choices, the history suggests that such failed relationships may constitute a reenactment of Juana's efforts to attract the notice of her father, who is described as caring though undemonstrative. As the oldest child and only girl in a sibship of four, Juana may also have unconsciously perceived her mother as the chief rival in her efforts to get closer to her father, a more or less classical oedipal scenario. If this dynamic premise is accurate, Juana's pattern of self-defeating behavior can then be understood to represent a masochistic solution, embodying the dual function of providing punishment for sexual guilt and, at the same time, offering a condition of safety for experiencing erotic pleasure.

The most important objectives in these early sessions, aside from helping the client to articulate her reason for seeking treatment, gathering pertinent history, explaining clinic policies, and the like, is, of course, to establish a basis for the therapeutic alliance and, where needed, to offer therapeutic holding. The therapist's warmth and concern for his client, which are here so evident, seem to have furnished Juana with a sense of optimism for what therapy may be able to offer her. Yet she also seemed to require a "homework assignment," which her therapist understood as the tangible expression of a desire for a "connection" that would sustain her until their next meeting. Noting that he is generally not disposed to make such "homework assignments," the therapist suggests that Juana "treat" herself to something special, such as "a topflight brand of cosmetic." This is an interesting and multifaceted message that not only offers Juana therapeutic "holding" but also subtly subverts her request for "homework"—within which may be contained a transference-born desire to surrender to the therapist—into an action for which Juana herself becomes the direct beneficiary.

As therapist and client continue to explore her self-defeating relationships in the next hour, Juana wonders why she experiences such great desire for unavailable men and again solicits direct guidance from the therapist. The therapist's gentle response underscores the collaborative nature of the treatment process that has now gotten underway. It further establishes the safety of the relationship with *this* man and, one might argue, offers Juana a different model for interaction with men in a more general sense. Clearly, Juana's comments at the end of this second hour, that she has "made a connection here," indicate that the level of trust and rapport sufficient to shape these early encounters into a more enduring therapeutic alliance has been attained.

In this chapter we have considered some of the more critical elements of the beginning phase of treatment. These elements include but are not limited to the establishment of a therapeutic holding environment and the different ways in which the concept of holding may be understood; the real relationship, and the cultivation of a therapeutic alliance. In the remainder of the chapter these aspects of relationship and their connection to the process of therapy as it gets underway were examined in greater detail, drawing from both the social work and psychoanalytic literatures. The concept of therapeutic alliance, particularly as it is represented in the work of Meissner and others, was explored in substantial depth. Finally, detailed clinical vignettes derived from both agency and private practice venues were presented to illustrate the process of initial engagement, therapeutic holding, and the development of a therapeutic alliance.

8

The Middle Phase of Treatment:
Resistance, Working Through, and Dynamic Technique

T HE PROCESS OF treatment cannot be easily divided into beginning, middle, and end phases, as those who have researched psychotherapy process will openly acknowledge. Nevertheless, most psychodynamic clinicians tend to accept the idea that there are important qualitative distinctions between the earliest encounters in treatment and those that herald its ending: an intermediate phase that lies between the establishment of a solid therapeutic alliance and the completion of the tasks of therapy.

The psychoanalytic term *working through,* which is often applied to this intermediate or middle phase of treatment, implies both a process and its intended result. But what is it, more specifically, that is "worked through"? Following the formation of a working alliance, as treatment enters this middle phase, the nature of the therapeutic task changes. A hallmark of traditional psychodynamic approaches to treatment is the presumption of *resistance,* a phenomenon linked almost indissolubly to the working-through process. According to classical theorists, resistance takes many forms, of varying intensities, but is fundamentally motivated by conflicting desires of which clients may be only partially aware. Certain contemporary psychoanalytic theorists, however, may view resistance as less a manifestation of neurotic conflict than an adaptive response to the threat of retraumatization, while others may understand resistance in exclusively intersubjective terms or as a realistic response to qualities or attributes residing in the therapist. Beginning with an overview of psychoanalytic perspectives on the working-through process and the nature of resistance, we will examine those "forces" subserving resistance—that interfere with or are otherwise in opposition to therapeutic progress or appear to be at variance with the therapeutic alliance. Later in the chapter various strategies such as circumnavigation, confrontation, and interpretation of resistance for promoting the working-through process are also explored.

Interpretation, regarded by most psychoanalytic clinicians as the central technique in the dynamic therapist's repertoire, assumes increasing importance with the deepening of the treatment process during the middle phase of dynamic therapy. Four basic kinds of interpretation are examined in this portion of the chapter, using representative case vignettes as illustrations. Several other basic dynamic techniques, such as exploration-description, clarification, and sustainment, are also described and illustrated.

In the final portion of the chapter, material derived from the middle treatment phase in two clinical cases is presented in detail, with particular attention to the actual therapeutic process and use of dynamic techniques and strategies in each instance.

HISTORICAL PSYCHOANALYTIC PERSPECTIVES

A basic assumption of classical psychoanalysis, and perhaps common in varying degrees to all psychoanalytic approaches to treatment, is that intrapsychic change generally requires both considerable effort and time. Freud first came to realize this in his early experiments with clinical hypnosis and the cathartic method, which, despite furnishing him with profound insights into the workings of the human mind, did not yield the clinical success he had anticipated. Although dramatic improvements often occurred early in treatment, more often than not the disabling symptoms and mental suffering of which his patients had originally complained seemed to recur with a disappointing predictability. Freud gradually recognized that at the center of such treatment "failures" was a phenomenon whose power and scope was equal to if not greater than his patients' desires to overcome their neurotic miseries. He termed it "resistance" and at first believed that, through persuasion and exhortation and the exercise of his physicianly authority, his patients might be induced to overcome this obstacle to therapeutic progress. These efforts, however, did not seem to bear fruit and ultimately led to the development of the structural hypothesis (Freud 1923) with its tripartite division (ego, id, superego) of the psyche. According to this model, resistance functions much like the defenses do, serving to protect the ego from unpleasures.[1]

Freud's work with patients suffering from hysteria, prior to his elaboration of the psychoanalytic method, furnishes one of the earliest reported clinical descriptions of resistance. Late in 1892 Freud had begun work with Fraulein Elisabeth von R., who had been referred to him for treatment of long-standing pain and difficulty in walking that did not appear to be of organic etiology. Freud began to use the "pressure technique" on Fraulein Elisabeth as a means of educing from his patient memories, thoughts, and other associations when these failed to arise spontaneously.[2] The procedure, which involved Freud placing his hand on the patient's forehead and the accompanying suggestion that the relevant thought or memory would occur to the subject as Freud released his hand, proved successful on a number of occasions. This early success, however, was not maintained as the treatment deepened. Freud became perplexed when, in spite of the pressure technique, Elisabeth remained silent, claiming that she "saw nothing." He ultimately determined, however, that the fault lay not in his procedure but rather somewhere else:

> I resolved, therefore, to adopt the hypothesis that the procedure never failed: that on every occasion under the pressure of my hand some idea occurred to Elisabeth or some picture came before her eyes, but that she was not always prepared to communicate it to me, and tried to suppress once more what had been conjured up. I could think of two motives for this concealment. Either she was applying criticism to the idea, which she had no right to do, on the ground of its not being important enough or of its being an irrelevant reply to the question that she had been asked; or she hesitated to produce it because— she found it too disagreeable to tell. I therefore proceeded as though I was completely convinced of the trustworthiness of my technique. I no longer accepted her declaration that nothing had occurred to her, but assured her that something *must* have occurred to her. . . . It often happened that it was not until I had pressed her head three times that she produced a piece of information; but she herself would remark afterwards: "I could have said it to you the first time." "And why didn't you?"—"I thought it wasn't what was wanted," or "I thought I could avoid it, but it came back each time." In the course of this difficult work I began to attach a deeper significance to the resistance offered by the patient in the reproduction of her memories and to make a careful collection of the occasions on which it was particularly marked.
>
> (Breuer and Freud 1893–95:153–54)

Freud's understanding of resistance gradually deepened, leading to significant modifications in both theory and technique. Eventually, the systematic interpretation of resistance assumed a place of central importance not only in the practice of psychoanalysis but also in that of psychoanalytic psychotherapy. But, before we consider various ways in which resistance can be addressed in treatment, it would be useful to answer a very basic question. What, more specifically, *is* resistance?

RESISTANCE: A WORKING DEFINITION

Broadly defined, resistance is *a phenomenon in which unconscious motives operate paradoxically, in opposition to the client's consciously articulated desire for therapeutic progress toward the resolution of intrapsychic conflicts, the repair of developmental arrests and defects, and the alleviation of distressing symptoms.* Such unconscious motives can interfere with the client's express objective for therapeutic change and may at times even culminate in a therapeutic stalemate. Resistance may assume any of a number of different forms (e.g., attitudes, verbalizations, or actions), though nearly always with the effect of preventing objectionable ideas, affects, ideas, memories, and other perceptions, or an admixture of such elements, from reaching conscious awareness and thus forming the basis for insights. Resistance may occur in any phase of treatment, from initial engagement to termination, and is usefully thought of as constituting an effort to preserve the status quo. The term *resistance* may also be legitimately applied to the phenomenon of transference, in which case it is specifically the subject's awareness of disturbing wishes or conflict-laden fantasies and thoughts associated with the person of the therapist that comprises the content of the resistance.

Although this usage differs somewhat from my own, it is also possible to define resistance more globally as "any observable phenomenon that interferes with . . . [a patient's] self-observation" (Weinshel and Renik 1996:436).

A PERSPECTIVE FROM SELF PSYCHOLOGY

As suggested in the introduction, psychoanalysts are not in unanimity in regard either to the nature of resistance or to its therapeutic management. Self psychologists, in particular, use the term to signify "an activity motivated by fear of injury to the self and designed to protect the self's structure and boundaries" (Wolf 1988:136). Kohut made a distinction, too, between resistances as they are manifest in the "conflict neuroses" (e.g., obsessive-compulsive, hysterical, and phobic neuroses) and in selfobject disorders.[3] He observed that the "hidden knowledge" of such neurotic individuals is focally concerned with "drive-wishes." The resistances encountered in their treatment, which arise from "unconscious infantile layers of the ego," are put forth in an effort to furnish protection to the subject's personality from experiencing castration anxiety (Kohut 1977:136). In disorders of the self the "hidden knowledge" involves aspirations of the subject's nuclear self, more specifically, "the need to confirm the reality of the self through the appropriate responses of the mirroring and of the idealized self-object" (Kohut 1977:136). In this instance resistances stem from the archaic nuclear self and constitute an effort to avoid reexposure to "devastating narcissistic injury" that would likely occur should basic needs for mirroring or idealization once again fail to evoke an attuned response. Resistance in this model is motivated by "disintegration anxiety."

It follows from this model that the therapist's failures in attunement are likely to give rise to new resistances or to exacerbate those that are already present. Although the therapist's contribution to the development or deepening of resistances was recognized long before Kohut's articulation of selfobject theory (e.g., Freud 1937; Greenson 1967), Kohut and those who have followed him have paid much closer attention to this theme (e.g., Stolorow, Brandschaft, and Atwood 1987).

FORMS OF RESISTANCE

Resistance can assume a variety of different forms, some of which seem almost transparent, others of which reveal greater subtlety and may prove far more difficult to recognize. As noted above, resistances have been specified according to their source (e.g., ego, id, superego, or self). They have also been classified according to points of fixation (e.g., oral, anal, or genital), types of defense, diagnostic category (Greenson 1967), and those that represent a "refusal to comply with basic requests" (Fine 1982; Strean 1985). Resistances have also been conceived as a function of character type (Fenichel 1945; Reich 1949), subdivided into those which are ego-alien and those that are ego-syntonic (Greenson 1967) and classified according to whether they are behavioral or communicative in nature (Langs 1981).

Greenson, in his multivolume work on psychoanalytic technique, noted a number of common clinical manifestations of resistance. These included the client's silence, the absence of affect, physical posture, avoidance of particular topics, the recounting of trivia or external events, lateness, missing hours, or forgetting to pay, secretiveness, acting out, and the client's "flight into health" (Greenson 1967). Excessive compliance, emotionality, undue emphasis on reality considerations, somatization, and dreams and fantasies used in the service of resistance are among other clinical manifestations reported in the literature (Strean 1985).

In the case of secondary gain, which has also been referred to as epinosic gain, the client's resistance is intimately bound up with advantages afforded by the very emotional problems for which relief has been sought. Although such gain did not enter into symptom formation itself, it may exert a powerful effect on the entrenchment of symptoms and the client's resistance to their resolution. An obvious example of this kind of resistance is that of the client suffering from agoraphobic symptoms whose family has assumed certain burdens for which the client was formerly responsible. Since he has become ill, he is no longer expected to take out the garbage, go shopping, or perhaps even go to work. In effect, his emotional problem offers a positively sanctioned route for regression and narcissistic satisfaction that would be far more difficult to obtain should psychotherapy be successful in helping him understand and resolve his emotional problems.

WORKING THROUGH

Prominent among those factors by which a psychodynamic treatment approach is differentiated from nonanalytic forms of treatment is the psychoanalytic concept of working through. The concept was formally introduced in 1914 in a brief essay, titled "Remembering, Repeating, and Working-Through" (Freud 1914b), to describe the dynamic process through which resistances are gradually overcome and insights achieved. The idea was at first linked closely to Freud's classical conception of the id. The deep structural changes that allow insight as well as the subject's capacity to make use of it were possible only if the "modes and aims of the instinctual drives" (Moore and Fine 1990:210) were altered, Freud maintained. Such alterations, Freud advised, would not be likely to occur simply because the client's resistance had been pointed out to him; rather, the client must be permitted repeated opportunities to digest and metabolize such information.

> One must allow the patient time to become more conversant with this resistance with which he has now become acquainted, to *work through* it, to overcome it, by continuing, in defiance of it, the analytic work according to the fundamental rule of analysis [free association]. Only when the resistance is at its height can the analyst, working in common with his patient, discover the repressed instinctual impulses which are feeding the resistance; and it is this kind of experience which convinces the patient of the existence and power of such impulses. (Freud 1914b:155)

Central to the notion of working through is the idea that a new pathway is being forged. However, such a new connection can only be reliably established over time and through the collective impact of repeated examinations of the client's essential dynamic issues. As to corresponding changes in the client's behavior, these are not typically immediate and are usually thought to represent the product of a successful working-through process.

In light of this characterization of the working-through process as intimately bound up with the client's instinctual impulses and their presumed source in the id, one might pose the question as to whether the notion is readily generalizable to other psychoanalytic psychologies. Does this idea have currency for the object relations theorist? For the self psychologist?

Apparently, this concept has proven less problematic than have others for Freud's theoretical successors, and it is well represented in the object relations literature as well as in self psychology. More contemporary views, however, "are less exclusively theoretical" and tend to "stay closer to phenomenology" (Weinshel and Renik 1996:435). The ultimate aim with respect to the content or material that is worked through differs, of course, among the various psychoanalytic psychologies. For psychologists of the self, working through must sooner or later penetrate to those "lethargies, depressions, and rages of early life via the reactivation and analysis of their archaic traumatic self-selfobject relationships in the transference" (Kohut 1984:5). For Winnicottians working through is closely bound to the revival of the client's "vital self," a possibility that depends on the therapist's success in creating an environment in which the client can "experience the treatment relationship . . . in the necessary mother-child terms" (Mitchell 1988:287). Still others may place greater importance on the narrational and constructivist process *within* which "working-through" occurs. In such a model of therapeutic process the "clinical psychoanalytic dialogue is best understood as a series of tellings and retellings by both parties to the dialogue" (Schafer 1997:189), and the existence of multiple truths is an implicit assumption.

TECHNIQUE IN DYNAMIC TREATMENT

Although the clinical illustrations in previous chapters have highlighted certain dynamic strategies and, to a limited extent, the various techniques embedded within them, we have not yet considered the technical dimension of dynamic treatment in explicit detail. Actually, many of the techniques presented and elaborated on here are applicable to any phase of treatment, though certain techniques, such as interpretation, tend to occur with greater frequency during the middle phase, as the treatment relationship deepens. Although the dynamic literature is filled with beautifully crafted case illustrations and intellectually satisfying excursions into theory, one criticism made of psychoanalytic authors is that they have tended to neglect the more practical domain of *how* one intervenes. Indeed, which tools are deemed essential for a dynamic approach to clinical work, and how does one use them? In the sections that follow, several essential dynamic treatment techniques are described, and brief illustrations of how they are actually employed in clinical practice are provided.

INTERPRETATION

Interpretation has been called the "central therapeutic activity" of the psychoanalytic clinician and represents the clinician's understanding of a client's mental life (Moore and Fine 1990). Interpretation is sometimes tied almost exclusively to the psychoanalytic notion of resistance, so that any interpretative comment made by the clinician is expressly designed to draw a client's attention to a resistance (Weinshel and Renik 1996). Others have defined the term somewhat less narrowly, viewing an interpretation as a "a statement of new knowledge" about a client (Moore and Fine 1990). Several different basic kinds of interpretation have been described in the dynamic literature. These are *genetic interpretations, dynamic interpretations, interpretations of resistance,* and *transference interpretations. Genetic interpretations* are designed to highlight the connection between intercurrent feelings, thoughts, behaviors, or conflicts and their historical origins, which, in many cases, involve experiences rooted in infancy and early childhood.[4] The raw data for such interpretations, which typically include the client's free associations, dream material, and transference fantasies, offers a basis for the analytic *reconstruction* of psychologically important early experiences. *Dynamic interpretations* focus more or less exclusively on conflicts and other salient emotional issues, as these are revealed in the client's ongoing life experience, though without reference to historical features.[5] *Interpretations of resistance* are used to test hypotheses regarding motivations that have interfered with the patient's self-observation. When a resistance is identified, the therapist forms a hypothesis to explain how a particular aspect of the patient's motivation, which, for the moment, remains outside of conscious awareness, has interfered with the self-observational function of the ego. *Transference interpretations* specifically address distortions arising in the therapeutic relationship due to the client's displacement of feelings, fantasies, attitudes, or behaviors associated with important figures from the client's past, such as parents and siblings (Moore and Fine 1990).

Although interpretation, especially transference interpretations and interpretations of resistance, play a measurably greater part in clinical psychoanalysis than in dynamic psychotherapy, the utility and legitimacy of dynamic and even genetic interpretations in such therapies has long been recognized by social work authors (e.g., Strean 1978; Woods and Hollis 2000).[6] In the following case vignettes, *genetic, dynamic, resistance*, and *transference interpretations* are illustrated with reproductions of the actual clinical process.

GENETIC INTERPRETATION

Dan E., a married forty-nine year-old businessman and father of two latency-aged children, had been referred for dynamic psychotherapy by his family doctor for symptoms of anxiety and depression that had proven refractory to several different medications. In the first several months of therapy, Dan revealed that his father, who had died six months earlier, had led a "double life" throughout most of his fifty-three-year marriage to Dan's mother. Dan's family lived in the suburb of a large city in the Pacific Northwest. The father, a successful attorney who until his mid-seventies was almost continuously involved in a series of extramarital affairs, maintained a downtown apartment in "the City" for his "trysts," apparently with his wife's full knowledge. Although Dan had only recently learned of his father's secret life from his older sister and mother, his relationship with his father had been deeply troubling to him for other reasons.

Despite repeated efforts to please him, Dan rarely if ever felt his father was able to acknowledge any of his accomplishments; in fact, he was exceedingly critical and demeaning, often lecturing him sternly on those occasions when Dan might approach him seeking fatherly advice. The picture of Dan's father that gradually emerged was that of a tyrant whose explosiveness, sadism, narcissistic entitlement, and insensitivity toward the rest of the family could prove almost unbearable. In social situations, he tended to "put on a good front," however, so that family friends rarely had a glimpse of what Dan, his sibs, and his mother witnessed daily. Although Dan believed that his mother had tried to offer him protection from his father, she was herself overburdened and depressed and often emotionally unavailable to him. Caught as he was between the Scylla of his father's narcissism and the Charybdis of his mother's beleaguered moods, Dan felt very alone during much of his childhood, and the specter of psychological abandonment loomed large in his thoughts. Dan reported that, on at least two occasions he could recall from his childhood, he had somehow gotten separated from his mother in a large public place; the second time this occurred he was actually briefly abducted by a man in an elevator, but he was able to struggle free. A far more recent, though, it proved, not unrelated concern for Dan had been his own marital relationship, which seemed to be unraveling after nearly twenty years. Dan had made repeated and seemingly desperate attempts to repair the relationship; marital counseling had not been particularly helpful, and his wife rejected the idea of individual work for herself. Nevertheless, Dan persisted, frightened at the prospect of losing his wife and at having to "start all over again." The following exchange, which took place during a therapy session approximately five months into Dan's sixteen-month-long treatment, illustrates how a genetic interpretation was formulated from the therapist's understanding of Dan's abandonment fears:

DAN: When I think about all of the changes I'd have to make, not to mention the fact that I'd be living alone, divorce just doesn't seem to be a very viable option. Besides, it's expensive, and I worry about my kids getting lost in the whole process.

THER: I certainly agree that there would be lots of changes, and no one ever said divorce is inexpensive, but I'm wondering about two things that you've just mentioned. One is the whole idea of being on your own, having your own place—

DAN: —well, it's just that I haven't really had my own place since college. I suppose I was always sharing . . . with someone. . . . It's probably silly, but it might take some getting used to.

THER: Uh hmm. The other thing you said was your concern about the kids "getting lost" in the whole process.

DAN: Right. . . . I think of my friend, H.L. He and his wife were so preoccupied with their divorce that their kids had a real rough time. It's as though they didn't have *either* parent for a while . . . and I don't want that to happen to Lizzie and Paul.

THER: Let me suggest a slightly different understanding of what you've been talking about these last few hours. My thought is that the prospect of divorcing your wife is unsettling for another reason as well. It brings up that whole issue of feeling "lost" in your own childhood because your Dad was so self-involved and angry and because your Mom had neither the presence of mind nor the energy to do much parenting a good part of the time. Who's going to look after *you* when you're divorced, when you're out there on your own? I'm thinking that this may be very reminiscent of that old danger situation from forty years ago. And when you think about your own kids and how they'd be affected, my guess is that you're probably using your childhood experience as a model. From what you've said about the sort of relationships you've cultivated with both Paul and Lizzie, you're very involved in their lives, and they know it. Even if you and your wife decide to get a divorce, I somehow think your kids are more likely to remain at the center of the equation . . .

DAN: Well, there's probably some truth in that, although I'm less certain about the part having to do with my childhood. . . . I'll have to think about that some more.

DYNAMIC INTERPRETATION

Rona J., a thirty-one-year-old lesbian graduate student pursuing an advanced degree in musical performance, sought crisis counseling through the university mental health clinic because of a rapidly escalating problem with stage fright and was assigned to a female social work staff therapist. Although Rona had never experienced stage fright until just three weeks earlier, she reported that she could barely perform as the piano accompanist for another student, a cellist, who was on that occasion giving her graduate recital. It turned out that Rona and the cellist were very close friends, although the relationship was a nonsexual one, since the other student was already in a monogamous lesbian relationship with someone else. In fact, Rona had never spoken to her friend of being sexually attracted to her and felt very ashamed over having such feelings. Shortly before she was to accompany her friend onstage to perform before the music school faculty and other students in the graduate program, Rona reported having had the passing thought that she and her friend would be "making beautiful music together." She then went onstage and was quickly seized by panic.

RONA: (*Sighing heavily*) I don't know how I got through that performance. I thought I was going to die.

THER: Yes, it must have been a terrible ordeal . . . I wonder . . . do you have any other thoughts about the phrase that you repeated just a moment ago, "making beautiful music together?"

RONA: (*Blushing slightly*) yeah, it's so corny . . . Well, I guess there's something sexual there, but I've never told anyone about my feelings for Cecily, so I don't really see what that's got to do with anything.

THER: (*Somewhat tentatively*) well, perhaps it doesn't. On the other hand, I'm thinking that here you are, "making beautiful music together" in front of everyone, shamelessly. I'm just guessing, but maybe for a moment that secret desire you've held for Cecily for so long felt as though it was right out there, on the surface, and it triggered an equally powerful feeling of shame.

I suppose you might even say that the "beautiful music" wasn't so "beautiful" any longer, once you froze and had so much trouble playing the piano part, as if a part of you was trying to prove that there wasn't any such feeling between the two of you.

RONA: Maybe. It is sort of true that I felt like everyone knew what I felt for Cecily once I was out on stage there, but that seemed silly.

INTERPRETATION OF RESISTANCE

Jamie was a slightly overweight, insulin-dependent diabetic woman in her early thirties, the oldest in a sibship of four, who had sought once-weekly treatment on the advice of her endocrinologist who, she offered, "is concerned because I can't follow a diet." Jamie's diabetes, first diagnosed when she was an adolescent, had become progressively worse since she reached her early twenties. At the time she entered treatment, she was showing early signs of diabetic retinopathy and had recently consulted a nephrologist because of worsening kidney problems. Jamie had also been hospitalized twice within the last eighteen months, once for an abdominal abscess and the second time with phlebitis. When I asked Jamie if *she* felt concerned about her health, she seemed to shrug off the serious nature of her condition, claiming that since "everyone else is so concerned, I don't need to be." As treatment got underway, Jamie was able to share some important personal and family history, including the circumstances surrounding a catastrophic family event, the loss of her younger brother, Tommy, following an automobile accident some nine years earlier. Jamie had been employed for several years in a community hospital as a dietician, although after her most recent hospitalization she left this position to assume the job of assistant manager at a fast-food restaurant. Jamie had returned to live with her parents after resigning from the hospital staff, although she complained that her mother continually "pushed" her to leave her managerial position at the fast-food restaurant and return to the dietetics field. Jamie was resentful of her mother's attempts to influence her but found it very hard to tell her directly. After a number of productive sessions during which she seemed to settle into the routine of therapy, Jamie rather uncharacteristically arrived for her hour nearly twenty minutes late.

JAMIE: I think that this hour is probably going to be a waste of time. I really didn't want to come in today, had to sort of force myself. I can't think of anything to say. . . . Let's see. . . . Oh, I did see something last night on cable that was kinda interesting. It was a made-for-TV movie with that same actor—I think his name is Harry Hamlin—who used to be on *LA Law* years ago. He was supposed to be a fire chief or something in this southwestern town with a rattlesnake problem. Did you ever watch *LA Law*? Well, he was far more believable in that role than in this thing last night. . . . Let's see (*exhaling audibly*), what else can I talk about? (*long pause*).

THER: I'm wondering if you have any other thoughts about being late today and your feeling that there's nothing much to talk about.

JAMIE: No, not really.

THER: Do you recall what we discussed in the last hour?

JAMIE: I dunno (*sounding annoyed*). Something about—well, I can't remember. Probably not very important.

THER: You know, you sound a bit irritated.

JAMIE: Maybe, a little, but I'm not sure what about.

THER: Well, something seems to be bothering you. Let's see if maybe we can figure it out. After all, being late isn't very like you, and—

JAMIE: —(*interrupting*) oh, I remember what I was saying, I think it was at the end of the hour. I was telling you about that history taking I had to go through with the guy, the second year nephrology resident, and how embarrassing it was when I had these thoughts . . . sexual . . . thoughts, about him. . . . God, I hated talking about that.

THER: So, maybe there's a connection between how you were feeling at the end of the last hour and your being late today, as well as with the problems you're having finding something to talk about and the irritation you're feeling with me?

JAMIE: OK, so there's a connection (*pause*). It has something to do with the sexual stuff, I'm guessing.

THER: I think so. I think it was also the feeling of embarrassment you had over having revealed more than maybe you felt comfortable telling me. After all, those were private thoughts.

JAMIE: I'm thinking maybe I was irritated at you last week, like I felt somehow that . . . oh, I'm not sure, that it was dirty, and I shouldn't have even said it. . . . You know, it reminds me how embarrassing that whole topic—sex—used to be for me around my parents. I'd do almost anything to avoid discussing it with them.

THER: Well, no wonder you were so peeved with me. And, I suppose the best way to avoid discussing a topic is—

JAMIE: —to not come in.

THER: Yes.

TRANSFERENCE INTERPRETATION

Hal was a tough-talking though very bright, obese fifteen year-old sopho-more, placed in a private high school, who had been referred to a family ser-vice agency by the school guidance counselor because of his hostile and uncooperative attitude toward classmates and his defiance of teachers and other school staff members. Hal was an only child whose parents had divorced when he was seven. He lived with his mother, a heavy woman who was over six feet tall and worked as the manager of a parking lot. He had spo-radic contact with his father, who had remarried several years after the divorce and quickly produced two children with his new wife. For a time Hal expressed interest in coming in for his therapy appointments and was even cooperative to a degree. Soon, however, he began to arrive for sessions late and became relentlessly critical of the therapist. In the following exchange, Hal's middle-aged male therapist attempts to make use of his deepening understanding of Hal's transference feelings and fantasies:

HAL: You know, this is stupid, and so are you. You're so fucking weak, too. Plus you're too old . . . I don't know why I'm still coming here, except my Mom makes me.

THER: I was just thinking . . . Your complaints about me have a familiar ring to them—

HAL: Yeah (*rolling his eyes*), that's because I've said them before. (Sarcastically) Good, at least your memory isn't shot yet.

THER: (*Continuing*) ahhh, what I meant is that you made almost the same complaint about your father a couple of weeks ago. Do you remember, you were saying that you haven't seen him much over the last few months, but that he's too old to do fun stuff with you, anyway; he can't play football any-more, doesn't have the strength or the endurance . . . and also, that he doesn't understand anything—

HAL: —he doesn't. So what? (*shaking his head*). Just my luck, I get a dumb-ass therapist who's *just* like my Dad.

THER: Well, there's another possibility, it seems to me.

HAL: Yeah? (*Challengingly*) I'm listening.

THER: Maybe I'm *not* so much like your Dad, but what you're feeling toward me—and maybe also toward the gym teacher and the principal—is the anger and disappointment you've felt toward your Dad but can't really talk about with him. Maybe those feelings are *so* strong that they end up getting stuck in places they don't even really belong.

HAL: No, actually, I really *do* think you're stupid, but maybe I'll keep coming in, just so I can listen to your ridiculous theories.

OTHER DYNAMIC TECHNIQUES: EXPLORATION-DESCRIPTION-VENTILATION, CLARIFICATION, SUSTAINMENT, AND SUGGESTION

Although interpretation as a therapeutic procedure is more or less exclusively tied to psychodynamic treatment approaches, dynamic therapy makes use of a range of other techniques. Some of these, such as exploration or empathy, are considered to be broadly generic or atheoretical and have also been incorporated into a number of nondynamic systems of therapy (e.g., cognitive treatment, gestalt therapy, transactional analysis, etc.).

Exploration-description is a term borrowed from what has come to be known as the "Hollis typology" (Hollis 1968b; Woods and Hollis 2000). The Hollis typology is a classification of client-worker communications originally extrapolated from intensive case studies and line-by-line examinations of clinical interviews. *Exploration-description*, which is used throughout the phases of treatment, beginning with clinical assessment, consists of communications made by the clinician designed to elicit both descriptive and explanatory material from the client. Such content may also be linked quite naturally, as the following example illustrates, with the client's expression of affect-laden material or what Hollis and others have termed *ventilation*. Although other, nondynamic systems of treatment (e.g., primal therapy, gestalt therapy, bioenergetics, and so forth) also place a high valuation on the release of powerful affects, dynamic approaches typically do not consider such *affectivity without accompanying insight* to represent the ultimate aim of treatment. Nevertheless, the release of suppressed, repressed, or dissociated affects and impulses constitutes a time-honored dynamic technique, originally termed *abreaction*, and used by Freud in his early treatment of hysterical patients (Breuer and Freud 1893–95).[7]

Ilona, a thirty-two year old African American attorney who was self-referred to a community agency, sought counseling because her husband had "walked out" on her several weeks before and was "shacking up" with a mutual friend. The clinician noted that over the first four or five interviews Ilona, in response to queries, had been able to furnish the clinician with a very detailed description of her marital relationship, her family background, even important events in her childhood. At the same time, the client had not really revealed her feelings about the breakup of her marriage; she seemed neither particularly angry nor saddened, although the therapist observed that Ilona tended to smirk slightly when she mentioned Darryl, her estranged husband, by name.

THER: I was just noticing, Ilona, that whenever you mention Darryl's name, you seem to smirk. Are you aware of doing this?

ILONA: Oh, yeah, I just think, what the hell . . . he sure had me fooled these past four years (*smirking again*). But, you know he's in marketing, so he's *really* good at selling things, even when he doesn't believe in the product.

THER: So you think he was selling you something?

ILONA: Oh, yeah (*smirking again*).

THER: You really haven't said very much about how all of this has made you feel, Ilona.

ILONA: Oh, I don't know . . . (*smirking again, but with her lips quivering slightly and tears forming in the corners of her eyes*). It's . . . I guess, I mean, I thought that he loved me (*crying very softly*).

THER: I can hear the hurt in your voice now for the first time.

ILONA: (*Tears streaming down her face*) it's not fair . . . we were in love, at least I loved him, and I just figured . . . that we'd be together, you know, for the rest of our lives.

THER: You're right, Ilona. It *isn't* fair, but I think it's important for you to be able to talk about your hurt and sadness over losing Darryl, and I expect there are more feelings where those came from.

ILONA: (*Nodding and crying softly.*)

Clarification is a term that has at times been used interchangeably with *interpretation* but is also closely linked to three forms of client-worker communication that in the Hollis typology are labeled, respectively, *person-situation reflection*, *pattern-dynamic reflection*, and *developmental reflection* (see notes 4 and 5). In the casework literature of the 1950s, *clarification* also represented one of two basic types of casework practice (the other being *supportive treatment*). *Clarification* was defined as "treatment aimed at modification of adaptive patterns" (Family Service Association of America 1953:19) and required "the use of techniques to help clients separate objective reality from distortions of the external world" (Woods and Hollis 2000:116). This usage is, however, somewhat at variance with that of Greenson, who describes *clarification* as one of four relatively distinct procedures for promoting the furtherance of insight, the others being *confrontation*, *interpretation*, and *working through* (Greenson 1967:37–39). Bibring considers clarification to constitute one of two basic technical principles of psychoanalytic treatment, the other being interpretation. The difference between the two, Bibring asserts, is that clarifying comments refer not to unconscious material or processes but rather to "conscious and/or preconscious processes, of which the patient is not sufficiently aware." but that are recognized "when they are clearly presented to him" (Bibring 1954:755). Clarification aims to assist patients in achieving greater self-awareness of typical patterns of conduct or how attitudes are related to behavior. In this sense clarifying remarks are designed to enable patients to view their difficulties from a new perspective—via their observing egos. Because clarifying comments are not aimed at unconscious material that has been subject to repression or otherwise warded off, they are also less likely than are interpretations to stimulate resistance. A therapist's observation that a patient seems to laugh when she is actually feeling angry, or is chronically late to family reunions because he wishes to avoid being alone with a particular sibling, or takes a bathroom break during a session because she feels anxious—each is an example of a clarifying comment.

I would define *clarification* as a procedure that is designed to highlight a specific intrapsychic process but that goes beyond *exploration-description* and precedes the work of interpretation; in effect, *clarification* prepares the client for interpretations that focus on dynamic or genetic components or that address aspects of resistance or transference.

Gabrielle, a bisexual woman in her early forties, sought therapy because she felt unable to make important decisions in her life involving career, where she ought to live, whether her current relationship was "the right one" for her, and so forth. Gabrielle was seen on a twice-weekly basis over a period of nine months, at which time therapy was discontinued by mutual agreement. Several months into her treatment, Gabrielle had been describing a childhood that, in spite of her parents' turbulent marriage, was mostly happy and carefree. Shortly after Gabrielle turned eight, on one bright summer day, she recalled purchasing with her own money a children's book with "beautiful color plates" from a local drugstore. She was very proud of this purchase and displayed it to everyone with whom she came into contact. Gabrielle then "made the mistake" of showing her newly acquired book to a neighbor, a young man in his late twenties, who invited Gabrielle into his house so that he could get a better look at the prized possession. Once she was inside, he shut the door and knelt down in front of her. He then quickly reached up beneath her dress, pulled her underpants aside, and placed his hand inside her vagina. She was too shocked to protest and simply stood there without uttering a sound until he had finished. The incident was never repeated, and Gabrielle believes that she never actually spoke of it until her first experience in counseling, which did not occur until she was a graduate student, some twenty years later.

At about the time she disclosed this traumatic incident, Gabrielle's transference feelings seemed to have intensified. She revealed that she sometimes thought about the therapist outside of her sessions and also that some of her lesbian friends had expressed surprise that she was willing to meet with a heterosexual male therapist. She was late for one particular session, an excerpt from which is reproduced below, due to the fact that she had "missed the highway exit and just kept going for a few miles."

GABI: It's funny, I *know* where the exit is, but I just blanked and kept going. Not sure where I would have ended up. . . .

THER: Well, that is unusual for you. I wonder if you have any thought about this being connected in some way to the experience you recounted a few sessions back?

GABI: Oh . . . do you mean the time I showed the book to Nate (the neighbor)? I guess I'm not quite seeing how that's connected.

THER: What occurs to me is that failing to make the highway exit may mean that coming in here to see me now triggers feelings of ambivalence not unlike those you've reported having in so many other parts of your life.

This material can be considered a *clarification* of the fact that Gabi's "forgetting" possessed a dynamic significance and is likely connected to her previous disclosure of childhood sexual molestation. The therapist's comments are something beyond being purely descriptive, but do not in themselves constitute an interpretation. The interpretative work, which followed later in this hour, made a far more explicit connection between Gabi's lateness and her fear of being retraumatized behind "closed doors" by an older heterosexual male.

Florence Hollis has described *sustainment* as "perhaps the most basic and essential of all psychosocial casework activities" (Woods and Hollis 2000:131). It consists of various clinical procedures designed to diminish a client's anxiety or lack of self-esteem or self-confidence through the clinician's expressions of understanding, interest, desire to help, confidence in the client's competencies or abilities, and reassurance to assuage anxieties or guilt (Woods and Hollis 2000:122). Some would argue that such interventions are not really psychodynamic at all and are more appropriately thought of as being supportive in nature. Dynamic therapists, they assert, should be far less interested in reassuring the anxious or guilt-ridden client, or in elevating the self-esteem of a client with poor self-confidence, than they should be in striving to understand the dynamic basis of such clinical phenomena. Others have noted that such interventions, though not "dynamic" in the more formal sense, are a commonplace and, perhaps, a necessary ingredient in achieving a balance between the client's *hope* and *discomfort* (Ripple, Alexander, and Polemis 1964).

Although *sustaining procedures* may still be somewhat less characteristic in psychoanalytic treatment than in dynamic therapy, there seems little argument of their ubiquity in the latter, especially early in the treatment encounter. In some measure this is because sustaining procedures actually cover a range of verbal and nonverbal responses to the client: a nod of the head, paraverbal expressions that convey interest or gentle encouragement to the client, in addition to very specific verbal remarks. Examples of verbal sustainment might include "I know that discussing your wife's illness is very hard for you, but perhaps it will be helpful for you to share some of this pain with another person" or "As depressed and hopeless as you're feeling at this moment, I believe that things will improve; if you've hit bottom, the only way you can go is up, right?"

Suggestion refers to the induction of ideas, impulses, emotions, actions, and other mental processes in the patient, whose position is one of relative dependence, by the therapist, who occupies a position of authority (Bibring 1954). Bibring considered suggestion to operate independently of a patient's rational, critical, or realistic thinking. Examples might include advice-giving, strong cautions against a particular course of action, proscriptions of negative symptoms or suggestions to manufacture positive behavioral changes, or the therapist's explicitly stated confident expectation that the patient will produce a dream in the following therapy session. In his early work with hysterical patients, Freud had often paired suggestion with hypnotic procedures, although he ultimately discarded both techniques because of what he regarded as their incompatibility with his new psychoanalytic method. Even years later Freud remained consistent in his caution to differentiate the "pure gold of analysis" from the "copper of direct suggestion" (Freud 1919b:168). Gradually, however, many of those trained in the classical psychoanalytic tradition realized that the technical orthodoxy adhered to in past generations was actually something of an illusion.[8] Indeed, Greenson observed over thirty-five years ago that the "'art' of psychoanalytic technique . . . is based on the blending of the analytic with the nonanalytic [e.g., abreaction, suggestion,[9] manipulation, etc.] procedures" (Greenson 1967:51).

In the two examples that follow, clinical process in the middle phase of treatment is examined in greater detail, with particular attention to resistance and working through. The first case is that of Ian, introduced in the last chapter, and the second is that of Jim, a physically abusive father whose treatment was court mandated.

CLINICAL CASE ILLUSTRATION 8.1: "IAN"

Ian, the twenty-one-year-old college senior originally referred for treatment of depression by a psychiatrist from his hometown, continued to meet with me on a three-times-weekly basis for three and a half months, and then twice-weekly for the next four months, until we reached the end of the academic year. Although he reported a continuing preoccupation with the idea of suicide, he never became acutely suicidal, and these disturbing thoughts gradually subsided over a period of some six weeks. Two of the most significant themes to emerge more fully in the middle phase of Ian's treatment were that of his sexuality and the dynamic tensions in the complex relationship between Ian and his father. Ian had previously described his father's cautions regarding sexually perverse older men early in the treatment encounter. The theme of sexual perversity, however, gradually expanded to include Ian's own sexual thoughts and fantasies, which he regarded as being abnormal. In one particular hour he remembered an experience dating to his twelfth year in which a close friend had approached him during a sleepover, wanting to engage in mutual masturbation and sexual play. Ian was horrified yet, at the same time, intensely curious. He declined the invitation, recalling that he tried to be careful lest he injure his friend's feelings. His sexual curiosity, however, seemed gradually to build from that time onward, to a point where he had become nearly obsessed with graphic portrayals of various sexual acts, principally between heterosexual partners. Despite feeling both guilt and self-contempt for what he described as an "addiction" to pornographic films and videos, Ian confessed that he found the image of a strong, macholike guy "fucking" a girl to be very arousing. In this same hour Ian spoke once again, though with far greater feeling, of his great disappointment when, at the age of six, two of his older siblings moved in with his father, but Ian was forced to stay with his mother. His mother tended to infantilize him, and, although he liked it some of the time, he longed to be with his big, strong father.

In the following hour he reported that his depression had returned, he had felt nearly overcome with a feeling of weakness, and had once again entertained the thought of suicide. He was at a loss to explain the return of these feelings.

THER: Do you think there might be some connection with what we were talking about in the last hour?

IAN: (*Sounding irritated*) you know, therapy isn't the only thing going on in my life. It might not have anything to do with Monday's session. (*Pausing*) I don't even remember what we talked about Monday.

THER: Listen, I know there are a lot of other things going on in your life. But your memory is usually pretty sharp. I wonder if there might be some reason for your not remembering. . . .

IAN: Reason? Not sure I'm following you.

THER: My thought is that something may have come up Monday that you found disturbing. Are you having a thought?

IAN: (*Sighs*) yeah, sort of, but it feels so distant, like that session could have been a year ago. I remember that I was . . . it was something about Dad having Jon and Rebecca come and live with him . . . and—oh, I know—the sexual stuff. God, it's really sort of foggy. . . .

THER: I'm thinking two things: that you revealed things about yourself, sexual things, that you consider shameful and perverse, and this was very difficult. And that we may have touched more deeply on the *feelings* you had when your Dad wouldn't let you come live with him. You've told me the story before, but this time it was different; this time you really felt the longing for him and the tremendous disappointment and . . . maybe something else too.

IAN: Like what? (*Without noticeable irritation and in a slightly playful tone*) go ahead—why don't you tell me what else I felt.

THER: (*Silence.*)

IAN: Anger? Are you saying that I felt angry?

THER: Actually, I didn't say that, but *what if* you did. Suppose you felt angry at your Dad. We know that's an even more difficult feeling for you than disappointment. And I think it's a feeling that you find very difficult to tolerate in yourself . . .

IAN: Well, yeah, it just brings *you* down. I mean, being angry at someone just makes you look bad. It doesn't help.

THER: But it's there—it's real, isn't it?

IAN: I don't know. . . . Maybe. Listen, it's not so important. You're blowing it out of proportion.

THER: See, I'm thinking that you got depressed and then started thinking about killing yourself because you had to get rid of the guilt those angry feelings triggered. I think it's *that* hard to be mad at him. But, to make matters more complicated, we know that you also feel a tremendous sense of shame over the porno stuff, and view this as a weakness in yourself. So, perhaps you actually had two reasons.

IAN: (*Reflectively, and with a distant expression*) I'm not really thinking about the whole pornography thing right now. It's odd, but I'm feeling mad at Dad . . . now. You know, I hated him for it, I think. I *really* didn't want to stay at my Mom's . . .

At the beginning of the next hour, Ian told me that he was still depressed, although he wasn't feeling as troubled by the suicidal thoughts, which now seemed to be "less a preoccupation, more a nuisance." He revealed that he and his girlfriend, Michelle, whom he'd started seeing again shortly after entering treatment, had finally begun to have sex after a long lapse. Ian told me, however, that the sex wasn't that good. After having intercourse, he often had the sensation of inner emptiness, as though he had lost something and couldn't get it back. In fact, he sometimes had the thought that perhaps he was gay, and maybe that was the root of his unsatisfactory sexual relations. Ian then recalled having been encouraged at around the age of six to dress up as a girl on at least several different occasions and remembered that his sisters and his mother thought of this as being "cute." Ian enjoyed the attention, although after being teased on a few occasions by John, his older brother, he began to feel self-conscious and subsequently gave this up.

I asked him to tell me a bit more about past sexual relationships. Ian then described his earliest sexual experience with a girl. He was fifteen, a sophomore in high school, and had met a nineteen-year-old girl who worked as a salesperson in the same stationary store in which Ian was employed part-time. They started to hang out together and dated a few times, although Ian kept the relationship a secret. This young woman was apparently also quite sexually aggressive and "sort of told me what to do." After a few months, however, they seemed to lose interest in each other, and the relationship ended. He had had one other "serious" relationship, during his sophomore year of college. For about six months, he dated Abbie, a freshman girl who, interestingly, suffered from a chronic neurological condition with very distinctive symptoms. Ian felt intrigued and excited by this girl, whom he described as "exotic," a reaction that was further strengthened by Abbie's nearly insatiable appetite for adventure and risk taking. "She'd say and do almost anything; in fact, sometimes she'd dare me to do things that I'm sure I never would have done otherwise, like taking her Dad's Porsche up to 110 mph on the highway."

A few sessions later, Ian began to talk about a recurring fantasy he had not previously reported in treatment. In this fantasy he is sexually penetrated *per annum* by another man. Recounting the fantasy led him back to the feminine/gay theme that had emerged several sessions previously and to a more complete recollection of the life-threatening illness his father had developed when Ian was a teenager.

IAN: It should have been so painful to watch him like that. He probably thought he was dying. But I didn't feel anything, really.

THER: You don't remember feeling anything at all?

IAN: Well . . . I didn't feel sorry for him. He was so weak. I guess I felt disgusted, but that's awful—how could I have been so callous?

THER: I think your perception of him as being weak is a central element here. You longed for a strong father, and here you get this weak, feminized guy who can't even feed himself; can't go to the bathroom without help. But I think that he disappointed you long before his illness.

IAN: You mean all the stuff about his moving away after my parents' divorce, and not letting me move in with him when Rebecca and Jon got to. Yeah, I guess I know all that already.

THER: OK, let's talk about the fantasy of being penetrated by a guy. Do you have any thoughts about this?

IAN: Yeah, it's sick, perverse. I don't know where it comes from.

THER: I'm thinking that it seems to tie a few things together. First, it allows you to be in a nonthreatening position, a "feminine" position, if you will. You know, in thinking about your childhood, it must have felt good, at least for a while, to have your Mom and your older sisters "baby" you. And not only did you get a lot of attention when they dressed you up as a girl, but that stuff was happening right around the time you were becoming more aware of your sexuality. Furthermore, your older brother then leaves to move in with your Dad. You were the only guy in the house—

IAN: —So, it's some sort of oedipal thing. . . . I studied that in my personality theory class. Sorry, but I don't really buy into it.

THER: There's actually another part. I think that your fantasy doesn't reflect an active homosexual desire so much as it points to a remedy for the feelings of being weakened and "feminized." Semen equals strength, the strength you sought throughout childhood from your father but never seemed able to count on.

IAN: So, when I saw him all fucked up and sick, it just brought everything home. But I also think of him as being strong. He's a good athlete, and there were other times when I was small and he used to tickle me and throw me around, and I loved it.

THER: Of course, there wasn't total privation. But maybe it's because you *knew* what you were missing that it made things that much more difficult with your Dad and the disappointment that much greater.

IAN: Well, maybe, but I think the oedipal stuff is too facile.

In this and subsequent hours we examined Ian's competitive relationship with his older brother, Jon, as well as a childhood aggression he had not previously described. It turned out that by the time Ian was in second grade he had developed not only a "rotten, nasty little mouth" but had become very physically aggressive. During this same period his mother was briefly married to a rather unstable and "very self-centered guy" whom Ian despised. When his mother's second marriage ended in divorce after less than two years, Ian felt as though he had been in part responsible and "shut down" his aggression more or less permanently. Several other themes also emerged in the middle phase of Ian's treatment. These included the reactivation within the transference relationship of his early fear of emotional abandonment, anxieties related to the thwarting of his childhood longing for contact with a strong, idealized male, and increasing awareness of a deeply felt anger and distrust of women.

DISCUSSION

This clinical summary and reconstruction from the middle phase of Ian's treatment is instructive insofar as it furnishes a revealing illustration of the ebb and flow of the process of psychotherapy. At times therapist and client seem to be in a sort of dialogic synchrony, engaged in a collaborative endeavor in which the deepening of the client's dynamic understanding appears as an orderly if not inexorable process. New memories surface, new insights are forged, and symptoms recede. At other times the client seems determined to resist the ideas his therapist presents for his consideration, dismissing them on theoretical grounds or for other reasons—the client has already thought of that, the therapist is making too much of a trivial matter, and so forth. By this point in Ian's treatment the therapeutic alliance has solidified, and to all outward appearances Ian seems unambivalently committed to his treatment. However, appearances, especially insofar as dynamic treatment is concerned, can deceive. To be certain, Ian arrives consistently and nearly always punctually for his appointments. He no longer seems preoccupied with the thought of killing himself and wants to feel better, to be rid of his depression and the disturbing fantasies he reports. But, as we see, Ian isn't ready to give up his "illness" just yet.

Ian has a session in which he returns to the theme of being disappointed by his father and discloses substantially new material regarding his "addiction to pornography" as well as a sexual trauma from middle childhood. In the follow-ing session he reports that his depression has returned, he feels a sense of "weak-ness," and he has thought again about suicide. Inferring some dynamic associa-tion between the content of the last hour and what has followed in its wake, the therapist asks Ian to consider the possibility that a relationship exists between the two. Ian first minimizes the importance of the therapy with a display of petu-lance and then cannot seem to remember any details from the previous session. The therapist, however, is persistent and thereafter combines *gentle confrontation with interpretation of the dynamic basis for the client's resistance*. At several junc-tures in the unfolding interpretative sequence, the client's input is sought, since such work is typically far more successful when the interpretative work is a joint endeavor. The most salient element in this portion of the vignette is the client's dawning recognition of his feelings of hatred toward his father for favoring the two older siblings and forcing him to remain in his mother's house. Another ele-ment illuminated by this dialogue is the relationship between angry feelings, guilt, self-contempt, and suicidal preoccupations. Although initially uncon-vinced, perhaps feeling as though the therapist "expected" a particular response from him, Ian then seems struck by the idea that he has been defending against full awareness of the powerful hatred he has felt toward his father for events that occurred so many years before. In fact, although Ian's shame over what he has regarded as evidence of his own perversion is a critical unconscious motivation for his "forgetting," the material relative to his relationship with his father appears to possess even greater presence here.

Over the next several weeks Ian begins to discuss a series of interrelated themes. He and Michelle have started having sexual relations once again, although he feels depleted rather than fulfilled after sex. What Ian adduces from this is further evidence confirming his fear that he is either gay or sexually per-verted. He then recalls having been dressed up to look like a girl by his mother and older sisters when he was about six and how much he enjoyed their atten-tion. However, his brother's taunts as well as his own recognition that cross-dressing made him different than other little boys soon led him to resist his mother's and sisters' entreaties. He describes a mid-adolescent encounter with a girl several years his senior who seems to have sought him out as a casual sexual partner, initiating him into a new and exciting world of postpubertal sexuality. He also mentions a relationship with another girl, one who was aggressive and independent, whose risk taking he found especially intriguing and sexually excit-ing. Unlike Ian, Abbie seemed to experience little guilt in connection with her flaunting of parental injunctions; indeed, she seemed to thrive on such danger-ous forms of excitement as drag racing. Ian also spoke of his recurring fantasy of being sexually penetrated by another man, which seemed to serve as a bridge to thoughts about the life-threatening illness his father developed shortly after Ian finally went to live with him as a high school freshman.

In this second excerpt Ian seems to question if not reject outright the thera-pist's efforts to help him piece together these seemingly disparate ideas and memories. Ian doesn't challenge the therapist's reiteration of the feminized father theme but reacts strongly to what he assumes to be an oedipal interpreta-tion. Rather than pressing the point here, which would serve little purpose other than to further crystallize Ian's resistance, the therapist *circumnavigates* the oedi-pal material, instead focusing on a different dynamic component: the *selfobject* dimension. Ian's subjective dread of being weakened or feminized has another discrete meaning: it also offers a disguised method for counteracting a series of traumatic disappointments in the idealizing realm. Ian's fantasy effectively per-mits him to acquire strength by incorporating the paternal semen via anal inter-course. Ian's subtle resistance to this *genetic interpretation*—that he can also think of his father as strong and athletic—is *joined* by the therapist. If Ian's father was sometimes strong, athletic, dependable, it makes him even more acutely aware of what it was Ian *wasn't* getting from him. Ian's apparent acceptance of this particular component of the interpretation (reconfirmed some time after the fact, with the reemergence of this theme later in treatment) may also be inferred, in part, from his explicit rejection of the oedipal hypothesis.

Ian later rediscovered his capacity for anger, acquiring a critical insight into his original motives for "shutting it down" as a third grader. This seemed to coa-lesce around an inner conviction that his "bad" behavior had led his mother's second husband to divorce her. As these historical issues emerged more fully and were gradually *worked through*, Ian's depression seemed to lift, and his nearly reflexive tendency to assuage his guilt through self-contempt, suicidal thoughts, or other forms of self-punishment was gradually, incrementally exchanged for more adaptive solutions.

CLINICAL CASE ILLUSTRATION 8.2: "JIM"

Jim, a twice-divorced forty-five-year-old Caucasian male, was court ordered to obtain individual and family therapy as a prerequisite for having unsu-pervised visitation restored with his then nine-year-old daughter Kate. Jim's involvement in the court system followed two incidents in which he was physically abusive toward his daughter while she was in his care. During the second incident, which stemmed from a minor infraction, Jim's punishment of Kate was so severe that she sustained bruises on her backside from head to toe. Kate's mother, Jane, and the court were understandably concerned, the more so because Jim denied the severity of his actions and justified them on the basis of his Christian beliefs and practices. The court-appointed psychological evaluator recommended both individual and reunification therapies as a means of assisting Jim to acknowledge the severity of his actions and gain insight into his aggressive behaviors and attitudes as well as to develop an understanding of and appreciation for his daughter's developmental needs. The stakes were high, inasmuch as therapy was considered to be the only means of ensuring Kate's safety and well-being.

Jim selected his female therapist's name from a list of referrals provided by the evaluator, later indicating that the therapist's designation as a theologically trained clinician had influenced his choice. She has now seen Jim individually for nearly three years in her private practice, for the most part on a once-weekly basis; recently, they began to meet every other week. Six months into therapy Jim and his daughter began seeing a reunification therapist. Jim's individual therapist was appointed to monitor his progress and ordered to furnish the court with semimonthly reports as well as periodic recommendations so that a schedule for a graduated reunification process between father and daughter might be developed.

Jim, who currently lives alone, works out of his home as a salesperson. He is of medium height and large muscular build, a bodybuilder, whose tight clothing accentuates the strength and definition of his body; a loud, booming voice seems to further underscore Jim's intimidating physical presence. Jim's thinking is very concrete and rigid; he is, moreover, oriented toward rules, which are characteristically interpreted literally. Initially he had very limited capacity for regulating or containing strong affects, particularly anger, a character deficiency magnified by his tendency toward impulsiveness. Although Jim was rarely at a loss for words, he experienced great difficulty in identifying his affective experience and in expressing emotions in an appropriate and measured manner. Until rather recently he neither demonstrated much awareness of or appreciation for the impact of his presence on others, nor did he show much understanding of others' needs. He generally evinced little insight into his own behavior or the conflicts that shaped it.

Reluctantly, Jim complied with the court ordered treatment. For the first year he approached therapy with tremendous resistance, alternately hostile and defensive. Jim's transference, which was negatively valenced, seemed to embody what has been referred to as a *habitual mode of relating*, the client's "typical, automatic, and characteristic ways of relating to others . . . [which] are not specific to the therapist" (Tyson and Tyson 1986:31). So far as Jim was concerned, his therapist was part of the enemy camp, along with his ex-wife, her attorney, and the court system, engaged in a sort of conspiracy to take his money and infringe upon his rights as a Christian American and father. He felt that she was twisting his every word to provide evidence to the court of his depravity. Interestingly, this belief didn't seem to deter him from an oft-repeated insistence that the biblical injunction "spare the rod and spoil the child" was a greater law than any order imposed by the court. Despite strong philosophical and spiritual objections, however, he was willing to comply with the court's recommendations as a "law-abiding citizen" who loved his daughter.

These were exceedingly difficult circumstances upon which to build a therapeutic alliance and reliable working relationship, although the challenge did not prove insurmountable. Jim, while still viewing the therapist with suspicion and exercising great caution over what he would reveal openly, gradually began to utilize the therapeutic relationship differently, venting frustrations with the "system" and developing greater understanding of his daughter's unique developmental needs as a child with emotional and learning difficulties. Despite his reluctance, Jim also became more curious about himself in relationship to others; he became increasingly open to examining his intimate relationships with women, in particular his mother, sisters, ex-wives, and daughter, and to considering his impact on those he loved. Another prominent theme in Jim's treatment was that of the effect of childhood experiences on his own development. Although at times he continued to resist the exploration of difficult content and remains suspicious of the court mandated treatment, Jim acknowledged the usefulness of the process and came to consider his therapist an ally.

A significant theme, which emerged early in treatment and remained a focus of their work ever since, is Jim's apparent lack of sensitivity to his daughter's needs and his reactivity toward her. Jim's defensiveness and resistance to examining his thoughts, beliefs, feelings, and actions in relation to Kate appeared at first to be so rigidly codified as to be impenetrable. However, as he began the second year of therapy, Jim demonstrated growing self-awareness and an openness to engage in conversation regarding this rigid position. In one particular hour Jim described several recent interactions with others in which his rigidity was at issue. In the same hour his newly developing capacity to be curious and playful in exploring his interactions with others was also evident.

JIM: Well, I saw Dr. Fink (the court-appointed evaluator) today.

THER: Oh, yes. How did that go?

JIM: I don't know. I guess I'll find out tomorrow.

THER: Oh? How so?

JIM: Well Dr. Fink is supposed to have the report done tomorrow.

THER: And he is getting the results to you?

JIM: No. He will be sending them over to the lawyer.

THER: Well, what was the experience like for you this time? I know you were anticipating it with some concern.

JIM: That guy (referring to Dr. Fink) . . . I don't know what he thought. I just think he's . . . well, you know. Anyway, he asked these questions like he was trying to trip me up. Like, he asked if I thought Kate should be on medication. I said, "I don't know. I am not a doctor." He asked again, "Do you think Kate should be on medication?" I said, "I don't know. I am not a doctor." He kept getting more frustrated and he said again, "I am going to ask you one more time. Do you think Kate should be on medication?" He looked like he was going to lose his cool. He kept moving forward in his chair and his voice got louder and louder. I said, "If you are trying to get me to say that I have something against psychiatry and that I will be unsupportive of Kate taking her medication, I am not going to, because it isn't what I think."

THER: Well, what do you make of that interaction between the two of you?

JIM: Well, if Dr. Fink wanted to know something, he should just ask. I think he was trying to trick me so that I would lose it and say something that would prove Jane's (Jim's first ex-wife and Kate's mother) accusation that I keep Kate's medication from her. I told Dr. Fink that I learned in therapy that sometimes when I say things people hear something totally different from what I intend. So I am just trying to be totally clear about what I think. I am not a doctor, so I do not know if Kate should be on medication. I don't know what he is getting all honked off about.

It is the same kind of thing with my minister. I got this email from him. He got all over me telling me what a pain in the neck I am. I guess he was really frustrated with me. He said I needed to work on my bull-headedness in relationships. I told him that I wouldn't be continuing to talk with him and that I have a perfectly competent therapist that can carry on from here. My minister! I was like—where is this coming from? I am *not* going to put up with that!

THER: And do you have any ideas about where he was coming from?

JIM: I don't know. He got all emotional with me like Dr. Fink. You know how I am with emotions.

THER: Yes. So, you got similar reactions from both of them, and there have been some other recent circumstances you've talked about in which you described people becoming frustrated with you and then you became frustrated and confused by their reactions toward you.

JIM: Like when?

THER: You have been talking recently about your interactions with Jill (Jim's most recent ex-wife). The tussles you've had with Jill over the car and the television. Then there are those times that you get into it with Kate. For instance, at your visitation last week when she wanted to play a game with you and you had something else in mind. You seem to get into a position and you won't budge.

JIM: (*Laughing*) well, yeah, that is what I have been trying to tell my minister. I am human. I am a big baby and I am stubborn. I have never denied any of that. But what is it that happens in my relationships? I don't know. Is it communication problems? Like, is it that I am not understanding them and they aren't understanding me because we don't know how to talk to one another, or is it that perception thing where people perceive me as saying or meaning one thing and that isn't what I mean at all?

Jim's need to hold rigidly to a position despite his knowledge that to do so leads to frustrations and fractures in his relationships has been an ongoing point of discussion in his treatment, particularly as it applies to his relationship with Kate. While he continues to be "stubborn," as he himself has acknowledged, Jim has made great strides in developing his capacity for self-observation, particularly insofar as his ongoing interactions with others are concerned. A natural consequence has been his notable efforts to alter long-held and maladaptive behavioral patterns in his interpersonal relationships. The transference relationship has also evolved into one *predominantly of past experiences* (Tyson and Tyson 1986) in which Jim's historical experiences, wishes, conflicts, defenses, and attitudes have gradually acquired dimensionality as they have been revived in the context of this ongoing relationship. More specifically, the transference is now ambivalently maternal; at times the therapist represents Jim's critical and dangerous mother, though now, increasingly, the mother whose approval he seeks. In general, however, his experience of her appears to be growing more positive.

Some months later, in another therapy hour, Jim's enhanced capacity both to identify with his daughter and experience a sort of empathic resonance for her emotional position led to an important recollection from his own childhood experience. This moment in treatment demonstrated a major shift in Jim's self-understanding as well as in his capacity to relate to others. Six months previously Jim had resumed unsupervised visitation with Kate, and, in the week preceding this particular session, he accompanied Kate's class on a three-day field trip to an educational camp. During the trip he was able to observe Kate and her interactions with her peers. In the excerpt that follows, Jim described his observations to the therapist.

THER: So, how have things been going with you and Kate?

JIM: Great! Really great. I been spending quite a bit of time with her lately. Last week I went with her class to Camp Mitchell for three days.

THER: (*Surprised*) on an overnight field trip?

JIM: Yep. With her whole class. I was one of the only dads.

THER: Really? What was that like?

JIM: Three days with a bunch of sixth-grade boys and girls. Of course, I had to sleep with the boys. So, you can guess how it was. Actually, it went pretty well.

THER: What was it like for you and Kate?

JIM: Fine. (*Defensively*) what do you mean?

THER: I was just wondering what it must have been like to have the chance to be with Kate in that setting and have the opportunity to observe Kate with her peers.

JIM: Well, she seemed to always have kids around her. I think she does fine.

THER: I know you have heard reports from her mom and her teachers that she has trouble in that area, and you have said that in the past that hasn't been your experience of her. So, you thought things went OK between Kate and the other children? I'm just wondering what it might have been like for the two of you to be together like that.

JIM: I think Kate really loved it that I was there. I'm strong, so I got to be the macho dad and impress the boys. I think she got a kick out of it. She seemed to be really glad I was there. . . . But, you know, now that I am thinking about it, Kate did spend a lot of time off to herself. She can be a real motor mouth. She comes by that naturally (*laughing*). I think the other kids get annoyed with her and she gets excluded. I don't think she gets it at all. She doesn't really fit in. I had to go to the school this week because there was a meeting. Kate supposedly wrote an inappropriate note to some kid. Apparently, this kid feels like Kate is "stalking" him. They didn't save the note, so how am I suppose to put any stock in what they are telling us? But I went home and yelled at her and told her she couldn't do stuff like this, and she acted like she didn't know what I was talking about. Then I felt terrible because I yelled at her.

THER: It must be so painful to watch your daughter struggling and not know how to help her.

JIM: (*Crying for the first time in session*) I don't know what to do. She tries so hard, but she just doesn't fit in. And they are calling her a stalker. You don't know what it is like to see your kid hurting and wonder if she is always going to have trouble like this and not know how to make it better. Yelling at her isn't going to help. She *is* a good kid. I guess she just doesn't get it. Her mother says it is part of her disorder. It just hurts. It is a terrible feeling. I don't want this for her. I want her to have so much more.

Later in the hour Jim was able to connect the hurt he felt as he watched his daughter suffer to his own childhood disappointments and pain; Jim too had never felt as though he fit in with peers and often found himself getting into trouble at school for inappropriate behavior. Rarely had he displayed this level of emotional honesty or empathic attunement with the experience of others. Previously it had been far too threatening for him to tolerate the profound sadness and pain that came with acknowledging his daughter's difficulties as well as the disappointments and suffering he had endured in his own life. Only recently has he been able to link his insensitive, aggressive behavior toward Kate and others to his own childhood experiences. Jim is desperate to provide his daughter with a different experience of parenting than he received from his own parents. However, as the child of an overwhelmed, critical mother, who was a harsh disciplinarian, and a violent and largely absent, mentally ill father, Jim until recently felt unequipped for the task of parenting. He is working very hard to change that fact.

DISCUSSION

Although both Ian and Jim were seen privately, Jim's treatment differed in a number of important respects from that of Ian's. Unlike Ian, whose psychological development placed him somewhere in that epoch developmentalists have termed the "bridge to adulthood," Jim was well into middle age, a twice-divorced parent with a nine-year-old daughter. Perhaps more significantly, Jim's character development, for better or worse, was essentially complete. Changes in personality structure, while certainly possible at virtually any age, are likely to present a greater clinical challenge, in general, for middle-aged clients than for older adolescents or young adults. This seemed even more likely to be the case for Jim, whose character structure appeared to lack resilience and whose hostile mistrust of others was so deeply entrenched as to border on paranoia. Another important issue was that of motivation for treatment. Although entering therapy may not have been Ian's idea, neither was he coerced or forced into attending; he did so, more or less of his own volition, to seek relief from moderately severe depressive symptoms. Jim's therapy, by contrast, was court mandated, making him what in social casework has traditionally been termed an "involuntary client." Entering treatment reluctantly, he questioned not only the legitimacy of the court's judgment, but remained unconvinced that his behavior had been hurtful or problematic to his daughter. A further complication, especially insofar as the nature of Jim's transference relationship was concerned, was the presence of a third party in the consulting room, the "court," with which his therapist was in periodic communication. Collectively, such factors would not appear to bode well for significant or lasting change in Jim's life.

Nevertheless, as the clinician's narrative reveals, Jim's treatment appears to have been moderately successful, at least to date. The therapist, who observed to me that she was often drawn unwittingly into the reenactment of early life scenarios with Jim via this primitively functioning client's tendency to employ projective identification, had for the most part been able to furnish Jim with the affective containment he sought so desperately from others. Rather than responding out of her own countertransference to his blustery, provocative manner, paranoidlike reactions, and dismissive responses to her attempts at interpretation, she managed to use her countertransference reactions to therapeutic advantage, although this was often extremely difficult. In effect, she was not only able to offer Jim *containment* of disturbing thoughts, affects, and other toxic mental contents but also an opportunity for renewed growth, for developmental rerailment, to which Jim's deepening capacity for empathy with his daughter's psychological pain so eloquently attests.

Containment is largely an internal and subjective experience for the clinician and hence difficult to represent in any reconstruction of the verbatim exchange between client and therapist. However, a closer examination of the transcript does reveal evidence of the therapist's use of several important techniques discussed earlier: *pattern-dynamic reflection, clarification,* and *exploration-description-ventilation.* In the first session excerpt, Jim complains that Dr. Fink, the court-appointed evaluator, attempted to provoke him into revealing an underlying hostility toward psychiatry and psychiatrists. He steadfastly resists what he believed to be the doctor's efforts to ensnare him, believing such a critical response would do little more than lend strength to his ex-wife's claim that he intentionally withheld medication from their daughter. Without directly challenging the unconscious conspiratorial premise behind Jim's account, the therapist instead helps him to reflect on dynamic similarities between the encounter with Dr. Fink and his interactions with others that had been similarly confusing and troubling. In this manner, the client's resistance is *circumnavigated* and, in a state of lowered resistance, he is able to consider possible explanations for the interpersonal pattern his therapist has identified.

The second excerpt is derived from an interview that took place several months further into Jim's treatment. By this time the therapeutic alliance has further solidified, Jim's core maternal transference relationship has become more firmly established, and the process of working through has intensified. Consequently, the therapist is able to gently confront her client's denial about Kate's behavior during the field trip, something that would not have been possible earlier in the treatment without jeopardizing a tenuous alliance and engendering massive defensive hostility on Jim's part. This intervention proves especially propitious inasmuch as it leads to a critical genetic understanding of the relationship between Jim's own childhood pain and his reaction to his daughter's distress. The significance of this therapeutic "moment" is further underscored by Jim's deepening capacity to identify and express sadness and grief, to *ventilate*; he can cry now without feeling either weakened by it or as though it might signal a loss of control.

Clinical social work practice often involves work with court-mandated clients such as Jim. At times, owing as much to the involuntary nature of their involvement in therapy as to time limitations or other external conditions imposed on their treatment, such clients may not be thought of as good candidates for insight-oriented work. Although this is undoubtedly true in many instances, Jim's case illustrates the way in which a dynamic treatment framework may be used advantageously with a client whose character rigidity, basic mistrust, hostility, impulsiveness, and massive resistance would ordinarily disqualify him from further consideration.

Insofar as the process of dynamic treatment may be usefully understood as occurring in phases, the middle phase of therapy appears to hold a unique distinction setting it apart from that which precedes and follows. In this intermediate phase, treatment is well underway: the therapeutic alliance has already been established; significant dynamic issues have been identified and are now explored in greater depth; the client's transference has gained in both complexity and importance; and the client has typically begun to exhibit *resistance*. The resistance may be to exploration of the meaning of attitudes or behaviors, to the examination of transference, or to new insights or knowledge about the self, but, fundamentally, it is always about a change in the status quo and underscores the intimate relationship such changes have to the *working-through* process. We have described several different ways of understanding and working with resistance, a concept whose definition, like that of so many other concepts in dynamic theory, has been adjusted to fit to the requirements of various psychoanalytic theoretical frameworks. The history of the idea of working through, a feature of the clinical process that may be altogether absent in nondynamic treatment approaches, has also been examined in depth. In addition, we have discussed and illustrated several important dynamic techniques, focusing on the four basic kinds of interpretation, clarification, exploration, description, ventilation, sustainment, and suggestion. Two detailed clinical illustrations were then presented. The first involved a young adult male struggling with introjective depression, the second a middle-aged man mandated by the court to seek treatment so that his right to unsupervised visitation with a nine-year-old daughter might be restored.

9

Termination: The Endgame

ENDINGS ARE ARGUABLY as important or perhaps more so than are beginnings, and all things, not good things alone, must come to an end. The thought of an experience or a relationship ending often generates a variety of emotional reactions: sadness, grief, longing, anxiety, and regret, to name but several. An ending frequently signifies a transition from one state or developmental phase to another. Consider the nearly universal lament of the mother whose mischievous older toddler, intoxicated with her emerging autonomy, eschews the earlier maternal dependence that made her so cuddly, cute, and "easy" to care for. Or, the excitement and anxiety that attend the young adult's departure from the "womb" of the university to full-time employment and the beginning of a career. Or, on the other end of the developmental spectrum, the elaborate rituals associated with an individual's retirement from active work life. Oftentimes ambivalence is a hallmark of endings, a reaction that accompanies even manifestly happy occasions—marriage, the bestowal of honors or special recognition, and promotions—and accounts for a unique affective reaction that we have termed "bittersweetness." Denial and reversal may also be at work: we are asked to "celebrate the life" of the recently departed rather than to immerse ourselves in grief and despair; graduation, we are advised, isn't an ending but rather a "commencement," and so forth.

In virtually every culture throughout human history, the emotional significance imputed to endings has also led to the creation of rituals to mark their observance. In this sense the process typically referred to in dynamic psychotherapy as "termination" may be conceived as a farewell ritual marking the conclusion of a treatment experience for both client and therapist that cannot but reflect the influence of a greater culture of which it is part. At the same time, leave-taking in dynamic psychotherapy must also accomplish certain aims and objectives at variance with those defenses and fantasies whose aim is to disguise, distort, or subvert the reality of termination or of the treatment process that has preceded it.

When possible, psychodynamic practitioners prefer to plan the conclusion of treatment and, when indicated, post-termination follow-up. As treatment draws to a close, clients may experience a recrudescence of their symptoms and request additional sessions, they may "shut down" emotionally, so that they are going through the motions but no longer affectively involved in the work, or they may take flight into health, asking that treatment end abruptly. We begin with a review of various psychoanalytic conceptions of the termination process, ranging from classical to contemporary, and then consider the history of this concept in the social work literature. Two carefully developed clinical vignettes are then presented to illustrate the ending process in a dynamic treatment encounter. The first involves a thirty-two-year-old single man in weekly treatment who sought therapy because of difficulty in asserting himself with women and whose termination, initiated by the client, occurred after fourteen months. The second involves a middle-aged professional woman with a history of traumatic losses, initially seen once weekly, later on an intensive (twice-weekly) basis, and, still later, in three-times-weekly psychoanalysis. Her treatment ended by mutual agreement after four and a half years.

THE CONCEPT OF TERMINATION IN PSYCHOANALYSIS

The idea of termination as a phase in psychoanalytic treatment, preceded by a beginning and a middle phase, is evidently a relatively recent one, dating only to the postwar years (Novick 1990). Seldom was the topic of termination addressed in the literature before that time, nor does it appear to have been taught to analytic candidates in the standard sequence of required institute courses on psychoanalytic technique. And, to judge from historical evidence emerging from early case narratives, one cannot even make the assumption that the ending of an analysis occurred with any real forethought or planning. Muriel Gardiner, who trained as a psychoanalyst prior to WWII, described the termination of her analysis with Ruth Mack Brunswick, an early adherent of Freud's, as having taken place without warning at the end of her third year of analysis, just before the usual break for summer vacation.

> She and her analyst shook hands, as was customary, at the end of the last session before the summer vacation. Dr. Brunswick said goodbye in such a note of finality that Gardiner asked, "Do you mean it's the end? My analysis is over?"

Brunswick smiled and said yes. Gardiner wrote, "I was overjoyed. 'Oh how wonderful! I'm so happy' I exclaimed, then I remembered to thank her."

(Gardiner 1983, cited in Novick 1990)

Freud's first reference to termination, in his 1913 paper on technique, is metaphorical and allusive; he likens the practice of psychoanalysis to a game of chess in which "only the openings and end-games admit of an exhaustive systematic presentation" (Freud 1913:123). The remainder of the essay, however, is focused exclusively on the process of beginning an analysis, without further consideration as to what rules might guide its conclusion. It was not until 1937 that Freud returned in a more substantive way to the topic of termination, in his essay "Analysis Terminable and Interminable."

It is here that Freud advances the idea that a successful psychoanalysis rests on the satisfaction of three requirements. The first of these is that the client no longer suffers from the symptoms, "the anxieties and inhibitions" that plagued her or him at the time the analysis began. Second, there is good reason to believe the pathological processes that had caused the original symptoms are unlikely to be repeated inasmuch as "so much repressed material has been made conscious, so much that was unintelligible has been explained, and so much internal resistance conquered" (Freud 1937:219). Finally, were the analysis to continue, the likelihood is that no further change would occur; in effect, the analyst's influence has been so extensive and complete that additional treatment would be redundant. An important basis for this last criterion for analytic termination rests on the assumption that the analytic client has gradually acquired an ability to resolve conflicts or to perform additional exploratory work on his or her own, what Freud and others since have referred to as the "self-analytic function" (Kupers 1988).

Some authors have observed that Freud's 1937 essay is not fundamentally a technical guide to the process of termination (Bergmann 1997) and that it fails to frame termination as a distinct phase in the psychoanalytic treatment process. It has also been argued that Freud's paper furnishes no technical recommendations either on how analysts might initiate or successfully conclude such a phase, focusing instead on "the inherent limitations of the technique, the patient, and the analyst" (Novick 1997:145). In fact, the overarching theme of Freud's paper can legitimately be characterized as pessimistic in its view of the therapeutic efficacy of psychoanalysis, simultaneously revealing the dispassionate scholarship of the scientist and the reflective, philosophical perspective of the leader of a movement at the end of a long career.

It has been suggested that Freud's handling of termination issues, as these are revealed in several of his better-known cases, may have been complicated by his failure to remain sufficiently attentive to his clients' unresolved transference issues and feelings about termination (Kupers 1988). This seems particularly true in his treatment of Dora, although it must be noted that Freud himself recognized the problem in his commentary on the case (Freud 1905a). There has also been speculation that countertransference issues, some of them characterological, may have accounted for what one researcher has described as Freud's occasionally "disastrous" management of treatment terminations (Kupers 1988).

Nunberg, a disciple of Freud's and author of an early work on the theory and practice of psychoanalysis, in the early 1930s enumerated six criteria whose satisfaction he thought coextensive with the aims of successful termination. As summarized by Bergmann (1997), these were: 1. previously unconscious material becomes accessible to consciousness; 2. representations of the instinct enter consciousness, resulting in less tension for the id; 3. a strengthening of the ego occurs in light of the decreased need for deployment of ego energies on the defenses; 4. primary process thinking is replaced by secondary process thinking; 5. an enrichment of the ego occurs by virtue of the assimilation of repressed material; and 6. the superego's severity is mitigated.

Other conditions or criteria were also suggested, such as the full capacity for free association (Ferenczi 1955 [1927]), the client's capacity to take responsibility for insight (Rangell 1982), and the establishment of psychological mindedness/capacity for self-analysis (Panel 1969; Siegel 1982; Shane and Shane 1984). A number of writers have emphasized resolution of the transference neurosis (Bridger 1950; Buxbaum 1950; Ferenczi 1955 [1927]; Firestein 1978; Greenacre 1954, 1971 [1966]; Held 1955; Kramer 1967; Kubie 1968; Macalpine 1950; Novick 1976, 1982; Panel 1969; Rangell 1982; Stone 1961; and Ticho 1967), although others have suggested that complete resolution may be an illusory goal (e.g., Reich 1950).

The termination phase of the treatment process has a special significance that differentiates it from all that has preceded it, owing to the fact that the conclusion of treatment invariably represents a loss. The client's opportunity and capacity to mourn the separation from and loss of the therapist, and to experience and work through a range of affective reactions linked to this unique aspect of the therapeutic process, is deemed essential to the overall success of the therapeutic effort. In fact, some have suggested that failure to address and resolve various difficulties encountered during the termination phase, or to complete the process of termination, may influence the final resolution and outcome of an analytic or therapeutic process and thereby render such efforts incomplete (Glover 1955; Rangell 1966; Tyson 1996). In psychoanalysis as well as in longer-term and more intensive psychotherapies, there is also a greater likelihood that the therapist will become "a central figure around which derivatives of childhood wishes, fantasies, and yearnings are revived during treatment" (Tyson 1996:503). In consequence, as treatment moves closer to termination, these conflict-laden childhood wishes and fantasies and the affective reactions associated with them are increasingly likely to be reawakened. Evidently, such wishes may have their origin in any developmental epoch or experience, although the termination process frequently seems to reactivate those unresolved wishes and conflicts associated with separation-individuation as well as with the oedipal period and adolescence (Tyson 1996).

Separation-individuation issues may arise at any time in the course of psychotherapy or analysis: the therapist's or client's illness, vacations, cancellations, and even missed appointments furnish a basis for the reevocation of feelings of helplessness, vulnerability, and other reactions associated with object loss. Yet termination carries with it the inescapable reality that the treatment relationship will now finally end. As a result, archaic fantasies and powerful affects, heretofore submerged, masked, or otherwise defended against, may rise to the surface in an undisguised and potent form (Tyson 1996). Although such reactions might occur more commonly in psychoanalysis, where a focus on the transference relationship and associated issues is an ongoing feature of the clinical work, this is by no means invariantly true. Consider the following brief clinical example:

George, a forty-two-year-old man of Polish Catholic ancestry, was seen on a once-weekly basis for treatment of work-related stress. In recounting his childhood as the oldest in a sibship of six, George joked that he could never recall a time "when there wasn't a rugrat around with a runny nose or a stinky diaper." George's mother became pregnant again shortly after his birth, but miscarried late in her first trimester. When several months later she again became pregnant, her obstetrician strongly advised bed rest beginning in the first trimester of this her third pregnancy in fewer than sixteen months. One consequence of his mother's condition was a pronounced disruption in the mother-child relationship. Although George later extracted some pleasure from serving as his mother's "sergeant at arms," he had few opportunities in infancy and early childhood to enjoy his mother's undivided attention. George had never felt especially close to his father, a telephone lineman who had often worked overtime to supplement the family income. Both of his parents, George also revealed, had died some years before.

George was seen at an outpatient mental health clinic by a female clinician in her early thirties to whom he soon became very attached. His therapy seemed to make a difference in work relationships, particularly with his female supervisor, and George appeared to make impressive treatment gains over a period of nine months. At that point his therapist informed him that she would be leaving the clinic in two and a half months' time, in order to pursue doctoral training out of state. Although taken by surprise, George quickly regained his equilibrium and congratulated his therapist. Therapist and client agreed to continue meeting until just before the therapist planned on leaving the agency. Significantly, although George had reported having occasional sexual thoughts about his therapist, whom he found very attractive, these fantasies were not central to the transference relationship that evolved in his treatment, which seemed to organize more along mirroring lines. George was rarely late to his appointments and even attended once when he was sick, despite having a fever of 101 degrees. He often expressed how much he looked forward to his appointments, what a good listener his therapist was, and how comfortable he felt in her "cozy little office." Not long after his therapist's announcement, however, he began to arrive late and then missed an appointment without canceling. Initially resistant to exploring his reaction to the impending termination, George minimized any unconscious meaning but then remarked that he didn't "really feel the need to see this out to the bitter end." Following her intuitions, his therapist gently persisted in exploring the dramatic alteration in George's experience of his therapy. George subsequently revealed his great disappointment with the therapist, whose unilateral decision to end his treatment had shocked and angered him. "I kept thinking, here we have this nice little meeting time for just the two of us, and you have to spoil it all by leaving," George finally confessed. It seemed unfair, although he also was ashamed that he was behaving in such a childish way, feeling that he should just "get over it." These thoughts and affective responses then led to further revelations about his mother's physical and emotional absences, his younger siblings' unceasing demands for her attention, and the sense that he had been "cheated" then much as he felt he was now being deprived by his therapist's decision.

Contemporary theorists have noted that it may be useful to consider the termination process with respect to the psychological challenges it poses for clients. These include the reworking and synthesis of previously acquired insights (Ekstein 1965; Tyson 1996) that can then become a basis for effective and enduring change (Greenson 1967; Tyson 1996). As noted earlier, old symptoms may resurface, occasionally to a magnitude that is distressing for both client and therapist. In many instances such problems are short-lived. When regressions do occur, and often they possess a transferential cast, they are usually counterbalanced by a treatment alliance that by the termination phase is well-developed and operating at peak efficiency (Ticho 1972; Tyson 1996).

However, this is not always the case. At times, clients will insist that there has been very little if any improvement in their condition or remediation for the problems for which treatment had originally been sought. The clinician faced with this challenge may decide on one of several courses of therapeutic action. One option would be to extend the date of closure, to allow for sufficient time to determine whether the client's distress is more directly a function of the process of termination rather than representing a more substantive complaint about overall therapeutic efficacy. A second possibility, should the clinician be disinclined to alter the termination date, would be to ask the client to contact the therapist for a post-termination interview after a period of a few months, at which time the client's current adaptation and additional need for therapy might be assessed.[1] Should the client desire further treatment, this might be furnished either by the clinician, himself or by a colleague the therapist has recommended. A third option, one far less likely either to assuage the client's anxiety or the therapist's guilt over treatment apparently having held such limited value for the client, is to "stay the course." The clinician, acknowledging that the client's problems have not been solved, nevertheless expresses confidence that the client is far better equipped than she or he was at the beginning of therapy to struggle with these same issues. To the extent that the therapist is able to adduce support for such claims by citing the client's earlier treatment successes, insights, and new adaptations, this argument is somewhat strengthened. Individual circumstances, of course, may call for completely different responses. It is always sensible to err on the side of caution when the client's distress involves severe regression, a loss of impulse control, or suicidal thoughts, for example. In such crises, which are atypical and likely reflect significant miscalculations on the therapist's part, preserving the integrity of the termination process becomes a moot point.

Insofar as termination may evoke powerful anxiety as well as other strong affects, equally strong defenses may also become activated. The client's denial of the significance of the relationship with the therapist may propel him or her toward new love interests, a change in employment, or even lead to a decision to become pregnant. In such cases the client unconsciously seeks alternate sources of gratification to compensate for the anticipated loss of the therapist (Reich 1950). Although denial of the loss and avoidance of the mourning process is clearly evident in these cases, Tyson suggests that such displacements also "betray complex compromise formations involving the expression of derivatives from" preoedipal, oedipal, and adolescent conflicts that have been reactivated during the termination (Tyson 1996). Other defensive maneuvers include the client's fantasy of becoming friends with the therapist after the therapy has been concluded, a desire to abridge the termination process by leaving treatment as soon as the topic of termination is broached, or an inability to set a specific termination date (Tyson 1996; Novick 1982; Dewald 1982).

Termination is, of course, an intersubjective reality rather than one existing solely within the province of the client. We have focused for the most part on issues of separation and loss from the client's perspective, although the therapist too must be able to relinquish any emotional attachments to the client and mourn the loss of the relationship. The therapist's discomfort with termination, which typically contains a countertransferential meaning, may prolong the treatment process unnecessarily (Tyson 1996). Furthermore, it may signal to a client who is otherwise inclined to bring treatment to closure that the therapist is somewhat less confident of the client's readiness for termination.

A related question is of course who actually makes the determination that treatment should be brought to closure. In an earlier generation psychoanalysts made such decisions more or less unilaterally, as the earlier example of Muriel Gardiner's analysis with Ruth Mack Brunswick clearly illustrates. Ferenczi and Rank (1925) and Glover (1955) were among the exponents of this position, which may have been time and culture bound, reflecting a somewhat more authoritarian view of the therapeutic process. Many contemporary analysts would now take exception to such a perspective, instead believing clients to be better equipped to make this determination as they become healthier and able to function with relative freedom from neurotic needs or conflicts (e.g., Ticho 1972; Kris 1982).

The question whether or not the clinician's technique should be altered during the termination process formed the basis of a protracted debate in the psychoanalytic literature. Some have proposed variations in the frequency of meetings to "wean" clients gradually from the consulting room, or taking active steps to achieve dissolution of the transference relationship (e.g., self-revelations on the therapist's part), in addition to other modifications in therapeutic technique (Held 1955; Saul 1958; Stone 1961). Others have argued it is essential that there be no departure from the usual therapeutic modus operandi, a position for which there may now be considerable unanimity among analytic practitioners (Tyson 1996). The decision not to deviate from one's usual clinical approach to a client may have important ramifications, as the following brief vignette illustrates.

Rebecca, an attractive Jewish woman in her late thirties, sought therapy because of chronic interpersonal difficulties encountered both at work and in her personal relationships. A transplanted New Yorker, she had originally left the East Coast some ten years earlier to attend graduate school in Madison, Wisconsin. Rebecca complained that people didn't understand her, that they were unaccustomed to her directness and assertiveness, and that this was probably the cause of her interpersonal problems. She had been in a number of short-lived relationships with men, the most recent of which ended in a "huge confrontation" when her boyfriend accused her, unjustly she thought, of being too aggressive in a social situation. Gradually she began to express dissatisfaction with her therapist. At first she would simply disagree with his comments, but she became increasingly critical, to the point of ridiculing what he had said. Attempts to point out the similarities between what Rebecca seemed to be reenacting in her therapy and the pattern of interpersonal problems she reported on the outside were largely unproductive. After eight months of once-weekly treatment, Rebecca announced to the therapist that she was "finished" with therapy, had found him to be unhelpful, and wished to terminate. The therapist, who was aware of experiencing some relief at the prospect of not having to continue to meet with this difficult client, nevertheless suggested that they get together for at least four or five additional interviews. He believed that these sessions were necessary to explore more completely the client's experience of the therapy and her insistence on bringing the treatment to unilateral termination. True to form, the client rejected this recommendation, consenting only to a final interview. During this last meeting Rebecca almost continuously berated the therapist for his inadequacies and for ruining her therapy. Near the end of this hour, she stopped abruptly and expressed surprise that the therapist seemed largely unperturbed by her endless, if (in her view) fully justified, criticisms. Why hadn't he finally put aside all of that "professional abstinence stuff, and become more candid and real" with her? Why hadn't he defended himself? Although the therapist was acutely aware of an equally strong, aggressive counterreaction induced in him by the client's provocations, he made a conscious effort not to retaliate, in the belief that this was precisely what his client both expected and dreaded. Instead, he told the client that he saw no reason to deviate from his customary way of relating to her simply by virtue of this being their last session. He also observed that she seemed to want him to retaliate and wondered whether such a response might furnish her with additional evidence of the therapist's incompetence or, worse, a lapse in professionalism. Perhaps needless to say, the client rejected this idea completely, although she seemed somewhat calmer as the session drew to a close. At the end of the hour the client and therapist shook hands, and the therapist wished her well.

Several years later the therapist and client met by chance at a large social gathering. The client, upon recognizing the therapist, approached him privately and embraced him warmly. She then told him that she had always marveled at the self-restraint he had shown in their termination session and wanted to thank him for it. Although at the time she had dismissed the value of their work, she had later reconsidered some of the therapist's ideas and believed this process would not have been possible had the therapist simply responded to her provocations in kind. Furthermore, she had started in treatment once again and felt she was making good progress.

In our discussion of termination we have focused largely on the arousal of unpleasant affects and the defensive reactions they may initiate. Several authors, however, have noted that other, fundamentally pleasurable affects such as relief, joy, and the feeling of emancipation are also linked to the termination phase (Panel 1975; Loewald 1962; Tyson 1996). A client's awareness of a greater capacity for intimacy, enhanced sense of effectance or mastery, or even the greater ability to tolerate guilt and to shoulder personal responsibility all carry a positive valence. As such, they may exert a mitigating influence over more negatively valenced affects stemming from the experience of separation and loss (Tyson 1996).

SOCIAL WORK PERSPECTIVES ON TERMINATION

Among social work theorists, representatives of the functionalist school may have been the first to give careful consideration to the concept of termination. This was undoubtedly due in good measure to the early influence of Otto Rank on his colleagues at the University of Pennsylvania School of Social Work during the 1930s. Rank, as we noted in part 1, had placed considerable emphasis on the psychological meaning of separation, linking a range of human experiences to what he considered to be the prototypical trauma—that of birth. This position appears to have been gradually incorporated into the functionalist view of both clinical process and phases of treatment. Smalley observed that although a great deal of attention had been paid to beginnings—intake procedures, the process of getting started, and the like—social work theorists seemed to have neglected endings, "which have their own feeling and quality. Just as beginnings are psychologically imbued with the feelings of birth, so endings are imbued in varying proportion and degree with the feeling of death—of separation" (1970:102). The historical neglect of the theme of termination in the clinical social work literature has been noted by others as well (e.g., Fox, Nelson, and Bolman 1969; Levinson 1977; Strean 1978).

Perlman, whose problem-solving approach was premised on the idea that "life is an ongoing, problem-encountering, problem-solving process" (Perlman 1970:139), focused more on the client's overall adaptation and the fulfillment of short-term goals than on the psychological meaning of termination or its clinical management. Other more contemporary social work authors have devoted far greater attention to the process and technical management of termination (e.g., Fortune 1985; Shulman 1992). Such techniques as "booster interviews," or follow-up sessions, which are "included as an integral part of practice with all clients," have also been advocated (Hepworth, Rooney, and Larsen 1997:614), although, as noted earlier, such practices may be of questionable value for particular clients. Some social work authors have, in fact, questioned the assumption that termination necessarily involves a process of mourning. They suggest that the strongest reactions of many clients to termination were positive, "including affect (a sense of pride, accomplishment, and independence)" and their evaluation of the treatment experience (Fortune 1987; Fortune, Pearlingi, and Rochelle 1992, cited in Woods and Hollis 2000). It is noteworthy, however, that the research on which these findings are based also revealed the reactions of clients to vary "depending on who made the termination decision, on the treatment outcome, and on the difficulty of terminating" (Fortune, Pearlingi, and Rochelle 1992:171).

CLINICAL CASE ILLUSTRATION 9.1: "DOUGLAS"

Douglas, an unmarried, thirty-two-year-old Catholic man residing with his mother, initially sought therapy at an out-patient mental health clinic because of difficulty asserting himself with women and fears that his failure to commit to a heterosexual relationship might indicate either homosexuality or perhaps some sort of gender identity disorder. Soft-spoken and meticulously attentive to detail, he was employed full-time as a computer software analyst for a large corporation. Douglas had previously participated in several groups, including a "men's" group, although he had not previously been in individual treatment. Although his parents had planned on having other children, within a few years of Douglas's birth his mother developed uterine cancer and was forced to undergo a complete hysterectomy. While her physical recovery from the cancer surgery was good, her psychological health seemed to deteriorate over time. There were few memories of his father during this period, and his mother's psychological problems prevented her from offering attentive, attuned care to Douglas. We surmised that he must have felt very lonely, a view that seemed to echo in Douglas's earliest memory at age three of being alone in his crib, trying either to "break out" or attract the attention of the family dog. When Douglas entered the first grade, his mother suffered the first of several psychotic breaks, ultimately being diagnosed with schizophrenia. During much of the next eight years, he lived on and off with his maternal aunt and her family. In the first hour Douglas also mentioned that his relationship with his father had always been a "tense" one and that his father had kicked him out of the house following an argument shortly after his seventeenth birthday. Although he lived on his own for over seven years, Douglas moved back into the family home to live with his mother in his mid-twenties after his father died somewhat unexpectedly following a short illness.

Therapy was initiated on a once-weekly basis. Over the next several months a picture of significant family pathology began to emerge. Douglas's mother had one brother who committed suicide in his early twenties, another who had also been diagnosed as schizophrenic. Douglas remembered being told that his father had "accidentally" broken both his arms lifting him out of his crib when he was fourteen months old. Although he had never questioned this explanation before, he felt a growing uncertainty now. Might this have been physical abuse rather than an accident, as his parents had always claimed? It then emerged that his father frequently criticized him, took virtually no interest in his accomplishments at school, and had actually thrown him out of the house at least twice before the incident that occurred when he was seventeen. His father had even threatened on several occasions to kill him, putting an adolescent Douglas on notice that "the day your mother dies, that's the day I shoot you." Douglas was terrified of his father but also wondered in therapy what he may have done to warrant his father's continuous insults, criticisms, and threats. When he finally returned to his parents' home immediately after his father's death, Douglas recalled that there were a number of relatives gathered in the living room. He mentioned "feeling embarrassed that I was crying in front of all my relatives." Feeling rather puzzled, I said, "But your father had just died," to which Douglas responded, "Yes, but I'm not sure I was crying because I felt sad. . . . I cried because I felt relieved. I knew that he couldn't kill me anymore." As deeply injurious as these early experiences and the powerful reactions they induced in Douglas appeared to have been, he exercised great vigilance over his characterization of his father and of his feelings toward him. His descriptions of even the most reprehensible acts were muted and downplayed, with whatever additional protection such defenses as isolation, reaction-formation, ambivalence, and denial might confer in his efforts to bar such strong feelings from consciousness.

Other memories then began to resurface. Douglas recalled that when he was very young his father had bathed him, and once Douglas had inadvertently become sexually aroused as his father dried off his genitals. In retrospect he found this to be both confusing and anxiety arousing. On the one hand, these intimate experiences were among very few where Douglas felt as though his father loved him, where he was the exclusive focus of his father's attention. On the other hand, it disturbed him greatly that he might experience sexual arousal on such an occasion. Could this be evidence that, indeed, something was wrong with him? Why would a boy have such feelings for his father? Over several sessions we explored the possible meanings this memory might hold for Douglas as well as its transference implications. Perhaps his father had intentionally aroused Douglas, although the likelihood of this representing an act of incest seemed small inasmuch as he had no recollection of similar experiences from childhood. I thought it somewhat more likely that Douglas, who was chronically understimulated because of the unresponsive parental milieu in which he was raised, had no way of modulating the overwhelming excitement he felt when his father, who was alternately distant and aggressive, behaved lovingly toward him. Suddenly and inexplicably, he became the sole object of father's attention and care, which aroused both intense pleasure and anxiety. At about this time Douglas also revealed having masturbated to a fantasy in which he is nude and another man holds him tenderly. The allusion to his experience with his father seemed fairly transparent to us both. I suggested that within the transference relationship I might have come to represent these aspects of his father to Douglas. Therapy offered him a certain intimacy that he had sought without notable success in relationships with women and with both his parents as well as other extended family members. However, the prospect of intimacy with me, even within the structure of our therapeutic relationship, may have stimulated powerful homoerotic feelings against which Douglas felt the need to defend himself. We were then able to identify a pattern that had emerged: it was precisely following those sessions in which Douglas felt most understood that he would begin to complain of the futility of "dredging up material from the past." Perhaps it was not only his panicked reaction to the sensual feelings evoked by his transference fantasies but also the very real prospect that I might behave as his father had, abandoning him or, perhaps even worse, behaving in a critical and rejecting way.

Another major theme in Douglas's treatment had to do with his efforts to modulate his involvement with his mother, with whom he resided. Douglas's mother, who was fifty-eight years old at the time he entered treatment, was extremely dependent on him, though within the context of this mother-son relationship his own psychological needs seemed nearly as prominent. At the same time, he deeply resented his mother's gratuitous advice and assumptions, which were often markedly colored by her own strongly held, quasi-delusional beliefs. In one particularly unsettling discussion between the two, his mother had asserted to Douglas that same-sex relationships were invariably more successful than heterosexual relationships, advancing the rather outrageous claim that incontrovertible proof of this could be found in the Scriptures. Although his first inclination was to disagree with her, he found himself paralyzed by his own ambivalence as well as his fear that he might somehow injure her by taking exception to something she had said. He also wondered momentarily whether or not to disclose to her that he himself might be either gay or bisexual, while ultimately deciding against it. Such incidents, in a more general way, added to his worries that he might be forever trapped in this unfulfilling and isolating symbiosis with his mother and, several months into treatment, Douglas began to talk seriously of his desire to move out and become independent of his mother.

The same ambivalence seemed to prevent Douglas from making any sort of lasting commitment to his then girlfriend Jenny, an office worker in her late twenties whose interest in Douglas evidently far exceeded his affection for her. In fact, although they had dated for well over two years, Douglas had seemed more comfortable limiting their contact to one date each week, a condition that his girlfriend had thus far been willing to accept. After six months of therapy, Douglas revealed that he and Jenny had never attempted sexual intercourse, nor even discussed the possibility, and, on those rare occasions when there was anything resembling intimate contact between them, both kept their clothes on. From time to time Jenny would introduce the idea that the two might intensify their involvement. Since Douglas expressed such conflict over the prospect, however, she would quickly apologize and turn to other topics. It is difficult to speculate as to what motives may have influenced Jenny to remain in what cannot have been a very satisfying relationship for her, though Douglas and I gradually identified several factors that seemed to explain his own reactions. In the first place, a deeper commitment to his girlfriend would constitute a betrayal of his mother, whose needs he had placed above everyone else's—his own included—for many years. A more frankly sexual relationship would also constitute a test of his masculinity and heterosexual prowess, which, for two reasons, further troubled him. First, he might be found wanting, thereby confirming his greatest fears about being "unmanly," or incapable of a heterosexual relationship, or, for a very different reason, given such an opportunity, he might behave as his father did, in an insensitive, aggressive, or brutish manner. Finally, there was always the prospect that Jenny would excite him, as his father had done, only to abandon him emotionally. Douglas's description of several previous relationships with women suggested a similar pattern. The sole exception was a professional relationship he had maintained over a period of several years with a masseuse named Janika who was trained in the Reiki method. In this relationship the "conditions of safety" for experiencing erotic pleasure could be satisfied. Since the relationship was a professional one, a firm boundary appeared to exist; moreover, he could decide to see her as often or as infrequently as he wished; finally, he was not asked to perform but simply to be the recipient of Janika's gentle ministrations. The image of Douglas, unclothed, on the massage table certainly also suggested the devoted and loving care of a parent doting on a small child. The massage was nonsexual in nature, although Douglas noted that he would occasionally have an erection during his sessions, which, to his relief, Janika never mentioned explicitly. He fantasized about her frequently.

After nearly twelve months of treatment, Douglas had made genuine progress in overcoming his ambivalence about moving out of his mother's home and in his relationship with Jenny and had experimented with ways of asserting himself without feeling overly aggressive. He occasionally fantasized about having sex with men, though this seemed almost invariably to follow disappointing experiences with Jenny. He believed that therapy had furnished him with a belated opportunity to work through the emotional quagmire resulting from his father's unexpected death years earlier. Although his essential obsessive-compulsive character remained unchanged, there was compelling evidence of his growing capacity to use defenses more adaptively and with greater flexibility. Clearly, additional work lay ahead, but, upon reaching the one-year mark, Douglas announced his intention to conclude his treatment.

DOUGLAS: I have thought about this quite a bit, and I think that I should stop coming in for therapy. I feel like I have accomplished a lot, and it seems like a good time to stop. Yes, I think it's time to stop coming in.

THER: Well, of course this isn't the first time you've talked about ending treatment. I wonder if you've had other thoughts that might give us a better idea about the timing of your decision to end therapy now.

DOUGLAS: Well, I'm not sure, really, but I'm very definite about wanting to stop now. Actually, I was thinking that this could be the last visit.

THER: Well, I will certainly respect your decision to bring your therapy to an end. However, I think it might be helpful for us to give the idea of termination a bit more time, since endings have just as much importance as any other part of therapy. After all, we haven't really rushed through any other phase of your treatment—why begin now? I'm also thinking that endings sometimes give us a valuable opportunity to discuss things that are left over from earlier in treatment, to take stock of the work we've accomplished, and talk about life after therapy. I would suggest that we do this in a more leisurely way, say over seven or eight additional meetings.

DOUGLAS: That sounds like too many, although I suppose I would be willing to meet at least a couple more times (*long pause*).

THER: You seem to be mulling something over. Can you say what it is you're feeling or thinking about?

DOUGLAS: Well, I'm feeling upset. I've found myself being too aggressive with Jenny, and I said something last week to the man who brings in the bottled water to the office . . . that was too sharp. I surprised myself, actually, by speaking so sharply to him.

THER: What happened exactly with the bottled water man?

DOUGLAS: Nothing, really. It wasn't a big deal, but he was being really noisy with the empties, and I couldn't concentrate in my office. I walked out and told him he needed to try and be quieter.

THER: It sounds to me as though you were being assertive, but what you've described doesn't sound especially harsh.

DOUGLAS: (*In a flash of anger*) I think you are talking down to me, and . . . you sound smug.

THER: (*Slightly surprised*) you know . . . I'm not really aware of behaving any differently than usual toward you. . . . However, your reaction does remind me of the way you've described your father—his condescension and smugness—and makes me wonder if there might not be a transference aspect to it.

DOUGLAS: I don't understand. How would what I said be transference?

THER: Well, a few moments before you reacted to my comments about assertion, we were talking about your decision to end your therapy. I think that this is a very big decision for you, since it represents your taking a stand and being very clear about what you want—not what I want or anyone else might want for you. So you weren't asking my advice; you were telling me what you had decided on your own.

DOUGLAS: (*Somewhat more calmly*) I guess I was, now that you mention it. That's different; it does feel different (*pause*). I probably wouldn't have been able to do this earlier; no, I'm sure I wouldn't have said this. Maybe I'd have just stopped coming in, like I did with the men's group.

THER: Yes, this seems to have been the old pattern for handling differences of opinion. But I think there's another element as well. In your relationship with your father, you were not only discouraged for thinking independently or making decisions for yourself, but there might also be severe consequences. And here you were, telling me that you don't need me anymore, probably thinking in the back of your head that I am going to be furious with you.

DOUGLAS: (*Laughing out loud*) yes, I suppose that I was bracing myself for something along those lines. But, I don't really understand why I got angry with you then and accused you of something you didn't even do.

THER: Let's think about that for a moment.

DOUGLAS: (*After a moment's silence*) could it have been that I was, I don't know, attacking you because I was still expecting you to be mad about my wanting to end therapy?

THER: I think that's right on target. The best defense is a good offense. But, it's also true that, as you've become more assertive in social situations, this new behavior is at times disconcerting. So, I guess in that respect, our work has complicated your life somewhat.

DOUGLAS: Sometimes, it just feels like it'd be easier if things would go back to the way they were.

THER: The choice is yours.

DOUGLAS: Yeah, I know (*reflecting momentarily*). I don't *really* want things to go back to the way they used to be (*pause*). How many sessions did you say we should meet for before I end?

THER: I was thinking seven or eight.

DOUGLAS: OK, why don't we meet seven more times.

THER: Agreed.

DISCUSSION

In spite of the fact that I was not in accord with Douglas's decision to terminate therapy, perhaps it was unrealistic for me to have anticipated a different kind of ending. Owing to his history, replete as it was with painful separations, maternal schizophrenia, paternal abuse, and profound concerns about the loss of autonomy, this was one threshold that Douglas may well have needed to cross on his own. Interestingly, the termination phase of Douglas's therapy proved to be an especially fertile one in his treatment overall. For the most part freed of his unconscious fear that I would force him into a submissive position where I made the final determination of his readiness to terminate, he became far more reflective, and new material emerged. In the very next hour he spoke of feeling ambivalence in agreeing to accompany his mother on her biannual visit to the cemetery where her husband was buried, a reaction of which he had not previously been aware. Being at his father's gravesite represented an accommodation to his mother's wishes, but it was for him an empty ritual dictated solely by his mother's interpretation of Catholic dogma. Furthermore, it always made him feel worse, not better, and he now actively questioned whether it made sense to continue to subject himself to this unnecessary pain. He began to speak spontaneously of another loss, this one involving a young woman colleague at his office, of whom he had been very fond, who accepted employment out of state. He was "heartbroken" when she left and spoke with deep longing of this kind person who had listened so attentively to his personal anecdotes and stories as well as offering him valuable advice.

In subsequent meetings Douglas spoke for the first time about his historical difficulty, back in high school, in allowing himself to feel pride in his accomplishments as a swimmer and cross-country runner. Because these successes brought him notice from some who, out of their own envy, criticized him or even ridiculed him, he decided long ago that it was simply easier "not to shine" or dominate in social interactions. I interpreted to Douglas that much of this difficulty seemed to have arisen as a result of his father's disdainful attitude toward him as well as his intolerance of Douglas's boyish aggressiveness. This led to further discussion of the separation-individuation theme and Douglas's struggles to find his own voice when others, such as his mother, her sister, or her friends make strong suggestions to him about his career, getting married, and so forth.

DOUGLAS: My Uncle Dave died last week, and we had the wake yesterday. I saw my aunt there, and she was pretty sad. But then she comes up to me and says something about how she's hopeful that I'll follow her advice and call things off with Jenny. Other people who were present seemed to disagree . . . but I didn't want to differ with her, didn't want to cross her.

THER: How come?

DOUGLAS: Well, I suppose because her husband had just died, and I didn't want her to disapprove.

THER: How did it feel *not* to disagree with her?

DOUGLAS: Not good. I think that it's really up to me to decide if and when I want to break up with Jenny. It's really *my* business.

THER: Yes, I agree with you. It does remind me, however, that you risked my disapproval in telling me that you'd decided to end your treatment.

And yet, I was supportive of your decision. How do you know that your aunt is going to be so critical and unforgiving?

DOUGLAS: I guess I don't, really. I've just always been this way with her (*pause*). I suppose she might even have some respect for me for taking a real stand—you know, a position that's different from hers.

THER: It's always a possibility, though I suppose you'll never know until you give it a try.

DOUGLAS: But, suppose she *is* disappointed or angry.

THER: Then you'd need to ask yourself if that seems like a reasonable response. Are you disappointed or angry when people don't follow your advice?

DOUGLAS: No, not usually. . . . You know, I feel like I have a better idea now what to do.

The termination process, as it often does, seemed to throw several of the most important themes from earlier in treatment into sharper relief. In preparing to bid me farewell, Douglas's life-long struggle to achieve psychological separation from his mother and her family and his efforts finally to admit to the tremendous disappointment and rage he felt in relation to his father seemed to rise to the surface. He had finally acknowledged how strong his need for approval was, but, having done so, seemed interested in achieving a better balance with his desire to be true to himself. Douglas's voice, however small—and still he seemed more like a timid adolescent than a thirty-two-year-old adult—had emerged during these final eight hours. In our last meeting he expressed gratitude not only for the work we had accomplished together during fourteen months of once-weekly treatment but specifically because I had been consistent in giving him the message that his self-knowledge was reliable and that this extended to the termination process as well.

CLINICAL CASE ILLUSTRATION 9.2: "JODY"

Jody, a Caucasian, forty-one-year-old married mother of three employed part-time as the office manager of a general medical practice in a suburb of Boston, was referred by a colleague four weeks following the unexpected death of her younger sister, Katherine. Although she seemed uncertain about entering treatment, Jody indicated that she had been struggling with a great deal of guilt over her sister's death and, after contacting her former therapist, decided it might be helpful to talk to someone. Raised in a semipracticing German Catholic family, Jody was the eldest in a sibship of four, although only she and a thirty-five-year-old younger brother, Jason, survived. Several years before Katherine's death, another brother had succumbed to a cerebrovascular accident. Jody's sixty-three-year-old father, who suffered from diverticulitis and congestive heart failure, had recently been diagnosed with metastatic oral cancer. Her husband, Jeb, a construction supervisor, was forty-eight years old. Jody had been twice married and divorced prior to meeting Jeb, whom she had married some fifteen years earlier. Joshua, nineteen, was her oldest son by a previous marriage; Bobby, thirteen, and Jimmy, eight, were born after she and Jeb married. Two years after Bobby's birth, Jody again became pregnant, but was not able to carry the pregnancy to term. Her tiny baby girl, born nearly two and a half months premature, was unable to survive and died within twenty-six hours of delivery. At the time Jody had been "heartbroken" over this loss, for which she strongly believed she bore at least partial responsibility, having indulged in "wild sex" with her husband the evening before her waters broke and the contractions began.

Jeb, who had suffered a moderately serious heart attack several years earlier, often worked long hours in his supervisory position. He also drank excessively on occasion, placing himself at considerable risk for another, possibly fatal, heart attack. Jody believed that his pattern of drinking and denial strongly suggested early-stage alcoholism, a perspective that I shared. Although an improvement over her earlier relationships with men, Jody described her marriage to Jeb as "cold," detailing a long history of frustration and disappointments. He had little to offer her in the way of psychological support and often withdrew from family life, leaving Jody to raise their three children and manage the household affairs on her own. Although often enraged at her husband for his abdication of his parental role, Jody seemed unconvinced that she herself was doing a good job of parenting and commented early in her treatment that her kids "might do just as well without her." Moreover, Jody was critical of her own motives, furnishing as an illustration the fact that she had married Jeb "for his money," making her nothing less than a "whore." In fact, she often followed criticisms of Jeb or her parents with such intropunitive comments, lest I or others be left with the impression that she thought herself any better than anyone else. If Jeb was a poor husband and father, so this argument seemed to go, perhaps Jody didn't really deserve any better. Jody had demonstrated, by the same token, that she had the ability to overcome such masochism and ambivalence, which hinted at the health inside her. Hoping to escape the rigid confines of the role she had been cast in for so many years, Jody had taken two graduate-level courses as a nondegree student in counseling psychology. She found this experience liberating but was also conflicted over whether it would be realistic for her to enroll formally in such a graduate program.

Jody and I met by mutual agreement on a once-weekly basis for a period of ten months. During this time she complained of her frustration in never being able to aspire to "certain things because I don't have a dick between my legs." She confessed that she often felt hatred and contempt for her husband and, in fact, had very little use for men in general, though beneath such hostile and depreciating remarks appeared to dwell a good deal of envy. In her sexual relations with Jeb, she often felt dehumanized, that sex was primarily in the service of her husband's needs.

Jody began having sex when she was fourteen years old with her mother's blessing, or so it seemed. Jody's mother actually introduced her to a married man in his mid-twenties, with whom she subsequently became sexually involved, and permitted her to sleep in an isolated bedroom in the family home where she might enjoy some privacy from her younger siblings when "entertaining" boyfriends. Furthermore, Jody could come and go as she pleased from the time she was in her mid-teens. She often stayed out all night and began to use a variety of drugs, including cocaine. Jody's father, who was detached, didn't seem to be aware of the seriousness of his daughter's behavior and her mother "took a sort of vicarious thrill" in what she was doing. Once, at age fifteen, she was forced into having sex with an "older guy," a man perhaps twenty years older than she whom she had originally believed to be trustworthy. We considered the possibility that Jody's liaisons with older men may well have been an effort to compensate for what was missing in her relationship with her father or perhaps a disguised effort to force him into action. Unfortunately, if the latter was her unconscious intent, it proved largely ineffective. Jody continued on a downhill course involving drugs and sex. She witnessed the death of a young male friend whose lifeless body was dumped by dope addicts in front of a local hospital after he succumbed to a drug overdose and the near death of a very close girlfriend, also from an overdose. Increasingly out of control at home, she spent several weeks in juvenile detention. This, she reported, was a terrible experience, although it did not immediately convince her to abandon her self-destructive lifestyle. When, some years later, her younger sister became heavily involved in drug use, Jody blamed herself, ultimately believing that she bore responsibility for her sister's demise. Her younger brother, Dan, had also experimented heavily with alcohol and drugs and eventually began to abuse intravenous drugs. Once again Jody felt she was to blame, since Dan looked up to her and "must have concluded that whatever I was doing was cool." Although the doctors did not attribute Dan's death to his drug use, Jody felt that his short life might have been far better had he not followed her lead.

We had just completed ten months of weekly treatment when a mind-numbing catastrophe occurred. Jody's oldest son, Joshua, was out driving with several friends late one night when the car in which he was a passenger collided at an intersection with another vehicle that had run a red light. Police estimated that the other vehicle was traveling in excess of forty miles per hour. Joshua, riding in the front seat without a seat belt, was thrown from the car and struck a light pole. He died instantly from massive head trauma, as did the driver; another friend was seriously injured. Investigators at the scene determined that the driver of the second vehicle, who was not seriously injured, was legally intoxicated, and he was later convicted and sentenced to prison. Postmortem tests revealed that both Joshua and the driver of the car in which he had been riding apparently had also been drinking, although neither beyond the legal limit. Jody was devastated. Soon after, her husband began to drink more heavily, and both of her surviving sons developed emotional and academic difficulties.

With little resistance on Jody's part, I suggested that we increase the frequency of her appointments to two times a week. During the next year Jody's treatment focused on the work of mourning. Unable to see Joshua's death as a case of being in the wrong place at the wrong time, which I believed to be the only reasonable explanation, Jody instead experienced overwhelming guilt, believing once again that she bore final responsibility for yet another family tragedy. Every so often the profound anger she felt toward Joshua would come to the surface, although this was so unbearably painful that it usually caused her to redouble her self-directed criticisms. Jody never became acutely suicidal, although at one juncture, some five months after the accident, she took a double dose of codeine cough syrup "in order to feel closer to Joshua and Katherine." This action, which Jody did not repeat, was only moderately successful. Drugs, she reported with almost palpable resignation, offered neither an avenue of escape from her nearly unremitting pain nor the subjective gratification they had for her some years earlier.

As Jody began to emerge from this period of intensive mourning, I introduced the possibility of further intensifying her treatment through psychoanalysis. Jody was highly motivated, demonstrated a good potential for insight based on the work we had already completed, and seemed intrigued at the prospect of entering psychoanalytic treatment. By this time she had also applied for formal admission to the graduate program in counseling psychology and believed that psychoanalytic treatment would be of benefit not only to her personally but also in her future work as a clinician. We subsequently agreed to meet on a three-times-weekly basis, a regimen that continued for the most part without variation until her analysis was brought to closure some thirty months later.

The analytic work seemed to focus on several interrelated themes. Jody spoke often of Joshua and of her deceased sister, although now with an admixture of guilt and anger. Though it was painful, she was able to acknowledge that she and Katherine were not alike. She had been stronger than Katherine and had stopped using drugs in early adulthood, although Katherine was unable to overcome her drug habit, finally succumbing to an overdose at the age of thirty-three. After Katherine's death Jody's parents had adopted Katherine's troubled adolescent son, Teddy, who soon stopped attending school regularly and became increasingly involved in drug use, shoplifting, and eventually burglary. Jody admitted that she felt little sympathy for Teddy; indeed, she felt anger and resentment at him for monopolizing her mother's attention. This anger, she realized, was a displacement both of powerful and largely unconsciously held feelings toward her sister as well as anger toward her mother for abdicating her role as a parent many years earlier. Jody now began to consider the possibility that neither of her parents had offered her the protection and guidance that she needed as an adolescent and, perhaps, even as a younger child. A number of important memories surfaced, many of them disquieting. Jody recalled that when she was five or six she was once sleeping with her maternal grandmother, who suggested that Jody remove her underpants so that she could "ventilate." Although her grandmother hadn't touched her, Jody was embarrassed and upset. She also realized, despite her complaints about her husband's tendency to withdraw from family life and the additional burdens this created for her, that Jody was often secretly pleased when he worked long hours, spent weekends hunting, or stayed out drinking with his buddies. When he was around, Jeb was more like another son, helpless and dependent on her to satisfy the most basic needs; when he left Jody felt able to claim a degree of freedom for herself that was not otherwise legitimately hers. Just as her mother had secretly celebrated Jody's father's absences, Jody had in effect derived both primary and secondary gain from her own husband's detachment from family life.

We considered the possibility, too, that Jody frequently seemed to sexualize relationships with men as a means of "keeping them interested." This had been literally enacted in a number of earlier relationships, although as a married woman Jody had been careful to confine such sexual expression to metaphorical allusions, double entendres, and sexualized teasing. She often found herself engaging in such sexualized banter with her physician-employer, Dr. Kramer, a man many years her senior. It also reminded her of how she had once "vamped around" as an adolescent, eager to stir her father out of his complacency. As she gradually accepted the fact that Dr. Kramer's interest in her was sustainable without her needing to libidinize their discourse, Jody expressed both surprise and a sense of deep satisfaction.

Midway through her analysis, Jody's father became gravely ill and required several major surgeries. Unable to eat or drink normally, he eventually was forced to wear a prosthetic headpiece and, later, a colostomy bag. Although Jody and her family had originally placed complete trust in the surgeon, a very self-confident and reassuring man in his mid-fifties, complications arose from one of the surgeries, which the surgeon had not bothered to inform the family was quasi-experimental in nature. Jody was furious and, after much consideration, began to contemplate the possibility of bringing a malpractice suit against the surgeon, whom she concluded had conducted himself unethically and unprofessionally.

Not surprisingly, the predominant transference configuration in Jody's treatment, one that had presaged the beginning of the analysis proper, was a paternal one.[2] At times idealizing features had prominence, as Jody spoke of the safety of the analytic situation or of my benevolent and reassuring presence. At other times she seemed more interested in ensuring that she had captured my undivided attention. She recalled that during her childhood her father was not only detached but also depressed. Although he appeared to be strong, he was not. Wishing to help him, she had sometimes felt as though she tried to "take on his discomfort" in order to enliven him. Indeed, perhaps she had done something similar in her marriage with Jeb, assuming responsibilities for him despite feeling growing resentment. She often seemed concerned at what she perceived to be my discomfort, and I sensed that she might all too willingly rush in to offer assistance, should I permit the opportunity to arise. At one point I attempted to renegotiate her fee, which I felt was too low. Jody was angry. She complained that she was already spending a great deal of money on the analysis and simply could not afford more, especially with graduate tuition and all of her other expenses. I decided not to push the issue, partly because of the strength of her resistance but also because I believed that she was not at the point where she could fully claim all to which she was entitled. Analysis remained somewhat of an extravagance in her mind, not as yet on par with her husband's discretionary pursuits, which were certainly no less expensive. Interestingly, Jody apprehended my willingness to let the matter rest neither with relief, nor as constituting a victory. Instead, she began to talk about her abiding belief that I might now even be more inclined to abandon her emotionally, much as she felt her father (and her mother) had done many years earlier. Though the ensuing hopelessness and depression she now felt were surely colored by the recent losses of her sister and son, there also seemed to be an undeniable transferential basis for these feelings.

As our work continued, Jody's mood seemed to brighten, although awareness of any pleasures she might experience often brought renewed guilt and self-blame. At such times it was as though she were not deserving of good things and, not unlike the fairy tale swordsman who must overcome yet another adversary in order to claim his reward, expiation for Jody's "sins" was never quite within reach. Nevertheless, her graduate studies were fulfilling; she enjoyed doing clinical work, and once again she was socializing, though mostly with girlfriends. She had also begun to travel for the first time beyond metropolitan Boston, making her first trip to New York despite having lived her entire life within a four-hour drive of the city.

Jody brought up the matter of termination for the first time some nine months after we had begun her analysis. This followed closely on the birth of my third child, which served as a painful reminder that I had gained what Jody had lost and that she had now been in treatment with me for over two and a half years. An additional motive, one tied to her transference-born fear of emotional neglect or abandonment, was that her unique position in our analytic relationship would now be superseded by my growing attachment to the newest member of my family. A closely related dynamic theme was of course that of sibling rivalry. Much as Jody had been forced from the limelight with the birth of each younger sibling, she now seemed destined to suffer from the birth of her analyst's child. These themes were interpreted and discussed, and Jody continued to make progress.

Two months later—approximately twenty-three months after Joshua's death—Jody decided that she needed more intimate knowledge of her son's final moments in order to obtain some semblance of closure, to come as close as possible to "bearing witness," albeit after the fact. This would only be possible, she felt, were she to visit the scene of the crash, read the accident report in its entirety, and actually view the police photos taken at the time of the crash. I questioned whether all of this was necessary—indeed, I felt it would be more likely to retraumatize her than lead to a resolution—but Jody was determined and went ahead with her plan. It was also something she felt strongly that she must accomplish on her own. This was, in part, because she didn't believe her husband shared her depth of feeling for Joshua, whom he hadn't known from infancy. However, it was also because she needed to "close the circle"—as though, by sharing in the moment of his death, a symmetry might be created to match the celebration of his birth twenty years earlier. As we had both anticipated it to be, the experience was horrific, worse even than she had imagined. Gazing at the images of Joshua on the sidewalk, his bloodied head disfigured by the force of the impact, she reported that she had sobbed deeply and uncontrollably for what seemed like hours. And yet, to my surprise, she also reported that she had now seen the worst and felt able to move forward with her life; guilt, her constant companion for so many years, seemed to take a back seat both in her analysis and in other parts of her life.

Jody now spoke more often of the length of her treatment and of her accomplishments and began to share thoughts and fantasies about when it might conclude. On the one hand, she felt as though analysis might continue indefinitely; how would she know, or I know, when her treatment was complete? Who would make the final decision? Jody expected to graduate from her counseling psychology program in seven months and wondered whether this might also be a good time to end her analysis. She also had continuing concerns about the cost of three-times-weekly treatment. Spending so much money on her psychoanalysis seemed supremely selfish, and at times she worried that her two children might be disadvantaged in consequence. At other junctures, however, she saw the analysis as her salvation and expressed pride in the commitment and investment she had made so that this important work might continue during a difficult time in her life.

Although I had decided not to inform Jody of my plans until they were certain, I had applied for sabbatical leave about three years into Jody's therapy. At the end of academic year, I learned that my sabbatical had been approved and, a few months later, firmed up plans for a semester abroad. Once everything was in place, and I knew with certainty that I would be unable to continue to meet with Jody during this period, I introduced the topic in an analytic session.

THER: Now that I know this for sure, I wanted to let you know that I'll be on sabbatical leave beginning about four and a half months from now. Although it's mostly to do research, I won't be staying in the area.

JODY: Oh (*surprised and a bit confused*). But are you coming back, then?

THER: Oh, yes. I'll be back about a month after the end of the spring term at my university. Although we won't be able to meet during those five months, we could start meeting again when I return or, as you have recently suggested, bring the analysis to closure before I leave.

JODY: OK, although I'm not sure. Where are you going to, if that's OK for me to ask?

THER: I'll be traveling to England, doing research at several libraries and institutes there, as well as a little teaching.

JODY: That sounds so exciting. I've hardly been out of Framingham, I mean, aside from going to our summer cottage and that trip I took a while back to New York (*pause*). You know . . . I've been subbing for Jenny at Dr. Kramer's, and Dr. K and I have been swapping books. He's reading two books I gave him, *Why People Believe Weird Things,* and *Molecules of the Mind.* We were talking about the gender stuff, and I'm thinking about Dr. Clark's class— remember my mentioning her? And it's as though I feel that women are being attributed these abilities: intuition, connectedness, and all. But does that mean that they can't be objective? You know, like I want it *all.* I've started asking myself for the first time. . . . Do I need to have a man to call in order to function—do I really need to be this dependent? I'm not sure what it all means, but I'm starting to feel more confident that I *can* make it on my own. But, it's sort of like throwing in the towel, in a way. I feel sad about it.

THER: Well, I think that there *is* a sense of loss involved in acting on one's own initiative, in acting autonomously. As exhilarating as it is to feel liberated and self-confident, it's also a loss of the familiar. . . . I gather you were talking more about Jeb and perhaps your father just now, but I wonder if you might also be reacting to what I've just said about the sabbatical?

JODY: Oh. Maybe, although I wasn't really conscious of doing that.

Over the next several weeks Jody and I discussed the potential advantages and disadvantages of terminating her analysis prior to my sabbatical. Although she was saddened at the prospect of ending a process that she had found so helpful, she also acknowledged feeling a sort of giddy excitement when she thought about "making it" on her own. We tentatively agreed to a termination date three months hence, a few weeks before my departure. Several sessions later, Jody reported that her father was again in the hospital and had taken a turn for the worse.

JODY: He's got some sort of bacterial infection, and they're having difficulty with the feeding tube. He kept vomiting, and, wouldn't you know it, it was a weekend, a holiday, and there were no doctors around. . . . I guess the timing's never great. Jeb got really angry at me after we had a fight about his hiding the liquor bottles in the cabin we own up in Gloucester, and he went out in the backyard and threw a log against a tree. I was watching from the kitchen. Well, it bounced off the tree and hit him in the groin, so he was like in agony, writhing on the ground. He was OK afterward, and it's terrible of me, but it was really sort of funny to watch. Then later he comes inside and he's depressed, and says something like, "Maybe you'll just get lucky and I'll get sick and die."

THER: I notice that illness, death, dangers, and the inaccessibility of doctors when they are most needed seem to be the pervasive themes today.

JODY: I suppose that's right, now that you mention it.

THER: I'm wondering, too, if you aren't also talking about the process of terminating? There's a way in which termination represents the death of a relationship, a process, and then there's also the matter of doctors who aren't around when you really need one, and that makes you mad.

JODY: I really hadn't thought of it that way. . . . I'm not sure.

THER: Well, maybe you're thinking of me now as being less reliable, like your Dad's doctors or your husband, who keeps secrets from you.

JODY: I've never thought of you as unreliable, although . . . I was sort of surprised when you told me about your plans to leave. I mean, what right would I have, anyway, to be upset with you?

THER: An interesting question.

JODY: (*Pause*) so you're saying that all of that stuff about the doctors and Jeb—that I'm sort of mad at you, too? Maybe, I can kind of see that, but it's hard to hold onto.

Shortly after this session, Jody's father lapsed into a coma from which he never regained consciousness and died a few days later. For a number of sessions Jody reflected on her father's life and death. Although deeply affected by the loss, Jody felt that she had worked through much of her ambivalence and was able to mourn his passing. Saddened, but neither despairing nor traumatized, she viewed his death as an expected event, a normative part of the family life cycle and consequently very different from the loss of her son or those of her two younger siblings.

Not quite a month after her father's death, Jody began a session by recounting a dream from the night before in which her husband sends her off on a plane. She had the sense once on board that she was beginning a "great adventure." On one end of the plane were high-powered corporate executives from General Electric, on the other end were uneducated and "sexualized women." Although she felt fraudulent in staying in the business-class section with the GE executives, she was aware of feeling that she didn't really belong in the other section either. Her first association to this dream was that "I could go places . . . not wait for things to happen." She then joked, "I'm also thinking that . . . if Jeb plays his cards right, maybe I'll keep him around for a while." We explored the dream and its significance for the remainder of the hour. I suggested to Jody that the dream seemed to herald the termination phase of her treatment. In the first place, just as her analysis has signified a journey, so too does what lies beyond. Nearing graduation

and the beginning of her career as a professional woman, she had acknowledged feeling for the first time that she was no longer on the same "plane" as
her husband, though she could still express gratitude for his help in financ-
ing her education. Even though she didn't yet "fit in" with the smartly
dressed men and women in "business class," the regression implied in join-
ing the "sexualized women" at the other end of the cabin no longer seemed
to hold much appeal. Perhaps, also, General Electric signified a "bright" and
stimulating future filled with new "ideas."

Shortly thereafter, Jody noted for the first time that she was feeling there
was "less to say" in her analytic hours. At the same time, she seemed preoccupied with family crises, particularly involving her nephew and husband,
and a number of sessions were devoted to these issues. Should she place her
nephew, who had gotten so out of control following her father's death, in a
residential treatment facility? Would this be a good time finally to leave Jeb,
whom she believed to be so poor a role model for her sons and whom she
had, in a sense, outgrown? I interpreted Jody's use of these hours as being
motivated in part by a wish to achieve resolution of important issues before
her analysis ended but also as a way to avoid any exploration of our impending termination and what it meant to her. She did not directly acknowledge
the accuracy of these interpretations, although she soon asked that we
extend our meetings until just before I was to leave, a request to which I
acceded.

In the final two months of her analysis, Jody seemed somewhat less preoccupied with her marital relationship, which had improved slightly. She
had essentially convinced her mother to place Teddy in a residential school
for adolescents with severe behavior disorders and was both pleased and
relieved by this. She traded in an old and unreliable car for a shiny new van,
finally convinced that she deserved to drive as nice a vehicle as did her husband. Jeb had, from time to time, spoken of relocating the family to rural
New Hampshire or Maine, where they could live in a sort of "splendid isolation." Although Jody never found such an idea terribly appealing, she had
only been vaguely aware of the reasons. She now knew with a sense of conviction that it was because she and Jeb were very different. Jody was drawn
toward people, culture, and, increasingly, intellectual stimulation, whereas
Jeb preferred solitary pursuits, was often critical of "high-mindedness" in literature and the arts, and at times seemed to eschew social contacts outside
those he shared with a close group of male drinking and hunting companions. When he had again proposed this idea in a recent conversation, Jody
was able, for perhaps the first time, to articulate her position without feeling
unduly anxious. We focused increasingly on "endings." Now that her father

had died, Jody had also become more acutely aware of her mother's limitations, which were more starkly revealed in his absence. She noted with sadness that her mother had never really "been able to walk" in her shoes. Jody reflected on the historical tensions between her mother and maternal grandmother and then mentioned for the first time that her mother had been placed temporarily in an orphanage as a young girl. Perhaps her mother's difficulties in empathic attunement had their origin in this early trauma as well as the more chronic disappointments her mother had experienced in her own childhood. She also decided that she no longer wished to maintain a relationship with the young man who had sustained severe head injuries in the same accident in which Joshua was killed. Since the accident Jody had agreed to periodic visits with this young man, whose name was Kyle, mostly out of a sense of obligation, though these visits were painful for her. Kyle's head injuries, moreover, had left him without the normal capacity to inhibit or modulate impulses; on a couple of occasions his efforts to extract physical comfort from Jody had felt awkward and uncomfortable. She eventually came to understand that her willingness to suffer through these meetings with Kyle had been driven primarily by guilt, and she no longer felt so guilty. She also dreamt that she and an ophthalmologist were fitting her husband with "new eyes," although Jody's role was to distract her husband while the surgeon completed the procedure. This seemed to reveal a wish that the two of us, Jody and myself, work in a secret alliance to furnish her husband with needed insights into his behavior and role in their marital problems.

In the final three analytic hours Jody spoke of her respect and admiration for the daughter of an old friend, a gutsy young woman who had declined an experimental procedure for her lymphatic cancer because she feared becoming helpless and dependent on her doctors. She also mentioned that since she had, in effect, completed all course requirements (though not yet been awarded her diploma), she was beginning to job hunt. In fact, she had been offered a job, although she felt uncertain about her prospective employer, who struck her as rather "controlling" in an interview. The theme suggested by these associations was that of extricating oneself from relationships with doctors on whom one might become dependent—a clear analogue to the analysis and Jody's transference feelings toward me. Early in her analysis Jody had expressed concern that she might become helplessly dependent on me, although this infantile helplessness never materialized in the transference. We decided that these thoughts signified anxiety stemming from Jody's unconscious desire to replace the analytic relationship, which was nearly over, with something or someone else. Jody also talked about her sense that the analysis had provided her with a set of "tools" for dealing with family crises and other anxiety-generating situations she would be likely to face in the future. Asserting herself to her husband, or her mother, or to others, no longer triggered guilt or made her feel as though she was being arrogant or condescending. Finally, she thanked me for having helped her work through the traumatic loss of her son and come to terms with the earlier losses of her sister and brother as well as the more recent death of her father. Rising from the couch, she embraced me warmly and bid me farewell.

DISCUSSION

Jody's treatment, of course, differs in several significant respects from the clinical work with Douglas described earlier in this chapter. In the first place, Douglas was seen face-to-face on a once-weekly basis. Although Jody's therapy began at the same session frequency, significant, ongoing changes in her life necessitated an increase in the frequency of our meetings and ultimately led to a mutual decision to convert her treatment from intensive psychotherapy to psychoanalysis. Although Douglas's early development had been affected by significant parental pathology and environmental turbulence, one of the most important treatment objectives for Douglas had been that of achieving psychological separation from his mother and her family, so that he might determine what he wanted for himself and in his own life. Jody, in contrast, had been pressured into becoming independent of her family when she was far too young—experimenting extensively with drugs and drifting in and out of sexual relationships in adolescence and early adulthood in desperate search of the comfort and stability unavailable to her at home. Finally, Douglas had made a unilateral judgment to end his treatment after fourteen months. The termination of Jody's analysis, on the other hand, was ushered in by my announcement that I was leaving the country for five months.

Jody had actually introduced the topic of termination many months in advance of my frank discussion of my sabbatical plans and had already considered the possibility that the analysis could end at the same time she completed her degree requirements in counseling psychology. Nevertheless, she seemed surprised and, I believe, saddened at the prospect of our work coming to an end. I suspect that Jody had used the analytic relationship to test out her unconscious assumptions about men, whom she had experienced as either exploitative or abandoning. Feelings of deep distrust and guilt commingled with a seething anger of which she at first had little awareness were the intimate psychological partners to this history of thwarted and unsatisfying relationships with men.

Although she had benefited from an earlier course of treatment with a female therapist, her adaptations before beginning treatment with me seemed largely unsuccessful. In our work together Jody was able both to identify salient elements in her family history that may have contributed to these problematic relationships and to reflect on her motives in having sought out partners who were infantile, psychologically abandoning, or even abusive. She became far more self-confident, believing for perhaps the first time that she possessed a good intellect and no longer needed to libidinize relationships with men in order to feel acceptance. Of course, the traumata, both historical and ongoing, of multiple losses involving her son, her younger siblings, and her father often eclipsed other issues.

Interestingly, the termination process seemed to have reawakened Jody's feelings about her mother, so that in the final weeks of her analysis this relationship and the profound disappointments associated with it became far more focal than perhaps at any other time in our collaboration. Apropos of Tyson (1996), whose work was summarized earlier in this chapter, one is tempted to understand such a development in relation to the separation-individuation themes that seem to surface with some predictability during the termination phase of treatment. Furthermore, in Jody's case analytic reconstruction of her early history strongly suggested that both the original separation-individuation process of infancy and early childhood as well as its recrudescence in adolescence were strongly affected by the limitations of both her parents. We had surmised that her mother, in part owing to burdens of parenting for which she felt unprepared, relied heavily on young Jody for emotional support, which had the likely effect of dampening or discouraging Jody's experiments with autonomy in the extramural environment. At these times her father, rather than fulfilling what Herzog (2001) has characterized as the paternal role of actively extricating the child from the symbioticlike attachment to her mother, was instead detached and uninvolved. By the time she had reached early adolescence, both parents had "cut her loose," with profound ramifications that we have already detailed. Although Jody lamented her mother's inability to "walk in her shoes," she no longer simply complained about her mother's failings. Rather, she evinced curiosity about her mother's past and how it may have shaped the failures in attunement that she had experienced so often growing up. These observations, which reflected both creative thinking and mature compassion, present perhaps the most persuasive evidence of Jody's increased capacity for insight as well as of her readiness to terminate her analysis.

Endings in therapy, as in any other realm of human experience, represent what has already been lived as well as the potential for new variations on a familiar theme. Our review of the psychoanalytic literature has highlighted the evolution of this concept, which, we noted, seemed to lag behind other psychoanalytic ideas about the process of treatment and its methodology. Rarely discussed by psychoanalytic writers before the mid-1940s, termination seems only recently to have been accorded a place in the literature equivalent to other treatment phases and the phenomena associated with them. As I suggested earlier, termination, like any other ending, is bittersweet. It is the embodiment of the client's accomplishments over the course of treatment as well as the therapist's and client's shared belief that the latter has now demonstrated a readiness to disengage from the psychotherapeutic relationship. However, crossing this threshold can also be expected to evoke powerful affects, foremost among them sadness, anxiety, and pleasure. Through a series of short vignettes as well as lengthier case illustrations, we have examined the phenomenology of termination, its technical handling, and its overall significance in the process of dynamic therapy.

PART 3

Special Clinical Populations and Adaptations of the
Psychodynamic Approach

10

Children

SOCIAL WORK WITH children and their families in this country can be traced back to the settlement house movement, antedating the emergence of the earliest psychodynamic treatment model by nearly a full generation. However, once psychodynamic practice principles became more widely applied to clinical work with children in the 1920s and 1930s, social work endorsement was enthusiastic, and social work clinicians today are the largest single group among the major mental health professions involved in working with this population.

We begin with a concise history of the origins of the concept of child treatment in the early psychoanalytic movement, discussing the specific contributions of two prominent psychoanalytic theorists and clinicians, Melanie Klein and Anna Freud. Next we explore the essential components that make any child treatment "psychodynamic." Inasmuch as previous chapters have examined important developmental theories, as well as transference and countertransference considerations in the treatment of children, this chapter will focus more on the basic method of psychodynamic child therapy and the time-honored play techniques associated with it. One such representative play technique, reciprocal storytelling, is discussed somewhat more extensively and illustrated with a clinical vignette involving an eleven year old. Other topics and themes, such as the *dynamic assessment* process and the basic method of *dynamic listening*, are also briefly addressed, though the reader is cautioned that this chapter and the following one, on adolescent treatment, are intended to be introductory. As such, a number of topics, especially those having to do with other specialized treatment methods or techniques, treatment approaches to discrete psychopathologies, work with children at different developmental stages, and so forth, are not included. Finally, a detailed treatment case is used to illustrate both the clinical process and technical dimensions of child therapy, in this instance with a traumatized latency-age child.

A BRIEF HISTORY OF CHILD ANALYSIS

Most accounts detailing the history of child analysis begin with Sigmund Freud's treatment of a five-year-old phobic patient referred to as "Little Hans" (Freud 1909b) whose parents were early adherents of psychoanalysis and whose mother had actually been analyzed by Freud some years earlier (Jones 1955). Freud, in fact, served as more of a consultant than analyst in this boy's treatment, much of which was carried out by the boy's father under Freud's guidance. However unorthodox such an arrangement may be considered by contemporary standards, the treatment of Little Hans, nevertheless, represents the earliest known therapeutic application of psychoanalysis in work with a young child. Moreover, it was likely the first opportunity afforded Freud to test the validity of theoretical premises about infantile development, arrived at retrospectively from the psychoanalysis of adults (Jones 1955). Interestingly, despite his pioneering achievement in extending psychoanalytic therapy to so young a patient, Freud was not sanguine about the future prospects of psychoanalytic work with children. In fact, according to Ernest Jones, Freud considered his success with Little Hans a "lucky exception . . . from which no general therapeutic conclusions" could be drawn (Jones 1955:260) and later described child analysis as possessing certain "limitations" to which the psychoanalysis of adults is not subject (Freud 1918). Even Hug-Hellmuth, a disciple of Freud's and an early advocate of child treatment, cautioned against psychoanalytic work with children prior to age seven or eight, expressing a general concern for the potential of psychoanalysis to disrupt development (Hug-Hellmuth 1921).

Melanie Klein and Anna Freud, whose respective contributions as developmental theorists are described in chapter 3, were the first psychoanalysts to apply clinical psychoanalytic concepts in a systematic way to the treatment of children. As mentioned previously, Klein's early clinical encounters with children led her to take the position that children's play is the equivalent of the adult patient's free associations and could therefore be interpreted in much the same way. She also believed children to be capable of developing a transference neurosis and that this too was interpretable, a controversial position to which others in the psychoanalytic movement, most notably Anna Freud, did not adhere. Klein's theories were controversial in other respects as well. Largely discounting the role of the environment in the creation of psychopathology in children, she instead attributed its development to the child's own aggression. She also advocated psychoanalysis for all children—whether or not they suffered from psychopathology—believing that it would one day be considered an indispensable tool for promoting healthy child development. Furthermore, her vision of infantile object relations was predicated on the existence of a complex fantasy life of which she believed infants capable, but for which there has never been compelling scientific support (Mishne 1986).

Klein's approach to child psychoanalysis strove to establish "contact with the child's unconscious fears and wishes . . . [and] to interpret the child's communications" (Pick and Segal 1978:433), rather than to offer guidance or education or assume psychological surrogacy for the child's mother or father. Klein paid especially close attention to the internalized object relations of her child patients and made frequent deep interpretations of a child's anxieties as well as defenses erected to guard against their awareness—splitting, introjection, projection, and projective identification, in particular. She met with child analytic patients at a frequency of five sessions per week, the same standard as for adult analytic patients, in a playroom stocked with an assortment of toys sufficiently nonspecific so as to "enable the child to endow them with properties from his fantasy world" (ibid.).

Anna Freud's vision of child analysis was radically different than that of Klein. For one thing, she did not accept Klein's basic premise that children's play was truly equivalent to adult free association, such that symbolic significance could be reliably inferred from virtually every play action or other event occurring during the treatment hour. Anna Freud believed this assumption was unwarranted both because child patients are incapable of attaining the mature "analytic attitude" of adult patients and because their play may sometimes "admit of a harmless explanation" (Freud 1946:29). For example, the interest shown by a three-and-one-half-year-old girl who opens up a female visitor's handbag may well signify the symbolic expression of a wish to view the contents of her mother's womb to determine whether it "conceals another little brother or sister" (29–30). On the other hand, such an action suggests other, competing explanations, such as the simple repetition of an act performed the preceding day with a similar play item.

Anna Freud, unlike Klein, viewed child analysis as consisting of educational as well as psychotherapeutic aims. She tended to pay much closer attention overall to the child's environment and to important relationships with parents and siblings, and was among the first child analysts to recognize the value of analytic consultation in early childhood educational settings. Her clinical approach, in sharp contrast to that Klein and her followers, enlisted the child's active participation in the treatment process. Furthermore, Anna Freud seemed to attach far more importance to the child's ego defenses, which led her to interpret children's play and unconscious conflicts more conservatively (Kessler 1966; Mishne 1983).

Although she acknowledged the existence of powerful transference reactions and fantasies in child patients, and even a phenomenon resembling transference neurosis, Freud never completely accepted Klein's view that children were capable of developing a full transference neurosis, chiefly because of the ongoing part played by their parents in their lives. She also believed that the "really fruitful" work of analysis with children occurred when the child's transference attachment was positively valenced, "however revealing" the child's negative impulses toward the analyst might prove to be (Freud 1946).

CHILD PSYCHOTHERAPY VERSUS CHILD ANALYSIS

Although the influence of child analysts such as Melanie Klein and Anna Freud, as well as D. W. Winnciott, Rene Spitz, and others, has been keenly felt in the psychoanalytic field, child analysis as a therapeutic method has never achieved a level of acceptance and practice commensurate with adult psychoanalysis.[1] Dynamic child psychotherapy, on the other hand, achieved wide acceptance as far back as the 1920s, originally in connection with the burgeoning child guidance movement in this country. While dynamic child psychotherapy shares a common theoretical ancestry with child psychoanalysis, the two methods differ significantly in other respects.

Child psychotherapy, to begin with, is more delimited in objective than its analytic counterpart. Treatment goals, which include symptom resolution, the modification of behavior, some modicum of personality change, and the return of the child to a normal developmental trajectory, are therefore more modest in scope (Sours 1978). Child psychotherapy tends to place greater emphasis on the child's ongoing environmental interactions independent of the treatment relationship, so that parents and siblings, school personnel, and other important figures in the child's life assume a greater importance and may, at times, become directly involved in a child's treatment. While there is of course interest in the child's past, ongoing issues and conflicts are typically accorded somewhat greater significance. Regressions may occur, although the therapist, generally speaking, does not promote these.

With its emphasis on the structural alteration of the personality, the child psychoanalytic process strives for a "deeper" and more encompassing kind of change. Child analysis invariably involves the promotion of regression via the child's transference attachment to the analyst, and these transference fantasies and other displacements are thoroughly analyzed. Furthermore, genetic-historical elements are accorded at least as much importance as are intercurrent issues and conflicts. Its basic method bears an essential similarity to those concepts and principles associated with the analysis of adults: "an overall emphasis on the patient's intrapsychic life entailing interpretation of resistance, defense and transference, reconstruction and working through" (Moore and Fine 1990:40).

Traditionally, child analysts also adhere to the rule of abstinence, so that direct gratification and advice giving, to the degree that they exist at all, are greatly minimized.

BASIC PRINCIPLES OF DYNAMIC CHILD TREATMENT

A number of significant differences separate the psychotherapy of children from work with adults, or for that matter, with adolescents. As a general rule, few children begin therapy with an expression of their interest in discussing wishes, intrapsychic conflicts, or defensive accommodations, nor are they likely to be very receptive to the therapist's efforts to introduce such ideas. This observation rests on several assumptions. The overwhelming majority of children and most adolescents do not usually seek out psychotherapy for themselves independently; rather, they are brought, sometimes quite unwillingly, into treatment by their parents. Furthermore, younger children may be uncomfortable entering into such discussions, since they have yet to acquire full mastery of spoken language and therefore rely far more extensively on primary process communications than do adults, who operate principally in the secondary process domain. A third factor is that the capacity for both reflective thought and for *mentalization* (Fonagy and Target 1998),[2] may not be especially well developed in many children entering treatment.

Another difference is that children (and adolescents) are in the process of negotiating in *real time* those conflicts and crises that for the adult patient are only variously accessible memories. In effect, children and adolescents are still heavily engaged with both parents and siblings in multiple discourses that for the majority of adults may have come to exist solely at the level of the imaginary. Yet another fundamental distinction between child and adult therapy lies in the repertoire of treatment techniques suitable for clinical work with either population. As we have noted, children, unlike their adolescent and adult counterparts, have yet to achieve mastery either of expressive speech or secondary process thinking and logic, so that use of the full adult range of verbalized communication is rarely possible for them (Lieberman 1983). Thus doll play, puppetry, modeling, therapeutic games, mud and clay, painting and drawing, computer and video games, and other "play" techniques are used either alone or in conjunction with elicited narratives, which, in turn, involve either direct verbal exchange or communications *per metaphor.*

In the sections that follow, two aspects of dynamic child treatment are examined, clinical assessment and dynamic listening, after which a specialized technique of dynamic child therapy, reciprocal storytelling, is described.

DYNAMIC ASSESSMENT OF CHILDREN

A great deal has been written on the process of dynamic child assessment, although Henry Coppolillo's book, *Psychodynamic Psychotherapy of Children: An Introduction to the Art and the Techniques* (1987) contains one of the most readable and comprehensive introductions to this topic available in the literature. Many others (e.g., McDonald 1965; Lieberman 1979; Greenspan 1983; and Chethik 2000) have also addressed this aspect of child work in a general way, and some have focused on the assessment of particular forms of psychopathology, such as learning disorders (Palombo 2001), personality disorders (e.g., Kernberg, Weiner, and Bardenstein 2000), and affective disorders (Bemporad and Lee 1988).

The instrument presented in chapter 6 is a useful framework for organizing data in the dynamic assessment of children, although the assessment *process* in child work is very different than in work with adults. In the first place, child assessment typically begins with contacts made by the parent(s) on the child's behalf; rarely does a child initiate contact with a therapist, although this may occasionally occur in schools and other community settings. It is therefore generally advisable to begin by helping the parent(s) to articulate the reasons that have prompted the referral, which may range from anxious concern about developmental delays to complaints about hyperaggressive behavior. Reassurance that is provided prematurely is seldom helpful to anxious parents, although the importance of forming a *parental alliance* at this early juncture in the child's evaluation cannot be emphasized too strongly. One method of helping bring about such an alliance—without which the evaluation process and subsequent treatment efforts are likely to fail—is to demonstrate empathy for the parents' guilt, anxiety, and perplexity as well as genuine interest in their explanations or theories. Coppolillo has wisely recommended that the child clinician undertaking an assessment bring with him to the interviews liberal quantities of *curiosity*, willingness to be *taught* by the parents *and the child* without feeling resentful or denigrated, and, above all, *humility* and respect for the enormous complexity of human development and mentation (Coppolillo 1987:94).

One assumption that seems to underlie many instruments or frameworks for dynamic assessment in child treatment is the availability of parents or other historians to furnish historical data, developmental, family, medical, educational, or otherwise,[3] as well as the overriding importance of such information. However, it might occur that the child to be assessed does not reside with her or his biological parents, since many children whom social work clinicians are asked to evaluate are placed in residential treatment facilities, group homes, foster or respite care. Contact with biological parents in such instances may be impossible or, even when possible, fraught with logistical or legal complications or clinically contraindicated. Indeed, there may be no primary source from whom to gather such information. This highlights two interrelated points about the process of child assessment. First, although clinicians may strive to stay as close as possible to the data in their effort to understand historical features that have contributed to or otherwise shaped a child's current difficulties, it is imperative to remember that this process is rarely, if ever, conclusive. Rather, it is designed to lead to the construction of *hypotheses* and reasonable clinical *conjectures*. Second, the single most important source of diagnostic data, even when parents are readily available and history is very complete, is the child her or himself.

If the clinician's failure to form a parental alliance can virtually guarantee the partial or complete failure of any future therapeutic efforts with a child, it is equally true that the neglect of the *diagnostic alliance* during the earliest child interviews bodes poorly for future therapeutic success. Optimally, the diagnostic alliance with the child actually begins in advance of the first clinical contact, as Coppolillo has suggested, with a phone call placed by the child to the clinician to "set up" the first appointment (Coppolillo 1987). Such a move, useful even with very young children, would ordinarily begin in consultation with the child's parents, who may then convey to their son or daughter the therapist's interest in talking with them over the phone to arrange a date and time for a first meeting. Such contact not only furnishes the child with an opportunity to become briefly acquainted with the clinician prior to the first in-person contact, and thus to allay some anxiety, but also empowers the child. It is through such a gesture that the clinician establishes respect for the child's sensibilities, initiative, and autonomy; furthermore, it may serve to model a critical distinction between the therapist and other adults in the child's life. For the child therapist, unlike parents, teachers, guidance counselors, ministers, soccer coaches, and other grown ups with whom children daily come into contact, is far more interested in *listening to and understanding* the child rather than in giving advice, proscribing unacceptable behavior, or furnishing him or her with morality lessons. Why not convey this message from the very beginning of the diagnostic relationship by respectfully soliciting the child's opinion as to when a convenient first meeting time might be?

Clinical child assessment optimally should be spaced out over several sessions, although when agency or managed care constraints make this impossible, even one or two interviews may be used to advantage. Data gathering in dynamic child assessment must always be counterbalanced by the clinician's sensitivity to the child's anxiety over the newness of the clinical situation, concerns about confidentiality, and need for information about the therapist and the nature of the therapeutic process. One is also interested in actively soliciting the child's own explanation for the problem that prompted her or his visit, if this information is not volunteered, since it may well be that in the child's estimation there *is* no "problem." Or, perhaps the existence of a problem is acknowledged, but the child identifies its locus as the parents, the school, or the other kids in the neighborhood. Although some of this information may already be known to the therapist, questions about the child's interests and leisure time activities, favorite subject(s) in school, closest friends, favorite foods, and so forth, may not only furnish useful data, but also serve a relationship-enhancing function. Particularly with younger children, there may potential projective value in asking such questions as, "If you could be any animal, what animal would you most/least like to be? If a genie magically appeared and granted you three wishes, what would your wishes be?" The child's investigation of the therapist's office/playroom is also of importance, especially in the first hour. Most children are naturally curious to see the therapist's toys or games, a request to which the therapist will, of course, wish to accede. Should this request not be forthcoming owing to shyness or anxiety, the therapist may wish to raise the question her or himself or offer to take the child on a "tour."

Children's artistic productions constitute a rich source of clinical data, and, in this regard, the clinician may make use of such time-honored techniques as the house-tree-person or the kinetic family drawing. In more specialized clinical cases various projective tests (e.g., Robert's Apperception Test, Children's Apperception Test, Rorschach) and other psychological tests may prove useful, although limited resources in many social service settings have made their use far less common. Winnicott's *squiggle* technique (Winnicott 1971), which calls for the therapist and child to take turns drawing "squiggly" lines and completing each other's squiggle drawings, may also be used in diagnosis, although it serves equally well as a technique of child therapy. The squiggle, which is as elusively simple a technique to use as it is clinically generative, is made with one's eyes closed, although the other subject always completes the drawing with her or his eyes open. Autogenic (stimulus-independent) stories may also be used for diagnostic purposes. Such stories have long been recognized as important sources of information about intrapsychic structure, characteristic conflicts, and defensive adaptations, and also furnish information about disturbing wishes and fantasies, interpersonal relations, the development of the self, and other aspects of character.

Perhaps the most critical task of clinical child assessment is achieving and maintaining the proper balance between the need for information and the *cultivation of a meaningful affective tie* with the child. Optimally, the treatment relationship evolves, as we have noted previously, from a rudimentary to mature therapeutic alliance shaped by realistic and transferential forces. However, with a proliferation of diagnostic inventories, symptom checklists, and assorted "rapid assessment" instruments measuring everything from bipolar depression to eating disorders to psychosis, the focus seems increasingly to have shifted from the *child* to the child's *problem* (although such "problems" are often defined for the child by others). The remedicalization of psychiatry, the burgeoning interest in neuroscience, and the dicta of managed care have undoubtedly also contributed to this perspective.

DYNAMIC LISTENING

The narrative discourse that commences with the earliest diagnostic contact and continues throughout the entire course of a child's treatment creates a fertile environment for the evolution of the child's unique and personal story. Although in clinical assessment a greater emphasis is placed on the historical-developmental context of a child's problems, a subtle shift must occur as the treatment process gets underway. In the first place, child treatment occurs in an ahistorical context, which requires the emphasis on time and sequence and on the developmental framework that guides the history taking to assume a secondary role. Time gradually gives way to time*less*ness, which means that the rational, chronological ordering of events no longer retains its superordinate status. Indeed, child treatment involves a continuous interweaving of themes and fantasies, and of conflict and defense, without particular attention to the logic of sequence. As we have noted, children, particularly young ones, are uncomfortable operating within the adult secondary process domain; nor are they capable of inductive or deductive logic and reasoning, instead preferring what Piaget (1969) has termed "transductive logic" (operating from particular to particular).

A more demanding task for the child therapist is creating and maintaining the necessary therapeutic ambience to enhance and promote the unfolding of the child's narrative. Permitting a child to express primitive fantasies, regressive desires, fears, or conflicts is a necessary prerequisite for such narration, although it is not sufficient. The therapist must then extract the child's story from such fragmentary and often confusing communications. It is useful to point out that even when the child's narrative seems to bear little resemblance to the historical facts, its importance is not thereby diminished. The therapist's *willing suspension of disbelief* in such an instance may mean the difference between mutual attunement and alliance and therapeutic misalliance.

Understanding and responding therapeutically to the language of children's play is not altogether dissimilar to dynamic work with adult clients. Children's play and verbalized fantasies, it may be argued, bear certain fundamental similarities to the dreams of adult clients. Both are anchored in a more primitive language, that of the primary process, and therefore not typically governed by the logic and consistency of the secondary process domain. Both may be understood as possessing a *manifest* content as well as *latent* meanings, both strive for the avoidance of unpleasure or the fulfillment of wishes, and each relies heavily on the use of metaphorical and symbolic elements (although such elements, unless interpreted, generally remain outside the subject's awareness). Finally, children's fantasies and adults' dreams may evince preoccupation with an intercurrent problem or issue, though, on closer examination, they sometimes also reveal earlier, historically important dynamic patterns, themes, or issues.

I have found the clinical task of doing effective dynamic child treatment is enhanced when the therapist is alert to several key aspects of the clinical encounter. These include the dynamic theme or issue, the representation of self and object(s) in children's play scenarios and fantasies, the child's affective tone, paralinguistic, visual, and kinesic cues, and, finally, the child's use of defensive behaviors, discrete defenses, defensive strategies, and conflict-free solutions.

- *The dynamic theme or issue.* What is the most salient issue, theme, or focal conflict in the child's communications? Childhood is filled with a range of normative problems and conflicts even when it is not disrupted by environmental crises or pathology. Various needs predominate at different phases of psychosocial and psychosexual development, encompassing everything from preschoolers' requirements for affirmation of their normal exhibitionism to the struggles of adolescents to combat the regressive pull of the nuclear family in an effort to extend their radius of social relationships. Typical focal conflicts (see also chapter 14) revealed in children's fantasies, stories, and productions might include *hostility versus guilt,* the wish for *intimacy versus fear of engulfment,* the wish to be *assertive versus fear of criticism,* or the desire for *autonomy versus fear of abandonment/rejection.*
- *Representation of self and object in children's play scenarios.* Children's play and fantasies sometimes portray a unique object relational experience derived from important, affectively charged early encounters with parents, siblings, and others. Such an experience may then serve as a lens through which all subsequent object relations may be understood. For example, the fantasy narrations of a ten-year-old boy whose mother tended to be overprotective as well as somewhat intolerant of his efforts to achieve psychological autonomy often involved a small, rather helpless character (usually a squirrel or other small animal) dominated by a larger and more powerful character. Every autonomous effort of the smaller character was somehow thwarted or undermined by the larger one, who, like the patient's mother, tended to discourage the smaller character from venturing out, being more assertive, and so forth. Even when such an object relational configuration

cannot reliably be identified, it is always useful to determine which characters in play scenarios may represent the child and which character(s) appear to represent other important figures in the child's life (e.g., parents, siblings, or the therapist).

- *Affective tone.* Another important element in therapeutic play is the child's affective or hedonic tone. Does the child enter into play with interest, pleasure, vigor, and enthusiasm? Or is she phlegmatic, cautious, depressed, or simply going through the motions? Does the child sound mildly annoyed, angry, hurt, frustrated, anxious, agitated, fatigued, or confused? Does the child's play seem to match his mood or is there a notable discrepancy?

- *Paralinguistic, visual, and kinesic cues.* Children's play is usually accompanied by a variety of sublingual utterances, distinctive facial expressions, and other, sometimes quite revealing bodily movements. Although such cues are generally consonant with the play themes and actions, they are at other times rather asynchronous or poorly matched. For instance, a very depressed nine-year-old girl, whose father abandoned the family, had quite a fanciful imagination. Her fantasy play often involved larger-than-life characters that embarked on high adventures in exotic locales. At the same time, her manner was remarkable for its *economy* of movement, and she looked and sounded depressed, her demeanor at striking variance with the content and themes of her play.

- *The child's defensive behaviors, discrete defenses, defensive strategies, and conflict-free solutions.* Children's play narrations often contain compromise solutions to conflict, typically activated by the ego's defensive function, which recognizes the danger of direct expression or fulfillment of a disturbing wish and seeks to disguise it in some manner. These accommodations include defensive behaviors in very young children (e.g., transformation of affect), discrete defenses (e.g., denial, undoing, isolation, or withdrawal), and wishes used defensively (e.g., hostility directed against the self, defensive intimacy, or defensive assertion). Relatively conflict-free adaptive strategies emerge as the child acquires more capacity for self-observation and insight, usually during the latter phases of treatment.

RECIPROCAL STORYTELLING

The use of allegories, fables, parables, myths, and legends in the intergenerational transmission of important values and moral precepts has been traced to virtually every culture since the beginning of recorded history, underscoring the effectiveness of storytelling as a mode of communication with the young. Developmental psychology also tells us that children experience themselves from an early age "through the symbols they use to apprehend, encode, change, and describe experience" and that self-composed stories may serve as the "most essential symbolic process" for reflecting on and describing such experiences (Engel 1999:185).

Reciprocal storytelling was specifically designed as a means of both eliciting children's self-composed or autogenic stories and providing a therapeutic response to them in the context of psychoanalytic child psychotherapy. Compared to the dreams and free associations of adult clients, such stories and fantasy productions may indeed be less subject to the processes of censorship and distortion and to other influences that obscure or disguise dynamic meaning. Autogenic stories, which of course are projective in nature, provide children with an opportunity to give expression to disturbing wishes, fears, and defensive adaptations in a "safe," though largely unconscious, metaphorical form. Because such stories are composed without specific thematic direction or guidance from the therapist or the use of storytelling "props," they are far more likely to represent faithfully the children's concerns, conflicts, and resolutions than are stories linked either to specific play materials or to themes suggested by the therapist. The technique of reciprocal storytelling calls for the child's creation of an imaginary story with make-believe characters. The story must be original and there must be a beginning, some development, and an ending; sometimes, but not necessarily, a lesson or moral can be appended. The therapist then discerns the dynamic meaning of the story and responds within the story metaphor with a therapeutic version of his or her own. The responding story provides healthier, relatively conflict-free alternatives to the child's original conflict-laden solutions (Brandell 1988; Gardner 1993).

One distinct advantage to the technique of reciprocal storytelling is the manner in which it shapes the client-therapist discourse. Without creating a rigid structure that is inimical to both the clinical process and the basic objectives of sound psychodynamic treatment, the stories enhance the therapist's ability to apprehend and decode important primary process communications; at the same time, they offer a natural vehicle for therapeutic responses. The reciprocal storytelling process thus establishes an intersubjective discourse that can be maintained throughout treatment and serve as an undeniably powerful therapeutic tool for the child clinician.

WHEN IS RECIPROCAL STORYTELLING USEFUL
AND WITH WHICH CLIENTS?

Storytelling procedures can be used selectively with children as young as three and as old as fifteen years, although the most effective age range seems to be school age to early adolescence (roughly five to twelve years). Reciprocal story-telling, in particular, appears to be therapeutically effective across a wide spectrum of childhood problems and emotional disorders: phobias, anxiety disorders, depression, obsessive-compulsive problems; chronic depletion states, *who* selfobject disorders, and difficulty in the regulation of self-esteem; sequelae of *for ?* emotional neglect and physical and/or sexual abuse. It is especially helpful in work with children of divorce and those suffering from other environmental crises (e.g., loss of a parent or sibling, life-threatening illness of a close family member). In addition, children who have experienced trauma—that is, in cases where a massive paralysis of ego functions has occurred—may be receptive to the use of such story communications *per metaphor*. Therapists may also find reciprocal storytelling a useful adjunct in their clinical work with children suffering from chronic or life-threatening illnesses or with those who have developmental disabilities. Even schizoid children or those with nascent borderline personality disorders may be good candidates for reciprocal storytelling.

Storytelling also seems to work well with resistant children. It may, in fact, provide the therapist with a vehicle for circumnavigating or surmounting initial resistance and establishing a basic working alliance despite the children's disinclination to reveal much of themselves in more direct verbal discourse or even through other play activities. Owing to the fact that stories are "make-believe," children seem reassured that they are not actually revealing anything of great import about themselves. So far as they are concerned, any disturbing wishes, conflicts, secrets, and the like are safely obscured from view. Precisely—and paradoxically—because the story is ostensibly about *someone else*, it permits the *most* important unconscious conflicts and disturbing fantasies, as well as other closely guarded or otherwise hidden parts of the self, to emerge in a disguised though decodable form.

On the other hand, storytelling isn't for everyone; nor is it invariably effective even for the same client at different points in the treatment process. Certain children with developmental disabilities may be incapable of the minimal cognitive organization required for even the most elementary story. Others whose expressive language is compromised by developmental or organic factors may prefer play activities that do not highlight spoken language. Still others may enjoy the reciprocal storytelling process early in the treatment relationship but later express a preference for alternative play activities. This is especially true over long courses of treatment that begin in preadolescence. In such instances the child's increasing developmental sophistication makes storytelling as well as other play activities seem infantilizing. Indeed, like any other technique in the child therapist's repertoire, storytelling should be deployed with sensitivity and in accord with a particular child's preferences.

It is not essential for a child to be highly verbal in order for such techniques to be used successfully. Even a short, three-line story from a very young or self-conscious child may prove quite revealing, in much the same way that adult clients' dream "fragments" often seem to be. Furthermore, when children express little confidence in their ability to compose a make-believe story, the therapist may suggest the use of a pictorial adjunct to the storytelling procedure to help them "get started." Winnicott's *squiggle* technique, described previously, is ideally suited for such occasions, inasmuch as it provides a natural lead-in to story making without suggesting specific themes or story-content to the child. Winnicott characteristically used the squiggle content as a springboard for analytic investigation. He did not always work within the metaphor of the drawing in the discussions that followed, nor did he ask the child to use the picture to compose an original story, although some of his subjects did this spontaneously.

When the goal is a story, however, it should always be based on the child's completed drawing rather than on the therapist's. The same ground rules apply: The story must be original, the characters must be imaginary, and there must be a beginning, some development of the story, and an ending. I don't require a moral or lesson since I don't believe this to be absolutely essential, but I will sometimes suggest that one be included. Years of personal observation confirm that even children who at first claim to be poor storytellers or unable to "think of one" to tell will suddenly launch into a story without any further prompting. In these instances the process of creating a drawing from the squiggle somehow liberates preconscious fantasies and their accompanying affects in such children. In fact, some children prefer to base their stories on such drawings, even though they may already have demonstrated an ability to compose their stories independently of this technique. The therapist is well advised to honor the child's wish to combine these two media and, indeed, may be rewarded for doing so with particularly fertile results.

ELICITING THE CHILD'S STORY

Because storytelling is for most children a mode of narrative interchange that is both experience-near and entertaining, they are typically more than pleased to provide an autogenic story at the clinician's request. Inasmuch as original stories are a more accurate measure of the child's issues, conflicts, and adaptations, the clinician may wish to emphasize that telling *made-up* stories is more fun than simply repeating something one has seen on a children's show or a video. (Although there is undoubtedly always some contamination of the content from exposure to movies, videos, and television, it is generally not pronounced.) Most children at six or seven years of age are able to provide reasonably well-integrated stories without a specific injunction to include a beginning, a middle, and an end. The use of a tape recorder frequently serves to enhance the children's storytelling, allowing them the narcissistic satisfaction of hearing their own voice played back. And at least one author has suggested that the storytelling process can be "framed" as a television show, in which the therapist serves as the interviewer/moderator and the child is introduced as a "special guest" (Gardner 1977). Such an approach may be quite appealing to some children and, in any event, establishes a somewhat more natural linkage with audio or videotape. Certain children, however, are resistant to the idea of audio recording or video-taping their stories and may experience such technology as intrusive or anxiety generating. The recording of stories and perhaps even the therapist's note taking may be contraindicated with these children or with others who exhibit paranoid ideation or fears.

Occasionally, a child will ask the therapist to construct a story collaboratively. Although the likelihood of the therapist's influence over story theme and content is undoubtedly increased in such instances, there are ways to minimize this effect; one might, for example, consent to help with the introduction though not with the rest of the story. Certain children, especially those who lack self-confidence, or who are extremely anxious or perhaps decompensation prone, may require this parameter until they are sufficiently self-assured to create a story without the therapist's active collaboration.

THE LESSON OR MORAL

For many, a well-told children's story is one that ends with a moral or lesson— certainly a time-honored and integral feature of numerous cautionary tales, fables, fairy tales, and other kinds of stories. The lesson or moral is particularly helpful, too, because it identifies for the listener what the story is intended to teach. Among younger listeners less able to accomplish this task without some assistance, a carefully articulated lesson or moral may make the story both more memorable and more meaningful.

Although it is true that asking the child to draw a lesson or moral at the conclusion of an *autogenic* story (Gardner 1977) may sometimes enable the therapist to select the most salient theme or clarify the meaning of ambiguous story content, that lesson or moral will not always be especially well matched to story theme or content. In fact, it may be chosen not for reasons having any obvious connection to its dynamic meaning but, rather, because the child knows a particular proverb and tosses it in as a way of pleasing the therapist. (Instead of specifically requesting a moral from a younger child, the therapist may find it more helpful to ask "what the story teaches.") Even those therapists who do not believe that doing without a moral from the child results in a significant loss of data may wish to include a moral or lesson at the conclusion of their responding story. In such cases the moral or lesson creates an additional opportunity for the therapist to demonstrate alternative strategies or new ways of thinking about problems that enhance the child's adaptive evolution of his or her narrative account.[4]

POSTSTORY DISCUSSION

It is often beneficial to explore the child's understanding of the stories at the conclusion of storytelling. This practice permits the therapist to test the child's awareness of particular story elements that may differ between the two story versions. It can also serve as a natural segue to other play activities. And, at times, poststory inquiry can provide a point of departure for discussing the child's conflicted feelings, fantasies, or thematically relevant recent experiences. Note, however, that although therapists do not generally find it problematic to use the stories as a springboard for discussion, perhaps even to suggest a certain similarity between some feature of the story and a recent experience of the child, direct interpretation is best avoided.

THE THERAPIST'S ROLE IN THE STORYTELLING PROCESS

The therapist's role in using stories is not appreciably different than it would be for any other activity in the therapeutic playroom. Listening carefully while remaining empathically attuned, discerning meaning in the child's play and verbalizations, and conveying such understanding in a form that the child can grasp and ultimately internalize—all of these capacities apply equally to the storytelling process.

Composing make-believe stories—like drawing, painting, or clay modeling—involves the child's creative imagination. The story is, in this sense, a creative product that the child has shared with the therapist. It should also be humbling. No matter how skilled or clever the therapist's response to this creation of the client's, the response must *always* be based on the *child's* material. Children recognize this connection right away and may even comment that the therapist's story sounds very much like their own (a creative debt that the therapist should graciously acknowledge).

As suggested earlier, it is important for the integrity of the storytelling process that such creative products generally not be approached via direct interpretation.[5] In other words, the therapist should respond *within the child's story-metaphor* rather than interpreting story themes, conflicts, or other content to the child. When the therapist's immediate response to the child's story is made outside the metaphor, not only are the "ground rules" violated and the therapist's trustworthiness called into question but the child may become convinced that the therapist has special extrasensory abilities.

Nevertheless, it can be quite useful to engage in a sort of poststory dialogue in which the therapist seeks to clarify ambiguous elements of the child's story and also to establish parallels between the story characters or themes and experiences or issues in the child's life. Such discussion can occur immediately, later within the same session in connection with a different play activity, or even in a subsequent session.

Due to the reciprocal nature of this play technique, the child will expect to hear a therapeutic response to his or her story. Although it is clinically optimal for the therapist to offer a story-response within a few minutes of the conclusion of the child's presentation, this is not always possible. Sometimes the content of the child's story will be ambiguous; at other times the clinician, whether due to fatigue or perhaps a countertransference reaction, will simply be unable to grasp the meaning of a given story. Under such circumstances the therapist might wish to consider three alternatives:

1. After the therapist explains that he or she is unable to tell a responding story right away, therapist and client engage in a different activity and return to the storytelling at a later point in the treatment hour. Because the dynamic meaning of a child's story is often played out in other activities during the session, the therapist will have additional opportunities to apprehend whatever had proven elusive about the child's story earlier in the session.

2. Another technique involves asking the child to create a "commercial" (Gardner 1977), the premise being twofold: a) It permits the therapist to "stall for time," providing a few precious minutes to pore over the child's text in a search for meaning and b) whatever pertinent dynamic issues are contained in the autogenic story are also presumed to be present in the commercial. This technique has proven beneficial at times, although nearly as often the child seems to view it as an open invitation to make undisguised use of actual television commercials. In consequence, it may frequently be more a source of distraction than a means of enhancing the therapist's understanding of the child's narrative.

3. A third solution is to admit defeat and not attempt a therapeutic response, at least within that particular therapy hour. In this instance the therapist may offer a simple apology for being unable to tell a good story in response to the child's offering. Important dynamic themes are, after all, likely to resurface in subsequent interviews. The frank admission of inability to come up with a story-response despite the desire to do so typically elicits a sympathetic reaction; it may even pave the way for less inherently ambiguous revelations from the child. Indeed, those children locked in competitive

struggle with the therapist may welcome such an admission as confirmation of a successful sortie against the enemy. This development can be viewed as an opportunity to comment on the obvious pleasure the child appears to have derived from outwitting the therapist. Should the comment prove evocative for the child, the therapist may then wish to explore the transference meaning of such competitive behavior in further dialogue.

Also, there are times, typically near the end of a successful course of therapy, when the therapist finds it difficult to improve upon a child's story, in which case common sense dictates that the therapist not even try. Earlier in the course of therapy, too, the repertoire of strategies a child deploys to resolve conflict may include both maladaptive or conflict-laden elements as well as somewhat more adaptive solutions *in statu nascendi*. The latter, of course, should always be validated and supported in the therapist's story-responses. When, at a later point in treatment, these nascent adaptive solutions are more fully evolved and have supplanted less adaptive strategies, the therapist can simply explain that the child's story is so well told that it can stand fully on its own. This situation is golden: In fact, it is a goal of the whole treatment process that the child internalize new and increasingly adaptive strategies for solving conflicts, develop new capacities for emotional growth, and, in so doing, make the therapy and the therapist superfluous. Insofar as highly adaptive, well-told stories serve as evidence that the child has "brought it all together," they provide reassuring confirmation of his or her readiness to consider termination of therapy.

WHAT ARE THE MOST IMPORTANT COMPONENTS OF CHILDREN'S STORIES?

As with any play activity or fantasy elaboration, the child therapist should strive to identify several key components, as previously discussed, in each autogenic story. Among these are the dynamic theme or issue, the object relations scenario and key self and object representations, the affective tone of the story, paralinguistic, visual, and kinesic cues, and, finally, the child's defensive behaviors, discrete defenses, defensive strategies, and conflict-free solutions.

CLINICAL CASE ILLUSTRATION 10.1: "TONY"

Eleven-year-old Tony, attractive if somewhat overweight, was originally referred for treatment because of poor academic performance and behavioral problems at home. His mother anxiously described their relationship as highly conflicted and admitted in a rush of words to feeling both helpless and exasperated in her attempt to parent him. Although Tony typically did

not openly challenge her authority, he often subverted, ignored, or sabo-
taged her efforts; that pattern, and in particular its impact on his two
younger siblings, had become a source of growing concern. Tony's almost
characterological tendency to procrastinate had negative ramifications for
his performance in school and especially irritated his mother. His father, an
academician and research scientist, often worked long hours at his lab and
traveled extensively to lecture at scientific conferences; he was, and always
had been, much less involved with Tony than she.

Tony's mother's portrait of her son's infancy and early childhood contrasted markedly with the presenting picture: She remembered him as an
active, happy toddler who smiled at strangers and was captured on home
video repeatedly and gleefully running circles around his tired mother—but
she now complained about his inactivity, passivity, and dislike of doing
physical things. Tony had been a poor eater, and, because he seemed to gain
weight so slowly, his mother switched from breast milk to formula and
began to force-feed him early on, although she admitted this was partly in
response to pressure from her husband's extended family. By age two Tony
had become "a better eater," but an early and significant pattern had clearly
been forged in the relationship between mother and son.

Although later developmental milestones were unremarkable, Tony did
not react well to the birth of his two siblings. His brother was born when
Tony was twenty-two months old, and a sister came along some three years
later. According to his mother, Tony's problems at home often seemed connected to his dislike and jealousy of David and, to a lesser degree, Patty. By
sixth grade Tony's school performance had deteriorated so markedly that
consideration was being given to either special classroom placement or
grade retention. Because subsequent testing revealed Tony to be a very bright
youngster whose intelligence clearly exceeded the cognitive and intellectual
requirements of the work he was being asked to do, such solutions didn't
seem particularly viable and were therefore dismissed.

Tony was a very agreeable client and appeared to enjoy a number of activities in the playroom, in his rather quiet and understated way. One of these
playroom pursuits was reciprocal storytelling, an activity in which we
engaged to very good effect over the entire course of his sixteen-month-long
therapy. At the time that Tony told me the following story, approximately
nine months into therapy, we had been discussing the anger and jealousy he
felt toward his younger brother. Tony had made some progress in his school
performance and there was moderate improvement in his relationship with
his mother, but the rivalry with his younger siblings continued to be a
problem.

TONY'S STORY

Once upon a time there was a fireplace, but it hadn't been used in a long time. These people who lived there were going to knock it down in order to put in a heating system. Well, this builder came by and said to them, "Don't knock it down. I'll take it and put it in my house." Except he really didn't use it much. Well, one day, he was sitting by it, and it cracked, and the bricks started to fall. It was falling apart. He tried to fix it, but it just fell apart again. Finally, he sold it to some people who turned it into a new fireplace, one that was worth more money than the old fireplace.

Moral: *Just because things are old doesn't mean they're worth a lot of money.*

ANALYSIS

Nowhere among Tony's remarks were the twin themes of sibling jealousy and narcissistic injury more poignantly expressed than in this story, although they were repeatedly reprised in Tony's other stories and play activities. The way in which he chose to represent himself here, as an old fireplace, makes for a densely packed metaphor really quite ingenious in its economy of expression. It emblematizes at once his passivity, his seething anger, and his desire to "shine brightly" before an admiring mother and father.

An old fireplace is scheduled for demolition, to be replaced by a newer, more modern heating system (Tony's younger siblings). Tony believes that the birth of his younger siblings has made him obsolete, like the old fireplace; not only does his mother seem endlessly preoccupied with the needs of his younger brother and sister, but his father is similarly unavailable, running laboratory experiments or away from home at professional conferences. Tony has suffered a series of narcissistic and oedipal defeats in relation to both siblings, although his "fall from grace" is more clearly connected to David's birth when Tony was not quite two. Although there is a certain degree of *secondary gain* to be extracted from his school-related problems and his conflicts with his siblings and his mother, the gratifications prove to be fleeting.

Interestingly, the "builder" in his story, who appears to have been introduced as a therapist-representative, seems at first quite genuinely interested in the fireplace. He prevails upon the house owners, the parent-representatives in this story, to permit him to take the fireplace home with him, thereby rescuing it. Sadly, however, the fireplace once again falls into disuse. The transference significance of this plot development is inescapable: The old fireplace is simply incapable of evoking any sustained interest, even from the well-meaning builder-therapist. Tony will eventually suffer the same sort of oedipal and narcissistic defeats with the therapist that he has experienced with his own parents.

In his story the most prominent maladaptive solution the fireplace adopts is to shake itself apart.[6] Not even the builder is able to repair the fireplace, so he sells it to someone else who proceeds to turn the old fireplace into a new one, enhancing its value in the process. The story's moral simply repeats the passive and masochistic solutions present in the story itself: Old things (fireplaces, older siblings) aren't worth much to anyone and, sooner or later, will need to be replaced or rebuilt. In keeping with the helpless and passive voice that pervades the story, it seems almost futile to attempt to counteract this eventuality.

Based on this understanding, I responded with a story of my own, using many of the same story elements. But there are also critical differences.

THERAPEUTIC RESPONSE

Once upon a time, there was a fireplace that used to be the center of attention. Then the people who owned it decided to create a new heating system. The fireplace became neglected, and no one sat by it anymore. One day a builder saw that the fireplace wasn't doing well and suggested that the fireplace come to his shop so that he could repair it. Well, the fireplace worked better for a while, but then it started to fall apart again. The fireplace felt neglected and displaced by the heating system, and didn't even care anymore, although it didn't know why it wasn't working well.

However, there were things about the fireplace that made it unique. First, it could burn logs, and the heating system couldn't. That meant that even if there was a power failure the fireplace could always provide warmth to the family as long as they brought logs in from the outside. The fireplace was also unique in that it was really cozy on cold nights, and people liked to curl up next to it as long as its flame didn't burn too brightly. People actually seemed to enjoy spending time at the fireplace, but it is true that the heating system demanded more attention from the family at times.

Anyway, the builder told the fireplace that it needed to remember that it couldn't always provide all the heat for the house, but it certainly could sometimes. He also said that if the fireplace could control its flame better, then people would probably be more likely to want to sit near it. Sometimes, of course, it's important to burn brightly so that people know you're still there, as long as your sparks don't fly out of the fireplace (since that can upset or scare people). The fireplace found these ideas interesting and agreed to try the builder's suggestions.

Moral: If you're a fireplace and people neglect you, try doing these things: Remember that you have to share heating the house with the more modern heating system, try to control your flame so that people will want to sit by you, and, if you're feeling like people aren't paying enough attention to you, try burning brightly for a little while, but without making sparks fly since that upsets or even scares people.

DISCUSSION

In my story-response I attempted to address several interrelated story elements. First, while preserving the fireplace metaphor, I tried to confer a sense of agency on the fireplace. In effect, a fireplace doesn't have to be completely passive or helplessly dependent upon others all the time, as the fireplace in Tony's story was. The fireplace can work with the builder in arriving at a better and more adaptive solution for its problems. Second, it is possible for a fireplace to use aggression constructively (heating up the room for the rest of the family), rather than for the purpose of acting out against others (letting sparks fly), or defensively (punishing itself by shaking apart). I believe that this idea, even after many months of therapy, remained a relatively novel one for Tony and was obviously a perspective he had yet to internalize fully. Finally, my builder counseled the fireplace to "burn brightly" as a way of vigorously announcing its needs, suggesting—aside from the issue of how aggression can be harnessed and used adaptively—that the fireplace deserves and is entitled to the appreciation of others. Others will admire its warmth and uniqueness, at least some of the time. By the same token, one cannot always be the center of attention; sometimes others will have the spotlight, and one must be tolerant and sufficiently flexible to sustain the corresponding narcissistic slights.

As he had countless times before, Tony participated in this storytelling exchange in a quiet, intently focused manner. He received my story-response with interest, although in our poststory discussions it was rarely possible to make direct connections between our narrative exchanges and his experiences outside of therapy. Tony would simply shrug, indicating that he had "made up a story" in accordance with the rules I had introduced in our first session. In essence, the stories were "make-believe," having nothing to do with him—a claim made relatively often by children when asked about the relationship of their stories to events or circumstances in their lives. Nevertheless, Tony gradually became quite invested in his therapy. This wasn't always clear from his predictably low-key presentation during our treatment hours; however, he often arrived early for his sessions, and he became far more interactive as we neared the termination phase of his therapy (occasioned by a family move out of state). Although Tony's treatment ended prematurely, he had already begun to show considerable improvement in his academic performance, and his mother reported significant strides in his tolerance for his younger siblings as well as in his relationship with her.

Although stories and storytelling have long been utilized as a means of therapeutic communication with children, storytelling activities have generally not been formalized, usually occurring in conjunction with other therapeutic activities such as doll play, puppetry, or therapeutic board games. Storytelling, however, can be used to considerable therapeutic advantage when it involves autogenic content and occurs within a reciprocal exchange. In such a procedure the therapist must identify the most salient dynamic issues or themes in the child's version, offering a therapeutic rendering of the child's story that preserves the basic theme, plot elements, and characters from the child's autogenic story. The therapist's story is intended to offer dynamic interpretations of the child's original version, *within the metaphor.* Such a procedure establishes safety in the therapeutic dialogue, permitting the child therapist to make important dynamic communications and to suggest increasingly adaptive alternatives for the resolution of conflict without educing the resistance that so often accompanies more direct interpretation of dynamic issues and intrapsychic conflicts.

Reciprocal storytelling is most valuable as a *technique* rather than a *method* of child treatment. Other playroom activities, including those traditionally associated with psychoanalytic child psychotherapy, are no less generative or useful; the process of child treatment, however, can be enhanced by the addition of reciprocal exchanges *per metaphor.*

TREATMENT OF COMPLEX PSYCHOSOCIAL PROBLEMS

Within the last generation, child analysts and therapists have gradually become more involved in working with a nontraditional clientele consisting of children suffering from moderately severe, long-standing, and complex psychosocial problems (e.g., those associated with nascent disorders of character, traumatization, patterns of familial violence, and drug and alcohol use). In the clinical illustration that follows, the dynamic treatment of one such child, conducted on a three-times-weekly basis, is presented in detail.

CLINICAL CASE ILLUSTRATION 10.2: "MARK"

Mark, a nine-year-old Caucasian child, resided with his mother, Ms. B., who was employed full-time in the equestrian field and also attended college part-time in pursuit of a teaching degree. Mark was an only child and had no contact with his father.[7]

A referral from school, following Mark's suspension for disruptive, aggressive, and defiant behavior, led to his evaluation at the child and adolescent psychiatry outpatient clinic. His behavior had, in fact, been so upsetting to school personnel one teacher declared to Mark's mother that she "never" wanted "to see him again" in her classroom. In school Mark was extremely disruptive, often running around the room during class; when redirected to sit down, he would bolt out of the classroom and barricade himself in the bathroom. During one such episode, it took nearly three hours to get him out.

Mark exhibited a pattern of hyperactivity and impulsivity. He frequently acted without deliberating consequences and engaged in high-risk behaviors without consideration to his safety. He became easily overstimulated by his emotions and had difficulty settling himself down. As his behavior escalated, he often required physical restraint.

Not surprisingly, Mark's emotional and behavioral problems exacted a toll from his relationships with peers. He tended to dominate in play interactions with other children and often bullied them. Mark became easily frustrated and made self-critical remarks when unable to complete his schoolwork. He was hypersensitive to criticism and easily demoralized, often acting out or becoming aggressive or destructive in response to others' critical remarks.

In the two months prior to referral for treatment, Mark's unrestrained behavior intensified owing to an accumulation of environmental stressors. Following the breakup of an extended relationship, Ms. B and Mark moved out of Ms. B's boyfriend's home, where they had resided for almost four years. This was painful for Mark, as he had become very attached to Mr. R., his mother's boyfriend. At the same time, Mark's maternal grandfather, who had been in ill health for some time, was hospitalized, after having suffered a major heart attack, and given an uncertain prognosis. Ms. B. and Mark then relocated to another part of the state so that they would be closer to other members of the family. Mark had difficulties before the move, but the cumulative effect of the loss of Mr. R., his forced adjustment to a new community, and fears about his grandfather's health gave rise to behavior that was increasingly unmanageable both at home and at school.

After the evaluation was completed, several recommendations were made, including individual psychotherapy, placement in a specialized self-contained classroom, and adjunctive psychotropic medication. In the completion interview, when the therapist attempted to schedule another appointment for Mark, Ms. B. informed him that, due to other obligations, she would be unable to bring her son in for several weeks. Several days later, he received an urgent message from Ms. B. stating that Mark was in the hospital under observation following an explosive episode in which he had made repeated suicidal threats and then run into the street. The physician at the hospital recommended inpatient psychiatric care for Mark. Ms. B., however, had grave concerns about hospitalizing her child and implored the therapist to provide outpatient services for him. The therapist informed Ms. B. that, given the high risk and potential for self-harm, he would only consent to meet with Mark if she agreed to bring him in immediately and to follow his recommendations very closely. She acceded to these conditions, and Mark was seen the following day.

Mark was an only child, the product of a five-year relationship. Although Mark remembered little of his father, Ms. B. described him as an explosive and cruel person, recounting numerous tales of severe abuse at his hands. When she was pregnant with Mark, he beat her "mercilessly." Especially while under the influence of alcohol or cocaine, he could become cruelly sadistic and violent. Following Mark's birth, the abuse did not cease but rather intensified, and the beatings, according to Ms. B., occurred almost daily.

According to Ms. B., Mark's father was involved in drug trafficking and had served several jail terms. He would disappear from home for weeks at a time. When Mark was two, Ms. B. finally left the relationship; in the middle of the night Ms. B's sister came and took them back to the family home. Reports from family members describe Ms. B. as having been extremely depressed and isolated during the time she was with Mark's father. When the therapist wondered what had finally led Ms. B to flee that abusive relationship, she replied, "I would hold Mark and look at him, knowing that he was the reason I would have to leave."

Ms. B. subsequently involved herself in another relationship and shortly thereafter moved in with this man. During this period, Ms. B. distanced herself from her family and essentially refused contact, although the reasons for this disaffection were unclear; furthermore, little is known about this period in Mark's life, since his mother resisted discussing it in detail. Ms. B's sister did say that, once the family discovered where Ms. B. was living, they went to see her. The sister described Mark as disheveled and the house as being in a "state of chaos." Mark, then merely five years old, had been left to tend to a younger child from the boyfriend's previous marriage. Mark's aunt commented that "it just didn't feel like he (Mark) had much of a chance to be a kid."

Once this relationship dissolved, Ms. B. soon moved in with another man in the same city. This relationship, while not abusive, was marked by frequent conflict and arguments. It was after the breakup of this relationship that Ms. B. and Mark moved to the metropolitan area and Mark was seen in the clinic.

For Mark, witnessing his mother being assaulted and humiliated resulted in vicarious traumatization. Due to his dependence on her, any danger to Ms. B. also constituted a peril to his own survival, thus arousing fears of annihilation. Furthermore, Ms. B's absence or chronic distress interfered with her ability to contain Mark's anxiety; consequently, there was an absence of consistent maternal modulation for Mark's intense affectivity and paniclike reactions. As a result, Mark's capacity for affect tolerance and drive regulation was minimal, and his defensive repertoire was limited to defensive behaviors (Fraiberg 1982) and primitive defense mechanisms. Owing to early traumata and developmental derailments, Mark possessed little or no capacity for signal anxiety, so that he often became rapidly flooded with dangerous affects, but with little capacity to defend against such internal states when they arose. A further complication, one that had severely compromised his psychosocial development, was a corresponding depletion of ego resources that might otherwise have been used in the service of age-appropriate developmental tasks.

Posttraumatic disorders may, of course, be exhibited even in young children who have neither attained fluency in expressive language nor in the capacity for autobiographical memory. Mark repeatedly experienced nightmares, persistent avoidance of stimuli related to the trauma, and heightened arousal. He spent an enormous amount of time hiding in small, confined places, had difficulty falling asleep, and would wake intermittently throughout the night reporting nightmares about tornadoes with spiked balls killing his family. Like many traumatized children, Mark's concept of chronological time was distorted, and he demonstrated a severely limited capacity to construct a coherent narrative of his past.

It is important to note that the domestic violence was only one of several traumatogenic experiences later to surface in Mark's therapy. When Mark was three, he and Ms. B were involved in a head-on collision; although no one sustained life-threatening injuries nor suffered permanent disabilities,

Mark had vivid recall of the tractor-trailer truck rolling over them. His aunt also described how, when he was hospitalized at age five to have his tonsils out, he desperately tried to keep his mother from leaving by attempting to scream, but could barely utter a sound because of the excruciating postoperative pain.

Mark persistently reenacted traumatic events through his play. For a period of time he would repeatedly smash toy cars together. This continued until Mark and the therapist made up a game in which cars had to be passed back and forth without having them turn over or hit any other toys. At times, when his behavior would escalate, the therapist would take a toy car and roll it to him. He in turn would pass it back. This soothed Mark. Perhaps it allowed, through play, some semblance of mastery over the car accident.

Mark displayed excessive gross motor activity, shifting from one activity to the next without interruption. He was excessively hypervigilant, surveying his environment in great detail. In his play and storytelling, exaggerated tales with self-preservation themes surfaced repeatedly. He would talk of battling large armies of ninjas out of his forts and of conquering them single-handedly. Through the displacement of play Mark would project feelings of rage and aggression. His depictions were marked both by extreme vividness and gross violence. In building his Lego fortresses, Mark would bang and scatter toys all around. He would pretend that his forts were forever being attacked. As this play continued, Mark became more anxious and unable to compose himself.

Traumatized children will use "violent hypermotor discharge" to ward off "toxic objects"- people who may pose a threat to overwhelm or destroy them (Parson 1995). For Mark, his frequent boasts of invulnerability accompanied by aggressive hyperarousal may have served this purpose. Excessive motility, too, may serve to protect against unbearable depressive and anxious affects. Mark's capacity to modulate affects and regulate impulses through higher order cognitive strategies was very limited; thus he relied on more primitive motoric discharge to achieve this, although the results were rarely successful.

Mark had difficulty conveying his thoughts and affects through words. He displayed mainly primary process thinking characteristic of a younger child. Although it was unclear whether he consciously chose fantasy over reality or retreated unconsciously into fantasy as a defense, Mark's excessive avoidance and retreat from any unpleasant external situation seemed certain.

Mark displayed arrests at each psychosexual phase of development, especially in connection with oedipal conflicts. Although Mark had few if any conscious memories of his father, he understood his father to be a "monster" who hurt his mother. He developed a fear that because his father was "the devil," he would return on October 30 (Devil's Night) and hurt him and his mother. For little boys the resolution of the Oedipus requires that an identification be forged with the father, who is, in consequence, no longer experienced either as malevolent or as a rival to be vanquished. In Mark's case such an identification became tremendously complicated because of the vicarious trauma of witnessing his mother beaten by his father, the later disappearance of his father, and repeated losses of male figures.

As a result, Mark had difficulty regulating his aggressive and sexual drives. Frightened by both external and internal threats, he often projected his hostility onto others, since it proved far too disturbing to locate within himself. Mark would frequently complain of being rejected and picked on at school; he lacked any insight, however, into how his aggressive behaviors perpetuated his alienation.

Mark was seen in individual psychotherapy on a three-times-weekly basis for a period of seven months, and the treatment was roughly divided into three phases. The first phase involved the establishment of trust, rapport, and structure. During the middle phase, therapist and client worked to develop a coherent narrative of Mark's traumatic past and to repair developmental arrests. The final phase focused on the experience of termination.

In the first three weeks of treatment, Mark was extremely anxious and motorically driven. He would frequently request to meet in a location close to the waiting area where his mother or aunt would stay, remaining hypervigilant and exhibiting "startle" reactions to noises outside the therapy room. During the sessions he was quite conscious of the therapist's movements and proximity. In these early sessions, Mark continuously built and rebuilt Lego fortresses, which were often very elaborate, with several layers of insulation. Mark would make reference to their invulnerability and impenetrability. The therapist gradually began to comment on his play.

THER: Mark, why is there such a big wall around your fortress?
MARK: It keeps people away.
THER: Does that make things safe?
MARK: Yeah.
THER: Mark, I don't see any doors or windows in your fortress. I'm wondering how friendly people come in and out?

Mark's "walls" served to protect against external as well as internal threats. He was terrified of aggression, both in others and in himself. His ego was extremely vulnerable and he would often disintegrate in therapy sessions. He seemed to lose touch with his surroundings, becoming so explosive that the therapist would sometimes intervene physically to help him regain control. Mark would throw toys across the room, repeatedly knock the chair against the wall, and scream.

In the early sessions Mark continued to build Lego forts without any doors or windows. In discussing fortresses, the therapist clarified distinctions between different kinds of walls. If they were too weak, then anyone could get through, "even dangerous soldiers." If they were too strong, then nothing could get through, resulting in isolation. The therapist then began to build fortresses alongside Mark's, except that his structures had doors through which he might selectively allow various toy figures to enter. Soon after, Mark added doors to his own fortresses. In one session he took a toy figure and handed it to the therapist. He then said that the figure could come into his fortress. After the figure entered, Mark again became verbally explosive and disorganized. However, since no one was being hurt and nothing was being destroyed, there was on this occasion no need to limit Mark's behavior. Instead, the therapist allowed time for Mark to compose himself, which he was gradually able to do. Perhaps Mark was overstimulated because of the anxiety of allowing another to get close or perhaps he was showing the therapist what his internal world was like—a place of chaos, anxiety, and confusion.

In one memorable hour Mark brought in a box of pogs.* Therapist and client played with them briefly, and then Mark asked if the therapist could outline him on the floor using the pogs. As the therapist traced him, they began to talk:

MARK: It feels like you're throwing knives at me (referring to the therapist's outlining him with pogs).
THER: You mean like in a circus, when the knife thrower throws knives around a person but doesn't hit him?
MARK: Exactly.
THER: What do you think it's like for the person to just stand there and have knives thrown at him?
MARK: That person has to be really brave.
THER: You're absolutely right. They do have to be very brave. You know, they also have to have a lot of trust in the person throwing the knives.
MARK: The day my hamster died, I just really hurt. So bad that I wanted to jump out the window.

---

*This is a game played with disklike objects that have pictures on their face side and a heavier disk, called the "slammer," used to strike stacks of pogs.

Up to this point Mark had resisted disclosing any information about himself. In fact, the therapist had felt both frustration, believing that the treatment was not progressing, and anger, sensing that he was not able to "contain" Mark. With Mark's acting out, the therapist had also been feeling as though he didn't have control of the sessions. Thus, Mark's invitation to the therapist to "subdue" him was gratifying. However, the image of the therapist driving knives into his client was unsettling and frightening, causing the therapist concern over his own aggressive feelings toward this young client. By shifting the scenario into a more benign one in which he intentionally pinned Mark down without hurting him, the therapist was able to create a safe metaphor that reassured them both that neither the therapist's words nor his actions were intended to be hurtful. Greater trust became evident as Mark began to talk about the painful loss of his pet.

Approximately three months into therapy, a major development occurred. Up to this point Mark had briefly mentioned his father but would quickly retreat from the subject as his anxiety escalated. Therapist and client began a particular hour by playing cops and robbers, continuing a play scenario that had begun several sessions earlier. Mark was the robber and the therapist was the kidnapped cop. With each successive session it appeared that Mark became more and more focused on the dynamics of the game. Everything had to be just so—the chairs, the toy guns, the pattern of events. Gradually, it was becoming more ritualized, and Mark registered distress when the therapist tried to lead him out of the fantasy. Any attempts to inject elements of reality were met with stern opposition. Mark's game had assumed a life of its own, and the characteristics of his play seemed increasingly compulsive, joyless, and driven—what has been referred to as "post-traumatic play" (Terr 1990).

At one point in the play, Mark aggressively held a toy gun to the therapist's head and commanded him to follow his directions. When asked why, he told the therapist not to ruin the game by talking. While Mark had been aggressive when angry in the past, in this play he seemed cruel. He displayed a meanness that was controlled and sadistic. When the therapist commented on it, Mark would insist, "It's only pretend." The therapist, who felt as though he could almost picture Mark's father through this play, questioned whether Mark was reenacting his father's abusiveness.

Although he did not stop Mark's play, the therapist continually commented on and questioned why the robber needed to kidnap the cop and boss him around. He then introduced a revision of this cop and robber scenario which, at first, frustrated Mark.

THER: I don't think the cop wants a gun pointed at him and to be told what to do.

MARK: Well, he has to.

THER: Why?

MARK: Because I'm the robber and I have the gun.

THER: So you're telling the cop that he has no choice because if he doesn't do what you want, you'll hurt him?

MARK: Yeah.

THER: Even if the cop has to do what the robber wants, how do you think he feels about it?

MARK: (*Stops playing.*)

Mark had dictated the therapist's actions and responded to any opposition with anger and resentment. However, it was through the therapist's persistent efforts to understand and modify the play scenario that Mark finally became conscious of a disturbing though previously unconscious core sadism, a critical development that served to weaken the fantasy.

After a few sessions Mark began to elaborate on his play. Mark wanted the therapist to pretend that he was " a [good] cop turned bad." The therapist would pretend to kill him to camouflage their escape. Once the authorities believed him to be dead, the therapist was to "break him out" of prison and together they would make a getaway. Upon reaching the hideout (a semicircle of chairs against the wall) Mark shut off the lights and began to flash a flashlight. Therapist and client then made shadow puppets on the wall. Throughout the last few sessions Mark and his therapist had talked about trusting others. It was in the context of this shadow puppet play that the therapist eventually became the "father" puppet and Mark the "son" puppet. Mark then began to attack the therapist's puppet with his own.

THER: Why is the son attacking the father?

MARK: Because he's angry.

THER: Why?

MARK: Because it's my fault. It's all my fault that Dad left. Mom was beat up because she wanted to have me. If I hadn't been born, they would be together and happy. Dad left because Mom had me.

In Mark's play his wish for the therapist to become a robber and rescue him reflected a fantasy that his father would return. Through the transference the arrival of Mark's father was met with an array of emotions. For the first time in their sessions, Mark addressed the rage and sadness he felt toward his father for leaving. Mark could tell his father how guilty and responsible he felt that his father was gone and his mother was unhappy. In previous sessions Mark had made reference to seeing himself as a "bad" child, and the therapist often questioned whether his delinquent behaviors were related to his disturbed self-image. In the weeks that followed, Mark began to ask his mother more questions about his father and then questions about his own childhood. Not only did he inquire about the historical events but he also began to question why things occurred.

As treatment progressed, Mark began to discuss how he never felt safe. In one session Mark feverishly attempted to climb into a toy car much too small for a child his age. The therapist interpreted Mark's wish to return to being smaller. Mark quickly informed him that he wanted to be a baby again so that he could always stay safe in his mother's arms. In another session Mark spoke of his recurring nightmare in which a tornado swept everyone away. Before Mark began to talk, therapist and client had constructed a plastic chain. While Mark spoke, they each held on to an end of the chain. For Mark the chain may have served to keep him connected and safe as he talked about his separation fears. Following this session, the nightmares stopped. As termination approached, Mark was integrating much better both at home and in school. Ms. B indicated that Mark was showing greater impulse control and a considerably higher threshold for frustration. He also had become more caring. Ms. B., in turn, was experiencing more pleasure and satisfaction from her relationship with Mark and, in consequence, was investing more energy and time with her son. At school Mark was nearly ready to be mainstreamed into a regular classroom. He was receiving As and Bs in his classes. Mark was also developing friendships with children his age and had begun to participate in a soccer club and Cub Scouts, excelling in both.

DISCUSSION

In a case such as this, which is described in unusually rich detail, a number of possibilities suggest themselves. We might focus on differences in how treatment is conducted with a neurotic or characterologically disturbed child (Chethik 2000) versus one with a posttraumatic disorder. Or we might focus exclusively on the transference-countertransference, which became such an important aspect of this treatment process. Then, too, it would be tempting to explore various elements in the therapeutic alliance and how these were shaped or, perhaps, from a more technical side, the therapist's interpretive comments and any immediate and cumulative effects these appear to have had on the client. Or, we might proceed in a somewhat different direction, by examining Mark's *play* in greater depth and use this as a point of departure in our consideration of other questions about his treatment.

Perhaps one of the most striking aspects of Mark's treatment was the *way* in which he played. Early in treatment Mark's play was, qualitatively speaking, compulsive, driven, and lacking in pleasure, a triad of characteristics often associated with posttraumatic adaptations in children. The *form* of Mark's play also differed from that we associate with normal children or those who, in any event, have not suffered trauma. Herzog (2001), for example, has suggested that such children are unable to engage in the normal form of play, which developmentalists refer to as "symbolic." Symbolic play involves displacement, which generally means that the point of origin for play themes, scenarios, and their infinite variations is the child's own imagination. These dynamic themes, which are rooted in real experiences, are ultimately played out with toys and other play materials. In the usual course of development, children "move from action, to action with another, to displacement in which the action happens between the characters in the play" (Herzog 2001:135). However, traumatic experiences tend to throw this sequence in reverse, so that play moves "from displacement to enactment to an obligatory mutual enactment" (ibid.). Play, in effect, suffers a *deformation*.

We see this most vividly in two play scenarios, the first involving the pogs, the second Mark's game of "cops and robbers." Mark's play in both instances seems to involve what Herzog has termed the "shift to the left," the reversal of the usual symbolization process (Herzog 2001:135). During the pog play the therapist became aware of a powerful, induced countertransference reaction to retaliate against this difficult-to-manage child. Such a development in the play seems virtually to define the notion of "obligatory mutual enactment." Play in this context, rather than serving as a displacement through which *symbolization* and *working through* may occur, instead leads to an aspect of the *original traumatic experience*, which is then reenacted with the therapist.

A somewhat different way of understanding Mark's play and the powerful reactions and fantasies it seemed to elicit from his therapist is suggested in Bion's concept of therapeutic projective identification (Bion 1959) and Ogden's more contemporary treatment of this concept (Ogden 1982). According to Bion, the therapist's intuitive understanding and containment of the client's projected mental contents—rage, violent projections or other fantasies, anxieties, and various internally arising dangers—makes possible metabolization and detoxification, after which the "contained" material is offered back to the client, though in a therapeutically useful form (Bion 1959, 1962; Ogden 1982).[8] The therapeutic effect of such containment is to assure the client that the therapist cannot be destroyed and that he is a "good" container for such dangerous thoughts, wishes, or impulses, thus furnishing the client with a "safe context for emotional discharge" (Meissner 1966:20). Employing Bion's idea of projective identification and therapeutic containment, Mark's play scenarios take on additional meaning. We may now understand Mark's play reenactments to contain elements not only of paternal sadism and his own helplessness in the face of it but several additional elements as well. Mark seems to project overwhelming guilt over having caused his father to leave, rage at the paternal abandonment, and fantasies of his father's return. At various times the therapist is induced to feel, among other things, enraged, helpless, discounted, and terrorized. These feelings are perhaps more usefully thought of as the therapist's inner experience of the split-off and projected psychic contents that Mark has placed in him for safekeeping. Rather than acting on these disturbing impulses, Mark's therapist has been able, in the main, to contain them successfully, offering Mark a detoxified, therapeutic product instead. As one example, Mark's therapist "pins him down" without injuring him, demonstrating the therapist's capacity to alter and modulate Mark's unconscious desires to be injured/punished. In the later play session in which the therapist/cop is subjected to the client/robber's sadism, the therapeutically metabolized, projected material is offered back to the client in a new form, one that disrupts the posttraumatic quality of the play by emphasizing the emotions of the characters. It is perhaps of additional significance in this play scenario that the police officer, a guardian of order often used to symbolize authority, power, and control, is, at least at the outset, a helpless victim of sadism and violence. This seems to reinforce a basic view of the world as not simply being filled with dangerous forces, but one in which benevolent authority has ceased to exist. This session and the variations of the cop-and-robber play that followed, indeed, seem to have been pivotal, ultimately paving the way for important fantasy revelations about Mark's father's return, his mother's unhappiness, and the centrality of his own guilt in relation to both his parents.

In this chapter we began with a necessarily condensed history of the origins of the concept of child treatment within the psychoanalytic movement, focusing, in particular, on the Little Hans case and the contributions of Anna Freud and Melanie Klein. We then examined differences between child psychoanalysis and dynamic child psychotherapy, describing some of the most essential elements of a dynamic approach to child treatment. Particular attention was given to two topics: *clinical assessment* and *dynamic listening*. This discussion was followed by a detailed description of a specialized dynamic play technique, *reciprocal story-telling*, illustrated with a clinical vignette involving a passive-aggressive latency-aged boy originally referred because of poor academic performance and behavioral problems at home. The chapter concluded with the presentation and discussion of a detailed treatment case involving a traumatized child. This case highlighted such topics as symbolic play versus mutual obligatory enactment and notions of projective identification, countertransference, and therapeutic containment.

11

Adolescents

A LTHOUGH THE ADOLESCENT treatment literature has probably never been fully equivalent to its child treatment counterpart and, even today, remains somewhat of a "stepchild" to child psychotherapy, a review of the psychoanalytic literature reveals long-standing interest both in adolescence as a unique developmental stage and in the treatment of teenagers. The earliest references to adolescence in the psychoanalytic literature appear in "The Transformations of Puberty," the last of Freud's *Three Essays on the Theory of Sexuality* (Freud 1905b). This essay presented Freud's view that the changes set in motion by the arrival of puberty lead, inexorably, to the final shape of infantile sexuality. He noted that genital sexuality assumes a superordinate significance relative to the other "erotogenic zones" (i.e., oral and anal), new, gender-distinctive sexual aims are established, and the adolescent looks beyond the family for new sexual objects. Although Freud's essay and the subsequent contributions of a handful of followers (e.g., Jones 1948b [1922]; Bernfeld 1995 [1923]; Aichorn 1948 [1925]) conferred an early legitimacy on the topic of adolescence and adolescent treatment, this new field developed only gradually. Even twenty-five years later (Spiegel 1951) a comprehensive review of psychoanalytic contributions to the topic of adolescence yielded only eight publications dealing specifically with treatment issues.

Interest in adolescent psychotherapy began to gain momentum in the early 1950s, and in the last half-century the adolescent treatment literature has expanded significantly.[1] Authors have examined various forms of adolescent pathology (e.g., Lorand 1950; Mason 1954; Blos 1961; Rie 1966; Kernberg 1978; Kohut 1980; Rinsley 1980; Altschul and Pollock 1988; Kernberg 1991; Kernberg, Weiner, and Bardenstein 2000), salient developmental issues and conflicts (e.g., Erikson 1956; Spiegel 1961; Perret-Catipovic and Ladame 1998), and special applications/adaptations of psychoanalytic technique for teenagers (e.g., Lorand 1961;

Ekstein 1966; Sandler, Kennedy, and Tyson 1980; Meeks and Bernet 1990; Wilson 1997).

Inasmuch as dynamic conceptions of therapy with this clinical population correspond closely to our understanding of adolescent development, we begin with a review of adolescence as a unique developmental epoch, a time of rapid growth and change. Following this, a brief review of psychoanalytic ideas in the adolescent psychotherapy field is provided, highlighting the special challenges faced by therapists as well as modifications of dynamic technique required for effective work with this clinical population and the potential limitations such a treatment approach may possess. Case illustrations include an anaclitically depressed seventeen-year-old boy seen in an outpatient mental health clinic and a severely depressed, suicidal fourteen-year-old African American boy treated in a children's residential program.

AN OVERVIEW OF ADOLESCENT DEVELOPMENT

Interestingly, there has been little unanimity in the field of adolescent development as to the universality of adolescent turmoil or Sturm und Drang. Although many psychoanalytic developmentalists have offered strong endorsement of this concept (e.g., Erikson 1950; Freud 1958), others have questioned the presumption of universal turbulence in the lives of adolescents (Offer 1969; Rutter et al. 1976; Eccles et al. 1993) and, in some cases, the very notion of adolescence as a developmental phase (Musgrove 1965; Offer, Ostrove and Howard 1981). In the last two decades adolescent turmoil has been reconceptualized as occurring in conjunction with particular bodily changes, any of which might precipitate emotional upheaval (Fonagy et al. 2002). The specific biological changes that lead to such emotional reactions, however, are thought to vary considerably among adolescents and, furthermore, to depend heavily on what such changes represent or symbolize to the particular subject (Paikoff and Brooks-Gunn 1991). Nevertheless, a view of adolescence as a time of rapid physical, intellectual, and socioemotional growth and change, frequently though not invariably accompanied by turbulence and perplexity, seems largely to have prevailed.

The biological transition from late childhood to early adolescence is marked in both genders by the appearance of secondary sexual characteristics; in pubertal girls, this coincides with the onset of menarche and, in boys, with the capacity to produce semen. Neurocognitive changes in adolescence make possible the capacity for abstract reasoning and logic, which Piaget referred to as the stage of "formal operational thinking" (Piaget 1969). A coterminous development with this leap in the adolescent's intellectual prowess is a decline in the pervasiveness of primary process thinking—the language of play—which up until preadolescence had so dominated mental life. Other significant changes occur in the sphere of moral development, development of the ego and superego, and internalized object relations. The firming up of personal identity, which some theorists have termed the adolescent's "sense of self," also takes place during this developmental period.

Although the psychology of adolescence had been a subject of scientific interest since the beginning of the twentieth century (Hall 1904), it wasn't until the 1950s that psychoanalysts began to regard adolescence as a distinct developmental phase. Erikson's psychosocial epigenetic theory, which examined ego development across eight life span stages (described in greater detail in chapter 3), is considered one of the earliest systematic efforts to explore adolescent development. Erikson believed healthy ego development to be contingent upon the mastery of specific developmental tasks and normative crises in each stage of development, and his theory seemed to accord adolescence a special significance. Adolescence, Erikson theorized, ushered in the stage of *identity versus identity diffusion*, a developmental stage far more extensively developed in his epigenetic framework than were any of the other seven. Successful negotiation of this stage required the integration of formative experiences to furnish the child with "the sense that he is a person with a history, a stability, and a continuity that is recognizable by others" (Holzman 1998:163). The adolescent's failure to achieve identity consolidation, Erikson's theory suggested, might be considerable and could include developmental arrests and derailments as well as specific forms of psychopathology. It is, in fact, frequently observed that depressive symptoms, characterological disorders, and disturbances of sexual identity are among those forms of psychopathology often manifest during early to mid-adolescence.[2] Anna Freud, too, had referred to adolescence as a prolonged "normative crisis" (1969), and Winnicott had written of the need for a "moratorium for youth" (1964, 1984 [1963]) in recognition of the vital developmental tasks in which adolescents were engaged (Lanyado 1999).

The environment and, more specifically, relationships occurring within each adolescent's family both influence and reflect many of these changes. Blos asserted that the adolescent's struggles over autonomy, considered by many to be a hallmark of this developmental stage, mark the reemergence of the separation-individuation matrix (Blos 1962). Adolescent requirements for independence, and the parental responses that they educe, may at times become the modal topic of discourse within families. Even as the dependency of earlier childhood is shunned, adolescents in some important respects resemble the very childhood selves they believe have been safely relegated to the historical past. Although determined not to permit their parents a role of continuing importance in their lives, this very denial may arouse anxiety. The result is an intense feeling of ambivalence, since the availability of parents to assist in "listening, containing, setting boundaries, and limits, and providing a structured family" to which they may return, as the need arises, is still required (Jarvis 1999:118). Adolescent struggles with frustrations and disappointments, which may lead to a sense of personal inadequacy, humiliation, or shame, suggest a further parallel.

Others have suggested that the emphasis on autonomy and individuation associated with developmentalists such as Blos and Erikson may obscure the importance of *attachment*, the "dialectical counterpart" of the adolescent's struggle for independence (Fonagy et al. 2002). These authors note that "real separateness implies an ability to recognize both difference *and* similarity" and that this capacity presumes a secure attachment. Psychic autonomy and consolidation of self-identity, they suggest, may not be fully attainable without a "secure sense of connection and likeness to the caregiver" (321).

The bewildering forces typically unleashed in adolescent-parent interactions, object relations theorists assert, may be the result of mutual projective processes involving both emotions and the internal representations of both parties (Jarvis 1999). In the face of seemingly endless provocations by adolescents, the capacity of parents to "contain" adolescent fears and anxieties becomes crucial in this regard, ultimately permitting such distressing feelings and reactions to be modified, managed, and transformed into something far less malevolent. As we have seen, each psychoanalytic theory may explain this transformative experience in somewhat different terms. However, a central idea appears to be common to them all: that containment, and the stabilizing, calming, and soothing effects it implies, permits adolescents to internalize and develop their *own* capacity for containment. Through a transmutative process the object relationship with the containing or soothing and calming object (the parent) is incrementally taken in and gradually made part of the adolescent's enduring intrapsychic structure (Trzcinski and Brandell 2001–1).

The adolescent's capacity for self-containment is associated more generally with self-regulation, which evolves from a matrix of biological forces and alterations in intrapsychic structure that occur in tandem with parent-child interactions and other environmental influences. Various theorists, among them Kohut, Winnicott, and Lichtenberg, have addressed the phenomenon of self-regulation in both normal development and psychopathology. Novick and Novick (2002) have asserted that parents play a significant mediating and, at times, explicit role in promoting healthy self-regulation in children and adolescents. In their estimation a healthy system of self-regulation, which is further defined as one that

is "competent and effective," is "based on mutually respectful, pleasurable relationships formed through realistic perceptions of the self and others" (9). Moreover, such a system is "open to experience from inside and outside and thus generative of creativity in life and work" (ibid. This is contrasted with a closed,
omnipotent, sadomasochistic system of self-regulation in which developmental
foreclosure and related pathology occur as a consequence of serious medical
conditions, losses, or other psychological traumata for which there is inadequate
compensation. Despite the diminished scope of parental influence in the daily
lives of adolescents as compared to younger children, early developmental
injuries and failures may become telescoped to later development; when exacerbated by environmental limitations or parental inadequacies, a range of problems and clinical symptoms will be the likely result.

PSYCHODYNAMIC TREATMENT OF ADOLESCENTS:
AN INTRODUCTION

Over forty-five years ago Anna Freud observed that the unique developmental
position of the adolescent patient is in fundamental opposition to the psychoanalytic situation (Freud 1958). As we have suggested earlier, the adolescent is
engaged in almost ceaseless efforts to liberate herself from parental influence.
This need to diminish or otherwise alter relationships with parental figures is
reflexively translocated to the treatment situation, where the struggle plays out
once again with respect to the therapeutic alliance and the transference. Partly in
response to fluctuating internal pressures, teenagers are notoriously inclined to
favor action over reflection, often characterized in the psychoanalytic literature
as the tendency to make disproportionate use of "experiencing" over observing
ego. Adolescent self-esteem, which is defined by its fragile and mercurial qualities, seems to predispose adolescents to externalization rather than introspection
(Lerner 2002). There is also the problem of identifying an appropriate vehicle for
therapeutic communication. Play therapy techniques, which perhaps just a year
or two earlier would have been experienced as natural, serving as an effective
channel for therapeutic communications, are now felt to be inappropriate and
infantilizing. At the same time, in spite of the adolescent's newly emerging capacities for complex cognitive operations, abstraction, and logic, these capacities are
as yet, unconsolidated. The result is that many adolescents are incapable of the
sustained self-observation required for the use of free association. The challenge
of adolescent psychotherapy is further compounded by other factors, some of
which reside in the patient, others of which belong more properly to the family,
and still others, to the therapist.

Challenges:

Among those factors residing in the patient are a reluctance to acknowledge *pt*
distress, the propensity of externalization, and the frequent shifting character
of mental organization. Complicating factors residing in the family revolve
around the powerful forces of denial and the intergenerational transmission of
psychopathology. Complicating factors in therapists revolve around a lack of
clarity about developmental norms and expectations and a clear conceptual
framework for understanding adolescent psychopathology. (Lerner 2002:124)

Although previous chapters have explored issues germane to child and adolescent therapy, such as transference and countertransference (chapters 4 and 5),
the real relationship (chapter 7), and transference interpretation (chapter 8), we
have not commented specifically on the notion of alliance in the psychotherapy
of adolescents. While the adolescent's direct expression of a wish for assistance in *the*
coping with conflicts and other internal problems may represent the most psy- *alliance*
chologically mature basis for a therapeutic alliance, such an occurrence, as a general rule, is unusual. Indeed, as I have already suggested, Anna Freud was not at all
sanguine as to the prospect of successful psychoanalytic treatment of adolescents,
in large measure owing to the significant obstacles posed to alliance-formation
with this clinical population. Even a predominantly positive attachment to the
therapist and an articulated wish for assistance in being able to overcome internal conflicts and problems, elements integral to an effective therapeutic alliance,
might prove insufficient to counterbalance an adolescent's "mistrust, suspicion,
skepticism, and doubt" so often experienced "in association with . . . efforts to
break ties with the parental figure" (Sandler, Tyson, and Kennedy 1980:50).

Not all threats to alliance formation with adolescents, however, are confined
to internal dangers or to the treatment relationship proper. Various factors extraneous to the alliance may also play a central role, the most common of which is
the influence exerted by parents, who may consciously or unknowingly sabotage *Parents*
the treatment relationship for a variety of reasons (Meeks and Bernet 1990). Par- *in*
ents may become resentful of the strongly positive or affectionate tie that devel- *ther.*
ops between child and therapist or they may attempt to enlist the therapist as an *alliance*
agent of their own hostility or manipulative control. Some may even be threatened by an adolescent's improvement should this prove disruptive to well established though pathological patterns of family interaction (Meeks and Bernet
1990). There are other factors extrinsic to the alliance that also may restrict or
otherwise interfere with its stability. The illness or death of a parent or other
emotionally significant individual in the adolescent's life may necessitate an
emotional withdrawal or need to mourn. Likewise, narcissistic injury stemming
from an overwhelming defeat or traumatic disappointment may also temporarily interfere with the stability of the alliance (Meeks and Bernet 1990).

Some adolescent therapists believe strongly that their role within the thera-peutic alliance is to enable young patients to understand the relationship between intercurrent feelings and behavior rather than to focus extensively on early conflicts and other genetic determinants of current problems. The argu-ment advanced in support of this position is that many adolescents, particularly younger ones, cannot tolerate the regression that genetic interpretations may call forth and that such a focus will likely threaten the adolescent's progressive devel-opment (Meeks and Bernet 1990). Other therapists, in conceiving of dynamic interpretation as a process that may ultimately unearth earlier conflicts or devel-opmental arrests, may be more inclined to employ such genetic interpretations, though in a cautious and parsimonious manner (Coppolillo 1987).

Some adolescents fail to develop a treatment alliance, which usually leads to a generally unsatisfactory therapeutic result. However, the failure to develop a treatment alliance is not invariably associated with therapeutic failure, as the fol-lowing brief vignette will illustrate.

Ricky T. was thirteen years old and in the eighth grade when he was referred for treatment by the school psychologist. Ricky, who had been adopted along with his sixteen-year-old brother in early childhood, exhibited a disturbing range of symptoms that suggested an emerging disorder of character. He had few friends, had several times been reprimanded for bullying younger chil-dren at school, and was emotionally volatile and hyperaggressive. His rela-tionship with his adoptive mother was especially troubled, in significant part owing to her own character pathology. He was also "accident-prone." On one occasion, while his parents were away, he was operating a power saw without adult supervision and sliced off a portion of his finger. He often arrived late for his sessions and expressed nearly unceasing resentment at having to come for therapy. A talented artist, he sometimes drew caricatures of the therapist and invented a game called "Guess the Feeling," which became another vehicle for Ricky to express his disregard both for the idea of treat-ment and his therapist. In spite of Ricky's apparent failure to develop any-thing much resembling a therapeutic alliance, he demonstrated some gains outside of treatment. In particular, his acting out at school seemed to dimin-ish and he also found more adaptive ways to extricate himself from his adop-tive mother's intrusive influence. It is possible the adversarial transference that developed in Ricky's treatment may have enabled him to accomplish certain developmental tasks that had been derailed or that an alliance did exist, but not in the more traditional sense of the term. However, it may also be argued that his failure to develop an alliance in which observing ego eventually played a prominent role rendered such improvement more "symptomatic" in nature and less the result of the structural alterations believed necessary for more enduring change. Nevertheless, characterologically disturbed youngsters such as Ricky may "benefit materially from a psychotherapeutic interaction in spite" of their inability to form a traditional therapeutic alliance (Meeks and Bernet 1990:118).

Although resistance in both children and adolescents may serve a similar *function* to that in adults (discussed in chapter 8), its *form* may be dissimilar from that observed in older clients. We have already noted the inherently less stable nature of the therapeutic alliance in adolescents. This, in combination with adolescents' tendency to utilize a sort of action language in place of introspection and self-observation and their less fully developed capacity for tolerating disappointments and delays in gratification, may fuel both conscious and unconscious resistance (Freud 1958; Sandler, Tyson, and Kennedy 1980; Mishne 1986). Where the adult patient may struggle with a disinclination to show up for an appointment and be able to overcome such a resistance, the adolescent patient may simply refuse to come. Although such resistance may stem from a variety of different sources, one common scenario may involve the therapist's invitation to the adolescent to discuss matters about which there may be a considerable burden of guilt. The adolescent "opens up" to the therapist and discusses a forbidden matter but then fails to arrive for the next appointment, having experienced the therapist as seductive and dangerous (Sandler, Kennedy, and Tyson 1980). Such resistances, Anna Freud observes, can sometimes be anticipated, and interpretations given "in advance" to prepare the patient for the possibility. In the instance described above, the therapist might warn the patient that a guilt reaction might be anticipated following the revelation of a conflictual idea or memory not previously discussed (ibid.).

Various treatment options exist in clinical work with adolescents, although, regrettably, clinical decisions to offer a particular kind of treatment are now based as often on the judgment of health care managers or other third parties as they are on the prerogative of clinician and patient. It may, nevertheless, be useful to identify and briefly describe three major forms of individual treatment employed in adolescent therapy: *expressive* or *insight-oriented psychotherapy*, *supportive psychotherapy*, and *psychoanalysis*.[3]

Clinicians have sometimes suggested that expressive or insight-oriented psychotherapy, which tends to be long-term and more intensive (often two and sometimes more sessions week), is more useful for patients demonstrating discrete areas of internal conflict, a sound ego structure, and the capacity for insight and psychological mindedness (Mishne 1997). Such a treatment approach is typically more anxiety-arousing than is supportive treatment and requires that the patient be motivated and have some capacity for tolerating frustration, an inevitability in the course of an intensive therapy. Furthermore, therapists employing such a clinical approach would be more likely to make some use of interpretation and to promote introspection, self-understanding, and the adolescent's adaptive resolution of conflicts or other problematic issues. A higher valuation, too, may be placed on the role of transference fantasies, reactions, and the more enduring transference relationship; moreover, the gradual acquisition of insight into some aspects of the adolescent's transference may also be considered a goal of this treatment approach.

Very disturbed adolescents, such as those presenting with nascent or diagnosable disturbances of character, habit disorders, posttraumatic sequelae, and psychoticlike disorders, are oftentimes thought, at least initially, to require treatment that is of a fundamentally supportive nature. Supportive treatment may also be useful with clients who are in an acute crisis precipitated by environmental events (e.g., loss of a home due to fire, recent death of a family member, or exposure to a traumatic experience). It may additionally be indicated for those who are experiencing acute anxiety or depression for which there is no discernible external precipitant. Such a supportive treatment framework aims to do one or more of the following: restore previous levels of adaptive functioning, prevent regression in adaptive functioning, maintain adaptive functioning through environmental manipulation as a means of enhancing the adolescent's continuing adaptation, or expand the adolescent's repertoire of healthier adaptations and coping strategies.

There is undoubtedly some degree of overlap between these basic treatment approaches. Indeed, many treatments may begin as principally supportive in nature, though they may later evolve into expressive psychotherapy. As a rule, in supportive treatment there is far less emphasis on the use of interpretation, the relationship of earlier conflicts, issues, injuries, and other developmental problems to the client's current complaints, transference phenomena, the development of insight, and so forth. Furthermore, alterations in intrapsychic structure, while theoretically possible, are neither expected nor a legitimate focus of a supportive treatment approach. Improvements often occur without the client's full awareness and, in any event, do not require a significant enhancement in the adolescent's capacity for self-observation or self-knowledge. From the side of the clinician, supportive work may involve deliberate and greater use of oneself as an "auxiliary ego" for the client. The term *auxiliary ego* refers to a therapist role in which missing or deficient ego functions, such as judgment or the ability to break large tasks down into smaller, more manageable units (partializing), are made available to the client. The therapist may, similarly, feel less constrained in the context of supportive treatment, in serving as a "selfobject" for an adolescent client. In this role, which differs significantly from that of selfobject transference (as described in chapter 4), the therapist *actively* furnishes "narcissistic supplies" or selfobject functions to the adolescent client. Such "supplies," which are linked to particular selfobject domains (i.e., idealizing, mirroring, and partnering), may consist of affirmation or praise to a discouraged client or reassuring, calming, and soothing remarks to one who is anxious or upset.

Psychoanalytic work with adolescents, which generally involves a minimum of three sessions per week, and often as many as five, is most usefully seen as a special variant of expressive or insight-oriented treatment, as previously described. Traditionally, psychoanalysis was reserved for a smaller subset of disturbed adolescents. These individuals mostly suffered from psychoneurotic conditions, evinced good capacity for relatedness to others, demonstrated the ability to observe and report their feelings and fantasies, and possessed a threshold for frustration sufficient to allow them to discuss impulses before converting them into action (Coppolillo 1987). Optimally, they also resided in environments that were stable enough to support frequent treatment sessions, and sufficiently healthy to preclude the possibility of massive environmental traumata (e.g., physical or sexual abuse, life threatening illnesses, or parental abandonment). Pathology stemming from regressions rather than developmental arrests in consequence of psychological trauma was also thought more likely to respond to psychoanalytic treatment (ibid.). The promotion of a transference neurosis, an arguable criterion for psychoanalytic work with younger children, appears to have greater conceptual legitimacy in the psychoanalysis of adolescents, especially older ones. However, even therapists who question the clinical salience of transference neurosis for adolescents in psychoanalytic treatment agree that the transference clearly gains in importance with the intensification of a treatment that is offered at a frequency of three to five sessions per week.

In more recent times, the boundaries between intensive psychotherapy and psychoanalysis have become more indistinct, especially insofar as the criteria for inclusion are concerned. This may be due, in part, to clinical and research literature that appears to demonstrate the effectiveness of a psychoanalytic approach with patient populations at one time thought to be untreatable with psychoanalysis (e.g., borderline or narcissistic individuals). Furthermore, posttraumatic cases involving developmental arrest no longer appear to be a contraindication for psychoanalysis; adolescent patients who suffer from dissociative disorders and those with dependent and schizoid personality features have also been successfully treated psychoanalytically. Nevertheless, the correspondingly greater and more consistent emphasis on the transference relationship, the understanding and interpretation of resistance, and the comparatively greater use of both dynamic and genetic interpretations highlight continuing distinctions between the method and treatment objectives of psychoanalysis and those of insight-oriented therapy.

CLINICAL CASE ILLUSTRATION 11.1: "DAN"

Dan L, a seventeen-year-old Caucasian high school senior, was originally referred to an outpatient mental health clinic by his high school guidance counselor, following his disclosure to her that he had made a suicidal gesture the preceding weekend. The immediate precipitant was Dan's anxiety and helplessness in the face of a difficult assignment given by his favorite teacher. Feeling overwhelmed and as though he could not see a favorable outcome to what seemed like a formidable challenge, he downed six or eight valium with some gin and fell into a deep sleep. He did this on a Sunday afternoon with the knowledge that his mother and younger sisters, who were out shopping, would be returning within two or three hours. When they discovered him, they found it odd that he was asleep, but did not awaken him. After awakening on his own several hours later, Dan told his mother and father what he had done, although neither parent made an effort over the next several days to contact a therapist or counselor. It was only after Dan's conversation with his academic adviser that a referral process was initiated.

In early work with Dan, due to his suicidal gesture, the treatment plan to which he and his family agreed called for meetings to be held on a three-times-weekly basis (later reduced to two times weekly). He also underwent an evaluation by an experienced adolescent psychiatrist who concurred with my recommendation for multiple sessions conducted on an outpatient basis. The possibility of hospitalization was briefly considered, although the nature of the gesture as well as the patient's willingness to abide by the treatment plan and his denial of further suicidal ideation supported the plan for intensive outpatient work.

Dan and his parents, Mr. and Mrs. L, initially denied the significance of what had occurred and, in a separate interview, continually referred to their "concern" for Dan and his distress in an emotionally distant way. Mr. and Mrs. L attempted to form a "false alliance" with me, in which the three of us were to engage in a sort of collaboration to assist their son. This needed to be repeatedly pointed out to them, their denial of the significance of the suicidal gesture interpreted.

Dan was very depressed, quiet, passive, and secretly condescended to me and to the idea of treatment. He felt he was being scrutinized and analyzed in therapy and soon began to complain in his individual sessions that I expected things of him that he was unable to provide. Becoming increasingly agitated on several occasions, Dan denounced the whole process. He also indicated that I must ask him questions and that he would otherwise refuse to say anything. My reactions at this time consisted of perplexity and exasperation, a real concern that the family's denial could potentiate further denial in the patient and lead to a flight into health, or to an intensification of the client's considerable resistance, and, later, that the client felt abject hatred for me.

During family meetings, which were conducted every six weeks or so, the client would typically remain passive and uninvolved in discussions. The parents were quite happy to talk to each other and to me, but it was only with great effort that I was able to bring all three back to the issue of Dan's depression and his suicidality. In later family interviews Dan became openly critical of me to his parents, referring to me in the most unflattering language. Although my initial reaction to Dan's derogatory comments was something akin to narcissistic mortification, I gradually came to understand these pronouncements by Dan as an oblique expression of his deepening transference feelings toward me.

As a primitive therapeutic alliance was gradually forged and Dan became somewhat more expressive during interviews, he began to talk about his relationships with both his parents. His father, a successful entrepreneur, was an imposing physical figure, with a deep and sometimes rather booming voice. Mr. L came from a lower-middle-class background and had created opportunities for himself in spite of the fact that little money was available from his family to support him in college or law school. Dan's mother had a similar family background; she had attended though never graduated from college and now worked in a paraprofessional capacity in the same suburban high school her son attended. Ms. L observed, with some pride, that her energies had been focused on raising Dan, his older brother, and his younger sisters and that the gratifications of family life more than offset whatever she may have sacrificed in the way of a professional career. Dan described his father as a very accomplished and successful attorney. Their early relationship was a good one; Dan observed that his father could be very tolerant, especially when it came to his protracted difficulty in sleeping through the night in his own room, a developmental milestone not reached until age six or seven. There was some indication, in fact, that Dan may have suffered from *pavor nocturnus* (night terror), inasmuch as he sometimes awoke screaming and was difficult to arouse during these episodes. Despite this early closeness between father and son, Dan's relationship with his father had gradually grown more distant, he noted. Mr. L was a highly competitive individual who "always has to have the last word." Dan's mother, on the other hand, tended to be overly concerned and overinvolved with him, to which he responded ambivalently. At times it was reassuring if not gratifying; at other times, however, he felt "repelled" by it.

In the early phase of treatment, which lasted roughly seven months, the effort was to stabilize Dan's functioning and assist him in developing greater capacity for expressing angry affects and for being assertive without feeling reactive shame. Therapy had begun in mid-December, although by mid-summer Dan seemed very eager to end his treatment. Some weeks earlier he had been notified of his acceptance by a local college, a rather prestigious private school whose letter of acceptance had both surprised and delighted him. We talked about the prospect of Dan either continuing treatment with me (since he would still be within commuting distance) or accepting a referral to a therapist closer to campus. Dan was not amenable to either possibility; and although I was far less confident as to his readiness to bring his treatment to closure, I finally acceded to his wishes, and we terminated in the first half of August.

Less than three weeks after his matriculation in college, Dan contacted me at home, asking to be seen as soon as possible. He was in an agitated state and reported feeling both anxious and depressed. He had been unable to leave his dormitory room except to attend classes and had returned to his parents' home each weekend. He finally decided to contact me when he found himself thinking about suicide the evening before; he couldn't bear the thought that the despair he had originally experienced some ten months earlier might return full force. Dan agreed to arrange for a consultation with the psychiatrist in the student health center, who placed him on an antidepressant; we then began to meet on a once-weekly basis, an arrangement that continued for three months. The following excerpt, derived from a session held about six weeks after Dan returned to therapy, is focused both on the historical antecedents of his ongoing difficulty with depression and the way in which these conflicts had found expression in his transference relationship with me.

DAN: You asked me a few sessions back if these feelings that I had right before I called you, if I'd ever felt anything like this before . . . not just when I first came to see you last year, but like when I was a kid? Well, I couldn't really answer then, but I was thinking a little about it over the weekend. It did sort of remind me of how I used to feel when my mom would leave me at preschool, even at kindergarten and first grade. I would get panicked, thinking that . . . I don't know what I thought. That maybe she'd forget to come back for me or something. I'd get so scared sometimes, I'd even hurt myself so that she'd have to come to school and pick me up; sometimes she would anyway. But, then, later, she'd want to hold me, or stroke me, or something . . . and I wouldn't want her to. I'd be mad at her, although I'd try not to show it.

THER: Well, I think this is important. Of course, you've talked before about how difficult separations were for you when you were little, including play dates with friends, the night terror, and so forth. These early feelings, it seems, have never gone away completely. It's as though a part of you feels the same sort of panic when you're in a situation, even now, as an eighteen-year-old, where you're expected to handle things on your own.

DAN: And then getting mad at her . . . where does that fit in?

THER: It's the other side of the same coin. This dependency thing isn't a good feeling, and even when you were successful in getting her to come to school, you felt resentment—in the first place, at her not being there when you needed her, and then, when she finally did arrive, because you wanted to be a big boy, someone who doesn't need mommy always to be there, who can manage problems on his own. *[interpretation]*

DAN: (*Sounding irritated*) you know . . . all of this sounds good, but it doesn't really make me feel any better. If it's so accurate, how come I still feel depressed? Why am I still coming home on weekends? Really, I don't think you've said anything that I couldn't have figured out on my own.

(*Pause.*)

THER: Actually, something occurs to me about the pattern we've just talked about. First, you felt panicked and needy, and then you'd experience either despair if your mother failed to respond quickly enough, or resentment when she did and tried to help you. Right?

DAN: Yeah, OK.

THER: That pattern is now a part of *our* relationship. You begin to feel panicked, as though you can't make it on your own. Then, you contact me, asking to come in right away. You even tell me that you've been thinking about hurting yourself, just like you used to do to get your mom to come to school. So, I give you an appointment, except by the time we meet the crisis is already over. And, then, everything I have to say seems self-evident to you; furthermore, it doesn't help. And you start to feel resentment, just like *[Transference interpretation]* you used to at your mother. After all, you're a big boy now—you can do this by yourself. Who needs a therapist?

DAN: OK. I think I see where you're going with this. Only, knowing this *still* doesn't make me feel any better.

A few weeks later, another family meeting was held. Perhaps not too surprisingly, Dan complained at this session that, after an entire year of treatment, he didn't feel any better and thought of therapy as "a joke," although he also recognized that he felt "stronger" and more self-confident now than he had earlier. He didn't think he needed to continue, especially since he was now taking an antidepressant. It seemed clear that, once again, Dan had made a unilateral decision to discontinue his treatment. Perhaps wishing to believe that Dan's insistence on ending his treatment represented a healthy expression of autonomy, his parents were supportive; they mentioned only that it was up to Dan to take the initiative in contacting me should he feel the need.

Somewhat to my surprise, Dan again contacted me shortly after the December holiday break and asked if he might return for treatment. He attended regularly for nearly five months, during which time his academic performance became stronger, he started dating a girl on a regular basis, and stopped returning to his parents' home every weekend. But, once again, in late May, Dan expressed his desire to quit therapy, believing it no longer to be necessary now that he had made it through his freshman year of college. Confronting him directly, I observed that there was a pattern in his participation in treatment that required closer examination and that this was very central to his struggle with depression. I then strongly advised Dan to give himself more time to think about his decision or at least to give us an opportunity to discuss the process of terminating. Although we were now concluding our work together for the third time, the ending phase had always been an abbreviated one, a more or less immediate and unilateral decision on Dan's part, leaving little time for discussion. Once again, Dan refused, and treatment ended. I heard from Dan on one subsequent occasion. About four months following our last session, several weeks into his sophomore year at college, Dan contacted me, in crisis, to request an immediate appointment. By this time, however, having relocated, I was not able to meet with him. In our phone conversation Dan seemed both surprised and hurt, but he did accept the names of several colleagues I recommended to him.

DISCUSSION

Dan suffered from what has been termed an *anaclitic depression*. The usage of the term *anaclitic* dates to Freud's seminal paper on narcissism in which he describes the the "original attachment . . . [to] persons who are concerned with a child's feeding, care, and protection . . . that is, to say . . . the mother or a substitute for her" (Freud 1914a:87). Spitz and Wolf (1946) first used the term *anaclitic depression* to describe the reaction of infants to severe maternal deprivation in the second half of the first year. Later, Blatt (1974) suggested that most depressions in adolescents typically fall into one of two major types: anaclitic and introjective. We have previously discussed introjective or superego depression in connection with the case of Ian (in chapters seven and eight). Anaclitic depression, unlike introjective depression, entails psychopathology that is the consequence of difficulties in achieving psychological separation from one's family of origin (Bemporad and Gabel 1992). Because such teenagers have not become sufficiently individuated so as to function adequately without a parental figure, environmental demands that require autonomy may evoke despair, anxiety, and depression.

> When strong atavistic dependency needs arise in times of stress, the adolescent, who is trying hard to see himself as an independent adult, feels ashamed of and humiliated by his own dependency. These youngsters continue to require an omnipotent, need-satisfying parental substitute and are exceedingly frightened by the changes that transpire in their social expectations and psychological functioning as a result of their maturation. They typically decompensate when they are forced to venture out on their own and realize their limitations, which had been previously hidden or compensated for by family and its attendant security. (Bemporad and Gabel 1992:120)

Zaslow's (1992) description of anaclitic depression also emphasizes such features as clingy dependency, helplessness, ego regression (in the form of disordered concentration or work inhibition), a heightened potential for suicidality, and denial of aggression. Such adolescents tend also to relate to others, including the therapist, in a fundamentally narcissistic way and are constantly in search of nurturance, so that therapists working with them experience the therapeutic relationship as one-sided and nonreciprocal. The teen's expectation is that the therapist will furnish him with a "cure," but one that requires little work on the patient's part. The combination of the depressed adolescent's whiny demandingness and his inability to forge a mature therapeutic alliance, one characterized by an acceptance of mutual responsibility, is often further compounded by counterdependent behavior and devaluations of the therapy and therapist.

So it was with Dan, whose depression had first arisen during his senior year of high school over what at first appeared to be a trivial problem—his belief that he would be unable to complete a difficult assignment for a teacher whose good opinion he valued highly. Dan's dramatic decompensation, which led to the suicidal gesture, was likely the end point in a sequence of events, however, each of which served to underscore his deficiencies in negotiating the important developmental tasks of late adolescence. For example, Dan had recently begun submitting applications to college programs, which proved to be a tension-filled process for both him and his family. And then graduation loomed on the horizon, representing yet another milestone in a rapidly expanding universe of social relationships and setting the stage for new experiences. Dan felt unprepared for the social, emotional, and intellectual challenges he now faced.

It is of considerable interest, to judge from the developmental data that Dan and his family furnished me, that his struggle with dependency antedated this adolescent crisis by a good number of years. In fact, this was an old issue, one that seems to have begun in early childhood and that may have accounted for his *pavor nocturnus* as well as a continuing problem with separations at school and elsewhere. To use the language of attachment theory, Dan seems to have made what is termed an "ambivalent attachment" to his mother. On the one hand, he felt an almost continuous need for contact with her, yet, on the other, he experienced resentment over his difficulty in extricating himself emotionally from her. Ms. L may, unwittingly, have fostered this dependency by too readily complying with Dan's dependent wishes rather than promoting his efforts at individuation and separation, tentative though those may have been.

In treatment the pattern of thwarted dependency and counterdependent behavior was recapitulated in the transference. Environmental demands for autonomous action represented a danger situation for Dan, and such demands took many forms. The challenge might be intellectual in nature, as the homework assignment proved to be, or it might be a social one, such as asking out a girl for a date; it might also involve a more significant life transition, as would the move from high school to college. Dan had urgently sought out my assistance, unable to summon the strength necessary to confront these tasks on his own. Yet, he felt resentful of me, of needing to ask for my help. Consequently, he devalued my role and the value of therapy more generally, even as he continued to complain that he felt no better and could do everything that therapy was doing on his own. At times his resentment felt more like hatred, though he consistently denied having such feelings toward me. I also began to consider the likelihood that commingled within the maternal transference was the old rivalry with his father; perhaps he felt that I, like his father, must also have the "last word." When I suggested this explanation, Dan acknowledged the possibility, though he minimized its importance.

As I noted in the clinical summary above, Dan, on several occasions, made unilateral decisions to withdraw from treatment, though each time he returned in a panic, overwhelmed with anxiety and depression and on the verge of despair. My efforts to interpret the revival within the transference of this early pattern of anaclitic attachment were for the most part unsuccessful. However, despite Dan's insistence on innumerable occasions that psychotherapy had not helped him at all, he had managed successfully to complete a year of college at a highly competitive Ivy League school and had started to date a girl regularly by the end of the spring semester. Although, like Anthony (1970), I felt drained by this patient's neediness and inability to assume his share of the responsibility in our work together, I noted with some satisfaction these areas of improvement in Dan's life.

CLINICAL CASE ILLUSTRATION 11.2: "MALCOLM"

Malcolm, a thirteen-and-a-half-year-old African American male, was referred to a children's residential program following an episode of acute depression and suicidal behavior. His suicidal gestures had resulted in two previous hospitalizations, though without discernible improvement. Other behaviors that led to his need for residential placement included threats to poison his grandmother with bleach, a preoccupation with the idea of setting his house on fire, and escalating physical aggression. The intensity of Malcolm's behavioral difficulties prevented him from living with his maternal grandmother, whose deteriorating health left her physically and emotionally unable to care for him. Thus there was essential agreement among the several mental health professionals working with Malcolm and his grandmother that residential placement was required. His highly charged emotions and nearly continuous struggle to manage powerful impulses that threatened to go careening out of control necessitated a more contained and structured environment that could offer him safety, security, and greater understanding of his emotional difficulties.

Malcolm's early childhood history was laden with chaos and disorganization. His mother, a chronic substance abuser, was suspected of having abused alcohol, marijuana, and possibly crack cocaine while Malcolm was in utero, although he did not suffer from fetal alcohol syndrome, nor is there a record of his having been treated for perinatal cocaine addition. However, his well-being was, in an important sense, already compromised and damaged by his mother's self-destructive actions and her inability to "hold" him either during her pregnancy or after his birth. Emotional deprivation and neglect shaped his very early life, and it appeared that Malcolm had never been cared for with warmth or emotional sensitivity. When he was a year old, Malcolm and his older brother went to live with their maternal grandmother, who had been awarded their guardianship. His biological parents, who never married, visited him infrequently, which only seemed to heighten his feelings of rejection, abandonment, and loss. Malcolm verbalized intense hatred of his mother and father, often referring to them as "crack lovin' junkies, who were fucked in the head." In an earlier treatment Malcolm had reported that he had on a number of occasions actually witnessed his mother "using drugs" and she "looked like a skinny, ugly crack junkie." As he approached mid-latency, Malcolm lived for a time with his father, who regularly exposed him to hard-core pornographic literature and who would also bring home prostitutes. Malcolm's grandmother likely provided him some sense of security; however, she had difficulty in remaining empathically attuned to his intense and unending emotional needs. Disharmony and conflict loomed large within their relationship. Eventually, Malcolm's difficulties were more than she could handle, as he became increasingly difficult to control, challenging and offending school authorities, reporting suicidal preoccupations and making suicidal gestures, and threatening his grandmother. By the time Malcolm arrived at the children's residential program, he was in desperate need, though not surprisingly he at first seemed completely unenthusiastic about the therapeutic program or, for that matter, the very *idea* of residential placement. Gaining his trust and establishing an effective therapeutic alliance under such distressing circumstances would prove to be challenging for the milieu staff as well as his therapist.

Malcolm, who was tall and attractive though thin-framed, conveyed both strong anxiety and hypervigilance. He rapidly established an intensive relationship with his therapist, whom he saw twice weekly, that wavered between feelings of deep love and deeply felt hatred. He interacted wildly with his therapist and others in the therapeutic milieu, behaving in a reckless and impulsive manner and often shouting "I hate you," "fuck you," and "nobody cares about me" somewhat indiscriminately to various staff members. He had tremendous difficulty containing angry affect, which often took the form of degrading insults and vicious comments. Never in short supply, these noxious epithets seemed always to issue forth during efforts by staff to establish a positive, meaningful interaction with him. It became increasingly apparent that Malcolm's internal world was overflowing with terrifying affects and fantasies that he neither understood nor was able to stop. He was suspicious to the point of paranoia of any attempt the therapist or others might make to be gentle or comforting. He seemed far more comfortable in a situation in which he might provoke someone into trading invectives with him—even though such exchanges might leave him feeling injured or worthless—than one in which positive interactions occurred. Malcolm perceived the world as a place filled with mistrust, suspicion, and badness. Yet, in spite of this, it was the impression of the staff and his therapist that Malcolm yearned for something else: a positive, reassuring encounter with another human being.

The following excerpt is derived from a session that took place within several months of Malcolm's arrival at the children's residential home. It is fairly representative of the tireless efforts made by his therapist, an attractive female clinician in her late twenties, to develop a trusting therapeutic alliance despite Malcolm's resistance and provocative nature. Shortly before the interview, Malcolm had learned of the possibility that his biological father might gain custody of him because of his grandmother's decision to sever her guardianship.

CLIENT: (*Angrily*) so when am I gonna be discharged?

THER: This seems to be the question that is always on your mind, and, for the time being, you will stay here until we hear from your worker. Your worker, Ms. Davis, is still trying to get in touch with your father to figure out if you will eventually live with him. What are your thoughts about living with your dad? It's been a long time since you've lived with him or even had contact with him, for that matter.

CLIENT: Well, fuck him. He doesn't care, give a shit. I hate him, I can't stand him. I hate you, you white bitch. You are always telling me the same answer, same story that I'm never gonna leave here. I hate it here! No one is helping me. My real therapy is going to begin once I leave here.

THER: I know that this is real disappointing and that my answer is always the same. Unfortunately your situation won't be changing anytime soon. Maybe we could try to understand all the angry and disappointed feelings you have . . .

CLIENT: I come from a goddamn dysfunctional family. How do I even know I'm my mother's baby? I betcha' she stole me from the hospital! They never shoulda' had me in the first place. My parent's don't want me, my grandma don't want me, you don't even like me.

THER: It seems you want me to understand, really understand, how rejected you feel by your mother, father, and grandmother. And you're also wondering if I'm going to leave you, give up on you, the way everyone else has.

Malcolm was nearly obsessed with these abandonments and losses, which had left him feeling so massively injured and enraged. He perceived people as threatening and insulting toward him, dishonest, and cruel. Even when one attempted to say a kind word, or make a heartfelt gesture, Malcolm was immediately dismissive, mounting defenses so as to wall himself off from any further such efforts. Paradoxically, in a life filled with insulting, humiliating, and hurtful experiences, negatives often felt far more familiar and were much more easily tolerated than loving, positive experiences.

During Malcolm's residential stay, he continued to hold to the position that others were "out to get him" and would consequently reject all efforts of the milieu staff and his therapist at meaningful contact. Within the context of his therapy, the clinician worked to establish a relationship with Malcolm in which "trust" was not contingent on fulfillment of the other's emotional needs, or subject to expediency or whim, but was rather the consequence of a slowly evolving therapeutic process. After a time, Malcolm showed the first signs of real progress, and the therapeutic relationship deepened. But then, in a rather sudden shift, his transference took on an erotized form. Malcolm began to reveal very explicit sexual fantasies about the therapist, even boldly inviting her "onto the couch—where we could be more comfortable." Ruminative sexual thoughts and fantasies accompanied by powerful affects and desires now regularly found their way into the therapeutic discourse. As the therapist sat with Malcolm, at times perplexed or even shocked by the frankness of his sexual revelations, she, nevertheless, sought to decipher their significance. What might such thoughts and fantasies represent in terms of his past experiences? What was Malcolm trying to convey to her about their relationship? Naively, Malcolm's therapist began to question whether she had inadvertently invited these explicit, sexualized expressions of intimate desire, especially since she had never before been the object of such intense longing. Retrospectively, she wondered whether a boundary had been violated, whether she had somehow given Malcolm the wrong message in their encounters.

At the height of his erotized transference, Malcolm brought in his journal and read an entry that revealed more details than had previously emerged regarding the nature of these sexual fantasies about the therapist.

CLIENT: "Ms. E is so pretty and nice. I have thoughts of Ms. E when I lay awake in bed. I think about making love, having sex with her. I want to make her feel good. I want to undress Ms. E and have her undress me. When we make love, I want to be on top of her. I wonder if Ms. E has a boyfriend or a husband. I love Ms. E. and want her to love me back."

THER: You seem to have very strong feelings and thoughts about me, my life. Could you tell me more?

CLIENT: I just want to be with you. You know . . . I'm not a virgin. I've been with other women, older women. I know how to make a woman feel good.

THER: I wonder if by telling me about the thoughts you have about us, you're trying to figure out how I am going to react to you and what you have to say. Will I still like you for *you* or be upset with you?

CLIENT: So what do ya think Ms. E, can we get somethin' goin'?

THER: No, Malcolm, we're *not* gonna get something going. Ours is a different kind of relationship, with special rules that we have to work by. It's important for you to feel safe and know that your thoughts and feelings will be listened to and understood. It seems that, for a very long time, you have felt that everyone in your life has ignored you, discouraged you, or was down right cruel. This makes our relationship very different . . . from what you're used to.

CLIENT: But, don't you like me?

THER: Of course I do. But liking you can also mean being with you in safe, caring, and supportive ways. . . . What do you think?

CLIENT: (*Timidly*) well, uh . . . OK . . . Ms. E. That's a lot different than life with my fucked up parents. They don't care about me at all.

Malcolm's therapist, anxious and confused over her patient's frankly sexual revelations, reported feeling helpless in the face of such powerful imagery and its accompanying affects, although she persisted, valiantly, in a struggle to determine the underlying meaning of his fantasies. It was very difficult for her not to feel enraged, disgusted, or insulted by such vulgarity, however, and soon she found herself rejecting Malcolm in much the same way that everyone else had. What gradually became apparent was that Malcolm elicited in his therapist the very feelings both therapist and client knew to have caused him such profound pain and emotional trauma in relationships with his parents and maternal grandmother.

The therapist was saddened by a painfully acute awareness that, in spite of Malcolm's sexual bravado, he was still very much a child. In desperate search of closeness and intimacy with another human being, he seemed to be going about it in all the wrong ways, largely owing to the cumulative impact of past traumas compounded by deficient social skills. Although Malcolm's thoughts continued to run wild within the individual therapy sessions, the structure of the sessions seemed at times to furnish him with a modicum of containment for impulses and feelings that constantly threatened to overwhelm him. The constant challenge was somehow to stay engaged and connected with Malcolm in a positive, meaningful way despite his provocative and off-putting behavior, since it would only be through the therapist's emotional availability and compassion that a truly therapeutic ambience could be created and maintained.

Regrettably, Malcolm was not unable to confine his sexual fantasies to a "virtual" existence within the verbal domain of psychotherapy and was discovered to have had sexual intercourse with an eleven-year-old girl who had recently been placed in the children's residential program. He became even more confused and disoriented following this sexual experience, a flagrant violation of the center's "ground rules," and appeared to decompensate. Ashamed and embarrassed, Malcolm steadfastly refused any attempts by either his therapist or other staff to involve him in discussion surrounding the distressing incident. Malcolm had claimed all along that he wanted to leave the children's residential program, and perhaps this was his way of ensuring that outcome, although it is difficult to conceive of the prospect of yet another abrupt transition in his life as possessing any adaptive value. Following the incident, staff determined that Malcolm required a more restrictive setting, and, after eighteen months of treatment at Bakersville, he was subsequently transferred to another children's residential program. His therapist, Ms. E, accompanied him to his new placement, giving them the opportunity to reflect on their time spent together. Just before Ms. E bade him farewell, Malcolm surprised his therapist one last time, hurriedly telling her as she put on her coat to leave how appreciative he was that she "never gave up" on him.

DISCUSSION

Countertransference rarely embodies greater intensity than in the residential treatment of children and adolescents. Complex and multifaceted, the countertransference reactions and attitudes of staff members in such settings arise from elements of their own personality as well as specific interactions with the coresidents. The perceptions of many such adolescent patients are often primitive, evincing significant distortions that may tend to evoke correspondingly primitive countertransference reactions in the caregiver. In fact, the attitudes of staff members are determined to a considerable extent by the disturbed adolescent's perceptions. An important characteristic of milieu treatment involves adolescents' efforts to recreate real or fantasied aspects of their pasts, including the pathological relationships that have contributed to their misery. Such repetition invariably provokes environmental compliance, so that the emotions and attitudes of the caregivers around the patient coincide with their regressed expectations. Although at times virtually impossible to fulfill, staff responsibilities include the recognition and apprehension of precisely what it is these patients are attempting to recreate from their real or fantasied past. Such understanding may then accomplish two interrelated therapeutic aims: 1. it precludes destructive or countertherapeutic enactments of countertransference and 2. enables staff to continue to view the patient as an unhappy person who both needs and wants to receive the staff's help, despite behavior or attitudes that may suggest the contrary (Borowitz 1970).

As the foregoing narrative of Malcolm's treatment suggests, these aims are not easily achieved. In a now-classic paper, Ekstein and his associates might well have been discussing Malcolm when they made the following observation:

> Children who are constantly threatened by catastrophic continuity from within and without, and who therefore need our assurances the most, are those whose treatment is most likely to be disrupted. For they successfully assail in us that which they need most desperately—our sustained capacity for treatment continuity.　　　(Ekstein, Wallerstein, and Mandelbaum 1959:217)

In retrospect, it is interesting to note that it was shortly after the transference relationship began to deepen and assume maternal qualities that the transference became erotized, ultimately leading to Malcolm's extratransferential enactment with the eleven-year-old girl. However, Malcolm's therapist had noted his treatment did appear to stabilize for a time as he grew more trusting of her and seemed to put aside his most strenuous objections to residential placement. His desire to share experiences with her, in much the same way a child and mother would, was not in itself remarkable and might even be considered an important development in the evolution of the transference relationship. Accordingly, the therapist wasn't particularly uncomfortable taking Malcolm's picture near the flowers they had planted together, or celebrating his fourteenth birthday with him, or even in making arrangements for the two of them to visit a former school of which he had especially fond memories. However, Malcolm's deep maternal longings, and what might be termed the "role responsiveness" (Sandler 1976) of his therapist, set in motion a complicated sequence of events. Ms. E's acceptance of Malcolm's transference-activated dependency might have comforted and reassured other adolescent patients, serving to enhance basic trust and to deepen the therapeutic alliance, although Malcolm responded with profound mistrust and as though this signified an abject danger situation. Perhaps it was inevitable that he would misinterpret the therapist's acceptance of his maternal longings as

a *prelude to her abandonment of him*, but it was this development that led ultimately to the derailment of Malcolm's treatment.

But what, more precisely, went wrong? It seems likely that Malcolm, whose
representational world was populated by disappointing, frustrating, and reject-
ing/abandoning objects, could neither readily accept a fundamentally different
kind of object encounter nor tolerate the possibility of earlier traumata compounded by yet another object failure. I believe there is little question Malcolm
experienced deep, dependent longings for Ms. E, but found this to be terrifying
insofar as it signaled the repetition of an all-too-familiar scenario, one as predictable as it was inexorable, that had always followed the expression of such
desires. Like his mother, his father, and his grandmother, Ms. E would eventually
forsake him, somehow, at some time, and this he dreaded. Malcolm's urgent need
to disengage from a relationship where such deep feelings of dependency had
been reactivated through his growing attachment to a warm and caring adult
woman then took the form of an erotized transference.

Because Malcolm is an adolescent with a poor, urban, African American
background, the possibility that cultural determinants played a significant part
in shaping his transference cannot be discounted, nor can we assume the therapist's countertransference reactions and attitudes to have been unaffected by
such cultural differences. In the psychoanalytic literature, these reciprocal phenomena have been referred to as "ethnocultural transference" and "ethnocultural countertransference." In summarizing the work of Comas-Diaz and Jacobson, Bonner notes a range of transference reactions that are likely to occur when
therapist and patient are from different cultural backgrounds. These include
"overcompliance and friendliness, denial of ethnicity and culture, mistrust and
hostility, and ambivalence" (Bonner 2002:64). Interethnic *counter*transference
reactions may include the therapist's denial of ethnocultural differences, pity,
guilt, aggression, or ambivalence, and what has been termed the "clinical anthro-
pologist syndrome," a posture in which the therapist, operating from an intellectual vantage point, seeks to "understand" the unique cultural experience of a
client (Bonner 2002).

The existence of unconscious attitudes in therapist and patient involving
both negative and positive racial or ethnic stereotypes is a related phenomenon,
and one that we may assume was very much alive in this clinical encounter. In
this connection we recall that Malcolm referred to the therapist as a "white
bitch," whose main job, as he saw it, was to deny him an opportunity to leave residential treatment. She is perceived not only to possess institutional authority by
virtue of her position, that of an adult staff member, but also to be a representative of the dominant Caucasian culture, with all of its associated power and priv-

ileges. Malcolm's dependency on her may have reinforced his sense of helplessness not only with respect to a history of painful, recurrent object loss but also because of his status as a member of an underprivileged minority group—all the more reason from his perspective to disavow such dependent longings.

The rapidly evolving, sexualized transference may in part represent a splitting process in which a positive image of mother, that of a loving, nurturing caregiver, has been exchanged for a more ambivalently held image—a sexual object, who has become more an equal and therefore less a threat to Malcolm. It has also made it possible for Malcolm to exchange the passive position of victimization for a far more appealing one, that of a sexual aggressor. In some measure he here identified with his father, whose sexual interests reflected primitive aggression and debasement of women, in addition to other pathology.

A less obvious contribution to Malcolm's erotized transference, however, is from the side of the therapist. At the time she was working with Malcolm, Ms. E had become involved in an "unfulfilling" sexual relationship with a male friend. Even as she reacted with disgust and anger to Malcolm's shocking sexual overtures, she also found herself feeling excited and sexually aroused and several times entertained the fantasy of accepting this tall, attractive black adolescent's offer of sexual intimacy. Momentarily, she also wondered whether he would be as virile as he had claimed. Although she never intended to act on her fantasy, Ms. E felt both guilty and self-contemptuous: how could she, a twenty-eight-year-old adult professional woman, have such thoughts about a fourteen-year-old boy—a patient, no less? Thus, although Ms. E didn't "create" her patient's erotic transference, she probably unwittingly contributed to it, inasmuch as it seems to have stimulated a countertransference response touching not only on personal issues of her own but also on an unconsciously held stereotypical belief about the sexual prowess of black males.

It may also be argued that Malcolm, whose provocative behavior, severely limited capacity to contain or otherwise modulate powerful affects, and flagrant use of primitive mechanisms of defense such as splitting, projection, projective identification, and omnipotence, would be likely to educe similar counterprojective reactions and responses from any therapist. In fact, other child care staff responded in much the same way to Malcolm's aggressive and defiant behavior. At first staff members were sympathetic, and efforts were of a more therapeutic nature, with the aim of offering Malcolm guidance and understanding, supporting rudimentary social skills, or providing him with affect containment when he seemed in danger of losing control. Gradually, however, as these measures proved unsuccessful, futility seemed to replace the earlier optimism, and Malcolm's provocations elicited hateful retaliatory responses, though under the guise of "behavioral management." Finally, many staff members simply "gave up" on Malcolm and distanced themselves from him emotionally in such a way as to recapitulate his earlier parental rejections and other object losses.

Although Ms. E experienced powerful countertransference reactions, some of which led to disjunctive responses, her affective involvement with Malcolm remained strong for the duration of their work. With the exception of guilt, an affect not yet available to her client, Ms. E experienced a range of powerful emotional reactions that seemed in many ways to parallel Malcolm's, among them perplexity, helplessness, anger, dread, hatred, and shame. She often discussed the case in clinical supervision, hoping for any new insights that might assist her in this challenging work. Interestingly, although she may at times have become quite angry with Malcolm, she never actually *disliked* him, a critical distinction of which Malcolm was acutely aware. This may have enabled him, as they parted company for the last time at Malcolm's new residential placement, to tell her he knew that, unlike most other staff, she had never "given up" on him. Perhaps it is too early to know what aspects of this therapeutic work Malcolm was able to internalize and how he may be able to draw on his experience with Ms. E in the future. One can only hope that Malcolm's eighteen months of therapy with Ms. E has provided him with a new model for object relations, one previously unavailable to him, that may now be elaborated.

It has been nearly a century since Sigmund Freud published the first psychoanalytic paper on adolescence, setting in motion a process that has led to the establishment of a substantial literature focusing on various aspects of adolescent development and treatment. In this chapter we began by reviewing the work of several prominent psychoanalytic authors who have addressed both developmental and treatment themes, including Anna Freud, Erikson, Blos, and the Novicks. A concise summary of psychoanalytic conceptions of adolescent treatment followed, with a focus on ideas such as resistance and alliance formation. We then described three basic clinical frameworks for work with adolescents— *expressive* or *insight-oriented treatment, supportive therapy,* and *psychoanalysis*— and the components and characteristics that distinguish these three approaches from one another. Finally, two highly detailed clinical illustrations were provided, each representing a unique presenting complaint, treatment venue, and set of clinical challenges.

The Meter's Running:
Dynamic Approaches to Brief and Time-Limited Therapy

IN A PRACTICE CLIMATE transformed by the requirements of managed health care and the ubiquitous use of biological interventions, brief and time-limited dynamic treatment approaches have become ever more attractive both to agencies and the clinicians who staff them. In fact, in many settings the luxuries of limitless time and resources are often not available to social work practitioners and their clients, nor are these always necessary or even desirable. In this chapter the essential characteristics of a dynamic approach to working with clients briefly is presented and discussed.

Historically, the concept of brief treatment and the use of time limits have been neither revolutionary nor exceptional in the practice of social casework. In fact, it has been argued that most social casework has been short-term in nature (Parad 1971). The presumption of time limits, for example, is an almost invariant feature of certain social service settings, such as hospitals, the courts, or schools (Shechter 1997), and in such venues as Traveler's Aid the duration of contact has rarely been longer than a single meeting. A number of social work practice models, in recognition of this fact, have either treated the idea of brief or time-limited contact as a central organizing feature or may be easily adapted for such time-sensitive work (e.g., Perlman 1957; Reid and Shyne 1969; Rapoport 1970; Golan 1978; Goldstein and Noonan 1999).

This chapter begins with a history of the concept of brief treatment in the psychoanalytic literature, focusing on Freud's use of brief and time-limited methods with several patients, among them "Katharina," the first published example of brief dynamic therapy. Others in the early psychoanalytic movement, most notably Sandor Ferenczi, Otto Rank, and Franz Alexander, subsequently experimented with brief dynamic interventions, and these contributions are also reviewed. In the last thirty-five years several distinctive clinical models of brief dynamic psychotherapy have emerged, and in the next portion of the chapter each is briefly summarized. Following this, a review of the principal techniques common to most contemporary models of brief dynamic psychotherapy is outlined. In the final portion of the chapter, a detailed discussion of Mann's integrative model of *time-limited psychotherapy* is presented, followed by its application to a treatment case involving a female graduate student in her mid-twenties seen at a university counseling center.

CLASSICAL PSYCHOANALYSIS AND THE IDEA OF BRIEF TREATMENT

SIGMUND FREUD

Although psychoanalysis has gradually come to be identified almost reflexively with such terms as *intensive* and *long-term,* it may be instructive to note that historically, even within the psychoanalytic community, factors such as session frequency and the overall duration of treatment were far from being immutable givens. In fact, despite being conducted on a six-times-weekly basis, the average length of a psychoanalytic treatment in Freud's day was probably closer to one year than to the contemporary standard of four to seven years. Furthermore, Freud had himself worked with at least several patients within what can be legitimately described as a brief-treatment framework. Miss Lucy R., a hysterical patient of Freud's whose complaints included chronic suppurative rhinitis, recurrent olfactory hallucinations, diminished energy, and dysphoria was seen on a weekly basis for just nine sessions, although apparently with enduring results (Breuer and Freud 1893–95).[1] In 1906 the pianist and conductor Bruno Walter consulted Freud when other specialists failed to cure a partial paralysis of his right arm, presumably a conversion reaction. Freud met with Walter for a total of six sessions, following which the then thirty-year-old musician was able to resume his duties as Gustav Mahler's assistant at the Vienna Court Opera. Whether this treatment can be termed "dynamic" is a matter of some dispute, however, inasmuch as Freud's approach with his patient may have been less interpretive than suggestive in nature and relied rather heavily on the patient's positive transference (Fonagy 1999). A few years later Freud met with Walter's mentor, famed composer and conductor Gustav Mahler, for a single session of four hours' duration, most of which took place on a stroll through the town of Leyden, Holland. Evidently, Freud was able quickly to establish a connection between Mahler's presenting complaint, which was sexual impotence, and a powerful and conflict-laden, unconscious association the composer had made between his mother and his wife, Alma. Mahler's sexual potency, according to Jones (1957), was fully restored after his brief meeting with Freud.

Freud had actually conducted a single-session dynamic treatment some years earlier, most likely in the summer of 1893, that he later included in the *Studies on Hysteria* (Breuer and Freud 1893–95). The case involved a young woman, Katharina, whom Freud had met while vacationing in the Austrian Alps. After discovering that Freud was a physician, the eighteen-year-old approached him, beseeching him for help with her "bad nerves." The origin of Katharina's panic attacks, Freud was able to adduce from her story, lay in a traumatic experience from her fourteenth year in which her father had sexually molested her.[2] However, Katharina's symptoms only began two years later, after she had witnessed her father molesting a girl cousin. At that time Katharina recognized the sexual nature of her father's behavior and made the connection to what she had experienced at the age of fourteen. She reported feeling disgust at this memory, and soon thereafter developed a posttraumatic neurosis in which hysterical symptoms played a prominent part. Although Freud's contact with Katharina was limited to a single meeting, the case record reveals a fundamentally dynamic treatment encounter, in which latent meaning is derived from manifest content, the patient's associative material is encouraged, emotional catharsis is promoted, and genetic interpretation is employed. The effects were dramatically evident. As Gay has observed, Katharina's "artless recital helped to discharge her feelings, [and] her moody manner gave way to sparkling, healthy liveliness" (Gay 1988:73). Although Freud expressed hope that Katharina might derive some enduring benefit from their brief encounter, he never again came into contact with her.

SANDOR FERENCZI AND OTTO RANK

Ferenczi is generally acknowledged as being the first psychoanalyst to experiment more systematically with methods intended to shorten the duration of psychoanalytic treatment (Crits-Christoph and Barber 1991). Ferenczi first presented his ideas in a 1920 paper given at the Sixth International Congress of Psychoanalysis (Ferenczi 1950b [1926]), concerned over what he regarded as a trend toward increasingly longer psychoanalyses and correspondingly greater passivity on the analyst's part. In his paper he recommended that both analyst and analysand increase their activity so that the latter might be helped to "comply more successfully with the rule of free association," which, in Ferenczi's view, might facilitate "or hasten the exploring of unconscious material" (Ferenczi 1950b [1926]:198). The "active technique" that Ferenczi advocated might involve the analyst's prescription to the patient for the enactment of certain behaviors or, conversely, injunctions made against their performance (Crits-Christoph and

Barber 1991). In fact, he believed that, with certain kinds of patients such as obsessional neurotics, the analyst's failure to intervene more actively would likely culminate in the patient's use of the basic psychoanalytic method, free association, in the service of resistance (Tosone 1997). He asked patients to associate to specific topics and themes and advocated that the analyst consciously and deliberately provoke affective experience in the transference (Messer and Warren 2001). Ferenczi maintained that his "active technique" might serve as a basis for rapid amelioration of the patient's resistance, which could also contribute to shortening the overall duration of the analysis. Despite his contention that the active technique was intended to be employed judiciously and selectively, and only as a supplement to psychoanalysis, the psychoanalytic community was, generally speaking, rather unreceptive to Ferenczi's paper (Tosone 1997).

Otto Rank has also been credited with introducing important ideas that are seen as developmental precursors to modern concepts of brief and especially, time-limited therapy. Rank had theorized that the whole of human development is characterized by a continuous tension between emotional attachment and dependency, on the one side, alternating with separation and autonomy, on the other (Messer and Warren 2001). In Rank's estimation, much that had been designated "resistance" by classical psychoanalytic theory could be defined more accurately as a natural opposition that existed between the "will" of the therapist and that of the patient. In his view the therapeutic process in classical psychoanalysis, shaped by the analyst's confrontations and interpretations, might ultimately lead patients to acceptance of a new view for their behavior, but at the expense of their own "will" (Messer and Warren 1995). Rank chose, instead, to assist patients to become more self-accepting, with an enhanced capacity to take responsibility for themselves without experiencing guilt (O'Dowd 1986). As soon as the patient's will was sufficiently motivated for change, she might assume greater responsibility for her treatment, thereby leading to a more efficient and shorter analytic process (Crits-Cristoph and Barber 1991). Rank's theory, which emphasized the salience of the ongoing, immediate experience of the analytic relationship over that of past events, also introduced the idea of establishing an end point to treatment. However, termination, in the Rankian framework, was intimately associated with the patient's "will to individuate," so that a termination date was finally set only once Rank sensed the patient to be struggling with issues of dependency, separation, and relatedness. "The key aspect of this process," O'Dowd has suggested in summarizing Rank's views on the topic of termination, "is maintaining the connection, the sense of belonging and attachment, along with a new-found capacity to will and to create a separate individual" (O'Dowd 1986:146).

In 1925, Ferenczi and Rank published a jointly written book, *The Development of Psychoanalysis*, now widely acknowledged as the conceptual predecessor to Alexander's volume on brief treatment, *Psychoanalytic Therapy*, which appeared twenty years later (Crits-Christoph and Barber 1991). Adumbrating many of the brief and time-limited models that were to follow, Ferenczi and Rank's work emphasized the immediate "here and now" aspects of the patient's relationship with the analyst and placed less importance on reconstruction of events and experiences from the patient's childhood past (Messer and Warren 1995). Moreover, they maintained that the power of the unconscious was fully revealed to patients only after unconscious wishes and affects were revived in the context of the patient's ongoing transference to the analyst. It is at this juncture, they believed, that genetic reconstruction would be far more likely to be therapeutic and effective (Tosone 1997). Ferenczi and Rank did acknowledge the significance of the genetic perspective, and the self-understanding that might be derived from reconstructive work, but they also believed undue emphasis on reconstruction of the past could lead to a strengthening of intellectual defenses (ibid.). Indeed, having identified the ultimate goal of an analysis as the substitution of "affective factors of experience for intellectual processes" (Ferenczi and Rank 1925:62), their work traverses a very different road than did classical conceptions of the psychoanalytic process prevailing in the mid-1920s.

This fact was not lost on others in the psychoanalytic movement, and Freud, despite certain misgivings, lent Ferenczi and Rank his qualified endorsement. He remained unconvinced that "one can penetrate to the deepest layers of the unconscious and bring about lasting changes in the mind" in four or five months, as he believed Ferenczi and Rank's modification of psychoanalytic technique sought to accomplish (*Rundbriefe*, cited in Jones 1957:61). However, he also believed such an experiment, with its aim of a shortened analysis, to be "entirely justified" and, in any event, undeserving of condemnation as a theoretical heresy (ibid.). Others, such as Karl Abraham, demonstrated far less equanimity in their appraisal of Ferenczi and Rank's work, and mounting criticisms of Rank's ideas within the psychoanalytic movement, particularly as these were developed in his controversial book on birth trauma (Rank 1973 [1924]), added to the developing controversy. Ultimately, the modifications of technique proposed in *The Development of Psychoanalysis* seemed to suffer a fate similar that of many other psychoanalytic innovations, namely, marginalization.

FRANZ ALEXANDER AND THOMAS FRENCH

Two decades after the publication of Ferenczi and Rank's controversial book, Franz Alexander and Thomas French, in collaboration with colleagues at the

Chicago Institute for Psychoanalysis, published *Psychoanalytic Therapy*. They readily acknowledged their intellectual debt to the authors of *The Development of Psychoanalysis*, noting their own work to be "a continuation and realization of ideas first proposed by Ferenczi and Rank" (Alexander and French 1946:23). In particular, their work may be seen as an endorsement of Ferenczi and Rank's view of the comparatively greater importance of emotional experience over that of insight derived from intellectual understanding.

Corrective emotional exp

Alexander and French are arguably best known for their concept of "corrective emotional experience." This principle holds that the most important changes in psychotherapy occur when historical conflicts are revived in the context of a new relationship, that between analyst and patient. However, the potential for such change is only realized, in Alexander and French's view, insofar as the analyst's response offers something new to the patient.

Corrective emot experience

> Because the therapist's attitude is different from that of the authoritative person of the past, he gives the patient an opportunity to face again and again, under more favorable circumstances, those emotional situations which were formerly unbearable and to deal with them in a manner different from the old. . . . This can only be accomplished through actual experience in the patient's relationship to the therapist; intellectual insight alone is not sufficient.   (Alexander and French 1946:67)

Thus the corrective emotional experience is "corrective" only to the degree that the analyst understands the motives embedded in the patient's transference behavior and is able to assume an attitude toward the patient that is different from that of the original transference object (Crits-Christoph and Barber 1991).

Alexander and French placed emphasis on the ongoing, contemporary aspects of the treatment relationship, rather than viewing it from the classical vantage point, in which the relationship is principally a projection screen for patients' fantasies of the analyst. This feature, according to some, anticipates the perspective of modern relational therapies in which the treatment relationship has assumed a central role for the overall improvement of the patient (Messer and Warren 1995).

post/ present

In their view of treatment as "a process of emotional reeducation," Alexander and French tended to be far more concerned with the patient's adjustment to the circumstances of the present, placing correspondingly less emphasis on the genetic origins of the patient's difficulties. While they did not dismiss such genetic understanding as unimportant, their interest in the patient's past was limited to the degree to which it illuminated the most immediate concerns in the present. Indeed, much of what Alexander and French wrote in 1946 presages

French's later work on the concept of "focal conflict" (explored in greater depth in chapter 14). Alexander and French also believed that exclusive reliance on classical or "standard" technique might ultimately hinder therapeutic progress and adopted a flexible approach to the use of treatment techniques, in which tactics were adjusted in accord with the requirements of individual cases. Among the modifications they proposed were

> using not only the method of free association but interviews of a more direct character, manipulating the frequency of the interviews, giving directives to the patient concerning his daily life, employing interruptions of long or short duration in preparation for ending the treatment, regulating the transference relationship to meet the specific needs of the case, and making use of real-life experiences as an integral part of the therapy. (Alexander and French 1946:6)

Such treatment strategies and techniques, Messer and Warren (1995) have suggested, can be linked to later developments in the brief therapy field; these include the use of behavioral techniques and suggestion (Garfield 1989), direct guidance, support, and advice giving (Bellak and Small 1965), and a focus on the patient's family circumstances (Gustafson 1986).

Alexander and French's framework for brief treatment ultimately did exert a profound influence over the "next wave" in the brief treatment field, those brief and time-limited systems that were introduced beginning in the late 1960s. However, at the time their book was published, condemnation from the psychoanalytic establishment was perhaps even sharper than the reaction Ferenczi and Rank's work had elicited twenty years earlier. The concept of the "corrective emotional experience" evoked a particularly strong reaction from many psychoanalysts of which Phyllis Greenacre's criticism was representative. Greenacre dismissed the idea as "little more than the old-fashioned habit training with especially strong suggestive influencing" (Greenacre 1954:676; Tosone 1997) and concluded that it involved a "working out" rather than a "working through" process. The former involved therapeutic procedures whereby the patient's emotional reactions might be reshaped into new patterns "without paying too much attention to the old," while the latter aimed to loosen "neurotic tendencies at their source" (Greenacre 1954:676). Then, too, Alexander and French's willingness to exchange the traditional role of analytic neutrality and abstinence for a far more active stance, in which the analyst makes specific therapeutic accommodations to the patient's transference needs, seemed further to intensify opposition to their treatment model. With recommendations for once-weekly sessions, a far more flexible use of analytic technique, diminished importance attached to reconstruction of the past, and the seeming abdication of analytic neutrality, Alexander and French's ideas regarding brief treatment, however laudable, were destined to remain outside the psychoanalytic mainstream for nearly another generation.

THE "SECOND WAVE": MALAN, SIFNEOS, AND DAVANLOO

After the publication of Alexander and French's book, the psychoanalytic establishment appeared once again to close ranks in its dismissal of brief treatment as a legitimate form of dynamic psychotherapy. However, this negatively valenced reaction was not universal among psychoanalysts, and, beginning in the early 1960s, several new approaches to brief dynamic treatment were introduced. These brief therapy methods, each of which is grounded in the theoretical assumptions of classical psychoanalysis and/or psychoanalytic ego psychology, have been collectively referred to as the *drive/structure model* (Messer and Warren 1995:2001). This term is actually borrowed from Mitchell and Greenberg, who, in their pioneering review of the psychoanalytic psychologies (Greenberg and Mitchell 1983), made a distinction between psychoanalytic theories organized according to the classical schema of drive/structure and those based on a relational/structure model. David Malan, Peter Sifneos, and Habib Davanloo are the principal exponents of this model, each of whom, independently, had developed an approach to brief treatment predicated upon such basic Freudian postulates as drive and defense, the ubiquity of intrapsychic conflict and its mediation by the ego, the centrality of the Oedipus complex, the notion of symptoms as "compromise formations," and so forth (Messer and Warren 2001).

Malan's approach, which he termed *brief intensive psychotherapy* (BIP), is perhaps closest to "standard" psychoanalytic technique within the drive/structure group of brief treatment approaches. It appears to be most effective with healthier patients who are motivated for insight, have attained a higher quality of object relations, and are able to employ "mature" or higher-level defenses (Piper, de Carufel, and Szkrumelak 1985; Messer and Warren 1995). Unlike psychoanalysis or long-term psychoanalytic therapy, however, brief intensive psychotherapy imposes a time limit (twenty to thirty sessions), has a specific dynamic objective (resolution of the conflict/conflicts identified in the initial meeting), and applies specific therapeutic interventions to maintain a focus on the area of conflict (Malan 1976). As a means of organizing treatment interventions, Malan developed two intersecting conceptual schemata (Malan 1976), the triangles of conflict and person (see figure 12.1 below). The elements in the triangle of conflict are impulse or feeling (I-F), anxiety (A), and defensive reaction or response (D). The triangle of person includes the objects targeted by a patient's impulses or feelings—the therapist (T),

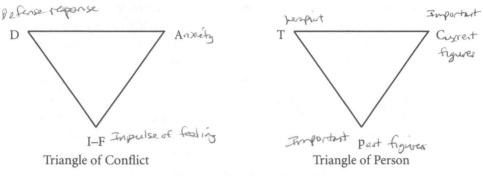

Defense response

D ▽ Anxiety

I-F Impulse of feeling

Triangle of Conflict

Therapist

T ▽ Important Current figures

Important Past figures

Triangle of Person

FIGURE 12.1   *Triangles of Conflict and Person*

significant individuals in the current life of the patient (C), and important figures from the past (P). Malan's intent was to systematically link the pattern of conflict identified in the triangle of conflict with each corner in the triangle of person (Messer and Warren 1995). Although the therapist makes active use of interventions tailored to address elements of the focal issue, Malan's treatment approach is not on that account a superficial one. Indeed, *brief intensive psychotherapy* is intended to "go as deeply as possible" into the psychodynamics and origins of the patient's core conflicts (Messer and Warren 1995:84). Research on this model has suggested "good evidence" for its efficacy, although this is apparently linked to capacity for higher-level object relations as well as to maturity of defensive style (Messer and Warren 1995).

Research

Sifneos

STAPP

Short-term anxiety-provoking psychotherapy (STAPP), the therapeutic approach developed by Sifneos, also seems most effective with healthier patients, in particular those with neurotic disorders or symptom constellations that include anxiety, mild depression, grief reactions, and interpersonal problems. Evidence of a capacity for insight or "psychological sophistication," is also judged to be important (Nielsen and Barth 1991). One of the most striking features of this method of brief treatment is an unrelenting focus on triangular or oedipal issues, which Sifneos believed to be the focal issue in the majority of patients he treated (Nielsen and Barth 1991). In stark contrast to the usual procedure in traditional psychoanalytic treatment, interpretation of the patient's defense does *not* precede the therapist's interpretation of the impulse or wish. In fact, therapists are encouraged to confront and interpret underlying wishes or impulses directly, and Sifneos consistently pushed patients to take responsibility for their fantasies, actions, wishes, and feelings. This represents a radical departure from psychoanalytic tradition although, Sifneos claims, it is not without justification. In short-term anxiety-provoking psychotherapy the early effort to craft the therapeutic alliance and promote the patient's positive transference makes possible a concentrated focus on "specific areas wherein most of the patient's dynamic conflicts exist" (Nielsen and Barth 1991). Moreover, Sifneos believed that the therapist's use of anxiety-provoking clarifications, confrontational questions, and direct interpretations often yielded significant new data. Although there has been some research on STAPP showing it to be effective in promoting patient self-understanding, symptomatic relief, new learning, and the acquisition of problem-solving abilities (Sifneos 1968, 1987; Sifneos et al. 1980), methodological and other problems may cast doubt on the validity of these results (Messer and Warren 1995).

Davanloo's *intensive short-term dynamic psychotherapy* (ISTDP) was developed as a confrontational method of breaking through a patient's defensive structures to promote "the examination of repressed memories and ideas in a fully experienced and integrated affective and cognitive framework" (Laikin, Winston, and McCullough 1991:80). This method is intended for use not only with higher-functioning neurotic patients but also with those suffering from personality disorders (e.g., avoidant, dependent, obsessive-compulsive, and passive-aggressive), as well as for some presenting with more severe psychopathology, such as borderline or narcissistic conditions. The duration of treatment may vary according to the degree of patient pathology, but in no case should it exceed forty sessions. Davanloo adheres to a more or less traditional psychoanalytic model in which abstinence and analytic neutrality are observed, personal inquiries are deflected, and the therapist refrains from offering direct guidance, advice, and praise (Laikin, Winston, and McCullough 1991). Davanloo's method is somewhat unique among drive/structure model brief treatment approaches in its focus on "cognitive restructuring," a pre-interpretive phase of ISTDP in which the triangle of conflict is outlined for the patient, though without interpretation of underlying psychodynamics. This variation in Davanloo's approach is intended principally for patients who are more resistant and difficult to treat—patients who would likely not be considered suitable candidates for either BIP or STAPP. Acknowledging his intellectual debt to both Malan and Sifneos, Davanloo also cites Wilhelm Reich's ideas regarding character resistance as an important influence. Like Malan, Davanloo's ISTDP is a dynamic model for intervention initially based on the therapist's understanding of the "two working triangles"—those of conflict and person. Although outcome effectiveness research on this method of brief treatment has been limited to a single study

(McCullough et al. 1991), results have been promising, particularly in light of the fact that certain personality-disordered cases deemed untreatable by other dynamic therapy approaches were included (Messer and Warren 1995).

THE "THIRD WAVE": RELATIONAL APPROACHES TO BRIEF PSYCHOTHERAPY

The fact that all psychoanalytic theories, as Greenberg and Mitchell maintained, tend to be organized in conformity with either *drive/structure* or *relational/ structure* assumptions, points to the existence of a basic and fundamentally irreconcilable theoretical chasm (Greenberg and Mitchell 1983; Mitchell 1988; Messer and Warren 1995). As we have noted previously, the relational/structure model, rather than accepting the classical notion of the primacy of the drives and the role they perform in the development of object relations, posits that psychic structure evolves from the interactions of the individual with other people. Or, put somewhat differently, in classical theory the object was in a sense "created" to "suit the impulse," whereas in relational theories the infant is *object seeking*, and the development of psychic structure very intimately linked to a subject-environmental matrix.

Several important approaches based on the theoretical assumptions of the relational/structure model have been widely applied to the practice domain of brief treatment. These include the Penn Psychotherapy Project's *short-term expressive psychoanalytic psychotherapy*, closely linked to an overarching concept referred to as the *core conflictual relationship theme* (Luborsky and Mark 1991); the model developed by Horowitz and the Center for the Study of Neuroses, *short-term dynamic therapy of stress-response syndromes* (Horowitz 1991); the Vanderbilt Group's *time-limited dynamic psychotherapy* (Binder and Strupp 1991); and the Mount Zion Group's method, which is based on the principles of *control-mastery therapy* (Weiss, Sampson, and the Mt. Zion Psychotherapy Research Group 1986).

Interestingly, none of the methods of treatment represented by these four psychotherapy research groups was originally conceived or promoted as a brief psychotherapy model. In fact, some authors have suggested that the distillation of brief treatment principles and their application to this conceptual domain was, in each case, a by-product of a more general program of research on psychodynamic theory and psychoanalytic therapy. Nevertheless, all four are judged to have made important contributions to the brief treatment field. Common themes seem to link these four methods with one another:

- With certain variations, each adopts the perspective that psychopathology is rooted in a maladaptive, interpersonal matrix;
- each accords a greater role to the real experience and to "real" failures of the environment;
- the adaptive function of defenses is emphasized, as contrasted with the more classical conceptualization of defense activation as a consequence of anxiety that arises from unacceptable impulses or wishes;
- the role of "real" experience, actual failures of the environment, and so forth are generally accorded greater importance in the formation of psychopathology;
- in varying degree, each presumes the existence of internalized self and object representations in its theories of personality functioning and psychopathology;
- more emphasis is placed on the role of intercurrent variables in the perpetuation of psychopathology than on the classical notion of genetic causality (Messer and Warren 1995:119–20)

TECHNICAL DIMENSIONS COMMON TO ALL METHODS OF BRIEF DYNAMIC TREATMENT

In the preceding sections we have highlighted significant differences between brief treatment approaches, organized in accordance with the theoretical premises of the drive/structure model, and those that are based on relational/structure assumptions. However, five technical dimensions common to all methods of psychodynamically based brief treatment have also been identified (Woods and Hollis 2000; Messer and Warren 2001). These are the use of a central dynamic focus or issue, setting of a time limit, significance attached to termination, active posture of the therapist, and establishment of attainable goals and treatment objectives.

USE OF A CENTRAL DYNAMIC FOCUS OR ISSUE

The therapist's formulation of a central dynamic theme or issue is not unique to brief therapy methods but, owing to the time-limited nature of such engagements of patient and therapist, is imbued with a special significance. Such a formulation, which is most usefully considered a clinical working hypothesis, accomplishes three objectives. It conveys the therapist's understanding of the underlying meaning of a patient's presenting complaints, provides an organizing framework for all subsequent clinical data collected over the course of treatment, and serves as a guide for specific clinical interventions.

SETTING OF A TIME LIMIT

In some brief therapy methods the duration of the treatment and date of the terminal interview are established by the therapist in an explicit manner from the earliest point of contact, as exemplified by James Mann's *time-limited psychotherapy*, which has a fixed number of sessions. Mann's treatment approach, however, differs from most others that specify the total number of sessions and date of the terminal interview in its emphasis on the themes of separation and loss relative to the time limit (see next section). In other brief therapy methods the time limit may be implicit and subject to negotiation by therapist and patient at some point after treatment is already underway. A basic assumption of all time-limited dynamic therapies is that a time limit, whether explicit or more implicit, serves to sharpen the focus on treatment objectives by heightening the "sense of urgency, immediacy, and emotional presence of the patient" (Messer and Warren 2001:76).

SIGNIFICANCE ATTACHED TO TERMINATION

It seems only natural for any treatment method in which a mutually acknowledged time limit exists, that the issue of termination assumes greater importance from the outset. In fact, therapy conducted briefly may afford unique opportunities for therapist and patient to consider the impact of termination, with its attendant themes of separation, loss, and death, throughout the duration of therapy. In psychoanalysis or in psychotherapy, where therapeutic engagement is often of an indeterminate length, resistance to termination is rarely manifest until treatment is well underway; moreover, such resistance, frequently signifying issues of separation-individuation or loss, may be permitted to unfold gradually. In the context of brief treatment, however, such resistances may appear in the very first session and become an ongoing focus of the clinical discourse over the entire term of therapy.

ACTIVE POSTURE OF THE THERAPIST

Brief therapy methods have long experimented with ways to hasten the pace of the clinical process, beginning with Ferenczi's *active technique* (Ferenczi 1950b [1926]). The establishment of time limits, confrontation, direct interpretation of underlying wishes or impulses, early and aggressive interpretation of transference reactions, and direct suggestion and guidance are other techniques employed to attain treatment objectives within the abbreviated framework of time-sensitive treatment. More recent, relational brief treatment approaches have also tended to emphasize the therapist's awareness of transference patterns, as these are manifest in the evolving relationship with the patient. With active reference to his experience of the patient in the present, the therapist is then able to make "here and now" interpretative linkages between past relational patterns and the ongoing treatment relationship (Messer and Warren 2001).

ESTABLISHMENT OF ATTAINABLE GOALS AND TREATMENT OBJECTIVES

Another important difference between longer-term dynamic psychotherapy and brief dynamic treatment is in the setting of treatment goals and objectives. Owing in part to the use of a central dynamic focus, the therapist's and patient's awareness of a time limit, and the special meaning that attaches to termination in brief dynamic therapy, goals and objectives tend to be stated with more explicitness than in longer-term treatment. Even when the setting of goals is not formalized, however, it is often implied in brief treatment, which in the main tends to be more symptom- or problem-focused (Messer and Warrren 2001). As a general rule, goals should also be realistic and attainable; time-sensitive treatment would not be an appropriate therapy in cases where significant alteration of character structure has been identified as the central treatment objective.

MANN'S TIME-LIMITED PSYCHOTHERAPY

Each of the methods of brief dynamic treatment we have thus far reviewed possesses certain strengths and weaknesses, although only James Mann's time-limited psychotherapy (TLP) offers an integrative theoretical framework in keeping with the transtheoretical outline of this book. As Mann has previously articulated, TLP approaches psychopathology from four complementary theoretical vantage points: 1. the structural hypothesis, 2. the theory of narcissism and development of self-esteem, 3. object relations theory, and 4. the developmental perspective (Mann and Goldman 1982). His treatment method also places a special emphasis on the concept of time and on the universal experience of loss as it is recapitulated within the frame of time-limited treatment.

Mann has observed that time is conceived in both "categorical" and "existential" terms (Mann 1973, 1991). We measure the first, categorical or real time, with timepieces and calendars. The second, existential or limitless time, represents a more archaic mode of psychic experience and signifies both immortality and infinitude. Our understanding of categorical time evolves only gradually, as secondary process thinking begins to supplant the primary process experience and the reality principle claims a greater share of what was once the exclusive province of the pleasure principle. An almost six-year-old boy, in a quiet moment at bedtime, suddenly becomes painfully aware of his father's mortality. "I don't want you to die," he whispers. "Can't you and me always be together—

forever?" Although categorical time gradually organizes our waking lives, our early pleasure of timelessness is never completely surrendered; indeed, we often seek to deny the effects of the passage of time, in ways both subtle and flagrant.

Unlike many other brief treatment methods, Mann elevates the universal experience of separation and loss to programmatic status. In fact, he declares that "the recurring life crisis of separation-individuation is the substantive basis" upon which TLP rests and proceeds to outline four "basic universal conflict sit-uations," all of which are linked to the individual's lifelong efforts to manage object loss. These *are independence versus dependence, activity versus passivity, adequate self-esteem versus diminished or loss of self-esteem,* and *unresolved or delayed grief* (Mann 1973:24–25). In keeping with the theme of object loss and separation-individuation, Mann's approach focuses on preoedipal rather than on oedipal issues, which reflects his belief that such issues are more amenable to time-limited treatment. At the same time, Mann has clearly noted that psycho-analysis continues to be the most effective method of treatment of oedipal issues, which in his view cannot ordinarily be resolved without the establishment of a transference neurosis, consistent attention to resistance phenomena, and so forth (Mann and Goldman 1982).

According to Mann, TLP is suitable for patients who are judged to have the ego strength necessary for rapid affective engagement and equally rapid disen-gagement, with the latter considered a measure of their capacity for tolerating object loss. Beyond this, Mann believes that his approach may be of benefit to a variety of patients presenting with maturational crises, neurotic disorders (e.g., anxiety, hysterical, obsessional, and depressive problems), and some personality disorders (e.g., mild narcissistic and some borderline patients). Mann's treat-ment method is contraindicated, however, for more seriously disturbed character-disordered patients, severe psychosomatic problems, bipolar affective disorder, and schizoid disorders (Mann 1991).

COMPONENTS AND PROCESS OF TIME-LIMITED PSYCHOTHERAPY

THE CENTRAL ISSUE

As quickly as feasible, and almost always within the first or second meeting, Mann endeavors to formulate a statement of the patient's *chronic and presently endured pain.* Such pain encompasses both a negative feeling about the self and also the patient's fundamental belief of having been victimized (Mann 1991). Because the central issue spans the patient's entire experience "from the remote past to the immediate present and into the expectable future," its formulation by the therapist will, with rare exceptions, differ markedly from those problems the

*Therapist &
Patient differ*

*Central
issue*

patient has given as the motive for seeking help (Mann 1986:123). The therapist's formulation of the central issue includes three basic parts: 1. acknowledgment of the patient's ongoing efforts to obtain recognition and to satisfy her or his needs, 2. the failure of these efforts, which has culminated in the patient's negative feelings about her or himself, and 3. some statement outlining the task of treatment (Mann 1973, 1991; Messer and Warren 1995). Eliciting the patient's reactions, if they are not immediate, to the formulation of the central issue becomes the very next task of treatment.

EARLY PHASE

In marked contrast to adherents of the drive/structure model (e.g., Davanloo or Malan), Mann's approach, particularly in first several sessions, is nonconfrontative, with the intent of establishing a rapid working alliance and engaging the patient through such techniques as mirroring, affirmation, and delicate probing (Mann and Goldman 1982; Messer and Warren 1995). Rather than interpreting aggressively, or challenging defenses, Mann endeavors to make the treatment experience a gentle, empathically attuned, and accepting one, which places the patient at ease. In such an ambience the therapeutic equivalent of the symbiotic orbit of mother and infant is (re)established (Rasmussen and Messer 1986). In Mann's words, "the warm sustaining golden sunshine of eternal union" is restored and the patient reports significant diminution of the presenting complaints (Mann 1973:33). In this environment it also becomes an increasingly difficult and greater challenge for the therapist and client to remain focused on the central issue.

MIDDLE PHASE

As therapy reaches the fourth or fifth session, the patient begins to experience disappointment, and the "honeymoon" is over. There may be a recrudescence of the original symptoms or complaints, and the recognition that not even the new relationship with the therapist, which seemed to hold so much promise, can solve all the patient's problems. The prospect of yet another separation from a "meaningful, ambivalently experienced person" becomes painfully evident at this midpoint in the treatment, and manifestations of negative transference become more obvious (Mann 1973). The task for the therapist at this stage is, through greater use of clarifications, mild confrontations, and interpretations, to encourage "further elaboration of the patient's ambivalence" so that associations to past separations and the feelings these evoked might be understood relative to the patient's central issue (Mann 1991).

*Task for
therapist*

ENDING PHASE

*pt feels
sad @
end of
Tx*

Mann has commented that termination may be considered satisfactory when the patient leaves treatment feeling sad. "Ambivalence, which previously had always led to feelings of anger or depression with concomitant self-derogation, has changed into awareness of positive feelings even in the face of separation and loss. Sadness in place of depression allows for separation without self-injury" (Mann 1991:36).

Mann assumes that by this juncture in treatment the therapist has amassed a good deal of clinical data to support the link between the patient's experience of past significant figures and the recapitulation of these fantasies and feelings in regard to the therapist. In the final three to four sessions, therefore, Mann feels confident in stepping up the frequency of transference interpretations, all the while continuing to highlight the central issue with fairly explicit references. The therapist's use of direct suggestions and of educational and supportive interventions also increases at this time. The intent of such interventions is to promote the patient's self-esteem as well as his efforts to master anxiety and to employ progressively more adaptive and independent actions.

LIMITATIONS AND RESEARCH SUPPORT FOR TLP

Several authors have been critical of TLP for its extension and generalization of the theme of separation-loss to all forms of psychopathology. Westen, in particular, has described Mann's model as a "single-cause theory of neurosis," problematic insofar as object loss may or may not be relevant to a given patient's central dynamics (Westen 1986). Others, as we have previously discussed (in chapter 9), have noted that the concept of termination as a negatively valenced, anxiety-ridden time for clients—in effect, a time of crisis—may be lacking in empirical support in the psychotherapy research literature (Marx and Gelso 1987). Mann's assumption that a definitive termination, with its accompanying object loss, is necessary to promote the process of internalization has also been challenged. Some (Quintana and Meara 1990; Qunitana 1993), for example, believe that the *dosing* of termination, where patients are invited to return for additional interviews on an as-needed basis, is more likely to lead to internalization than Mann's approach, which views relinquishment of the relationship as a necessary precondition for internalization.

Though relatively little systematic research on TLP exists, several studies offer support for its efficacy and for the durability of its therapeutic effects. Furthermore, retention of clinic patients seems to be enhanced through the use of a specified number of sessions and the setting of a terminal interview date (Messer and Warren 1995). One study involved thirty-three psychiatric outpatients, aged twenty-three to forty-two years, who had completed their secondary education, worked in white-collar professions, and had presented with symptoms of anxiety or depression (Shefler, Dasberg, and Ben-Shakhar 1995). They were randomly assigned to an experimental group, which received TLP immediately, or to a control group, in which case they received TLP, but only after a delay of three months. Patients were evaluated on the basis of outcome measures at termination, and subsequently at six and twelve months posttermination. Significant improvement was noted in the experimental group after TLP, but control group patients failed to demonstrate systematic changes after three months; once TLP was initiated for the control group, however, these patients also improved significantly. Gains achieved posttermination appeared stable for both groups at six- and twelve-month follow-up.

CLINICAL CASE ILLUSTRATION 12.1: "CARLA"

Carla, an attractive twenty-four-year-old single woman of Welsh and Italian ancestry, sought treatment for anxiety and depression of approximately six weeks' standing at University of Y Counseling Service. When asked what she was seeking help for at the time, Carla, without hesitation, said that she had been feeling fine until her boyfriend had broken up with her two months earlier. Now, however, she was feeling very depressed and discouraged. Furthermore, she wasn't sleeping well and was finding it increasingly difficult to concentrate on her schoolwork. At the time of her evaluation she was completing a master's level graduate program in engineering and anticipated leaving the area within several months to accept an out-of-state offer of employment. Carla, who was self-referred, had been in psychotherapy for approximately four months on one previous occasion several years earlier, an experience she found helpful. At that time she had also been depressed, and her treatment had focused on issues in the relationship with her father and with another boyfriend. Carla's parents were divorced when she was less than two years of age, at which time her father moved to a distant part of the country and, shortly thereafter, remarried. Although she visited her father during summers and other vacation periods, she typically had far more contact on these visits with her stepmother than with her father, a busy attorney whose work week often exceeded fifty hours. She often felt that he barely noticed her and reported that these visits were a "lonely time" for her, in contrast to the "happy times" she spent living with her mother, whom she now thought of as being almost like "a sister." At this time her eyes welled up, and she began to cry softly, warning me with a laugh that there would probably be a lot more of this to come, but that "it always looks worse than it is." Particularly when she was younger, Carla continued, the preparations for these visits with her father were an upsetting time, with tearful protests almost until the hour of her departure. But "each time," Carla sighed, "I ended up having to go. Even if she'd wanted to, Mom couldn't do anything about it" owing to the terms of the postdivorce custody arrangement.

When asked to say more about her parents, Carla first talked about her mother, who had recently turned forty-nine. She and her mother had a "very close relationship," and this had been so "as far back as I can remember." Carla had decided to attend college very near her mother's home and then remained in the same geographical area (though she attended a larger university) for her graduate studies. Mother and daughter spent a good deal of time together and often confided in each other. In fact, Carla worried "a little" about her mother now that she was preparing to graduate, with a firm job offer from an engineering firm in the southeast, many hundreds of miles from her mother's Midwest home. Carla's father, now fifty-five, led an active lifestyle and was a well-respected public prosecutor in the northern California community where he and his family resided. He had one son, seven years older than Carla, from a marriage antedating his relationship to Carla's mother; there were two other children, offspring of his current marriage, a twenty-year-old son and a seventeen-year-old daughter. Carla continued to spend at least one vacation with him each year. Although she had long before stopped feeling anxious in preparation for these visits, she also observed that "you're pretty much on your own when you go out there. You just have to fit in; that's what I try and do, anyway."

I noted during this first meeting that, although Carla often spoke of feeling sad, upset, or lonely both now and in the past, she often seemed to force a smile, playing down her distress. In fact, her disposition had been so cheerful when I greeted her in the reception area, and even during the first several minutes of our initial meeting, that I found it hard to imagine this young woman having any *real* problem at all. Even when she cried, the effect was minimized both by her laughter and her comment about having a penchant for such dramatic reactions.

Carla seemed highly motivated for time-limited treatment and appeared to be a strong candidate. This assessment was based on several factors: 1. she was able to engage rapidly, demonstrating good capacity for an affective relationship; 2. generally speaking, she demonstrated good ego strength, including evidence of a capacity for tolerating both anxiety and guilt; 3. despite feeling anxious and depressed, she seemed reflective and appeared capable of introspection and insight; 4. she had reported having been helped by her previous experience in psychotherapy; and 5. there were no obvious contraindications for TLP such as suicidality, the presence of a severe characterological disturbance, or bipolar affective disorder.

Following this initial evaluation, I suggested to Carla that we meet once a week on Fridays for twelve sessions, at which time we would conclude her therapy. She was agreeable to this, and so we decided on a regular meeting day and time as well as a specific date for termination. After our diagnostic session and prior to the first therapy session, I formulated Carla's central issue in this way: *"You have always tried very hard to please the men in your life, although their response is often disappointing, and that has caused you a great deal of pain. First there was your father, but there have been others, like your boyfriend, who've seemed to lose interest in you. Our job will be to figure out what's happening so that you always end up feeling hurt in this way."*

With a clear statement regarding Carla's *present and chronically endured pain*, this formulation of the central issue also addresses the three components outlined earlier: her ongoing efforts to obtain recognition and to meet interpersonal needs, the apparent failure of these efforts, and the task or objective of her therapy. It may be argued that the central issue can be reformulated in such a way as to acknowledge the importance of Carla's relationship with her mother, toward whom she has always felt overly responsible. Along these lines, one might understand Carla's relational difficulties with her father and boyfriend as being motivated by the need to remain loyal to her mother. If one were to proceed along these dynamic lines, the central issue could be restated as follows:

"From the time you were little, you and your mother have always had a very close relationship, and you've always felt a special sort of responsibility for her happiness. Sometimes this concern has been so great that you haven't been able to enjoy other relationships or activities, and this makes you feel depressed and upset."

Such a problem, for which the clinical data offers a moderate level of support, is however, largely unconscious. As such, it might be expected to arouse resistance, which, in the framework of TLP, becomes problematic. As Mann and Goldman have noted, "the central issue as posed by the therapist must be one that, among other things, will bypass defenses, control the patient's anxiety, and stimulate the rapid appearance of a therapeutic or working alliance as well as a positive transference" (1982:20).

SESSION 1

When Carla arrived for her appointment, she noted right away that she had been feeling a little better since talking with me last week, despite having felt "sort of sad" after leaving the session. Although she had wanted very much to call her ex-boyfriend, Chris, she had managed to hold off, socializing with other friends over the weekend and trying to write a term paper. She then reported with sadness that her father had not sent her any flowers this year on Valentine's Day (which had fallen earlier in the week), which led to a memory of another disappointment dating to her senior year of high school. At that time she had been admitted to X College, a rather prestigious school that she had convinced herself would not even seriously consider her application. When she received the letter of admission, she was elated, and that evening called her father to tell him the good news. Carla was deeply hurt when her father, rather than responding with pride at her accomplishment, summoned little enthusiasm at the news, "which he knew meant so much to me." He then immediately focused on the cost and "began to tell me what he could and couldn't afford, how Mom would have to pay for part of it, and stuff like that." Carla then did something very uncharacteristic that she had not done before and which she has not repeated since. Rather than simply holding onto her hurt, or "trying hard to act nice" when she was feeling exactly the opposite, she instead became very angry with her father and accused him of not caring about her, of never being supportive, and so forth. "He said he wouldn't even dignify it with a response," and the conversation ended. Again, she became tearful, but noted that it helped to be able to talk about this with someone other than her mother. At this juncture I presented my formulation of the *central issue* to Carla, which she readily accepted.

SESSION 2

Carla talked more about her parents during this hour, filling in many details of her childhood as well. She mentioned that her mother maintains close ties with her family. She was third oldest in a sibship of seven, and several brothers and a sister reside nearby. Her father was the oldest of three boys, but is not particularly close to his family. She produced an early memory, dating from her fourth year, of spending the summer with her mother on Cape Cod at a "sleep-away" camp. Although her mother worked part-time as an administrator at the camp, Carla remembers getting "lots of attention" from the other staff members, who often played with her when her mother was unavailable. "I was always the number one priority in her life," Carla observed. She returned to the theme of feeling "cut loose" at her father's house. It was so hard for her as a little girl; her stepmother wasn't very helpful either. "They expected me to be able to do things that no four or five-year-old should be expected to do. . . . Really, I tried so hard to do what I thought he wanted me to, but he never seemed happy." At this point Carla began to sob. Referencing the central issue, we discussed how Carla might have interpreted her father's long absences during these visits as an indication that he was disappointed in her or didn't care about her, when it was his professional responsibilities that drew him away. She hadn't considered this before, although it seemed to make some sense to her.

SESSION 3

In this hour Carla seemed to focus once more on her ex-boyfriend. Although he had promised to call her, he had not contacted her. She waited for days, hoping to hear from him, finally deciding that she couldn't wait any longer. He didn't seem pleased to hear from her, which was depressing to her. She keeps trying to be accommodating, but doesn't know what she's doing wrong. I point out the connection between what she had discussed in our last session—her feeling that she could never do enough or figure out what she was doing wrong with her father—and the feeling she has with Chris. This is beginning to make some sense to her. Almost as an aside, she tells me that she remembered something following her last session that she thought might be worth mentioning. Following vacations spent with her father and his family in California, she would always feel "a little strange" coming back to her mother's house. Although she couldn't explain why, she had to "touch everything" in her bedroom. In this regard, we discuss how disconnected these two parts of her life were and how abrupt the transitions between her parents' homes must have felt to her. Possibly, the "touching" was a way of reestablishing this connection; it may also have signified that all of *these* things, unlike the things in her father's house, belonged to *her*. Carla now looks forward to coming in for her weekly sessions. She is finding it a little easier to concentrate on schoolwork, even though matters with Chris feel unresolved.

SESSION 4

Today I noted what seemed to be a pattern in the beginning of Carla's treatment sessions. Not only is she cheerful when I greet her, but Carla always asks, with genuine interest, how I have been. This seems to go beyond the usual exchange of amenities, however, as though a more detailed response is anticipated. In fact, I have resisted the impulse on a couple of occasions to furnish her with more information than I ~~would customarily provide~~ a patient in response to this query. As the hour began, she reported that her closest girlfriends have told her "it's time to move on" and start dating other guys. She thinks that maybe they have a point inasmuch as she and Chris are no longer technically dating. However, Carla continues to pursue some sort of relationship with Chris, believing that since he has not become seriously involved with anyone else a rapprochement might yet be possible. Chris claims he just wants more time apart to do things with his male friends, but Carla needs more from him; although she knows it's "totally unreasonable," she nevertheless feels jealous when he hangs out with his roommates or parties with other friends. We ~~discuss the parallel between this issue and Carla's~~ *Connection* childhood jealousies over her half-siblings, with whom she always felt she was in competition on visits to her ~~father~~'s. I then commented, "So your dad wasn't just leaving you to go to work; you felt you couldn't hold your own against your half-sibs, and this made it even more hurtful." Carla thought this might be a possibility, since she has always felt this way with guys, not just with Chris. The conversation then shifted to a recent experience Carla had during a family get-together at her maternal grandmother's house. Her mother's older sister, Jenny, an unhappy woman in her mid-fifties who had never enjoyed as close a relationship to Carla's grandmother as had Carla's mother, had been critical of Carla for not offering to help with the food preparation. As a matter of fact, Carla had earlier told an uncle that she would be happy to help but had been reassured that no further help was needed. Nevertheless, she felt "awful" when her aunt pulled her aside to lecture her and began to feel that she had been wrong. As we examined her reaction, however, it soon became clear that Carla didn't really feel the criticism to be a fair one; furthermore, she felt angry toward Aunt Jenny. We then *punishing* talked about her need to "contain" and detoxify such angry feelings, even to *self* the point where she punishes herself for reacting normally to an unreason- *unreasonably* able provocation. Carla found this idea intriguing and wondered how often she might do this with others, such as her father.

SESSION 5

The evening before this session, a surprise winter storm had dumped six inches of snow on the ground. Carla arrived promptly for her session but asked whether any of my other patients had been unable to come in for their sessions. I had two thoughts about Carla's comment. The first was that here she was, whether or not anyone else showed up; she was reliable, committed, and so forth. I also recall thinking at the time that perhaps Carla had been concerned that *I* might not have been at my office when she arrived. She began the hour by talking about her recent tendency to behave in a sort of friendly though negativistic way. She finds herself challenging things her friends have said, even when she is in essential agreement with them. I suggest that perhaps she is displacing feelings that belong elsewhere, such as toward her father or her boyfriend. Carla seems slightly taken aback by this idea but admits that it offers "some sort of explanation, anyway." Pausing for a moment, she continues:

[margin note: displacement]

CARLA: I suppose I have a problem believing in relationships. Down deep, I feel that relationships don't last and that you can't count on guys.

THER: Perhaps you were wondering when you mentioned my patients not showing up whether I would be here when you arrived, whether you could count on me?

CARLA: Oh. No, I don't . . . I hadn't . . . no, I guess I thought you'd call me. . . . I don't think I thought that.

[margin note: here and now transference]

Although Carla didn't accept my "here and now" interpretation of transference, her ambivalent reaction suggested that something had "hit home." In retrospect, this may have been the first indication that the positive transference was beginning to shift, revealing Carla's expectation that I, like her father, her boyfriend, and other men in her life, will sooner or later lose interest in her. In the remainder of the hour, Carla focused on the theme of "untrustworthy" men, in particular, another former boyfriend she had dated during her freshman and sophomore years in college, who had "cheated" on her.

SESSION 6

Carla has been feeling a little more depressed recently. She begins the session wondering what "therapy is all about." She was feeling better a couple weeks back, but she's having trouble sleeping again, can't concentrate as well, and so forth. She had another conversation with Chris, and he seems to be distancing himself from her. The more he distances himself, the harder she tries. She then begins to talk about her parents' marriage. Her mother was so accommodating toward her father before their divorce. When he was admitted to law school, she moved halfway across the country with him. She kept house, worked part-time to help make ends meet, took care of his son,

Sandy, when he would visit periodically. She really "put herself out." She then mentions for the first time that her father had been involved in an affair just before he broke up with her mother, the woman he eventually married following their divorce. I commented that her mother had seemed to want to keep the momentum in the marriage going at virtually any cost and yet this somehow wasn't enough. I asked Carla if she felt a parallel existed between her description of her own tendency to make accommodations and her mother's behavior while she was married to her father. "Yeah," she replied with a long sigh, "and look what happened to her. She says she's happy and all, but, I mean, after she and my dad got divorced, well . . . she's never gotten seriously involved with another guy." I suggested that Carla's mother had good reason to feel betrayed by her father, although her solution—steering clear of deep commitments altogether—may not have been a terribly adaptive one. I also suggested that these solutions seemed to represent two extremes: either a woman behaves in an incredibly accommodating and self-sacrificing fashion or she has no relationships at all with men. Carla didn't reject this idea, but neither did she seem to embrace it. Toward the end of the hour I asked whether she knew how many sessions we had remaining. Carla paused for a moment, and then, sounding just a bit surprised, said, "Six. I guess we're at the halfway point, right? Don't worry, I still have things to talk about."

Beginning in the fifth session and intensifying in this hour, Carla's reactions seem to embody what Mann has characterized as the "return of ambivalence both about the therapist and the possible outcome of treatment" (Mann and Goldman 1982:11). The anxiety revealed in her last comment suggests that a) she will try hard to keep me interested even though she may be feeling that there is less to say and b) the end of treatment and of the treatment relationship is not far off, although unresolved issues remain.

SESSION 7

Carla has been feeling increasingly desperate about the relationship with Chris. They went out to talk about their relationship ("It wasn't really a date") and wound up at a bar that Chris frequents. They ran into two of Chris's friends, spending an hour or so chatting with them. Carla wanted to spend more time together afterward, but Chris decided to go home. I suggest that just as Carla could not "give up" on her father, even when he seemed so preoccupied with other things, she feels unwilling to relinquish her relationship with Chris. On the other hand, it is hurtful to feel that she is not as important to Chris as he is to her. She then revealed that when Chris was a junior in high school his mother developed a serious illness that left her bedridden for many months, and she became dependent on Chris, her only child. Although he wasn't resentful, once it came time to look for schools, he applied only to colleges that were out of state. I commented that perhaps Chris felt as though an important part of his adolescence was somehow derailed because of his mother's illness and that he was making up for lost time. She then observed, "Yeah, maybe that's one of the reasons he's distanced himself from me. Maybe it's less about me and more about some sort of fear of involvement he has. . . . But it still doesn't make me feel good."

Carla's insight is a poignant one, since it involves a dawning realization that Chris's reactions to her also reflect his own unique history, which makes it harder for Carla to attribute them simply to a recapitulation of her past experience with her father. In fact, the contrast between Chris and Carla is rather striking: Chris needed to escape from the regressive pull of his mother and her illness, while Carla has tried to hold onto the relationship with her father, in constant fear that his interest in her will otherwise wane. Her comment that it "doesn't make me feel good" to have arrived at this understanding is also important, since it represents both a more realistic appraisal of the relationship and a decline in the strength of the magical fantasy that she alone is responsible for keeping men interested in her.

SESSION 8

Carla began this hour by discussing a vacation she was going to be taking with two girlfriends to Miami Beach (which she had mentioned several weeks previously). It was spring break week, and she felt "determined" to have a good time. Both of the other girls had boyfriends, but this was to be just a "girl thing." She then reported a dream in which "I was trying on a pair of socks. The socks were black with gray squares, definitely men's socks. But then, after I got them on, the color changed, and they seemed to have pink polka dots, like the socks I'd wear." I encouraged Carla to associate to the dream, and she began to talk about her older half-brother, Sandy, whom she had previously described as being "a lost soul," having been married and divorced by his mid-twenties, drifting from one job to the next, without a steady girlfriend. The socks reminded her of the kind he might own, with sort of an argyle pattern. She had always found it hard to understand him before, and they had never been especially close. In fact, she felt that he resented her and, when they were younger, considered her "spoiled," perhaps because he knew how close a relationship Carla had with her own mother. But she knew that he had suffered; Sandy's mother had severe emotional problems, he had often been on his own during his childhood and adolescence, and he didn't seem comfortable during visits to his father's California home. In my interpretation I emphasized her newly emerging capacity for trial identification, first with Chris, reflecting on her comments during the last session, and now with Sandy. She was, in effect, "trying his socks on" for size. This is further underscored when the socks temporarily morph into "girl's socks" as she pulls them onto her feet; it is as though this is *her* experience, at least for the moment. She seemed to confirm the accuracy of this interpretation by noting, "I guess I do want to know what guys think and feel."

SESSION 9

Carla reported that her trip had been a lot of fun and that she had actually met a guy one night while with her girlfriends in Miami Beach. He was good-looking and also very attentive and interested in her; the two "hung out" together on and off for a couple of days, although Carla also wanted to spend time with her girlfriends. I asked her how it had felt to be in the position of telling a guy that *she* had other friends to hang with and wouldn't be able to spend all her time with him. Carla smiled, looking only slightly embarrassed, and said, "It was OK. Actually, it felt sort of good. One of the nicest parts was that I didn't feel like I was working that hard. It was more . . . spontaneous." She continued to think about Chris, but she was beginning to feel that maybe things would have to wait, especially since it looked as though they would be living in different parts of the country after both graduated. (Chris was also completing a master's degree, though in a different field.) Perhaps they would become reinvolved, although maybe not. In any event, she wasn't feeling nearly as desperate at the prospect of moving on and not being with Chris. The night after she returned, she was still feeling very good about herself and decided to go to a singles bar downtown, where she met yet another interesting and attractive man, also in his mid-twenties. He has been calling her ever since, although she doesn't want "to encourage him too much." Making reference to the central issue once again, I commented that Carla didn't seem to be experiencing the old anxiety with either of these two men and sounded far more relaxed and self-confident than she has typically reported having felt in similar situations in the past. Perhaps most important, she had also been able to enjoy herself "in the moment." She replied that, while this was possibly true, she wasn't ready to give up on her idea of finding a "true love," as silly as that might sound. However, she now accepted the possibility that the time might not be right for this.

SESSION 10

Carla began this hour by telling me that although she had been feeling better, she was beginning to realize that there were still significant issues that she had not worked through. She is about to graduate, and yet, she still feels very confused about Chris; he emailed her a nice note a few days back, and it stirred up all sorts of feelings she thought she had finally put aside. She also mentioned feeling upset as she began to think about leaving the area and moving away. She was concerned about her mother. For the first time, they wouldn't be within a few hours' drive of each other. She then wondered if maybe some of her problems with men could be related in some way to how she felt about her mother. I sensed that Carla was introducing what was, in essence, a new theme. It was actually somewhat along the lines of the alternate central issue mentioned earlier. However, its introduction at this time, along with her renewed anxiety, was more likely related to Carla's awareness of the nearing termination date. She seemed to be presenting me with new problems and a recrudescence of her original concerns as a sort of unconscious protest over our contract, as if to say, "Can't we continue to meet while I sort these things out?" However, since Carla had introduced the topic of her relationship with her mother, I thought it might be worthwhile to pursue.

THER: It's a big responsibility when someone tells you that you're "the number one priority" in their life.

CARLA: You know, sometimes, it wasn't that bad at my father's house. Actually, they do a lot of hiking, camping, and outdoorsy kind of things. As I got a little older, it could even be fun.

THER: Did you tell your mom about those parts?

CARLA: Well, I think she knew. . . . But, no, I mostly complained to her; I'd tell her how much I missed her.

THER: So maybe you felt as though it would be hurtful to your mom if you were to have positive experiences with your dad?

CARLA: Yes. I think I must have felt this way, at least sometimes.

THER: And every time things go well with a guy, perhaps you are thinking that this is another betrayal of your mom, who hasn't had the same sort of success you've had in relationships?

CARLA: Maybe. I'm not sure.

In the remainder of the hour, we returned to the termination issue. Carla's thoughts about being "cut loose," with all that this implies for her historically, as well as her deepening transference to me, seem to have combined to make her separation anxiety far more evident in this hour.

SESSION 11

By the time we met for the eleventh session, Carla had graduated from University of Y and spent the first part of the hour discussing this. Her mother, as well as a number of other relatives from her mother's family, came to see her graduate, although her father had told Carla he wouldn't be able to because "he was trying a very big case or something like that." Carla's eyes filled with tears and, sobbing, she said, "It's still hard at times like this not to have him there. I don't know, I just really wanted him to see me graduate. I don't think that's asking too much, is it?" We then discussed her wish to be seen as special in her father's eyes. On this occasion, however, the desire for recognition appeared much less tied to the childhood rivalries with her half-siblings than to Carla's desire for affirmation or mirroring. I commented that she had experienced many such disappointments in this relationship and that such a need for recognition, to be seen as "special" in her father's eyes, struck me as being both reasonable and healthy. Carla agreed that this was true, reflecting that this also seemed to be an important theme in her relationships with other men. She then paused and said, "I guess maybe I'm so convinced that other guys are going to act just like my dad that, even when they don't, I can't really believe it. Like, it's going to happen, sooner or later." I commented that this seemed to be an important insight and wondered whether Carla might yet expect a similar outcome in her relationship with me. She replied that this might have been true in our first few meetings; she had been aware of feeling slightly apprehensive before those first several appointments wondering if I were really interested in her. However, she had gradually become more comfortable talking with me and now actually looked forward to coming in for her sessions. This theme, which of course had brought us back to the central issue, was then elaborated. Carla observed that, although she now understood herself much better than she had when therapy began and had begun to notice changes in the way she behaved with her family as well as male friends, she was anxious at the prospect of falling back into her old routines. Without dismissing the possibility, I told her that I believed she had made a good deal of progress and that she was now armed with knowledge about herself and the strength and courage to put it to good use. She smiled weakly, but said, "Maybe, but I don't feel like I have very much courage." I told her that I had to disagree, and not just based on the hard work that she done in therapy. In fact, when I thought of Carla as a four or five-year-old, flying two thousand miles across the country to spend vacations with her father, in an unfamiliar place, where she often felt isolated and alone—*this* took courage. She registered surprise at this, noting that she would never have thought of this as courageous but thought, perhaps, I was right. As the session drew to a close, I mentioned that the next was to be our final session. Although Carla appeared sad, she smiled and, in a soft voice, said simply, "I know."

FINAL SESSION

Although Carla had always been talkative in our therapy sessions, she confessed that she felt there wasn't as much to say today. She did offer that, for the most part, she wasn't feeling very anxious or depressed, nor was she having much difficulty sleeping, the problems of which she had originally complained. But there seemed little else to say. This seemed just a bit odd to her, inasmuch as just two weeks ago she was feeling that much remained unresolved, but also because this was to be our last meeting. I commented that perhaps she was now beginning the posttreatment task of relying more upon herself to work through problems and didn't need me in the same way. I took the opportunity to review some of what she had accomplished in therapy. She now understood the basis of her chronic feeling of disappointment in her father. Although it saddened her, she could now recognize that this was a result of his limitations in combination with environmental factors that were beyond her control. Furthermore, her wish to feel "special" in his eyes represented healthy entitlement, not the unreasonable reaction of a "spoiled" child. She had gradually come to understand that this dynamic had persisted in a largely unmodified form and was present in other important relationships, particularly with boyfriends. I also commented on Carla's concern that she not betray her mother, both with respect to any positive aspects of the relationship with her father as well as in her own relationships with men. I suggested that she might now find it more difficult to blame herself for the shortcomings of others. Furthermore, she now possessed a greater range of adaptive solutions and strategies, so that "bad" feelings such as anger no longer need to be "contained" at all costs or turned into their opposite. Carla found this review helpful, although, as we neared the end of the hour, she grew tearful and told me how much she would miss her sessions with me. I, too, was moved and told her I would miss her as well. She embraced me warmly, handing me a card as she left my office for the last time. The card thanked me for helping her to rediscover the inner strength she must have had all along and for being such a good listener. She wrote also that she felt greater confidence in being able to make her relationships with men "more of an equal partnership" and was hopeful, too, that the relationship with her father might continue to evolve. Finally, she felt much better able to take on the challenges that lie ahead, knowing that in difficult times—if she listened carefully—she could still hear my "little voice cheering" her on.

Beginning with a historical overview of the concept of short-term treatment in the psychoanalytic literature, this chapter has examined a number of different approaches to the challenge of conducting therapy briefly. The pioneering contributions of writers such as Sigmund Freud, Sandor Ferenczi, and Franz Alexander were discussed in some detail, followed by summaries of the work of those representing the next two generations of brief-treatment theorists. The various brief treatment methods emerging within the last thirty-five years appear to reflect more generally observable trends in psychoanalytic theory formulation and can be ascribed to two basic conceptual models: namely, the drive/structure model and the relational/structure model. In the next portion of the chapter, technical parameters common to all forms of time-limited and brief dynamic psychotherapy were summarized. Following this, what has been termed the only truly "integrative" model of brief dynamic treatment, James Mann's time-limited psychotherapy, was presented in greater depth. Finally, a case illustrating this method of time-limited treatment was offered in substantial detail, complete with process summaries of each treatment session.

13

Psychodynamic Case Management

JERRY E. FLOERSCH AND JEFFREY L. LONGHOFER

IN THIS CHAPTER we briefly consider the rise of the case manager, case management, and community support services in the era after closure of mental hospitals. We then argue that concerns about service coordination, medication monitoring, money management, skill development, and resource acquisition came to dominate practice models and thereby elided the need for psychodynamic approaches. Although service coordination is essential to good case management, engagement and recovery require practices that alleviate the *external* deprivation (i.e., lack of access to resources) and the *internal* struggle caused by severe mental illness. Behind coordinated and uncoordinated services is the person—the individual or self. We consider approaches to case management that sought to redress the absence of clinical theory by describing a "clinical case management" approach that a small and dedicated group of practitioners and scholars have developed since 1985. Finally, derived from our research on case management and using a case study to illustrate our theory, we present a practice language that offers a synthesis of resource acquisition, skill development, and clinical approaches to case management but with a psychodynamic and developmental foundation.

THE RISE OF THE CASE MANAGER, CASE MANAGEMENT, AND COMMUNITY SUPPORT SERVICES

The emptying of mental hospitals presented formidable challenges to the world of patients, practitioners, and policy makers. Needs were many: housing, education, jobs, medication, mental health and social services. By 1979 the National Institute of Mental Health (NIMH) convened a series of meetings that culminated in new policies and practices, known collectively as community support services (CSS). Deinstitutionalization policy and practice desegregated hospital patients by shifting the site of service to the community (Floersch 2002). Community care did not eliminate institutional boundaries, however, as imaginary walls called "catchment areas" denoted a county or zone within which each discharged patient would be served. Although it was often the case that many lived independent of community institutions, nationwide, many discharged patients were placed in intermediate-care facilities, residential-care facilities, nursing homes, jails, halfway houses, and transitional-living apartments (Torrey 1997). In short, community support services represented a mobilization of resources that coordinated the movement of discharged hospital patients through variously organized community spaces (e.g., group homes, supervised temporary apartments, crisis facilities) to "higher levels of independent living" in "the least restrictive environment," that is, to an independent apartment or home. It has been common for individuals to cycle through community-based residential sites. Ex-patients often relapsed, returned to the hospital for days or weeks, left, returned to their apartment—if their case manager was lucky enough to pay the rent—or, if not, moved into a group home, then into an apartment; consequently the movement through space and time became cyclical. Asylum policy fixed the patient to one service site, the closed system of the hospital. Deinstitutionalization policy encouraged client mobility in the open system of the community; homelessness has highlighted this point as the severely mentally ill wandered through our streets and mobile crisis units have had to provide street-level services.

Community support service administrators and policy makers correlated successful deinstitutionalization with the reduction of hospital utilization, resource acquisition, skill development, and service coordination. This narrow view limited deinstitutionalization practice because it privileged the social world and forced clinical practices that focus on the internal world (or self) to the background. The National Institute of Mental Health, in the late 1970s, together with a host of activists, researchers, and practitioners, defined fragmented community services and the lack of service coordination as the critical failure of deinstitutionalization. As a result, case managers, or service coordinators, were named the professional most essential to successful community living.

In the early years of community support services (1970–1985), case managers created their own practice model by relying upon a "learning by doing" modality (see Floersch 2002). However, in the second phase of case management development (1985–2000), administrators, policy makers, and researchers sought to standardize community work for reasons of accountability; they promised standardization through implementation of single "model" perspectives and approaches. Researchers facilitated the process of standardization by investigating the "learning by doing" practices of managers and through their scientific work (re)presented these as "empirically based" (and now "evidence-based") practice. Floersch has demonstrated how the latter process, from field to the university, worked in establishing the dominance of "strengths" case management (see Floersch 2002:42–82). Throughout the 1980s, and at various sites, others fashioned "Rehabilitation" (Boston Center for Psychiatric Rehabilitation), "Assertive Community Treatment" (Wisconsin ACT or PACT), "Broker," and "Consumer" models. And in general there was a strong movement away from clinical, medical, or psychological theories, which were labeled illness-saturated or deficit models. Consequently, case managers, equipped with newly minted practice models, offered the many CSS stakeholders the promise of coordinating resource acquisition and skill development. State departments of mental health, national organizations (i.e., National Alliance for the Mentally Ill), federal policy makers, and local mental health organizations adopted one or another model (e.g., assertive community treatment, strengths, rehabilitation, clubhouse model, family psychoeducation, and medication management) and case managers were subsequently trained in the model's specialized language. It was generally argued that psychological theories and associated clinical practices did not assist the manager in making sure that the mentally ill stayed out of hospitals.[1]

Also contributing to the suppression of psychodynamic theory in mental health was the 1980s application of social constructivism to clinical practice. Social constructivists sought in important and unique ways to confront the problem of mental illness stigmatization by carefully examining the way in which concepts, theories, classifying or diagnostic schemes, or narratives, *construct* mental health reality; it was hoped that social work could avoid medical-scientific languages that labeled and "objectified" their clients. Included among these problem-saturated discourses were psychodynamic theories and practice. Dennis Saleebey, for example, wrote that what may be

> happening in the helper-client interaction is that the helper, clumsily or deftly, imposes his version of the situation or recasts the client's version into professional cant and canonical, not common, sense. That is the theory. Clients surrender their own narratives (or suppress them) and accept the professionals' theory, thus becoming more receptive to technique and more compliant with regimen.   (Saleebey 1994:355)

Many in social work turned to social constructivism, where the individual has no necessary developmental tasks and presocial (e.g., impulses) characteristics. Instead, individuals were simply mirrors of the social environment (Archer 2002:5) and they were determined by the culturally and historically dominant values and attitudes (i.e., discourses) on gender, ethnicity, sexual orientation, and social class, for example. The tendency to view clinical language and theory as an intrinsically "pathologizing" and "cultural" discourse led some to under-emphasize the everyday nature of clinical work so that, for example, managers were taught to focus on an individual's strengths without awareness of what within the client was being strengthened. Bypassing psychological theory, management theorists argued for a "wide-pool of people (professionals, BA-level generalists, students, consumers)" from which managers could be selected (Rapp 1998:187). Unfortunately, and through no fault of their own, this "wide pool of people" were put into case management positions with minimal clinical training and supervision.

Consequently, independent of comprehensive psychological services, case management theorists, policy makers, and administrators focused the central aim of management on facilitating independence from institutional environments. Yet it was here that the theorist and practitioner of management models confronted a most puzzling question: if the goal of deinstitutionalization and community support service was to produce client self-maintenance, what aspects of the client was the manager to work on? Management models provided no theory or language of the self that could account for self-observing, self-monitoring, or self-regulating practices. Instead, they tended to focus solely on resource acquisition and the production of appropriate community and social manners.

More recently, growing numbers of policy makers, activists, and practitioners have turned to the idea of "recovery." Although recovery is a recent concept in mental health services, it has received enough consideration that it can be easily summarized. Advocates find consensus that recovery from severe mental illness requires self-mastery, self-control, empowerment, hope, a nonlinear and small-step approach, self-responsibility, partnership, and renewed social roles (Acuff 2000; Anthony 1993; Bradshaw, Roseborough, and Amour 2003; Jacobson and Greenley 2001; Liberman et al. 2002; Marsh 2000; Ralph 2000; Roth et al. 2000; Spaniol et al. 2002; Townsend et al. 2000; Turner-Crowson and Wallcraft 2002; Warren and Lutz 2000). The definition of recovery has purposely encompassed a broad internal and external territory. From 1993 to the present, for example, the Ohio Department of Mental Health (ODMH) has engaged in a discovery process to define and construct a recovery practice model. Together with the Center for Mental Health Services, the ODMH effort started with a National Forum on Recovery for Persons with Severe Mental Illness and these early findings provided the groundwork for the policy maker's definition: "Recovery is an *internal, ongoing process* requiring adaptation and coping skills, promoted by social supports, empowerment and some form of spirituality or philosophy that gives hope and meaning to life" (Beale and Lambric 1995:8; emphasis added).

Another commonly reported definition is William Anthony's, director of the Boston Center for Psychiatric Rehabilitation. He writes that recovery is

> a deeply personal, unique process of changing one's attitudes, values, feelings, goals, skills and/or roles. It is a way of living a satisfying, hopeful, and contributing life even with limitations caused by the illness. Recovery involves the development of new meaning and purpose in one's life as one grows beyond the catastrophic effects of mental illness.   (Anthony 1993:15)

Note that these definitions mark a significant conceptual shift in CSS models toward the identification of client "internal," "personal," "unique," and "meaning" aims orientation. These ideas—internal, personal, unique, and meaning—suggest that CSS and case management theory will need psychodynamic theory to help fulfill the promise of recovery: self-mastery, self-control, empowerment, hope, a nonlinear and small-step approach, self-responsibility, partnership, and renewed social roles. Informed psychodynamic case management can conceptually and practically identify how the caregiving relationship does the work of promoting the overall goal of recovery: meaningful work, lives, and relationships.

CLINICAL CASE MANAGEMENT APPROACHES

Fortunately, a small but committed group of practitioner-scholars has written about the clinical skills that case management requires (Hagman 2001; Harris and Bergman 1993; Harris and Bachrach 1988; Harris and Bergman 1987; Kanter 1987, 1988, 1989, 1995, 1996, 1999, 2001; Lamb 1980; Surber 1994; Walsh 2000). Harris and Bergman note that service coordination and resource acquisition are important, but too often management focuses "on its managerial rather than its clinical elements" (Harris and Bergman 1987:296). Walsh uses an ego psychology and symbolic interactionist approach in his comprehensive book, *Clinical Case Management with Persons Having Mental Illness*. He writes that "the power relations inherent in helping require therapeutic theory and skill in order to effectively carry out the six core management activities: assessment, planning, linkage, advocacy, monitoring, and evaluation" (Walsh 2000:9–16). The reality of the lived experience of a helping (or clinical) relationship is that the professional relationship itself is often hidden from the researchers' fidelity or the policy makers' outcome measures. After all, it is difficult to measure something as complex, open, elusive, and productive as a clinical relationship; therefore, most case management models have overlooked the influence of interpersonal relations. Empirical research has instead focused on readily observable outcomes such as the reduction of hospital utilization; therefore, most management research fails to study how professionals use the self when helping clients satisfy their most basic needs while also helping them develop their internal world.

By excluding the work of therapeutic or clinical relationships, management models lack a clinical understanding of how to *actualize* the idea of choice, partnership, and self-mastery in recovery relationships. Although numerous researchers and client advocates have consistently argued that a trusting and continuous therapeutic alliance is fundamental to recovery (Bradshaw, Roseborough, and Amour 2003; Chinman et al. 1999; Fenton, Blyler, and Heinssen 1997; Dubyna and Quinn 1996; Deegan 1996; Solomon, Draine, and Delaney 1995; Frank, Kupfer, and Siegel 1995), case management models fail to explain how participants, in caregiving relationships, voluntarily develop trusting therapeutic alliances (or partnerships). Joel Kanter, moreover, has written that

> while various models of case management . . . have emphasized various aspects of case management practice, case managers involved in personal, ongoing interactions with long term clients implement five underlying principles: 1) continuity of care, 2) use of the case management relationship, 3) titrating support and structure in response to client need, 4) flexibility of intervention strategies (i.e., frequency, duration and location of contact), and 5) facilitating client resourcefulness or strengths.   (Kanter 1996:259)

Thus it is time the field of community support services incorporates clinical case management insights into its practice conceptualization for understanding how management relationships produce recovery effects.

In *Personal Therapy for Schizophrenia*, for example, Gerard Hogarty (2002) borrows language from psychodynamic theory. Hogarty writes, "in times past, most of this initial period of recovery occurred in the context of a hospital (asylum), but today it falls to the outpatient therapist to create a "holding environment" in what is often a stressful and unaccommodating world" (137). Like others (Surber 1994; Kanter 2001), Hogarty borrows the holding environment concept from object relations theorist Donald Winnicott (1965b), who argues that practitioners must consciously create a safe environment for change. The clinical case management we outline below fits the relationship-oriented, clinical case management tradition, yet we are taking the tradition into a new era by promoting a common sense management language that is uniquely tied to psychodynamic and development theories. We believe our research underscores the importance of viewing recovery as rooted in safe clinical (or helping) relationships. Safe and trusting relationships are extremely powerful tools because they are portable and transferable to many situations and community settings. Clinical relationships empower by helping clients *name* feelings and desires—particularly those that often lie outside awareness and beyond everyday functional needs. Although one is not always aware of hidden feelings, this does not mean they are less real. Otherwise only consciously stated wants, needs, and desires would be significant and this, perhaps, was the biggest mistake most management models enacted. When a theory of human behavior posits the existence of external and internal characteristics of clients, then case managers need a theory and language that can access both levels of everyday reality. The efficacy of strengths-based case management, for example, is at the external level of mental health community support work: identifying strengths, goals, wants, and taking resource-acquisition action. In actual practice, however, managers necessarily probe into less accessible issues. And by probing we will not be pointing to the psychoanalytic conception of the unconscious but rather deeper into the everyday psychological issues that clinical relationships inevitably serve up.

A CASE ILLUSTRATION OF PSYCHODYNAMIC THEORY AND CASE MANAGEMENT

We use findings from our participant-observation research to describe the case management relationship.[2] Using a case study, we illustrate four ways participants in case management relate to those with severe mental illness. We call these the *four forms of relatedness:* 1. "doing for," 2. "doing with," 3. "standing by to admire," 4. "doing for oneself."[3] These, in turn, are correlated to the service recipients' emotional states (Spaniol et al. 2002). Internal states, overwhelmed by (the disability), struggling with (the symptoms of disability), living with (the symptoms of disability), and living beyond (the disability),[4] combine with social relations of caregiving to constitute what we call the *zone of recovery relatedness* (ZRR).

According to clients using the recovery model, *overwhelmed by* the disability is an ongoing and recurrent debilitating anxiety; it often begins at the onset of illness and can last for months or years. "Daily life can be a struggle mentally and even physically. The person tries to understand and control what is happening, but often feels confused, disconnected from the self and others, out of control, and powerless to control his or her life in general" (Spaniol et al. 2002: 328). In *struggling with* the disability "the person recognizes the need to develop ways of coping . . . in order to have a satisfactory life" (330). *Living with* the disability is exemplified, according to Spaniol and colleagues, by a stronger sense of self and the idea that a confident "self" is recovered from illness. In *living beyond disability*, the fourth, a person feels well "connected to self, to others, to various living, learning and working environments, and experiences a sense of meaning and purpose in life" (331). Understanding these complex relationships and processes, however, requires psychodynamic theory, and, where it is absent, we have argued (see Floersch 2002), it will inevitably be reinvented.

With the ZRR we see the unfolding processes wherein service providers and related caregivers interact with clients in multifarious ways, recursively engaging in the four forms of relatedness. We argue that the four forms of relatedness can be correlated with aspects of the self and internal experience and conceptualized in each instance as a unique ZRR.[5] Vygotsky called the relationship between external (social) relations and internal (mental) development the "zone of proximal development" (Vygotsky 1978:84–91). He argued "that higher mental functions appear first on the "interpsychological" (i.e., social) plane and only later on the "intrapsychological" (i.e., individual) plane" (Wertsch 1979:2). In the client's external environment they would be represented by a teacher, parent, or peer who provides help. The person being helped (the person with severe mental illness) internalizes what helpers offer, describe, or perform. For Vygotsky and for Furman (2001) self-mastery (or confidence) is a process of converting the external environment into an internal one. While there is recursive movement and the possibility of relapse, there is always potential for recovery. Vygotsky and Furman show us how an individual's capacity to function, learn, or relearn depends not only on present relationships but also on past ones.

Below we represent the case of Marilyn through the zone of recovery relatedness informed by psychodynamic theory. In this case you will see not only how caregivers function in relation with Marilyn at different levels within the ZRR but also how caregivers use the self differently and recursively throughout. As well, you will see how object relations, drive, ego, and self psychologies can be used to augment the work of case management in the zone of recovery. Marilyn's ZRR experience was not predictable or linear. In fact, at times it appeared as if she were simultaneously experiencing different levels of recovery relatedness.

CLINICAL CASE ILLUSTRATION 13.1 "MARILYN"

Marilyn, age twenty-three, was living in a supervised group home with other women and men of various ages and diagnoses at the time our research began. She had been diagnosed with dysthymia (Axis I) and learning disabilities in reading and math (Axis II) and was taking medication for anxiety and depression. She voluntarily entered the group home three years prior to the study and described the decision as one of consensus between her mother, her older sister, and herself, all of whom were living in a three-bedroom-one-bath bungalow in a working-class suburb. There were also two coresident small children, girls, ages six and nine, both daughters of Marilyn's sister.

Marilyn was working a part-time, supported employment position at a woodworking shop where she split the required weekly eighteen hours between clerical and other jobs. The woodshop, operated by the agency that owned the group home, was one among several recent stints in fast-food restaurants (e.g., Pizza Hut) and related work at an amusement park. Cooking for Marilyn was meaningful in both work and social life; and she hoped the agency would help find her employment in food service or hospitality. When she spoke of cooking she beamed with pride and reported that peers at the group home enjoyed what she prepared: with them she felt admired and often praised. And by assisting others less comfortable in the kitchen, she achieved much needed peer support. Early on Marilyn identified the following personal recovery goals: 1. to move out of the supervised environment of the group home into her own apartment, 2. to find a more meaningful and satisfying job, and 3. to learn how to drive.

MARCH 18

Marilyn, while *struggling with disability*, was sometimes able to *do for herself*. On this day, however, *unable to take action*, she turned to others. She called Lisa (the field researcher, who was acting as a case manager) and informed her that she wanted to talk. Her voice was heavy; it seemed she had a lot on her mind. She asked Lisa to join her for coffee; Lisa, *doing for* Marilyn, made arrangements to pick her up. At coffee, because Marilyn was not eager to talk, Lisa initiated the conversation. Soon she was reporting that the group home manager had become concerned about her ability to keep her room orderly and to perform required cooking and cleaning. Marilyn was informed that noncompliance could jeopardize eligibility to remain in the home and to qualify for an apartment. The manager enlisted a housing specialist to *do for* (help with household tasks) Marilyn; at this point, *overwhelmed*, she was helped to regain confidence to perform *actions* necessary for group living. In taking this *action*, Lisa was *doing with*. Marilyn engaged, and a successful alliance formed. Note here, in the application of the ZRR, Marilyn is overwhelmed.[6] Moreover, using the ZRR language, a case manager is confronted with the need to both understand and to assess the individual experience of anxiety. *Overwhelmed* may mean in this specific context that she feels a "terror that the self will be overwhelmed, will be engulfed by another, will cease to exist" (McWilliams 1999:79). In psychodynamic theory this is called annihilation anxiety, though it may also be described as a variant of separation anxiety. Both forms of anxiety entail threats to the self and are especially important for managers when working with those who have severe mental illness and who often face overwhelming realities in community living.

Marilyn, *struggling with disability*, also worked with an employment specialist who was *doing with* her in taking *action* to identify a training program in culinary arts as a way to find more meaningful work. Here Marilyn did not talk with Lisa about feelings that pertained to employment or housing. And, when asked, she remained silent; *overwhelmed*, she turned to Lisa for help *with feelings*. Lisa was *doing for* by *feeling for* Marilyn, by encouraging her feelings, and responding to her feeling needs (Furman 1992:67–84). Here, "having and communicating feelings became a tool for understanding a situation and knowing what to do about it" (68). As well, case managers work in a world of intense affect, especially among those struggling everyday to meet even the most basic human material needs. And with this intensity of affect comes a special need to understand and assess the ability to express feelings in words. Or are these feelings expressed in bodily ways? Or are they acted out? We cannot possibly help those living in communities with recovery unless we can describe their affective experience accurately. Where, for example, affect can be separated from action, the work of case management will be quite specific. Some, who cannot do this, may find relief in hitting; obviously the goals, resources, and efforts of case managers will be differently trained under these circumstances; more "doing for" will be necessary. In this instance it will be feeling for. And case managers must be especially cautious in asking for the expression of feeling in words when this capacity is missing (see McDougall 1989 for discussion of this problem). In other cases, affects may be used defensively.

Individuals with severe mental illness report that feeling, thinking, and actions are often constrained by overwhelming hopelessness, powerlessness, and despair (Spaniol et al. 2002). When case managers, or members of caregiving networks, engage in doing for activity they offer hope and safety, experiences that are at first entirely external. The client joins the caregiver in a dependent relationship, not taking responsibility for thoughts, feelings, or actions but engaging instead in a communicative act in which the caregiver offers an auxiliary ego to name (or describe) what is happening.

JULY 14

Lisa met with Marilyn in a park to talk about the upcoming move and the support network necessary for the task. *Working with* Lisa, Marilyn developed a "to do" list to prepare for the move from the group home to an apartment (*living with the disability*). With Lisa's help, Marilyn identified priorities. First, she needed to work alongside the case manager and contact Consumer Protection Services (CPS) so that they could help with money management (at this time Marilyn's mother was her legal payee). Second, Marilyn needed to save money to buy household items, yet she seemed eager to spend (she was quick to name specific needed items and thrift stores). Third, they compiled a list of network members who could help on the moving day. Marilyn, now prepared to take action, *living with her disability,* was *doing for herself.* After the "to do" list was completed, Lisa asked Marilyn about the status of her relationship with family (mother, sister, and nieces) and, after talking about the relationships, she invited Lisa to a church festival in her mother's neighborhood. "It would be a good opportunity for you to meet them," Marilyn said. Throughout the work Lisa struggled to define and maintain management boundaries. Often case managers are caught in a maelstrom of transference and countertransference (see chapters 4 and 5). And although it may be necessary for managers to meet and engage family members (to perform assessments and so forth), the client's transference and the worker's countertransference reactions may complicate these contacts. Effective management requires awareness of these feelings and how they affect the work of helping Marilyn do for herself.

JULY 25

Lisa met with Marilyn in a park, where she talked about troubles with her boyfriend and thoughts about moving. "I am feeling more anxious and more stress about the uncertainty of the move. I am really anxious to move out," she said, adding that the group home supervisor had informed her that she was still on a waiting list but there were no apartments available. Marilyn also talked about the job, how she disliked it, and reported that she had applied on her own for a job at a video store. She was restively waiting to receive word about the status of the application and talked about the fear of not being able to keep a time commitment of more than eighteen hours per week. "Work really stinks," she said. "I'm afraid I'll never be able to get a job outside of there." Lisa encouraged Marilyn's expression of feeling. Though here *struggling with the disability*, Lisa was listening, feeling, and *standing by to admire* as Marilyn described her fear and anxiety about moving into an apartment and finding a new job. Because Marilyn talked more about her feelings, Lisa asked questions in an attempt to learn more about how she had typically dealt with them. *Struggling with her disability,* Lisa (feeling) asks Marilyn about her expression of feeling. With this, the third form of relatedness, *standing by to admire,* Marilyn named the feeling, thinking, and action needed to achieve her goals and, as a result, built self-confidence.

The client internalizes the safety the caregiver represents and gradually depends less on the auxiliary function of the caregiver's ego. Or one might see Lisa as a mirroring selfobject, responding to and confirming Marilyn's sense of accomplishment (see the discussion of self psychology in chapter 3). And though the relationship is still interdependent, it moves closer to independence. With independence one might usefully describe what Kohut calls the *nuclear self,* that is, the client communicates personal awareness with "I did" statements and takes a significant share of responsibility for the task. The caregiver no longer, or minimally, has to *do with* or *do for* and uses admiration of the client to produce *within* a feeling of personal accomplishment. At this point, the desired outcome is for the client to internalize the admiration of the other and to use it as a scaffold (Hagman 2001) for building personal pride, self-respect, safety, and confidence: the nuclear self. These are necessary internal states that provide protection from overwhelming feelings of powerlessness and helplessness.

JULY 31

Lisa took Marilyn to a coffee shop, where they talked. Marilyn reported a break with her boyfriend; she was still working at the same job and was on a waiting list for an apartment. Asked about how she was coping with the turmoil and uncertainty, she replied, "I'm distracting myself with video games and movies. I'm keeping myself busy preparing for the move. I still need to shop for household things." Marilyn defensively copes with the breakup and uncertainty about the move with video games and though here *struggling with her disability,* she is *doing for herself.*

Case managers inevitably face the challenge of understanding the range and intensity of defenses. It may not be within the clinical case manager's purview to interpret defenses. However, knowing how and when to recognize them (especially those that place clients in jeopardy living in communities or may be crucial for functioning) is essential for effective management and necessary for engaging in the four forms of relatedness. Some managers, not recognizing defenses, may engage unnecessarily and unproductively in an intermittent or even continual cycle of doing for. Also, recognition of the nature of defenses helps managers understand the possibility for and changing nature of the alliance at each level of relatedness; if defenses are rigid, the alliance may be difficult or impossible to achieve or maintain. Lacking this knowledge and sensitivity, it would be impossible for managers to recognize defenses that get in the way of promoting independent living in communities and contribute to a lack of motivation or responsibility necessary for the kind of living *expected* in the era after deinstitutionalization. This, as well, is one source of case manager burnout: incessant doing for without recognition of the possible underlying defenses supporting client dependency leads to a management cul-de-sac.

AUGUST 2

Lisa met with Marilyn in the dining room at the group home, where Marilyn noted that she and the case manager had completed the paperwork to transfer SSI and SSDI checks from her mother to CPS, which would now pay monthly bills and provide a stipend for other expenses, like transportation and entertainment. The change in payee was a step closer to the independence Marilyn sought. Now living *with her disability*, the case manager is *doing with* (taking action) Marilyn in the completion of paperwork necessary to get help from CPS. To specific questions about medication and money, she responded that her mother, psychiatrist, pharmacist, and Medicaid (because they paid the bills) helped monitor medications and that, until recently, her mother and the group home supervisor helped manage money. Here, *struggling with disability*, Marilyn's mother, the group home manager, and CPS took *action to do with* in the management of money. Likewise, with Marilyn, her mother, psychiatrist, pharmacist, and Medicaid helped manage medication.

SEPTEMBER 26

Marilyn reported that the housing specialist (see March) helped complete the application for a new apartment and that she would be meeting with a case manager on October 3 to review it. Marilyn told Lisa, "I never heard back from the video store [about my job application]. I hate my job . . . and I am afraid I'll be stuck there forever." Now *living with the disability*, the service agency was taking *action*, *doing with* Marilyn to complete paperwork for the new apartment. Marilyn, however, expresses frustration about her employment situation and, while struggling *with these feelings and her dis-*

ability, she is *doing for herself*. In doing for herself, the fourth form of relatedness, she completes the process of internalizing the hope, safety, trust, and confidence represented by the caregiver and detaches from her. She now enters into relationships with others that are self-determined and independent and, consequently, takes over the problem-solving effort from them. The caregiving relationship shifts from the interpsychological to the intrapsychological plane and the transition from regulation by other to regulation by self is exemplified. Marilyn masters the task. In other words, Marilyn internalizes her caregivers. As previously discussed (in chapter 3), this might also be usefully described as a process of *transmuting internalization*, that is, where a "function formerly performed by another (selfobject) is taken into the self through optimal mirroring, interaction, and frustration" (Elson 1986:252).

While the case manager, in the many hours of negotiating urban and exurban worlds, focuses on meeting the materials needs and wants of clients, they simultaneously exist in a world of intense affects, transference, and countertransference. As case managers go about the business of doing for and doing with in the realization of these, they face the uncertain and complex nature of how the relationship is to be used (Walsh 2000:96–97). It is the manager, for example, who works in the transference, often in intense daily interactions with clients in sometimes familiar settings (e.g., automobiles and the privacy of homes). It is especially in the client's relationship with the case manager that the client is most likely to repeat situations of feeling and impulse that have been experienced earlier, in their relationships with those in their present lives and personal histories.

OCTOBER 10

Lisa picked up Marilyn from the group home for shopping and coffee. Marilyn talked about her concern for a friend from the group home who had been hospitalized. She bought music CDs and video games ($40), a coffee mug ($12), a cup of coffee, a pastry ($5), and lunch at Burger King ($5). At the coffee shop Lisa asked Marilyn if she was concerned about the upcoming move. *Struggling with the disability*, Marilyn spends money and has little concern about budget. She responded, "It's the challenge of the unknown. The 'what ifs.' There are fears and there could be problems with my roommates. I wonder how much dish TV costs. I'd like to get that." Marilyn expressed concern about being able to access convenient transportation because the group home had a van that took residents shopping for groceries and clothing necessities and occasionally on social and recreational outings. Living on her own, she would have to rely on public transportation. Here, *standing by to admire* and *doing with*, Lisa asks Marilyn how she feels about moving, listens, and applauds her thinking ahead about public transportation (struggling with disability). In working with the severely mentally ill, case managers inevitably challenge a person's self-esteem; they must confront and sometimes cajole; they are in the business of managing people's lives. Some of what they say and do will wound. How, then, without psychodynamic concepts, do managers work with clients in such a way as to convey what is necessary without producing terrible blows to self-esteem? It is only done with knowledge of how self-esteem is produced.

OCTOBER 23

Moving day. Lisa arrived in the morning at the group home with her pickup truck to find Marilyn's room a complete mess. There were clothes, papers, stuffed animals, toys, video games, CDs, and trinkets piled everywhere. Moving boxes were empty. Most of the morning, Marilyn sat on the edge of the bed, *overwhelmed*, while Lisa and one of her friends (a resident at the group home) packed boxes and carried them down the stairs and into the truck. Marilyn sat silent most of the time and, when she spoke, she did not refer to the task of moving. She said, for example, "since I don't have cable yet and don't have an antenna for my TV, I'm wondering if my new roommates will let me watch *Roswell* [a television show] tonight." *Overwhelmed by disability*, Lisa and her friend pack (action) and move boxes for Marilyn. They *do for*. Here, Marilyn had difficulty understanding how the relationship should function, that is, toward helping to establish independence in *action*; in many cases clients remain incapable of making the move from doing for to doing with, no doubt related to crucial developmental tasks, unrealized in earlier forms of relating, where the need for manager doing for became exaggerated by the severity of the client's current experience with mental illness.

Finally, Marilyn commented on the move. She complimented Lisa on her ability to pack efficiently. She said, "Wow. You're good at this." Fifteen minutes later she asked, "Am I being helpful?" Lisa said, "No, not especially, but I'm guessing that maybe you are feeling really overwhelmed or something else like that and it is making it very hard for you to help with the move." Marilyn did not acknowledge her feelings. She simply said, "I guess." Here, *overwhelmed by disability*, Lisa monitors and names feelings. She is *doing for* and feeling with Marilyn. While she sits on the edge of the bed, overwhelmed, and watches her friend and Lisa pack and move belongings, the caregiver names the feeling state and its relationship to the task at hand. Here the client leans on (or depends upon) the hopefulness and initiative of the helper.

OCTOBER 24

Lisa picked up Marilyn from the new apartment for grocery shopping. In the supermarket Marilyn wandered up and down the aisles filling a grocery cart with more items than could possibly be stored in the refrigerator. Because she knew Marilyn had to share the refrigerator with two roommates, Lisa monitored the shopping; she had been allocated one shelf only, but had purchased enough food to fill an entire refrigerator. Lisa brought this to Marilyn's attention, which she continuously ignored. Still *overwhelmed*, Lisa monitors Marilyn's spending. She is *doing for*, in *thinking and acting*. Like Marilyn in this instance, clients sometimes need an auxiliary ego; others have memory but occasionally lack good judgment. Marilyn needed ego supports and often needed help in developing the capacity to test reality and to engage in effective action. Lisa offered an auxiliary ego to help with actions involving decisions as to what behaviors were appropriate in these circumstances. Lisa helped as well in identifying possible courses of action and anticipating and weighing the implications or consequences of Marilyn's behavior (judgment) in order to engage in appropriate action, that is, behavior directed to achieving desired goals with minimal negative consequences.

To get Marilyn's attention, Lisa stepped in front of her and said, "Please don't take this the wrong way, but I've never seen you this disorganized and I'm really concerned. The past two days I've been trying to point out the reality of your new living environment, like how you're going to get your groceries home from the store and how you're going to put them away and how you are going to get to and from work." Marilyn replied, "Oh, I kind of try to avoid reality." Here, *still overwhelmed*, Lisa gets Marilyn's attention and *does thinking for her*, by stepping into her physical space.

On the way back to the apartment, Marilyn reported that she had sensed that something had been going wrong but was not sure what it was. She then reported that she had missed the last appointment with the psychiatrist, had run out of medication, and had not told anyone because she was afraid the case manager, psychiatrist, and the manager of the group home would yell at her. Lisa spent a lot of time assuring Marilyn that she was not going to get in trouble and helped develop a plan for getting in touch with the psychiatrist. Though still *overwhelmed*, Marilyn is reporting that she missed her last appointment with the psychiatrist and has stopped taking meds. She reports being afraid of getting into trouble. Overwhelmed, she requires the case manager to do *this with her* (feeling). Lisa helps Marilyn develop a plan to contact her psychiatrist to get medication (thinking, *doing with*). With this second form of relatedness, the client can name the feelings and thoughts and connect them with actions by standing alongside others and "doing with." Here, having understood that the client can differentiate feeling from action, the work of management takes a different course. In this interaction, though the client still depends on the caregiver, she begins to experience the relationship as interdependence; she begins to participate, but her feeling, thinking, and action is still dependent on the caregiver. While the client is not functioning as an independent problem solver, she is developing a sense of what is necessary for independent activity. For example, Lisa helped Marilyn develop a plan to contact her psychiatrist and get more medication. This is a necessary step in the ZRR because it allows the individual to experience interdependency as positive. The desired outcome of this form of relatedness is a sense of pleasure in "doing with" others. By making "doing with" activities pleasurable, a positive internal feeling state becomes attached to relationships, and this offers protection against feelings of alienation and social isolation.

DISCUSSION

Marilyn's ability to accomplish recovery tasks was not predictable, linear, or consistent. Nor was her mood. Mood correlated with the ability to accomplish tasks. When *overwhelmed by* or *struggling with* symptoms, confidence was low; she was unable to think about the future, consider consequences, or make choices to minimize stress and resolve conflict, internal or external (see October 23, for example). However, when in control or *living with symptoms*, she recovered self-confidence and assertiveness; she accomplished what she wanted and needed with minimal negative consequence (see July 14). In short, there was a correlation between the internal environment (feeling and thinking) and mastery of her external environment (action). Although we observed Marilyn *doing for herself*, she never performed these actions in an emotional state of *living beyond* disability. She typically made decisions and took actions by herself when she was struggling with or living with the symptoms of her disability, drifting toward an over-whelmed emotional state and a relapse into dependency on care providers.

Our research suggests that internal (emotional/mental) functions affect and are affected by social relationships and that the transition from external moni-toring by others (i.e., case manager, psychiatrist, family members) to internal monitoring by the self can be positively affected by competent application of the ZRR. For instance, when Lisa helped Marilyn create a "to do" list for moving, Marilyn's confidence and self-satisfaction increased (see July 14). Also, when Lisa monitored and named Marilyn's sadness—during and after her move—her con-fidence and satisfaction increased. She made the effort to refill her medication as Lisa worked *with her* and *stood by to admire*.

Not only did we observe the correlation between Marilyn's internal and external worlds, we also observed that both were irregularly mediated by profes-sionals in her recovery network. In addition, mediation was not focused on help-ing Marilyn transform dependency on others into independence, even with those recovery goals in which Marilyn demonstrated interest and competency (e.g., cooking as meaningful employment). At best, her relationships with providers were sporadic; they were certainly uncoordinated, and managers stayed stuck in what we call "doing for," managerial or monitoring functions.

Marilyn's experience with various levels of self-mastery at preparing for and securing a new apartment occurred in a treatment (or therapeutic) environment that we are calling the ZRR. Self-control or self-mastery outcomes that are attrib-uted to the use of the four forms of relatedness are more likely when associated with trusting, hopeful, and mutually responsive relationships. As in the case of Marilyn, mutuality required negotiating dependence on "doing for" work. This necessary dependence attached the internal (emotional) environment of Marilyn to the safety embodied in the external (social) environment represented by Lisa. Dependence on an individual that represents safety is an essential component not only in the process of learning but also in the process of recovery in mental health. Why? We speculate that the conscious use of the four forms of relatedness facili-tates the process of transforming the external helping relationship into an inter-nal (emotional) and cognitive capacity for self-help.

Placing yourself in a "doing for" recipient position is a critical step, yet it can be a frightening one because it makes the recipient vulnerable to manipulation and control by others. We think that those who refuse the case manager's "doing for" work resist dependence because they often mistrust the helper; they may, per-haps, fear an engulfing type of dependence. In other words, they resist attach-ment because they are protecting themselves. Many do not perceive the helping relationship as safe, nor do they see the hope that a measured and conscious dependence on "doing for" will produce a movement toward interdependence and, eventually, independence. Hope and trust, moreover, are integrally connected. Feelings of trust mitigate the perceived external threat of the helper (too much "doing for" activity) by creating a safety net, and a potential relationship of conflict is therefore transformed into a relationship of care. We anticipate that persons with severe mental illness may be more likely to receive help if they can perceive the positive outcome of receiving all four types of relatedness. We are confident that the ZRR will provide that hope because it offers a recovery context (a movement toward independence) in a commonsense language that can be understood by everybody participating in a recovery network, including those who give help and those who receive help: 1. clients, 2. caregivers, 3. service professionals, 4. family members, and 5. agency supervisors. Most important, the commonsense language is rooted in psychodynamic and development theory.

Policy makers and professionals in health and human services continuously seek new ways to encourage mental health clients to live as independently as possible. This is a challenging task because the capacity for independence varies from person to person. Our capacity for independence, because of illness, can be compromised or the capacity may not be there in the person's developed self. The ZRR provides service professionals with a structure and language to develop a continuum of relationships to help persons with mental illness develop and/or recover self-confidence and capacity to perform everyday tasks.

Psychodynamic theory will help the professional understand the complexity of mental health caregiving. With the potential for the ZRR to be incorporated into client records, supervisors can use the ZRR as an instrument to track professional (usually case manager) intervention strategies and professional uses of self. Such a development would (re)introduce appropriate clinical theories from the past, which are badly needed in today's work. We speculate that professional caregivers experience burnout when they begin to feel overwhelmed by too much "doing for" activity. Consequently, the ZRR provides an opportunity for supervisors to examine the relationship between front-line practitioners and clients and identify the causes of burnout from both directions. We anticipate that case managers, for example, feel overwhelmed by work if they become stuck in "doing for" and "doing with" activity alone. For instance, if managers are constantly "doing for" clients and not moving toward "doing with" and "standing by to admire," they may be encouraging unnecessary dependence and, thus, creating too much work for themselves. From another perspective, supervisors might use the ZRR to help managers understand why clients might be resisting their attempts to "do with." A careful analysis of a client's interpersonal history might reveal that those who keep themselves dependent have had few positive, if any, long-lasting interpersonal experiences.

Because case management professional and specialty jargon is often inaccessible to clients and does not prepare managers to think clinically about caregiving relationships, many clients remain unengaged or dependent. The language of the ZRR would maximize client and family participation; it would promote partnerships (i.e., therapeutic alliances) resulting, hopefully, in independence from CSS. Although the ZRR is cast in everyday language, it does not eliminate the *judicious* use of abstract, discipline-specific, psychodynamic theory. The ZRR was constructed out of phenomenological, interrelational, developmental, and psychodynamic informed research, so the resultant commonsense language is rooted in psychodynamic theory. By starting with the "near" experience of both caregivers and clients, the ZRR enables professionals to utilize their specialized language but to *reserve* it for *specialized* situations—in conversations with other professionals and with caregivers and clients who have the capacity to understand the nuance and complexity of abstract, professional theory.

PART 4

Research on Dynamic Treatment

14

Research on Clinical Process and Outcomes in Psychodynamic Therapy and Psychoanalysis

STUDIES OF THERAPEUTIC efficacy involving psychoanalysis and other psychodynamic therapies, taken as a subset of all empirical research on psychosocial treatments, are vastly underrepresented. The reasons for this are multiple and involve such factors as the historical isolation of psychoanalytic institutes from the behavioral sciences and from academia, in general; the deemphasis in clinical psychoanalysis on manifest symptomatology and corresponding emphasis on latent processes and phenomena as well as the difficulty in developing suitable operational definitions for many psychoanalytic concepts; the frequently long course of psychodynamic therapies; and the impressionistic and probabilistic nature of the psychoanalytic treatment endeavor, which is not measurable with the same efficiency as are other forms of treatment. This historical trend, regrettably, has led to a widening chasm between psychoanalysis and the other behavioral sciences, specifically to assertions that psychodynamic principles are not researchable and hence unscientific. But is there, indeed, a substantive basis for such claims?

In this chapter we will begin by revisiting the issue originally raised in this volume's opening chapter—the scientific status of psychoanalysis. Can psychoanalytic treatment processes be measured, and are they quantifiable? Is psychoanalysis an empirical science, or is it more properly regarded as a hermeneutic discipline and therefore not subject to the same evidentiary rules required of empirical disciplines? Research on psychodynamic psychotherapy has typically been of two principal types: investigations of the process of therapy and studies designed to measure treatment effects or outcomes.[1] In the next two sections a concise summary of current psychoanalytic research on therapeutic outcomes, followed by a discussion of existing research examining the treatment process, are provided. In the final portion of the chapter, a particular instrument for measuring client verbal process, termed the *focal conflict model*, is presented and illustrated with several case vignettes and interview excerpts.

THE SCIENTIFIC NATURE OF PSYCHOANALYSIS

For more than one hundred years, influenced by Freud's early allegiance to the principle of scientific rationality, psychoanalysis has aspired to the empirical method. However, the question of the scientific status of psychoanalysis has yet to be satisfactorily resolved. As I noted earlier, some analysts believe that psychoanalysis adheres to the basic tenets of empiricism in its methods but is not experimental (Holzman 1998). Wallerstein (1988) has taken the position that psychoanalysis is indeed a science, and that it is governed by the usual scientific canons. However, he believes this definition is applicable only to "experience-near" clinical theory (e.g., resistance and defense, impulse and anxiety, transference and countertransference, conflict and compromise formation) rather than to "general" or "metapsychological" theory. Others, however, have argued that psychoanalysis is neither experimental nor truly empirical. These writers consider psychoanalysis to be a "linguistic discipline" whose province is meaning and interpretation rather than "mechanism and explanation" (Home 1966; Rycroft 1985; Bateman and Holmes 1995). Spence has taken this position somewhat further, arguing that psychoanalysis is the study of *narrative* truths rather than *historical* truths. In Spence's view the most salient criterion may not be whether a psychoanalytic interpretation corresponds to a verifiable reality but rather the degree to which it is internally consistent and can provide a satisfying and coherent explanation (Spence 1982).

Still other psychoanalytic writers, including the author of this book, believe that while psychoanalysis is not exclusively empirical, investigations that rely on empirical methods are possible and have "given us psychoanalytically valuable information" (Galatzer-Levy 1995). Studies of various psychodynamic and psychoanalytic processes, such as Luborsky's research on the *core conflictual relationship theme method* (Luborsky and Crits-Cristoph 1990), as well as important large-scale investigations, among them the Menninger Foundation Psychotherapy Research Project (Wallerstein 1986), may be offered in support of this position.

At the same time, there is widespread acknowledgment that empiricism often seems far removed from the central interests of psychoanalysts. As Galatzer-Levy has observed, "Most analysts are primarily interested in explaining the psychology of people in depth, and derive their principal reward from the detailed description of how particular people function psychologically" (1995:401). Such research interests have led rather naturally to a high value placed on *narrative case study*, a topic that we explored in some depth in the beginning of this book. In spite of the compelling reasons that support continued use and refinement of such single case investigations, too exclusive reliance on this methodology may also be problematic. Fonagy, for one, has been critical of the undue emphasis psychoanalysis has placed on anecdotal clinical data, which

> left the epistemology of psychoanalysis and psychotherapy dependent on an outmoded epistemic paradigm: enumerative inductivism [i.e., extrapolating and generalizing from a number of examples]. Enumerative inductivism, finding examples consistent with a proposition, is at most an educational device and not a method of scientific scrutiny. The almost universal application of this epistemic tool in psychoanalytic writings has created a situation where, currently, psychoanalysis has no method of discarding ideas once they have been proposed and made to sound plausible.   (Fonagy 1993:577)

However, I would argue that psychoanalytic research is no longer as exclusively defined by such anecdotal clinical data—to which the work of researchers such as Horowitz, Weiss, and Fonagy himself attests. Does psychoanalysis conform to the current definition of empirical research, which requires that data be obtained through "systematic observations capable of being replicated (i.e., verified) by other individuals and subject to evidentiary standards" (Thyer and Wodarski 1998:2)? Perhaps not fully, although there is mounting evidence not only of increasing research sophistication but also of far more attention to research, in general, among psychoanalysts.[2]

RESEARCH ON TREATMENT OUTCOME

Ever since the publication of Hans Eysenck's research claiming psychoanalytic patients demonstrated no more improvement than did untreated controls (Eysenck 1952), psychoanalysts and others interested in the therapeutic efficacy of psychoanalysis and dynamic psychotherapy have endeavored to develop methodologies and instruments to demonstrate its therapeutic effects. Although in the early 1950s research studies in psychoanalysis were greatly outnumbered by clinical and theoretical publications, Eysenck's controversial conclusion about the efficacy of psychoanalytic treatment was a challenge that analysts could not ignore and may well have contributed to a renewed interest in researching clinical outcomes in psychoanalytic treatment.[3] As Bateman and Holmes note,

By the 1980s this view had been conclusively refuted with several well-controlled studies and meta-analyses showing the effectiveness of psychotherapy compared with untreated controls (Smith et al. 1980; Lambert et al. 1986). About 30 per cent of the people on waiting lists improve spontaneously, compared with the 70 per cent of treated patients who benefit from psychotherapeutic treatment. Also the *rate* [emphasis in the original] among "waiting list controls" is slower than for those in active treatment (McNeilly and Howard 1991). Howard et al. (1986) studied the "dose-effect curve" in psychotherapy, and found that, in general, the more prolonged the treatment the greater the benefit. (1995:246)

Although such findings appear to strengthen the claims of psychoanalysts and dynamic psychotherapists that dynamic treatments are efficacious, other therapeutic methods, some at striking variance with the theoretical premises, methods, and techniques of psychoanalytic therapy, seemed to be as effective. This problem, termed the "equivalence paradox," was explained by one researcher (Frank 1973; Parloff 1986) as arising from the confluence of three "common factors" that are present in all therapies: "'remoralization,' or the giving of hope; the offering of a relationship with the therapist; and providing a rationale and a set of activities which suggest a pathway towards health" (Bateman and Holmes 1995:247). However, treatment efficacy in psychoanalysis is not fully explained by such nonspecific "supportive" factors alone, but is more likely the result of "common factors" in combination with factors that are specific to the psychoanalytic situation, such as interpretation, promotion of the transference, and so forth (ibid.).

In chapter 1, where we first considered the question of psychoanalysis and its relationship to the empirical method, several significant second-generation studies of therapeutic efficacy were briefly mentioned. Among these were the Menninger Foundation Psychotherapy Research Project (Wallerstein 1986), the Boston Psychoanalytic Institute Prediction Studies (Kantrowitz, Katz, and Paolitto 1990a, b), and the Anna Freud Center Study (Fonagy and Target 1994, 1996; Target and Fonagy 1994).

The Menninger Foundation Psychotherapy Research Project, which began in 1954, has yielded more than sixty papers and five books and is generally regarded to be the most comprehensive and systematic of all psychoanalytic outcome investigations. Originally led by psychoanalysts Robert Wallerstein and Lewis Robbins, this landmark investigation of forty-two psychoanalytic patients was conceived as a naturalistic, longitudinal, prospective study whose aim was to identify the kinds of change that occur in psychoanalysis and psychoanalytic psychotherapy as well as the specific processes that yield therapeutic change. The contributions of analyst, patient, and various environmental features were all assessed, together with basic precepts of psychoanalytic therapy. The Menninger project is also considered exceptional for its detailed study of the lives of disturbed adults and of adult development more generally (Galatzer-Levy et al. 2000). The project is credited with important methodological advances and innovations, among them the adaptation of Fechner's method of paired comparisons (Fechner 1966) to complex clinical data, which permitted researchers to render such data in a quantifiable form. There were several important study findings. First, as a group, patients with severe illness tended consistently to fare poorly when analyzed by inexperienced psychoanalysts. Another finding, one since replicated in other investigations, is that the most likely mode of therapeutic action in analysis and analytic psychotherapy is not via the interpretation of unconscious conflict but rather through supportive elements in psychotherapy (Emde 1995). Finally, data from the Menninger project suggested that initial evaluations, however detailed and comprehensive, are nonetheless of limited predictive value when considering the outcome of an analysis (Galatzer-Levy et al. 2000). Although heralded as a landmark investigation, this study also had several major limitations. Among them were its recruitment of severely ill patients not ordinarily thought to be suitable for psychoanalytic treatment, use of modified analytic techniques, the relatively small sample size, and use of student analysts in conducting treatment (ibid.).

The Boston Psychoanalytic Institute Studies (Kantrowitz, Katz, and Paolitto 1990a, b), which began in 1972, were designed to assess suitability for psychoanalytic treatment using a prospective methodology. Led by psychoanalyst Judy Kantrowitz, these studies relied on both clinical assessment techniques as well as psychological tests (e.g., Rorschach, TAT, and Draw-A-Person) and were evaluated with respect to the subjects' reality testing, level and quality of object relations, motivation for treatment, affect availability, and affect tolerance (Galatzer-Levy 2000). Clinical outcomes were judged on the basis of therapeutic benefit and according to whether an analytic process had evolved. Therapeutic benefit, based on a follow-up interview with the original analyst, was tied to changes in reality testing, object relations, and so forth. Analyzability, also determined on the basis of a follow-up interview, was determined according to a four-point scale: 1. analyzable with resolution of transference neurosis; 2. analyzable with partial resolution of transference neurosis; 3. analyzable with variations, partial resolution of transference neurosis, and 4. unanalyzable. Of the twenty-two cases followed, 75 percent demonstrated improved outcome at termination, although raters judged only 41 percent to have developed an analytic process. Significantly, neither clinically based pretreatment data nor clinical interviews conducted prior to the beginning of analysis predicted analyzability or therapeutic benefit

(Galatzer-Levy 2000). Another interesting finding was that clinical judgments made by the subjects' analysts and members of the intake committee as to the severity of the subjects' impairment differed markedly from the psychological test data. Although at intake each of the twenty-two subjects was judged by the committee to be functioning in the "neurotic range," test data found only eight subjects to be neurotic. Others were identified as "narcissistic characters," "borderline," "borderline with psychotic process," or "psychotic characters" (90). Despite serious limitations, such as the small sample size, use of candidate analysts in the conduct of treatment, lack of precision in operationalizing psychoanalytic precepts, questionable validity associated with some of the psychological tests as instruments for evaluating psychoanalytic results, and adequacy of the follow-up data, this study has important strengths. Its methodology was prospective, and it examined a clinical population judged to be representative of typical clinical practice in psychoanalysis. Furthermore, there was an attempt to examine the analyst's contribution to the treatment process as well as a focus on the salience of posttermination follow-up. Kantrowitz and her colleagues also attempted to differentiate *analytic process* from *therapeutic benefit*, concentrating on dimensions of the patient-analyst match (91).

If research on psychoanalysis and psychoanalytic psychotherapy outcomes with adults is greatly underrepresented among all research on psychosocial treatments, investigations involving child and adolescent outcomes are even less prevalent. Several factors may account for this. One is a methodological dilemma, common to all research on psychosocial treatments with children, termed the "maturation effect," which, simply put, suggests that change might have occurred without any intervention, as a function of continued development. A second, related problem has to do with the view, originally advanced by Anna Freud, that the *capacity to continue development* is the best measure of children's psychological health and, moreover, constitutes the major aim of psychoanalytic treatment (Galatzer-Levy et al. 2000). Although not completely without controversy, the notion that adult patients might attain some sort of psychological maturity as a function of successful psychoanalytic treatment rests on an ideal of psychological well-being. As difficult as measuring the adult patient's "developmental level" might prove, demonstrating the *capacity for continued development* in children and adolescents represents an even more formidable challenge in research on clinical outcomes (Galatzer-Levy et al. 2000). Yet another problem for the researcher interested in clinical child and adolescent outcomes resides in the continuing lack of consensus among child and adolescent analysts as to the central features that constitute psychoanalytic treatment with this population. Even today, analysts working with the young are not in unanimity regarding such fundamental questions as the existence of transference, whether interpretation can be successfully employed via play metaphors or must be made directly, and so forth.

Although their study was retrospective in nature, Fonagy and Target's (Fonagy and Target 1994, 1996; Target and Fonagy 1994) stands out as one of the most detailed investigations of clinical outcomes involving children in psychoanalytic treatment. Theirs, in fact, is the only study to have attempted to 1. identify factors predicting success in psychoanalytic child treatment and 2. differentiate those disorders that would fare better in analysis versus nonintensive treatment or dynamic psychotherapy (Galatzer-Levy et al. 2000). With access to detailed records involving 763 cases treated at the Anna Freud Center, Fonagy and Target were able compare children who had been treated psychoanalytically with others seen less intensively, controlling for children's age, diagnosis, and other salient variables. Major findings included the following:

1. Younger children improve during psychodynamic treatment and do even better with four-to-five-times weekly sessions.
2. Anxiety disorders, with particular specific symptoms rather than pervasive symptoms, are associated with a good prognosis even if the primary diagnosis is a disruptive disorder.
3. Children with pervasive developmental disorders do not do well even with prolonged intensive psychodynamic treatment.
4. Children with emotional disorders with severe and pervasive symptomatology respond well to intensive treatment but much less well to nonintensive psychotherapy (Galatzer-Levy et al. 2000:110).

The study had a number of limitations, the most significant of which was its retrospective methodology. Other problematic elements involved the preparation of outcome data by the children's own therapists rather than by independent clinicians, treatment of cases by trainees, and the failure to account fully for changes in how analytic child technique is conceptualized (ibid.). Nevertheless, the Anna Freud Center study, particularly when paired with earlier research comparing intensive psychoanalytic with less intensive work in the treatment of school-age children (Heinicke 1965), makes a compelling case for psychoanalysis as an effective treatment for children suffering from emotional disorders.

RESEARCH ON TREATMENT PROCESS

Research on process is generally conceived as a means for understanding how change is achieved and for learning more about the intrinsic nature of the therapeutic endeavor. Process research has typically been contrasted with outcome research investigations, which are designed to measure client change once treatment has been concluded.[4] Although the distinction between process and outcome in treatment research has been rejected by investigators who view process measures as "interim measures of outcome" (American Psychiatric Association 1982:39), other researchers have emphasized the focus on internal changes in the clinician's or client's behavior over time, phenomena that are often more obliquely related to treatment outcome.

In vivo studies of treatment process generally involve some form of *content analysis*. According to Marsden, an early writer on the topic, content analysis

> denotes a research technique for the systematic ordering of the content of communication processes. Typically, it involves procedures for division of content into units, for assignment of each unit to a category or to a position on a metric, and for summarizing or otherwise manipulating coded units to provide a basis for inference concerning their significance. The basic contribution of content analysis is that it makes public the grounds on which an investigator makes inferences about the significance of a body of communication.   (Marsden 1971:345–46)

Marsden identified several different kinds of process instruments. The *classical* model emphasizes "quantification of the manifest content of communication" and is designed to restrict the analysis of content to the semantic and syntactic aspects of communications. The *pragmatic* model, rather than coding units to categories descriptive of the content itself, as in the classical model, uses categories "descriptive of some condition of the communicator, or of the relationship between him and his communication." The pragmatic model focuses on the dynamic motives of the client, which can be either conscious or unconscious. The *nonquantitative* model has been used in linguistic, acoustic, and kinesic analyses of content (382–84). Over a quarter century ago, Davis suggested that both the classical and pragmatic models hold great promise for the investigation of treatment process in clinical social work (Davis 1976). The Hollis typology, one of the better-known process instruments developed for use in clinical social work, appears to have certain characteristics of both the pragmatic model and the classical model, although the relatively low level of inference required to use the typology establishes it as predominantly a classical process instrument (Hollis 1968a, 1968b; and Woods and Hollis 2000).

Process data can be collected in several different ways. Process recordings, audio tapes, and audiovisual tape recordings are the most commonly used methods for data collection. Although process recordings have a time-honored place in clinical social work education and occasionally have served as the principal means of data collection in research investigations in both social work (Hollis 1968b) and psychiatry (Wolfson and Sampson 1976), most investigators reject them as an unacceptable methodology because of the inevitable omissions, condensations, and distortions of content and sequence typically associated with their use (Wallerstein and Sampson 1971; Davis 1976; Gill et al. 1968; Lustman 1963; and Shakow 1959).

Although various instruments and research methodologies for the analysis of treatment process currently exist (Kiesler 1973; Shapiro and Emde 1995), few adaptations for use in either clinical supervision or instruction have been reported in the social work, psychoanalytic, or psychological literature. One major problem with many systems of process analysis is the length of time required of those who wish to learn how to use a particular instrument. Competence in applying the instrument to process data is almost invariably measured by observing the degree of agreement or interrater reliability between two or more coders (Jones 1995). An acceptable level of agreement may require many hours of training. Satisfactory agreement among raters is also rather predictably associated with the level of inference required in a given system of process analysis. Training raters to code data according to more or less objective criteria (for example, rate of speech, number of references to a specific theme, frequency of a particular behavior) is relatively simple. However, when the categories to be coded require a greater degree of inference (expressions of specific affect, use of defenses), agreement is somewhat more difficult to achieve.

Another possible obstacle to adaptation is the difficulty that is frequently encountered in data preparation. Although computer software programs are now available for speech-to-text conversion, the ability of even the most technologically sophisticated software to recognize verbal nuances, paraverbal utterances, exclamations, idiosyncratic expressions, and the like remains limited. Secretarial or other staff are often more accurate in transcribing such therapy data, although, when a system of process analysis requires the transcription of entire treatment sessions from audio recordings, this procedure is both time consuming and costly. Moreover, patient privacy is increasingly cited as an issue in both clinical and educational venues, although informed consent procedures, disguising of data, and adherence to professional ethics in using treatment data have proven to be fairly reliable safeguards against compromising the client's confidentiality. The use of audio recorders or camcorders has occasionally also been criticized as constituting a "parameter" in the treatment situation and thereby undermining treatment effectiveness. One pertinent finding in treatment research, now more than a generation old, is that, generally speaking, therapists seem to be more affected by the presence of the recorder than do their clients (Marsden 1971). Nevertheless, some clients feel anxious about the presence of the recorder or feel that it is disruptive. In such cases, recording is, of course, absolutely contraindicated (Brandell 2000:13).

It is sometimes suggested that the kinds of variables and phenomena many content-analysis instruments are designed to assess are those that are "immediately observable and obvious"—a situation leading to "superficial and mechanistic" research on the process of treatment (Davis 1976:6). One might then also conclude that such analysis would have a correspondingly limited value for clinical supervision or instruction.

A final problem in using process-analysis instruments is the amount of time involved in *coding* material. Although computer-assisted coding of clinical process dimensions have made possible multivariate analyses of a range of process dimensions inconceivable just thirty-five years ago, the computer is unable to analyze certain kinds of information. Such data tend to be ambiguous, and judgments about them inferential. However, it is precisely these data in which psychoanalysts and psychodynamic clinicians and researchers tend to be most interested. Once again, however, when coding requires a great deal of time, the applicability of such instruments for didactic use is even further restricted.

Issues such as those described above represent significant obstacles to the successful adaptation of many of the existing instruments of process analysis for use either in clinical supervision or for instruction. One apparent exception to this general rule is the *focal conflict model*, which has been used not only for supervisory and instructional purposes but has also demonstrated some potential as a single-system methodology for researching clinical outcomes in dynamic treatment.

THE FOCAL CONFLICT MODEL: A BRIEF HISTORICAL ACCOUNT

The *focal conflict* model is a concept firmly anchored in the structural hypothesis of psychoanalytic theory. According to Thomas French (probably somewhat better known for his role as Franz Alexander's coauthor in *Psychoanalytic Therapy*), the focal conflict is "the problem with which the patient's ego is preoccupied" (French 1954:378). Each focal conflict is described as consisting of three parts: *a disturbing wish or motive*, which generates a *reactive motive*, which in turn activates an *orienting hope* designed to alleviate or resolve the conflict. Disturbing wishes are generally conceived to possess either an aggressive or a libidinal cast. The disturbing wish gives rise to a specific emotional reaction, such as fear, guilt, or some other form of anxiety. These two components, the disturbing wish and reactive motive, constitute the focal conflict. French described the third component in his paradigm as the orienting hope, the problem-solving mechanism that is activated by the focal conflict. French focused his attention on adaptive (hope-oriented) solutions to the focal conflict, largely ignoring the role that defenses, symptoms, and solutions that are otherwise *conflictful* play in the ego's effort to resolve the focal conflict (Kepecs n.d.:19). French viewed the focal conflict as a preconscious phenomenon, although he did hypothesize a relationship between focal conflicts and a deeper, underlying nuclear conflict. Nevertheless, French was more interested in arriving at the correct understanding of the client's focal conflict during a therapy session:

> Our task is first to understand and then to lend support to the ego's problem-solving efforts. We should try to identify with the patient's ego, to imagine ourselves in the situation of one who has the same problem to solve. It is not enough that we recognize one or another fragment of his problem, that we discover the infantile wish that is disturbing him or the guilt or shame with which he is reacting to that wish, or that we recognize some single repressed thought or fantasy. On the contrary, our task as therapists is to understand how all of these fragments fit together. Identifying with the patient's ego, *we should always try to keep in touch with the problem in adaptation to present reality with which the patient's integrative mechanism is already preoccupied.*
>
> (French 1954:378; emphasis added)

French was also careful to note that the focal conflict of an interview was always " a reaction to the patient's emotional situation in the immediate present . . . the precipitating situation" (382). He advocated that the therapist explore psychologically meaningful events both inside and outside the consulting room and not be overly intent on consistently fitting the client's emotional reactions to the template of transference. Later, in a jointly written text on dream interpretation, French and Erika Fromm systematically applied the focal conflict method to dreams (French and Fromm 1964).

Although French's focal conflict method was an important contribution to theoretical psychoanalysis and held value as a didactic instrument, it never actually achieved the status of a research instrument for analyzing process. Joseph Kepecs, who had been a student of French's at the Institute for Psychoanalysis in Chicago, later successfully adapted the focal conflict paradigm into a research instrument for the study of therapeutic process (Kepecs 1977; Kepecs n.d.). He retained the focal conflict idea, originally described by French, but modified it by expanding the *wish* category to include *mastery* and *assertion*, both of which further emphasize the ego psychological nature of the focal conflict instrument. Kepecs also dealt with efforts at conflict resolution that are unsuccessful or mal-

TABLE 14.1 *Focal Conflict Model Checklist*

Wishes:

Select one or two (if applicable)

___ PHR Positive human relations: statements that refer to the self supporting, praising, expressing desire for sexual/nonsexual intimacy, expressing need for dependence on others. Also statements that refer to others doing, expressing, or wishing to express similar interests, or performing similar actions.

___ HO Hostility out: Statements that refer to the self attacking, belittling, humiliating, criticizing, or teasing others, ranging from simple angry statements to murder. Can apply to therapist. Covert hostility (others wishing to act or performing similar actions on other individuals) is also coded HO; denial of hostility is coded HO and denial, if appropriate.

___ M Mastery: Statements that clearly represent the individual's desire to take adaptive action. Includes wish to be autonomous, achieve goals, achieve self-understanding, control own life, change, succeed. To be considered mastery the wish should be stated in a declarative form, which implies adaptive action. Statements of having overcome difficulties are coded as ADAC, not as mastery.

___ A Assertion: Statements that represent a wish, stated explicitly or implicitly, for power and control over others. Assertion is interpersonal, rather than intraindividual (as is Mastery).

Reactions:

Select one or two (if applicable)

___ Fear of overstimulation

___ Fear of abandonment

___ Fear of merger

___ Fear of loss of autonomy

___ Fear of separation

___ Fear of rejection

___ Fear of bodily harm

___ Fear of death

___ Fear of loss of control

___ Guilt

___ Shame or embarrassment

___ Nonspecific anxiety or fear

___ Other (to be specified)

Maladaptive Solutions:

Check all that apply

___ INT Intropunitiveness: Statements characterized by self-criticism, self-blame, suicidal or parasuicidal thoughts, disappointment in oneself, self-initiated threats to self; self held to account for all failures and dissatisfactions in life; self seen as unworthy, depressed, or in despair; also, statements that are reports of self-injurious or self-destructive behavior (drug and alcohol abuse, self-mutilation, accident-proneness). Differs from masochism primarily in that self, not others, is making critical and/or denigrating remarks.

___ MAS Masochism: Statements in which self is harmed, threatened, criticized, misunderstood, abandoned, rejected, neglected, punished, abused, or otherwise victimized by others. Note: Care must be taken to differentiate chronic reliance on the masochistic defense from circumstances in which the report of abuse is not a solution, but an anxiety-generating situational precipitant.

___ HS Helplessness: Statements that reflect helplessness, confusion, weakness, inability to cope, sleepiness, impotence, inability to focus or succeed. HS implies an inability to act and does not clearly represent internal conflict.

___ IHB Inhibition: Some awareness of conflicting forces reflected in patient's statements, in that helplessness or inability to succeed, for example, are connected with an anxiety state—a sense of something that causes the individual to feel inhibited.

Adaptive Solutions:

Check all that apply

___ ADAC Adaptive activity: This category includes solutions that are relatively conflict-free, as in the following:

___ Self-observation

___ Neutralization

___ Liberation

___ Maturation

___ Sublimation

___ Self-approval

___ Self-confidence

___ Realistic self-appraisal

___ Self-calming and self-soothing

___ Hope

___ Humor

___ INS Insight: Statements characterized by a dynamic understanding of the self and one's own motives, including awareness of the focal conflict and the efforts made to resolve it.

___ DRV Driveness: Statements referable to the individual's feeling that he/she ought to/should be doing something. An implied objection to the pressure and a feeling of constraint should both be present in order to code DRV. The implication is that should the driveness be given up, dire consequences will result.

Other maladaptive solutions:

___ UND Undoing   ___ AMB Ambivalence

___ SOM Somatization   ___ DEP Depersonalization/ Derealization

___ ISO Isolation   ___ DEN Denial

___ REG Regression   ___ RFM Reaction Formation

___ REP Repression   ___ SUP Suppression

___ WTH Withdrawal   ___ Other (to be specified)

Wishes used defensively:

___ DHO Defensive hostility directed outward: Often used after a PHR statement but can follow other wishes. Any wish met by rejection or attack can lead to DHO. The attack or rejection should precede or be otherwise closely connected to the use of DHO. An HO wish requires that there be no identifiable precipitating attack or rejection.

___ DPHR Defensive Positive Human Relations: Usually occurs in connection with an HO or DHO statement.

___ DM Defensive mastery: A refusal or wish to refuse to submit to internal intrapsychic intimidation or criticism.

___ DA Defensive Assertion: Refers to interpersonal action and is a refusal or wish to refuse to submit to influence, intimidation, or control.

adaptive such as defenses, wishes used defensively, and symptoms. These were added to French's original orienting hopes category, which Kepecs renamed *solutions*. The rating system in Kepecs's model borrows terminology from the Gottschalk-Gleser Content Analysis Scales (Gottschalk 1995; Gottschalk 1979; Gottschalk and Gleser 1969; Gottschalk, Gleser, and Winget 1969) and is influenced by Roy Schafer's action language (Schafer 1976).

Kepecs described the focal conflict model in the following manner:

> The assumptions underlying a focal conflict formulation are: A person wants to act or do. He has learned through many experiences that some kinds of actions or potential actions will get him into difficulty with others around him; or, will upset inner balance—homeostasis; or, when external relations have been internalized, will get him into trouble with his conscience (superego and ego ideal). To avoid these difficulties, which are mainly feelings of fear or anxiety, the person will use a variety of solutions some of which are compromises or defenses and others of which have varying degrees of adaptive value. The particular focal conflict is likely to predominate through a particular therapeutic hour, though it may sometimes change within the hour. When it can be identified, it serves to orient the therapist and is a guide to interpretations and interventions. (Kepecs n.d.:384–85)

Kepecs advocates the use of a ten-minute verbatim transcript of an audiotape treatment interview.[5] According to Bachrach and coworkers, the use of interview segments for the investigation of therapeutic process is somewhat limited (Bachrach et al. 1981). They observed that judgments about the treatment relationship and transference are much less reliably made from interview segments than from complete session transcripts. Both Bachrach and colleagues and Mintz and Luborsky, however, suggest that the brief segment can serve quite admirably for understanding other dimensions of therapeutic process, such as client affect, reflectiveness, receptivity, and therapist activity (Mintz and Luborsky 1971).

Kepecs observed that the brief, typed interview excerpt, which is arbitrarily selected from the interview, is valuable both because it "gives focus and precision" to the interview data and because it provides student and instructor with a representative piece of the treatment interview (Kepecs 1977:383). For these reasons, he believed it was preferable to other instructional and supervisory methods, such as anecdotal reports and nontranscribed audio recordings. He also states that the use of sequential transcripts provides a "good map of the course of therapy" and that the typescripts can be used to demonstrate "empathy, parallel process . . . tracking errors of the therapist" and "the power of the text." (Kepecs n.d.:13–14).

Kepecs's coding scheme (reproduced with some modification in figure 14.1) is intended to be used in the following manner:

1. A transcription is made of the brief (five- to ten-minute) excerpt from an audio recorded session.
2. The transcript is independently scored by the student(s) and the instructor on a line-by-line basis.
3. A formulation of the focal conflict is made based on the wish(es), reaction(s), and solutions identified in the transcript.

Since ratings, when compared line by line, do not always show a high rate of concurrence, the final formulation of the focal conflict has more value as a measure of interrater agreement.

Kepecs does not provide interrater reliability statistics, although he does state that a "very satisfactory degree of consensus" can be reached between independent coders (41–42). The possibility of chance agreement in the first two categories (wishes and reactions) must be eliminated, however, before one can confidently discuss the level of agreement between raters. In my own research, interrater agreement in both the wish category ($k = .58$, $p < .005$) and the reaction category ($k = .41$, $p < .005$) between trained raters lent some support to Kepecs's contention. Because the "solutions" category can involve a variable number of designations between raters, it is much more problematic to assess the level of interrater agreement in this component. My research data demonstrated that consensus existed on at least half the identifiable solutions in better than four out of five (82 percent) ratings. Although this is not exceptionally high agreement, it does suggest the existence of a substantive basis for recorded agreements in the coding of solutions.

HOW THE FOCAL CONFLICT MODEL CAN BE USED

I have actually used the focal conflict instrument in several different ways in my work as an educator and clinical supervisor. Over the years I have conducted a number of seminars on process analysis using a continuous case format for which the focal conflict instrument has proven quite durable. I have also taught focal conflict theory in both graduate-level psychopathology courses and advanced clinical practice courses as a way of introducing students to basic psychoanalytic concepts. I often ask trainees to reproduce a verbatim or reconstructed process excerpt and then analyze the content using a focal conflict approach, and I have used focal conflict analysis in both individual and small group supervision of graduate students and postmaster's degree clinicians. Although not all trainees find this method of approaching clinical data appealing, many have found it to be a useful adjunct to their clinical education. Students have sometimes told me, in fact, that using the focal conflict theory to guide their analysis of process has helped demystify or elucidate various psychoanalytic ideas that had proven elusive. The seminars were viewed as nonduplicative of other classroom, research, and field internship experiences, and students also felt that focal conflict analysis enhanced their psychodynamic understanding of clients as well as their overall understanding of the therapeutic process.

Many trainees observed that the focal conflict instrument contributed to their dynamic understanding in a manner that process recording did not. Participants seemed to find seminars most useful when they had the opportunity to present a particular case over a three- or four-week period. After preliminary discussion of the case material, the taped segment was played back for the other seminar participants; each then scored his or her copy of the audio transcription. All seminar participants then compared notes, and the typescript was read back again in order to see how global agreement (that is, the formulation of the focal conflict) compared with line-by-line agreement.

It may also be helpful to make selective use of the literature on dynamic theory and treatment in conjunction with cases presented to the seminar. If, for example, the case under discussion has a diagnosis of dysthymic depression, it is useful to assign several readings that specifically address this disorder to the seminar as a means of enriching the case presentation. The focal conflict model, unlike the Gottschalk-Gleser Content Analysis Scales (Gottschalk, Gleser, and Winget 1969) and other sophisticated "pragmatic" instruments for researching and studying process, does not involve a complicated scoring procedure. Although some training is required before competence in using focal conflict analysis can be achieved, most of the concepts and terminology associated with this model are also associated with psychodynamic theory and practice, thereby making the trainee's task somewhat easier. Because the unit of study is the five- to ten-minute treatment segment, data preparation does not usually exceed one and a half to two hours on the average. Since the focal-conflict instrument requires a substantial degree of inference, the data it yields serve to complement and deepen the trainee's understanding of her or his case as well as the way in which treatment can most successfully be conducted.

One major limitation of focal conflict analysis is that it is exclusively designed for analyzing client verbalizations. Therapist verbalizations are not coded and focus on the therapist-client dialogue is limited. According to Kepecs, however, this limitation may, paradoxically, serve as an advantage in the instruction of anxious beginning-level trainees. Insofar as the focus of focal conflict analysis is not principally on clinical acumen or technical competence of the therapist but on the nature and meaning of the client's communications, trainees may be somewhat less defensive or guarded. The focal conflict model is, furthermore, designed only for use in analyzing client process in *individual* treatment.[6]

The following clinical examples illustrate how the transcript is actually scored (note that abbreviations for the codings are displayed in the margin):

EXAMPLE 14.1

CLIENT: I just felt like *I wanted to make a pass at her—just*	PHR ♀ (erotic)
wanted to try it and just wanted to figure out—well, you	PHR ♀ (erotic)
know, what would happen. I was sort of practicing, well,	
I'll try it and I couldn't . . . and I was trying to look for	
signs, you know, cues from her behavior, on her part, and	
stuff. It was really not. . . . I stayed there until midnight	
or so, and then I became really tired and wanted to leave	
and she was getting tired, too, so I started to leave. *I*	PHR ♀ (erotic)
turned around and I kissed her and *it was really the coldest*	rejection
kiss I have ever had. It's like *she puckered up her lips and*	rejection
turned away, and *I asked if I could kiss her again,* and *she*	DA
just smiled and shook her head, and I said, "All right," and	rejection
said goodbye and left. *It wasn't that painful— didn't get*	DEN, INT
that much out of my efforts and they weren't very reward-	INT
ing at all. . . . I felt like . . . how I tried [unintelligible]. I	
don't know . . . I feel . . . today I feel, I feel really . . . *I'm*	HS
partially tired, but *I just feel tense* and *I don't know why.*	ANX, HS
THER: I noticed when you came in here today that you	
seemed tired, and you sounded . . . almost grim when	
you began to talk back at the beginning of the session.	
CLIENT: Yeah . . . again that's . . . a different feeling. *I don't*	HS
recognize it as any specific feeling. It's partly that *I feel tense,*	ANX
angry—at what, *I don't know.* It's just a whole combina-	DHO, HS
tion of . . . but it's sort of a feeling that I don't recognize	
having had before. I just feel—*it's not very good.*	ANX
THER: How does it make you feel? What do you feel like	
today?	

CLIENT: *I feel like being by myself.* Listening to music . . . WTH
just do that or . . . work on my classes. *I just feel like being* WTH
alone. I want to go back to the apartment, but *I don't* WTH
want anyone to be there. I don't feel like talking to any- WTH
body.

FC = PHR ♀ (erotic) vs. rejection → HS, DA, INT, DHO, WTH, DEN

In example 14.1, the focal conflict is the client's wish to develop a sexual relationship with a woman. When the client approaches her at the last possible
minute to kiss her, he experiences her as cold and *rejecting*, which in turn leads
to various defensive strategies, including *helplessness, denial, withdrawal,
intropunitiveness,* and *defensive assertion.* (It is helpful to indicate gender, when
possible, in a client's use of wishes and solutions.)

EXAMPLE 14.2

CLIENT: *I do want to help her. I was able to help myself to a* PHR ♀, ADAC
point, but *I had other people to help me, too. You.* My boss. PHR (dep)
You know, *all of those people telling me they cared.* You PHR (dep)
know, *they could have just fired me and put me out the* MASO
door, and . . . *I did a lot of it myself,* but but *I had a lot of* ADAC, PHR
help, too. And I know it takes help. Before, I was always
so adamant—"*I'll do it myself, I'll do it myself*" . . . You DA
can't do it yourself. Not all the way. *If I hadn't been com-* (PHR♀)
ing here, I think I probably would be shooting up again, INT
you know. It just wasn't . . . me alone.

THER: Perhaps you're feeling that once you stop coming in
to see me that it will happen all over again.

CLIENT: I sometimes sit and wonder . . . what's going to
change, and are any of my ideas going to change. I mean,
I have a lot of confidence in you. In fact, *I feel I can talk to* PHR(ther), PHR (ther)
you about everything and anything, and *I wonder whether* ANX
I'm going to feel that with the next person. Uh, yeah, *I have* ANX
a lot of misgivings, but *I'm going to try to work at it* . . . try DM
to see what happens . . . *try to go with it* and . . . who DM
knows. *I don't really know. It's like going into a new job,* HS, ANX
some kind of new situation, or whatever. ANX

FC = PHR (ther) vs. ANX (separation) → MASO, DA, DM, INT, HS, ADAC

Example 14.2 illustrates the client's considerable conflict over ending treatment with her therapist. She wishes for continued support from the therapist, which in light of the agreed upon termination, is not possible. This stimulates *anxiety* (over the separation); various solutions, predominantly maladaptive, are employed as a means to diminish the client's anxiety. Despite the predominance of mechanisms such as *masochism*, *defensive assertion*, and *intropunitiveness*, the client shows some indication that she has more *self-confidence* (ADAC) as therapy comes to its conclusion, an important prognostic sign.

EXAMPLE 14.3

CLIENT: *I don't know how else to describe it to you, and I*   HS, HS
don't know why it happens. It's very scary and it frightens   ANX
me.

THER: You feel a sense of emptiness, as if you are alone even when you are with others?

CLIENT: Yeah. My mom and Aunt Rose and I were in that little cottage, and it was very small. Both my mom and Aunt Rose were there at the time. *I feel very close to them*   PHR ♀
both. We were just having something to drink, and I was getting warmed up, and *all of a sudden it came over me*   ANX
and I became terrified. I can't even describe what it feels   ANX, HS
like except . . . that *everyone seems so foreign and distant*   DEP
from me. It's the only way I can describe it. . . . It has happened whenever I was around my mom, about five times, although I hadn't felt like that in a long time.

THER: When you feel that way, what do you do?

CLIENT: *I try to snap out of it* . . . you know, right away.   DM
Sometimes I try praying, but I guess I don't concentrate   DM, INT
enough because it doesn't work.

FC = PHR ♀ vs. ANX → HS, DEP, INT, DM

In example 14.3 the focal conflict appears to involve this female client's wish *for intimacy with a woman* and the *anxiety* that her wish generates. Although the specific nature of the reaction is not revealed in this excerpt (the therapist strongly suspected that the client had been sexually molested in childhood), the client makes prominent use of *derealization* and *defensive mastery* in her efforts to diminish the massive anxiety that she reports.

EXAMPLE 14.4

CLIENT: *I was very hot-tempered*, very . . . *very aggressive without being . . . totally aware of . . . other people's feelings.* Um, or you know, I see this lady sitting at a desk, a receptionist, you know, and I go in and say, "*I want to speak to so-and-so about something.*" You know, ah, well, "*Can you tell me what you're talking about?*" "*Well, don't you know, you work here?*" You know. It's that kind of thing . . . *very smart-assed attitude.*	INT, INT A Fear of criticism, DHO INT
THER: OK. OK. I thought that maybe what you meant is once you got angry, then you could say what it was you were intending to say. But you couldn't do it until you got angry.	
CLIENT: Noooo, *I just think it's just being lazy,* that . . . taking the time to . . . use the right words, so that I could save a whole lot of time. You know. *And that's why I'm more assertive on the phone,* because I don't want to . . . *why beat around the bush about what I want and waste their time and my time?*	INT A RAT
THER: But somehow it took courage for you to be able to be that way.	
CLIENT: Oh, yeah. *It always takes a little bit of courage to be able to stand up to other people and tell them exactly what you want* even though it might not be . . . um . . . for instance, OK, Atlantic Bell. I used to talk to them and they'd say, "Well, we can't do something until so-and-so or such-and-such." "*Well, you turned it off. Why can't you turn it back on? You messed up the bill, I didn't.*" You know. "I'm paying my phone bill and *you're cutting off my service. Now, that is not right and you can't tell me that it is.*" You know. And they'd say, "Well, we'll get out there in a couple of days." And I'd say, "*Couple of days, my foot!*"	A DA DHO, DEN MASO DA DA

You know, I'm still paying for those two days. *You're*   MASO
*making my life miserable 'cause I got to walk two blocks to
the damn phone,"* you know, and they just . . .

THER: Uh-huh. . . . So, before, it couldn't have been that
way.

CLIENT: Uh-huh. . . . *I let everybody just run over me . . .*   MASO
and walk all over me, you know . . .   MASO

THER: You didn't have much self-esteem . . .

CLIENT: Um. That could very possibly be it.

THER: You said you let people walk all over you.

CLIENT: Yeah.

Ther: So you felt like . . . you were . . . that you were shoved
around?

CLIENT: Yeah. . . . And then *that would just give me some-*   DHO
*thing to scream and yell and rant and rave about, be mad
about, you know.*

FC = A vs. fear of criticism → INT, DHO, DEN, MAS, DA, RAT

In example 14.4 the client, a woman in her mid-thirties, expresses a wish for
assertion. This gives rise to her fear over being criticized and leads to various
efforts to diminish this anxiety. These include *intropunitiveness, defensive hostility directed outward, rationalization, denial, masochism,* and *defensive assertion.*
Although the client is making an attempt to assert herself in ways that were not
previously possible for her, she nevertheless falls back on conflict-laden solutions.

EXAMPLE 14.5

CLIENT: Sometimes I just feel like . . . I wish . . . I don't
know . . . *I wish she were dead.*   HO ♀

THER: Uh huh.

CLIENT: *I don't even know if it would help me or not*   HS
(pause). *I'm so tired.* . . . Like I've said before, I wish she   HS
never was . . . *I never really felt like she cared about*   MASO
me. . . . Well, now the letter is written, *so I don't really*   DEN
care what's going on.

THER: Did they contact you after you sent the letter?

CLIENT: No, *but I really don't care.* You know, when I was   DEN
    still living at home, *I really tried to kill myself, to commit*   INT
    suicide a bunch of times. *I took an overdose of my nerve*   INT
    pills. That didn't do any good, so *I tried a different medi-*   INT
    cine, but that didn't work either. I guess when you've
    taken medicines and you're used to them, *you must really*   INT
    need a lot to kill you.

THER: Did anyone know about your suicide attempts?   RIP

CLIENT: No, they were all gone. The times I tried it, I just
    came out of it by myself. But *I don't remember what hap-*   REP
    pened to me, if anything did, you know.

THER: You wanted something to happen?

CLIENT: Yeah. Like I said, *I wanted to die.* Like I said, *life*   INT, INT
    was miserable.

FC = HO ♀ vs. (?) → HS, MASO, DEN, INT, REP

It happens every so often that it is impossible to locate a particular focal conflict component (generally the *wish* or the *reaction*) in a brief excerpt. In example 14.5 no clear evidence of a reaction exists, although both the wish and the defensive accommodations are easily identified. The client, a young woman, expresses *hostility* against her mother, which subsequently stimulates some as yet unidentifiable reaction in her (in all likelihood, *guilt*). A variety of maladaptive solutions are then used to attenuate the conflict she is experiencing, with fairly heavy reliance on her self-directed (suicidal) aggression (*intropunitiveness*).

Although interest in empirical research on psychoanalytic treatment outcomes and process dimensions has not always occupied a high berth among psychodynamic clinicians, a body of research—some of it relatively sophisticated—has gradually accumulated over the last fifty years. Many psychoanalytically oriented clinicians are only vaguely aware of the existence of this research literature, however, which is all the more unfortunate in an era of treatment accountability and dwindling resources for psychotherapy services. Thus, the first portion of this chapter was devoted to surveying this research literature and to examining several landmark investigations in slightly greater depth. Following our discussion of clinical process research, a particular research instrument, the *focal conflict model*, was described in substantial detail. Unlike many other instruments for measuring aspects of therapy process, focal conflict analysis can be used to capture important elements within a therapy hour as well as across interviews. For this reason it may elucidate important dynamic themes in a given interview and, when used over the course of treatment, may also reveal significant changes in the client's repertoire of adaptive solutions to conflict and strategies for handling stress.

1. Enter Freud: Psychodynamic Thinking and Clinical Social Work

1. Even the somewhat later, more widely accepted James and Alix Strachey translations of Freud's books and essays, which culminated in the mid-1950s publication of the *Standard Edition of the Complete Psychological Works of Sigmund Freud*, have not gained universal acceptance among Freud scholars. See, for example, Bruno Bettelheim 1983.

2. In fact, by the late 1920s the bearded Viennese alienist (a term ultimately superceded by that of *psychiatrist*) was already so readily recognizable a cultural icon that the cameo appearance of a "Dr. Max Egelhofer" in Hecht and McArthur's play, *The Front Page* (1928), seemed perfectly natural.

3. Those searching for evidence of a continuing split between the micro- and macro-level traditions need look no further than Specht and Courtney's recently published book, *Unfaithful Angels: How Social Work Has Abandoned Its Mission*, which excited a firestorm of controversy when it was released in 1997. In it the authors claim that the contemporary focus on psychotherapy among social work practitioners represents an abandonment of social work's original mission to aid and serve the underprivileged.

4. Psychoanalysis offered a radically new perspective, one that augmented and complemented the caseworker's understanding of how social forces contribute to the client's maladjustment with a unique emphasis on the client's motives, conflicts, disturbing wishes, defensive adaptations, and personal history (Strean 1993:6–7).

5. A number of other psychoanalytic theorists also influenced the psychosocial school, including Karl Abraham, Anna Freud, Thomas French, Franz Alexander, August Aichorn, Ernst Federn, Abram Kardiner, Erik Erikson, Heinz Hartmann, Ernest Kris, Rudolf Loewenstein, Rene Spitz, Margaret Mahler, W. R. D. Fairbairn, Donald Winnicott, Harry Guntrip, Edith Jacobson, Robert White, Otto Kemberg, and Heinz Kohut (Hollis 1970:39; Woods and Hollis 2000:31–32).

6. Although ideas regarding brief treatment are not often thought of as "psychoanalytic," some psychoanalytic historians (e.g., Shechter 1997), citing Freud's treatment

of the eighteen-year-old hysterical patient "Katharina" (Freud 1893–95) and his brief consultation with Gustav Mahler (Jones 1955:70–80), argue that Freud himself experimented with such adaptations (for additional discussion, see chapter 12). Ferenczi and Rank's work, *The Development of Psychoanalysis* (1924), revealed a more deliberate modification of psychoanalytic technique in the interest of shortening patients' psychoanalyses. This work, however, was not well received by analysts of the period who, like Freud, believed that such brief analytic therapy would likely "sacrifice analysis to suggestion" (Gay 1988:474).

7. Rank's book, *The Trauma of Birth,* first published in 1924, was at first favorably received by Freud (Jones 1957). Within two years, however, with the publication of *Inhibitions, Symptoms, and Anxiety* (Freud 1926), Freud had completely reversed himself, rejecting Rank's thesis in toto.

8. Prior to the 1970s such institutional training for social workers and psychologists was available in only a few places, primarily in New York, that were unaffiliated with the American Psychoanalytic Association. In practice, psychoanalytic training for nonphysicians tended to be informal, often "bootlegged" (Edward and Rose 1999:5), despite Freud's early insistence that psychoanalysis should never become the exclusive province of medicine. Historically, this resistance to the training of nonphysicians led to the infamous refusal of the New York Psychoanalytic Society to grant psychologist-analyst Theodore Reik, who had been trained and analyzed by Sigmund Freud, full membership in its organization. It was not until 1988, the year in which the settlement of a lawsuit brought against the American Psychoanalytic Association by the American Psychological Association's Division of Psychoanalysis was reached, that nonmedical candidates could finally be admitted to psychoanalytic training without the need for special waivers.

9. This "technical paramater," proposed by Sandor Ferenczi and his coauthor Rank in their book, *The Development of Psychoanalysis* (1924), has been cited as one of the earliest experiments in brief treatment (Bauer and Kobos 1987; Crits-Cristoph and Barber 1991; Flegenheimer 1992; Tosone 1997). See also note 6, this chapter.

10. In an internet site displaying many of the exhibition's historical documents, photographs, and commentaries, this controversy is acknowledged, and the following description offered: "Our notions of identity, memory, childhood, sexuality, and, most generally, of meaning have been shaped in relation to—and often in opposition to—Freud's work. The exhibition examines Freud's life and his key ideas and their effect upon the twentieth century." http://www.loc.gov/exhibits/freud.

11. Many of Freud's psychoanalytic writings, according to Holzman (1998), can be seen to reflect two very differerent traditions: the physicalism of Helmholtz, Brucke, and others and the *Naturalphilosophie* of mid-nineteenth-century Western Europe, in which the focus is on romantic and philosophical themes embodied in grand metaphysical systems.

12. The scientific status of psychoanalysis has probably not been helped by the fact that it has, as a discipline, operated largely outside the mainstream of academia, principally in freestanding training institutes, which, in the main, have relatively little commerce with other academic disciplines or the universities that support them.

13. In Freud's original theory he had claimed mature femininity and with it, the capacity for vaginal orgasm, could only occur with the renunciation of clitoral sexuality. He believed that this critical shift paved the way for the female's acceptance of her ultimate sexual role, that of propagation. Of course, both Horney and Freud were wrong in their emphasis on vaginal erotism, as contemporary human biology has demonstrated. According to Masters and Johnson, *both* the clitoris and the lower one third of the vagina are aroused during orgasm (1970); furthermore, clitoral and vaginal orgasm cannot be differentiated biologically (Coen 1996).

14. Donald Spence notes that the classical psychoanalytic model relied heavily on such positivistic assumptions, and therefore emphasized reconstruction in its quest for *historical truth,* but that it is now more accurate to say that psychoanalytic inquiry coalesces around the capture of *narrative truths,* which may or may not possess veridicality (Spence 1982).

15. Several authors have recently noted that an ideological chasm now exists between those who view psychoanalysis as a hermeneutic discipline and those who believe it should be conceived of as positivistic science (Mitchell and Black 1995; Palombo 2000).

16. They are far more applicable to the medical model in American psychiatry, with its overarching emphasis on pathological symptoms and the disorders to which they are linked, definitively represented in the APA's *Diagnostic and Statistical Manual.*

17. The *reality principle* is one of two regulatory principles postulated by Freud, the other being the *pleasure principle.* The pleasure principle posits that human organisms strive for the most direct route through which pleasure may be obtained and unpleasure avoided. When such gratification is not possible, owing to environmental or intrapsychic impediments, or simply the individual's knowledge of the cause-and-effect conditions of everyday life, a modification of the pleasure principle, termed the reality principle, occurs (Freud 1911c).

18. Kohut used the term *selfobject* to refer to a particular kind of object relationship in which the object is actually experienced as an extension of the self, without psychological differentiation (for a more complete discussion of this concept, see chapter 3).

19. Even as this demedicalization of psychoanalysis has continued, a very different trend, one that attempts to link psychoanalysis with the neurosicences, has recently emerged. It is represented in the pioneering work of Schore (1994, 1997, 2001) and others (e.g., Kaplan-Solms and Solms 2000; Pally 1998; Westen and Gabbard 2002) and is seen by some as an important future direction for dynamic thought and practice, both within social work (e.g., Applegate, in press) and for the profession of psychoanalysis in general.

2. Psychoanalytic Theories of Development and Dysfunction: Classical Psychoanalysis

1. This tendency, despite recent and notable exceptions (see, for example, Stern 1985; Beebe and Lachmann 2002; and Main 1995), has contributed to the resistance of the

scientific community to acceptance of psychoanalytic theories, in general, and theories of human development, in particular.

2. It was at this time (late 1897) that Freud, with reluctance, relinquished what is now commonly referred to as his "seduction theory"—in which a veritable occurrence of sexual molestation perpetrated on the child by an adult is presumed to have occurred—in favor of a more purely psychological explanation for the psychogenesis of such mental disorders as hysteria. Nevertheless, even years later, he continued to believe that "seduction has retained a certain significance for etiology," observing that in the cases of Katharina and Fraulein Rosalia H, the patients had been sexually assaulted by their fathers (Gay 1988).

3. Although psychoanalysis is legitimately regarded as an empirical science, it is also a naturalistic one. Some authors have suggested that it is most usefully thought of as *post*dictive—seeking to explain behavior and its antecedents—rather than making any attempt to predict behavior (Holzman 1998:5).

4. Defined fundamentally as the "individual's interactions with external and internal (real and imagined) other people, and to the relationship between their internal and external object worlds" (Greenberg and Mitchell 1983).

5. Self psychologists, following Kohut, might be inclined to focus on Captain Ahab's injured narcissism in this particular example and view his hatred as constituting a *dis-integration* or *breakdown product* (see chapter 3 for further discussion of these concepts).

6. From the Greek, literally translated as "abnormal or faulty actions."

3. Psychoanalytic Theories of Development and Dysfunction: Ego Psychology, Object Relations Theories, the Psychology of the Self, and Relational Psychoanalysis

1. If the infant's mother was able to resume her maternal functions during the first three months, the downward spiral that otherwise often led to retardation, marasmus, and death could be reversed.

2. Masterson and others have hypothesized that adolescents and adults with borderline pathology have experienced a derailment in the normal separation-individuation process during the critical rapprochement phase; this leads to what has been described as the core dilemma of the borderline character: fear of loss of self versus fear of loss of the other.

3. *Epigenesis* is a term that Erikson expropriated from the field of embryology. It is defined as "the predetermined sequential development of the parts of an organism" (Holzman 1998:160). Each part follows an internal organismic timetable, permitting it to emerge and then to become successfully integrated with the rest of the organism. In such a developmental schema the earliest stages of growth have an inherently greater vulnerability to environmental disruption than the later ones; moreover, the earlier the disturbance, the more profound the effects on all subsequent later developmental stages.

4. Grotstein (1996:95) observes that Hermann's work seems to have adumbrated the well-known experiments of H. F. Harlow (1959) in this regard.

5. In their assertion of such an instinct the Balints repudiated Freud's concept of primary narcissism and the idea that infants only gradually develop attachments to objects (Grotstein 1996).

6. It is not difficult to see a clear parallel between Sullivan's use of the term *organism-environment complex* and the social work emphasis on the person-in-environment matrix; interestingly, however, Sullivan is not often cited by social work historians as having had a significant influence on the development of social work theory.

7. Chapter 10 includes a more detailed discussion of the contributions of Anna Freud and Melanie Klein to child psychoanalysis and dynamic child psychotherapy.

8. In Kleinian theory the regulation and containment of aggression has the quality of a leitmotif, though with specific meanings at various developmental stages.

9. Ernest Jones (1879–1958), a pioneer in the early psychoanalytic movement, was a close friend and disciple of Freud. The contribution for which he is most often remembered is his three-volume biography of Freud (Jones 1953, 1955, 1957).

10. See King and Steiner (1991) for a detailed account of these meetings.

11. Erikson had, of course, addressed this particular phenomenon (though from an ego psychological perspective) in his description of "ego integrity versus despair," the eighth and final normative crisis in the human life cycle.

12. Kohut has referred to this as the need for "uplifting care," both literally and figuratively speaking, from the idealized selfobjects.

13. Akhtar (1988) also notes that self psychology has made contributions to the study of sociopolitical processes and the philosophy of human nature.

14. The key elements in the sequence of transmuting internalization are, in order, *optimal frustration, increased tension, selfobject response, reduced tension, memory trace,* and *development of internal regulating structure.*

15. Defensive structures, another term Kohut used, are differentiated from compensatory structures in that the defensive structures "cover over" the primary defects in the self; compensatory structures actually compensate for the defect rather than simply disguise it.

16. Such concepts are traceable in some measure to Kohut's ideas about the formation of the self (Kohut 1974), as well as to psychoanalytic research on infant development (e.g., Beebe 1986; Stern 1985), intellectual debts that relational theorists freely acknowledge (Gordon et al. 1998).

17. This idea is a direct descendant of Heisenberg's "uncertainty principle," originally developed within the framework of the experimental sciences to account for the influence of the observer over her/his observations.

18. Please see chapters 4 and 5 for significantly expanded reviews of these concepts.

4. Transference

1. The "pressure technique," by which Freud originally sought to penetrate the resistance, involved him placing his hands on the patient's forehead, with the suggestion that something would then occur to the patient—a thought, image, or memory—that would contain the objectionable idea (Freud, 1893–95:109–10).

2. Freud, however, partially due to the mixed results he had obtained from hypnotic treatments, professed skepticism as early as the mid-1890s over the utility of a hypnotic approach in his work with hysterical patients (Freud 1893–95:284–85).

3. Such an approach to unraveling the meaning of transference posed far less difficulty for Freud than for his senior colleague, Josef Breuer. After Breuer's famous patient, "Anna O," developed a sexualized transference toward him that culminated in her hysterical pregnancy, Breuer abruptly ended his involvement with her, and went on a second honeymoon with his wife, during which she became pregnant (Strean 2002).

4. In point of fact, Freud never advocated *total* and *complete* abstinence, perhaps recognizing that such a rarefied analytic posture, even were it possible, might preserve the integrity of the analysis, but likely at the expense of losing the client.

5. This topic will be explored in far greater depth in chapter 7, which is devoted to issues of initial engagement and the development of a working alliance.

6. The temptation in working exclusively from one theoretical position is that of making the data conform to the theory even when the fit is poor, the so-called Procrustean bed phenomenon.

7. In chapter 10 we will examine the treatment of children in greater detail, although brief sections devoted, respectively, to the themes of transference and countertransference in clinical work with children are presented here and in chapter 5.

5. Countertransference

1. Gradually, however, our view of the analytic process and of the analyst's contribution to it has been transformed by postmodern assumptions about what constitutes science and scientific inquiry. Constructivist approaches to the study of clinical process, for example, assert that no one has access to a singular, stable, and fully knowable reality (Niemeyer 1993a:2–3), and that our understandings are instead embedded in social and interpersonal contexts, therefore delimiting them in perspective, depth, and scope. Such a view is consistent with *coherence theory*, which sees "truth" as deriving from internally consistent assumptions or experiences "rather than from a correspondence with facts which are conceived as absolute, independent and/or external" (Hamilton 1993:64, cited in Hanna 1998).

2. Hanna 1998 has also argued that this view is likely a result of the considerable emphasis placed on internalized object relations by exponents of the English and independent traditions, groups that are heavily represented in the totalistic literature.

3. Though Lacan does not typically receive credit for his early contributions to the idea of intersubjectivity, this may be due less to poor scholarship on the part of psychoanalytic historians than to the almost mystical quality of his writing, which at times appears to invite misunderstanding.

4. Ogden's theory of intersubjectivity, however, relies upon the theoretical principle of mutual projective identification. In the view of others, particularly those who adhere to basic tenets of selfobject theory, this is a problematic model insofar as it

retains an objectionable theoretical assumption: that the translocation of mental contents from one subject into another is developmentally possible for borderline or other developmentally arrested patients, when such projection should only be possible after there has been some consolidation of selfobject boundary differentiation (cf. Stolorow, Brandchaft, and Atwood 1987).

5. I am grateful to Robert Hooberman, Ph.D., for his suggestion that Dirk's need to sleep in his father's bed as well as the commingling of paternal and twinship transference elements at different stages in the treatment may point to a developmental arrest in the negative oedipal position. Furthermore, my patient's dreams and waking fantasies of sexual intercourse and his associations to his father's prostatectomy and the murder-suicide, images invaded by violence, may also reveal a homoerotic theme. Though understandably conflicted over his homoerotic desires, Dirk may, nonetheless, have sought the love and intimacy from me that he so desperately desired from his father but was unable to obtain.

6. Dirk did remain in treatment briefly with the therapist who assumed responsibility for my clinical caseload at the family service agency, but soon requested that his sessions be held on alternating weeks. The therapist, who may have interpreted Dirk's proposal as resistance, was unreceptive to this idea and remained firm in his insistence that sessions occur on a weekly basis. Shortly thereafter, Dirk severed his relationship with the agency.

6. Dynamic Assessment

1. Although the model presented here can be readily adapted for use with children, readers may also find it helpful to review Timberlake and Cutler's (2001) text on developmental play therapy for a more detailed exposition of this theme (especially chapters six and seven).

2. These terms are similar to those originally used by Perlman (1957), although here defined somewhat differently.

3. Timberlake and Cutler (2001), in their well-written text on developmental play therapy, impute general significance to a child's *choice* of play materials. In addition, they suggest a number of vehicles through which children's play and fantasies may be explored (e.g., controlled and free-play scenarios: dreams and daydreams, three wishes, happiest/unhappiest times, fables, writing, television, movies, music, drawings, and so forth).

4. An individual's proclivity for adversarial self/selfobject relatedness may also be considered here, though there is less agreement among self psychology theorists as to the developmental significance of such selfobject experiences.

5. This framework for dynamic assessment is adopted in part from several different sources: Ray Vassar, Ph.D. (unpublished), Bellak's (1984) model of ego function assessment [EFA], and Greenspan and Cullander's (1973) framework for metapsychological assessment.

6. Mediate catharsis, a term introduced by Leopold Bellak, involves the clinician's use

of him/herself in a hypothetical manner to portray affective reactions the client has not expressed but that the therapist deems useful for the client to consider. An example might be, " I was thinking that, if I were you, and Sally told me that she didn't want to see me any longer, I'd feel really sad and hurt, and then I might want to get even by saying something hurtful back to her too."

7. Beginning Treatment:
Initial Engagement, the Holding Environment, the Real Relationship, and Formation of the Therapeutic Alliance

1. With the advent of the child guidance movement in the 1930s, it became an increasingly common practice for intakes to be assigned a particular clinician for whom this represented an exclusive and sometimes permanent agency role; when therapy was recommended, a different clinician would subsequently become involved. Although this model is still used in certain settings (e.g., medical inpatient), it is no longer modal in social service agencies, residential treatment facilities, or outpatient clinics. In such settings it has probably become at least as common for the same clinicians to conduct the clinical assessment as therapy proper, so that clinical assessment serves as a sort of prologue to the treatment that follows. Even in cases where an intake assessment has already been performed, the information furnished to the clinician may be primarily descriptive and behavioral; in such an instance, dynamic assessment remains the province of the therapist assigned responsibility for treatment. In effect, the clinician always serves two masters.

2. An even greater motive was the gradual movement toward professionalization within social work, which required greater conceptual clarity as well as the substitution of a new "scientific" terminology for the experience-near language of casework pioneers such as Mary Richmond.

3. *Empathy, positive regard,* and *congruence* constituted the original "facilitative conditions" identified in the Rogers' seminal research (Rogers 1957), although this list was later amended to include *nonpossessive warmth* and *genuineness.*

4. Meissner (1996) and others (Spruiell 1983; Arlow and Brenner 1964) have all cautioned against the "implicit appeal" of such a model, with its "parental, even maternal view" of the therapeutic relationship. Holding is a very legitimate and, in many instances, essential component in the therapeutic relationship, but one that also has the potential to expand beyond what is clinically necessary. It may become the basis of a "gratifying transference fantasy" that ultimately replaces the collaborative relationship of therapist and client, leading to a therapeutic impasse or otherwise subverting the psychotherapeutic process (Meissner 1996).

5. *Handling* is a specific term sometimes used to denote the structural arrangements that contribute to the maintenance of a therapeutic holding environment. Agency policies and procedures, the setting of fees, cancellation policies, appointment times, and so forth constitute such "containing boundaries of clinical work" (Applegate and Bonovitz 1995:112–13).

8. The Middle Phase of Treatment:
Resistance, Working Through, and Dynamic Technique

1. Although the defensive efforts of the ego were hypothesized as the principal source of resistance, Freud also attributed a role to both the id and the superego. In the case of the id, such resistance was theorized to explain the operation of the "repetition compulsion" at times well beyond the point at which insight is first achieved. When resistance emanates from the superego, it is caused by the sense of guilt and need for punishment, which may undermine treatment "successes" and, in certain cases, result in what has been termed the "negative therapeutic reaction" (Freud 1923; Asch 1976; Moore and Fine 1990).

2. Freud's abandonment of the hypnotic method, thought to have occurred in 1896, apparently presaged by several years his abandonment of the "pressure technique" and the instruction that analytic patients keep their eyes shut during analytic sessions (Breuer and Freud 1893–95:110n).

3. By 1984, the date at which Kohut's final (posthumously published) work appeared, the expanding theoretical and clinical domains of psychoanalytic self psychology may have rendered such distinctions less salient for self psychologists than they had been in 1971, when Kohut published his first book.

4. The social casework concept of *developmental reflection*, which "includes procedures of encouraging the client to think about the development of his or her psychological patterns or tendencies" and focuses very specifically on early life experiences, is very compatible with that of *genetic interpretation* (Woods and Hollis 2000:124).

5. Similarly, Hollis's definitions of *person-situation reflection* and *pattern-dynamic reflection* seem to be a rather close parallel to what is here described as *dynamic interpretation*: "[Person-situation reflection] consists of communications designed to draw clients into reflective consideration of their situations and of their functioning within them," with a focus on "current and relatively recent events, exclusive of early life material," [whereas pattern-dynamic reflection] "consists of procedures for encouraging clients to think about the psychological patterns involved in their behavior or responses and the dynamics of these patterns and tendencies" (Woods and Hollis 2000:123–24).

6. Moreover, as we will explore in somewhat greater detail in chapter 12, interpretative interventions may be used to advantage even in brief and time-limited dynamic treatment approaches.

7. In a now classic 1954 paper reviewing therapeutic principles and techniques in psychotherapy and psychoanalysis, Bibring relegated abreaction to "a rather insignificant curative role in psychoanalysis." He did, however, acknowledge that abreaction could provide relief from emotional tensions and, furthermore, that it was useful in "offering evidence for the correctness of the interpretations and constructions and in providing conviction through emotional reliving" of the patient's past conflicts (762–63).

8. Although formally advocating "strict and untendentious psycho-analysis" (Freud

1919b) based upon such ideas as analytic abstinence and neutrality, no less an exponent of the psychoanalytic method than Sigmund Freud was also observed "bending his rules and at times breaking them, with a sovereign sense of mastery and in the interest of sheer humaneness" (Gay 1988:303). Freud sometimes reduced the fees of analysands in times of personal financial hardship, permitted himself to make cordial comments during treatment sessions, and even "made friends with his favorite patients" (ibid.). Such activities strongly suggest not only that Freud was relatively comfortable in deviating from the "basic method" of psychoanalysis but also that he possessed a technical repertoire that was far richer than his papers on technique would have led readers to surmise.

9. Suggestion, which is similar but not identical to what Hollis terms "direct influence," undoubtedly does occur in dynamic treatment. However, it is generally used as a temporary measure and with great caution, since "whenever possible, it is far more respectful and supportive of clients' sense of competence to foster their reflective consideration" than for the clinician to give them directions (Woods and Hollis 2000:122–23).

9. Termination: The Endgame

1. Post-termination follow-up remains a somewhat controversial idea among some psychoanalytically oriented clinicians because it suggests that closure is an illusion. It can also fuel transference fantasies of endless access to, or continuing dependence on, the therapist or convey to the client that the therapist is not fully confident of the client's capacity to make adaptive use of what has been learned in the course of treatment.

2. A secondary transference theme, one that emerged on only a few occasions in the course of her analysis, was that of extracting good supplies from me and, in the process, of "using me up" so that I had nothing left to offer her—a fantasy that seems unequivocally maternal.

10. Children

1. In fact, it has become a relatively rare and esoteric form of treatment in more recent years, likely because of its intensive (three to five sessions per week) nature, the overall length of treatment, and the associated expense.

2. *Mentalization* has been defined as the ability to create and make use of mental representations of one's own and others' emotional states (Fonagy and Target 1998).

3. It is pertinent to note here that even when parents *are* available to furnish such historical data, retrospective omissions and other inaccuracies are relatively frequent; sometimes these are inadvertent, though, on occasion, they may be unconsciously motivated.

4. It has been my experience that some children assign titles to their stories, some supply morals, some furnish both, and others neither. It may be a measure of the elasticity of this technique that the child's disinclination to title a story or include a les-

son or moral rarely has a negative consequence for the therapeutic discourse. An analogy can be drawn to the use of dreams in the psychotherapy of adults, whereby the raw data—the dream content and dreamer's associations—are far more valuable than the need for imposing an invariant set of organizing principles to aid in their interpretation. In effect, then, the therapist works with the child's stories in the form that the child is most comfortable with and capable of supplying.

5. Although it is unusual, children occasionally reveal situations in which harm to oneself or others has either occurred already or is anticipated. In such an instance any minor therapeutic breach that might result from a clinical decision to explore story metaphors in a more direct manner would of course be fully justified.

6. Although one might argue that this element represents the experience of disintegration anxiety, I am more inclined to view it as an example of self-directed hostility owing to Tony's relatively stable self-cohesiveness.

7. This case vignette is an adaptation of a case originally published in Theodore Varkas, "Childhood trauma and posttraumatic play: A literature review and case study," *Psychoanalytic Social Work* 5.3 (Summer 1998): 29–50.

8. Ogden's "analytic third" further extends this concept by formulating the existence of a "subject" that is neither therapist nor client but a "third subjectivity unconsciously generated by the analytic [therapeutic] pair" (Ogden 1997:9).

11. Adolescents

1. A great deal of the adolescent literature is "embedded" in books and articles that nominally address both child and adolescent psychopathology and treatment but, in reality, focus to a somewhat greater degree on children. This may be part of a larger issue that has led "conceptual trends in adolescent psychotherapy . . . to be somewhat delayed in their appearance because of resistances among child therapists" to addressing issues pertaining to adolescents (Gartner 1985:195).

2. Some theorists have asserted that not only adolescents but also children may exhibit personality disorders and other forms of psychopathology more commonly associated with adults (e.g., Kernberg, Weiner, and Bardenstein 2000), although this idea continues to generate controversy in the child and adolescent mental health field.

3. That group treatment and family therapy, both of which boast a sizable literature and are considered viable and effective treatment methods for troubled adolescents, are not discussed here is solely because to do so would extend this book beyond its purview.

12. The Meter's Running: Dynamic Approaches to Brief and Time-Limited Therapy

1. Having encountered his patient by chance some four months after treatment was concluded, Freud found Miss Lucy R. to be "in good spirits" and her recovery apparently maintained.

2. In the original case history Freud had disguised this fact, substituting Katharina's

uncle for her father. In a postscript added to the case some thirty years later, this distortion was finally corrected.

13. Psychodynamic Case Management

1. Floersch (2002:202) has shown how a resource acquisition language dominated the strengths model and compromised the possibility of working on internal resources, including strengths.

2. The research reported here was funded by the Ohio Department of Mental Health. In our research—not an outcomes study utilizing predetermined survey (questionnaire) instruments—we used participant-observation methods to understand relationships among clients and participants in helping (or recovery) networks. We selected case studies using a convenient sampling technique. Case managers identified clients, who consented to our accompaniment as they received help or services from anyone in their social networks, including formal (e.g., health and human service professionals) and informal caregivers (e.g., family members, friends, employers, etc.). In client networks we became *participant-observers*. First, we *participated* as case managers in transporting clients to appointments, helping them access resources (e.g., grocery shopping), and staying in continuous contact to experience everyday life. Second, we *observed* service providers and other caregivers as they interacted with clients. We then coded activities to determine how Recovery goals, self-mastery, and empowerment were actualized in the caregiving relationship. The data presented here comes from one case study. The larger case study and analysis will be published by Columbia University Press (forthcoming) as *On Being and Having a Caregiver*.

3. This theory, first articulated by Erna Furman in her discussion of development, has since been elaborated into a theory of the caregiver relationships; see Furman 2001.

4. We adapted the four subjective experiences of recovery, or internal emotional states, from a qualitative study of recovered individuals. See Spaniol et al. 2002.

5. For Vygotsky, mental development is "the distance between the actual development level, as determined by independent problem solving, and the level of potential development as determined through problem solving under adult guidance or in collaboration with more capable peers" (Wertsch 1979:2). The quality of mental development (internal subjective processes) is positively related to the quality of social interactions (external relational processes).

6. Spaniol and associates, for example, write that "daily life can be a struggle mentally and even physically. The person tries to understand and control what is happening, but often feels confused, disconnected from the self and others, out of control, and powerless to control his or her life in general."

14. Research on Clinical Process and Outcomes in Psychodynamic Therapy and Psychoanalysis

1. My exclusive focus on outcome research and studies examining various process dimensions reflects the unique relevance each has with respect to the clinical enter-

prise, which is, of course, the subject domain of this book. Readers, however, should be aware of the existence of other kinds of psychoanalytic research, no less important than the studies I have described. These studies are focused on a variety of themes and issues, such as human attachment (Main 1995), developmental psychopathology (Fonagy 1995), and clinical phenomena not strictly related either to process or outcome (e.g., Bornstein and Masling 1998).

2. The recent publication of an entire issue devoted to psychoanalytic research in a major psychoanalytic journal, *Journal of the American Psychoanalytic Association* 50.2 (Spring 2002), is one such example.

3. The earliest studies of outcome in psychoanalytic treatment, admittedly unsophisticated by the standards of contemporary psychotherapy research, were conducted in such psychoanalytic centers as Berlin, London, and Chicago, beginning nearly a full generation before Eysenck's paper appeared (Alexander 1938; Knight 1941; Bachrach et al. 1991; Bateman and Holmes 1995).

4. There are, however, significant exceptions to this general rule, which may reflect the current dominance that the concept "evidence-based practice" has over the entire psychotherapy field. A recently published collection of research articles exploring various components of the therapy relationship (e.g., the treatment alliance, empathy, transference, countertransference, attachment style, and so forth) emphasizes the fact that such relational features—traditionally classified as process dimensions—exert as much influence as do particular treatment methods in determining treatment outcomes (Norcross 2002).

5. In my own research I have found a five-minute segment to furnish data comparable in most respects to that of a ten-minute excerpt.

6. Somewhat different distillations of French's original focal conflict theory have been developed and applied heuristically to marital couples treatment (Wallace 1979), outpatient group treatment (Whitman and Stock 1958; Yalom 1975), the integration of individual and group-level phenomena (Whitaker 1982), group treatment in the context of partial hospitalization (Karson 1991), and art therapy (Jadi and Trixler 1980).

SELECT GLOSSARY
OF PSYCHOANALYTIC TERMS AND CONCEPTS

Adaptive point of view: The metapsychological perspective, associated with ego psychology, that refers to the intercurrent and reciprocal relations between organisms and environments. Although both are changed in consequence of such ongoing interaction, the presence of conflict is not necessarily implied.

Analysand: A psychoanalytic patient.

Cathartic method: A therapeutic procedure, originally introduced by Freud's associate, Josef Breuer, whose aim was the release of suppressed emotions. The cathartic method was "superseded by psychoanalysis" where understanding and insight were accorded a status equal to that of catharsis (Holzman 1998).

Cathexis: A term with a Greek derivation, selected by Freud's English translators (the Stracheys) as a substitute for the German word *Bezetzung*—which is, in turn, roughly equivalent to the English word *occupation.* Indicating interest, attention, or emotional investment, this term is generally used in conjunction with the word *libidinal*; libidinal cathexis thus refers to an individual's "erotic interest in a specific person or item" (Moore and Fine 1990).

Cohesive self: The essential self-structure of a well-adapted, healthily functioning individual whose self-functioning evinces the harmonious interchange of ambitions, ideals, and talents with the events of everyday life.

Conversion: A defensive process through which functional somatic symptoms resembling organic pathology (e.g., functional paralyses, palpitations or other cardiopulmonary symptoms, tics, and so forth) are produced. Freud explained such symptoms as being the result of "unconscious fantasies whose psychic energy (libido) had been withdrawn and converted into somatic symptoms" (Holzman 1998).

Countertransference: The broad range of subjective reactions, whether conscious or unconscious, educed from the therapist in the context of ongoing therapeutic interaction with a client. These reactions may consist of fantasies, thoughts, atti-

Adapted in part from the work of the following five authors: Fenichel (1945); Moore and Fine (1990); Goldstein (1995); Holzman (1998); and Meissner (2000).

tudes, affects, counterreactions, counterresistances, behavior, and behavioral enactments. Although specific countertransference reactions may involve displacements of affective or ideational phenomena from historically important relationships of the therapist, this is neither a universal feature nor a requirement.

Denial: A mechanism of defense, which involves a negation or disavowal of an aspect of reality or of one's internal experience.

Depressive position: In Kleinian theory the depressive position (the second developmental organizer of infancy) is initiated by the infant's growing concern for the welfare of the libidinal object that has been the recipient of hateful fantasies of vengeance and annihilation characteristic of the paranoid-schizoid position. Concomitant with the infant's newly emerging capacity for whole object relations is an ability to experience ambivalence or both good (loving) and bad (hateful) feelings toward the same object, which represents a critical developmental achievement for the infant, according to Klein.

Disintegration anxiety: The fear of breaking up of the (nuclear) self, described by Kohut as the deepest form of anxiety an individual can experience, its origins traceable to the earliest preverbal stages of psychological development.

Displacement: A defense mechanism that consists of transferring a quantity of cathexis from an anxiety-provoking idea to an innocuous one. The result is that the previously innocuous idea receives a heightened significance while the anxiety-provoking idea loses its importance.

Dissociation: A defense mechanism involving an altered state of consciousness, designed to protect a subject from experiences of an overwhelmingly traumatic nature. When the experience involves distortions of the subject's bodily self experience only, the term *depersonalization* is sometimes used; when the distortions involve apprehension of external stimuli, the term *derealization* is sometimes employed. *Fugue states* and *hysterical conversion reactions* are also dissociative in nature.

Drives: Freud identified two drives or instincts, sex (libido) and aggression, to which he ultimately attributed the most basic internal motivations for behavior.

Dynamic point of view: That metapsychological principle that refers to the existence of motives underlying behavior. The dynamic perspective asserts that all behavior is lawful and purposive, regardless of whether it is conscious and deliberate or unconsciously enacted.

Economic point of view: The metapsychological viewpoint that posits a quantitative basis for human behavior and accounts for the strength with which motivational aims are held.

Empathy: Vicarious introspection or the feeling of oneself into the experience of another. The capacity for empathy is regarded as a crucial sine qua non for healthy development of the self; chronic and sustained lapses or failures in (parental) empathy are believed responsible for various kinds of structural pathology.

Epigenesis: An embryological concept that explains development as involving gradual differentiation of a substance that was initially undifferentiated, affected by environmental circumstances; later expropriated by Erik Erikson as the basis for his eight-stage theory of human psychosocial and psychosexual development. According to epigenetic theory, "early damage to the growing entity results in greater general impairment than does later damage" (Holzman 1998).

Experience-distant: As used by Kohut, this term pertains to those observations that are a) made from the perspective of an outside observer, b) based upon assumptions about human growth and development, c) formed at a level of abstraction higher than those that are "experience-near," and d) made from a morally tinged position (Kohut 1984). See also *experience-near.*

Experience-near. A theoretical principle used by Kohut to refer to observations and knowledge whose character is fundamentally introspective and that rely upon subjective and empathic processes. See also *experience-distant.*

Externalization: A mechanism of defense, often thought of as the counterpart of *internalization,* by which the subject's internally arising fantasies, fears, and other intrapsychic phenomena are attributed to the external world. Externalization differs from *projection* inasmuch as the latter is intimately associated with specific introjects, whereas *externalization* is more broadly defined. *Externalization* does not exist exclusively within the province of psychopathology and, for example, may also be used for adaptive purposes by artists and writers.

False self: The false self, in Winnicottian theory, is a facade that the infant-child erects so as to achieve compliance with mother's inadequate adaptations, whether these maternal failures take the form of deprivations or impingements on the child's growth (Goldstein 1995). Applying this concept to adult development, Winnicott came to think of certain patients as suffering from psychopathology whose most central feature was such a false self.

Fantasy: A mental activity that most often represents an effort at wish fulfillment but may also subserve various other mental aims, including the primarily defensive (Freud 1936) and those functions associated with empathy and the creative process (Arlow 1969; Sachs 1942). Fantasies may be conscious (e.g., daydreams or reveries) or unconscious (e.g., forbidden wishes of a sexual or aggressive nature toward significant people in one's life).

Genetic point of view: That metapsychological principle that identifies historical antecedents as the distal causes of intercurrent human behavior and psychopathology.

Identification: A mental process, associated with normal development of the personality, whereby a person takes on certain attributes, such as values, attitudes, or personality characteristics, of another person who is loved, admired, feared, or hated. When the identification involves a feared or hated object, it is referred to as *identification with the aggressor.*

Incorporation: A form of *internalization* that operates at a relatively low level of differentiation and was originally based on an oral model implying swallowing or ingestion.

Internalization: Refers to those processes that contribute to the development of an internal world (sometimes termed the *representational world*) and to the consolidation of internal structure. Includes *incorporation, introjection,* and *identification.*

Interpretation: Called the "central therapeutic activity" of the psychoanalytic clinician, *interpretation* represents the clinician's understanding of a client's mental life.

Some psychoanalysts link the concept almost exclusively to the psychoanalytic notion of resistance, believing that any interpretative comment made by the clinician should be expressly designed to draw a client's attention to a resistance. Others, however, have defined the term somewhat less narrowly, viewing an interpretation as a "a statement of new knowledge" about a client (Moore and Fine 1990). Several different basic kinds of interpretation have been described in the dynamic literature. These are *genetic interpretations, dynamic interpretations, interpretations of resistance,* and *transference interpretations.*

Introject: A term commonly used by object relations theorists to refer to a sort of psychic "residue" or imprint that forms in consequence of critical exchanges with significant objects in the individual's life. These exchanges with others "leave their mark" and become the basis of the individual's attitudes, reactions, and perceptions (Greenberg and Mitchell 1983:11).

Introjection: Another variant of *internalization* "in which part properties and functions of the object are appropriated but not fully integrated into a cohesive and effective sense of self" (Moore and Fine 1990:102–2). Developmentally speaking, introjection is considered to be more sophisticated than *incorporation,* but generally thought of as somewhat less advanced than *identification.*

Isolation: A defense mechanism whose effect is a loss of awareness of the connection between an idea and the emotions originally associated with it. In *isolation* or *isolation of affect,* as it is often termed, ideas that would otherwise be very disturbing or anxiety producing—such as death wishes of a parent toward a newborn—are able to remain in awareness because the accompanying feelings have been repressed and are not available to consciousness.

Libido: One of two basic forms of psychic energy, the other being the aggressive drive.

Metapsychology: The theoretical structure of psychoanalysis, within which psychopathology and other mental phenomena may be understood. The term *metapsychology* was selected to distinguish psychoanalysis from other extant psychological systems of the late nineteenth and early twentieth centuries, none of which offered comparable explanations for either psychopathology or normal behavior. The psychoanalytic metapsychology includes six axiomatic perspectives or viewpoints (dynamic, economic, topographic, genetic, structural, and adaptive).

Naturalphilosophie: A romantic philosophical tradition represented in the work of such individuals as Goethe, Schelling, and Schopenhauer that arose in Europe during the eighteenth century. Its basic tenets were 1. that intuitive understanding, rather than solely objective or empirical knowledge, was necessary to understand the natural world and 2. that the world was defined by conflicts embodying basic polarities. *Naturalphilosophie* is often identified as one of the two major forces, the second being the physicalist tradition, to have shaped Freud's vision of normal and pathological mental operations.

Object constancy: Perhaps the most widely accepted definition of object constancy is the infant's capacity to maintain a positive, reassuring, and comforting image of the mother in her absence, irrespective of the presence of frustrating or gratifying experiences. Object constancy signifies a resolution of earlier psychological problems that necessitated the *splitting* of gratifying and frustrating images of the object. The psychoanalytic usage of this term always implies a *libidinal object* and is therefore *not* the equivalent of the Piagetian concept of *object permanence*, which involves a cognitive representation only. It is, moreover, often associated with the concept of *self constancy*, in which an individual has attained a comparable capacity for holding constant a representation of the self that, once again, is more or less invariant despite external conditions and the vicissitudes of inner life.

Object relations theory: A network of theories, represented in the work of such authors as D. W. Winnicott, Melanie Klein, W. R. D. Fairbairn, and Michael Balint, addressing the development of the personality, psychopathology, and specific therapeutic interventions. *Object relations theories* tend to place a high valuation on the role of early attachments and on relationships, more generally, in the evolution of the personality, focusing on the "development from primitive relatedness in the infant to complex mental functioning and relationships in the mature adult . . . and the structured aspects or enduring and distinctive patterns of relationships that characterize individuals" (Moore and Fine 1990:131–32).

Paranoid-schizoid position: Termed the "first and most primitive organization of the mental appartus" (Moore and Fine 1993). In the paranoid-schizoid position "*paranoia* refers to the central persecutory anxiety, the fear of invasive malevolence, coming from the outside . . . (while) *schizoid* refers to the central organizing defense: splitting, the vigilant separation of the loving and good breast from the hating and hated bad breast (Mitchell and Black 1995:93). Infants operating out of the paranoid-schizoid position have a bifurcated and fragmented experience of objects.

Persecutory anxiety: According to Melanie Klein, infants as young as three weeks experience a primitive form of anxiety that she called persecutory anxiety. She believed this configuration of anxiety was linked to schizoid mechanisms (e.g., splitting, projective identification, idealization, and magic omnipotent denial) and that such intrapsychic experience culminated in the infant's first developmental organizer, the *paranoid-schizoid position.*

Pleasure principle: One of the two most basic regulatory principles of mental functioning in classical psychoanalysis, the other being the *reality principle*. The pleasure principle refers to the individual's efforts to discharge tensions—whether endogenously arising or from the external environment—through the most expeditious route. Put somewhat differently, this principle stipulates that the pursuit of pleasure and the avoidance of unpleasure constitutes the ultimate aim of all psychic activity.

Postdiction: In psychoanalysis, the idea that one operates retrospectively, by making inferences about probable antecedent conditions from an assessment of intercurrent circumstances.

Primary autonomy: A concept introduced by Hartmann that refers to such ego functions as motility, perception, intelligence, thinking, speech, and language, which are relatively free from the influence of the drives and therefore unencumbered by conflict.

Primary or paranosic gain: The gratification of those unconsciously motivated infantile aims that are directly linked to the appearance of neurotic symptoms.

Primary process: The earliest "language" of infancy and childhood, characterized by such phenomena as a disregard for the rules of logic, the coexistence of opposites, and the use of imagery. Though a primitive mode of thought more often linked to such thought products as dreams, symptoms, or slips of the tongue, primary process may also be associated with "higher" ego functions. Examples might include the ability to use metaphor in literary products, artistic creativity, or the capacity to understand and appreciate literary or artistic products.

Projection: A defense mechanism whereby an unacceptable impulse or idea (i.e., one that is painful, dangerous, or otherwise unwelcome) is attributed to another person and felt to be directed against oneself.

Projective identification: Originally attributed to Melanie Klein, the concept of projective identification is believed essential by many for understanding and treating borderline and other character pathology. Projective identification is considered by many psychoanalysts to constitute an interpersonal defense as well as a significant, though developmentally primitive, mode of interaction. In projective identification the subject projects unwanted parts of the self into others for "safekeeping." This concept addresses the mechanism by which "feeling states corresponding to the unconscious fantasies of one person (projector) are engendered in and processed by another person (the recipient) . . . [thereby constituting] the way in which one person makes use of another person to experience and contain an aspect of himself" (Ogden 1982:1).

Reaction formation: A defense mechanism whose principal action consists of the substitution of one set of painful or anxiety-producing feelings for its opposite, as, for example, in the transformation of a desire to play with one's own feces into a compulsion to clean.

Reality principle: The second of two basic modes of action and thought, the other being the *pleasure principle.* The *reality principle* stipulates that gratifications or pleasures sometimes be deferred in order to meet the requirements of external reality.

Regression: Although this term is used in various ways by psychoanalysts, the defense of regression usually implies a return to more primitive or developmentally immature mental functioning and relies heavily on the notion of successive developmental stages.

Repression: A defense mechanism that excludes a psychologically painful or conflict-laden idea from conscious awareness. *Repression* is regarded as the prototype for defenses insofar as all defensive operations are designed to protect the self from conscious exposure to objectionable ideas, impulses, attitudes, and wishes. In Freud's early writings *repression* was used more or less interchangeably and synonymously with the concept of defense, although, as other defenses were elaborated, it came to be more narrowly defined.

Resistance: A phenomenon in which unconscious motives operate paradoxically, in opposition to the client's consciously articulated desire for therapeutic progress toward the resolution of intrapsychic conflicts, the repair of developmental arrests and defects, and the alleviation of distressing symptoms.

Secondary autonomy: Ego functions or mechanisms that originally developed within the sphere of conflict, subserving defensive purposes, but that have gradually acquired independence from the drives and have been deployed for other functions (e.g., synthesis or adaptation).

Secondary or epinosic gain: The additional gratifications that already formed neurotic symptoms bring to the sufferer. Although not a factor in the formation of the neurotic problem, such gain may entrench existing symptomatology or contribute to a client's resistance to treatment.

Secondary process: The "language" of adulthood, the developmental successor to *primary process*. Secondary process operates at the behest of the ego and the *reality principle* and is characterized, inter alia, by logical thinking and an understanding of chronological time.

Selfobjects: A term devised by Kohut to refer to a particular kind of object relationship in which the object is actually experienced as an extension of the self, without psychological differentiation. According to the theory, there are at least three distinctly different though equally necessary kinds of selfobject experiences: *mirroring* selfobjects, "who respond to and confirm the child's innate sense of vigor, greatness and perfection"; *idealized selfobjects*, "to whom the child can look up and with whom he can merge as an image of calmness, infallibility, and omnipotence" (Kohut and Wolf 1978:414); and *alter ego* or *partnering* selfobjects, who provide a range of experiences through which children acquire a sense of belonging and of essential alikeness within a community of others.

Self psychology: A treatment orientation within psychoanalysis that encourages the growth of an integrated and cohesive intrapsychic structure through empathic attunement and the internalization of particular functions initially proffered by the therapist.

Separation-individuation: A theory formulated by Margaret Mahler to explain the gradual emergence of infants from a hypothesized objectless or nonrelated stage at birth (to one month) to the development of self and object constancy. Other stages include a period of *maternal-infant symbiosis* (one to five months) followed by four relatively discrete stages of separation and individuation: *differentiation* (five to nine months), *practicing* (nine to fifteen months), *rapprochement* (fifteen to twenty-four months), and the development of *object constancy* (twenty-four to thirty-six months and beyond).

Splitting: Associated with both normal and pathological development, splitting may signify normative developmental processes whereby the infant separates psychological representations of self from others or of self from others according to *hedonic valence* (good versus bad self, good versus bad object). It may also be used for defensive purposes, as a means of separating two mutually opposing feeling states. Along with *projective identification*, *omnipotence*, and *denial*, splitting constitutes a principal defense of borderline and other characterologically disturbed individuals.

Structural viewpoint: A metapsychological viewpoint that asserts conflict is inherent in all mental activity and hypothesizes the existence of specific mental structures for its mediation. The structural viewpoint was more fully elaborated in 1923 with the introduction of Freud's tripartite model of mental functioning (i.e., id, ego, and superego).

Sublimation: Although its status as a defense has been questioned, sublimation involves the conversion of a formerly anxiety-arousing or objectionable impulse into a socially unobjectionable aim. Because sublimation permits the attainment of the original goal, a modicum of pleasure associated with the original (sexual or aggressive) impulse is also retained. Along with such mechanisms as *self-observation, insight, humor, stoicism,* and *altruism,* sublimation constitutes a relatively nonneurotic or conflict-free adaptation.

Topographic point of view: The metapsychological perspective that posited a layering of consciousness (unconscious, preconscious, and conscious) and dominated Freud's thinking from the 1890s until the elaboration of the *structural viewpoint* in 1923.

Transference: A reflexive, unconscious repetition or revivification of varying combinations and patterns of ideas, fantasies, affects, attitudes, or behavior, originally experienced in relation to a significant figure from one's childhood past, that have been displaced onto an intercurrent interpersonal relationship.

Transference neurosis: The point at which, in the course of psychoanalytic treatment, the locus of attention has shifted from intercurrent problems and issues to the major, unresolved issues of childhood. These are subsequently reproduced in their original, infantile form in the transference, with the psychoanalyst being cast as the central figure.

Transitonal object: Perhaps the best known of Winnicott's ideas, the transitional object, typically a blanket, teddy bear, or other inanimate but nevertheless cherished possession of the infant, is endowed with soothing and calming qualities that are especially evident during stressful separations from caregivers and at bedtime (Winnicott 1958b [1951]); in mother's absence it is such objects that enable infants to sustain the illusion of a calming, comforting mother. Although the concept of the transitional object and transitional experience was originally applied to the context of early infant development (1959b [1951]), Winnicott later broadened this framework to include aspects of adult experience. The *transitional experience* for the child is embedded in a capacity for play, whereas, for the adult, transitional experience is a "protected realm" where there exist opportunities to "play with" new ideas and fantasies and cultivate one's own creative impulses (Greenberg and Mitchell 1983).

Transmuting internalization: The developmental process whereby a function formerly performed by another is taken into the self and becomes an aspect of the enduring, unique psychological structure of that individual, occurring via optimal frustration and optimal gratification and characterized by incremental accretion and consolidation.

True self: In Winnicottian theory the true self is an "inherited potential" that represents the infant's core self or essence.

Tripolar self: The intrapsychic structure linking particular kinds of self/selfobject relationships with corresponding poles of self experience, composed of the *grandiose-exhibitionistic self,* the *idelaized parent imago,* and the *alter ego.*

Turning against the self: Also termed *intropunitiveness*, this is a defense mechanism in which the self is exchanged as the target for a hostile or aggressive impulse originally directed at another object.

Undoing: A defense mechanism in which an objectionable or forbidden act is carried out but then compulsively undone, as when hostile or aggressive language or behavior is subsequently "taken back" via expiatory or conciliatory behavior or gestures.

REFERENCES

Abend, S. 1981. Psychic conflict and the concept of defense. *Psychoanalytic Quarterly* 50:61–76.

—— 1984. Sibling love and object choice. *Psychoanalytic Quarterly* 53:425–30.

—— 2000. The problem of therapeutic alliance. In S. Levy, ed., *The therapeutic alliance,* pp. 1–16. Madison, CT: International Universities Press.

Abraham, K. 1921. Contributions to the theory of the anal character. In *Selected Papers of Karl Abraham,* pp. 370–92. London: Hogarth, 1973.

—— 1922. Manifestations of the female castration complex. In *Selected papers on psycho-analysis,* pp. 248–79. New York: Basic, 1952.

—— 1924a. A short study of the development of the libido. In *Selected papers on psycho-analysis,* pp. 418–50. London: Hogarth, 1948.

—— 1924b. The influence of oral eroticism on character formation. In *Selected papers on psycho-analysis,* pp. 393–406. London: Hogarth, 1948.

—— 1925. Character formation and the genital level of libido development. In *Selected papers on psycho-analysis,* pp. 407–17. London: Hogarth, 1948.

Abrams, S. 1993. The developmental dimensions of play during treatment: A conceptual overview. In A. Solnit, D. Cohen, and P. Neubauer, eds., *The many meanings of play,* pp. 221–38. New Haven: Yale University Press.

Acuff, Catherine. 2000. "Commentary: Listening to the message." *Journal of Clinical Psychology* 56(11): 1459–1465.

Adler, A. 1927. The practice and theory of individual psychology. New York: Harcourt.

Aichhorn, A. 1948 [1925]. *Wayward youth.* New York: Viking.

Akhtar, S. 1988. Some reflections on the theory of psychopathology and personality development in Kohut's self psychology. In J. Ross and W. Myers, eds., *New Concepts in psychoanalytic psychotherapy,* pp. 227–52. Washington, DC: American Psychiatric.

Alexander, F. 1938. Psychoanalysis comes of age. *Psychoanalytic Quarterly* 7:299–306.

Alexander, F., and T. French. 1946. *Psychoanalytic therapy: Principles and application.* New York: Ronald.

Altman, N. 1992. *Relational perspectives in psychoanalysis.* Hillsdale, NJ: Analytic.

Altschul, S., and G. Pollock. 1988. *Childhood bereavement and its aftermath*. Madison, CT: International Universities Press.

American Psychiatric Association. 1982. *Psychotherapy research: Methodological and efficacy issues*, p. 39. Washington, DC: American Psychiatric.

Anastasopoulous, D., J. Tsiantis, and A. Sandler. 1996. Countertransference issues in psychoanalytic psychotherapy with children and adolescents: A brief review. In J. Tsiantis, D. Anastasopoulous, A. Sandler, and B. Martindale, eds., *Countertransference in psychoanalytic psychotherapy with children and adolescents*, pp. 1–35. Madison. CT: International Universities Press.

Anthony, E. 1970. Two contrasting types of adolescent depression and their treatment. *Journal of the American Psychoanalytic Association* 18:841–859.

Anthony, E., and B.Cohler. 1987. *The invulnerable child*. New York: Guilford.

Anthony, W. 1993. Recovery from mental illness: The guiding vision of the mental health service system. *Psychosocial Rehabilitation Journal* 16(4): 11–23.

Applegate, J. In press. Full circle: Returning psychoanalytic theory to social work education. *Psychoanalytic Social Work* 11(1).

Applegate, J., and J. Bonovitz. 1995. *The facilitating partnership: A Winnicottian approach for social workers and other helping professionals*. Northvale, NJ: Aronson.

Archer, M. 2000. *Being human: The problem of agency*. New York: Cambridge University Press.

Arieti, S. 1974 . *Interpretation of schizophrenia*. New York: Basic.

Arlow, I. 1969. Unconscious fantasy and disturbances of conscious experience. *Psychoanalytic Quarterly* 38:1–27.

Arlow, I., and C. Brenner. 1964. *Psychoanalytic concepts and the structural theory*. New York International Universities Press.

Asch, S. 1976. Varieties of negative therapeutic reactions and problems of technique. *Journal of the American Psychoanalytic Association* 24:383–407.

Atwood, G., and R. Stolorow. 1984. *Structures of subjectivity: Explorations in psychoanalytic phenomenology*. Hillsdale, NJ: Analytic.

Bacal, H. 1985. Optimal responsiveness and the therapeutic process. In A. Goldberg, ed., *Progress in self psychology* 4:202–27. New York: Guilford.

——— 1996. The essence of Kohut's work and the progress of self psychology. *Psychoanalytic Dialogues* 5:353–56.

Bacal, H., and K. Newman. 1990. *Theories of object relations: Bridge* to *self psychology*. New York: Columbia University Press.

Bachrach, H., H. Curtis, P. Escoll, H. Graff, H. Huxster, P. Ottenberg, and S. Pulver. 1981. Units of observation and perspectives on the psychoanalytic process. *British Journal of Medical Psychology* 54:25–33.

Bak, R. 1943. Dissolution of the ego: Mannerism and delusions of grandeur. *Journal of Nervous and Mental Diseases* 98:457–64.

Balint, A. 1949. Love for the mother and mother-love. *International Journal of Psychoanalysis* 30:251–59.

Balint, M. 1949. Early development states of the ego. Primary object love. *International Journal of Psychoanalysis* 30:265–73.

——— 1959. *Thrills and regressions*. London: Hogarth.

——— 1968. *The basic fault: Therapeutic aspects of regression.* London: Tavistock.

Basch, M. 1986. "How does analysis cure?" An appreciation. *Psychoanalytic Inquiry 6,* 403–28.

——— 1988. Doing psychotherapy. New York: Basic.

Bateman, A., and J. Holmes. 1995. Introduction to psychoanalysis: Contemporary theory and practice. London: Routledge.

Bauer, G., and J. Kobos. 1987. *Brief therapy: Short-term psychodynamic intervention.* Northvale, NJ: Aronson.

——— 1995. *Brief therapy: Short-term dynamic intervention.* Northvale, NJ: Aronson.

Beale, V., and T. Lambric. 1995. The recovery concept: Implementation in the mental health system. A report by the Community Support Program Advisory Committee. Columbus, OH: Ohio Department of Mental Health.

Beebe, B. 1986. Mother-infant mutual influence and precursors of self- and object representations. In J. Masling, ed., *Empirical Studies of Psychoanalytic Theories,* 2:27–48. Hillsdale, NJ: Analytic.

Beebe, B. and F. M. Lachmann. 2002. *Infant research and adult treatment: Co-constructing interactions.* Hillsdale, NJ: Analytic.

Bellak, L. 1984. Basic aspects of ego function assessment. In L. Bellak and L. Goldsmith, eds., *The broad scope of ego function assessment,* pp. 6–30. New York: Wiley.

Bellak, L., and L. Small. 1965. *Emergency psychotherapy and brief psychotherapy.* 2d ed. New York: Grune and Stratton.

Bemporad, J., and K. Lee. 1988. Affective disorders. In C. Kestenbaum and D. Williams, eds., *Handbook of clinical assessment of children and adolescents.* New York: New York University Press.

Bemporad, J., and S. Gable. 1992. Depressed and suicidal children and adolescents. In J. Brandell, ed., *Countertransference in psychotherapy with children and adolescents,* pp. 105–26. Northvale, NJ: Aronson.

Benjamin, J. 1988. *The bonds of love: Psychoanalysis, feminism, and the problem of domination.* New York: Pantheon.

Bergmann, M. 1997. Termination: The Achilles heel of psychoanalytic technique. *Psychoanalytic Psychology* 14:163–74.

Berlin, I. 1987. Some transference and countertransference issues in the playroom. *Journal of the American Academy of Child and Adolescent Psychiatry* 26:101–7.

Bernfeld, S. 1995 [1923]. Concerning a typical form of male puberty. *Adolescent Psychiatry* 20:51–65.

Bettelheim, B. 1983. *Freud and man's soul.* New York: Knopf.

Bibring, E. 1954. Psychoanalysis and the dynamic psychotherapies. *Journal of the American Psychoanalytic Association* 2:745–70.

Bibring, G. 1936. A contribution to the subject of transference-resistance. *International Journal of Psycho-Analysis* 17:181–89.

Biestek, F. 1957. *The casework relationship.* Chicago: Loyola University Press.

Binder, J., and H. Strupp. 1991. The Vanderbilt approach to time-limited dynamic psychotherapy. In P. Crits-Christoph and P. Barber, eds., *Handbook of short-term dynamic psychotherapy,* pp. 137–65. New York: Basic.

Bion, W. 1959. Attacks on linking. *International Journal of Psycho-Analysis* 40:308–15.

———— 1962. *Learning from experience.* New York: Basic.

Blanck, G., and R. Blanck. 1974. *Ego psychology: Theory and practice.* New York: Columbia University Press.

———— 1994. *Ego psychology: Theory and practice.* Rev. ed. New York: Columbia University Press.

Blatt, S. 1974. Levels of object representation in anaclitic and introjective depression. *Psychoanalytic Study of the Child* 29:107–57.

Blos, P. 1961. Delinquency. In S. Lorand, ed., *Adolescents: Psychoanalytic approach to problems and therapy,* pp. 132–51. New York: Hoeber.

———— 1962. *On Adolescence.* New York: Free.

Bonner, C. 2002. Psychoanalytic theory and diverse populations: Reflections on old practices and new understandings. *Psychoanalytic Social Work* 9:61–70.

Borden, W. 1995. Making use of theory in practice: Legacies of the independent tradition. Unpublished manuscript.

Bornstein, R., and J. Masling, eds. 1998. *Empirical perspectives on the psychoanalytic unconscious.* Washington, DC: American Psychological Association.

Borowitz, G. 1970. The therapeutic utilization of emotions and attitudes evoked in the caretakers of disturbed children. *British Journal of Medical Psychology* 43:129–39.

Bowlby, J. 1969. *Attachment and loss.* Vol. 1: *Attachment.* New York: Basic.

Bradshaw, W., D. Roseborough, and M. Amour. 2003. Recovery from severe mental illness: The lived experience of the initial phase of treatment. Paper presented at the meeting of the Society for Social Work Research, Washington, DC.

Brandell, J. 1988. Storytelling in child psychotherapy. In C. Schaefer, ed., *Innovative interventions in child and adolescent therapy,* pp. 9–44. New York: Wiley.

———— 1992. Countertransference phenomena in the psychotherapy of children and adolescents. In J. Brandell, ed., *Countertransference in psychotherapy with children and adolescents,* pp. 1–44. Northvale, NJ: Aronson.

———— 2000. *Of mice and metaphors: Therapeutic storytelling with children.* New York: Basic.

———— 2002. Discussion: The countertransference controversy. In H. Strean, ed., *Controversies on countertransference,* pp. 88–97. Northvale, NJ: Aronson.

Brandell, J., and T. Varkas. 2001. Narrative case studies. In B. Thyer, ed., *The handbook of social work research methods,* pp. 293–308. Thousand Oaks, CA: Sage.

Brenner, C. 1974. Depression, anxiety, and affect theory. *International Journal of Psychoanalysis* 55:25–32.

———— 1975. Affects and psychic conflict. *Psychoanalytic Quarterly* 44:5–28.

———— 1979. Working alliance, therapeutic alliance, and transference. *Journal of the American Psychoanalytic Association* 27 (Supplement): 137–57.

———— 1981. Defense and defense mechanisms. *Psychoanalytic Quarterly* 50:557–69.

———— 1982. *The mind in conflict.* New York: International Universities Press.

Breuer, J., and S. Freud. 1893–95. *Studies on hysteria.* Vol. 2. Trans. J. Strachey. London Hogarth.

Bridger, H. 1950. Criteria for the termination of analysis. *International Journal of Psychoanalysis* 31:202–3.

Bridgman, P. 1945. Some general principles of operational analysis. *Psychological Review* 52:246–49.

Brown, D., and E. Fromm. 1986. *Hypnotherapy and hypnoanalysis.* Hillsdale, NJ: Erlbaum.

Buhle, M. 1998. *Feminism and its discontents: A century of struggle with psychoanalysis.* Cambridge: Harvard University Press.

Buxbaum, E. 1950. Technique of terminating analysis. *International Journal of Psychoanalysis* 31:184–90.

Chapman, A. H. 1976. *Harry Stack Sullivan: The man and his work.* New York: Putnam.

Chethik, M. 2000. *Techniques of child therapy.* 2d ed. New York: Guilford.

Chinman, M., M. Allende, P. Bailey, J. Maust, and L. Davidson, 1999. Therapeutic agents of assertive community treatment. *Psychiatric Quarterly* 70(2): 137–62.

Chodorow, N. 1978. *The reproduction of mothering: Psychoanalysis and the sociology of gender.* Berkeley: University of California Press.

———— 1989. *Feminism and psychoanalytic theory.* New Haven: Yale University Press.

Christ, A. 1964. Sexual countertransference problems with a psychotic child. *Journal of Child Psychiatry* 3:298–316.

Chrzanowski, G. 1977. *Interpersonal approach to psychoanalysis.* New York: Gardner.

Chused, J. 1988. The transference neurosis in child analysis. *Psychoanalytic Study of the Child* 43:51–81.

———— 1992. The transference neurosis in child analysis. In *Saying goodbye: A casebook of termination in child and adolescent analysis and therapy,* pp. 233–64. Hillsdale, NJ: Analytic.

Coen, S. 1996. Sexual disorders. In E. Nersessian and R. Kopff, eds., *Textbook of psychoanalysis,* pp. 345–90. Washington, DC: American Psychiatric.

Cole, L. M., V. John-Steiner, S. Scribner, and E. Souberman, eds. 1978. *Mind in society: The development of higher psychological processes—L. S. Vygotsky.* Cambridge: Harvard University Press.

Coles, R. 1986. *The political life of children.* Boston: Houghton-Mifflin.

Cooper, A. 1987. Changes in psychoanalytic ideas: Transference interpretation. *Journal of the American Psychoanalytic Association* 35:77–98.

Coppolillo, H. 1987. *Psychodynamic psychotherapy of children: An introduction to the art and the techniques.* Madison, CT: International Universities Press.

Cournoyer, B., and G. Powers. 2002. Evidence-based social work: The quiet revolution continues. In A. Roberts and G. Greene, eds., *Social worker's desk reference.* New York: Oxford University Press.

Crits-Christoph, P., and J. Barber, eds. 1991. *Handbook of short-term dynamic psychotherapy.* New York: Basic.

Davis, I. 1976. Social treatment process research: Some thoughts and viewpoints. *Occasional Paper* no. 7. Chicago: University of Chicago School of Social Service Administration.

Deegan, P. 1996. Recovery as a journal of the heart. *Psychiatric Rehabilitation Journal* 19(3): 91–97.

Dewald, P. 1982. Serious illness in the analyst: Transference, countertransference, and reality responses. *Journal of the American Psychoanalytic Association* 30:347–63.

Dubyna, J., and C. Quinn. 1996. The self-management of psychiatric medications: A pilot study. *Journal of Psychiatric Mental Health Nursing* 3(5): 297–302.

Eccles, J., C. Midgely, A. Wigfield, C. Buchanan, D. Reuman, C. Flanagan, and D. Mac Iver. 1993. Development during adolescence: The impact of state-environment fit on young adolescents' experience in schools and in families. *American Psychologist* 48:90–101.

Edward, J. 2002. A tribute to Gertrude Blanck. *Newsletter of the National Membership Committee on Psychoanalysis in Clinical Social Work* (Spring).

Edward, J., and E. Rose. 1999. Playing in time and space: An interview with Jean Sanville. In J. Edward and E. Rose, eds., *The social work psychoanalyst's casebook*. Hillsdale, NJ: Analytic.

Ekstein, R. 1965. Working through and termination of analysis. *Journal of the American Psychoanalytic Association* 13:57–78.

——— 1966. *Children of time and space, of action and impulse: Clinical studies on the psychoanalytic treatment of severely disturbed children*. New York: Appleton-Century-Crofts.

Ekstein, R., J. Wallerstein, and A. Mandelbaum. 1959. Countertransference in the residential treatment of children: Treatment failure in a child with symbiotic psychosis. *Psychoanalytic Study of the Child* 14:186–218.

Elson, M. 1986. *Self psychology in clinical social work*. New York: Norton.

Emde, R. 1992. Social referencing research: Uncertainty, self, and the search for meaning. In S. Feinman, ed., *Social referencing and the construction of reality in infancy*, pp. 79–94. New York: Plenum.

——— 1995. Epilogue: A beginning—research approaches and expanding horizons for psychoanalysis. In T. Shapiro and R. Emde, eds., *Research in psychoanalysis: Process, development, outcome*, pp. 411–24. Madison, CT: International Universities Press.

Engel, S. 1999. *The stories children tell: Making sense of the narratives of childhood*. New York: Freeman.

Epstein, L., and A. Feiner. 1979. Countertransference: The therapist's contribution to treatment. *Contemporary Psychoanalysis* 15:282—303.

Erikson, E. 1950. *Childhood and society*. New York: Norton.

——— 1956. The problem of ego identity. *Journal of the American Psychoanalytic Association* 4:56.

——— 1959. *Identity and the life cycle*. Vol. 1: *Selected papers, psychological issues*. New York: International Universities Press.

Erle, J. 1979. An approach to the study of analyzability and analyses: The course of forty consecutive cases selected for supervised analysis. *Psychoanalytic Quarterly* 48:198–228.

Erle, J., and D. Goldberg. 1984. Observations on assessment of analyzability by experienced analysts. *Journal of the American Psychoanalytic Association* 32:715–37.

Esman, A. 1990. Introduction. In A. Esman, ed., *Essential papers on transference*, pp. 1–14. New York: New York University Press.

Eysenck, H. 1952. The effects of psychotherapy: An evaluation. *Journal of Consulting Psychology* 16:319–24.

Fairbairn, W. 1952. *An object relations theory of the personality.* New York: Basic.

Family Service Association of America. 1953. *Scope and methods of the family service agency.* New York: Family Service Association of America.

Fechner, G. 1966 [1860] *Elements of psychophysics.* Ed. H. Adler, D. Howes, and E. Boring. New York: Holt, Rinehart, and Winston.

Fenichel, O. 1929. Dread of being eaten. In H. Fenichel and D. Rapaport, eds., *The collected works of Otto Fenichel, first series,* pp. 158–59. New York: Norton.

———— 1945. *The psychoanalytic theory of neurosis.* New York: Norton.

Fenton, W., C. Blyler, and R. Heinssen. 1997. Determinants of medication compliance in schizophrenia: Empirical and clinical findings. *Schizophrenia Bulletin* 23(4): 637–51.

Ferenczi, S. 1950a [1913]. Stages in the development of the sense of reality. In *Sex in psychoanalysis.* Trans. E. Jones. New York: Basic.

———— 1950b [1926]. The further development of an active therapy in psychoanalysis. In E. Jones, ed., *Further contributions to the theory and technique of psycho-analysis,* pp. 198–217. Trans. I. Suttie. London: Hogarth.

———— 1955 [1927]. The problem of the termination of an analysis. In M. Balint, ed., *The selected papers of Sandor Ferenczi: Problems and methods of psychoanalysis,* 3:77–86. New York: Basic.

Ferenczi, S., and O. Rank. 1925. *The development of psychoanalysis.* New York: Nervous and Mental Diseases.

Figes, E. 1970. *Patriarchal attitudes: The case for women in revolt.* New York: Fawcett.

Fine, R. 1975. *Psychoanalytic psychology.* New York: Aronson.

———— 1982. *The healing of the mind.* New York: Free.

Firestein, S. 1978. *Termination in psychoanalysis.* New York: International Universities Press.

Firestone, S. 1970. *The dialectic of sex: The case for feminist revolution.* New York: Morrow.

Fischer, C. 1954. Dreams and perception The role of unconscious and primary modes of perception in dream formation. *Journal of the American Psychoanalytic Association* 2:389–445.

Fischer, J. 1976. *The effectiveness of social casework.* Springfield, IL: Thomas.

Flegenheimer, W. 1992. *Techniques of brief psychotherapy.* Northvale, NJ: Aronson.

Floersch, J. 2002. *Meds, money, and manners: The case management of severe mental illness.* New York: Columbia University Press.

Fonagy, P. 1993. Psychoanalytic and empirical principles to developmental psychopathology: Can they be usefully integrated? *Journal of the Royal Society of Medicine* 86:577–81.

———— 1995. Psychoanalytic and empirical studies to developmental psychopathology: An object relations perspective. In T. Shapiro and R. Emde, eds., *Research in psychoanalysis: Process, development, outcome,* pp. 245–60. Madison, CT: International Universities Press.

———— 1996. Il transfert e la sua interpretazione (On transference and its interpretation). *Richard e Piggle* 4:255–73.

———— 1999. The process of change and the change of processes: What can change in a "good" analysis. Keynote address to the Spring Meeting of Division 39 of the American Psychological Association, April 16, New York, New York.

———— 2000. Points of contact and divergence between psychoanalytic and attachment theories: Is psychoanalytic theory truly different? Paper given at Michigan Psychoanalytic Institute.

Fonagy, P., G. Gergely, E. Jurist, and M. Target. 2002. *Affect regulation, mentalization, and the development of the self.* New York: Other.

Fonagy, P., and M. Target. 1994. The efficacy of psychoanalysis for children with disruptive disorders. *Journal of the American Academy of Child and Adolescent Psychiatry* 33:45–55.

———— 1996. Prediction of the outcome of child psychoanalysis: A retrospective study of 763 cases at the Anna Freud Center. *Journal of the American Psychoanalytic Association* 44:27–77.

———— 1998. Mentalization and the changing aims of child psychoanalysis. *Psychoanalytic Dialogues* 8:87–114.

Fortune, A. 1985. Planning duration and termination of treatment. *Social Service Review* 59:647–61.

———— 1987. Grief only? Client and social worker reactions to termination. *Clinical Social Work Journal* 15:159–71.

Fortune, A., B. Pearlingi, and C. Rochelle. 1992. Reactions to termination of individual treatment. *Social Work* 37:171–78.

Fosshage, J. 1994. Reconceptualizing transference: theoretical, clinical considerations. *International Journal of Psychoanalysis* 75:265–80.

Fox, E., M. Nelson, and W. Bolman. 1969. The termination process. *Social Work* 14:53–63.

Fraiberg, S. 1982. Pathological defenses in infancy. *Psychoanalytic Quarterly* 51:612–35.

Frank, E., D. Kupfer, and L. Siegel. 1995. Alliance not compliance: A philosophy of outpatient care. *Journal of Clinical Psychiatry* 56(1): 11–17.

French, T. 1954. *The Integration of Behavior*, 3:378. Chicago: University of Chicago Press.

French, T., and E. Fromm. 1964. *Dream interpretation: A new approach.* New York: Basic.

Freud, A. 1926. *The psychoanalytic treatment of children.* London: Imago.

———— 1936. *The ego and the mechanisms of defense.* London: Hogarth.

———— 1946. *The psychoanalytical treatment of children: Technical lectures and essays.* New York: International Universities Press.

———— 1958. Adolescence. *Psychoanalytic Study of the Child* 13:255–78.

———— 1963. The concept of developmental lines. *Psychoanalytic Study of the Child* 18:245–65.

———— 1965. *Normality and pathology in childhood.* New York: International Universities Press.

———— 1969. Adolescence as a developmental disturbance. In *The Writings of Anna Freud.* Vol. 7: *1966–1970.* New York: International Universities Press.

Freud, S. 1894. The neuropsychoses of defense. *The standard edition of the complete psychological works of Sigmund Freud,* 3:45–61. Trans. J. Strachey. London: Hogarth.

———— 1895a. On the grounds for detaching a particular syndrome from neurasthenia under the description "anxiety neurosis." *SE* 3:87–113.

———— 1895b. Project for a scientific psychology. *SE* 1:283–387.

———— 1900. *The interpretation of dreams. SE* 4 and 5.

———— 1901. *The psychopathology of everyday life. SE* 6.

———— 1905a. *Fragment of an analysis of a case of hysteria. SE* 7:1–122.

———— 1905b. *Three essays on the theory of sexuality. SE* 7:125–245.

———— 1908. Character and anal eroticism. *SE* 9:169–75.

———— 1909a. Family romances. *SE* 9:235–41.

———— 1909b. *Analysis of a phobia in a five-year-old boy. SE* 10:1–149.

———— 1909c. *Notes upon a case of obsessional neurosis. SE* 10:153–318.

———— 1910. The future prospects of psychoanalytic therapy. *SE* 11:139–53.

———— 1911a. Psycho-analytic notes on an autobiographical account of a case of paranoia (dementia paranoides). *SE* 12:1–82.

———— 1911b. The handling of dream interpretation in psycho-analysis. *SE* 12: 89–96.

———— 1911c. Formulations on the two principles of mental functioning. *SE* 12:213–26.

———— 1912a. The dynamics of transference. *SE* 12:99–108.

———— 1912b. Recommendations to physicians practicing psycho-analysis. *SE* 12:111–20.

———— 1913. On beginning the treatment. *SE* 12:123–44.

———— 1914a. On narcissism: an introduction. *SE* 14:67–102.

———— 1914b. Remembering, repeating, and working-through. *SE* 12:147–56.

———— 1915. Observations on transference-love: Further recommendations on the technique of psychoanalysis. *SE* 12:158–71.

———— 1916. Some character types met with in psycho-analytic work. *SE* 14:159–71.

———— 1917a. Mouming and melancholia. *SE* 14:237–60.

———— 1917b. *Introductory lectures on psychoanalysis: General theory of the neuroses.* Part 3. *SE* 16:431–47.

———— 1917c. On transformations of instinct as exemplified in anal erotism. *SE* 17:125–34.

———— 1918. From the history of an infantile neurosis. *SE* 17:7–122.

———— 1919a. "A child is being beaten": A contribution to the study of the origin of sexual perversions. *SE* 17:175–204.

———— 1919b. Lines of advance in psycho-analytic therapy. *SE* 17:157–68.

———— 1920a. Beyond the pleasure principle. *SE* 18:7–64.

———— 1920b. The psychogenesis of a case of homosexuality in a woman. *SE* 18:145–72.

———— 1923. The ego and the id. *SE* 19:12–66.

———— 1925. Some psychical consequences of the anatomical distinction between the sexes. *SE* 19:241–58.

———— 1926. Inhibitions, symptoms, and anxiety. *SE* 20:75–175.

———— 1933. New introductory lectures. *SE* 22:1–182.

———— 1937. Analysis terminable and interminable. *SE* 23:209–53.

——— 1940. An outline of psychoanalysis. *SE* 23:139–207.

Friedan, B. 1974. *The Feminine Mystique.* New York: Dell.

Friedman, R., and J. Downey. 1995. Biology and the Oedipus complex. *Psychoanalytic Quarterly* 64:234–64.

Frings, J., R. Kratovil, and B. Polemis. 1958. *An assessment of social case recording.* New York: Family Service Association of America.

Fromm-Reichmann, F. 1939. Transference problems in schizophrenics. *Psychoanalytic Quarterly*, 8:412–26.

——— 1950. *Principles of intensive psychotherapy.* Chicago: University of Chicago Press.

Frosch, J. 1970. Psychoanalytic considerations of the psychotic character. *Journal of the American Psychoanalytic Association* 18:24-50.

Furman, E. 1992. On feeling and being felt with. *The Psychoanalytic Study of the Child* 47:67–84. New Haven: Yale University Press.

——— 2001. *On being and having a mother.* Madison, CT: International Universities Press.

Gabbard. G. 1995. Countertransference: The emerging common ground. *International Journal of Psycho-Analysis* 76:475–85.

——— 1996. *Love and hate in the analytic setting.* Northvale, NJ: Aronson.

——— 2000. A contemporary psychoanalytic model of countertransference. *Journal of Clinical Psychology* 57:983–91.

Galatzer-Levy, R. 1995. The rewards of research. In T. Shapiro and R. Emde, eds., *Research in psychoanalysis: Process, development, outcome,* pp. 393–410. Madison, CT: International Universities Press.

Galatzer-Levy, R., H. Bachrach, A. Skolnikoff, and S. Waldron. 2000. *Does psychoanalysis work?* New Haven: Yale University Press.

Gardiner, M. 1983. *Code name "Mary."* New Haven: Yale University Press.

Gardner, R. 1977. *Therapeutic communication with children: The mutual storytelling technique.* New York: Aronson.

——— 1993. *Storytelling in psychotherapy with children.* Northvale, NJ: Aronson.

Garfield, S. 1989. *The practice of brief therapy.* New York: Pergamon.

Gartner, A. 1985. Countertransference issues in the psychotherapy of adolescent. *Journal of Child and Adolescent Psychotherapy* 7:187–96.

Gay, P. 1988. *Freud: A life for our time.* New York: Norton.

Gedo, J. 1989. An epistemology of transference. *Annual of Psychoanalysis* 17:3–16.

Ghent, E. 1992. Foreword. In N. Skolnick and S. Warshaw, eds., *Relational perspectives in psychoanalysis,* pp. xiii–xxii. Hillsdale, NJ: Analytic.

Gill, M. 1979. The analysis of the transference. *Journal of the American Psychoanalytic Association* 27 (Supplement): 263–88.

——— 1983. The point of view in psychoanalysis: Energy discharge or person? *Psychoanalysis and Contemporary Thought* 6:523–52.

Gill, M., and M. Brenman. 1959. *Hypnosis and related states: Psychoanalytic studies and regression.* New York: International Universities Press.

Gill, M., J. Simon, G. Fink, N. Endicott, and I. Paul. 1968. Studies in audio-recorded psychoanalysis: I. General considerations. *Journal of the American Psychoanalytic Association* 16:8–27.

Gill, M. and I. Hoffman. 1982. A method for studying the analysis of aspects of the patient's experience of the relationship in psychoanalysis and psychotherapy. *Journal of the American Psychoanalytic Association* 30:137–67.

Giovacchini, P. 1975. Productive procrastination: Technical factors in the treatment of the adolescent. In S. Feinstein and P. Giovacchini, eds., *Adolescent Psychiatry,* 4:352–70. New York: Basic.

————— 1992. The severely-disturbed adolescent. In J. Brandell, ed., *Countertransference in psychotherapy with children and adolescents,* pp. 141–62. Northvale, NJ: Aronson.

Glover, E. 1941. Problems of psychoanalytic technique. *Psychoanalytic Quarterly.*

————— 1955. *The technique of psychoanalysis.* New York: International Universities Press.

Goldstein, E. 1995. *Ego psychology and social work practice.* New York: Free.

————— 1997. To tell or not to tell: Self-disclosure of events in the therapist's life to the patient. *Clinical Social Work Journal* 25:41–58.

————— 2001. *Object relations theory and self psychology in social work practice.* New York: Free.

Goldstein, E., and M. Noonan. 1999. *Short-term treatment and social work practice.* New York: Free.

Gordon, R., L. Aron, S. Mitchell, and J. Davies. 1998. Relational psychoanalysis. In R. Langs, ed., *Current theories of psychoanalysis,* pp. 31–58. Madison, CT: International Universities Press.

Gottesfeld, M., and F. Lieberman. 1979. The pathological therapist. *Social Casework* 60:387–93.

Gottschalk, L. 1979. *The content analysis of verbal behavior: Further studies.* New York: Spectrum.

————— 1995. *Content analysis of verbal behavior: New findings and clinical applications.* Hillsdale, NJ: Erlbaum.

Gottschalk, L., and G. Gleser. 1969. *The measurement of psychological states through the content analysis of human behavior.* Berkeley: University of California Press.

Gottschalk, L., G. Gleser, and C. Winget. 1969. *Manual of instructions for using the Gottschalk-Gleser content analysis scales: Anxiety, hostility, and social alienation-personal disorganization.* Berkeley: University of California Press.

Grayer, E. and P. Sax. 1986. A model for the diagnostic and therapeutic use of countertransference. *Clinical Social Work Journal* 14:295–307.

Greenacre, P. 1954. The role of transference: Practical considerations in relation to psychoanalytic therapy. *Journal of the American Psychoanalytic Association* 2:671–84.

————— 1971 [1954]. Problems of infantile neurosis: Contribution to a discussion. In *Emotional Growth: Psychoanalytic studies of the gifted and a great variety of other individuals,* 1:50–57. New York: International Universities Press.

————— 1971 [1966]. Problems of overidealization of the analyst and of analysis: Their manifestations in the transference and countertransference relationship. In *Emotional growth: Psychoanalytic studies of the gifted and a great variety of other individuals,* 2:743–61. New York: International Universities Press.

Greenberg, J., and S. Mitchell. 1983. *Object relations in psychoanalytic theory.* Cambridge: Harvard University Press.

Greene, R. 2002. *Resiliency: An integrated approach to practice, policy, and research.* Washington, DC: NASW.

Greenson, R. 1965a. The problem of working through. In M. Schur, ed., *Drives, affects, behavior,* pp. 277–314. New York: International Universities Press.

———— 1965b. The working alliance and the transference neurosis. *Psychoanalytic Quarterly* 343:155–81.

———— 1967. *The technique and practice of psychoanalysis.* New York: International Universities Press.

Greenspan, S. 1983. *The clinical interview of the child.* New York: McGraw-Hill.

Greenspan, S., and C. Cullander. 1973. A systematic metapsychological assessment of the personality—its application to the problem of analyzability. *Journal of the American Psychoanalytic Association* 21:303–27.

Greenspan, S., and W. Polk. 1980. A developmental approach to the assessment of adult personality functioning and psychopathology. In S. Greenspan and G. Pollock, eds., *The Course of Life,* pp. 255–97. Washington, DC: NIMH.

Grossman, W. 1991. Pain, aggression, fantasy, and concepts of sadomasochism. *Psychoanalytic Quarterly* 60:22–52.

Grotstein, J. 1996. Object relations theory. In E. Nersessian and R. Kopff, eds., *Textbook of psychoanalysis,* pp. 89–125. Washington, DC: American Psychiatric.

Guntrip, H. 1968. *Schizoid phenomena, object relations, and the self.* New York: International Universities Press.

———— 1971. *Psychoanalytic theory, therapy and the self.* New York: Basic.

Gustafson, J. 1986. *The complex secret of brief psychotherapy.* New York: Norton.

Hagman, G. 2001. Scaffolding the self: A self-psychological perspective on case management. In National Membership Committee on Psychoanalysis in Clinical Social Work, *Conference on Dynamic Social Work.* Arlington, Virginia (March).

Hall, G. 1904. *Adolescence: Its psychology and its relations to anthropology, sex, crime, religion, and education.* New York: Random House.

Hamilton. V. 1993. Truth and reality in psychoanalytic discourse. *The International Journal of Psycho-Analysis* 74:63-80.

Hanna, E. 1998. The role of the therapist's subjectivity: Using countertransference in psychotherapy. *Journal of Analytic Social Work* 5:1–24.

Harlow, H. 1959. Love in infant monkeys. *Scientific American* 200:68-74.

Harris, M., and H. Bergman. 1987. Case management with the chronically mentally ill: A clinical perspective. *American Journal of Orthopsychiatry* 55(2): 296–302.

———— 1993. *Case management for mentally ill patients: Theory and practice.* Langhorne, PA: Harwood Academic.

Harris, M., and L. Bachrach. 1988. *Clinical case management.* San Francisco: Jossey-Bass.

Hartmann, H. 1939. *Ego psychology and the problem of adaptation.* New York: International Universities Press.

Hartmann, H., E. Kris, and R. Lowenstein. 1949. Notes on the theory of aggression. *Psychoanalytic Study of the Child* 3–4:9–36.

Havens, L. 1976. *Participant observation.* New York: Aronson.

———— 1986. *Making contact.* Cambridge: Harvard University Press.

Havens, L., and I. Frank Jr. 1971. Review of P. Mullahy, *Psychoanalysis and Interpersonal Psychiatry* 127:1704–5.

Heimann, P. 1950. On countertransference. *International Journal of Psycho-Analysis* 31:81–84.

Heinicke, C. 1965. Frequency of psychotherapeutic session as a factor affecting the child's developmental status. *Psychoanalytic Study of the Child* 20:42–98.

Held, R. 1955. Les critères de la fin du traitement psychanalytique. *Revue Française Psychanalyse* 19:603–14.

Hendrick, I. 1942. Instinct and the ego during infancy. *Psychoanalytic Quarterly* 11:33–58.

—— 1943. Work and the pleasure principle. *Psychoanalytic Quarterly* 12:311–29.

Hepworth, D., R. Rooney, and J. Larsen. 1997. *Direct social work practice: Theory and skills.* Pacific Grove, CA: Brooks/Cole.

Hermann, I. 1933. Zum Triebleben der Primaten. Bemerkungen zu S. Zuckerman: Social life of monkeys and apes. *Imago: Zeitschrift fuer Psychoanalyse auf die Geistswissenschaften* 19:113.

—— 1936. Sich-Anklammern-Auf-Suche-Gehen. *International Zeitschrift fuer Psychoanalyse* 22:349–70.

Herzog, J. 2001. *Father hunger: Explorations with adults and children.* Hillsdale, NJ: Analytic.

Hoffer, A. 2000. Neutrality and the therapeutic alliance: What does the analyst want? In S. Levy, ed., *The therapeutic alliance,* pp. 35–54. Madison, CT: International Universities Press.

Hoffman, I. 1983. The patient as interpreter of the analyst's experience. *Contemporary Psychoanalysis* 19:389–422.

—— 1991. Discussion: Toward a social-constructivistic view of the psychoanalytic situation. *Psychoanalytic Dialogues* 1:74–105.

—— 1992. Some practical implications of a social-constructivistic view of the analytic situation. *Psychoanalytic Dialogues* 2:287–304.

Hogarty, G. 2002. *Personal therapy for schizophrenia and related disorders: A guide to individualized treatment.* New York: Guilford.

Hollis, F., 1968a. A profile of early interviews in marital counseling. *Social Casework* 49:35–43.

—— 1968b. *A typology of casework treatment.* New York: Family Service Association of America.

—— 1970. The psychosocial approach to the practice of social casework. In R. Roberts and R. Nee, eds., *Theories of social casework,* pp. 33–75. Chicago: University of Chicago Press.

Holzman, P. 1998. *Psychoanalysis and psychopathology.* New York: McGraw-Hill.

Home, J. 1966. The concept of mind. *International Journal of Psychoanalysis* 47:42–49.

Horner, T. 1985. The psychic life of the young infant: Review and critique of the psychoanalytic concepts of symbiosis and infantile omnipotence. *American Journal of Orthopsychiatry* 55:324–44.

Horney, K. 1967 [1924]. On the genesis of the castration complex in women. In H. Kelman, ed., *Feminine psychology,* pp. 147–61. New York: Norton.

———— 1926. The flight from womanhood: The masculinity complex in women as viewed by women and men. *International Journal of Psycho-Analysis* 7:324–39.

———— 1951. Tenth anniversary. *American Journal of Psychoanalysis* 11:3.

Horowitz, M. 1991. Short-term dynamic therapy of stress response syndromes. In P. Crits-Christoph and P. Barber, eds., *Handbook of short-term dynamic psychotherapy,* pp. 166–98. New York: Basic.

Hug-Hellmuth, H. von. 1921. On the technique of child analysis. *International Journal of Psycho-Analysis* 2:287–305.

Hurvich, M. 1989. Traumatic moment, basic dangers, and annihilation anxiety. *Psychoanalytic Psychology* 6:309-23.

———— 1991. Annihilation anxiety: An introduction. In H. Siegel, L. Barbanel, I. Hirsch, J. Lasky, H. Silverman, and S. Warshaw, eds., *Psychoanalytic reflections on current issues,* pp. 135–54. New York: New York University Press.

Jacobs, T. 1999. On the question of self-disclosure by the analyst: Error or advance in technique? *Psychoanalytic Quarterly* 68:159–83.

———— 2000. On beginnings: The concept of the therapeutic alliance and the interplay of transferences in the opening phase. In S. Levy, ed., *The therapeutic alliance,* pp. 17–34. Madison, CT: International Universities Press.

Jacobson, E. 1964. *The self and the object world.* New York: International Universities Press.

———— 1971. *Depression: Comparative studies of normal, neurotic, and psychotic conditions.* New York International Universities Press.

Jacobson, J. 1994. Signal affect and our psychoanalytic confusion of tongues. *Journal of the American Psychoanalytic Association* 42:15–42.

Jacobson, N., and D. Greenley. 2001. What is recovery? A conceptual model and explication. *Psychiatric Services* 52(4): 482–85.

Jadi, F., and M. Trixler, 1980. The use of focal conflict model in art therapy. *Confinia Psychiatrica* 23:93–102.

Jarvis, C. 1999. Adolescence: A personal identity in a topsy-turvy world. In D. Hindle and M. Smith, eds., *Personality Development: A Psychoanalytic Perspective.* London and New York: Routledge.

Jones, E. 1948a [1911]. The psychology of morbid anxiety. In *Papers on psychoanalysis.* 4th ed. London: Bailliare, Tindall, and Cox.

———— 1948b [1922]. Some problems of adolescence. In *Papers on psychoanalysis.* 4th ed. London: Bailliare, Tindall, and Cox.

———— 1953. *The life and work of Sigmund Freud.* Vol 1: *1856–1900, the formative years and the great discoveries.* New York: Basic.

———— 1955. *The life and work of Sigmund Freud.* Vol. 2: *1901–1919, years of maturity.* New York: Basic.

———— 1957. *The life and work of Sigmund Freud.* Vol. 3: *1919–1939, the last phase.* New York: Basic.

Jones, E. 1995. How will psychoanalysis study itself? In T. Shapiro and R. Emde, eds., *Research in Psychoanalysis: Process, development, outcome,* Madison, CT: International Universities Press.

Jung, C. G. 1967b. *Collected works of C. G. Jung. The relations between the ego and the unconscious,* 7:1–201. Princeton: Princeton University Press.

———— 1967b. *Collected Works of C. G. Jung. On the psychology of the unconscious,* 7:202–406. Princeton: Princeton University Press.

Kanter, J. 1987. Mental health case management: A professional domain? *Social Work* 32(5): 461–62.

———— 1988. Clinical issues in the case management relationship. In M. Harris and L. Bachrach, eds., *Clinical case management, New directions for mental health services,* 40:15–28. San Francisco: Jossey-Bass.

———— 1989. Clinical case management: Definition, priniciples, components. *Hospital and Community Psychiatry* 40: 361–68.

———— 1995. *Clinical issues in case management.* San Francisco: Jossey-Bass.

———— 1996. Case management with long-term patients: A comprehensive approach. In S. M. Soreff, ed., *Handbook for the treatment of the seriously mentally ill.* Seattle: Hogrefe Huber.

———— 1999. Clinical issues in delivering home-based psychiatric services. In A. Menikoff, ed., *Psychiatric home care: Clinical and economic dimensions.* San Diego: Academic.

———— 2001. Being there: The transitional participant in case management. Paper presented at the National Membership Committee on Psychoanalysis in Clinical Social Work, Conference on Dynamic Social Work, Arlington, Virginia.

Kantrowitz, J., A. Katz, and F. Paolitto. 1990a. Follow-up of psychoanalysis five to ten years after termination. Part 1: Stability of change. *Journal of the American Psychoanalytic Association* 38:471–96.

———— 1990b. Follow-up of psychoanalysis five to ten years after termination. Part 2: The development of the self-analytic function. *Journal of the American Psychoanalytic Association* 38:637–54.

———— 1990c. Follow-up of psychoanalysis five to ten years after termination. Part 3: The relation between the resolution of the transference and the patient-analyst match. *Journal of the American Psychoanalytic Association* 38:655–78.

Kanzer, M. 1981. Freud's "analytic pact": The standard therapeutic alliance. *Journal of the American Psychoanalytic Association* 29:69–87.

Kaplan-Solms, K., and M. Solms. 2000. *Clinical studies in neuro-psychoanalysis: Introduction to depth neuropsychology.* New York: Karnac.

Karson, A. 1991. The application of group focal conflict theory to partial hospitalization: An integrative model. *International Journal of Partial Hospitalization* 7(2): 137–54.

Kepecs, J. 1966. Theories of transference neurosis. *Psychoanalytic Quarterly* 35:497–521.

———— N.d. Focal conflict and other guides to therapy. Department of Psychiatry, University of Wisconsin Medical School, Madison, Wisconsin. Unpublished manuscript.

———— 1977. Teaching psychotherapy by use of brief transcripts. *American Journal of Psychotherapy* 31:383–93.

Kernberg, O. 1978. The diagnosis of borderline conditions in adolescence. *Adolescent Psychiatry* 6:298–319.

———— 1980. *Internal word and external reality.* Northvale, NJ: Aronson.

———— 1987. An ego psychology-object relations theory approach to the transference. *Psychoanalytic Quarterly* 56:197–221.

Kernberg, P. 1991. *Children with conduct disorders*. New York: Basic.

Kernberg, P., A. Weiner, and K. Bardenstein. 2000. *Personality disorders in children and adolescents*. New York: Basic.

Kessler, J. 1966. *Psychopathology of childhood*. Englewood Cliffs, NJ: Prentice-Hall.

Kiesler, D. 1973. *The process of psychotherapy: Empirical foundations and systems of analysis*. Chicago: Aldine.

King, P., and R. Steiner, eds. 1991. *The Freud-Klein controversies, 1941–1945*. London: Routledge.

Klein, G. 1976. *Psychoanalytic theory: An exploration of essentials*. New York: International Universities Press.

Klein, H. 1974. Transference and defense in manic states. *International Journal of Psychoanalysis* 55:261–68.

Klein, M. 1932. *The psychoanalysis of children*. London: Hogarth.

———— 1952. The origins of transference. *International Journal of Psycho-Analysis* 33:433–38.

———— 1964a [1935]. A contribution to the psychogenesis of manic-depressive states. *In Contributions to psychoanalysis, 1921–1945*. New York: McGraw-Hill.

———— 1964b. *Contributions to psychoanalysis, 1921–1945*. New York: McGraw-Hill.

———— 1975a [1946]. Notes on some schizoid mechanisms. In *Envy and gratitude and other works, 1946-1963*. New York: Delacorte.

———— 1975b [1952]. Some theoretical conclusions regarding the emotional life of the infant. In *Envy and gratitude and other works, 1946-1963*. New York: Delacorte.

Knight, R. 1941. Evaluation of the results of psychoanalytic therapy. *American Journal of Psychiatry* 98:434–46.

Kohon, G., ed.. 1986. *The British school of psychoanalysis: The independent tradition*. London: Free Association.

Kohrman. R., H. Fineberg, R. Gelman, and S. Weiss. 1971. Technique of child analysis: Problems of countertransference. *International Journal of Psycho-Analysis* 59: 487–97.

Kohut, H. 1966. Forms and transformations of narcissism. *Journal of the American Psychoanalytic Association* 14:243–72.

———— 1971. *The analysis of the self*. New York: International Universities Press.

———— 1972. Thoughts on narcissism and narcissistic rage. *Psychoanalytic Study of the Child* 27:360–400.

———— 1974. Remarks about the formation of the self. In P. Ornstein, ed., *The search for the self*, 2:737–70. New York: International Universities Press.

———— 1977. *The restoration of the self*. New York: International Universities Press.

———— 1980. Diagnosis and treatment of borderline and narcissistic children and adolescents. *Bulletin of the Menninger Clinic* 44:147–70.

———— 1984. *How does analysis cure?* Chicago: University of Chicago Press.

Kohut, H., and E. Wolf. 1978. The disorders of the self and their treatment: An outline. *International Journal of Psychoanalysis* 59:413–25.

Kramer, C. 1967. Maxwell Gitelson: Analytic aphorisms. *Psychoanalytic Quarterly* 36: 260–70.

Kris, A. 1982. *Free association: Method and process.* New Haven: Yale University Press.

Krystal, H. 1993. *Integration and self-healing: Affect, trauma, alexithymia.* Hillsdale, NJ: Analytic.

Kubie, L. 1968. Unsolved problems in the resolution of the resolution of the transference. *Psychoanalytic Quarterly* 37:331–52.

Kupers, T. 1988. *Ending therapy: The meaning of termination.* New York: New York University Press.

Lachmann, F., and B. Beebe, 1992. Representational and selfobject transferences: A developmental perspective. In *New therapeutic visions: Progress in self psychology,* 8:3–15. Hillsdale, NJ: Analytic.

———— 1994. Representation and internalization in infancy: Three principles of salience. *Psychoanalytic Psychology* 11(2): 127–66.

Laikin, M., A. Winston, and L. McCullough. 1991. Intensive short-term dynamic psychotherapy. In P. Crits-Christoph and P. Barber, eds., *Handbook of short-term dynamic psychotherapy,* pp. 80–109. New York: Basic.

Lamb, R. 1980. Therapist-case managers: More than brokers of services. *Hospital and Community Psychiatry* 31(11): 762–64.

Langs, R. 1981. *Resistances and interventions.* New York: Aronson.

Lanyado, M. 1999. "It's just an ordinary pain": Thoughts on joy and heartache in puberty and early adolescence. In D. Hindle and M. Smith, eds., *Personality development: A pychoanalytic perspective.* London and New York: Routledge.

Laufer, M., and E. Laufer. 1989. *Adolescent breakdown and psychoanalytic treatment in adolescence.* New Haven and London: Yale University Press.

Laughlin, H. 1979. *The ego and its defenses.* Northvale, NJ: Aronson.

Leider, R. 1996. The psychology of the self. In E. Nersessian and R. Kopff, eds., *Textbook of psychoanalysis,* pp. 127–64. Washington, DC: American Psychiatric.

Lerner, H. 2002. A two-systems approach to the treatment of a disturbed adolescent. In J. Brandell, ed., *Psychoanalytic approaches to the treatment of children and adolescents: Tradition and transformation,* pp. 95–122. Binghamton, NY: Haworth.

Lester, E. 1990. Gender identity issues in the analytic process. *International Journal of Psychoanalysis* 71:435–44.

Levenson, E. 1972. *The fallacy of understanding.* New York: Basic.

Levinson, H. 1977. Termination in psychotherapy: Some salient issues. *Social Casework* 58:480–88.

Liberman, R., A. Kopelowicz, J. Ventura, and D. Gutkind. 2002. Operational criteria and factors related to recovery from schizophrenia. *International Review of Psychiatry* 14:256–72.

Lichtenberg, J. 1983. *Psychoanalysis and infant research.* Hillsdale, NJ: Analytic.

———— 1989. *Psychoanalysis and motivation.* Hillsdale, NJ: Analytic.

Lieberman, F. 1979. *Social work with children.* New York: Human Sciences.

———— 1983. Work with children. In D. Waldfogel and A. Rosenblatt, eds., *Handbook of clinical social work,* pp. 441–65. San Francisco: Jossey-Bass.

Lifton, R. 1993. *The protean self: Human resilience in an age of fragmentation.* Chicago: University of Chicago Press.

Little, M. 1950. Countertransference and the patient's response to it. *International Journal of Psycho-Analysis* 32:32–40.

———— 1957. "R"—the analyst's response to his patient's needs. *International Journal of Psycho-Analysis* 38:240–54.

Loewald, H. 1962. Internalization, separation, mourning, and the superego. *Psychoanalytic Quarterly* 31:483–504.

———— 1971. *Journal of the American Psychoanalytic Association* 19:54–66.

———— 1980. *Papers on psychoanalysis.* New Haven: Yale University Press.

Lorand, S. 1950. The psychoanalytic contribution to the treatment of behavior problems in children. In *Clinical studies in psychoanalysis.* New York: International Universities Press.

———— 1961. Treatment of adolescents. In S. Lorand, ed., *Adolescents: Psychoanalytic approach to problems and therapy,* pp. 238–50. New York: Hoeber.

Lorenz, K. 1957 [1937]. The nature of instincts. In C. Schiller, ed., *Instinctive behavior.* New York: International Universities Press.

Luborsky, L., and D. Mark. 1991. Short-term supportive-expressive psychoanalytic psychotherapy. In P. Crits-Christoph and P. Barber, eds, *Handbook of short-term dynamic psychotherapy,* pp. 110–36. New York: Basic.

Luborsky, L., and P. Crits-Christoph. 1990. *Understanding transference: The core conflictual relationship theme method.* New York: Basic.

Lustman, S. 1963. Some issues in contemporary psychoanalytic research. *Psychoanalytic Study of the Child* 18:51–74.

Macalpine, I. 1950. The development of transference. *Psychoanalytic Quarterly* 19:501–39.

McCullough, L., B. Farber, A. Winston, F. Porter, J. Pollack, W. Vingiano, M. Laikin, and M. Trujillo. 1991. The relationship of patient-therapist interaction to outcome in brief psychotherapy. *Psychotherapy* 28:525–33.

McDevitt, J. 1996. The continuity of conflict and compromise formation: A twenty-five-year follow-up. *Journal of the American Psychoanalytic Association.*

McDonald, M. 1965. The psychiatric evaluation of children. *Journal of the American Academy of Child Psychiatry* 4:569–612.

McDougall, J. 1984. The "dis-affected" patient: Reflections on affect pathology. *Psychoanalytic Quarterly* 53:386–409.

———— 1985. *Theaters of the mind.* New York: Basic.

———— 1989. *Theaters of the body.* New York: Basic.

McWilliams, N. 1999. *Psychoanalytic case formulation.* New York: Guilford.

Mahler, M. 1968. *On human symbiosis and the vicissitudes of individuation.* New York: International Universities Press.

———— 1972. The rapprochement subphase. *Psychoanalytic Quarterly* 41:487–506.

Mahler, M., F. Pine, and A. Bergmann. 1975. *The psychological birth of the human infant.* New York: Basic.

Main, M. 1995. Discourse, prediction, and recent studies in attachment: Implications for psychoanalysis. In T. Shapiro and R. Emde, eds., *Research in psychoanalysis:*

Process, development, outcome, pp. 209–44. Madison, CT: International Universities Press.

Malan, D. 1976. *The frontier of brief psychotherapy.* New York: Plenum.

Malcolm, J. 1983. In the Freud archives. (Interview with Jeffrey Masson.) *New Yorker,* December 5 and 12.

Mann, J. 1973. *Time-limited psychotherapy.* Cambridge: Harvard University Press.

——— 1986. Transference and countertransference in brief psychotherapy. In H. Myers, ed., *Between analyst and patient: New dimensions in countertransference and transference,* pp. 119–27. Hillsdale, NJ: Analytic.

——— 1991. Time-limited psychotherapy. In P. Crits-Christoph and P. Barber, eds., *Handbook of short-term dynamic psychotherapy,* pp. 17–44. New York: Basic.

Mann, J. and R. Goldman. 1982. *A casebook in time-limited psychotherapy.* New York: McGraw-Hill.

Maroda, K. 1998. Enactment: When the patient's and analyst's pasts converge. *Psychoanalytic Psychology* 15:517–535.

Marsden, G. 1971. Content analysis studies of psychotherapy: 1954 through 1968. In A. Bergin and S. Garfield, eds., *Handbook of Psychotherapy and Behavior Change: An Empirical Analysis,* pp. 345–84. New York: Wiley.

Marsh, D. 2000. Personal accounts of consumer/survivors: Insights and implications. *Journal of Clinical Psychology* 56(11): 1447–57.

Marsh, J. C. 2002. "Learning from clients." *Social Work* 47(4): 341–43.

Marshall, R. 1979. Countertransference in the psychotherapy of children and adolescents. *Contemporary Psychoanalysis* 15:487–97.

Marx, J. and C. Gelso. 1987. Termination of individual counseling in a university counseling center. *Journal of Counseling Psychology* 34:3–9.

Mason, P. 1954. Suicide in adolescents. *Psychoanalytic Review* 41:48–54

Masson, J. 1998 [1984]. *The assault on truth: Freud's suppression of the seduction theory.* New York: Pocket.

Masters, W., and V. Johnson. 1970. *Human sexual inadequacy.* Boston: Little, Brown.

Masterson, J., and D. Rinsley. 1975. The borderline syndrome: The role of the mother in the genesis and psychic structure of the borderline personality. *International Journal of Psychoanalysis* 56:163–77.

Meeks, J. and W. Bernet. 1990. *The fragile alliance.* Malabar, FL: Krieger.

Meissner, W. 1992. The concept of the therapeutic alliance. *Journal of the American Psychoanalytic Association* 40:1059–1087.

——— 1996. *The therapeutic alliance.* New Haven: Yale University Press.

——— 2000. *Freud and psychoanalysis.* Notre Dame: Notre Dame Press.

Messer, S. and C. Warren. 1995. *Models of brief psychodynamic therapy: A comparative approach.* New York: Guilford.

——— 2001. Brief psychodynamic therapy. In R. Corsini, ed., *Handbook of Innovative therapy,* pp. 67–85. New York: Wiley.

Meyer, W. 2001. Why they don't come back: A clinical perspective on the no-show client. *Clinical Social Work Journal* 29(4): 325–39.

Miller, J. 1976. *Toward a new psychology of women.* Boston: Beacon.

Millet, K. 1970. *Sexual politics.* New York: Doubleday.

Mintz, J., and L. Luborsky. 1971. Segments vs. whole sessions: Which is the better unit for psychotherapy process research? *Journal of Abnormal Psychology* 78:180–91.

Mishne, J. 1983. *Clinical work with children.* New York: Free.

———— 1986. *Clinical work with adolescents.* New York: Free.

———— 1993. *The evolution and application of clinical theory.* New York: Free.

———— 1997. Clinical social work with adolescents. In J. Brandell, ed., *Theory and practice in clinical social work,* pp. 101–31. New York: Simon and Schuster/Free.

———— 2002. *Multiculturalism and the therapeutic process.* New York: Guilford.

Mitchell, J. 1974. *Psychoanalysis and feminism: Freud, Reich, Laing, and women.* New York: Pantheon.

Mitchell, S. 1983. Aggression and the endangered self. *Psychoanalytic Quarterly* 62:351–82.

———— 1988. *Relational concepts in psychoanalysis.* Cambridge, MA: Harvard University Press.

———— 1993. *Hope and dread in psychoanalysis.* New York: Basic.

Mitchell, S., and M. Black. 1995. *Freud and beyond: A history of modem psychoanalytic thought.* New York: Basic.

Moore, B., and B. Fine. 1990. *Psychoanalytic terms and concepts.* New Haven: Yale University Press.

Mullahy, P. 1970. *Psychoanalysis and interpersonal psychiatry.* New York: Science House.

Mullen, E., J. Dumpson, eds. 1972. *Evaluation of social intervention.* San Francisco: Jossey-Bass.

Muller, J. 1932. A contribution to the problem of libidinal development of the genital phase in girls. *International Journal of Psycho-Analysis* 13:362–68.

Musgrove, F. 1965. *Youth and the social order.* Bloomington: Indiana University Press.

National Association of Social Workers. 1958. *Use of judgment as data in social work research.* New York: National Association of Social Workers.

Nielsen, G. and K. Barth. 1991. Short-term anxiety-provoking psychotherapy. In P. Crits-Christoph and P. Barber, eds., *Handbook of short-term dynamic psychotherapy,* pp. 45–79. New York: Basic.

Niemeyer. G. 1993a. *Constructivist assessment: A casebook.* Newbury Park, CA: Sage.

———— 1993b. Defining the boundaries of constructivist assessment. In G.Neimeyer, ed., *Constructivist assessment: A casebook.* Newbury Park, CA: Sage.

Norcross, J., ed. 2002. *Psychotherapy relationships that work: Therapist contributions and responsiveness to patients.* Oxford, England: Oxford University Press.

Novick, J. 1976. The termination of treatment in adolescence. *Psychoanalytic Study of the Child* 31:389–414.

———— 1982. Transference varieties in the analysis of an adolescent. *International Journal of Psychoanalysis* 63:139–48.

———— 1990. Comments on termination in child, adolescent and adult analysis. *Psychoanalytic Study of the Child* 45:419–36.

———— 1997. Termination conceivable and inconceivable. *Psychoanalytic Psychology* 14:145–62.

Novick, J. and K. Novick. 2002. Two systems of self-regulation. In J. Brandell, ed., *Psychoanalytic approaches to the treatment of children and adolescents: Tradition and transformation,* pp. 95–122. Binghamton, NY: Haworth.

Nunberg, H. 1951. Transference and reality. *International Journal of Psycho-Analysis* 32:1–9.

O'Dowd, W. 1986. Otto Rank and time-limited psychotherapy. *Psychotherapy* 23:140–49.

Offer, D. 1969. *The psychological world of the teenager: A study of normal adolescent boys.* New York: Basic.

Offer, D., E. Ostrove, and K. Howard. 1981. The mental health professional's concept of the normal adolescent. *Archives of General Psychiatry* 38:149–52.

Ogden, T. 1982. *Projective identification and psychoanalytic technique.* Northvale, NJ: Aronson.

——— 1995. Aliveness and deadness of the transference-countertransference. *International Journal of Psycho-Analysis* 76:695–710.

——— 1997. *Reverie and interpretation: Sensing something human.* Northvale. NJ: Aronson.

Okun, B. 1992. Feminist perspectives of object relations theory. In L. Brown, and M. Ballou, eds. *Personality and psychopathology: Feminist reappraisals,* pp. 20–46. New York: Guilford.

Paikoff, R. and J. Brooks-Gunn. 1991. Do parent-child relationships change during puberty? *Psychological Bulletin* 110:47–66.

Pally, R. 1998. Emotional processing: The mind-body connection. *International Journal of Psycho-Analysis* 79:349–62.

Palombo. J. 1985. Self psychology and countertransference in the treatment of children. *Child and Adolescent Social Work Journal* 1:36–48.

——— 2000. Psychoanalysis: A house divided. *Psychoanalytic Social Work* 7:1–26.

——— 2001. *Learning disorders and disorders of the self in children and adolescents.* New York: Norton.

Panel. 1969. Problems of termination in the analysis of adults. *Journal of the American Psychoanalytic Association* 17:222–37.

——— 1975. Termination: Problems and techniques. *Journal of the American Psychoanalytic Association* 23:166–76.

Parad, L. 1971. Short-term treatment: An overview of historical trends, issues, and potentials. *Smith College Studies in Social* Work 41:119–46.

Parens, H. 1979. *The development of aggression in early childhood.* Northvale, NJ: Aronson.

Parloff, M. 1986. Frank's "common elements" in psychotherapy: Nonspecific factors and placebos. *American Journal of Orthopsychiatry* 56(4): 521–30.

Parson, E. 1995. Posttraumatic stress and coping in an inner-city child. *Psychoanalytic Study of the Child* 50:272–307.

Perez Foster, R. 1998. *The power of language in the clinical process: Assessing and treating the bilingual person.* Northvale, NJ: Aronson.

Perlman, H. 1957. *Social casework: A problem-solving process.* Chicago: University of Chicago Press.

———— 1970. The problem-solving model in social casework. In R. Roberts and R. Nee, eds., *Theories of social casework*, pp. 129–79. Chicago: University of Chicago Press.

Perret-Catipovic, M., and F. Ladame. 1998. *Adolescence and psychoanalysis: The story and the history*. London: Karnac.

Perry, H. S. 1982. *Psychiatrist of America: The life of Harry Stack Sullivan*. Cambridge: Harvard University Press.

Phillips, A. 1997. Interview with Adam Phillips [Adam Phillips/Anthony Molino]. In A. Molino, ed., *Freely associated: Encounters in psychoanalysis with Christopher Bollas, Joyce McDougall, Michael Eigen, Adam Phillips, and Nina Coltart*. London: Free Association.

Piaget, J. 1969. *The psychology of the child*. New York: Basic.

Pick, I. and H. Segal. 1978. Melanie Klein's contribution to child analysis: Theory and technique. In J. Glenn, ed., *Child analysis and therapy*, pp.427–49.

Pine, F. 1970. On the structuralization of drive-defense relationships. *Psychoanalytic Quarterly* 39:17–37.

———— 1985. *Developmental theory and clinical process*. New Haven: Yale University Press.

———— 1988. The four psychologies of psychoanalysis and their place in clinical work. *Journal of the Amencan Psychoanalytic Association* 36:571–96.

———— 1990. *Drive, ego, object, and self*. New York: Basic.

Piper, W., F. de Carufel, and N. Szkrumelak. 1985. Patient predictors of process and outcome in short-term individual psychotherapy. *Journal of Nervous and Mental Disease* 173:726–33.

Qunitana, S. 1993. Toward an expanded and updated conceptualization of termination: Implications for short-term, individual psychotherapy. *Professional Psychology: Research and Practice* 24:426–32.

Quintana, S. and N. Meara. 1990. Internalization of therapeutic relationships in short-term psychotherapy. *Professional Psychology: Research and Practice* 21:123–30.

Racker, H. 1953. The countertransference neurosis. *International Journal of Psycho-Analysis* 34:313–24.

———— 1957. The meanings and uses of countertransference. *Psychoanalytic Quarterly* 26:303–57.

———— 1968. *Transference and countertransference*. New York: International Universities Press.

Ralph, R. 2000. Review of recovery literature: A synthesis of a sample of recovery literature 2000. National Association of State Mental Health Program Directors and National Technical Assistance Center for State Mental Health Planning. http://www.nasmhpd.org/ntac/reports/ralphrecovweb.pdf, May, 3, 2003.

Rangell, L. 1966. An overview of the ending of an analysis. In R. Litman, ed., *Psychoanalysis in the Americas*. New York: International Universities Press.

———— 1982. The self in psychoanalytic theory. *Journal of the American Psychoanalytic Association* 30:863–91.

Rank, O. 1973 [1924]. *The trauma of birth*. New York: Harper and Row.

Rapaport, D. 1960. *The structure of psychoanalytic theory*. New York: International Universities Press.

────── 1967. *Collected papers of David Rapaport*. M. Gill, ed. New York: Basic.

Rapoport, L. 1970. Crisis intervention as a mode of brief treatment. In R. Roberts and R. Nee, eds., *Theories of social casework*, pp. 265–311. Chicago: University of Chicago Press.

Rapp, C. 1998. The strengths model: Case management with people suffering from severe and persistent mental illness. New York: Oxford University Press.

Rasmussen, A., and S. Messer. 1986. A comparison and critique of Mann's time-limited psychotherapy and Davanloo's short-term dynamic psychotherapy. *Bulletin of the Menninger Clinic* 50:163–84.

Reed, G. 1994. *Transference neurosis and psychoanalytic experience: Perspectives on contemporary clinical practice*. New Haven:Yale University Press.

Reich, A. 1950. On the termination of analysis. *International Journal of Psychoanalysis* 30:179–83.

Reich, W. 1976 [1933]. *Character analysis*. New York: Pocket.

────── 1949. *Character analysis*. New York: Orgone Institute Press.

Reid, W. and A. Shyne. 1969. *Brief and extended casework*. New York: Columbia University Press.

Reiser, M. 1990. *Memory in mind and brain: What dream imagery reveals*. New York: Basic.

Renik, O. 1993a. Analytic interaction: conceptualizing technique in light of the analyst's irreducible subjectivity. *Psychoanalytic Quarterly* 62:553–71.

────── 1993b. Countertransference enactment and the psychoanalytic process. In M. Horowitz, O. Kernberg, E. Weinshel (Eds.), *Psychic structure and psychic change: Essays in honor of Robert S. Wallerstein, M.D.*, pp. 137–60. Madison, CT: International Universities Press.

────── 1995. The ideal of the anonymous analyst and the problem of self-disclosure. *Psychoanalytic Quarterly* 64:466–95.

────── 1999. Playing one's cards face up in analysis: An approach to the problem of self-disclosure. *Psychoanalytic Quarterly* 68:521–40.

Richmond, M. 1899. *Friendly visiting among the poor*. New York: Macmillan.

────── 1917. *Social diagnosis*. New York: Russell Sage Foundation.

Rie, H. 1966. Depression in childhood. *Journal of the American Academy of Child Psychiatry* 5:653–86.

Rinsley, D. 1980. Diagnosis and treatment of borderline and narcissistic children and adolescents. *Bulletin of the Menninger Clinic* 44:147–70.

Rioch, J. 1943. The transference phenomenon in psychoanalytic therapy. *Psychiatry* 6:147–56.

Ripple, L., E. Alexander, and B. Polemis. 1964. *Motivation, capacity, and opportunity*. Chicago: University of Chicago Press.

Robinson, V. 1930. *A changing psychology in social casework*. Chapel Hill: University of North Carolina Press.

Rochlin, G. 1973. *Man's aggression: The defense of the self*. Boston: Gambit.

Rogers, C. 1957. The necessary and sufficient conditions of therapeutic personality change. *Journal of Consulting Psychology* 22:95–103.

Roth, D., D. Crane-Ross, M. Hannon, and G. Cusick. 2000. A longitudinal study of mental health services and consumer outcomes in a changing system: Time five results. *New Research in Mental Health*, 14:159–76. Columbus: Ohio Department of Mental Health.

Runyan, W. 1982. *Life histories and psychobiography: Explorations in theory and method.* New York: Oxford University Press.

Rutter, K., P. Graham, O. Chadwick, and W. Yule. 1976. Protective factors in children's responses to stress and disadvantage. In M. Kent and J. Rolf, eds., *Social competence in children.* Hanover, NH: University Press of New England.

Rycroft, C. 1985. *Psychoanalysis and beyond.* London: Chatto.

Saari, C. 1991. *The creation of meaning in clinical social work.* New York: Guilford.

——— 2002. *The environment: Its role in psychosocial functioning and psychotherapy.* New York: Columbia University Press.

Sachs, H. 1942. *The creative unconscious.* Cambridge: Sci-Art.

Saleebey, D. 1994. Culture, theory, and narrative: The intersection of meanings in practice. *Social Work* 39(4): 351–59.

——— 2002. *The strengths perspective.* Boston: Allyn and Bacon.

Sandler, J. 1960. The background of safety. *International Journal of Psychoanalysis* 41:352–65.

——— 1976. Countertransference and role-responsiveness. *International Review of Psychoanalysis* 3:43–47.

Sandler, J., H. Kennedy, and R. Tyson. 1980. *The technique of child psychoanalysis: Discussions with Anna Freud.* London: Hogarth.

Sanville, J. 1991. *The playground of psychoanalytic therapy.* Hillsdale, NJ: Analytic.

Saul, I. 1976. *The psychodynamics of hostility.* Northvale, NJ: Aronson.

Saul, L. 1958. Progression and termination of the analysis. In *Technique and practice of psychoanalysis,* pp. 224–31. Philadelphia: Lippincott.

Schachtel, Z. 1986. The "impossible profession" considered from a gender perspective. In J. L. Alpert, ed., *Psychoanalysis and women: Contemporary reappraisals,* pp. 237–55. Hillsdale, NJ: Analytic.

Schafer, R. 1976. Psychoanalysis without psychodynamics. Part 1. *International Journal of Psychoanalysis* 56:41–55.

——— 1977. The interpretation of transference and the conditions for loving. *Journal of the American Psychoanalytic Association* 25:335–62.

——— 1992. *Retelling a life.* New York: Basic.

——— 1997. *Tradition and change in psychoanalysis.* Madison, CT: International Universities Press.

Schamess, G. 1981. Boundary issues in countertransference: A developmental perspective. *Clinical Social Work Journal* 9:344–57.

Schore, A. 1994. *Affect regulation and the origin of the self: The Neurobiology of emotional development.* Hillsdale, NJ: Erlbaum.

——— 1997. A century after Freud's *Project*: Is a rapprochement between psychoanalysis and neurobiology at hand? *Journal of the American Psychoanalytic Association* 45:809–40.

——— 2001. The effects of early relational trauma on right brain development, affect regulation, and infant mental health. *Infant Mental Health Journal* 22:201–69.

Schowalter. J. 1986. Countertransference in work with children: Review of a neglected concept. *Journal of the American Academy of Child and Adolescent Psychiatry* 25:40–45.

Schwaber, E. 1992. Countertransference: The analyst's retreat from the patient's vantage point. *International Journal of Psycho-Analysis* 73:349–61.

Searles, H. 1965. *Collected papers on schizophrenia and related subjects.* New York: International Universities Press.

Shakow, D. 1959. Discussion. In E. Rubinstein, ed., *Research in psychotherapy,* 1:108–15. Washington, DC: American Psychological Association.

Shane, M., and E. Shane. 1984. The end phase of analysis: Indicators, functions, and tasks of termination. *Journal of the American Psychoanalytic Association* 32:739–72.

Shapiro, D. 1965. *Neurotic styles.* New York: Basic.

Shapiro, T., and R. Emde. 1995. *Research in psychoanalysis: Process, development, outcome.* Madison, CT: International Universities Press.

Sharpe, S., and A. Rosenblatt. 1994. Oedipal sibling triangles. *Journal of the American Psychoanalytic Association* 42:491–523.

Shainess, N. 1975. Authentic feminine orgasmic response. In E. Adelson, ed., *Sexuality and psychoanalysis.* New York: Brunner/Mazel.

Shechter, R. 1997. Time-sensitive clinical social work practice. In J. Brandell, ed., *Theory and practice in clinical social work,* pp. 529–50. New York: Free.

Shefler, G., H. Dasberg, and G. Ben-Shakhar. 1995. A randomized controlled outcome and follow-up study of Mann's time-limited psychotherapy. *Journal of Consulting and Clinical Psychology* 63:585–93.

Sherfey, M. 1966. The nature and evolution of female sexuality in relation to psychoanalytic theory. *Journal of the American Psychoanalytic Association* 14:28–128.

Shevrin, H., J. A. Bond, and L. Brakel. 1996. *Conscious and unconscious processes: Psychodynamic, cognitive, and neurophysiological convergences.,* New York: Guilford.

Shulman, L. 1992. *The skills of helping.* Itasca, IL: Peacock.

Siegel, B. 1982. Some thoughts on "Some thoughts on termination" by Leo Rangell. *Psychoanalytic Inquiry* 2:393–98.

Sifneos, P. 1968. Learning to solve emotional problems: A controlled study of short-term anxiety-provoking psychotherapy. In R. Porter, ed., *The role of learning in psychotherapy,* pp. 87–96. Boston: Little, Brown.

——— 1987. *Short-term dynamic psychotherapy: Evaluation and technique.* 2d ed. New York: Plenum.

Sifneos, P., R. Apfel, E. Bassuk, G. Fishman, and A. Gill. 1980. Ongoing outcome research on short-term dynamic psychotherapy. *Psychotherapy and Psychosomatics* 33:233–41.

Smalley, R. 1967. *Theory for social work practice.* New York: Columbia University Press.

——— 1970. The functional approach to casework practice. In R. Roberts and R. Nee, eds., *Theories of social casework,* pp. 77–128. Chicago: University of Chicago Press.

Solomon, P., J. Draine, and M. Delaney. 1995. The working alliance and consumer case management. *Journal of Mental Health Administration* 22(2): 126–34.

Sours, J. 1978. The application of child analytic principles to forms of child psychotherapy. In J. Glenn, ed., *Child analysis and therapy,* pp. 615–46. New York: Aronson.

Spaniol, L., N. Wewiorski, C. Gagne, and W. Anthony. 2002. The process of recovery from schizophrenia. *International Review of Psychiatry,* no. 14, pp. 327–36.

Specht, H. and M. Courtney. 1997. *Unfaithful angels: How social work has abandoned its mission.* New York: Simon and Schuster.

Spence, D. 1982. *Narrative truth and historical truth: Meaning and interpretation in psychoanalysis.* New York: Norton.

Spiegel, L. 1951. A review of contributions to a psychoanalytic theory of adolescence: Individual aspects. *Psychoanalytic Study of the Child* 6:375–93.

——— 1961. *Adolescents: Psychoanalytic approach to problems and therapy.* New York: Hoeber.

Spitz, R. 1945. Hospitalism: An inquiry into the genesis of psychiatric conditions in early childhood. *Psychoanalytic Study of the Child* 1:53–73.

——— 1965. *The first year of life.* New York: International Universities Press.

Spitz, R., and K. Wolf. 1946. Anaclitic depression. *Psychoanalytic Study of the Child* 2:313–42.

Sprung, G. 1989. Transferential issues in working with older adults. *Social Casework* 70:597–602.

Sterba, R. 1940. The dynamics of the dissolution of the transference resistance. *Psychoanalytic Quarterly* 9:363–79.

Stern, D. 1985. *The interpersonal world of the infant.* New York: Basic.

Stolorow, R., B. Brandschaft, and G. Atwood. 1987. *Psvchoanalytic treatment: An intersubjective approach.* Hillsdale, NJ: Analytic.

Stolorow. R. and G. Atwood. 1996. The intersubjective perspective. *Psychoanalytic Review* 83:181–94.

Stone, L. 1961. *The psychoanalytic situation.* New York: International Universities Press.

——— 1967. The psychoanalytic situation and transference: Postscript to an earlier communication. *Journal of the American Psychoanalytic Association* 15:3–57.

Strachey, J. 1934. The nature of the therapeutic action of psycho-analysis. *International Journal of Psycho-Analysis* 15:126–59.

Strean, H. 1978. *Clinical social work: Theory and practice.* New York: Free.

——— 1979. *Psychoanalytic theory and social work practice.* New York: Free.

——— 1985. *Resolving resistances in psychotherapy.* New York: Wiley.

——— 1993. Clinical social work: An evaluative review. *Journal of Analytic Social Work* 1:5–23.

——— 1996. Applying psychoanalytic principles to social work practice: An historical review. In J. Edward and Jean Sanville, eds., *Fostering healing and growth: A psychoanalytic social work model,* pp. 1–22. Northvale, NJ: Aronson.

——— 2002. Countertransference: An introduction. In H. Strean, ed., *Controversies on countertransference,* pp. 1–24. Northvale, NJ: Aronson.

Strouse, J. 1974. *Women and analysis: Dialogues on psychoanalytic views of femininity.* New York: Grossman.

Sullivan, H. 1940. *Conceptions of modern psychiatry.* New York: Norton.

——— 1953. *The interpersonal theory of psychiatry.* New York: Norton.

———— 1956. *Clinical studies in psychiatry.* New York: Norton.

———— 1962a. *Schizophrenia as a human process.* New York: Norton.

———— 1962b [1930]. Socio-psychiatric research. In *Schizophrenia as a human process.* New York: Norton.

Sulloway, F. 1979. *Freud, biologist of the mind: Beyond the psychoanalytic legend.* New York: Basic.

Surber, R. 1994. *Clinical case management: A guide to comprehensive treatment of serious mental illness.* Thousand Oaks: Sage.

Suttie, I. 1935. *The origins of love and hate.* New York: Matrix House, 1952.

Swales, P. et al. 1995. Letter to the Library of Congress. http://users.rcn.com/brill/swales/html.

Target, M., and P. Fonagy. 1994. Efficacy of psychoanalysis for children with emotional disorders. *Journal of the American Academy of Child and Adolescent Psychiatry* 33:361–71.

Terr, L. 1990. *Too scared to cry.* New York: Basic.

Thompson, C. 1964. *Interpersonal psychoanalysis: The selected papers of Clara Thompson.* New York: Basic.

Thorpe, W. 1956. *Learning and instinct in animals.* Cambridge: Harvard University Press.

Thyer, B. and J. Wodarski. 1998. First principles of empirical social work practice. In B. Thyer and J. Wodarski, eds., *Handbook of empirical social work practice,* 1:1–31. New York: Wiley.

Ticho, E. 1972. Termination of psychoanalysis: treatment goals, life goals. *Psychoanalytic Quarterly* 41:315–33.

Ticho, G. 1967. On self-analysis. *International Journal of Psychoanalysis* 48:308–18.

Timberlake, E., and M. Cutler. 2001. *Developmental play therapy in clinical social work.* Needham Heights, MA: Allyn and Bacon.

Torrey, E. 1997. *Out of the shadows: Confronting America's mental illness crisis.* New York: Harper and Row.

Tosone, C. 1997. Sandor Ferenczi: Father of modern short-term psychotherapy. *Journal of Analytic Social Work* 4:23–41.

Townsend, W., S. Boyd, G. Griffin, and P. Hicks. 2000. Emerging best practices in mental health recovery. Columbus: Ohio Department of Mental Health.

Trzcinski, E., and J. Brandell. 2000–1. Adolescent outcomes, poverty status, and welfare reform: An analysis based on the survey of program dynamics. Final report prepared for the Research Development Grant, U.S. Bureau of the Census, U.S. Health and Human Services and Joint Center for Poverty Research.

Turner-Crowson, J., and J. Wallcraft. 2002. The recovery vision for mental health services and research: A British perspective. *Psychiatric Rehabilitation Journal* 25(3): 245–54.

Tyson, P. 1978. Transference and developmental issues in the analysis of a prelatency child. *Psychoanalytic Study of the Child* 33:213–36.

———— 1996. Termination of psychoanalysis and psychotherapy. In E. Nersessian and R. Kopff, eds., *Textbook of psychoanalysis,* pp. 501–24. Washington, DC: American Psychiatric.

Tyson, P., and R. Tyson. 1986. The concept of transference in child analysis. *Journal of the American Academy of Child Psychiatry* 25:30–39.

———— 1990. *Psychoanalytic theories of development.* New Haven: Yale University Press.

Varkas, T. 1998. Childhood trauma and posttraumatic stress: A literature review and case study. *Psychoanalytic Social Work* 5:3, 29–50.

Wallace, M., 1979. A focal conflict model of marital disorders. *Social Casework* 60 (July): 423–29.

Wallerstein, R. 1985. Defense mechanisms and the structure of the mind. *Journal of the Amencan Psychoanalytic Association* 31 (Supplement): 201–25.

———— 1986. *Forty-two lives in treatment: A study of psychoanalysis and* psychotherapy. New York: Guilford.

———— 1988. One psychoanalysis or many? *International Journal of Psychoanalysis* 69:5–21.

Wallerstein, R., and H. Sampson. 1971. Issues in research in the psychoanalytic process. Part 1. *International Journal of Psychoanalysis* 52:12–50.

Walsh, J. 2000. *Clinical case management with persons having mental illnesses: A relationship-based perspective.* Pacific Grove, CA: Brooks-Cole.

Warren, B. and W. Lutz. 2000. A consumer-oriented practice model for psychiatric mental health nursing. *Archives of Psychiatric Nursing* 14(3): 117–26.

Weber, J., H. Bachrach, and M. Solomon. 1985a. Factors associated with the outcome of psychoanalysis: Report of the Columbia Psychoanalytic Center Research Project, part 2. *International Review of Psychoanalysis* 12:127–41.

———— 1985b. Factors associated with the outcome of psychoanalysis: Report of the Columbia Psychoanalytic Center Research Project, part 3. *International Review of Psychoanalysis* 12:251–62.

Webster's II new college dictionary. 1995. Boston: Houghton-Mifflin.

Weinshel, E., and O. Renik. 1996. Psychoanalytic technique. In E. Nersessian and R. Kopff, eds., *Textbook of psychoanalysis,* pp. 423–54. Washington, DC: American Psychiatric.

Weiss, J., H. Sampson, and Mount Zion Psychotherapy Research Group. 1986. *The psychoanalytic process: Theory, clinical observation, and empirical research.* New York: Guilford.

Wertsch, J. 1979. From social interaction to higher psychological processes: A clarification and application of Vygotsky's theory. *Human Development* 22(11): 122.

Westen, D. 1986. What changes in short-term psychodynamic psychotherapy? *Psychotherapy* 23:501–12.

Westen, D. and G. Gabbard. 2002. Developments in cognitive neuroscience. Part 2: Implications for theories of transference. *Journal of the American Psychoanalytic Association* 50:99–134.

Whitaker, D. 1982. A nuclear conflict and group focal conflict model for integrating individual and group-level phenomena in psychotherapy groups. In M. Pines and L. Rafaelson, eds., *The individual and the group: Boundaries and interrelations in theory and practice,* 1:321–38. New York: Plenum.

White, R. 1959. Motivation reconsidered: The concept of competence. *Psychological Review* 66:297–333.

———— 1963. *The ego and reality in psychoanalytic theory.* New York: International Universities Press.

Whitman, R., and D. Stock. 1958. The group focal conflict. *Psychiatry* 21:269–76.

Willick, M. 1985. The concept of primitive defenses. *Journal of the American Psychoanalytic Association* 31 (Supplement): 175–200.

Wilson, P. 1997. The problem of helping in relation to developmental breakdown in adolescence. In M. Laufer, ed., *Adolescent breakdown and beyond,* pp. 57–71. London: Karnac.

Winnicott, D. W. 1956. On transference. *International Journal of Psycho-Analysis* 37:386–88.

———— 1958a. *Through paediatrics to psychoanalysis.* London: Hogarth.

———— 1958b [1951]. Transitional objects and transitional phenomena. *Through paediatrics to psychoanalysis.* London: Hogarth.

———— 1963. Psychiatric disorders in terms of infantile maturational processes. In *The maturational process and the facilitating environment,* pp. 230–41. New York: International Universities Press.

———— 1964. Youth will not sleep. *New Society* (May).

———— 1965a [1958]. The capacity to be alone. *The maturational process and the facilitating environment.* New York: International Universities Press.

———— 1965b. *The maturational process and the facilitating environment.* New York: International Universities Press.

———— 1965c [1960]. The theory of the parent-infant relationship. In *The maturational process and the facilitating environment.* New York: International Universities Press.

———— 1971. *Therapeutic consultations in child psychiatry.* New York: Basic.

———— 1984 [1963]. Struggling through the doldrums. In C. Winnicott and M. Davis, eds., *Deprivation and delinquency.* London: Tavistock.

Witenberg, E., ed.. 1973. *Interpersonal explorations in psychoanalysis: New directions in theory and practice.* New York: Basic.

Wolf, E. 1972. Technique of child analysis: Problems of countertransference. Report of a paper delivered to the Chicago Psychoanalytic Society.

———— 1976. Ambience and abstinence. *Annual of Psychoanalysis* 4:101–15.

———— 1988. *Treating the self: Elements of clinical self psychology.* New York: Guilford.

Wolfson, A., and H. Sampson. 1976. A comparison of process notes and tape recordings. *Archives of General Psychiatry* 33:558–63.

Woodroofe, K. 1971. *From charity to social work in England and the United States.* Toronto: University of Toronto Press.

Woods, M., and F. Hollis. 2000. *Casework: A psychosocial therapy.* New York: McGraw Hill.

Yalom, I. 1975. *The theory and practice of group psychotherapy.* New York: Basic.

Yanof, J. 1996. Language, communication, and transference in child analysis. *Journal of the American Psychoanalytic Association* 28:657–88.

Young-Eisendrath, P., and F. Weidmann. 1987. *Female authority: Empowering women through psychotherapy.* New York: Guilford.

Zaslow, S. 1992. Depressed adolescents. In J. O'Brien, D. Pilowsky et al., eds. *Psychotherapies with children and adolescents: Adapting the psychodynamic process*, pp. 209–30. Washington, DC: American Psychiatric.

Zetzel, E. 1970 [1956]. The concept of transference. In *The capacity for emotional growth*, pp. 168–81. New York: International Universities Press.

Mind: adaptive perspective on, 42; and awareness, 21; conflict-free ego capacity in, 45; conscious, 39; as dyadic, 110; dynamic perspective on, 40–41; economic perspective on, 41, 48, 73; evolutionary development of, 28; Freud on, 26, 27, 55; genetic perspective on, 41; hierarchical organization of, 26; higher functions of, 27; Klein on, 55–56, 57; pleasure-unpleasure principle of, 28–29; and psychoanalysis, 27; in relational psychoanalysis, 110; strata of, 27; structural perspective on, 39–40, 44; three systems of, 39; topographical perspective on, 39–40, 73; in Vygotsky, 357

Mintz, J., 386

Mirroring: in adolescent treatment, 301; in assessment, 143; Kohut on, 64, 65, 190; in Mann, 334; and resistance, 190; in time-limited psychotherapy, 334; and transference, 71, 78–79, 101

Mishne, Judith, 10–11

Mitchell, Juliet, 18

Mitchell, Stephen, 21–22, 54, 68, 326, 329; *Object Relations in Psychoanalytic Theory,* 67

Moral condemnation, 36

Morality, 39, 40, 294

Mother: adaptations of, 59; and anaclitic depression, 307; and child, 16, 46, 47, 48–49, 50, 53, 54, 59, 60, 95, 162, 334; in developmental ego psychology, 46; and empathy, 59; evil, 53; girl's tie to, 16; and good-enough mothering, 59; and holding environment, 59, 162; inadequacy of, 59, 60; Jacobson on, 48–49; loss of, 34; in Mahler, 22–23, 47; male envy of, 17; in Mann, 334; needs of, 59; and omnipotence, 59; and primary maternal preoccupation, 59; in self-in-relation theory, 18; Spitz on, 46; subjectivity of, 59; Sullivan on, 53, 54; Suttie on, 50; and symbiosis, 59; in time-limited psychotherapy, 334; and transference, 71, 95, 96; Winnicott on, 58–60; *see also* Parent(s)

Motivation: in Boston Psychoanalytic Institute Prediction Studies, 377; for child treatment, 262; disturbing, 382; in dynamic perspective, 40; and focal conflict model, 382; Freud on, 54; genically determined, 28; from instinctual drives, 54; from interpersonal experiences, 54; in Mann, 334; and resistance, 189; Sullivan on, 51, 54; in time-limited psychotherapy, 334

Motor activity, 20, 45, 47

Mount Zion Group, 329

Mourning process, 36, 49, 227, 231, 297

Multideterminism, 136

Mutative interpretation, 73–74, 102, 163

Mutual regulation, 68

Narcissism: in adolescent treatment, 119, 301; Balints on, 401n5; in child treatment, 271; in Davanloo, 328; Freud on, 49, 56, 401n5; in intensive short-term dynamic psychotherapy, 328; Kohut on, 35, 62, 63; in Mann, 332, 333; and storytelling, 271; in time-limited psychotherapy, 332

Narcissistic injuries, 35, 297

Narcissistic pathology, 65

Narcissistic personality disorder, 62, 333

Narcissistic rage, 65

Narcissistic supplies, 301

Narrative, 19, 137, 144, 374; in child treatment, 263, 265, 267–74

Narrative case study, 14, 375

National Forum on Recovery for Persons with Severe Mental Illness, 353

National Institute of Mental Health, 350, 351

Need(s), 64, 78

Neurosis: in dynamic perspective, 40; Ferenczi on, 322; Freud on, 26, 56; Kohut on, 62, 189; in Mann, 333, 335; nuclear, 32; and resistance, 186; in short-term anxiety-provoking psychotherapy, 327; in Sifneos, 327; and therapeutic alliance, 171; in time-limited psychotherapy, 333,